This book aims to demonstrate that the changing relationship between humanity and nature is a key to understanding world history. Humans have been grappling with environmental problems since prehistoric times, and the environmental unsustainability of human practices has often been a decisive, if not immediately evident, shaping factor in history. Ironically, the measures that societies and states have adopted to stabilize the relationship between humans and the natural world have repeatedly contributed to environmental crises over the course of history. *Nature and Power* traces the expanding scope of environmental action over the course of history: from initiatives undertaken by individual villages and cities, environmental policy has become a global concern. Efforts to steer human use of nature and natural resources have become complicated, as *Nature and Power* shows, by particularities of culture and by the vagaries of human nature itself. Environmental history, the author argues, is ultimately the history of human hopes and fears.

Joachim Radkau is Professor of History at Universität Bielefeld in Germany. His books include *Die deutsche Emigration in den USA, 1933–1945* (1971), *Deutsche Industrie und Politik von Bismarck bis zur Gegenwart* (in collaboration with George W. F. Hallgarten, 1974), *Aufstieg und Krise der deutschen Atomwirtschaft* (1983), *Holz: Ein Naturstoff in der Technikgeschichte* (in collaboration with Ingrid Schäfer, 1987), *Das Zeitalter der Nervosität: Deutschland zwischen Bismarck und Hitler* (1998), and the biography of Max Weber, *Die Leidenschaft des Denkens* (2005).

PUBLICATIONS OF THE GERMAN HISTORICAL INSTITUTE
WASHINGTON, D.C.

Edited by Christof Mauch
with the assistance of David Lazar

The German Historical Institute is a center for advanced study and research whose purpose is to provide a permanent basis for scholarly cooperation among historians from the Federal Republic of Germany and the United States. The Institute conducts, promotes, and supports research into both American and German political, social, economic, and cultural history; into transatlantic migration, especially in the nineteenth and twentieth centuries; and into the history of international relations, with special emphasis on the roles played by the United States and Germany.

Recent books in the series

Andreas W. Daum, Lloyd C. Gardner, and Wilfried Mausbach, editors, *The Vietnam War and the World: International and Comparative Perspectives*

Detlef Junker, editor, *The United States and Germany in the Era of the Cold War: A Handbook*, 2 volumes

Roger Chickering, Stig Förster, and Bernd Greiner, editors, *A World at Total War: Global Conflict and the Politics of Destruction, 1937–1945*

Kiran Klaus Patel, *Soldiers of Labor: Labor Service in Nazi Germany and New Deal America, 1933–1945*

Andreas W. Daum and Christof Mauch, editors, *Berlin – Washington, 1800–2000: Capital Cities, Cultural Representation, and National Identities*

Peter Becker and Richard Wetzell, editors, *Criminals and Their Scientists: The History of Criminology in International Perspective*

Michelle Mouton, *From Nurturing the Nation to Purifying the Volk: Weimar and Nazi Family Policy, 1918–1945*

Jonathan Zatlin, *The Currency of Socialism: Money and Political Culture in East Germany*

Andreas W. Daum, *Kennedy in Berlin*

Nature and Power

A GLOBAL HISTORY OF THE ENVIRONMENT

JOACHIM RADKAU
University of Bielefeld

Translated by THOMAS DUNLAP

GERMAN HISTORICAL INSTITUTE
Washington, D.C.
and

CAMBRIDGE
UNIVERSITY PRESS

#123136850

CAMBRIDGE UNIVERSITY PRESS
Cambridge, New York, Melbourne, Madrid, Cape Town, Singapore, São Paulo, Delhi

Cambridge University Press
32 Avenue of the Americas, New York, NY 10013-2473, USA

www.cambridge.org
Information on this title: www.cambridge.org/9780521851299

GERMAN HISTORICAL INSTITUTE
1607 New Hampshire Avenue, N.W., Washington, DC 20009, USA

© Verlag C.H. Beck oHG, München 2002
English translation © Cambridge University Press 2008

First published in German as *Natur und Macht* by Joachim Radkau 2002
First English edition 2008

Printed in the United States of America

A catalog record for this publication is available from the British Library.

Library of Congress Cataloging in Publication Data

Radkau, Joachim, 1943–
Nature and power : a global history of the environment / Joachim Radkau.
   p.   cm. – (Publications of the German Historical Institute)
Includes bibliographical references and index.
ISBN-13: 978-0-521-85129-9 (hardback)
ISBN-13: 978-0-521-61673-7 (pbk.)
   1. Human ecology – History.   2. Nature – Effect of human beings on – History.   I. German
Historical Institute in London.   II. Title.
GF13.R34   2008
304.2–dc22   2007015238

ISBN   978-0-521-85129-9 hardback
ISBN   978-0-521-61673-7 paperback

Contents

Preface to the German Edition

The night before I began working on this book I had a nightmare: seated in a small, rickety airplane somewhere over Russia, I was going through one landing after another on bumpy runways. Aware that the plane had nuclear bombs on board, I was trembling in a state of constant panic. Fortunately, I soon awoke. The dream was not difficult to interpret as the barely concealed expression of a feeling of unease. I used to dismiss global overviews in environmental history and called for a "middle level." Now I myself was venturing into world history: would I find reasonable landing places along the way? Would the many years I spent in the field of nuclear technology prove to be risky baggage? What did the ecological and economic disaster of the communist bloc mean for that kind of environmental history whose basic assumptions would have led one to assume that a socialist state-run economy would be able to undo the environmental damage caused by the private profit motive?

Some time after my fiftieth birthday, I came across a reference in an article on the history of forestry in India to an ancient Indian ideal of the human life cycle. According to this idea, it behooves a person at the age of fifty to venture into the forest in search of the truth.[1] That idea appealed to me, since the history of the forest has long been one of my favorite topics. But what is the historical wisdom with which one returns from the forest? It is surely not as thunderous as that of the prophets who come from the desert; instead, it is quiet, restrained, occasionally muted, like light falling through the leaves. An environmental historian who has absolute certainty about what he does need not go into the forest at all.

Eric L. Jones once remarked that to write universal history, he had to transform himself from a hedgehog into a fox.[2] As for myself, ever since acquiring my own garden, I have turned increasingly into a hedgehog, intellectually too, and I have often had the feeling that the secrets of history are hidden above all in microcosms and therefore elude the habitual globetrotters. World history can achieve genuine breakthroughs only with the help of regional field research. Whenever there was a doubt in my mind as I was researching this book, I therefore tended to give credence to works with such a local flavor. But at times, even regional studies are constructed around more generalized images of history and are therefore often strikingly similar. Once in a while one must range further afield to discover local peculiarities. Even Oliver Rackham, who never tires of mocking a pseudo-universal environmental history that is built on sweeping preconceptions, has confessed that it was in Texas that he came to change his views about English hedges.[3] If one wanders over the terraced fields of Mallorca, the Himalayas, and the Andes, one gets a powerful, ambivalent feeling: in some ways everything seems very similar, but in some ways also very different. It is not a bad thing to acquire, on foot, a foundation of emotional insights into environmental history.

One thing that makes environmental history so attractive is that it encourages one to discover history not only at "historical sites," but also in the sweep of the landscape. It makes one realize that traces of human history are found nearly everywhere, even in what seems like wilderness: in eroded mountain worlds, in the steppe, in the jungle. In my own case, the joy of roaming about is heightened by the pleasure – too often suppressed – of wide-ranging reading: everything from the "commentaries" of the Inca prince Garcilaso de la Vega to the *Secret History of the Mongols*, depending on the landscape. Now and then, environmental history needs the "wandering gaze." Faith in nature includes the confidence that, in the end, all the colorful diversity will give rise to a new order – the outlines of a new kind of world history.

It has become clear to me, especially at conferences on environmental history in the United States, that however much I admire the productivity of American environmental historians, the time has come to incorporate the experiences of the Old World more thoroughly and consistently into the discipline: to examine not the cult of "wilderness," but questions about sustainability in old cultural landscapes; to analyze not the imagination of Native Americans, but institutional traditions.[4] I am indebted to Frank Uekötter[5] – my intellectual sparring partner of many years – for insights that institutions and organizations contain an important key to an environmental history that rests on solid ground, insights that I initially resisted.

The Global Environmental Conference in Rio de Janeiro in 1992 elevated sustainability – in the sense of a careful stewardship of natural resources to preserve them undiminished for future generations – into the guiding goal for the global economy. In German forestry, this principle has a history stretching back centuries. For critics today, "sustainability" is a linguistic shell that legitimizes the exploitation of nature; but history can help a great deal to impart color and substance to this concept. The history of the forests, in particular, reveals also the ambiguity of this concept, as well as its capacity to be manipulated. Still, a better alternative is not in sight.

I have repeatedly ridiculed the stereotypical thinking and unexamined contra-dictions within environmental history: for example, on the one side the refrain "We have seen all this before" (namely the destruction of the forests, overexploita-tion, river pollution), and on the other side the hymn to the Native Americans' primal harmony with nature. Or on the one hand the pessimistic image of "human history as the history of the destruction of nature," and on the other the revisionist concept of "humanity as an episode in the eternal transformation of nature": so far, these opposing positions exist in their own separate worlds, disconnected from each other. This absence of a discussion has its reason, however: the majority of empirical studies are so limited in their range that they never even get to the fun-damental questions. That is another reason why I believe it is high time to attempt to write environmental history in such a way that a wisdom of the woods becomes conceivable – if only through the countless shortcomings and weaknesses that are an inevitable part of such an endeavor.[6]

Joachim Radkau, Spring 2000

Preface to the English Edition

Some time ago I was talking about Rachel Carson with a German scientist who had been involved for decades in the environmental and women's movements. To my consternation, she asked: "Who is Rachel Carson?" I responded that she was to the American environmental movement what Joan of Arc was to French nationalism. This episode reveals how deeply the Atlantic still separates the environmental movement on its opposing shores and the degree to which that movement still lacks a global historical awareness – a genuine global awareness, not a putative one.[1]

Surprises of a very different kind are also possible. The Global 2000 Report to the American president about the state of the global environment appeared in 1980 in an affordable German edition (1,508 pages) and became a bestseller and the Bible of the German environmental movement. As it was generally believed that the report had a similar impact in the United States, I was greatly astonished to discover that Global 2000 had received far less attention in that country.

Many German opponents of nuclear technology know nothing about the American origins of the protest against nuclear installations. On the other hand, many American environmental activists seem largely unaware that this form of protest had far greater long-term effects in Germany than in the United States and that it was the origin of the environmental movement in West Germany, France, Italy, and even Taiwan. In Carolyn Merchant's comprehensive *Guide to American Environmental History* (2002), nuclear energy is not a major theme, nor was it in a previous textbook she edited, *Major Problems in American Environmental History* (1993).[2] The *American Encyclopaedia of World Environmental History* (2004) has no entry on "Chernobyl." By contrast, the catastrophic accident at the Soviet nuclear power plant in April 1986 was seen in parts of Europe as the most important event in the environmental history of modern times (a perception, however, that was not to last).

All of this shows us how different the ideas are about what is and is not part of the "environment" and how little the environmental movements of the various countries know about each another, even when they claim to be thinking "globally." And since environmental history grew out of the environmental movement, the same is more or less true for this discipline. Even when it believes that its perspective rises above national narrowness, its mental horizon is often shaped by national traditions, more so than it realizes. Environmental history is in for many surprises if and when it learns to transcend these mental barriers. By looking at other countries one can suddenly notice elements in one's own country that previously seemed perfectly normal. I myself was led to rethink my own positions through conversations with American friends. For instance, I became much more keenly aware that my book had been shaped, in its contemporary references, by a political situation in which the Green Party in Germany had entered the halls of power on the federal level and in many local and regional governments, giving rise to the concern that it might succumb too quickly to the temptations of bureau-cratic power. At present, the situation in the United States is very different, and things have also changed in Germany. As a result, the potential political function of environmental history has also been transformed. In Germany, environmental his-torians may have the future task of keeping alive the memory of the larger context that gave rise to environmental initiatives within a disintegrating environmental movement.

The present book owes an immeasurable debt to American and English environ-mental history, and it could not have been written without the model of a global approach that one can find in its scholarship. I hope that I have repaid at least some of that debt by revising the original German edition for this English translation. At the same time, I hope that some of the approaches typical of continental Europe can provide a stimulus to the international discussion. Unlike the Americans and the British with their immense colonial empire, continental Europeans have rarely lived with the illusion of unlimited resources. That there are "limits to growth" was self-evident to them most of the time: hence it was clear that prudence dictated a careful harnessing of limited resources. That does not mean that this bit of wisdom was always followed in practice. Still, a striving for sustainability has deep roots in Europe as well as in other old cultures.

Writing environmental history from the criterion of sustainability therefore does not mean projecting a modern slogan anachronistically back into past ages. Rainer Beck is surely right when he notes that long before German forestry administrations elevated sustainability into a doctrine in the eighteenth century, every peasant had to practice a more or less sustainable husbandry to ensure his very survival.[3] By contrast, the concept of "wilderness," the fascination with which has shaped the American environmental movement and environmental history, makes no sense in the environmental history of the Old World; indeed, it leads one astray. In the Old World, the environmental historian needs to enlighten his readers first and explain foremost that most putative "wildernesses" are in reality old cultural landscapes and that their beauty can be preserved only by continuing ancient practices.

In revising the original text, I have tried to explain names and facts that an American or English reader cannot be expected to know and to give English and American experiences and perspectives more space than I did in the German edition. I leave it to the reader to judge how successful I have been. I have also tried to consider, as much as possible, the many discussions and reviews generated by the German edition and have introduced many new details.[4] Above all, however, I have sought to bring out even more sharply the overall conception of the book, its basic lines and structures.

Reconciling all these intentions proved challenging. Again and again I felt torn between making the overall concept of the book more uniform and presenting the colorful diversity of environmental history in all its richness. In attempting to reconcile the two approaches, I learned much from working on a school textbook about environmental history, from the need to explain everything to the students as clearly and simply as possible to making the presentation vivid and colorful.

Impulses of a very different kind came from my work on a larger study of Max Weber's highly ambivalent relationship to nature. While Weber possessed a keen appreciation for the natural foundations of history, he was a vigorous opponent of "naturalism" in the social sciences – to be precise: of speculative and poorly thought-through naturalism. Engaging the ideas of Max Weber is therefore one of the hardest exercises one can imagine for a modern environmental historian, but Weber also offers a global environmental history a wealth of impulses to which the worldwide "Max Weber industry" has paid no attention. Perhaps most importantly, wrestling with Weber made me more keenly aware than ever before that for a historian, "nature" always means also human nature. There is a *natura prima*, which is unchangeable and shared by all humanity, and a *natura secunda*, which is subject to historical change, while never entirely breaking away from the first nature. This theoretical foundation of my environmental history, which I had initially absorbed more instinctively than consciously, along with all the consequences flowing from it, has become much clearer to me recently, in part also through the German–American conference "Turning Points in Environmental History" that I organized jointly with the German Historical Institute (Washington, D.C.) in Bielefeld in June 2005.

The vast majority and most surprising clues to hitherto unheeded aspects of American environmental history, and to a comparison between the United States and Germany, have come from my longtime friend and assistant, Frank Uekötter. For his magnum opus, a comparative history of how air pollution has been dealt with in the United States and Germany, he scoured archives from Stuttgart to Salt Lake City with a gargantuan appetite for sources. He uncovered differences in the American and German styles of politics, differences that reach back to the late nineteenth century and have received little attention so far, but also surprising commonalities, for example, in the early "environmental movement before the environmental movement." The prehistory of today's environmental awareness is far more extensive on both sides of the Atlantic than most people are aware of.

I would like to thank Christof Mauch, the director of the German Historical Institute in Washington, for supporting this American edition and Thomas Dunlap for his skillful and sensitive translation.

Finally, I would like to remedy an oversight in the original German preface: to express my abiding gratitude to my wife Orlinde, who has hiked the world with me for forty years, from the Andes to the Gobi desert, always urging her impatient husband to stop and observe the most minute details of nature. Many secrets of environmental history are hidden in these details: even with a global approach, that is something one should never forget.

Joachim Radkau, Bielefeld, October 2007

I

Thinking about Environmental History

I. BLINDERS AND DEAD ENDS IN ENVIRONMENTAL HISTORY

Although environmental history is an offspring of the environmental movement, the dream of uniting history and nature has enticed historians for a very long time, going back all the way to Herodotus.[1] The idea of history contained a connection between culture and nature at its very inception: writing history means grasping culture in its development, and it is here that natural processes of growth and decay come into play. Reinhart Koselleck has observed that "biological naturalisms were already rampant" in nineteenth-century historiography.[2] A reuniting of history and nature can tap into a deep current that has been running through historical writing since ancient times.

The relationship of historiography to nature, however, is burdened by the past. The natural, organic element that was projected into peoples and cultures was usually a product of the ideologies of the day, and scholarship took these intellectual constructs as its starting point. Kant proclaimed, in his *Idea of a Universal History in a Cosmopolitan Plan* (1784), "A philosophical attempt to compose a universal history in the sense of a cosmopolitical history on a plan tending to unfold the purpose of nature in a perfect civil union of the human species . . . is to be regarded as possible, and as capable even of helping forward this very purpose of nature,"[3] but his was an idealistic and teleological conception of nature, which asserted that humanity's progress toward reason was the intent of wise nature. Even Kant became entangled in contradictions with this conception of nature. Intellectual history as a whole shows that it is not easy to think clearly about nature. At times Max Weber made it his sole ambition to purge the social sciences of any and all "naturalism." Current environmental history writing must not suppress historical experiences with dead ends in the way humans have thought about nature. Contemporary environmental history, too, is grounded in the critique of the old naturalism, namely, in the recognition that society is something fundamentally different from a natural organism – indeed, that societies can destroy their own natural foundation.

Beginning in antiquity, a synthesis of history and nature occurred mostly along the lines of geographic and climatic determinism: the essence of a people, it was believed, grew from its landscape, including wind and weather. Arnold Toynbee, in contrast, interpreted the high cultures as a response to the challenges of an environment that was not always kind to its inhabitants. However, nature appears primarily when cultures are born. Their decline is, at its core, an internal cultural matter. Decline manifests itself as the end of growth and the loss of dominion over nature; the other idea, that growth and the domination of nature could itself prove fatal to a culture, was not yet on the horizon. Gazing on the overgrown ruins in the Yucatan peninsula, Toynbee thought that the "forest, like some sylvan boa-constrictor, has literally swallowed them up."[4] It did not yet occur to him that this civilization could have been destroyed by a self-inflicted deforestation. Or is this, too, merely a fashionable theory?

Fernand Braudel began his great work on the Mediterranean world in the age of Philip II with the primacy of nature, with mountains and plains. Confessing unabashedly that his love of the Mediterranean was one impulse behind his writing, he expressed the hope "that a little of this joy and great deal of Mediterranean sunlight will shine from the pages of this book." But this joy distracted him from the question about the ecological decline of the Mediterranean region; instead, he criticized Mediterranean peasants for not ploughing their soil more deeply – absurd criticism from an ecological perspective. And that was not all: steeped in the tradition of the belief in progress, he paid scant attention to the dangers of overpopulation; instead, like an eighteenth-century politician bent on increasing the population, he raged against the practices of birth control that began to spread in Enlightenment France.[5]

The ecological movement allows us to advance our thinking on a number of issues to which older historians were blind. But even contemporary environmental history has its blinders, and often it even seems unaware of them. Initially – and in the beginning this was a sensible strategy – environmental history sought out ecological niches within the scholarly world that were not yet colonized by any established discipline. This, along with the current ecological impetus, explains the focus on industrial water and air pollution, which was a marginal area in the history of industry and technology, little studied until the 1970s. But it also explains the fondness for the history of ideas about nature, an area largely disregarded by the history of philosophy until very recently. Unfortunately there is virtually no connection between these different ecological niches of environmental history. Above all, environmental historians – in Europe even more so than in the United States – have tended to avoid core areas of the historical relationship between humans and their environment – such as the history of fields and woods, of urbanization and traffic, of population movements and epidemics. These were already claimed by others and therefore not easily accessible to newcomers; moreover, the scholarly traditions established in these fields are somewhat suspect to the ecological movement. But if environmental history wants to become world history, it must push into these very areas. And perhaps even more importantly: it has to become a history of human nature.

Because it does not understand its real prehistory, the environmental movement often lacks historical awareness, caused by the fact that the environmental problems and the strategies to counter them have fundamentally changed in the twentieth century. Today, the overfertilization of fields is a major source of stress on the environment; for thousands of years, however, the *shortage* of fertilizers was humanity's most pressing environmental concern. In this case the landscape of our modern problems has blocked our view of the historical issues. Even Goethe, as State Minister of Weimar, at times did not have enough fertilizer for his gardens;

getting them properly fertilized was one of his last worries before his death.[6] On his travels to Italy, he did not consider it beneath him to observe how the cities were dealing with their waste. He gave the Venetians and the inhabitants of Palermo bad marks in this regard, but praised the Neapolitans, who fertilized their gardens intensively (diary entry of April 7, 1787).

Today, we are confronted in many parts of the world with the destructive consequences of rampant free market selfishness. Yet this situation should not blind us to the fact that, many times throughout history, a secure law of ownership and inheritance probably promoted the protection of the soil and the fruit trees growing in it. Two conservationists, after analyzing conditions in Southeast Asia, concluded that the problem of the environment was basically quite simple: wherever the local population does not have control over its resources and is unable to keep outsiders away, the environment degrades.

There are other blinders that spring from the current state of affairs. Under earlier conditions, a regulation of sexuality, which is today seen as a compulsive-neurotic repression of human nature given modern contraceptives, could function as a brake on population growth and promote a harmonious balance between humans and their environment. Xenophobia, today for many the very embodiment of political pathology, may well have served a purpose under premodern conditions, since the balance of the relationship between humans and their environment in agrarian-pastoral microcosms was indeed upset by migratory movements, and local knowledge and experience was lost when populations moved. John R. McNeill has rightly pointed out that the great "transmigration" project in Dutch Indonesia, which was supported in the postcolonial era not only by the World Bank but also by the Communist Party, was the source of large-scale environmental destruction.[7] Environmental historians who still regard mobility as progress and love for one's native land as reactionary are blind to such factors.

Another observation is perhaps more important still: the universal law of inertia, which today often promotes the thoughtless treatment of the environment, was frequently the best protector of the environment in times when cutting and transporting trees was a very laborious task. If historians are fixated on an idealistic notion of modern environmental awareness, they fail to see the everyday, environment-preserving behavioral patterns of the past, which often emerge only between the lines of written sources and which today's environmental movement tends to look at less than favorably. To be sure, the world of "zero growth," of thriftiness and endless recycling, was all too often not the pleasant world conjured up by the phrase "living at peace with nature." Rather, it was a world in which many accepted a high infant mortality with a certain equanimity, since they knew that the survivors would have more to eat if fewer hungry mouths crowded around a food supply that was exceedingly difficult to increase.

A serious obstacle for environmental history is also the demand by environmental fundamentalists for a kind of history in which nature is the focus, not humanity, and in which nature is not perceived from the perspective of human interests. In such a history, the struggle of humans for thousands of years to come to some kind of arrangement with their natural resources appears only as an interference factor – as the eternal attempt on the part of humanity to make nature serve humanity's ends. Thoughtful environmental historians are constantly assaulted by scruples: are they doing real environmental history if they study forest and water conflicts in the past? Is not all of this about human interests and not at all about nature? Between the lines one can often read the assumption that "real" environmental protection exists only where (1) it is selfless, (2) it is done out of an ecological understanding, and (3) it is done with a holistic view of nature.

A historian, however, cannot work with such uncompromising criteria. Like all powerful movements in history, environmental history is driven not only by noble but also by selfish motives; not only by wise understanding, but also by vague feelings and sometimes by baseless fears; not only by a holistic view of nature, but very often also by a fractured one. An environmental historian should not write comic book history, where heroes fight villains, but realistic history. It is not difficult to recognize that the clash between "biocentric" and "anthropocentric" environmental history is a sham. Written sources restrict the historian – provided he or she has an understanding of source criticism – always to the interests of those who produced them and handed them down. Is all of environmental history a history of crimes, the story of how human beings have raped virgin nature? We have long known from ecology that the ideal of "untouched nature" is a phantom, a product of the cult of virginity. An impartial environmental history does not recount how humanity has violated pure nature; rather, it recounts the processes of organization, self-organization, and decay in hybrid human-nature combinations.

Contemporary environmental history that is written in the Third World, which does not suffer from surfeit, deals with human conditions of life almost as a matter of course. Vandana Shiva, next to Wangari Maathai perhaps the most famous Third World "eco-woman" of our day, is vehemently opposed to separating environmental protection and the preservation of the human food supply. The cult of the wilderness has its origins above all in the United States. There it has a practical reason: the protection of the national parks, of the giant trees of the West, and of the remaining buffalo herds. But it has long since been shown that the "wild" nature glorified in the West was created under the influence of the slash-and-burn agriculture practiced by Native Americans: "The most damaging misconception that Europeans brought with them to California – as well as the rest of the continent – was the belief that they were entering a 'natural wilderness.'"[8] Thus they believed they had to expel the Native Americans from the national parks to preserve the beauty of what they thought was untouched nature. As William Beinart and Peter Coates have said, the presumed "virgin land" was in reality a "widowed land": a land whose Native American population had been decimated by epidemics.[9] In environmental history, the guiding notion of "wilderness" has the fatal effect of diverting interest away from improving the environment shaped by human beings. What is more, even if one believes that the eco-fundamentalists are not capable of harming a fly, there is good reason to be uncomfortable with a philosophy that regards humanity as the "cancer of the earth," a philosophy that should make one wish for nine-tenths of humanity to disappear from the planet.

It is rather strange how tenaciously such a contested concept as "wilderness" has persisted. Or is there a deeper reason behind it? The word "wilderness" often seems like the awkward expression of a deep-seated feeling that exists for a good reason: the feeling, namely, that human culture, if it wishes to retain the capacity to develop and prosper, needs quiet reserves, room to play, unencumbered spaces.

The "thought of seeing every scrap of earth dug up by human hands," Wilhelm Heinrich Riehl wrote long ago, "has something horribly eerie for the imagination of every naturally feeling person,"[10] and he may very well be right in a perfectly rational sense.

Not least for that reason, an environmental history worthy of the name deals not only with human beings and their works, but also with sheep and camels, with swamps and fallow land. One must notice that nature has a life of its own and is by no means only a component of human action, or the topic of human discourse. It is precisely the unintentional chain of effects that flow from human action, and in which natural contexts make themselves felt, that is worthy of special attention.

Universal history connects the historian with those disciplines that have practiced environmental history for a long time, sometimes with considerable public resonance: ethnology, anthropology, and prehistory (including paleobotany). So far, these disciplines and the research of environmental historians are all but unaware of each other. Much depends on bridging this gap, and uniting the still widely scattered knowledge about environmental history could set off powerful chain reactions. Until now, ecological forays into universal history have been undertaken more often by biologists and ethnologists than historians.[11] However, the ecological dimension in ethnology is usually the basic pattern of "adaptation of culture to the environment." In this way, culture's destructive impact on the environment is easily marginalized. Ethnologists are partial to isolated cultures little touched by modern civilization and to remote mountain villages: as a result they miss the ecological dimensions of modernization and the interconnectedness of the world. The common formula of "adaptation to nature" still conceives of nature too much as something given a priori, eternally the same. A history of human environmental awareness cannot be written as the history of a sense of nature's right to exist on its own terms, but only as the history of a coevolution of culture and nature: the feeling – shaped by the experience of crises – for the long-term natural foundations of one's own life and culture. This history does, in fact, exist, and many conflicts over resources lead into it.

An environmental history that is committed to the "environment as such" will invariably put on blinders about the other contexts of historical sources; as a result, it is reluctant to engage in source criticism and tends toward self-delusion. If one does reconstruct the contexts, one discovers that the real issue in many early modern complaints about the destructive exploitation of the forests was not the woods, but the assertion of forest rights, and that the lament about the neglected state of the commons was driven not by concern for the ecology of the pasture, but by an interest in the division of the commons and agrarian reform. In more recent times, the *Chipko* ("hug the trees") movement in northern India has become "the most celebrated environmental movement in the Third World" – yet a closer look reveals that it is primarily a peasant movement aimed at defending traditional forest rights.[12] But why deny or marginalize these contexts? If one conceives of environmental history not as a specialty but as an integral component of a *histoire totale*, one gains a deeper appreciation for all the other elements that come into play in environmental conflicts.

Let us take another concluding look at the blinders: environmental history could also get bogged down if, influenced by the ecological debates, it seeks to be overly refined and fails to develop sufficient appreciation for the mundane. Dunghills and cesspools are great themes in a realistic environmental history, for they were crucial to preserving the fertility of the fields. Eating and procreative behaviors are essential in the relationship between humans and their environment. The potato and coitus interruptus are key innovations of the eighteenth century that are environmentally relevant. For the environmental historian, the French Revolution of 1789 takes on special importance not least because by breaking the power of the church, it made contraception the rule in French families and established France as a pioneer in this area.[13] An excessively top-heavy environmental history ignores the fact that crucial things occur below the waistline. Exaggerated fear of the charge of "biologism" that is popular among social scientists also puts blinders on the way environmental historians think. The primary, elementary connection between man and environment is established by the fact that the human being is a biological organism.

The inner coherence of environmental history, which until now has presented itself often as a colorful potpourri of themes, is guaranteed, in the final analysis, by the reality that there are intimate connections between external nature and the inner nature of human beings, who have always been aware of this. It is strange that "nature in man" was more of an everyday theme a hundred, two hundred years ago than it is today, in the supposedly "ecological age." Environmental history should remember this old theme. It will become history on a grand scale only if it succeeds in grasping the "nature in humanity" in its historical changes, as well as in its biological and suprahistorical elements.

"Environmental awareness" is at its core largely a health consciousness, and as such it has a history that is thousands of years old. Disease is one of those basic experiences in which human beings, in a moment of crisis, repeatedly experience an intimate connection between external and internal nature. Hippocrates was one of the first to accord the environment great importance as a cause of disease. Hippocratic reflections about "air, water, places" established a "geo-medical" tradition stretching over millennia. That tradition lives on in the medical topographies of the early modern period and in the hunger for light and air driving the modern reform of housing and urban renewal; after being temporarily interrupted, it has been resurrected in the environmental movement. The fear of disease is one of the most potent phobias of world history, and its effects extend from the history of religion to the process of civilization. And it was no mere delusion to connect diseases with the constellations of humans and their environment. The history of many diseases begins with humans settling down in denser communities; great epidemics like malaria, the plague, cholera, typhus, and tuberculosis mark certain environmental conditions and phases in environmental history. There is some evidence to suggest that the fear of cancer stands at the very beginning of the modern environmental consciousness. A "nonanthropocentric" concept of environmental history runs the risk of obscuring the real interconnections.

2. THE SAMENESS OF VICIOUS CIRCLES AND THE COMPLEX WAYS OF ESCAPING THEM

Were it true, as many historians assert, that historical reality is infinite in its variety, universal overviews would be a scholarly dead end. But that is evidently not the case, least of all in environmental history. If you scan a great many studies on the regional history of forests, pasture, and irrigation, you experience the eternal return of the similar and get the sense that the problems are on some level rather simple. Jared Diamond maintains that "the pattern of ecological collapses of past civilizations is a familiar, almost banal, one."[14] Since natural laws come into play, this uniformity comes as no surprise.

While we are not dealing with a single story, we are dealing with a limited stock of stories, which in typical cases become intertwined and set a vicious circle in motion. Overpopulation leads to an overuse of pastures and forests: for many observers, this process, abbreviated as PPR (population pressure on resources), is the very essence of the entire global history of the environment from the beginning until today – the Malthusian effect completed by ecology and turned into a vicious circle. Desperate need spawns new troubles, as famines and unbridled competition over limited resources renders a sustained and forward-thinking form of economic life impossible – the present wins out over the future. Shortsighted self-interest prevails over the long-term, collective interest in survival. The forest pasture destroys the forest. The pasture develops into a nomadic or seminomadic economic form and deprives the arable land of fertilizer. Deforestation leads to soil erosion and the accelerated drainage of rainwater; in combination, the two effects produce in one area steppe and desert, in another swamps and malaria. Artificial irrigation causes an increasing salinization of the soil. Added to all of this are the effects of growing mobility and global interconnectedness. The balance between humans and their environment that was created over many generations is upset by external influences, by invasions and the loss of autonomy.

For two modern historians of China, the leitmotif of China's environmental history across the millennia is quite simple: it is population growth, which has led to an initially slow but then rapidly progressing degradation of Chinese soils.[15] For Robert Sallares, reproductive behavior is also the key to ancient Greek history. He applies the models of "r" and "K" strategies developed by ecologists for animal species: "r" strategy is the method for securing collective survival by producing a large number of offspring, even if they are mostly short-lived; "K" strategy is a way of adapting to a relatively inflexible food supply by producing a limited number of offspring that are given careful nurturance. The "K" strategy is most likely to occur where a clearly circumscribed living space is evident. By this reasoning, the progressive elimination of boundaries in the world is threatened by population pressure, struggle, misery, and mass death. Sallares recognizes all the signs of an "r" strategy in the ancient Greek colonial period; in the long run, though, since colonial expansion soon reached its limits, this strategy led to an ecological crisis. Sallares draws parallels with many other cultures of the world. John R. McNeill has noted that the environmental tragedy of the Mediterranean – whose main stages he places at a much later time, to be sure – is now repeating itself in the mountain systems of the tropics: overpopulation, overuse, deforestation, erosion.[16]

As we can see, the universal leitmotifs of environmental history for the most part boil down to crisis. But that is not the only story. These vicious circles are, first of all, ideal-typical processes in the Weberian sense. To write environmental history we need these kinds of ideal-typical models about the mutual interaction between humanity and the environment – yet no one should believe that perfect examples of these processes can be found in the sources. We must never forget that these are ideal types that must not be confused with reality. One must always take a very close look to determine whether a certain type of environmental destruction actually applies in a concrete case. Irrigation systems do not promote salinization and malaria under all circumstances: much depends on whether the irrigation systems are covered and protected from evaporation, whether drainage is functioning properly, and whether ponds and flooded rice paddies are home to fish and frogs who eat the larvae of the mosquito, the host of the malaria parasite. Population growth does not automatically lead to environmental degradation; rather, agricultural terraces, which protect against soil erosion, require a high population density for their maintenance: under such conditions, a decline in population leads to soil erosion.

There are other questions that need to be asked: How heavy was the "heavy plow"? How solid were the agricultural terraces, how tight were the fences, and how cheap were the pipes?[17] It is not unusual that small differences crucial to environmental history are found on a mundane technical level. A minor innovation like the motorized pump leads to an overuse of groundwater. The tractor allows farmers to plough more deeply than ever before in history: here the old identification of agriculture with the plow is given a new and fateful meaning.

In many cases it is not entirely clear whether a human population is autonomous or controlled by external forces, whether it follows an "r" or a "K" strategy in its reproductive behavior. Do human beings ever follow a single reproductive strategy in pure form, like whales follow the "K" type and lemmings the "r" type? Evidently they have always had some leeway to guide their population number; Hubert Markl has gone so far as to argue that humans are "biologically speaking the most strongly K-selected primates."[18] Sallares has noted that both strategies also existed in ancient Greek culture. Especially a meager environment sometimes promoted birth control, which produced more stable conditions than did population growth in response to more abundant environmental conditions.

The types of environmental degradation I have mentioned did not lead always and everywhere to a vicious circle. Precisely dense settlement and intensive agriculture can give rise to a careful cultivation of the soil, a kind of cultivation more expansive economic forms are not capable of: the Danish agronomist Esther Boserup (1910–99) founded a school of thought that studied the common sense and sustainability of intensive small-scale farming.[19] If human excreta are completely incorporated into the soil, population growth does not necessarily lead to soil exhaustion. If the garden is the prototype of a successful harmony between humanity and environment, a certain density of settlement is advantageous. An intensive use of the forests can lead to their destruction but also to a well-considered and sustainable silviculture; but even in Germany, with its abundance of files and documents relating to forestry, it is not always easy to determine when and where in the history of the forest the one or the other was the case.

The crisis-like causalities of environmental history do not unfold with the inexorableness of natural laws, for human beings are often able to pursue counter-strategies. However, it is possible to construct patterns of events that make it very difficult for human beings to take remedial measures. That is the case when the decline of the environment takes place slowly and nearly imperceptibly over centuries. But it can also occur when the decline is precipitous and a variety of factors combine to create a self-sustaining vicious circle. Both scenarios seem to have existed in typical cases, at times they are even found in the very same process. Erosion researchers have long observed "that erosion begins slowly and with the smallest, barely noticeable transformation of the soil, but it can very rapidly reach a large, indeed catastrophic, scale."[20]

In general, however, one can assume that human beings are aware – up to a certain degree – that they are destroying the basis of their own existence, and that they are in principle capable of taking steps against it. Precisely because many traditional environmental problems are thousands of years old and in essence rather simple, there has also existed since time immemorial a good deal of knowledge about how to deal with them. If one wanted to, it was not difficult to keep sheep and goats from destroying the forest; and much that is known about the usefulness of forests is not a new insight. But human beings were by no means always able – or encouraged by their living conditions – to act with an eye toward the long term; likewise, institutions and legal traditions capable of providing effective protection for the life-sustaining environment were not always present.

The crucial point is evidently that adequate strategies for remedying environmental problems do not follow a few simple basic patterns the same way that environmental problems do. This is where culture and society come into play. In many cases, effective solutions were not a recognizable response to a given problem, but a component of the culture that was presumably reinforced by environmental pressures, though not created by them. A cultural preference for homosexuality is consistent with the overpopulation of Attica in the classical period, whereas in Tibet much later, polyandry and the large number of unmarried monks correlate with the tightly circumscribed food supply. The solutions to environmental problems are often hidden within social and cultural history, and it is there that we must first decipher them. It would appear, however, that solution strategies in general were also not infinitely variable; rather, the more natural laws came into play, the more they were confined to a limited number of typical strategies. A comparative study of how drinking water was supplied and wastewater disposed of in Berlin and Istanbul concluded, by and large, that the most important determinants were found not in the differing cultures, but in the different natural conditions. From that perspective, Istanbul's greatest problem was always supplying water, while Berlin's greatest challenge was increasingly the disposal of wastewater.[21]

Typical patterns in solution strategies also arise from the fact that as the management of environmental problems moves to higher levels of the state, it becomes increasingly subject to the laws of power and the preservation of authority. In and of itself, the regulation of resource problems has had its attractive side for systems of political control since antiquity: one need only recall the building of canals and dikes and the supervision of the use of water, forest, and pasture. Environmental history is always also the history of political power – and the more it moves away from practical problems on the ground and into the sphere of high-level politics, the more that is the case.

It is here, especially, that we encounter what is probably the most important, elementary process in world history when it comes to how environmental problems have been dealt with. When we look at the problems themselves, there is a limited stock of leitmotifs that recur over and over; but there is historical development with respect to the geographic reach of environmental problems and how humans have dealt with them. Environmental history is invariably shaped also by the formation of ever larger political and even more expansive economic entities, and by the growing interconnectedness of the world. The geographic dimension of certain problems increases, and the competency to deal with them is claimed by higher political levels: territories, nation-states, and supranational institutions. Environmental knowledge, too, becomes more exclusive, turning into a matter for science and bureaucratic experts. This process has causes that are inherent in the phenomenon itself, but it is also driven by the power interests of the state and the professional politics of the experts.

The steady stream of forestry regulations that began to flow especially from the sixteenth century on served the growth and expansion of the early modern territorial state, and in its wake also of forest administration and the science of forest management. That is not to say that the impending shortage of wood, which was used to justify the forest regulations, did not exist at all; however, one must not assume that these decrees were always a direct and appropriate reaction to actual changes for the worse in the forests. The situation is much the same with many of the agricultural reforms that were pushed from the top and justified with reference to the dismal state of agriculture: in reality they were motivated by a quest to secure a greater income for the state or manorial lords, and in the end they actually increased the danger that some resources would be overexploited. There is reason to believe that this holds true also for the irrigation culture of the ancient Near East, for the agrarian reforms of the eighteenth and nineteenth centuries, and more recently for the "Green Revolution."

Historians, who are fascinated by long-distance trade, have often overlooked that, until very recently, humanity's food supply was largely dependent on local and regional subsistence, and that an effective response to environmental problems was most likely to occur at those levels – if at all. Fertilizing fields, maintaining terraces, desilting the many small irrigation canals, and caring for fruit trees – these tasks could not be organized centrally, but were a matter for villages and households. That is why the shift of important aspects of environmental preservation to higher levels raises some concerns. It is possible that the supposed management of the problems misses the real problems and ends up creating new ones.

In this context, importance attaches to another, special phenomenon. We often find in certain environmental sectors of a region *one* dominant problem that over-shadows all others. If one were to analyze the psychology of environmental history, one might arrive at a theory of the *primary trauma*. Since drought is *the* terror of humanity in many regions of the world, there is a tendency to engage in irrigation wherever possible and with no regard for unwanted long-term consequences. On the other hand, the myth of the Great Flood, which is found in several ancient cultures, indicates the extent to which flooding was the primeval danger associated with water in many other regions. Where the danger of flood dominates thinking, people pay no heed to the dangerous repercussions from a drastic drop in the water level as rivers are regulated. The fixation on drainage as the chief means of increasing agricultural yields had similar consequences. Many regions were once wetter than they are today. Whether in the Netherlands, France, or England: at the beginning of agrarian history we often find drainage. As late as the 1930s, the environmentalist Alwin Seifert complained about the extent to which

German hydraulic engineering was dominated by traditional "hydrophobia." A similar effect radiated from the fear of epidemics arising from swamps; the sanitationist Max Pettenkofer declared "war to the finish" even on subterranean swamps. In the valley of Mexico City as well, marshification and flooding was the primal trauma since the conquest of the Spaniards in the sixteenth century. For the mounted Spaniards, the Aztec capital Tenochtitlán – located in the middle of a lake – was a deadly trap; they let part of the lake silt up, which made the flooding worse. In the end, drainage was pursued with such obsessiveness that the city began to dry up and sink in the twentieth century. The environmental history of Beijing, too, was characterized by drainage, until the surroundings became threatened by desertification.[22] A monomaniacal environmental policy throws up new problems. In 1870 the French agronomist Jean Augustin Barral complained that politicians and farmers did not understand how important it was "to create a dual system of drainage and irrigation."[23] Hands-on people like simple thinking and action: they focus on either irrigation or drainage. This, too, needs to be kept in mind in environmental history: environmental knowledge is generally put into practice only in a very truncated, simplified form.

As the world becomes more tightly knit together, the transfer of knowledge and technology extends over increasingly greater distances. Technologies become detached from the environment in which they arose and to which they were adapted, and this creates a new kind of environmental risk. The heavy plow is used on soils for which it was not created and which it exposes to erosion. Water-intensive technologies that stem from water-rich Western and Central Europe are transferred to water-poor regions of the world. Of course, such technology transfer is not always blind to the regional conditions: the history of technology is not only a history of the diffusion of technology, but also of its adaptation. That history, however, is messier: it is more a history of details than of the great technological ideas, which is why only its rudiments have been written to date. Waste management technology, in particular, necessitates an adaptation to specific conditions. One member of the board of the Emschergenossenschaft (a cooperative association set up in 1899 to look after the river Emscher and its tributaries) wrote in 1925 that dealing with coal sludge required an "effective engagement with the peculiarities of the various types of sludge."[24] In the history of technology as well, the rule holds true that while environmental problems are triggered according to certain standard patterns, solutions to these problems demand specific strategies that are adapted to local conditions.

Excursus: The Liebig Thesis – The Sewage Question in the Subsoil of Environmental History

When all is said and done, is there not in fact *one* great and very simple leitmotif that runs through environmental history from the beginning of agriculture – namely, the inexorable decline of nature as it is increasingly subjugated by humanity? Is this the basic process behind all the singular dynamics of destruction? The majority of popular ecological literature suggests the conclusion that environmental history is the history of a fall from grace and its unending consequences. In the process, empirical concerns are usually mixed with theoretical ones, and this makes it more difficult to engage the subject. At the outset there is often the basic conviction that the mere human refashioning of nature as such is tantamount to interference in and destruction of nature. But we have known for quite some time that ecosystems are in constant flux even without human help, and that there is no such thing as an eternal harmony that is disturbed by humanity.

However, one should beware of taking this argument too far, as though there were no balance at all that man could destroy to his own detriment: rather, the possibility that a gloomy basic theme of ecological decline runs through all of human history deserves very serious consideration. Although the global threat to the atmosphere and to water resources is of fairly recent date, when it comes to the third great environmental medium, the soil, the assumption that the threat goes back thousands of years has much in its favor. That is another reason why the historical study of the environment must not limit itself to modernity, for if it did so, it would fail to fully grasp the most elementary problem of environmental history.

The pessimistic belief that the fertility of the cultivated soil slowly but surely declined over time already appears in antiquity. "Terra ipsa fertilior erat inlaborata et in usus populorum non diripientium larga," wrote Seneca: "The very soil was more productive when untilled, and yielded more than enough for peoples who refrained from despoiling one another." Columella, the Roman writer on agriculture, begins his opus on agriculture with a general attack on this complaint: "[I]t is unbecoming to a man of good judgment to believe that Earth, to whose lot was assigned a divine and everlasting youth, and who is called the common mother of all things . . . has grown old in mortal fashion." But even he recognizes a decline of agriculture as a result of the "mistreatment of the soil" by humanity; but humans are in a position to remedy this situation at any time – which is the very justification for his own book on agriculture.[25] This tenor of cheerful activism carries on in the agricultural reforms of modern times, but as a counterpoint complaints about mistakes also grow louder.

The chemist Justus von Liebig embodied the highpoint of this dialectic: using the insights of chemistry he sought to revolutionize agriculture while at the same time condemning the entire European tradition of soil cultivation as destructive exploitation. At its core, though, his argument sprang from chemical theory, not from history. The basic idea was simple: the fertility of the soil is based not on a self-regenerating life force, but on mineral components. Each harvest extracts minerals from the soil; if humans do not return them – all of them – to the soil in some form or another, the fertility of the soil will decline inexorably. It was a basic principle formulated along the lines of the model of the law of the conservation of energy (which was articulated at the same time) or monetary economics: if you spend more than you have or earn, you will become poorer.

According to Liebig, this gradual impoverishment of the soil had been going on for millennia, though at an accelerated pace since the agrarian reforms of modern times, which extracted ever higher yields from the soil. The circle of nutrients would be closed again if the excreta of humans and animals (including urine) were returned completely to the soil from which the food came. The "progress of culture," said Liebig, was a "question of sewage": at that time, he did not yet have access to chemical fertilizer as the seemingly perfect solution – which is fortunate, for given his single-minded fixation on mineral nutrients, he could have done a great deal of damage.

Liebig believed that the Chinese recycled excreta in exemplary perfection, and that this explained the singular continuity of Chinese culture across millennia. By contrast, the West usually neglected to do so, and the introduction of the water closet and the combined sewage system were about to put a complete stop to it. Though Europe might well look splendid in the eyes of many, in reality it was "in the position of someone suffering from consumption, whose mirror reflected back to him the picture of good health." The destructive exploitation reached its height on the farms of North America, which amounted to "murder of the fields." But what was referred to as the "intensive cultivation" of Europe was also a form of robbery, only more sophisticated, "robbery with self-delusion," concealed by a pseudo-scientific web of lies.[26] This, however, was not only a modern phenomenon, Liebig maintained: all older high civilizations, with the exception of China, had invariably fallen victim to the self-inflicted exhaustion of their soils.

The resonance of Liebig's warnings reached as far as the United States, where the importers of phosphatic guano used Liebig's mineral theory to advertise their product.[27] To this day the veracity of this theory, on which the interpretation of all of environmental history hinges, has not been thoroughly discussed among either agrarian or environmental historians. Modern ecological research is focused on the current problem of overfertilization and has shown little interest so far in the desperate fertilizer shortage that persisted for thousands of years. Liebig's contemporaries, by contrast, had the famines of the early nineteenth century in the back of their minds. What imbued Liebig's theory with suggestive power, however, was not empirical evidence, but its simple logic, the rigor of its formulation, and the seemingly simple clarity of the solution: the minerals taken from the soil had to be returned. Even Karl Marx adopted Liebig's thesis in *Das Kapital*, depicting the ruinous exploitation of the soil as a counterpart to the exploitation of the proletariat.

To this day, the Liebig theory is difficult to verify with exactitude, since there are also natural processes of soil exhaustion across the millennia. Soil formation processes are exceedingly difficult to grasp, primarily because of the ratio of microorganisms and a time frame that extends over centuries and millennia. Moreover, the degree to which the pace of these processes keeps up with the extraction of nutrients is difficult to determine for the present, let alone the past. An intense debate raged over these issues especially during Liebig's lifetime. Even the agrochemist Julius Adolph Stöckhardt, who has come back into favor as the pioneer of research into damage to forests and who was originally an ardent supporter of Liebig's, mocked the "specter of soil exhaustion." Others responded to Liebig that his contention that German farmers – unlike the Chinese – had engaged in a "terrible waste of human excreta" was simply not true. If they were right, the core of Liebig's argument would collapse. But even this counterclaim is open to question. It is not all that easy to uncover the history of how humans have dealt with sewage, which gets lost in the darkness of the latrines. Excreta are typically a taboo subject. In postwar Germany, which had a severe shortage of fertilizer, people fertilized their gardens with their own excreta, but they didn't talk about it.

In theory there could have been a perfect cycle of nutrients between city and countryside in preindustrial times, maintained by the land's hunger for fertilizer and the city dwellers' need to rid themselves of their sewage. Latrine archaeology indicates, however, that in real life this cycle functioned only in part: otherwise one would not find so many vestiges of earlier centuries in the latrines.[28]

The economist Wilhelm Roscher only half believed Liebig's theory of destructive exploitation and offered a simple counterargument: "Since no matter disappears entirely from the earth, the exhaustion of the soil can only be a dislocation of valuable soil elements." In fact, one can often assume that the soil that is lost in the mountains collects in the valleys; however, in earlier times it was no longer usable there because of marshification and epidemics. The use of such valley flood plains was a question of progress for drainage technology. As long as soil fertility – following Liebig's doctrine – consisted only of minerals, its decline was never irreversible. The issue becomes really critical once one regards humus as the crucial factor, since it is more difficult to replace than minerals. Liebig angrily opposed the humus theory, because he smelled in it the belief in the special status of living matter that escaped chemical formulas. But it is precisely when one transcends Liebig's lopsided perception of the soil that the fate of soils over the course of human history appears in an even more critical light.

The historian Heinrich von Treitschke, a younger contemporary of Liebig's who did not have a high opinion of chemists and dismissed the fear of soil exhaustion as an antiquated whim, considered it a fact that the great estates in the early nineteenth century had realized the perfect cycle of nutrients: "Each large estate was as it were an isolated entity, endeavoring to restore the exhausted energies of the soil without extraneous aid, depending upon a well-planned rotation of crops and upon a combination of tillage and cattle-breeding and sheep-farming."[29] But this was the type of farming that was barely producing for the market, a type that was long since obsolete in regions with a more favorable transportation infrastructure. The more the market orientation of agriculture progressed, and the more distant the point of consumption was from the point of production, the more the local nutrient cycle was dissolved. The inevitable conclusion is that the basic tendency of history has contained the potential for ecological crisis for a long time.

Do the agricultural advances in the modern age refute this historical picture? Not necessarily, for the pioneering work of Wilhelm Abel has shown that the living standard of the broad mass of the population in many parts of Europe declined drastically between the late Middle Ages and the early nineteenth century.[30] It is doubtful that population growth during this time was so strong that it alone can explain this deterioration in living standards. Liebig's gloomy scenario of decline was not entirely plucked out of thin air. The more the world's population grew, the more the failure to recycle human excreta affected the ecology of the soil. Since that time, the problem of the regeneration of soil fertility has been masked by the gargantuan use of energy in the manufacture of fertilizers.

Erosion was not a topic for Liebig, as it was of no concern to a chemist and hardly registered in Germany for a long time. But erosion is especially "insidious, since it typically occurs at a slow pace and generally accumulates unnoticed over time."[31] Not until the dust storms in the United States in the 1930s did people become aware of erosion as a major factor in the destruction of soil around the world. Initially it was seen as a phenomenon of the present; only soil archaeology discovered just how far what is believed to be anthropogenic erosion stretches back in time. Though there are many methods to guard against soil being carried away by wind or washed away by water, on the whole it would appear that increased erosion is – from a global historical perspective – simply the inevitable price of agriculture. Like a decline in soil fertility, erosion is often not noticed over a long period of time; and while in both cases there are a number of countermeasures, depending on local conditions, there is no reliable and generally known standard solution to the problem. In the face of the dust bowl of the 1930s, one American erosion scientist even went so far as to propose this thesis: "Soil erosion is altering the course of world history more radically than any war or revolution. Erosion is humbling mighty nations . . . and once and for all it has barred the way to the El Dorado that a few years ago seemed almost within reach."[32]

There is one fundamental objection: if the theory of the insidious decline of the soil as the result of human cultivation is correct, would humanity not have met its demise a long time ago? Is humanity's survival for thousands of years and its enormous growth in numbers since the invention of agriculture not proof enough that there must be elements of sustainability not accounted for by this theory? Clearly, insidious decline is not the only story; many other stories cut across it. However, it is not clear whether those stories are equally fundamental in nature. The question of fertilization and sewage remains a critical point of environmental history. An environmental historian should always pay attention to cycles of nutrients, even if he cannot reconstruct them in their entirety.

3. IN THE DEPTH OF TIME, AND THE MYSTERIOUS REGENERATIVE POWER OF THE NATURE IDEA

In his lecture on the "historical roots of our ecological crisis," delivered on Christmas in 1966, Lynn White reached far back to the beginnings of the Judeo-Christian religion and the commandment in the Old Testament by God that humans should "subdue the earth."[33] The lecture became a kind of "sacred text" for the emerging field of environmental history, and for a time it was very popular to go way back in time and to start with the Old Testament. Subsequently, however, it turned out that it was very difficult to translate this approach from the history of ideas into empirical studies. Once environmental history moved beyond preliminary essays and became more concrete, it limited itself overwhelmingly to the industrial era, when emissions have become the most urgent environmental problem. If one were to make water and air pollution the centerpiece of environmental history, only the age of coal and oil would in fact be truly important.

But it is historically narrow-minded to limit one's perspective in this way under the influence of contemporary issues and problems. Today there simply is no doubt any longer that human cultures have struggled with self-caused resource shortages for thousands of years. Drawing on the current state of scholarship, one of the very first steps forward lies in realizing that large-scale changes to the landscape by human hand have been taking place for millennia. Slash-and-burn agriculture and pastures changed the environment on a far more extensive scale than did the factories in the period of early industrialization. According to our current understanding, moors were typically created by erosion processes stemming from forest destruction and overgrazing in the Neolithic period. Prehistoric shifting of settlements indicates that human beings exhausted their resources time and again as early as the prehistoric age. To be sure, that did not create a global environmental problem; but if people lived within a narrow horizon, their world was certainly threatened by the danger of resource depletion. Even Karl Butzer, who studied primarily Egypt, the exemplar of a phenomenal continuity in the balance between humans and environment, was forced to acknowledge: "The geo-archaeological record of soil erosion and related cut-and-fill cycles demonstrates that homeostatic equilibrium has rarely been maintained over the long run." John R. McNeill, the historian of the mountains of the Mediterranean world who generally emphasizes the modern origins of deforestation, arrived at the conclusion that all adaptations to the environment – including those of the ancient world – are temporary.[34]

Is all of this prehistory irrelevant to the present? There is reason to believe that our current environmental behavior follows patterns that are in part very old, indeed, that our perception to some extent corresponds to the problems posed in earlier times. Why do human beings not register the highly toxic carbon monoxide (CO) with their senses? For the evolutionary biologist Franz Wuketits, the answer is quite simple: "Because CO was not present during that vast period when coal ovens did not yet exist."[35] The fact that we have such a deep attachment to an "Arcadian" landscape of pastures has very concrete reasons across millennia of pastoralism. The environmental historian must therefore go back deep into the past to find out how our current environmental behavior has been preprogrammed.

There are primarily two, widely separated paths by which one can arrive at continuities in the humanity-environment relationship that are thousands of years old: one takes us via objective remains – pollen, skeletons, soil structures – and employs scientific methods; the other stays with the semantic field surrounding the word "nature" and related concepts and draws on intuitive understanding, on the assumption that a good deal of human environmental history lives on in us.

The realization that the human interaction with the environment has a depth dimension stretching back many millennia is grounded not least in pollen analysis, combined with radiocarbon dating. It has shown that the thinning of the forests in Central Europe did not begin with the clearings of the high Middle Ages, and that Germania, contrary to earlier fantasies, was no longer covered with a dense primeval forest by the time of Arminius's battle against Varus (9 C.E.). It was not the use of wood by the Lüneburg saltworks that created the Lüneburg Heath; rather, analytical studies of pollen have shown that the process of heathification was already in full swing around 1500 B.C.E., the result, presumably, of slash-and-burn agriculture and pasturage. There are even indications that humans beings, even in prehistoric times, not only reduced the forests, but influenced its species composition in positive ways, for example, by promoting the spread of the oak and the ash, much sought after for the animal fodder they provided. However, pollen analysis also reveals that vegetation can change even without human influence.[36]

Of course, the evidentiary value of pollen has its own limitations. We can grasp only the areas surrounding lakes and moors in which pollen is preserved, that is, above all the wet regions rather than the dry ones. On the basis of pollen it is possible to both overestimate and underestimate the extent of the forest cover in earlier times. From the number of pollen one can draw only uncertain conclusions about the quantitative composition of extensive ecosystems.

Is it possible to journey back into the distant past by way of human ideas about nature? One immediately runs into the counterargument that what we today think of when we use the word "nature" is a modern construct, and that older conceptions of nature had nothing whatsoever to do with the environment. Joachim Ritter, in a widely noted 1962 essay on the nature aesthetic, argued that "nature as landscape" could "exist only under the condition of freedom on the basis of modern society." But this thesis is a prime example for the kind of optical illusion that is created when the gaze is narrowed down to encompass only the modern age. The young Max Weber, who was well versed in classical literature, assured his mother, a nature enthusiast: "It would never occur to me to regard the enjoyment of nature as the invention of the modern age."[37] One look at the wall paintings of Pompeii is enough to remind us how old the delight is in an abundant and flourishing nature and the song of the birds. Hildegard von Bingen believed in a green natural vigor (*viriditas*) that animated the trees and flowers as much as humanity and the animals. There is much to suggest the existence of a "biophilia" that is innate to humans. The medievalist Ernst Schubert regards the feeling for the beauty of nature as an "anthropological constant." From that perspective, environmental history possesses an inner center within human nature.[38]

The Greek word for "nature" – *physis* – is derived from "growth." To be sure, its etymological development in antiquity led not to wild growth, but into the essence of things, reasoned order, and abstraction, and this semantic thread runs right into the modern age. At the same time, the concept of nature always returned to its original meaning, to the world of growth, of luxuriant fertility. Even in the reflections and discussions about "nature" there are remarkably consistent elements. Aristotle's pupil Theophrastus questioned his teacher's teleological nature conception and saw no reason to assume that nature existed inherently for humans: the controversy of "nonanthropocentrism vs. anthropocentrism" is that old.

The ideal of a life in harmony with nature – external and internal nature – likewise reaches back into classical antiquity, as does the demand not to coerce nature. Seneca, who called nature a protective mother (*ut parens ita tutela omnium*), accused the rich of despoiling the landscape: "How long shall there be no lake unshadowed by your towering chateaux?" That comment could have been made about Lake Starnberg in the twentieth century – once again we see that one must not exaggerate the modernity of contemporary problems and the perception of problems. In the fourth century the Taoist Ko Hung, the founder of Chinese alchemy, has the anarchist philosopher Pao Ching-yen rail against behaviors that pretend nature existed for humans: "That the bark is peeled off the cinnamon tree, that sap is collected from the mountain pine, is not what these trees want. That pheasants are plucked and the kingfisher torn to pieces is not the wish of these birds. . . . The seeds of fraud and cunning lie in acting against nature, when such action is based on violence." Here, then, is the axiom of the modern environmental movement: violence against external nature produces violence against human nature.[39]

In antiquity we already encounter nature as something vulnerable though in the end unconquerable, which man struggles against merely to his own detriment: "Naturam expellas furca, tamen usque recurret" – Though you may drive out nature with the pitchfork, it will return: these are the words of Horace, who like no other ancient author praised the rural life. Since fertility is part of nature, erotic-sexual connotations are also very old. In the twelfth century, the scholastic Alain of Lille has the goddess Natura, whom he places into a garden of eternal spring surrounded by a forest, speak out against sodomy, which prevented procreation. The late-antique goddess Natura appears even in medieval scholasticism, though dressed up in Christian morality. Through her, as Ernst Robert Curtius said, "as through an opened sluice, the fertility cult of the earliest ages flows once again into the speculation of the Christian West." At times, Natura – amazingly enough – even holds Mary, the Mother of God, on her lap.

"Nature" describes not only an allegorical figure of a woman, but also a way of life where one feels good in one's skin. In the sixteenth century, the Lutheran preacher Johann Mathesius in the hill town of Joachimsthal taught: "Thus everything that is natural fares and lives better."[40] The experience of how pleasant it is to cast off constraints and to yield to the needs of body and soul is an ancient one. In the process, the inner nature led to outer nature. Botany begins as the study of medicinal plants.

For lovers of nature there is nothing more bewildering than the philosophical history of nature, especially since the most important factor is usually not found there: love. Studies of the concept of nature from the perspective of the history of philosophy mention the presence of "nature" in eroticism, medicine, the art of living, "natural law," the "natural sciences," and technology only as an aside – if at all. For that reason they miss a major part of the vigorous, normative, and practical significance of the concept of nature. From the perspective of most theoreticians, the history of the concept of nature is highly contradictory and muddled, and the confusion actually increases as the modern era progresses.[41] Nature as a being/nature as wilderness, nature as teacher/nature as the untameable, kind nature/terrible nature: what is one to make of this jumble of contradictions? It is very easy to deconstruct nature as norm and as philosophical category. The only puzzling thing is how indestructible this ideal is and how the concept of nature reemerges from every maelstrom of confusion and returns to original meanings. It would appear that this phenomenon has never been adequately appreciated. The concept must have preserved some kind of life meaning – whether symbolic or practical – over the millennia.

The basic mistake was undoubtedly that the influence of the philosophers led people into misunderstanding "nature" as a concept. In reality, it is something else. Norbert Elias called this word a "symbol that represents a synthesis on a very high level"[42] – a synthesis of long collective experience and reflection; an abstraction, to be sure, but one that time and again takes on concrete form and proves its worth as a useful guideline. It is in this direction that we are likely to find the answer to the mystery. How could one briefly describe the stock of experiences to which "nature" alludes? It is certainly an experience that our own well-being is interconnected in many different ways with the flourishing of the flora and fauna, with the purity and inexhaustibility of bubbling springs, and an inkling that all of this is subject to rules that one must not violate arbitrarily. The effectiveness of the ideal of nature is by no means always tied to the *concept* of nature. In general, most humans adapted to the natural conditions on a daily basis without having much to say about it.

There is probably a simple reason why the circle of ideas tied to nature has repeatedly proved useful, indeed vital: humans are biological organisms and are subject to the same laws as the other organisms they are reliant on to live. A human, too, dehydrates without water, starves without plants and animals, withers away without light, dies out without sex. "Nature" is not merely the product of discourse, but in the final analysis springs from humanity's animal nature. Trying to argue away humanity's biological nature as the foundation of human history is as absurd as denying the indissoluble connection of the mind to the body. "Nature" repeatedly proved its vitality as a counterpole to artificial orders and constraints invented by humanity.[43] That is why "nature" points not so much at a primeval harmony – it would not have required this kind of articulation – but at very old danger zones of human existence. Environmental history broadens into a *histoire totale* of humanity when it arrives at the history of human experience with our own nature.

Since ancient times, the intense experience of nature has frequently sprung from solitude, including the solitude of twosomes. One hears the singing of birds best if one is alone and quiet. Alexander von Humboldt found an especially early and marvellous description of nature in a letter from the Cappadocian hermit Basil the Great (died 379).[44] In medieval Europe and in ancient China and India, it was often the hermits who established an especially intimate relationship to nature; sometimes vagrants did so as well. The rise of the modern love of nature is internally connected with the increasing individualization of humanity.

Does the human being as an individual have an especially direct contact to nature, or is the nature relationship always mediated through society? "Of course it is mediated by society!" answers the chorus of social scientists. But every person possesses an elementary connection with nature through the body: it is his or her sole possession, in it takes place life and survival, and it is a more compact entity than all social systems. When Max Weber, in the name of individualism, fought against the naturalism in the social sciences that turned peoples and societies into organisms, he was himself the real naturalist.[45]

Society can block the perception of natural necessities. Those who were too deeply absorbed in their usual conversations in the salons on the *Titanic* noticed too late that the ship was sinking. The more complex societies become, the more self-absorbed they are, and the greater the danger that they become incapable of reacting to natural necessities. To be sure, environmental history and social history are connected, but they do not form a harmonious whole.

But biophilia, too, if it exists, is not a reliable, environment-sustaining instinct. Where should such an instinct come from in the first place? After all, it is not human behavior as such that is harmful to the environment, only its aggregation. In other respects, too, the reason inherent in the love of nature has its limitations: among many modern people it does not even go so far as the ability to appreciate rain, without which there would be no flourishing nature. The danger of one-sidedness and monomania exists not only in environmental policy, but also in the feelings for nature.

4. TREES OR SHEEP? THE PROBLEM OF VALUE JUDGMENTS
IN ENVIRONMENTAL HISTORY

Environmental history is usually written with a critical undertone, but the criteria of the critique are usually not identified, let alone discussed. The problem of finding legitimate norms was never resolved in the past, and contemporary environmental policy has yet to find a solution. I presume this problem is being avoided because many sense that behind it lies an irresolvable dilemma. In addition, the question itself contains a lot of fuel for ideological fissures. Whether or not to allow exotic animals in national parks can be debated with the same kind of bitter intensity as immigration policy; in the controversy over whether sheep may graze in parks, the ideal of wilderness clashes head-on with the ideal of protecting traditional ways of life for humans and animals. Environmental protection often wasted a good deal of its energy in controversies, all the more so because it did not know how to discuss them reasonably.

The judgments that are made in the process influence the perspective of all of environmental history, since species transfer and the pasture have been chief factors in environmental change for millennia. Incidentally the reluctance to lay the criteria of judgment on the table probably also stems from the fact that in matters of the environment, existential necessities are often intermingled with questions of personal taste: for instance, questions about the global atmosphere with those about urban green spaces. Today, people often simply regard as "ecologically valuable" what has become rare – even if it is the "heavy metal fields" on the old slag dumps of mining operations. In this regard, environmental protection is following the laws of the market. The neglected grassland poor in nutrients, which drew little attention even from environmentalists until the 1970s, is today sacred ground for environmental protection because it has become so rare and is home to rare flowers. In the era of overfertilization, nature lovers are discovering the charms of degraded soils and their special species–richness.

We have known for quite some time from the study of ecology that one must not think of "nature" as a stable organic unit in a state of constant harmony, but that nature changes continuously even without human help – not only in geologic, but also in historical, time. What this means for the problem of ecological value judgments has still not been clarified. Rolf Peter Sieferle has used this insight to argue that we should dispense with value judgments altogether, and that the supposed "destruction of nature" should be registered merely as the "transition from one state of order to another."[46] It is certainly true that an environmental historian should not rush into making value judgments. All of environmental history is not a struggle between good and evil. If one notes that swamps with their mosquitoes were for centuries the best protection of the tropics against the white intruders, there is no need, beyond this statement, to take a stand either for or against the mosquitoes. That is simply the way it was. On the other hand: even if the extinction of species is something entirely normal in the history of the earth, we are acting in a perfectly sensible manner if we do whatever we can to postpone our own extinction just a little, especially since extinction is often preceded by a long and unpleasant phase of decline. In the final analysis, only this goal offers a basis for value judgments. As long as one argues only with "nature for its own sake," with the preservation of the "balance of nature" and of biological diversity, one can – if one wants to – create an enormous confusion of values. There is any number of stories of how human interference in nature harmed certain species but gave others a chance to flourish. Clear imperatives arise – if at all – only from the interest in the survival of humanity under humane and decent conditions in specific historical situations.

Now and then one encounters a type of ecological interpretation of history which, by invoking environmental constraints, proclaims a revaluation of all values and relativizes not only technical progress, but human progress as well. Since the 1970s, eco-anthropologists have been seriously discussing the ecological justification of cannibalism, whether among the Aztecs in Mexico or the Papuas of New Guinea.[47] Cynicism sometimes erupts among environmental historians, probably as a reaction against the usual moral correctness. John Opie mentioned Jonathan Swift's *Modest Proposal* of 1729, which proposed that London's problem of poverty and overpopulation be solved by serving the babies of the poor as food at the tables of the rich, as an early idea of "environmental management." An "ecological history" of India turns the caste system into a model of "conservation from below": the fact that each caste had its special ecological niche, we are told, prevented a competitive exploitation and overuse of resources.[48] Whether cannibalism or the caste system: the claim that either one was a optimal form of resource management is not compelling in its logic. It is logical at best on the assumption that those cultures had no other strategies available to them, and that assumption still needs to be proved.

The environmental historian in search of concrete criteria for value judgments might hope that the *forest* is most likely to offer solid ground. Those who approach the subject from the perspective of the history of the forest have a tendency to hand out grades everywhere depending on how the forest is being treated. There are undoubtedly good – and not only romantic – reasons for this: one merely needs to recall the importance of the forest for the water cycle and soil protection. It is not without reason that the high forest, which demands action guided by the long term, is considered an indicator of the extent to which a society is capable of making provisions for the future. The Swiss writer and poet Gottfried Keller said: "Ein Forst zeigt wie ein blanker Schild / der Gemeinde Ebenbild" (A forest, like a polished shield, is / the community's mirror).[49] In many regions of the world, the destruction of forests triggers disastrous chain reactions: from this perspective it is by and large possible to justify seeing forest preservation as the heart of environmental protection.

Beginning in the nineteenth century, reforestation was regarded as a categorical imperative not only by foresters, but also by many other lovers of nature. No matter what the local conditions, the trees that were used, and the cost: reforestation was always good. Today, when a country wants to demonstrate that it is doing something for environmental protection, a public tree-planting action is an especially popular choice, even when these trees have little chance of surviving and flourishing. This, too, is a prime example of just how much humans beings tend toward simple maxims in practice. The discovery in the nineteenth century that the eucalyptus tree, a native of Australia, also thrives in all kinds of other environments, that it grows rapidly and is hardy against pests, sparked a global eucalyptus boom. The botanist John Crumbie Brown, one of the founders of conservation in South Africa, "used Darwinian arguments in his campaign for the introduction of the fittest, all-conquering eucalyptus." Portugal established eucalyptus plantations as early as 1850, and they are today among the oldest in Europe. As late as 1986, when Portugal and Spain joined the European Union, both countries experienced another eucalyptus mania funded by EU subsidies. Since the eucalyptus uses enormous quantities of water, it was planted in swampy areas to dessicate them, though in drier regions it was propagated with the standard argument that the trees retained the water in the soil. In reality, in dry regions the eucalyptus deprives other plants of water. As a result, virtual "eucalyptus wars" took place in recent years in Portugal and Spain, when the police moved against farmers who were destroying seedlings. Since eucalyptus leaves are slow to rot and suffocate plant growth around them, one Indian environmental journalist has described the eucalyptus as an "ecological terrorist."[50]

When it comes to the question of *which* forest should be preserved, one runs into fundamental conflicts in the past as well as today. Is the forest composed only of trees, or does it also live through its wildlife? On this point, in particular, the opinions and emotions of foresters and forest lovers are deeply divided. Equally burdened by old battles between foresters and peasants is the issue of forest pasture. The historian should not automatically take the side of the foresters. Especially former pasture forests enchant nature lovers today. The supposed "primeval forests" that still exist in Germany are usually former pasture woodlands; as late as the nineteenth century, the "primeval forest" (*Urwald*) at the Sababurg in the Solling forest was tended by cattle. The Windehäuser Woods near Nordhausen, an old peasant coppice in which nearly every type of German deciduous tree is found, is considered the *locus classicus* of Thuringian floristics. Until the nineteenth century, the peasant economy tended to increase "biodiversity." "Given equally favourable growing conditions," the ecologist Josef H. Reicholf has remarked, "the plant that is moderately pruned or nibbled by animals will bloom more vigorously than one that is left to grow entirely unharmed."[51]

Often, soil protection was all too simply equated with *tree protection* and reforestation, even though the planting of trees does not promote soil protection under all conditions. Some claim that the Mediterranean *garrigue* with its scrub heath is much better than the forest at retaining the soil in the mountainous region.[52] Does the ideal nature indeed consist of forest always and everywhere? Must we resent the goat for promoting the transformation of the forest in the Mediterranean region into *maquis* and *garrigue*? Many forest trees, whether beech or spruce, are decidedly intolerant and prevent the growth of other species in their environment. As Marvin Harris has noted, the advance of the forests after the end of the last ice age was an "ecological catastrophe" for many animals that lost their grazing lands. Others argue that, in many regions, the megafauna prevented dense forest from arising in the first place. According to this "megaherbivores theory," the open pasture landscape is primeval and was not created only under the influence of humans. This theory about the prehistoric landscape is well suited to mediating a typical quarrel among conservationists: the controversy over whether national parks should be left entirely to their own devices to allow a dense forest to grow, or whether the landscape should be kept open through pasturing.

An environmental historian would have every reason to appreciate not only forests but also meadows, which have so far been sorely neglected by historical scholarship. Meadows have a greater species variety than many forests; moreover, they were and are very important as a human-animal living space. As Braudel has written, in early modern France meadows could be worth ten times as much as arable land; in fact, in Thuringia in 1335 we hear of prices for meadows that were a hundred times higher![53]

In 1984 the Alpine geographer Werner Bätzing wrestled with the dilemma of value judgments in environmental history. He was puzzled – and for good reason – that with all the complaints about the exploitation of nature by humans, the alternative of a "nonexploitive relationship between humanity and nature" often remained "rather pale and abstract." (One might add: at least in Europe, which did not have the Native American alternative.) The often-quoted phrase "peace with nature," so Bätzing, was "at this time more a cipher than the articulation of substantive content."[54] Nothing much has changed since then; if anything, the exotic alternative of the original and natural peoples has become even more questionable. For his part, Bätzing offers a real historical alternative in the case of the Alps: Alpine farming (*Almwirtschaft*). It is not primeval and could develop fully only in more recent times, when trade had progressed to the point where mountain farmers were able to give up farming and shift entirely to dairying. Mountain pastures protect the soil better than does farming on the steep slopes. The division of labor between regions can lead to a better adaptation to environmental conditions.

There are extreme differences when it comes to the ecology of pasture farming, depending on geomorphological conditions, how it is regulated, and the types of pasture animals that are used. Goats have the worst reputation. For many forest people they are virtually the incarnation of evil – they have been called the "razor of the forest." In Europe during the Middle Ages we already find the maxim that goats must not be allowed into the forest, even though this did in fact happen. In 1908 a hydrological engineer who had been sent to Cyprus called the goat an even greater curse for the island than locusts. In 1992 the farmers of northern Cyprus were forced to sell all goats grazing in the mountains to the state, which slaughtered them.[55]

But even in the case of goats one hesitates to pronounce apodictic condemnations if one hikes through the mountains of Cyprus and sees on the one side the monotony of ailing pine forests, and on the other side the merry eyes and liveliness of the goats. Why should one be opposed to goats on principle? Why can't they embody nature, why must it always be trees, and only trees? As the literature shows, the verdict on the goat has always been an emotional topic where fundamental positions collide. As early as 1945, we hear reports from within circles of the British colonial administration of a "new cult of the goat" as a reaction against the image of the goat as the enemy. A leading member of the FAO spoke in 1970 of "irrational condemnation" if the goat was held solely responsible for soil erosion, and assured his readers that the people of the Peloponnesus defended the goat not out of stupidity, but because they knew it was useful and harmless. The "poor man's cow" was often protected for sociopolitical reasons against forestry administrations that were fixated on exportable building timber. Therefore the goat was one of the winners of the French Revolution of 1789, at least during the Jacobin phase. One study about the "Place of the Goat in Global Agriculture" praised the animal as a heroic defender of pasture landscapes against the regeneration of the forest. Even modern environmentalists learned to love the goat once they realized that protecting traditional heath landscapes against shrubbing could not be done with sheep alone, but required the help of goats. Shepherds, however, complain that goats corrupt the entire sheep herd along with the sheepdogs because they do not obey.

The verdict one renders on the goat is to a certain extent a question of interests, not ecology. Where the goat has been grazing for millennia – in some parts of the Near East, the goat has been present for eight thousand years – the goat pasture must possess a kind of ecological stability. And if the goat is particularly well adapted to barren soils and is therefore common there, it does not mean that the goat made the soil that way. One English prehistorian has dismissed the blame that has been heaped on the goat: "The evidence that the goat has browsed its way over the last ten millennia through a lush and fertile Eden is far from impressive."

Nonetheless, there is no denying that this omnivore, which climbs trees and nibbles on them, damages the vegetation cover in ecologically fragile areas and can destroy the young growth of trees in clear-cut areas. Here, too, it all depends on the limits that are imposed on the number of animals and their grazing range. One particular problem is that goats have a mind of their own and are much more difficult to control than cows and sheep. Only modern wire fences offer a perfect solution to the problem of control.[56]

An animal actor of far greater significance to global environmental history than the goat – perhaps the most important animal species as such – is the *sheep*. Today it is easy to forget that it was once highly important also to the German economy and landscape. As late as 1860, the Prussian statistician Georg von Viebahn highlighted wool as Germany's strongest bastion in the textile sector vis-à-vis England and France – at that time Germany still had 28 million sheep, almost as many as there were people. "Sheep farming has always been Germany's pride," it was said at the time, as though Germany were Australia.[57] The almost complete disappearance of sheep farming must have substantially altered the German landscape since then, not only in and around the Lüneburg Heath. How should we judge this change? Should we judge it at all?

This is where opinions diverge, even among committed nature lovers. For John Muir, the founder of the Sierra Club and of the American environmental movement, the sheep was a "hoofed locust" that should be banished from Yosemite National Park.[58] At the same time in Germany, Hermann Löns, Muir's spiritual kin in his cult of nature, venerated the Lüneburg Heath as a remnant of wild nature. Here one must remember that Muir encountered the sheep in the form of gigantic herds that were driven through the landscape in accordance with the profit principle, whereas Löns encountered heath sheep farming as an ancient way of life and was writing at a time when German sheep rearing was already in decline.

Reference to the Lüneberg Heath has become a standard argument in Germany to unmask the illusions of conventional environmental protection. George Sperber, from the perspective of a forester, points to the paradox that "a last piece of

Germany's most maltreated woodland landscape, the Lüneberg Heath, became the first 'nature park.'" Another writer went so far as to call the heath a "catastrophic landscape" from an ecological perspective. Today, however, we know from soil archaeology that the heath in that part of Germany has a 3,000-year tradition. Must one see the heath mixed with juniper as a maltreated forest rather than as a unique historical nature of great species diversity? The heath has its own biological communities, as, for example, the one including sheep, blossoms, and bees, which also enrich the human way of life; after all, humans need not only wood, but also honey. Did the sheep ruin the soil? As late as 1904, the botanist Paul Graebner expressed doubts whether the heath "can ever be suited to carrying a formation that deserves the name forest." Today, however, after the end of sheep farming, it has become very difficult to keep old heaths from being reclaimed by the forest. At times it would appear that people have forgotten the banal fact that sheep not only eat, but simultaneously fertilize the soil on which they graze. Even in the sixteenth century the manure from sheep pens was highly sought after, and right into our time, the saying that sheep have "golden hooves" means something in agriculture. In more recent times, sheep were sometimes driven into the woods in an effort to improve the forest soil.[59]

Possible detrimental effects from sheep farming – damage to useful plants, especially on hillside locations – have long been known and could be prevented without difficulty, if one wanted to. Herds of sheep can be much more readily contained by dogs than herds of goats. Peasants would cast a very suspicious eye on the wandering sheep herds to see if they were doing any damage, and sometimes peasants and shepherds came to blows.[60] Whether or not sheep farming created a sustainable combination together with farming and silviculture depended on social conditions. Where the owners of enormous sheep herds did not have to show any consideration, as in early modern Spain or Mexico, sheep pasture left behind correspondingly destructive traces in the landscape. But here, too, sweeping negative judgments are uncalled for. At a symposium on forest history in Paris in 2000 (*Forêts et troupeaux*), it was said that after centuries of unanimous condemnation of forest pasture by foresters, the pasture economy had been "completely rehabilitated" in contemporary environmental protection.[61]

One absolute measure for assessing a culture in economic-ecological terms is whether it guaranteed the subsistence of its population on a sustainable basis. To do that, a culture must possess reserves, which is one of the reasons why forests deserve special consideration. Where it gets complicated is when one demands that the environment should also be "socially compatible" by guaranteeing not merely naked survival, but the continuation of culture and society. It is here, especially, that "nature" turns into a norm grounded in culture and history.

In 1992 Rudolf zur Lippe argued that we should abolish the term "nature," since it was merely a "bag for unprocessed history."[62] But where a historian finds a "bag of unprocessed history," he responds with curiosity rather than disdain. If it turns out that nature does not exist as such, but only as a historical phenomenon, it may lose its charm for the intellectual who is looking for ahistorical structure – but for the historian this is precisely where the process of understanding begins. For a historian, to say that something has "become historical" does not mean that it has become "random." If people of a particular period perceive their own nature and the nature around them in a particular way, that does not mean that this type of perception is random and arbitrary. Constructs of nature will endure only if they contain useful experiences. Where pure constructivism repeatedly shifts the nature discussion in an ahistorical setting into a dead end, that is where the historian starts to think about historicized nature.

However, it is peculiar that environmental history has so far failed to seize the opportunity that is contained in the historicization of ecology. After all, it is only this new ecology that offers the possibility of conceiving of the history of the nature-humanity relationship not only as a gloomy, never-ending process of destruction, but as a suspenseful mixture of destructive and creative processes.

The anthropologist Colin M. Turnbull, who became known through his affectionate account of the cheerful forest culture of the Mbuti Pygmies (1961), described, by way of contrast, the physical and emotional misery of the Ik in northern Uganda: resettled from the Kidepo National Park, they were forced to trade in their roaming lifestyle as hunters for a settled way of life in a barren environment. The loss of their accustomed environment and way of life robbed them of any sense of friendliness, indeed of pleasurable sex.[63] An especially famous counterexample from European history for the planned preservation of an environment that, while difficult, was inextricably interwoven with self-identity is Venice. The city maintained its lagoon and its fragile island location with considerable effort, even though it would have been technically possible to drain large sections of the lagoon and convert them into fields and pastures; in fact, such an environmental correction would have offered a number of advantages. The Venetian archives are an overflowing treasure trove for a historical environmental awareness that reaches back into the Middle Ages.

German history – and it is not alone – offers a comparable example: it occurred when the Germans preserved their forests and restored them to a better state at the very time when the "age of wood" was coming to an end and wood was needed less and less as a source of energy. Wilhelm Heinrich Riehl uttered the warning: "Chop down the forest and you will smash the historical, civic [*bürgerliche*] society."[64] What he had in mind was evidently the burgher class in the sense of the old estates. Is this nothing more than an egregious lapse of archaicizing social romanticism? Yet his warning also had a very real purpose: forests offered social niches for the rural underclasses, and as such they dampened unrest and promoted the peaceful coexistence of the social estates. In addition, they offered space shielded from prying eyes to a burgher class that otherwise stood under excessive surveillance, and a quiet refuge from the growing stress of industrial civilization. Riehl was probably right that the social utility of forests was greater at his time than ever before, even as their economic significance was in decline.

Evidently "wild" nature is not a supratemporal value, but acquires its charm – and there is a certain logic in this – only in a society that has overcultivated wide swathes of its environment. Only a social stratum that hardly knows hunger any more has an eye for the aesthetic of the wasteland, the panorama of rocky crags. From that perspective it is questionable, however, to expect developing countries to exhibit the same appreciation for wilderness.

The biologist Jacob von Uexküll (1864–1944), who gave what was until then the sociological concept of "environment" (*Umwelt*) its modern, ecological meaning, took great pains to emphasize – very much in contrast to "hard" ecosystem theories – that every living thing has its own environment. Modern ecology does not know what to do with this concept of environment, but it is well suited to environmental history. To understand the sources correctly, it is important to remember that the forest looks different to the forester than it does to the peasant, the shepherd, and the city-dweller in search of rest and relaxation. One could conclude from this that it would be best to leave each cultural microcosm its ecological niche, in such a way that the greatest possible number of those living there feel comfortable in it. If it is not only the interests of industry that come into play along rivers, but also those of fishermen, boatmen, bathing children, meadow irrigation, and urban water supply, we could assume that the diversity of interests will guarantee a "good" environment. And what is true for a river is similarly true for the world as a whole. That environment is "good" that makes possible many small worlds, worlds that are as much psychological as ecological entities. "Environmental science [*Umweltlehre*] is a kind of externalized psychology [*Seelenkunde*]," Uexküll wrote.[65] Environmental history is also a history of mentalities – the mentalities that become humanity's second nature.

In this regard, environmental history can be grounded in a philosophy of the ecological niche: the niche created by nature, but also the niche created by humans. It is ecological niches that ensure the diversity of nature, but also of human culture and of happiness. This is the foundation of the nature philosophies of the garden, the hedge, the dry stonewall. There is good reason why the human love of nature often found its highest bliss in gardening.

Environmental history, however, revolves not around "ought," but first and foremost around "is." That is why it should not become too moralistic – not an endless confession of sins. Especially if one takes nature seriously as a historical actor, one must be prepared for unpredictable causal chains. Since nature is not anthropomorphic, the penetration of humans into it does not invariably amount to an injury that draws "nature's revenge." Even the enormous emissions of carbon and nitrogen in the industrial age have had not only negative effects on plant growth; rather, they have counteracted a centuries-old nitrogen depletion of the forest soil.[66] On the other hand, climate change unrelated to human activity *can* make history. Always injecting morality into environmental history can lead us astray and prevent an unbiased observation of unexpected developments. One spoils the potential of environmental history if one uses it solely to justify current environmental policies. Rather, the inner kinship between history and ecology lies in the fact that both disciplines train their practitioners to look beyond today at complex processes that are not discernible in a snapshot. And yet, environmental history would disavow its vital impulse were it to foreswear any and all interest in politics; but more about that later.

5. ECOLOGY AS HISTORICAL EXPLANATION: FROM THE COLLAPSE OF MAYAN CULTURE TO THE GREAT IRISH FAMINE

For environmental history to become grand history it must not only deal with the ecological *consequences* of human activity, but also introduce ecology as an *explanation* for historical processes: only then will nature become a historical actor, as it were. However, if one resorts too hastily to ecological explanations, one runs the risk of falling into all kinds of traps. In some scholarly circles, ecological explanations have been fashionable for some time now: without further ado, the environment is granted the status of a causal explanation, as though it were something clearly defined and given. This kind of ecological determinism appears so readily because it is often merely a new version of the old economic or geographic determinism, in the face of which Georges Bertrand called on environmental history to perform an "exorcism." "Ecological fallacy" became a standard concept in sociology in the 1950s, and it referred to the practice of making regional, secondary phenomena into primary causes. In 1969 the sociologist Erwin Scheuch expressed the view that a substantial part of what was presumed to be empirical knowledge in sociology was based on such "ecological fallacies."[67]

One must also ask with what right ecological circumstances are elevated into the final cause. From Istria to India, goats, which eat young growth, are regarded as the cause behind the destruction of vegetation and soil in the mountains. But goats eat only the young shoots to which they are given access. The great wandering herds of sheep are not natural but organized events. Anders Hjort, in a critical review of ecological models to explain the decline of the African pasture economy, has emphasized that ecology can become ideology, whereas in reality it has "little explanatory value" once it is disconnected from the economic, political, and social context.[68] If the cause of environmental problems is readily apparent to those concerned, and their solution is merely a question of social organization, then the factor "environment" makes sense only as a component of a historical explanation that is social and political.

In the current clashes over environmental policy, explanations are usually linked with the assigning of blame. In history, however, the question of blame should be initially set aside. If one discovers that broad regions of the Mediterranean and the Middle East have fallen behind as a result of self-caused processes of desertification, in many cases it is hardly possible to determine when and where there existed decision-making situations in which certain actors could have stopped this decline, and which social causes prevented a sustainable relationship with the environment. Because of this kind of ignorance, ecology remains a final ground of historical events.

Social and cultural history can also end up leading to ecological explanations, namely, if it makes clear a society's limited ability to act, for example when it comes to birth control, forest protection, or the preservation of soil fertility. It is precisely insight into the rigidity of society that moves the inherent power of natural circumstances that much more sharply into focus.

Some eco-anthropologists have discovered the Mormons as a modern exemplar of an ecologically conditioned religious community, especially since they invite monocausal ecological explanations by their isolated life in the desert of Utah. An affinity evidently existed between the strict communal organization of the Mormons and the demands of irrigation. More so than anywhere else in the American West, water distribution among the Mormons was regulated in such a way that it provided a solid foundation for a broad stratum of small and medium-size farmers. We can assume that the vital necessity of having a final authority in conflicts over water contributed to the powerful position of the Mormon Church.

But the religion of the Mormons was not born in the desert; and, needless to say, the ecological conditions of the desert do no automatically produce these kinds of religious communities. At least these conditions seem to have stabilized Mormonism. As William Abruzzi found, its stability also rests on a certain diversity within its ecological basis – and above all on the colossal energy of this community. In the long run, the Mormons did not remain an island unto themselves: from their circles came the initiators of the irrigation systems of the American West, which are today seen by many as the height of economic-ecological folly.[69] Environmental history is not exhausted by a one-time causality.

The factor "ecology" has always been especially impressive in connection with catastrophe theories, whether today or in the past. An especially long tradition attaches to the ecological explanation when it comes to interpreting the decline of Mayan culture. Decades before ecology became fashionable, some scholars were speculating that the Mayans had caused their downfall by torching the forests and subsequently overusing and destroying the fragile tropical soil. This, then, was a countertheory to the notion that the ancient American cultures had lived in a state of harmony with nature. The ecological explanation was undoubtedly boosted by the fact that Mayan script was undecipherable until the 1970s, and all we had before our eyes was the puzzling picture of the silent remnants of a high culture in the tropical forest.

Was this ecological disaster – if it did take place – an unavoidable fate, an unstoppable vicious circle? Theoretically speaking the answer is: not necessarily. At a colloquium on the "Maya Collapse" (1973), two anthropologists drew the conclusion that an expansion of food supply would certainly have been possible, and that Maya civilization collapsed in the final analysis from the elite's lack of innovative capabilities. This is the typical claim of those who believe in the ever-present possibility of innovation and effective crisis management. But to what extent did the Maya, such as they were, have a realistic chance? If that question could be answered at all, it had to await the decipherment of Mayan texts. And in fact, shortly after their decipherment there arose the thesis that the Maya's fatalistic-cyclical sense of history prevented vigorous crisis strategies.[70] The catastrophe came because a catastrophe was expected – a warning to contemporary fatalism about ecological catastrophe?

Recent work in the field has confirmed the sensationally high population density in the core regions of the Maya and the subsequent, abrupt demographic collapse without any apparent cause; it has also reinforced indications of a connection between population pressure and soil erosion. Others have countered that Maya culture lasted for well over a thousand years.[71] But that observation may well contain the answer to the puzzle: precisely because the Maya were so successful for so long with their environmental management (contemporary Mexican environmentalists have even elevated them into ecological exemplars!), they were all the more incapable of responding when their venerable and proven methods failed. It is hard to shake off the concern that modern industrial civilization may suffer a similar fate.

The geographer Herbert Wilhelmy, in an extensive study, sought to refute the thesis of the ecological suicide of the Maya by laying out in detail the elements of ecological stability that were contained partly in natural and partly in cultural conditions. It is an instructive opus, reminding the environmental historian how important it is to immerse oneself deeply in the study of the soil and the peculiarities of soil history for every region, and that one must gain a thorough understanding of a culture's functioning, including its ecological conditions, before one starts to talk about crises. But Wilhelmy retains this scenario: the Maya engaged mostly in slash-and-burn agriculture, whereby the population density of several core areas in the end exceeded the density of all other slash-and-burn regions of the world to a worrisome degree. Moreover, the dominant cultivation was that of maize, which is hard on the soil (even if traditional strains of maize were not as hard as the products of modern selective breeding), and the Maya never arrived at a developed fertilizer economy nor at erosion-preventing terraced cultivation on a larger scale. The hypothesis that "the Maya found themselves in a kind of ecological trap of their own making," while admittedly old-fashioned, is still more plausible than competing theories;[72] whether there will ever be a definitive explanation is doubtful.

The ecological argumentation gets especially tricky when it comes to explaining famines that affected only the lower classes and did not overlap with a crisis of an entire civilization. Does ecology in this case function as an antisocial sleight-of-hand by diverting attention away from the problem of distribution and the blame that belongs to structures of social power? Probably the best documented, extreme example is the "Great Hunger," the massive Irish famine between 1845 and 1850. The immediate cause is known: the potato blight, combined with an almost complete dependence of the poor on the potato. But why was there this dependence?

The demographic cause behind the famine is clear: between 1780 and 1840, Ireland's population grew by more than 170 percent. This was an enormous rate of growth by preindustrial standards, unparalleled in Europe and the kind of growth that only mighty metropolises, at most, could absorb without harm. The basis of this population explosion was the potato, which grew especially well in Ireland. It had a far greater nutritional value than grain grown on the same acreage of land, and it boosted both the fertility of women and the enthusiasm of men to have children, for children were useful in harvesting potatoes. In other regions, as well, one can observe "Irelandization": a combination of potato farming and population explosion.[73] The sudden improvement in the food supply led to growth whose limits were initially not recognized, and – since the potato does not compel the farmer to practice crop rotation – to a monoculture whose risks were also hidden for some time: in this respect, there is something paradigmatic about Ireland's fate.

Or was it possible to recognize from the outset that Ireland's path bore a high risk? Traditional peasant polyculture had something of an antirisk strategy about it; one did not put all one's eggs in *one* basket. In the eighteenth century it was above all agrarian reformers like Duhamel du Monceau and Arthur Young who heaped praise on the Irish for extracting the maximum nutritional value from the soil with their potato monoculture, while Malthus was already clear-sighted enough to realize that it is dangerous to practice agriculture without ecological reserves.[74] Sometimes well-intentioned reformers do more harm than a pessimistic skeptic.

Liebig saw in the rapid spread of the potato, which ploughed through the soil "like a pig" in search of remaining nutrients, the consequence of a preceding exhaustion of the soils. If he was right, the Irish famine would be the result of a fatal ecological decline that had already been going on for some time. Arthur Young, on the other hand, who traveled in Ireland between 1776 and 1779, emphasized that one should not be misled by the pitiable appearance of Irish agriculture, for the soil was "rich and fertile." For centuries, and more intensively as the population grew, the Irish fertilized the plowland with chalk-containing sea sand; unlike in the case of northern German plaggen fertilization, no soil is destroyed in the process. Other than that, however, it would appear that practices of soil improvement were hardly customary in Irish agriculture, which means that there is probably some truth to Liebig's thesis. At the heart of the traditional Irish way of life stood pasture farming, not agriculture; in the age of the potato, as well, the small farmers did not achieve a balance between agriculture and fertilizer-producing livestock. To that extent the Irish misery could be understood as the fiasco of an intensive agriculture without a corresponding tradition, a subsistence economy on a very small scale without the requisite ecological diversity.[75]

In Germany, poor small farmers fed their animals from the forest in times of need. Ireland, however, had lost its forests by that time, and with them an important social niche. In the nineteenth century, Ireland was among the European countries with the poorest forest coverage. That was a fairly recent development, for as late as 1728 Irish oaks were prized for their shipbuilding qualities. But neither the English nor the Irish paid much attention back then to preserving the forests; still today we hear complaints in Ireland that the country lacks a "forest awareness." Around 1800 the shortage of wood among the rural poor was in many places so acute that hedges had no chance to grow: this, too, was an ecologically detrimental effect of deforestation.[76]

To be sure, warnings against ecological determinism in explaining history are well taken. But it is possible to go too far in the other direction. If "explanation" in history (as elsewhere) means not merely deriving one event from another, but deducing historical processes from relatively permanent circumstances using logic that can be generalized, ecological patterns of explanation do not fare badly in many cases. Much the same is true if "explanation" means deduction from a level of causation beyond which historical empiricism cannot reach. Sometimes, interregional comparisons will reveal deductions based on social history to be pseudo-explanations. For example, while Dennis Mack Smith links the ecological decline of Sicily to sharecropping,[77] the stable polycultures of *mezzadria* in Tuscany or *métayage* in French regions show that the effect of sharecropping on the soil is not invariably destructive. However, often it is the paralysis of human action that makes nature into a determining factor.

Why did China, for thousands of years the largest and most stable culture of the world, fall behind Europe in the modern period? To answer this question, even Jared Diamond, who otherwise tends toward a universal-historical, ecological determinism, descends to the microlevel of political intrigue: in the fifteenth century, so we are told, opponents of the eunuchs who had until then dominated the imperial court brought shipbuilding to a halt and got China to turn its back on the sea; as a result, China entered into an inexorable decline against Europe. Although many European princes at the time also shrank from the risks of the ocean, thanks to the multitude of competing powers Columbus eventually found his backers. But is the struggle of political powers really such a productive principle in history? Was it in fact the absence of political rivals rather than a self-caused degradation of the environment that contributed its share to China's decline? Many scholars have argued that Chinese bureaucracy declined in the eighteenth and nineteenth centuries: Did it actually happen, or was the increasing impoverization of broad masses the result of overpopulation and the degradation of the soil? Institutional or ecological crisis: where is the heart of the matter?[78] This is one of the most exciting questions in environmental history, one that we shall be revisiting repeatedly.

6. TERRA INCOGNITA: ENVIRONMENTAL HISTORY AS SECRET HISTORY OR THE HISTORY OF THE OBVIOUS?

Honesty compels one to admit that there is a good deal in environmental history that one does not know or can recognize only faintly. Especially for antiquity or the premodern history of non-European regions, environmental history seems to consist of the art of getting around the deplorable reality that we have only a handful of sources; to make matters worse, it is unclear how certain we can be about what they tell us. To be sure, the scholarly literature is growing by leaps and bounds, but one can plow through ever-growing mountains of literature without finding solid ground. Anyone who handles the scholarly literature and sources critically must pass through a phase of agnosticism. Although Lynn White created the impression, in his programmatic essay of 1966, that he knew the "historical roots of our ecologic crisis," he was jumping back and forth between modern mass consumerism and the introduction of the heavy plow in the Early Middle Ages, between Bacon's "knowledge is power" and the Old Testament injunction "Be fruitful and increase, fill the earth and subdue it."[79] This is, in fact, a shortcoming of many surveys of environmental history: they gloss over immense gaps in our knowledge. The historical study of the environment will only make progress, however, if it admits to the open questions and articulates them with greater precision.

Fundamental questions of environmental history, in particular, are especially murky across broad stretches of time. That is true above all for the greatest environmental problem of humanity for most of history, namely the degradation of the soil. This is still a treacherous problem today, since the soil – even more so than water and the atmosphere – represents a sinkhole where harmful substances accumulate over very long periods. To some extent the unsatisfactory source material and scholarly literature pertaining to the past is the result of the fact that the maintenance of the soil was usually the business of those who worked it, and not of official agencies that produced written sources and research findings. But the problems of the soil are inherently intricate and complicated in and of themselves, if one considers the variety of soils and the great importance of the myriads of microorganisms they contain. "A handful of humus garden soil contains as many organisms as there are humans beings on the earth today!" No wonder that the soil was dirty matter for theoreticians. "Every soil has its own history – none is like another." As Rachel Carson observed in 1962: "There are few studies more fascinating, and at the same time more neglected, than those of the teeming populations that exist in the dark realms of the soil." A more recent historical study of the soil still emphasized the "cryptic character of the soil."[80]

Yet this very opacity is an important fact that allowed the soil to become a latent crisis zone that could never be entirely mastered. That is true of both plowland and woodland. The great forestry reforms of the eighteenth and nineteenth centuries still took place without much knowledge of forest soil; August Bernhardt was complaining as late as 1875 that "no other branch of the study of nature has been so sorely neglected until now."[81] For centuries and decades, humans around the globe had been using forest foliage as animal fodder, and forest reformers often fought against this practice of pruning. But to what extent the removal of leaves leads to an impoverishment of forest soils has been studied more closely only in recent times. There are now nature enthusiasts who are delighted by the sight of pruned trees, and who like to demonstrate that skillful pruning increases the vitality of trees.[82]

A relatively clear-cut process is erosion; under the soil conditions of Central and Western Europe, however, it could progress for a long time without notice. The issue is more complicated when it comes to desertification. Here, too, problems of definition get mixed up with those of empirical corroboration in the past. The United Nations Conference on Desertification (UNCOD), which met in Nairobi in 1977 with the catastrophic famine in the Sahel (1969–73) still fresh on everyone's mind and which was intended to provide practical impulses, placed human effects at the center of its conceptual definition. However, to what extent we were dealing with new or age-old forms of impact remains an open question; in the Sahara, some estimates put the human impact as far back as 18,000 years, others push it back 600,000 years! Still, there is no doubt that natural factors play a crucial role in desert formation. The question what part humans have played in the creation of the Sahara has not been definitely answered to this day, in spite of extensive literature on the topic. Moreover, the various theses are subject to the ebb and flow of political currents: when the Italians ruled Libya, the ancient Romans were the great model of how to make the desert fruitful; later, however, the Romans were blamed for desertification processes. The British archaeologist R. W. Dennell commented with a note of resignation that the evidence about land use during the last two millennia is so poor "that it can be used to support any claim."[83] And that is even truer, of course, for the last 20,000 or 200,000 years.

For many environmental historians the most uncomfortable unknown is the climate factor. To anyone who seeks a moral and a "message" in environmental history, it is a disruptive factor devoid of meaning, at least for most of history, when human influence on macroclimate can be ruled out. Historical climate research has evolved into a highly specialized discipline, and it is difficult for an outsider to judge how reliable and generalizable its findings are. According to David Landes, Ellsworth Huntington, who tried to explain much of global history with his climatological determinism, gave American geography a bad name.[84] In and of itself, the influence of climate on human affairs is the oldest factor that was identified among environmental influences: after all, the influence of weather on human health and on agriculture was always palpable. Ever since we have known that climate is subject to long-term fluctuations, we have had to reckon with climate as a historical factor, though it is difficult to weight this factor in a concrete case. It is clearest at the margins of human settlement: in the high mountains, at the edge of the large deserts, and in the arctic. As Christian Pfister has shown, in Switzerland since the nineteenth century, collective relief actions in response to natural catastrophes – especially floods – "triggered thrusts of national integration," indeed, they created "a new feeling of Swissness."[85]

Pfister created for Switzerland what is to this day by far the most thorough regional climate history by an environmental historian. Still, in his recent economic and environmental history of the canton of Bern, climate is not a major theme that determines structures and long-term trends. Scholars had just come to believe that the "Little Ice Age" offered us a striking macroevent in climate history that could be held partly responsible for many of the troubles of the early modern period from Western Europe to East Asia – when new studies showed, in Pfister's summary, "that the so-called Little Ice Age was by no means a single period of temperatures below those of the twentieth century, but rather a period with cool phases that lasted decades and were interrupted by warming intervals." That offers no solid basis for a new interpretation of environmental history. The Swiss agrarian historian Andreas Ineichen concluded, for the canton of Lucerne, that the peasants were already able in the sixteenth and seventeenth centuries to compensate for a cooling climate through improved irrigation. H. H. Lamb, the founder of the first Institute for Historical Climate Research, believed that he could make a lot of clear-cut statements about the "influence of weather on the course of history"; but occasionally he did admit that humans were "without a doubt" able to adapt to the lower temperatures of the Little Ice Age.[86] Over the short term, farmers were often helpless in the face of the vagaries of climate; over the long term, though, the crucial factor was not the weather, but the ability of rural society to respond to it. For example, beginning in pre-Christian times, European peasants responded to the cooling climate by stepping up the cultivation of rye and oats, which were also high-quality grains.[87]

For some time now it has been argued that the "Little Ice Age" caused the persecution of the witches, since the weather magic of witches was held responsible for the deteriorating climate. However, we also find evidence that the rise in lumber prices caused by the cooling climate put an end to witch burnings. Climate fluctuations as such do not trigger specific causalities in history.

Even where we find environmental information in the past, it is often scattered and random. To write environmental history, one needs theoretical models. This follows from the simple fact that when it comes to the history of the real relationship of humans to their environment, everyday behaviors and habits are far more important than large-scale and governmental actions. As a rule, however, everyday behavior patterns are not perfectly discernible in the sources; instead, a good deal must be reconstructed. In doing so one runs the risk of sliding off into speculative constructs and failing to distinguish them clearly from the empirical findings. In this context it is helpful to remind oneself that in many cases very different ideal-type constructs of the human–nature relationship are conceivable in purely theoretical terms. Given the ecological conditions of the steppe, one can construct nomadic societies that live in harmony with their environment, but also those that destroy it through an increase in the number of humans and animals and through overpasturing. Nor do the succession doctrines of botany yield laws that apply invariably at all times: sometimes, shifting cultivation produces a grassland steppe, while in other cases it alternates with reforestation. Still, the number of possibilities is usually limited, which is why attempts to reconstruct environmental developments from scattered evidence are legitimate, within limits.

What shapes the environment throughout history is not individual ideas and actions, but the persistent and large scale: in other words, the day-to-day, habitual, and institutionalized behavior by large masses of people over long periods of time. This is not something that can easily escape the historian's perception even when the sources are fragmentary and the behavior reveals itself only between the lines. Moreover, the ecological relevant effects of human actions are the long-term effects. That is one reason why environmental history recognizes in the longer span of time many things that escape a focused and singular examination.

Compared to the environmental history of older periods, the industrial age is faced with the opposite problem: at first, it seems like the history of the obvious. Sometimes, it is considered dull and boring, because the reader already knows the outcome of the story at the outset: namely, that industrial civilization advanced in the face of all concerns – over the protests of farmers, fishermen, nature protectors, and cultural pessimists. But do we really know all there is to know? What happened when and why? And what were and are the long-term effects? Here the open questions are not infrequently at the end rather than the beginning.

Many believe that history can be written best when the outcome is already known. But the historical method, of looking at the flux of historical phenomena and examining them from as many sides as possible, makes the most sense where the end is still open and one must be prepared for future surprises. Dyed-in-the-wool ecological optimists have turned the surprises and imponderables of nature into an argument against environmental worries, but this logic is anything but compelling. Leading critics of technology have confessed that what they find most disquieting is not what we know, but what we don't know; and they use primarily this ignorance to justify the categorical imperative that we must be cautious in our interactions with nature and in taking our guidance from the experiences of the past.[88] The historian, too, has no cause to deny the terras incognitas of the present and the future: what stands at the end of environmental history is not the illusion of final knowledge, but a mind open to the flux of things and to surprising experiences.

2

The Ecology of Subsistence and Tacit Knowledge: Primeval Symbioses of Humans and Nature

Max Weber opened his great work *Economy and Society* with an overview of the primeval forms of community, beginning with the house community, though this section was moved to a later place in the book in the posthumous edition.[1] He did not want the reader to understand this beginning in an evolutionary sense, with the progress of evolution invariably leading away from these communities; instead, he knew from personal experience the potent meaning that home and family still carried in the modern world. In a similar way, it makes sense to begin a global history of the environment with an overview of primeval forms of the relationship between humanity and nature. Here, too, I do not mean to suggest that some inherent law leads the historical development far beyond these forms. Rather, these forms reverberate down to the present, and it pays to reflect on their future significance. There is no linear progress in environmental history. But there are, without a doubt, profound processes of change that have marked off historical eras.

What are the eras of environmental history? Does it possess eras of its own that are distinct from the traditional epochs of world history? It would appear that there has never been a great debate on this question. Some environmental historians posit the existence of "ecological revolutions" that initiate new ages,[2] prime examples of which are the irruption of the Europeans into the New World or the transition from renewable to fossil energy sources. But the term "revolution" is derived from political history (and ultimately from astronomy) – to what extent it actually applies to events in environmental history is questionable. Whether or not the arrival of the Europeans in America or the transition to coal was a genuine "revolution" in an ecological sense – embracing all of nature – is difficult to say. When it comes to natural processes, one must also think in different categories: cycles, superimposed layers, and interconnections. "Revolutions" and turning points exist above all with respect to human problems in dealing with nature.

If one approaches environmental history as the history of environmental problems, it makes sense to delineate eras from the perspective of both the problems and the strategies for solving them, and ideally to combine the two. Sometimes, but not always, the eras that emerge overlap with those of economic history.

The structure I have chosen arises from the geographic reach of environmental problems, the level of social authority that deals with them, and the type of knowledge that is employed in the process. In the most basic state of affairs, environmental problems are usually local in nature and are resolved within the framework of the household economy and the neighborhood, and the solutions draw on an unwritten tradition of experiential knowledge. This is a time when subsistence economy is dominant, when humans produce for their own needs and the local market, when the cycle of nutrients is self-contained within local parameters. It is not possible to demarcate this era precisely; as a substrate it extends deep into later periods. Even the long-distance trade of more modern times usually rested on a broad foundation of subsistence economy; and the preservation of forests and of the fertility of the plowland still took place – if at all – within the framework of the household and village community. If higher powers asserted the need for regulation by the authorities, it does not mean that this need was real and that the regulation from above had the desired effect. The breakdown into eras should therefore not be misunderstood as demonstrating unavoidable progress: there is no law of evolutionary progress toward centralization in the history of the relationship of humanity and the environment. What keeps the history of that relationship fluid is, not least, the fact that the strategies for solving problems – which are often simultaneously strategies for preserving power – address the true problems only in part and in turn generate new problems. One prime example is nuclear energy, which was pushed forward with the argument that fossil energy resources are finite.

Perhaps the most important higher authority of that first, fundamental epoch is religion, with all its rituals and regulations governing the annual cycle. It is here that one can most readily grasp environmental notions. Incidentally, we are dealing largely with "tacit knowledge," with self-evident truths that are handed down orally: as they are committed to paper only under special circumstances, they are evident only between the lines of our historical sources. But even the "natural religions" were not in every respect effective answers to the early problems in humanity's interaction with the environment.

One must not imagine this first epoch as a self-contained time carried by a stable harmony between humanity and nature. It also included primeval experiences of a traumatic kind – of drought and cold, hunger and thirst, floods and forest fires. An alertness toward the environment is probably grounded not so much in a natural instinct as in such traumatic experiences. Again and again, times of famine made humans aware that the cushion in the food supply was small and fragile. In general, however, dealing with environmental problems was not a separate sphere of action, but an integral component of life. Women were more involved than they were in all later kinds of environmental protection: concern for the environment was directly connected to care for children and grandchildren – unlike in the late twentieth century, that connection did not have to be construed by philosophers. But there is surely a reason why humanity did not persist in that state. The environmental problems at the time were already threatening, again and again, to explode the boundaries of the primeval social cells and microcosms.

Let me raise one of the great, simple questions on which the interpretation of all of environmental history hinges: Is it correct to assume that human economic activity was, on the whole, environmentally sound whenever it took place in small, contained units and was aimed primarily at providing for oneself and the local market, not at accumulating capital and serving long-distance trade? Or is this merely a nostalgic illusion? Many modern strategists of development aid give subsistence farmers the lion's share of the blame for the destruction of forests

and soils. When it comes to this topic, we find ourselves caught in a web of funda-
mentalist positions and empirical findings that is difficult to disentangle.

To be sure, there is good reason to suspect that the predilection for subsistence
economy is really an ideological position dressed up in ecological garb. The oldest
among these positions is the moral condemnation of unbounded greed and the
philosophical preference for the kind of independence that springs from autarchy.
"Freedom is the greatest fruit of self-sufficiency," proclaims one of Epicurus's
maxims; American farmers in Jefferson's time would still have understood this
saying well. To this we must add the socio-philosophical sympathy for the economy
of self-sufficiency, because it eliminates intermediate trade, great capital, and thus
many opportunities for exploitation, and because it does not conceal an object's
utility value behind its trade value. Now we also have a feminist rehabilitation of
the subsistence economy, since the position of the woman is usually better within
it than in the market economy that is interconnected across regions. Under the
conditions of self-sufficiency, the important thing is not who has the money, but
who has the key to the larder. If women are accorded a special role as the guarantors
of human economic activity that is compatible with the environment, it can be
deduced especially well from their significance within the subsistence economy –
provided the latter was in fact ecologically sound.[3]

There are a few simple reasons why that was emphatically the case. Preserving
the environment is most easily accomplished where preservation does not need
to be organized from above but is inherent in a particular way of life, where the
environment that is affected by human activity remains small and easy to survey,
and where those who cause environmental damage must bear the consequences
themselves. Liebig's demand that all nutrients removed from the soil be returned
can be most readily accomplished in a subsistence economy on a small scale. The
wider the cycles become, the less complete they are. In a system where, to use
Wilhelm Abel's vivid language, "the further [oxen] had to go, the higher their
price," and the highest prices were paid at a great distance, manure did not reach
the fields. Henry Charles Carey (1793–1879), the American economist who also
pondered soil quality and changed from a free trader into a protectionist, warned
in his *Principles of Social Science* (1858) that under the dominion of free trade, good
harbors and fertile soils were the most dangerous things a country could possess,
because they turned it into a country of agricultural exports and thus into an object
that drained the soils.[4]

Karl Polanyi (1886–1964), whose description of the humanity and reasonableness of the subsistence economy is especially impressive, characterized this economic form not least by its closeness to nature. Because the economy of self-
sufficiency did not have to respond to the fluctuations of the market, it could
react that much better to the natural conditions on which it depended. Braudel
has written that in the Mediterranean world of the sixteenth century, the worst
famines occurred on the islands of Corfu, Crete, and Cyprus, which were part of
the Venetian trading empire, whereas the "poorer and more backward islands" –
"paradoxically," from Braudel's perspective – suffered less. When the Chinese
government suffered a loss of authority in the nineteenth century, "local armed
groups barricaded rivers at important posts to prevent grain supplies from being

sent out. . . . Official rhetoric condemned grain blockers as 'bandits,'" but the latter knew full well what they were doing.

Niger, one of the poorest countries in the world, improved its population's food supply when it halted the export of peanuts in 1972, until then the country's largest business: in this way, it became "the only country of the Sahel that was able to defeat hunger, at least in part." Nevertheless, "globalization" is today becoming the new religion even in countries that hardly stand a chance in the global market. The chief weakness of the subsistence economy was and is not ecological but political in nature: since it did not generate the potential for power on the same scale as economies geared toward the production of added value, it easily fell under foreign control, and self-sufficiency was disturbed by taxes and dues. "Rural indebtedness is the traditional plague of the peasant world." The pressure of debts forces peasants to go against their better wisdom by overusing the soil and cutting down the forest.[5]

One could raise the following objection to the thesis that the fundamental feature of the subsistence economy is its ecological soundness: Was the world of subsistence really that small and contained? Did the economic exhaustion of the soil not get out of control on the common pastures and forests? The theory of the "tragedy of the commons" is still being discussed. But no matter how much one might or might not agree with it, the fact is that a substantial part of traditional agriculture is not affected by it at all. The notion that the original state of the peasantry was a cooperative one is not tenable. In this case, historians often fall for an optical illusion: since only the larger social units – from landed lordships and village communities on up – produced files and documents, and since only those things that give rise to the need for regulation on a higher level are usually documented for historians, there was a tendency to regard these bodies as the elementary forms of economic life. However, the basic unit was usually the house. "Economy" is derived from *oikos* (Greek: "house") and originally meant "house economy." Otto Brunner, who rediscovered the "whole house" as the basic unit of the premodern economy, emphasized that "the old economy is not a doctrine of the market, but a doctrine of the house." The garden, the nucleus of the relationship between humanity and nature, was always part of the house, never part of the larger entity; the same was true for many fruit-bearing trees. Robert Netting, arguing against those theorists who posit a primitive communism, notes that he is not aware of any cases around the world where descent groups above the level of the household were the primary social units of production and consumption. Even the old English common fields were always worked individually, never collectively.[6]

Netting, in particular, has made us aware recently that alongside the type of agriculture that is far more familiar with extensive and cooperatively used areas, "smallholders," small farmers engaged in intensive cultivation, are also found all over the world – whether in Central Europe, China, or Africa. He is right to emphasize that it would be quite wrong to see "smallholders" as a backward, marginal phenomenon of agriculture; rather, we are dealing here with an economic way of life that is capable of economic and ecological perfection, and that could even tolerate a considerable increase in population density. The weak point of small farmers who are formally independent is their political and economic weakness. If, as happened so often in modern times, they are pushed onto poor soils and slopes threatened by erosion, where ecological stabilization requires considerable effort and persistence, it can easily happen that they promote soil erosion.[7]

However, it would not be correct to equate the subsistence economy with individualistic narrow-mindedness and to link it only with the individual farmer: the principle of providing for one's own need radiated far beyond the house economy and was, right into the modern age, a self-evident principle of the economy of village communities, landed estates, cities, and states. This principle meant that providing the local population with basic foodstuffs and with wood took precedence over export. But while the self-sufficiency of the single farmstead, without the need to purchase anything from the outside, was an old peasant ideal, reality was often very different. The kind of subsistence economy that was the rule in historical reality was not isolated and cut off from all higher culture, but contained elements of a local and regional division of labor. In many regions of the world we find old, "natural" trading relations between neighboring regions with different natural resources: between the pasture areas of the uplands and the agricultural regions in the valleys, between wetland areas rich in marine life and zones of deciduous forest in which pigs were pastured.

Only the exportation of grain and wood to "foreign realms" (which were often not far away) was still in the eighteenth century seen as immoral in many German regions if there was shortage at home, even if this was de facto done. E. P. Thompson has shown that the same "moral economy" existed in the consciousness of the English lower classes at that time. This attitude was connected with a nondynamic understanding of human needs. The old days of contentment with what one had is not a myth; it is evident in the irritation of the protagonists of industrial growth, both capitalist and socialist, as, for example, in Lassalle's polemic against the German workers' "damned lack of needs" (*verdammte Bedürfnislosigkeit*).[8] To be sure, Machiavelli had already claimed that "nature has so constituted men that, though all things are objects of desire, not all things are attainable; so that desire always exceeds the power of attainment, with the result that men are ill content with what they possess and their present state brings them little satisfaction" (*Discourse* I.37). Yet this was not an eternal and unchanging but a historically created human nature, which took shape especially early in the Italian trading cities.

The priority given to meeting one's own needs first held true even in the lumber policy of important commercial cities, and under the threat of a wood shortage it could reemerge and consolidate even in the course of the early modern period. In the Middle Ages, forest-rich Freiburg could afford to place its woods in the service of silver mining; but here, too, the subsistence principle won out after the decline of the mining wealth. Similar reasons prompted Besançon to engage in a tenacious fight throughout the eighteenth century against the establishment of new iron-smelting works and other large-scale users of wood in Franche-Comté.[9] None of these cities had the least ambition to become large industrial cities, and progress toward a growing use of energy would have struck them as an utterly absurd goal.

Economic historians used to allow themselves to be blinded by the triumphant progress of long-distance trade since the Middle Ages – all those stories about the rise of the splendid trading cities of Venice, Genoa, Bruges, Seville, and others. In the process they did not pay enough attention to the fact that the life and survival of most people was grounded, far into the nineteenth century, on local and regional self-sufficiency. And this is also where we should look for the strongest stabilizer of the balance between humans and their environment. "The trade in grain remains afflicted with such natural difficulties that no important land and hardly any province of greater significance could get around satisfying the need for bread for the most part through their own cultivation," the third edition of Roscher's *Nationalökonomik des Ackerbaus* (1903) still maintained. Even in England, at the time the most highly industrialized state in the world, regional self-supply was dominant into the nineteenth century. Before the age of the train, the steamship, and the truck, it was difficult to transport bulk commodities over long distances: at that time, "free trade" did not yet mean what it does today. Ivan Illich was probably right when he argued that the subsistence economy around the world was not destroyed on a broad basis until after 1945: this, too, an indication that one of the most profound turning points in the history of daily life and the environment occurred in the very recent past. Even in the time of famine after 1945, many people survived only because it proved possible to revive a remnant of the old self-sufficient economy. Polanyi's thesis that "previously to our time no economy has ever existed that, even in principle, was controlled by markets" is confirmed by a good deal of evidence.[10]

To be sure, individual households were never completely autonomous. The potential for conflict always existed in relations with neighbors; at the same time, one needed their help in times of need: "A bad neighbor is as great a plague as a good one is a great blessing" – this sentence by Hesiod surely encapsulates a timeless experience of village life.[11] Even the self-sufficient house economy created the need for regulation early on through its relations with neighbors. Neighbor law is one of the historical roots of environmental law, namely, its most restrictive tradition, which limited the environmental impact of a commercial enterprise strictly to the property of the proprietor and stipulated that it could not impinge on even the most immediate neighbors.

1. IN THE BEGINNING WAS FIRE: GLOBAL SLASH–AND–BURN AGRICULTURE AND PYROMANIA IN ENVIRONMENTAL HISTORY

Until the 1960s, slash-and-burn cultivation was a very obscure topic. Many foresters saw it as a criminal outrage, an act of arson. The Brandenburg-Prussian forestry codes of the sixteenth century opened with the battle against slash-and-burn agriculture; and since that time, the Habsburgs, too, waged a battle in the Alps against this "land-destroying waste." It was a battle that would repeat itself in many third world countries in the nineteenth and twentieth centuries, beginning with British India and Dutch Indonesia. Burning was destructive mischief also in the eyes of leading agrarian reformers who were trying to raise the peasants' conscious-ness about fertilizers. Arthur Young wrote in 1789 that slash-and-burn cultivation was the source of all agriculture in Brittany and at the same time the ruin of the province.[12]

John Wesley Powell, one of the great explorers of the American West, declared in 1879 that forest protection "is reduced to one single problem – Can the forests be saved from fire?"[13] But there were also dissenting voices. From the time Yosemite

National Park was founded in 1890, the prevailing opinion of foresters and environmentalists who had elevated the battle against forest fires to their highest priority
was opposed by those who defended the traditional "light burning" of the Indians,
which removed the underbrush without damaging the large trees. They pointed
out that the beauty of the Western forests with its big trees, the sequoias, was the
result of fire that enriched the soil, created space for the giant trees, and prevented
truly disastrous conflagrations by reducing the combustible debris.[14] But these
countervoices did not meet with a broad resonance until the critical climate of
the 1960s.

Since that time, the realization that slash–and–burn cultivation has been practiced
around the globe for thousands of years under various names (*Hauberg-*, *Schwend-*,
and *Egartenwirtschaft* in the Siegerland and in the Alps, *écoubage* in France, *slash-and-
burn* or *swidden* agriculture, and *shifting cultivation* in the English-language realm)
has placed environmental history on a new footing. As we can see, the myth of
Prometheus has a deeper meaning than people once suspected; Bernard Campbell
was right when he said that taming fire and putting it to use for hunting and agriculture was "one of the most outstanding leaps in humankind's conquest of nature."[15]
Virtually everywhere in the world, fire stands at the beginning of the drama of the
relationship of humans to their environment. It imbued human behavior toward
nature early on with a more active – indeed, a more aggressive – quality than the
idyllic image of "natural man's" harmonious integration into nature suggests.

Since the fertility of the soil produced by ash is only temporary, slash–and–
burn agriculture led in many regions to shifting cultivation. Still, it possessed its
own economic-ecological stability. In his outline of an ecological history, Georges
Bertrand characterized the Mediterranean mountain forests as the *royaume du feu*,
the realm of fire – a characterization that stands in curious contrast to today's
manic and desperate battle against forest fires in the Mediterranean region. The
hunters and farmers of earlier times did not set fire randomly; instead, burning
had its orderliness and technical culture, which is today being rediscovered, in
a modernized form, as the "technique of resource management." The author
of a history of French fire cultivation has emphasized that the techniques for
preparing the fire and working the soil afterward were highly developed: "Every
detail mattered."[16]

Slash–and–burn agriculture was humankind's primal experience with the fertilizing power of fire, the basis of fire mythology. It shows just how early there
existed an awareness that humanity could and had to do something for the fertility
of the soil. Ancient Chinese texts advised the burning of weeds and scrub to make
the soil fruitful; Columella believed that ash was even more effective than animal
manure. Alpine farmers knew how well grain grew on burned soils: "Fire grain
(*Brandkorn*) was better than field grain (*Feldkorn*)." Moreover, fire produced highly
prized seeds that were not contaminated with weed seeds: the weeds had been
destroyed by the fire, which functioned, not least, as an herbicide.[17]

Some scholars maintain that in all woodland areas that were not regularly des-
iccated by dry periods, slash–and–burn agriculture was able to spread only with
the iron axe: here the forest could be torched only after trees had been cut down.
However, in 1953, a Finnish expert demonstrated that a medium-sized oak could
be felled in half an hour even with a Neolithic stone axe. Soil studies in the

Alpine foothills point to a strong rise in fire-clearance husbandry as early as around 3,700 B.C.E.[18] Discoveries of this kind, which are supported by pollen analysis, have revolutionized the picture of the early history of the relationship between humans and the environment by revealing that large-scale changes of the landscape by human hand reach back far into prehistoric times.

Now and then the environmental historian is tempted to turn into a pyromaniac and to make fire into the driving force of all of environmental history right up to the present. Since fire has always fascinated humans, this opens up a glimpse into a myriad of cross-connections to the history of human passions and fantasies: what an enticement for an historian! Fire is linked with a primal human experience of the deadly threat posed by the forces of nature, but also of one's own power over nature: Prometheus is considered the mythological ancestor of industrialization.[19]

It is not possible to make sweeping statements about the ecological effects of slash-and-burn agriculture; the important thing is to distinguish various forms. There is simple *Rasenbrennen*, the burning of grass, weeds, and underbrush. And there is the burning of entire forests, after the trees have been first cut down or killed by "girdling" the bark. This, however, is not necessarily tantamount to the destruction of the forest, but can be part of a rotating field and forest cultivation.

The most ancient use of fire was undoubtedly for hunting. Fire was used to roust game, but another effect was more lasting: the lush, fresh greenery on burned soils attracted wildlife in large numbers, which made the difficult job of hunting much easier and less uncertain. According to a report from the late eighteenth century, Native Americans burned "immense tracts of land" for this purpose.[20] Shepherds also used to set fires to improve their pastures and prevent the growth of forests. The earliest plowland was presumably carved out by fire, and fire practices have remained in use into recent times in many regions of the world.

The crucial question in assessing fire-clearance cultivation is the extent to which humans knew how to keep fire under control. Of course, for many older periods we can do no more than conjecture and are forced to draw inferences from modern observations. An awareness that fire can be dangerous was surely present from the beginning. Natural fires can turn brushland (*Buschsteppe*) and dry forests into an inferno; experiences of this kind must have been traumatic for the survivors and are reflected in the idea of hell. The word "holocaust" is a common term in the relevant literature to describe gigantic conflagrations in historical periods. But it was precisely through small, controlled fires, which continuously burned up dried wood and underbrush, that one could reduce the risk of uncontrolled conflagrations. If one paid attention to the time of year, temperature, weather, and wind conditions, and if one knew the terrain, one could be fairly confident in the ability to keep a fire under control. Doing this usually required only family members and neighbors, no larger social entities. However, this applies primarily to forests, less so to heaths. We have repeated reports about Danish heath peasants in the eighteenth century who lost control of fires and destroyed the vegetation and the soil to the point where sandstorms arose and deprived them of the basis for their livelihood for one or two generations.

Farmers who practiced a rotating field-forest cultivation and made use of the woods as well knew how to secure the regeneration of the forests during burning. In

Master Guan, an ancient Chinese work about the art of governing from the fourth century B.C.E., we read the following: "It is the business of forest wardens to see that the rules about fires are enforced, so respect is shown to the hills, wetlands, forests, and thick vegetation. This is because these are the sources of materials." This is how far back there were already "rules about fires" that were posited as known. The Native Americans of California burned the chaparral, the typical shrubbery of the Sierras, only enough to promote the growth of new seedlings, which attracted deer. To this day the Kayapó Indians have their specific signs in nature to determine the right time for burning, which is carefully supervised by shamans experienced in the use of fire. But when the Portuguese landed on Madeira in 1420 and the first settlers torched the forest to create plowland, the fire raged out of control, eventually forcing the arsonists to run for their lives: one group had no choice but to escape into the sea, where they had to endure two days and nights standing in the water up to their necks. In more recent times, forest fires became in Madeira – much as they did in Cyprus and British India – an act of resistance to outside forest management. In the steppes of Russia, fires often got completely out of control and burned entire villages to the ground.[21]

As a growing number of observers came to realize over the past few decades that fire-clearance husbandry makes economic sense and was ecologically useful, a mood of pyromania spread among environmentalists and those enamored of the Native Americans. "Burn, burn, burn" an Australian national park manager told his U.S. colleagues at a meeting in Finland in 1992, and Finnish forest ecologists proudly showed off a piece of forest they had burned down, and from which the first tender green was already sprouting. Already at the beginning of the twentieth century, the Finnish national historian Väinö Voionmaa had worked hard to vindicate the slash-and-burn agriculture in the Carelian forests. Today the prohibition against slash-and-burn cultivation that was enacted in Finland in the nineteenth century under the influence of German writers on forest management is blamed for famines and the increasingly monotonous nature of Finnish forests. It would appear, however, that, in its last phase in the early nineteenth century, Finnish swidden agriculture led to an overuse and degradation of the soil when it was no longer used as part of a subsistence economy, but for the purposes of exporting grain.[22]

In 1997 the skies over wide areas of Southeast Asia darkened for weeks on end when fires set in the forests of Sumatra and Borneo to clear land burned out of control. Ecologists have long been horrified and outraged by gigantic conflagrations in the Amazon region that are deliberately set to open up plowland and pastures, and the full extent of which can be grasped only by satellite images. Where fire-clearance cultivation combines with the dynamic of the modern economy it becomes a public hazard. But there is reason to believe that slash-and-burn agriculture, in combination with sheep and goat rearing, contributed to the destruction of vegetation and soil in the Mediterranean regions in earlier times.[23]

There can be no doubt: swidden cultivation is not an entirely benign, inherently nature-friendly technique, and a sweeping ecological rehabilitation of the practice would be unrealistic. Fire contains an aggressive expansionary power that humans merely have to unleash, and that stimulates aggression in humans themselves; that is why the setting of fire has been overused in agriculture and abused as a weapon of war. If the minimal use of energy is the ideal, slash-and-burn cultivation does not fare well, as it is a visible waste of energy: a "high-input system" that, from the perspective of the energy flow, is analogous to chemicalized agriculture. Burning harms the humus layer, at least on the surface, and the enrichment of the soil with nutrients is only temporary. Fire-clearance cultivation is especially attractive in the tropical rainforest, where the nutrients are for the most part contained in the vegetation, not the soil, and are quickly introduced into the soil through burning. But the tropical rain also leaches the ash out very quickly, and the deceptive fertility of the soil vanishes again after only a few years.[24]

We are left with the realization that the ecological effect of slash-and-burn agriculture depends on the historical context. Even Clifford Geertz, who did much to rehabilitate this system of cultivation, admitted that swidden cultivation can become a factor that leads to the overuse and exploitation of the environment in traditional societies: "The reasons for this overcultivation are various, including an historically rooted conviction that there are always other forests to conquer, a warrior's view of natural resources as plunder to be exploited, a large village settlement pattern which makes shifting between plots a more than usually onerous task, and, perhaps, a superior indifference toward agricultural proficiency." The homo oeconomicus did not rule everywhere. Pyne concludes that while fire alone "has rarely destroyed a landscape," "fire and hoof, fire and axe, fire and plow, fire and sword" can very well do serious ecological damage, especially in ecologically fragile regions of the world.[25] No matter how much historical understanding one might have for slash-and-burn cultivation, there is no reason for ecological pyromania.

2. HUMANS AND ANIMALS: HUNTING AND DOMESTICATION

The influential book *Man the Hunter* (1968) by the Harvard anthropologists Richard B. Lee and Irven DeVore presents the hunting-gathering existence as an archetypal way of life that characterized 99 percent of human cultural history during the past two million years and optimized the relationship between humans and nature: "To date the hunting way of life has been the most successful and persistent adaptation man has ever achieved." If we assume that humanity has been deeply imprinted by its history and that hunting, with its powerful emotions, has left a stronger imprint than gathering, human beings – or more precisely: the male of the species – should be, by nature, above all hunters. The topic invites anthropological speculation: whether in the modern soldier or in the tourist, in the researcher or the philanderer – everywhere, we are told, one can recognize the millennia of the hunting tradition.[26]

At least the Native Americans are said to have derived all their ideas and institutions from the hunt. Yet even the Navajos, whose hunting rituals and taboos are especially famous, supported themselves in historical times primarily by agriculture. In the eighteenth century, the Franco-American Michel Crèvecoeur made famous the saying of an Indian chief "that the meat from which we live has four legs to run away, while we have only two to catch it."[27]

For some time now, the thesis that the human being is by nature a hunter has been subject to a wave of criticism. In all likelihood, plants played a large role in the human diet already in prehistoric times, and as wildlife stocks were decimated, that role grew and invariably led to a greater appreciation of women's work. The gathering of seeds, tree fruit, and roots turned almost invariably into planting and sowing: agricultural forms, as well, reach back far into the period of the hunting-gathering life. Agriculture most likely emerged from gathering and planting, not from animal domestication, as was believed in the nineteenth century. As the practice of slash-and-burn agriculture shows, hunter-gatherers and early planters not only adapted to the environment they found, but also actively changed it over large sections. Lévi-Strauss, noted that such tribes by no means had a purely traditionalist mentality, quoting a biologist who lived among the forest-dwelling pygmies in the Philippines: "The Negrito is an intrinsic part of his environment and, what is more important, continually studies his surroundings."[28]

In nature, the higher mammals are most similar to humans, and the relationship of humans to animals is often much more emotional than their relationship to plants; it is only in ecology and tranquil nature romanticism that the preferences are reversed. Many animals are superior to humans in strength and speed, or they possess abilities that humans lack. In many ancient cultures, the sense of superiority that humans felt toward animals was not very pronounced and mixed with an awareness of inferiority. Often a hunter would achieve superiority over his prey only with the help of domesticated animals – the horse, the dog, the hunting falcon. The distance between humans and animals was not as marked as it is today. Gods had animal shapes, and the mating of humans and animals was no rarity in mythology.[29]

It is striking that prehistoric art depicted animals more skillfully and naturalistically than it did humans. However, this art already was presumably about power over nature, about hunting magic and the acquisition of animal strength. During the bear dance of the Chumash Indians of southern California, the dancers, wearing bear paws around their necks, sang: "I am a creature of power. I stand up and begin to walk to the mountaintops."[30] To be successful in the hunt, one had to study the habits of animals with great care, to predict their behavior, in a sense to understand and imitate them. Outwitting animals in this way must have been a primeval experience of success for humans, and this triumph, outsmarting nature by understanding its hidden rules, was repeated time and again in the history of science and technology. For a long time, however, most victories were modest and were often followed by defeats.

Hunting large animals was most successful if done in groups that surrounded the prey. On the other hand, the danger of group organization was that it could be too successful and decimate the wildlife. The more perfect the technique, the lower the sustainability: the problem is an ancient one. Humans must have realized very early on that larger agglomerations of people were incompatible with the food supply derived from hunting. Many researchers believe that hunters and gatherers of the Stone Age already practiced forms of population control.

From the perspective of environmental history, the primary question is the extent to which populations of hunters developed a sense for sustainability, a concern not to overhunt their hunting grounds and not to prevent wildlife from reproducing. To this day there is no consensus about the answer. The apologia for the hunting way of life is countered by the thesis that the history of human hunting began in wide regions of the world with an ecological fiasco, namely, the extirpation of most large species of wildlife, whose reproductive behavior followed the K-pattern rather than the r-pattern – that is, they did not have the indestructibility of rabbits. A thesis that became especially widely known was that of Paul S. Martin (1973) about the "Pleistocene overkill," the eradication of the North American megafauna at the end of the first ice age within a period of about 600 years by newly arrived humans. In the meantime, scholars discovered also in other regions of the world that the first appearance of humans coincided with the eradication or precipitous decline of large animals: most strongly in Australia and on islands that humans reached relatively late, and comparatively the least in Africa and Eurasia, where humans evolved and animals were able to develop early flight instincts toward this dangerous neighbor.[31] By now, the notion of "first-contact extinctions" has become a fixture in the scholarly literature (there is already an abbreviation, "FC").

There is no end in sight to the debate about the "Pleistocene overkill," though exact and direct proof that human hunters caused the decline of the megafauna is not possible. All in all, however, the evidence for the human factor is quite strong, especially from a global comparative perspective. The usual counterargument, that the prehistoric population density was much too low and the hunting techniques much too primitive to make possible the extinction of entire species, does not hold up to careful examination. From an early period, we already find not only individual hunting, but also the mass slaughter of animals that were driven by fire and lured over precipices. At some Palaeolithic quarry sites, archaeologists have found enormous mounds of bones, for example, the remnants of over a thousand mammoths in Unterwisternitz in Moravia, or of more than 100,000 wild horses in Solutré in France. One French archaeologist recognizes a "brutal development of hunting" in the Palaeolithic era. Even if the "overkill" theory has been repeatedly challenged, there is a broad consensus that no natural instinct urges the human hunter to practice sustainability. The palaeontologist Niles Eldrige believes that hunters are by nature opportunists with a tendency to kill whatever they can get.

The dodo has long been the symbol of endangered animal species: a large, flightless running bird on the island of Mauritius, it was hunted to extinction in the seventeenth century by European invaders. More recently, another giant running bird attained some prominence: the moa, exterminated centuries ago in New Zealand by the Maori who arrived on the island. Even the Polynesians, once considered the world's happiest children of nature, had no instinct for sustainability if seized by the hunting fever. And although Werner Müller lists all the arguments that support the notion that the Native Americans of the New World treated nature with care, he also recounts the Gluskap myth of the Abenaki Indians in the far Northeast of the United States. The Hercules-like figure of Gluskap, who is central to Abenaki mythology and combines strength with cunning, cut down the primeval forest and killed the monsters of the oldest creation. Even among Indians there was not always the vaunted brotherly relationship to animals. Many, though by no means all, findings among modern-day hunting tribes support the "foraging theory," which argues that hunters behaved in accordance with the principle of "short-term maximum yield" (to use modern terminology).[32]

Once again one must be careful about making sweeping judgments. There is no lack of indications that hunters and gatherers were concerned to reduce the risk to their existence by taking precautions. Colin Turnbull, an expert on African forest peoples, even assures us that the hunter is the "the best of conservationists, knowing exactly how much he can take from where at any given time." To turn the life of the hunter into a precisely calculable existence goes decidedly too far, however, for there is much that argues against such a view. Ecological good sense should have led populations of hunters to always live widely dispersed: but much like what happened with the nomads, social and political motives could tempt them into concentrations that would result in an overhunting of the wildlife. There is an intimate link between hunting and war, hunting and domination. The trapper, the beaver hunter, became the pioneer of the American push into the West, and the sable hunters were the pioneers of the Russian expansion into Siberia. Around 1690, sable already had been hunted to extinction even around Yakutsk, far to the east: the constant overhunting became the motor of further and further expansion.

Of course, the hunter loves his game in his own way; but if one concludes from this that the hunter is the best conservationist, such a view contains a dose of modern hunting romanticism. Theories of this kind presuppose the sort of contained and manageable hunting grounds that arose only with the large-scale clearance of land and the cutting back of forests. Even in German national parks today, estimating wildlife density is difficult and provides ammunition for endless controversies over hunting quotas.[33]

The issue of sustainability is entirely different for animals than it is for plowland. Since animals reproduce on their own, it would seem that there should be no problem of regeneration as long as humans do not prevent animals from procreating. In a story from ancient India, a gazelle reproaches a king bitterly because he transfixed her with an arrow while she was mating. To preserve the abundance of wildlife, one must be familiar with the reproductive behavior of animals. To be sure, hunters have always gathered such knowledge with great curiosity. Still, even in the nineteenth century, German foresters could quarrel over whether a buck mates with a single doe or several, and whether bucks could thus be hunted at will and only the does needed to be spared to ensure offspring.[34]

Among many hunting peoples one finds the rule not to kill more animals than are needed to provide one's own group with meat. But here, too, it is not clear whether this rule was always observed in real life. A study of Mongolian nomads revealed a discrepancy between verbal rules and actual behavior: de facto it happens that hunting is done purely for pleasure. During the controversy over Martin's "overkill" thesis, one researcher among South American Indios reported that each one killed two pregnant cows a day only to eat the unborn calves, which were considered a delicacy. Roscher referred to a report according to which "a horde of Indians in a single afternoon drinks away the payment for 1,400 fresh buffalo tongues, having left everything else of the hunted animals behind."[35]

The many rituals surrounding the hunt have been used as a primary argument for the notion that hunting people were careful in their dealings with animals. Occasionally we are also told that the shamans set the hunting quotas during these rituals. Many times the rituals reveal that the animals to be hunted were seen as animate beings whose consent to the hunt had to be obtained. But anyone who allows himself to be overly impressed by these rituals forgets that the quarry could not answer, and that the purpose of the rituals was to instill confidence in the hunter and provide him with a clean conscience. When it comes to the native inhabitants of America, a demonstrable sustainability is presumably found least where it is most often looked for – in hunting. It is more likely found in the agriculture to which friends of the Native Americans pay much less attention, and which women typically pursued in the form of intensive gardening: this emerges from the great work of the English geographer David Watts about changes in the environment of the West Indies since 1492.

If one sees how much success in the hunt meant to men, and the intensity of the hunting fever that still seizes many hunters today, it is hard to imagine that a very considerate behavior toward animals was the rule. Instead, there is reason to assume that it was precisely when game became scarcer, and hunting down the quarry involved so much effort, that the concern over killing too much wildlife receded into the background. The extent to which one sees the decimation of wildlife as a loss to nature depends on how one defines "nature." Tree growth benefited from the decline of the megafauna. Graphic illustrations of this are found in more recent times: "Numerous valuable, beautiful stands of mixed pine in the Black Forest owe their appearance to the Revolution of 1848," when peasants hunted game without impediments.[36]

Fishing, with the exception of whaling, is a more peaceful art than hunting. But an animal-protecting instinct is least likely to be encountered here, since humans identify far less with cold fish than with warm-blooded mammals. The use of nets in fishing made mass killing routine early on. On the other hand, fishermen, at least in inland waterways, stay within a confined and definable space: here it is easier to imagine an awareness of the limited nature of resources and a concern for sustainability. Much the same is true also for fishing along the seacoast. In more distant times, most fishermen fished only within sight of their home and port. As Braudel has written, the fisherman "knows the waters outside his port like the peasant knows the plowland of his village; . . . he works the sea like the peasant works his field." A historical study of fisheries along the coast of California – one of the most thorough recent studies on the history of fishing – points to evidence that some Indian communities did die out because they depleted their fishing grounds; however, other communities learned from such experiences and avoided a similar fate by establishing rules, but above all by keeping down their own population numbers. These rules consisted not only of religious rituals, but also of property rights.[37]

In principle, sustainable fishing is quite straightforward: one simply has to make the nets wide enough to let immature fish escape. The Confucian philosopher Mencius taught that "[i]f nets that are too narrow are not allowed in ponds and lakes, there will be more fish and tortoises than can be eaten." Along the Dordogne, state officials and the owners of fishing rights in the eighteenth century used to sound the alarm because of the imminent depletion of fish stocks: the goal was to keep out illegal fishermen and to underscore the need for regulation, even though the Dordogne's wealth of fish still seemed inexhaustible at the time.

When it came to fishing on the high seas, however, any sense of sustainability was lost. Even Herman Melville, the author of *Moby Dick* (1851) who was fascinated by whaling as much as by the whales themselves, mocked the concern that whales could be hunted to extinction – even though by his day, and before the invention of the grenade harpoon, whales had been repeatedly exterminated in certain hunting grounds. Back then there was already a memory of a time when whales had been so numerous even in the Caribbean that it was hard to sleep at night on the Bermudas, so loud was their blowing. But new hunting grounds were discovered to make up for their loss, and the whalers knew no borders. Every reader of *Moby Dick* knows that the psychology of whale hunting does not exactly promote sustainability, and this psychology left its mark even on the author. Richard Ellis, a historian of whaling and member of the International Whaling Commission from 1980 to 1990, concludes: "The history of whaling is rife with repeated mistakes; it is an industry where greed has almost always displaced reason, and short-term profit-taking has invariably precluded anything approximating a sensible approach to resource-management."[38]

With the sea seemingly a place of endless bounty until recently, a pirate mentality has existed in deep sea fishing since ancient times, though it was only the tools of modern technology that made it calamitous. Werner Helwig, in his novel *Raubfischer in Hellas* (Predatory Fishermen in Hellas, 1939), which was based on personal experiences, offered a moving description of how poor Greek fishermen in the Aegean made unrestrained use of dynamite, even though they knew that they were destroying the abundance of fish in their sea, and even though many of them were themselves maimed by the explosions. At that time, the dictatorship of Metaxas took up the battle against these practices.

Some governments already fought against the overfishing of oysters from beds close to shore in the early modern period, when the eating of oysters became a status symbol for the upper classes. A maritime environmental awareness on the part of the French elites developed earliest out of the concern for the oyster stocks. In 1652 a veritable "oyster battle" broke out between oyster fishermen privileged by the Danish king and their competitors. Oyster beds were one of the places where ecological research originated. As late as 1701, the Swiss writer Louis Michel expressed his astonishment at what he saw in the Chesapeake Bay: "The abundance of oysters is incredible." There, oyster shells were used even as fertilizer and for road surfacing. But observers also noted that the shells were growing smaller with time.[39]

A historian with a fondness for nature who vacations at the seashore is often seized by the desire to elevate the seas into historical spaces, indeed, into historical actors. Fernand Braudel, to universal and enthusiastic acclaim, made the Mediterranean Sea into a great historical theme. But then he proceeded to unfold the Mediterranean scenery beginning with the mountains, not the sea! Following Braudel's model, K. N. Chaudhuri endeavored to make the Indian Ocean into a historical space, into a cultural unit that has existed for over a thousand years.[40] In fact, the coastal regions of both bodies of water are connected by a network of old trading links as well as shared climatic elements. The Mediterranean succession of winter rains and summer drought and the monsoons of southern Asia are cycles that create a specific experience of time and nature. In India the time of the monsoon was the terror of colonial officials, but the season of inspiration for poets. And yet, the great seas have still not become a unity in the sense of trade, institutions, and the practice of a sustainable treatment of resources. The dilemma of current international policy to protect the seas is precisely that, unlike other sectors of environmental policy, it has very few older institutional traditions it can connect to. To be sure, such traditions are not entirely absent. Today it has been all but forgotten that the League of Nations in the 1920s made the protection of the seas – especially against oil pollution – one of the areas in which it became active. The protection of whales was also one of the areas of wildlife conservation that saw some of the earliest international cooperation.[41] Environmental policy is most likely to be successful where it establishes simple and striking goals. Those include the largest animals on land and in the sea, elephants and whales. The issue gets more difficult with visually less impressive species.

Traditional water law also made few provisions against the pollution of rivers and lakes. Until the twentieth century, the discharge of wastewater into rivers was regarded everywhere as old customary law, occasionally even justified with the argument that this was the natural purpose of waterways. It was usually dying fish that first attracted the attention of humans to water pollution. Among the many ways that water was used in premodern times, flax-retting pools – ponds for rotting the flax fibers so they can be worked into linen – were most likely to become the target of prohibitions, as they instantly killed off the fish and spread a penetrating stench. The Constitutions of Melfi (1231) enacted by Emperor Frederick II for the Kingdom of Sicily forbade flax-retting pools in running water. In this case the prohibition was justified with the divine commandment to keep the air pure.

At this point one might ask: Would fishermen not always have been the natural monitors to control the purity of the water? Would they not have been able to exercise political influence, since fishing was often the right of the seigneurial lords? In his polemical essay "German Rivers or German Sewers?" (1907), the German physician Georg Bonne invoked among other things the threatened fisheries, "which provide a salutary and decent living to more than 50,000 German men." Until now, environmental history has paid scant attention to fishing. The Constitutions of Melfi issued this prohibition: "We also forbid yew or herbs of this kind, by which fish are killed or die, to be thrown into the water by fishermen" – the Middle Ages had precursors to dynamite fishing. The fishermen were thus not entirely reliable monitors against the discharge of fecal matter into the water, another reason being that the addition of nutrients to the water increased the fish stocks. When Lake Constance became cleaner than ever thanks to sewage treatment plants, fish stocks declined sharply, to the great regret of the fishermen.[42]

Is hunting, from a historical perspective, an appropriate ally of conservation and environmental protection? Old images of hunting, more so even than written sources, seem to reveal that the ideal of the wilderness originates with hunting, even if modern environmentalists prefer to deny this provenance of their own ideal. With a vividness of language that is well suited to charming modern environmentalists, the Sachsenspiegel, the most famous German legal code of the Middle Ages, describes the royal forest ban as peace for the animals: the image we get is one of wildlife threatened by hunters as the legal partner of humans. It is a tantalizing question whether the royal hunting prerogative should be interpreted as a response to the overhunting of game in prehistoric times, that is to say, as a prime example of the union of conservation and lordship. Robert P. Harrison, in his cultural history of the forest, has written that when it comes to the royal forest privilege, "an ecologist today cannot help but be a monarchist of sorts," and he enthusiastically quotes an old English poem about William the Conqueror: "He loved the stags as much / as if he were their father." The aristocratic hunters felt a bond with the "noble" game they alone were allowed to hunt, and the verdant green of the forest, which attracted the wildlife, was also part of the hunt. Many hunting pictures convey a fascinating insight into the extent to which the pleasure of the hunt and the enjoyment of the forest were connected: this was evidently one of the most potent historical sources for the enjoyment of nature. Above all, hunting was originally the strongest incentive behind the protection of forests. As late as the early nineteenth century, the forest reformer Wilhelm Pfeil, who was otherwise strongly focused on economics, proclaimed that the forester felt happiest in the solitude of his lodge when he was simultaneously a hunter. And nothing was better than hunting at teaching the forester to forget theories and "learn from nature."[43] Foresters tell us that they come to know even remote corners of their range through the passion for hunting.

Does any of this matter in terms of environmental history? It is surprising how little first-rate historical literature there is on hunting, considering that it was for centuries the great pleasure activity of the aristocracy. Not even the history of forestry has examined the influence of hunting on wildlife and forest in any great depth. To this day, the topic of hunting is wrapped in a great deal of passionate feelings that get in the way of a sober analysis. And since historical hunting often escaped rationalization processes, it does not seem to have been a school of woodland sustainability. Carefully considered wildlife protection, which took into account the carrying capacity of a forest, established itself only in the nineteenth and twentieth centuries, and even then often merely on paper. Sometimes it was large-scale capitalism that gave rise to the rationalization of hunting necessary for sustainability; one example is the Hudson Bay Company and Canadian beaver hunting already in the early nineteenth century. Or was the beaver in the end saved only by the fact that its fur went out of fashion? One root of Russian conservation was the wildlife protection undertaken in the interest of the fur trade. In the long run, however, a conflict between the interests of hunting and those of conservation was inevitable.[44]

There are many cross-connections between hunting and the origins of the environmental movement. During the era of colonialism it was, not least, influential large game hunters who promoted the establishment of nature and game reserves in Africa, and who loathed plans to sacrifice the habitats of large game to peasant settlers. Their initiative led to a first international conference on African wildlife in 1900, which agreed on rules that would govern large game hunting, at the expense, chiefly, of the indigenous peoples. With substantial participation from large game hunters, a wild game association was founded at that time, which the British press dubbed the "Penitent Butchers Club." When Robert Koch suggested that large game animals be decimated because they were hosts of the tsetse fly and thus promoted the spread of the sleeping sickness, a protest meeting was arranged in Berlin in 1908. One big-game hunter from South Africa launched a vehement polemic against bacteriology using ecological arguments: the tsetse fly, he proclaimed, was another one of nature's provisions to prevent Africa from being "overrun by herds of cattle."[45]

The American president Theodore Roosevelt, the founding father of American "conservation" policy, was a passionate hunter who once invited bear hunters from the Wild West to a "bear-hunters' dinner," assuring the readers of his autobiography that "no finer set of guests ever sat at meat in the White House." Around the same time, Aldo Leopold, an intellectual leader of the American environmental movement, sought to establish the new profession of "game management" from the perspective of hunting, assuring his contemporaries that the practice of a certain degree of wildlife management reached back to the beginnings of human history.[46] In the German Hermann Löns, who shared Leopold's views, a glowing love of nature was also intimately linked with a passion for hunting: his "Green Book" of 1901 contains hunting tales that usually end with a kill shot. In his mind, nature and love, love and the hunt are *one*.

Günther Schwab, the cofounder of the Weltbund zum Schutze des Lebens (World League for the Protection of Life, founded in 1960), wrote enthusiastic books on hunting and dogs. In the 1960s, Hubert Weinzierl, in his capacity as spokesman of the Deutsche Naturschutzring, sought an alliance with hunters, who, he believed, were feeling a growing sense of responsibility for endangered animals. On the other hand, Bernhard Grzimek, at the time the most popular advocate of animal protection in Germany, indeed, the world, clashed fiercely with large game hunters in his campaign for the Serengeti Nature Reserve. In the mid-1970s, the grassroots initiative against the nuclear power plant in Wyhl on the Rhine received financial backing from a regional hunters' cooperative. Since then, however, a hostile atmosphere has grown up between the environmental movement and hunters. Militant defenders of wildlife have been known to cut down the raised blinds of foresters. The fact is that hunting cannot be considered a prototype of a peaceful relationship to nature. In the seventeenth century, Wolf Helmhard von Hohberg praised hunting as "a veritable praeludium belli," the "prelude and mirror of war."[47] Historically, hunting and the art of war are closely connected.

Compared to hunting, which presumably wiped out many animal species, Marvin Harris has called the domestication of animals the "greatest conservation movement of all times."[48] The preservation of fertility emerged early on as the chief problem in the domestication of animals – in this regard it was similar to agriculture, and different from hunting – because a great many wild animals do not procreate in captivity. For that reason alone, only a small number of animals are suited for domestication. However, it was not only the promotion of fertility but also castration that became a basic innovation of animal domestication and animal breeding.

The domestication of most animal species is such a protracted process, and the economic success so uncertain, that it is hard to imagine domestication as simply a purposeful, economically motivated action on the part of humans. The ecologically highly advantageous combination of agriculture and animal husbandry was not planned from the beginning. To this day, Eduard Hahn's hypothesis (1896) that the domestication of animals began not in the service of agriculture, but in a playful way and perhaps also from religious motives, remains plausible. Successful domestication was a primal human experience of mastery over nature. The dog is

virtually everywhere the oldest human domesticated animal, and no other animal
can be trained to such a degree of attachment and submissiveness. The relationship
between man and dog became especially intimate through the hunt. Wherever in
history dominion is exercised, we very often find the presence of dogs. Dogs teach
their masters to shout sharp commands. In the eighteenth century, the bulldog
became England's national animal: "The courage of the bull-dogs," wrote David
Hume, "seems peculiar to England." Thomas Bewick (1753–1828), famous for his
depictions of animals, claimed that the domestication of the dog had led to the
peaceful conquest of the earth by man.[49]

Others would ascribe even greater importance to the horse. For Lynn White,
one of the founding fathers of environmental history, the discovery of how significant seemingly minor details such as the horseshoe and the stirrup were to
the emergence of feudalism was one of the turning points in his career as a historian. Alfred Weber believed that it was horse breeding that made history into
world history: beginning around 1200 B.C.E., he argued, the onslaught of horsemen throughout Europe and Asia created an elementary synchronicity of events,
indeed, a mental unity. Even the philosopher Karl Jaspers, who loved the spirit
more than nature, was reluctantly persuaded. Reinhard Koselleck, once a student
of Weber and Jaspers and not usually a friend of naturalistic elements in historical
scholarship, in his last years maintained that all of world history can be broken down
into three phases: the pre-horse age, the horse age, and the post-horse age. The
archaeologist Marija Gimbutas even links the spread of the Indo-Europeans – a
much-discussed puzzle of history – with the earliest horse breeding by the Kurgan
culture of southern Russia and speculates that with these mounted fighters, patri-
archy triumphed over older, matriarchal cultures.[50] The connection between the
horse and political dominion is plainly evident. Many princes throughout history
loved their horses more than they did their women. There is no other animal that
humans have understood to the same degree as a being of equal or even higher
rank. The rearing of horses was often more sensitive than the pedagogy intended
for human children.

The importance of the horse to environmental history is undoubtedly very
great, and yet we read very little about it. Any time there are discussions today
about whether or not nature preserves should be made a playground for wild
horses, it turns out that we know little about the ecology of the horse. For that
reason the present study cannot accord the horse the place it presumably deserves.
Books on horses have usually been written by horse lovers, who have little interest
in what their beloved animals excrete and how they influence the food niches
available to other creatures. Horse manure was the chief environmental problem
in American cities right into the twentieth century, so much so that the automobile
was seen as progress to greater cleanliness. And as late as the 1960s, the chief of the
Polish Communist Party, Wladyslaw Gomulka, complained that all of Poland was
disappearing into the bellies of its horses. There was food competition between
humans and horses for oats, which Udelgard Körber-Grohne called "biologically
the most valuable of our grains." In Central Europe, the cultivation of oats in
earlier times was a strategy of responding to a cooling of the climate and higher
precipitation.[51] Under such conditions, the "Little Ice Age" was – at least in the

long run – not necessarily an "environmental crisis," at least not from the horses' point of view.

The Church father Origines took the existence of domesticated animals as proof of human superiority. Pets offer children a creature they can order around and harass, but they have always created also an intimate relationship between humans and animals. Around 1800 the Bavarian agrarian reformer Joseph Hazzi found that wherever he went, domesticated animals were in a similar condition to their owners and were an indicator of whether the latter were doing well or poorly. When Descartes described animals as soulless machines he was not articulating a conventional belief, and he sparked vigorous disagreement. To this day the relationship between humans and domestic animals is an area beset with profound emotions, which poses the same difficulties to a sober analysis as does the human relationship to wild animals. Of one thing there is no doubt: humans have not only shaped domestic animals, the latter have also had a reciprocal effect on the *mentalités* of humans – but how so? Eduard Hahn, following a long discussion of the castration of domestic animals, warns us against playing up too much the human side of the human-animal relationship.[52] When all is said and done, the history of the relationship between humans and animals is certainly not benign and harmonious. That history bears animal traits also on the human side: it is pervaded by hunger and love, by power and the lust for power. To this we must add the broad and insidious terrain of a symbiosis with animals and life forms that was not intended by humans – with rats, fleas, and bacteria. Here the human relationship with the animal world turns into one of pure horror – but that is another story.

3. GARDENS AND FRUIT TREES

An environmental historian who is overfixated on the ideal of the wilderness fails to see the antiwilderness in which humans have cultivated an especially intimate and at the same time creative relationship to nature since time immemorial: the garden. More so than the field, the garden is characterized by the fence, the impenetrable demarcation against wilderness. The tradition of intensive working of the soil arrives early with the garden. Everything seems to indicate that gardening is older than agriculture, as it is found also in primitive cultures that do not engage in large-scale cultivation. It has been said that "all 12,000 cultivated plants probably ... went through a gardening stage before they were adopted by the branches of soil cultivation engaged in mass production."[53] In the early modern period, the garden became the laboratory for the intensification of agriculture. In a certain sense it stands not only at the beginning, but also at the end of agriculture. Today there are many who see in agroforestry the combination of garden-like cultivation and fruit trees, the future of agriculture and forestry in many parts of the Third World – if there is a future for them. There is little doubt that the garden, especially in conjunction with fruit trees, is one of the most elementary forms of human interaction with nature all over the world, from the earliest times to the present. In the garden was born a sense of sustainability as well as an ideal of beautiful nature. Ian Tyrrell has shown that garden idylls in the nineteenth century stood at the beginning of environmental politics in Australia as well as in California.[54]

In old German law, the fenced garden enjoyed a "peace of the garden" analogous to the "peace of the house": intruding animals – even persons – could be killed. The garden was always a private sphere that was part of the house; it was not subject to compulsory tillage and was unaffected by the "tragedy of the commons," wherever that "tragedy" in fact unfolded. From ancient times until today, the garden has offered people of all walks of life great delight and a purpose in life; gardening was an activity pursued with love and passion. "When all is said and done, is there any more marvellous sight, any occasion when human reason is nearer to some sort of converse with the nature of things, than the sowing of seeds, the planting of cuttings, the transplanting of shrubs, the grafting of slips?" asked St. Augustine. The Chinese emperor Quianlong (1736–96), who established the enormous gardens of the summer palace near Beijing, is described as having been possessed by a garden madness. Even Francis Bacon (1561–1626), whose relationship to nature at times assumed violent forms, raved that gardening was "the Purest of Humane pleasures," though he also had a clear appreciation of the charms of the seeming wilderness. "Paradise" as a pleasure garden is an ancient dream of humanity that can still be found at the foundation of the modern ideal of "biodiversity." Even the link between garden and health has a long tradition. In the nineteenth century, the economist Roscher felt that the lack of gardening around the outskirts of Madrid and in part also of Rome was a "symptom of disease."[55] However, in the past the fruits of the garden were not associated with good health as self-evidently as they are today: Alvise Cornaro, the author of one of the most famous books on the art of longevity, spurned fruits and vegetables. The herb garden, on the other hand, was the origin of the apothecary and of biology.

The significance of the garden to the peasant economy varied by time and place. In regions of intensive field cultivation on a small scale, the peasant becomes a gardener. However, it was a well-known fact in older times that the majority of German peasants "did not think much of the garden," looking on it "as a kind of necessary evil" that diverted fertilizer from the growing of grain. This was not true of peasant women, though. From the pueblos in ancient America to German farms in modern times, the garden has typically been the woman's realm and pride. Here there are traditions of female knowledge and experience that are often difficult to grasp in the sources. If one looks for a special role of women in environmental history, one finds a solid basis for it most often in the garden. In centuries past, this is especially well documented for noble women. The Electress Anna of Saxony (1532–87) knit a "dense and extensive social network – among them many women of the higher classes with botanical-economic interests, including nuns – in which plants and plant knowledge was continuously circulating"; her correspondence comprises ninety-one folio volumes. Among men, too, the passion for gardening created, beginning in the early modern period, entire networks of communication in which plants, seeds, and experiences were exchanged.[56]

How should we think of the special quality of what we experience in the garden? Without a doubt, it was here, above all, that the habit developed of taking a close look at the soil and crumbling it in one's hands. The spade and shovel are implements that virtually invite those wielding them to study the various layers of the soil in the utmost detail. It was the garden, more so than expansive fields, that nourished the feeling that the soil should be treated with care. Even at the time of the first great agrarian reforms, P. G. Poinsot, in his book *L'Ami des cultivateurs* (1806), emphasized, to the amazement of the historian Fernand Braudel, that "the earth is never so well turned over and shaken apart as with the spade." Early modern images often still show peasants with a spade, not a plow: Was this at that time already a mere archaicism, as the East German agrarian historian Ulrich Bentzien has argued? "The spade is the peasant's goldmine" goes a saying from Flanders, a region with a highly advanced agriculture.[57] Garden cultivation was *not* merely an area of retreat from agriculture, and the disadvantages of plowing are not a discovery of modern soil ecology.

Even in early times, it was possible to fertilize gardens generously on account of their limited size. In the garden, more so than in fields, it was possible to experiment with various kinds of fertilizer, discover the dangers of overfertilization, and gather experiences with new plants. It was in the garden that urine was first employed as a fertilizer. Subsequently, its systematic use by underpinning stables with masonry was one of the most important ecological achievements of the agrarian reforms of the eighteenth century. No compulsory tillage prevented individuals from trying out new things in the garden. With a multitude of plants growing in a confined space, it became apparent that not all species get along well, and these were fundamental insights of plant ecology. In addition, cultivators learned about successful and unsuccessful rotations of different species on the same plot of soil. One could observe how some plants fertilized the soil better than others, and how certain species spread at the expense of others as soon as the garden was left to grow on its own for only a few weeks.

All in all, the age-old tradition of gardening is one of the strongest arguments that humanity must have possessed a good deal of practical knowledge about ecological interrelationships since ancient times. It is not so clear, though, whether the garden gave rise to an awareness of processes that could lead to ecological crises, since it is easier to control the ecology in a small, fenced plot of earth than over large areas, and since a depletion of the soil could be easily remedied here. In any case, flowers need soil that is not too rich in nutrients. Especially in proximity to urban markets, peasants early on switched to garden cultivation on a larger scale, and the urban latrines provided plenty of fertilizer. Garden landscapes are, ecologically, the most pleasant side of the urbanization process, and they diverted attention away from the fact that the growing cities were upsetting the cycle of nutrients. Incidentally – precisely because gardens are such complicated ecological entities, causal connections cannot be clearly determined by experience alone, as there are usually more than one opinion on why one plant or another fails to thrive. What the garden promoted least of all was an understanding that it could be a good thing to leave nature to its own devices once in a while, and that natural ecosystems are self-regulating: to have the garden just the way one wants, one has to weed it frequently. The notion that nature is by itself a blooming garden is a typical illusion of those who do not work in a garden. Gardens gave rise to greenhouses. Beginning in the eighteenth century, cultivators in English, Dutch, and French gardens experimented ceaselessly with the "acclimatization" of exotic plants.[58] To this day, gardeners take special pride in plants that are found nowhere else in their area.

Many gardens include fruit trees, and they are often central to the cultivation scheme. This was certainly not the case from the very beginning, for their cultivation presupposes a sedentary way of life. In many areas of Central Europe, the great period of orcharding did not begin until the nineteenth century. But *fruit-bearing trees* in the older meaning of the words include also the oak, the chestnut, the olive, the carob, and in more southern climes the palm, the banana, and the mango – trees that often formed the core of entire peasant cultures. Growing and caring for these trees was *the* original silviculture, and it is here that one must look for the earliest arboreal consciousness. Victor Hehn, a pioneer of the cultural history of nature, came to believe that it was above all the cultivation of fruit trees that made humans sedentary and taught them how to labor with a long-term perspective.[59] When clouds of insects swarmed around the blooming fruit trees in the spring, it gave humans an inkling of the great interconnectedness of nature, even if the pollination of blossoms by insects was not discovered until the eighteenth century. It was one of those realizations that formed the basis of the belief in the divine wisdom of nature.[60]

Fruit trees often enjoyed special protection in written and unwritten law. Mosaic law forbade the cutting down of the enemy's trees in time of war (Deut. 20:19); Solonic legislation in ancient Athens outlawed the felling of olive trees on pain of death. For Saint Augustine, the groundless plundering of a pear tree was a special transgression, worse than sexual sins. In 1187 Emperor Frederick Barbarossa placed those who destroyed vineyards and orchards on a par with murderous arsonists. In the costumals of German forest communities (*Markgenossenschaften*) we repeatedly encounter the stipulation that he who "girdles" or strips a fruit tree – that is, kills it by removing the bark – should be disemboweled.[61] In more recent times as well, damage to fruit trees aroused strong emotions. Goethe's Werther became irate when the pastor's wife had the walnut tree in front of the parsonage cut down: "Cut down! I am furious and could kill the dog who struck the first blow with his axe."

Earlier than pasture and field, fruit trees were private property, even when the ground on which they stood was still seigneurial or cooperatively owned land. In Germany, in many regions of which orchards did not have a very long tradition, an "age of pomology" began around 1800, a time when orcharding entered into a phase of experimentation and intensification. Fruit tree monocultures are generally a phenomenon of modernity. But as the core element of polycultures, some fruit trees reach back into very ancient times. When Don Quixote is given a meal of acorns by some goatherds he launches into a rapturous account of the Golden Age, describing that "blessed age" as a time when "no one, for his daily sustenance, needed to do more than lift his hand and pluck it from the sturdy oaks that so liberally invited him to share their sweet and flavorsome fruit . . . the heavy curve of the plowshare had not yet dared to open or violate the merciful womb of our first mother." One archaeologist has calculated that the inhabitants of the Mayan city of Tikal in the ninth century derived 80 percent of their calories from breadnuts.[62]

In conventional history of the forest, fruit-bearing trees make at most a marginal appearance, and the situation is not much better in agrarian history. That is why there has been little recognition to date that the protection of fruit trees is a tradition of practical environmental awareness. When the colonial administration of British India laid hands on the woodlands, it turned parts of the local population into enemies of the forest; but many Indian villages have been cultivating their mango and palm stands since time immemorial. P. G. Madon, who organized the forest administration of the British colony of Cyprus after 1880, underscored the need for regulation by complaining that the "most instinctive hatred of trees is, perhaps, the only point of affinity between Greeks and Turks." He was forgetting the olive trees so carefully tended by their owners, and especially the carob trees, the "black gold of Cyprus." Much the same holds true for the alleged hostility to trees in many other traditional cultures. The conditions of the Mediterranean are more favorable for fruit-bearing trees than for ordinary forest cover: that is why the inhabitants were behaving in a rational way not only economically, but also ecologically, when their love was directed chiefly at fruit-bearing trees. In regions of sub-Saharan Africa, banana trees produced fifteen times the yield in food than the cultivation of wheat could have achieved on the same acreage.[63]

The olive tree and the grape have shaped the landscape and the way of life in the Mediterranean region since prehistoric times. Still today, one can see the "age-old marriage of oil and wine" along many Mediterranean coastlines, a sign that it must have developed ecological stability over thousands of years. The vine is grown both as a climbing plant and as a freestanding bush with a gnarled trunk. Columella deals with the vine at the beginning of his book on trees, writing that viticulture was more difficult than the cultivation of any other tree. In contrast to other fruit-bearing trees, the olive and the vine have not only an archaic, but also a modernizing, side, containing from early on an impetus to trade and to move beyond the subsistence economy. That is why viticulture and olive growing received a first, powerful impetus from the rise of Mediterranean trade in Greco-Roman antiquity. With the decline of the Roman Empire they receded, advancing once again in the high and late Middle Ages. Their spread came in part at the expense of the original forest cover of the Mediterranean region.

As early as the thirteenth century, France saw the *bataille des vins*, the battle between the wines of various regions; the production of wine for trade was a risky business from the outset. In the sixteenth century, a *fièvre de l'olivier* spread along some Mediterranean coasts, a feverish surge in the growing of olive trees, which reached the point where the dangers of monoculture became real, for the olive tree was otherwise only one part of a *cultura promiscua*. Beginning in the late seventeenth century, the vine and olive cultures of southern France were heavily damaged by the frosts that climate historians regard as part of the "Little Ice Age." The cultivation of the olive and the vine already prompted a marked sensitivity to changes in the climate in ancient times, leading Theophrastus to speculate that humans were causing a coarser climate by cutting down the forests.[64]

Viticulture and olive growing did not generate a concern for the soil in the same way, and in that regard one could hold them responsible for some of the ecological indifference of the Mediterranean peoples. To be sure, on many hillsides they called for laborious terracing, but vines and olives also flourish in barren, rocky, even eroded soils. It is possible to increase the yield of the vine with fertilizers, but too much fertilizer is not good, and the best wines often grow in poor soils. "Wine must suffer," say the vintners of Bordelais: what they mean is that the vine in barren soil must search out its nutrients with long roots. The olive tree with its deep roots and enormous resilience and life span could nourish the confidence that nature and humans could survive even in the barren world of the mountains. The cultivation of the olive tree as such does not promote the love of dense forest; on Mallorca, "trees completely exposed to the circulation of the air are considered to be superior." Grape growers, on the other hand, prefer to have a forest nearby that provides a supply of wood for stakes and wine barrels. That is why one often finds forest and viticulture in tandem in France. Woodland was not usually cut down to make room for viticulture, since grapes do not grow well in forest soil. In Madeira the vines snake up chestnut trees – hence the spread of the chestnut in the north of the island. The olive tree, which yields its first harvest only seven years after being planted but can live a very long time, also promoted and demanded a long-term focus. Asked why there were no olive trees in Brazil, an Italian answered: "Who in this country wants to wait one or two human generations for a harvest?"[65]

Since ancient times, the *oak* has enjoyed throughout Europe a prestige like no other tree, which probably has to do less with the hardness of its wood than with its fruit, the acorn, which was a popular symbol of fertility and served as food, above all for pigs, though occasionally even for humans. This made them exceedingly valuable to the old peasant economy in many parts of Europe. It was in relationship to the oak that the subsistence economy shifted early on into a commercial economy. In Solling around 1600, the raising of pigs on acorns yielded twenty times as much money as the use of wood. Veritable "pig wars" erupted over the right to pasture pigs in a forest.[66]

The spread of the oak tree in more recent times was often the work of man. Long before foresters carried out reforestation, peasants were planting oak trees and nursing seedlings, at a time when they were clearing forests. Palynological studies in the Bentheim forest have noted "a marked rise in Quercus pollen spectra from the first periods of forest clearing in the early Middle Ages." Sixty-one malters of acorns were sown in the Frankfurt city forest in 1398. Acorns were sown not only by humans, but also by jays and pigs, who, while they were digging *for* acorns, were also digging acorns *into* the ground and eating pests. Many beautiful oak groves we owe to pig farming: the pig, at the same time an excellent consumer of leftovers, is one of the unsung heroes of environmental history. When environmental historians occasionally describe pig farming as an element in the destruction of the forests, they are turning the real situation on its head. If we look at old pictures that show peasants using sticks to knock down acorns from the trees, the whole thing might seem violent, but this method, by which people sought to beat the jays and squirrels to the crop, did not necessarily harm the tree, in fact, it could stimulate the production of acorns. But the fact that squirrels still trumped humans when it came to harvesting of acorns is presumably one of the reasons, according to Jared Diamond, why humans in the end did not choose the cultivation of oak trees but the growing of grain.[67]

"Acorns account for the riches of many nations," remarked Pliny the Elder. People lived on them in times of grain shortages. When Virgil describes the happiness of pigs in a year with a good acorn harvest, it becomes clear how the cheerful grunting of the swine rubbed off on the mood of humans. In Westphalia, people prayed to Saint Antonius with the pig, whom they called the "Fickel-Tünnes" (Piglet Antonius), for a good acorn yield, and there was rejoicing in the villages if the prayers were answered. No less famous than the Nordic oak groves are the durmast oak and cork oak forests of Spain and Portugal, which peasants cultivated as pig pastures and for cork, and which contrasted with the bare landscape dominated by huge herds of sheep. In 1916 an American geographer concerned about preserving the resources of the world lauded the cultivation of the oak on the Iberian peninsula as a prime example for an optimal combination of economy and ecology, one that could become a model for the whole world. A modern geographer has maintained that "the web of laws and customs connected with the use of these oak forests is without parallel in its complexity." Since the oak is slow growing, the planting of these trees demonstrates a forward-looking behavior focused on the distant future. Heavy beams of oak wood were a sign of good economy in German farmhouses; traditionally there was a tendency to overestimate the value of oak as building timber.[68]

There are, however, very different oak stories, as well. As Per Eliasson has recounted, there was a veritable hatred for the oak among Swedish farmers in the nineteenth century. In Sweden the oak was not protected by the pig, since the pasturing of pigs in the forest was not a significant activity in that country. The Swedish crown, on the other hand, laid claim to the oak for shipbuilding. As a result, this tree became for the farmers the symbol of interference in their own rights: the battle over the oak pervades nineteenth-century Swedish forest politics. Here, as in so many other instances, we see the dialectic of governmental protection of the environment at work: it is precisely the protection compelled from above which makes the object of protection unpopular.[69]

The *chestnut* is one of those themes in environmental history whose importance is best grasped on hikes, whether through the Ticino, the Ligurian Appenines, the Cévennes, or the mountains of Catalonia and Asturia. There the chestnut was once, in many places, the chief food and center of a polyculture in combination with the growing of grain and the keeping of sheep and goats. As primeval as the chestnut forests seem to the observer, they all go back to human plantings; this, too, is a kind of peasant arboriculture that began thousands of years before forestry-based afforestation projects. In the mountain regions of the Mediterranean, the chestnut is an especially rich provider of nourishment and calories, richer than grain or even the potato. Even where it was not a major source of food, it was a reserve for emergencies: in 1653, when rye and barley "failed completely" in the Alps while chestnuts were raining down from the trees, hungry people were streaming down into the Valtellina. Since the chestnuts were growing nicely, wrote a landowner in Languedoc in 1586, the girls were "in full flower, strong and healthy." But many agrarian reformers in the eighteenth and nineteenth centuries did not like the chestnut and saw it as a symbol of backwardness and as a food that made people heavy of blood and sluggish.

How one should assess the cultivation of the chestnut from an ecological point of view is a question that is open to debate. Vito Fumagalli sees it as an early disturbance of natural ecosystems, since the chestnut did not allow other plants to grow up around it. On mountainsides, the chestnut tree does not retain the soil on its own, but requires the support of terrace walls. In some places it led to an impoverishment of the soil, which the peasants counteracted by burning sod (*Rasenbrennen*) and fertilizing with ashes. Typically, though, the chestnut was the backbone of a polyculture adapted to the Mediterranean environment: a triad of arboriculture, husbandry, and pasturing.[70]

From an ecological perspective, the silvo-agro-pastoral triad of tree, field, and pasture was in many cases far from an ideal trinity, and the role of trees in it is not beneficial in every regard. For example, trees deprive agricultural crops of light, water, and nutrients, and their leaves can lead to an unwanted acidification of the soil.[71] Still, the fact that the relationship to trees is regarded as a chief indicator of humanity's relationship to nature is not entirely unjustified. The cultivation of fruit-bearing trees in the broader sense of the word was in many regions of the world for thousands of years an important element in the stabilization of the environment, an element that has so far received too little attention. There is good reason why trees are a symbol of forward-looking stewardship: around trees there arises, with a certain natural inevitability, a mental outlook that is focused on future generations. In earlier times, trees usually promoted polycultures, not monocultures. By and large they helped to protect the soil and to store water. Since they do not depend on changing weather conditions nearly to the same degree as grain, and since they are difficult to replant, they direct the attention of humans to the enduring conditions of the local environment. They created a sense for "sustainability" long before this word was ever used. Within the world of plants, humans have had a special and frequent predilection for identifying themselves with trees. But that was by no means always an identification with nature growing wild. For arboriculture is also a culture of polling, grafting, and pruning, a partial taming of wild growth, no different from the art of gardening.[72] Columella (V.9.15) reminded his readers of the "old proverb" that "he who ploughs the olive-grove, asks it for fruit; he who manures it, begs for it; he who lops it, forces it to yield fruit." But this is not the only place in history where we find a close link between the manipulation of nature and the love of nature. From the perspective of ecology, as well, the gardener's basic experience that beautiful nature can not only be preserved, but also newly created, is not an illusion.

4. FARMERS AND HERDERS

The "origin of farming" is a classic theme in prehistory. Since 1928 scholars have tended to follow Gordon Childe in picturing this event as analogous to the upheavals of modernity: as the "Neolithic Revolution," the transition from nomadic hunter-gatherer ways to a sedentary life, to husbandry and animal keeping, to property and the accumulation of surplus.[73] From the bourgeois point of view this was the beginning of progress, from the Marxist point of view it was the beginning of exploitation. As the Fall of Man, the Neolithic Revolution also figures in a common ecological version of world history, namely, as the transition from humanity being part of nature to subjugating it.

In 1928, however, the "Neolithic Revolution" was not a process that could be empirically demonstrated, but a speculative construct. Modern archaeologists have called this process a "monumental non-event."[74] After all, agriculture did not arrive as a great new system; rather, gathering and the early working of the soil must have existed side by side for a long time. Hunters already intervened actively in their environment by using slash-and-burn cultivation. There were fluid transitions from the gathering way of life to cultivation involving planting, the digging stick, and the hoe: the road to early agriculture was not a great leap. The beginning of agriculture is found thousands of years earlier than was believed at the time of Gordon Childe.

That is why agriculture, like the garden, is in its early forms part of the primeval ways in which humans have interacted with their environment. The breeding of strains of grain that multiplied the crop yield many times over must have been a lengthy process, which began first in areas where promising strains grew wild. In all likelihood, it was an evolution that inched its ways forward with the help of experience, and not an abrupt change of the environment. Even a medieval field of grain would hardly be recognizable as such to a modern observer, so small was the grain and so densely was it pervaded by weeds.

There has been a good deal of speculation about how we should imagine the motivation that impelled ancient humans to transition from a hunter–gatherer life to agriculture and sedentism. Of course, speculation is all it can be. Both Jewish and Greek mythology suggest that the transition to agriculture occurred only reluctantly and under the pressure of necessity, and that the happiest time was when humans lived without much labor and from what nature offered freely of herself. Studies of modern "stone age peoples" have shown that unless they have been pushed into impoverished refuges, they do indeed possess a varied diet and a good deal of leisure: the myth of paradise, of the Golden Age, has a real foundation. Even today, one can observe that population groups, once land is available in abundance, revert from intensive agriculture back to "shifting cultivation," because they can feed themselves with less work.[75]

A combination of logical and empirical conclusions suggests the existence of a demographic-ecological chain reaction since the Neolithic period: under growing demographic pressure, extensive economic forms are replaced by intensive ones. However, since this increases the danger of overworking and degrading the soil, the dynamic triggered by the impending crisis is further accelerated, as a more intensive cultivation of the soil requires more people, who in turn increase the pressure on the soil. "If there was any flywheel that drove the history of this time," Hubert Markl observed, "it was no doubt the flywheel made up of fear of imagined and experienced shortages."[76] Note the wording: it is not only stark necessity that is the mother of invention, but equally so the fear of necessity – of a necessity that one may not have experienced oneself, but is merely anticipating.

Since the breeding of high-yielding strains of grain takes a long time, it is impossible to imagine it as a panic reaction. This is yet another case that shows that great innovations are done not only out of sheer necessity, but that opportunity, ambition, and available resources must be thrown into the mix. It is striking that the earliest agriculture arose in comparatively favored regions of the world. Reviewing the archaeological finds in the Old and New Worlds, Bruce D. Smith concludes that an "agricultural way of life appears to have emerged where societies were not immediately threatened, but nonetheless were encouraged by surrounding circumstances to search widely for ways of reducing long-term risk." One can imagine that the diffusion of agriculture was driven not only by the pressure of necessity, but also by the impulse of a social system seeking surplus products. Karl Butzer, himself a pioneer of environmental research in archaeology, has warned against using a one-dimensional "environmentalism that obscures the fact that the origin of agriculture is, in the first place, a cultural phenomenon." The more differentiated society becomes, the more humans respond directly not to natural conditions, but to the social definition of natural phenomena. For Jared Diamond, the inexorable spread of agriculture all over the world has to do above all with *power*: sedentary agriculture spawned greater concentrations of people with superior weapons and social organization.[77]

And yet, the rise of agriculture cannot be due solely to military superiority, since that superiority was slow to emerge. The hunter was actually a better warrior than the farmer. Agricultural societies often fell under the rule of an aristocracy that cultivated the tradition of the hunt.[78] Only the perfecting of heavy firearms in the early modern period established the conclusive military superiority of sedentary cultures. Prior to that, farming settlements were very vulnerable – much more vulnerable than nonsedentary hunter populations. Because farmers are much more exploitable than hunters, they offered a much more stable foundation for structures of political domination. But we must also ask whether the superiority of agriculture was not also grounded in a much more stable ecology: only sedentary farmers were capable of sustainable economic practices, sustainable in the sense of engaging in conscious planning.

Sedentism, however, creates – to an unprecedented degree – the danger that the soil will be overused. To be sure, it was only now that this danger was clearly seen and could be countered with specific measures: but were the solutions always at hand and were they successfully implemented? Only the sedentary farmer can ensure that the field does not lose any fertilizer – but did he actually do that? Moreover, the concentration of people in a single location increases the danger of disease and epidemics. Agriculture became a "bonanza for our microbes,"[79] as the rise of agriculture also ushered in a great age of mice, rats, and locusts.

It is striking that precisely the oldest agricultural regions in Central Asia are today largely barren, and the suspicion that agriculture destroyed itself there by exhausting the soil springs readily to mind. In these instances we are talking about regions that are already ecologically fragile by nature and threatened by desertification. But pollen analysis has shown that even in Central Europe the sedentary nature of farming settlements was not permanent. In southern Germany, Roman rule brought a first phase of settlement continuity, but when that rule came to an end, there was a return to shifting cultivation.[80] Political conditions evidently played a decisive role in the emergence of lasting sedentism. Was the previous migratory cultivation the result of necessity, the impoverishment of the soil? In the early period, farmers practiced single-field cultivation without crop rotation: if the plowed land was not rotated, yields invariably declined over the long run. All over the world, crop rotation and the combining of cultivation with fertilizer-producing livestock breeding emerged only gradually over the course of time.

An awareness that the environment is a potential problem is the inevitable result of a sedentary way of life. The fertility cults that are found throughout the world are an indication that an awareness of the fertility of the fields being constantly under threat has existed since very ancient times. Religion and rituals are not necessary for tasks that are routinely accomplished. And, needless to say, rituals do not accomplish any tasks at all. The remedy for soil exhaustion was well known in principle: a fallow period, fertilization, crop rotation. Pliny the Elder even encountered marling among the Ubii in the region around Cologne. Organized crop rotation was found among premodern sub-Saharan tribes, who generally did not fertilize their fields.[81] The simplest method of regeneration was the fallow, often combined with the pasturing of animals; the explanation for this effect was that the soil, just like humans and animals, needed rest from time to time. As late as the nineteenth century, the "tiredness" of the soil was a standard term.

Yet if the soil is a living organism, will it not be injured by the plowshare? Already in the consciousness of ancient times, the introduction of the plow, which cut the entrails of the earth, constituted a turning point that ushered in a harsher time. From the perspective of environmental history, that sentiment was not unfounded: plants were now no longer treated individually as they were with cultivation using the hoe. With looser soils and on sloping ground, the plow increases the danger of erosion. As plowing requires oxen and horses and considerable physical strength from the farmer, a farming economy takes on a more pronounced patriarchal quality. One can imagine how the heavy plow went hand in hand with a more imperious attitude toward nature.[82]

"Plough, plough, plough" was the advice that Cato the Elder hammered into the heads of Roman peasants. "What is good farming?" asked Pliny the Elder: "Good ploughing. What is second best? Ploughing. What third? Manuring." "Plough with all your might" was his advice. But even the realization that the plow must be used with caution depending on the lay of the land and must be adapted to the nature of the soil is, in principle, nothing new. Pliny knew that in "Syria they use a light ploughshare that cuts a narrow furrow, because the subsoil is rock which causes the seeds to be scorched in summer." Theophrastus also warned that plowing too deeply could be harmful since it caused the soil to dry out. Ancient Greek plows were of wood and were fashioned by the peasants themselves; they were surely light plows, more or less adapted to the light Mediterranean soils. The heavy plow with the iron plowshare emerged in Northern Europe with its heavy soils, where it is already attested in the early Middle Ages, and possibly even earlier. In the north it is useful for returning to the surface the nutrients that are washed down to the lower layers by the frequent rains; by contrast, in southern, semiarid climate the nutrients tend to rise upward through strong evaporation.[83]

However, when Lynn White believed that he could detect a technological revolution in the early Middle Ages that was partly caused by the plow, he was dramatically exaggerating the processes that took place. Even the "heavy" plows of earlier times were rather light by modern standards; as late as the early modern period, they penetrated the soil to a maximum depth of only 12 centimeters.[84] That explains why those agrarian reformers around 1800 who highlighted the importance of humus to the fertility of the soil were far from condemning the plow as the destroyer of the soil. In the beginning, the technological transition from the hoe to the plow was fluid, and the progress toward deeper plowing was a slow and protracted process in preindustrial times. A rapid acceleration became possible only in the age of mass-produced steel and mechanical traction power. In the twentieth century, the heavy plow was also used on soils where it was destructive over the long run; in older times, though, we can see only the beginnings of an inherent dynamic in plow technology that had gotten out of control. Wood as the material and animals as traction power imposed tight limits on how deeply the plow could penetrate the soil.

For thousands of years, maintaining the fertility of the soil was a question of fallow periods and fertilizer. That is why the relationship between agriculture and animal husbandry is one of the key themes of environmental history throughout the world. In many cases an optimal balance and combination was not achieved, with the two forms at loggerheads instead of coexisting. A great many deplorable conditions in the past are directly or indirectly connected with this relationship. To be sure, the plow compelled farmers to keep draft animals; other than that, though, even the peasants of Central Europe often regarded the keeping of animals as "useless and onerous." Even in the fertilizer-conscious nineteenth century, the advance of agriculture sometimes exacerbated the clash with cattle breeding: "In the end a battle breaks out between plow and herds," complained the agrarian reformer and pedagogue Stephan Ludwig Roth in Transylvania, where agriculture was often practiced by the German "Saxons," and pasture farming by the Rumanian Walachians. Often, though, there was enmity between farmers and herders even without the added clash of nationalities: "Improbable though it seems," remarked Braudel, "scorn for the shepherd and livestock-farmer has carried on down the ages into the present day." Roger Dion, the historian of viticulture, believes that the traditional difference between landscapes of northern and southern France results, not least, from the fact that the French north combined agriculture and animal breeding on its open fields, while the southern French type of field cultivation excluded animal herds.[85]

In regions with intensive, garden-like cultivation of agriculture on terraced fields, farmers do not need draft animals – in fact, animals tend to pose a danger to the terraces. Throughout the Mediterranean, agriculture and animal husbandry often did not form a reciprocally stabilizing unit, and one can see this failure as one fundamental shortcoming of Mediterranean history across centuries and millennia. In northern Italy, for example, an ancient hatred existed between farmers and herders. Here, as elsewhere, the pasture economy was often a world unto itself, with different owners, ways of life, and population groups. The Old Testament story of Cain, the farmer, and Abel, the herder, reflects an age-old clash. In this instance, the farmer killed the shepherd. Many times, though, the herders were more martial than the farmers and had the backing of powerful owners of herds. Where that was the case, they did not have to pay much heed to farmers, who tried to defend themselves. In German lands, seigneurial shepherds suffered "hatred and persecution, mayhem and murder" at the hands of farmers for centuries. In those regions of the Algarve in which the strawberry tree (*artubus unedo*) was cultivated, there was "open warfare" between farmers and herders. The agrarian ecology was thus in the final analysis a question of social structures and power relationships. But the pasture also promoted agriculture unintentionally, by, of all things, its destructive effect: by advancing the erosion on the mountain slopes, the pasture caused the fertile soil to collect in the lowlands, where it could be more conveniently cultivated.[86]

The pasture economy was furthest removed from agriculture among the *nomads*. The gap between the two had ecological as well as political consequences. In the nineteenth century, Senegal experienced an enormous surge in peanut cultivation under French rule, but the boom ended up exhausting the soil, which was not receiving any animal fertilizer: animal breeding was something nomads did, not farmers.[87] The eventful relationship between nomads and sedentary cultures is a leitmotif of world history from late antiquity to the early modern period, and it is of great importance for environmental history as well. This raises the question whether the conditions of the steppe permit a type of sustainability other than farming: a type of environmental regeneration precisely through a nonsedentary lifestyle and the frequent change of pastures. One could argue that the best kind of sustainability is that which requires no careful planning for the future at all, but is simply achieved by making sure that the ground remains covered with vegetation at all times. That was also the view of many nomadic leaders in the struggle with farming peoples. In 1892 the religious head of the Mongols called on his people "to destroy the many Chinese who are turning the soil yellow and dry with their ploughing." But does it make sense at all to speak of sustainability with respect to the nomadic way of life?

The Arab historian Ibn Khaldun (1332–1406) gave a classic description of the contrast between nomads and sedentary peoples, and he did so filled with admiration for the nomads, whom he described as some kind of "noble savages": they were healthier, stronger, and less corrupted than civilized people. That they lived such a frugal life and often suffered hunger merely contributed to their virtues. And yet: wherever they went, they left destruction in their wake, for "the very nature of their existence is the negation of building. . . . Furthermore, it is their nature to plunder whatever other people possess."[88] A forward-looking and sustainable economic behavior is hard to imagine among the sort of nomads described by Ibn Khaldun.

As sedentary peoples in many regions of the world have looked on nomads since time immemorial with fear and loathing, the environmental historian might be tempted to share this view in his own way. In fact, Bernard Campbell, in his universal survey of environmental history, concluded: "Overgrazing, the tragedy of pastoralism, has brought about chronic deterioration in the ecological communities of many areas of the world" and "has been a disaster for nature and a tragedy for humankind." Xavier de Planhol also tended to confirm this negative verdict in his sweeping, carefully researched synopsis of the historical geography of the Islamic world. He argued that Islam, itself a religion of the desert, had promoted "bedouinization" in an "unparalleled way," thereby also supporting the advance of steppe and the desert at the expense of field and forest, even if in certain areas – chiefly Spain – it led to the flowering of irrigation agriculture by introducing eastern technologies. On the whole, Islam spread the extensive pasture economy; moreover, it exacerbated population pressures, because nomadic society ceaselessly produced "humans, like locusts" – this was the result of the nomad's healthful way of life so praised by Ibn Khaldun and of the salutary climate of the desert.[89]

Today nomads around the world have turned from threatening into threatened peoples who enjoy the sympathy of ethnologists. In more recent times the environmentally friendly elements of pastoralism have been frequently highlighted, in part as a reaction against the traditional contempt that sedentary civilizations have felt for nomads. From an ecological perspective there is no need to regret that nomads over centuries retarded the advance of irrigation agriculture into dry regions. Horst G. Mensching, a student of desertification, believes that the Arab nomads of the Middle Ages helped to regenerate in North Africa the ecosystem of the steppe unhinged by Roman agriculture.[90] Since this question is of fundamental importance for the interpretation of all of global environmental history, it deserves closer examination.

Nomadism is not a primeval way of life, nor is it likely to have evolved directly out of the stone age hunting way of life; instead, nomads generally live from trade with sedentary cultures and already presupposes the domestication of animals. For those nomads who moved across the wide expanses of the desert, the fundamental innovation was the domestication of the camel, presumably achieved around 3,500 years ago. The camel, with its unique ability to go days without water and to give milk even in times of drought (it is also an excellent food utilizer), is today recommended in steppe regions as the ecologically preferable alternative to cattle and as a prophylactic against desertification. The growth and reproduction of the camel is fairly slow, which means that a temporary improvement in the food supply does not immediately lead to a rapid increase in numbers. Only the camel made possible a full nomadism that was highly mobile in desert regions, as a result, the nomadic warriors posed a much greater danger to sedentary peoples.

Nomadism presumably arose as a reaction to experiences of ecological crises, to desertification in the wake of climate change or overgrazing. Today we can watch as nomads who have been forced to settle down destroy sparse vegetation within a few short years with their pasture economy. In these regions only movement saves the pasture economy from an ecological disaster. The historian and diplomat Steven Runciman, who spent a good deal of time in the East, went so far as to comment that all nomadic tribes lived in constant "fear lest their pasture-lands and forests should be exhausted."[91] Herding peoples had the migrations of wild animals as their model. There are, however, many indications – admittedly, not always unambiguous – that nomads not only responded to the conditions of the steppe and the desert, but themselves contributed to the spread of these landscapes.[92]

If the nomads relied exclusively on the sparse and dispersed food supply of their habitat, they were consigned to an extremely decentralized form of society. In fact, nomads are said to possess a pronounced sense of individualism. Still, throughout history there have been nomadic concentrations of power. One Indian agrarian historian even believes that "militarization" is part of the very nature of distance-spanning nomadism, since nomads have to be constantly prepared for attacks. Herodotus thought that the great advantage of the nomadic mobility of the Scythians lay in its military superiority, and not, for example, in its adaptation to the environment, which he described as richly endowed with water.[93] Mobility was of the essence especially if one was amassing warriors and horses in the steppe: if one remained in the same place even briefly, the animals would run out of food. The great campaigns of conquest by the nomads were not a direct response to the nature of the steppe; however, once the massing of military power had begun, its dynamic was reinforced by ecology.

The sight of the desert, in particular, where the environment seems all-powerful, can seduce the observer into an ecological determinism. As a result, when it comes to the nomads, the ethnologist Karl Jettmar has warned of the danger that the "overall ecological concept" is "almost hopelessly overemphasized" and politics is neglected. Even current observations can seduce one into this perception, since today nomads everywhere lead a powerless existence in areas of retreat, where they have no other choice but to adapt to a sharply circumscribed environment. This is how the Tibetologist Melvyn C. Goldstein has described the nomads of western Tibet, whose grazing animals are restricted in number and their yearly change of pasture fixed – today by the Chinese administration, before that by the officials of the Panchen Lama. The nomads know that they cannot move into any other region, which is why they are always very careful not to overuse their grazing grounds. But even under these conditions, it is not easy to prevent overgrazing. And the nomads at the time of Mohammed or Genghis Khan are far less likely to have had a basic attitude of precautionary self-restraint. The Asia scholar Ferdinand von Richthofen believed as late as the nineteenth century that every nomadic tribe "has regarded the steppe as its property since time immemorial." The endless steppe did not promote a thinking in circumscribed spaces. Fighting over grazing grounds was constant, which explains the militant trait of pastoralism. It was only outside powers that drew fixed boundaries through the desert and the steppe.[94]

More recent scholars have emphasized that the nomads are not as "wild" as they seem to many sedentary people, but usually move within bounded spaces and are in principle perfectly capable of preventing their living space from being overtaxed. The old notion of an utterly unbounded nomadism contains an element of romanticism. But even Johannes Esser, who accentuates this "nonwildness," concludes that the system of rules in the nomadic pastoral economy contains only "a direct relationship of production to the sheep, the herd, but not to the soil or the steppe," and therein lies a fundamental difference to agriculture. To be sure, the nomads, too, observe the fertility of the soil, but traditionally they have no means of improving it. Animals are the possession in which nomads take pride, not land. And even if nomads had good intentions of adjusting their herds to the available pastureland, it would not have been easy for them to determine its carrying capacity. Defining ecological carrying capacity is difficult even today. As it is not possible to calculate the precise balance between the number of grazing animals and their pastures even in *theory*, it is easy to see why in historical *reality* there was often tension in that equation. It is true that camels reproduce only slowly, but even camel nomads often have sheep and goats. Sheep herds can double in size in three or four mild winters. And nomads certainly did not *always* move along fixed routes, but often sought out new pasture grounds. As John R. McNeill has observed for the Mediterranean region: "Instability is an inherent condition of pastoralism."[95]

The chief counterargument against the thesis of an inherent danger of overgrazing is climatic variability: periods of drought reduced the number of animals on a more or less regular basis. On the other hand, one strategy of protecting oneself against drought is precisely to increase the size of the herds so one could slaughter animals in times of famine. Herds were also increased for reasons of prestige, for in the logic of pastoralism, social rank is determined not by land, but by the size of the herd. Especially the omnivorous goat is affected the least by times of drought and cold. According to H. F. Lamprey, the "overwhelming evidence of continuous ecological degradation" in the African savannahs demonstrates that the adaptation of pastoralism to the environment, while it did exist, was not the rule, least of all in places where herds were not periodically decimated by winter and drought.

If there were regulatory mechanisms, that doesn't mean they were ecologically motivated. "The camel markets in Syria, Mesopotamia, and Egypt," observed T. E. Lawrence, "determined the population which the deserts could support, and regulated strictly their standard of living." The frequent use of dung as fuel already argues against the view that nomadic society was fundamentally sustainable. When Donald Worster, though not entirely unreceptive to the romanticism of the Wild West, highlights the destructive character of what he calls "Cowboy Ecology," he simultaneously indicates that this ecological fragility is inherent in extensive nomadic pastoral economies, even if this fragility was exacerbated by the dynamic of the capitalist pursuit of profit. All in all, a fundamentally negative assessment of sedentism and intensive land cultivation compared to extensive pastoralism *cannot* be sustained on ecological grounds.[96]

Sweeping value judgments are also difficult for the simple reason that in historical and contemporary reality we find numerous intermediate forms between pure nomadic pastoralism and completely sedentary agriculture. On closer inspection, many supposed "nomads" turn out to be seminomads, as, for example, the Kasaks of Central Asia. The ideal-type clash between farmers and nomads is in reality often blurred or overlaid by positive relationships. Over time, the contrast between farmers and nomads was not stable: under pressure of necessity, farmers turned into nomads and vice versa. No small number of peoples incorporate agricultural and nomadic elements, and their imagined identity is accordingly fluid: for example, the Old Testament Israelites, the Russians, the Rumanians, and the Tibetans. The yak herds, the foundation of both Tibetan agriculture and the nomadic way of life, embody the symbiosis of these two worlds. In Old Testament Israel, on the other hand, what Max Weber called the "old, cheerful Baal cults" with their sexual orgies, which were part of the agricultural world, were opposed by the prophets with an ascetic militancy that was the product of the barren steppe.[97]

Among the forms of migratory pastoralism based on sedentary herd owners, transhumance in Southern Europe is especially well known in modern times. Transhumance is a half-yearly alternation between summer pasture in the mountains and winter pasture in the valleys. Since the herds often belonged to influential landowners and entrepreneurs, the herders frequently showed little regard for the farmers. Transhumance thus offers prime examples of a calamitous clash of field and pasture. The potential for sustainability is greater – given the requisite geographical and climatic conditions – in a pastoral economy that is rooted in the soil and encompasses only a small and contained radius, examples being the Alpine pastures and the irrigated meadows. Types of mountain pasturing are found not only in the Alps, but also in Asian regions. It was here that a friendly and productive symbiosis of pasture and field was most likely to be achieved. Indian landowners even paid shepherds to have their animals fertilize the rice fields; similar arrangements are also found in German regions. All in all, there was probably far more peaceful exchange between farmers and herders than our historical sources, which record above all conflict, would have us believe, for the economic and ecological conditions favored coexistence, not conflict. The combination of agriculture and animal husbandry, not enmity between farmers and herders, seems to have been the rule even in ancient Israel, the story of Cain's murder of Abel notwithstanding.[98]

The ideal of a peaceful coexistence of field and pasture is evident right up to early modern European landscape painting.

In the industrial age, the cheap wire fence has made such a peaceful coexistence easier than ever. However, the historically unparalleled mass breeding of animals has disconnected stock raising from agriculture more profoundly than ever before, turning it into an ecological threat of global dimensions. It has been calculated that the total living weight of the more than 1.3 billion head of cattle in the world today exceeds the living weight of all humans by nearly threefold, and that the emissions from cattle approach those from cars in their effect on the atmosphere. James Lovelock believes that the pasture economy that is expanding at the expense of the forest constitutes today "the greatest threat to Gaia's health" (also by overburdening the atmosphere with methane gas), and he even recommends infecting the herds of the entire world with a viral disease and planting a tree on top of every dead animal.[99]

5. THE "TRAGEDY OF THE COMMONS" AND THE PLAGGEN PLAGUE: WAS PREMODERN AGRICULTURE "UNCONSCIOUS PLUNDER"?

Even when peasants combined agriculture and animal husbandry, that alone did not settle the issue of whether premodern agriculture was sustainable, for it was under these very circumstances that the problem of the commons – the communal pasture – emerged. It was this problem, especially, that attracted the critical attention of agrarian reformers and ecotheorists: more concretely, it was the question of whether the forests and pastures used by many farmers were not invariably subject to overuse and would thus sooner or later be ruined. The best known contribution to the debate was the essay "The Tragedy of the Commons" by the biologist Garrett Hardin, which was published in 1968 and challenged the anarcho-socialism of the sixties. Hardin created the impression that his thesis had a solid foundation in history. Historians actually paid little attention to it, while outside the historical profession it was often treated as a proven fact.

In Hardin's essay, the old commons with all its attendant problems becomes a metaphor, the prototype of a dynamic of ecological decline that is at work from prehistory to the present, from the village environment to the global atmosphere. The basic idea is quite simple and corresponds to the logic of game theory: since a person can never rely on the social sense of others, his behavior is most rational when he behaves selfishly, which means extracting as much as possible from common goods. Of course, in the long run these common goods will be ruined by such behavior; and yet, over the short run the advantage to the person acting in an unscrupulously selfish manner is far greater than the damage he inflicts. He who drives more cows onto the commons than is good for it still has the full benefit of these cows, but only a small fraction of the damage they cause, which affects all. Some individuals may act ethically, but it lies in the logic of things that the unscrupulous will triumph over the virtuous.[100] Hardin's conclusion: only selfishness can protect resources, which is why clear property laws – be they individual or state laws – are necessary everywhere.

To the extent that we are talking about the historical commons, this criticism is two centuries old, reflecting the polemic of the early modern agrarian reformers

against the communal peasant ownership of forest and pasture. "Quod communiter
posseditur, communiter neglegitur" (What is communally owned, is communally
neglected): in the eighteenth century, this originally Aristotelian polemic against
the communism of the Platonic polis was sometimes applied to the commons. The
bony and emaciated cows of the commons haunt the writings of those agrarian
reformers who preached barn feeding and the planting of fodder crops on what had
been the fallows and the commons. The scandal, however, was not necessarily the
overuse of the commons, but the shortage of fodder in the winter: "Covered in filth
like some kind of armor, with sharply projecting ribs and bones, the unfortunate
victims of human stupidity drag themselves along with crooked bodies" – this is
how Johann von Schwerz describes the return of the cows to the common pasture
in spring. One must bear in mind that each farmer was generally permitted to
drive as many cows onto the commons as he could bring through the winter,
which was one incentive to keep as much cattle as possible during the winter. The
emaciated cows are thus not necessarily evidence for the overuse of the commons,
but of the regulation of pasture animals by winter. In many old commons regions,
the soil was *not* destroyed. One modern plant ecologist fell into raptures studying
a common pasture that had been used since the Middle Ages, so great was the
diversity of its plant communities.[101]

As for Hardin, his interest was not in the old commons, but in the globally shared
resources of today, the oceans and the atmosphere. He sought to demonstrate that
it would be a fatal mistake to rely on the ecological conscience of good people
when it comes to the preservation of these resources; instead, harsh coercion was
necessary, above all coercive birth control. He had little confidence in the UN.
Taken to its logical conclusion, this scenario would essentially produce a global
ecodictatorship on the part of the United States, the last remaining superpower,
which also had the best sense of "property rights" for the task. So far, however,
it looks in many ways as though this amounts to putting the fox in charge of
the henhouse. A. T. Grove and Oliver Rackham have denounced Hardin's thesis:
"This pernicious notion was invented by an American with no experience of how
commons actually work. Despite a lack of evidence, it has been repeatedly used
by governments as an excuse to abolish or oppress commons, often with results
very different from those intended."

When it comes to the historical commons, many things were different. The
users were almost always a contained circle of individuals who knew each other
well and kept an eye on each other, kept out strangers, and – in spite of the
many quarrels within a village – were accustomed to varied forms of cooperation:
whether in the practice of multicourse crop rotation with its compulsory tillage,
the maintenance of irrigation systems, or the rendering of neighborly assistance
during emergencies or to ward off intruders. As long as the use of the commons
remained within the framework of the subsistence economy and was not seized
by the dynamic of income maximization, a customary self-limitation was in place.
When the commons showed signs of overuse, the Westphalian *Markgenossenschaften*
(forest communities) restricted the number of pasture animals. A "minor village
war" (Jon Mathieu) erupted in the Lower Engadin around 1700 over restrictions
on the keeping of goats. According to Werner Bätzing, "wherever the mountain
pasture economy was practiced collectively," the mountain farmers "fixed the

animal load of the pastures precisely and tried to adhere to it at all times." Well-organized village communities were frequently in a better position to care for the common forest in keeping with their needs than money-hungry lords who wished to fill their treasuries with the forests, and who often did not even know the woods they were supposedly protecting. A study of the canton of Lucerne has shown that peasant villages in the early modern period were able to improve the use of the commons in a prudent way: here we find nothing of the brutal indifference that – if some agrarian reformers are to be believed – led people to treat the common meadows like common whores. In the age of the commons, people had a very concrete conception of common goods that needed to be protected against private self-interest. It was first with nineteenth-century liberalism that the common good became a fiction.[102]

One can construct a logical argument that is the opposite of Hardin's argument, namely, that the care of future generations is in better hands with communities than with individuals who think only of their own life span. One could further add that world history certainly does not demonstrate that humans are by nature selfish beings who live only for the moment: on the contrary, not infrequently they display a frightening willingness to sacrifice themselves for larger communities and distant goals.

But caution is called for also with this counterthesis, for it is often evident that common practical reason is not automatic but functions only under favorable conditions, and even then by no means without friction. We can see this in the minutes of the early modern *Holthinge*, the court sessions of the type of forest cooperative especially common in northwestern Germany, which threatened those who transgressed against trees with terrible punishments, but in practice often allowed violations to be settled with beer for a communal drink. The transgressions dealt with at these sessions reveal how the supervision of the shared use of the forest functioned, but also its increasing shortcomings. The situation is similar with the communal property of Japanese village cooperatives: there, too, one can observe a "strong community identity" as a basic condition, with the effect that the villagers are very concerned with their standing within the community. Still, adherence to the rules in the use of the communal land had to be secured with punishments at all times, and the effectiveness of this system of sanctions is difficult to determine. And there is another aspect one must not overlook: if the driving of animals onto a mountain pasture is regulated, that certainly does not mean that this regulation is based on ecological criteria; most likely it is an expression of the distribution of power within a village. Regulatory action was taken only if there was conflict.

Ecological regulation certainly existed in premodern farming-herding societies, but we must not construct an exaggerated image of its stability and perfection. Within the old village communities, as well, people were often selfish and downright stubborn in their behavior. Indications of overgrazing are found even on Swiss mountain pastures: in 1849 the forest reformer Marchard decried that in the Berner Oberland, "six greedy mouths fight for each blade of grass." No less a friend of the farmers than Jeremias Gotthelf declared that the farmers "usually all do their own thing, each has first of all only his own interest at heart, no matter how the collective is faring." It was only in the twentieth century that the carrying capacity of the mountain pastures was precisely calculated and defined according to "large animal units" and "normal cow grazers."[103]

Roscher was "pleasantly impressed by the liberality with which nearly everywhere, if the population was not too crowded, use of the common pastures was permitted even to those who, strictly speaking, had no right to them." This liberality of the commons contained, however, a seed of ecological fragility: overuse of the commons was a factor in the development of a rural underclass. Moreover, the attacks on the commons that were gathering pace in the late eighteenth century were something of a self-fulfilling prophecy: if it was predictable in any case that the commons would be divided up sooner or later, a person behaved only rationally if he tried to quickly extract as much as possible from them. *That* was the true "tragedy of the commons," and it in fact seems to have been a global phenomenon that was repeated in the nineteenth and twentieth centuries on the pastures of Indian villages when state intervention, population pressure, and market incentives came together.[104] Prior to that, however, common pastures and forest constituted an ecological reserve that made the peasant economy more resistant to crisis.

Nineteenth-century Germany, like other countries as well, discovered – to the great disappointment of liberal forest reformers – that it was precisely the *division* of the commons that was often followed by the cutting of the forests. Moreover, in many cases the privatization of land did not lead to full ownership for farmers, but to tenancy. From an ecological point of view, tenancy comes with its own problem, since short-term leases favor the ruthless exploitation of the land. Although German leaseholding agreements from ancient times contained the stipulation that the land had to be returned well fertilized, in practice that could not be controlled with any accuracy. The agrarian reformer Albrecht Thaer, who opposed tenancy, described with withering irony in his "golden ABC for tenants" how one could, "with the utmost cunning," apply to the soil "all the arts of exploitation."[105]

Agrarian reformers usually attacked the *fallow* in conjunction with the commons – that is, the custom of leaving farmland uncultivated and opening it up for pasture at regular yearly intervals to restore its fertility, in keeping with the notion that tired soil needed a period of rest. But many times the anger directed at the fallow land was also driven by moral and economic rather than ecological motivations: the fallow embodied unused time, niches of idleness hidden within the old way of life. All over the world, the fallow was the primeval response to the exhaustion of the soil; in slash-and-burn cultivation, before the introduction of crop rotation, it often lasted many years. Around 1600 an English farmer using a two-field system – that is, leaving a field fallow every other year – achieved a ratio of 1:11 between seed grain and harvest grain, which was an excellent result by the standards of earlier times. In Andalusia farmers achieved a ratio of 1:8 by cultivating the land every third year. Julius Stöckhardt, a student of Liebig's, still proclaimed in his *Chemische Feldpredigten*: "Where nature is left to its own devices, we do not see a decline in the vigor of the soil, but a gradual increase. But we do see a clear impoverishment of the soil wherever man arrives with his drudgery (*Qual*)." This was an allusion to Schiller's verse from the play *The Bride of Messina*: "Die Welt ist volkommen überall / Wo der Mensch nicht hinkommt mit seiner Qual" ("Nature is perfect everywhere, that man does not get to with his drudgery").[106]

Around the heath landscapes of Northwestern Europe, the *plaggen system* held sway into the nineteenth, indeed the early twentieth, century. Soil archaeology has revealed just how widespread it was and how many centuries old. Many agrarian reformers, however, regarded the plaggen as a "plague" and a particularly flagrant example of the systematic destruction of the soil of the commons. Especially in regions that were not fertile by nature, it was the custom for centuries – if not millennia – to cut grass sod from the common land, enrich it with slurry from the barn, and apply it to the cropland as fertilizer. This even made possible a "permanent" cultivation of grain without crop rotation, while the commons deteriorated more and more and were transformed into a treeless heath, sometimes even into a dune landscape. Heinrich Christian Burckhardt, the longtime head of the Hannover forestry administration, complained in 1895 about the "Libyan desert" in the plaggen grounds of the Emsland.[107] Soils with sparse vegetation were additionally damaged from wind erosion and the leaching out of mineral components, which solidified into hardpan lower down and blocked the growth of roots and the groundwater supply. The plaggen system consumed an enormous amount of land: using plaggen to fertilize the cropland required an outfield area at least five times – if not thirty or forty times – the size of the cultivated fields. To anyone who measures the quality of agriculture by the intensity of land use, the plaggen system was an utter disgrace.

But did the plaggen economy necessarily constitute the destruction of nature, and is its four-hundred-year-old history that of an ecological time bomb? In some areas it lasted nearly a thousand years and left behind landscapes that delight modern nature lovers. The sods were very effective in regenerating the fertility of the fields. In northern Germany, the transition to the cutting of sod around 1000 C.E. was a "revolution in agricultural economy" (Ellenberg), which made possible an intensive cultivation of rye. Even the agrarian reformer Schwerz found it peculiarly difficult to render a verdict on the cutting of sod in his description of Westphalian agriculture (1836) and wavered on the issue: on some level he was appalled at how humans kept destroying the "work begun" by nature and left behind large tracts of land in a "despoiled state." On the other hand, this kind of agriculture seemed to be based "not only on happenstance and mere sloppiness, but was also grounded in the very nature of the thing itself." To all appearance, the sustainability of a plaggen soil economy was a question of settlement density, the available wasteland, and – resulting from this – the rest periods allowed the soil between the cutting of sod. The sheep that grazed the plaggen grounds during this time also fertilized the soil. As several historians of the Lüneburg Heath have noted, the heathland was subject in earlier times "to a constant rejuvenation through pasturing, mowing, sod-cutting, and burning."[108]

If one reproach leveled against premodern agriculture was that it lived at the expense of the heath, another was that it lived at the expense of forest and destroyed the forest soil through the use of leaves and litter: in this case, as well, the sustainability of agriculture was merely an illusion. "Without deadfall, the cultivation of grain" would have long ago "disappeared" in many parts, Liebig assured his readers. "Instead of robbing the soil, people are robbing the forests for as long as possible!"[109] From a modern perspective there is indeed reason to suspect that the removal of leaves and deadfall deprived the forest floor of far more nutrients than the cutting of wood; this particular criticism should be taken more seriously than many sweeping judgments regarding the harmfulness of forest pasture.

On the other hand, in more recent times we have come to understand – far more clearly than did the forestry teachers in the early nineteenth century – the danger of the overacidification (what Otto von Bentheim called the "plague of the forest") of the soil from raw humus; in fact, around 1900 some foresters wished to revive the declining litter use as a way of maintaining the forest floor. Even the use of foliage through "pruning," the cutting of lateral branches, can constitute a form of sustainable forest use if done to trees that leaf vigorously, whether in the German Mittelgebirge or in the Himalayas.[110]

The more the peasants restricted the fallow period, the more the preservation of soil fertility became a question of fertilizers. Damage was done not only by a lack of fertilizer, but also by a one-sided fertilization. A special hidden danger lay in those methods that raised the yield of the soil over the short term, while exhausting it all the more thoroughly over the long term: in environmental history, it is often the pseudo-successes of environmental policy that mask a most calamitous decline of the environment.

The classic example of this in the history of premodern agriculture is *marl*. When the lime and silicic acid–containing marl is applied to lime-deficient soils, other nutrients are initially activated and high yields are achieved. However, these other soil components are depleted, and if they do not regenerate and are not added back, the soil becomes exhausted and the rich harvests are followed by years of poor crops. As soon as farmers used "marling" on a large scale and tracked the impact over decades, they were able to recognize the baleful long-term effects. "Marl makes rich fathers and poor sons" was an often-quoted piece of peasant wisdom in the eighteenth century in Germany and Denmark, which experienced a virtual marl boom after 1750. The saying contains a primal expression of what is today seen as "environmental awareness": the concern that the present generation is living at the expense of posterity, as was done most visibly in taking on debts and cutting down the forests.

A guilty conscience, however, has certainly not always been able to keep humans from living at the expense of the future. Marling was already a widespread practice in areas rich in marl in the Middle Ages. As early as 1277, a lease contract of the Gereon monastery in Cologne mentioned "marling" (*mergelare*) as commendable work. Carl Sprengel's *Lehre vom Dünger* (A Treatise on Fertilizer) (1845) declared that marl was without a doubt the mineral fertilizer "through which fields on a large scale could be most quickly and inexpensively put into vigor and improved cultivation"; Sprengel himself experimented a good deal with marl: "The most infertile lands," he maintained, "were often improved by marl in a miraculous way." How tempting it was to dismiss that pernicious peasant saying! Many farmers regarded marl as the "non plus ultra of all fertilizers" and even believed "that using it allowed them to do without manure." "The marl pit is the farmer's goldmine!" declared Wilhelm Hamm in 1872.[111] Even today, the attentive hiker can discover many one-time marl pits in regions with calciferous subsoil. Marl fertilization was the historical pioneer of mineral fertilization. In the period before the American Civil War, Edmund Ruffin – the editor of the *Farmers' Register* and one of the most influential publicists on agrarian matters in the United States who was influenced by Liebig's obsession with minerals – tried unsuccessfully to use marl to save the exhausted soils of the South and with them its social system.[112]

To be sure, there was within agriculture a good deal of traditional knowledge about the careful handling of the soil. Around 1600, Johannes Colerus, in his *Oeconomia ruralis et domestica*, assured his readers that a good farmer above all had to recognize "rightly and properly the nature of his land and soil"; in that way he would "abstain from forcing his fields to grow and produce one thing or another that was contrary and abhorrent to them," "especially since the saying goes that the person who forces the land is not well thought of."[113] Farmers used to have more visible clues to the nature of the soil back when weeds grew on their fields: corn poppy indicated soil rich in lime, sorrel was evidence of acidic, chamomile of wet, and chickweed of excellent soil. Even if most farmers did not understand the value of worms to the soil as late as the nineteenth century, not everything that has been imagined about the natural instinct of old-time farmers is a nostalgic myth. Quite often it was the political, economic, and legal conditions that prevented farmers from making use of their collective, experiential knowledge about cautionary behavior. The pressure of taxes, high rent dues, uncertain inheritance rights, overpopulation promoted by a governmental policy of boosting human numbers, outside control exercised in distant metropolises, invading armies, the socially conditioned separation of farming and herding, but also the incentives of the advancing market economy: all these things together probably contributed far more to unsettling the balance between humans and the environment than did a lack of knowledge about soil and fertilization. It is likely that environmental history, too, once it starts to penetrate its subject deeply, will often encounter processes of general history.

6. MOTHER EARTH AND THE FATHER IN HEAVEN: ON THE ECOLOGY OF RELIGION

Anyone who paints the closeness to nature of "natural peoples" in glowing colors usually reveals a particular preference for their "natural religion," for nature elements in magic, myth, and ritual. Even the sociologist Niklas Luhmann, who scoffs at modern ecoromanticism, maintains that an environmental awareness that was holistic and pervaded all of life did in fact exist in archaic times, when society had little differentiation and was still regulated by religion: "These societies were able to present supernatural matters better than natural ones and therefore they sought ecological self-regulation in mythico-magical ideas, i.e., in taboos and rituals dealing with the environmental conditions of survival."[114]

The history of religion tempts one to adopt an evolutionary view: it would appear that the horizon of religion developed from the earth up to the heavens. The oldest layer of religion, under headings such as "nature religion," "hunting magic," "agrarian religion," "fertility cult," is intimately linked to the relationship between humans and nature. However, the practical significance that nature elements in religion and myth had for how humans dealt with their environment has still not been elucidated very much; only too often this issue is not even recognized.

In same cases, a practical meaning aimed at the preservation of living conditions is evident in sacred taboos and ritual laws. A famous example is the "pig cycle" of the

New Guinea Maring, where every twelve years a year-long ritualized slaughter of pigs (supposedly) reestablished the balance between humans and their environment. In the mythology of ancient Egypt, the sycamore, a kind of date palm, was revered as the world tree and the tree of the goddess Hathor; the simple and obvious explanation for this lies in the varied usefulness of this tree to the inhabitants of the land of the Nile. The Wanika of East Africa believed that every coconut palm had its own spirit: "The destruction of a coconut palm was to them tantamount to matricide, since this tree gave them life and food like a mother did to her child." As late as the 1970s, a Protestant missionary in New Guinea thought he was a new Saint Boniface, who had felled the sacred oak of Thor worshipped by the pagan Saxons, when, against the "superstitious" warnings of the natives, he cut down "holy" trees to make room for a landing strip. Western Mongols believe that lightning will strike them in punishment if they pick certain medicinal plants without cause. Nonetheless, this kind of protection of nature through religious taboos remains scattered, much like modern environmental protection that is limited to certain "natural monuments" and preserves.[115]

The modern-day tourist in Nepal is charmed when, amid the urban sprawl that now disfigures the environs of Katmandu, he discovers the sacred forest of Deopatan. And he is delighted to hear the mythological reason for this surprising sylvan idyll: Shiva, in the shape of a male gazelle, is said to have withdrawn there with his consort Parvati, in the form of a female gazelle, for a thousand-year coitus. But a millennial coitus is not common even among the gods, and it did not lead to a large-scale protection of the forest.[116]

Marvin Harris takes pleasure in finding concrete ecological pragmatism every-where in the history of religion, from Aztec human sacrifice to the Hindu vener-ation of the cow. But he, too, refers to indications that the Mayans hurled human beings and ritual objects into a famous water hole "to appease the water gods."[117] This ritual sacrifice is unlikely to have promoted the protection of water. The point is that religion is not a mere function of either economy or ecology.

Scholars who trace the ecological notion of the "revenge of nature" to the primeval belief in natural deities often commit the methodological mistake of taking nature references in ancient cults out of context and interpreting them from the perspective of modern "nature" contexts. The ritual engagement with nature – whether in hunting magic or agricultural fertility rites – often contains an element of magic and thus the attempt to gain *power* over nature: this is an old dream of humankind, one that has been partially fulfilled only in modern times. Some passages from the "Collection of the Nagas," the most popular book of the old Tibetan Bon religion, are well suited to delight modern nature lovers. These stories repeatedly relate how the earth and water deities punish humans with disease for inflicting violence on the earth and waters through the plow, the axe, the quarry, and canals. The idea of the revenge of nature is an old one and found around the world. However, the real point of the stories is that an expert, a shaman, was needed who would placate the gods and ensure the success of the cultivation of the soil, which was beneficial to humans. Nevertheless, to this day the Tibetans have retained a reluctance when it comes to hydraulic construction projects.[118]

In the year 15 C.E., following a catastrophic flood, the Roman Senate debated a project devised on orders from Emperor Tiberius to reduce the volume of water in the Tiber by redirecting the course of rivers and lakes that fed it. Part of the water would have flowed into the Arno, which sparked a fear among the Florentines that their city would face an even greater threat of flooding. As Tacitus reported (*Annals* I.79), religious concerns were also raised: "Nature had made the best provision for the interests of humanity, when she assigned to rivers their proper mouths – their proper courses – their limits as well as their origins. Consideration, too, should be paid to the faith of their fathers, who had hallowed rituals and groves and altars to their country streams. Besides, they were reluctant that Tiber himself, bereft of his tributary streams, should flow with diminished majesty." But by no means all rivers enjoyed that level of respect. Newer archaeological work has unearthed, especially in ancient Rome, an astonishing number of river diversions, even through tunnels in mountain regions.[119]

Niklaus Luhmann's assertion that archaic societies "were able to present super-natural matters better than natural ones" is hard to believe. The notion that religion constantly pervaded all spheres of life in premodern and non-Western cultures betrays the influence of modern tourism, which, to the extent that it focuses on "culture," has a pronounced penchant for sacred architecture and cultic dances and ceremonies – these provide the best entertainment and photographs. Hans Peter Duerr has grumbled that "only middle class citizens enamored of luxury" could believe that consciousness and not material existence determined the "life of a society." As soon as one is tormented by pangs of hunger, he goes on, one feels the truth of Brecht's sarcastic comment: "First chow, then morals" (Erst kommt das Fressen, dann kommt die Moral) – we should occasionally remind ourselves of this also in environmental history. Clifford Geertz, well versed in the study of the interconnections between religion and ecology, noted: "But no one, not even a saint, lives in the world religious symbols formulate all of the time, and the majority of men live in it only at moments." Everywhere there existed, alongside religion, also a world of practical experience, without which no one could survive. Geertz saw "man as moving more or less easily, and very frequently, between radically contrasting ways of looking at the world."[120]

Found throughout the world are tree symbolism and the veneration of sacred trees, whether in Christian or non-Christian religions. These tree cults are far better documented than the cult of "Mother Earth"; it is here that what we today call "environmental awareness" is especially palpable in the older religious notions. The thirteen-volume work by James Frazer on ancient nature cults and tree magic (*The Golden Bough*) was so intensely devoted to the cult of the tree that Frazer, in his radically abbreviated version of 1922 (still nearly a thousand pages long), had to defend himself against the charge that he saw tree worship as the core of the history of religion. Frazer dedicated an entire chapter to the "Killing of the Tree-Spirit": the priests of Diana at the small forest lake of Nemi in the Alban hills seemed to believe that the Forest King had to be killed to keep him from the ravages of old age; in Frazer's view this belief had something archetypal about it. To be sure, fruit-bearing trees were protected as long as they bore fruit, but they were also threatened: "Will you now bear fruit or not?" a Malay sorcerer asks a barren tree and strikes it with a hatchet: "If you do not, I shall fell you."[121]

The legal records of the northern German Holthinge repeatedly admonish woodcutters to thank the forest once their work was done. There are reports from as late as the nineteenth century that many woodcutters in Switzerland and the Upper Palatinate would ask a tree for forgiveness before cutting it down – but then they went ahead and did it, for the tree could not deny their request. Among the Mayans, judging from their art, the tree cult was richly developed: the World Tree embodied royal power, and certain trees were presumably spared. Still, there is much to support the hypothesis that deforestation was one cause behind the downfall of the Mayan culture. In China, bleeding trees crying out in pain and outrage when they are cut or burned appear fairly often in Chinese literature – and yet, China early on became a land poor in forests.[122]

Shaftesbury (1671–1713) imported the tree cult into modern European romanticism; writing that every spirit had a tree, he inspired the Goethean cult of nature. Still, eighteenth-century England was by no means exemplary in its treatment of the forest. "Find me a new religion – a religion of which the chief rite is tree planting," proclaimed Atatürk, the founder of modern Turkey – but to this day, Turkey suffers grievously from deforestation.[123] One must never confuse the history of religious ideas with the real history of the environment.

The cult of "Mother Earth" or of the "Great Mother" who embodies the fertility of the earth is often invoked as evidence that humans were once imbued with a loving and reverential awe toward nature. "The earth also, as we all know, is a mother," wrote Philo of Alexandria,[124] though it took Deucalion and Pyrrha, in the myth recounted by Ovid, some time to arrive at this insight when the goddess commanded them to "throw behind you the bones [namely, the rocks] of your great mother." It would appear that these kinds of ideas did not characterize the earliest phases of human history, but rather the late stage of the hunter–gatherer way of life, when the gathering of plants had become the mainstay of the food supply, and early agriculture before the introduction of the heavy plow and draft animals, which made agriculture more patriarchal. Oswald Spengler believed that it was only agriculture that made the earth into "Mother Earth," giving rise to "a new devoutness" that "addresses itself in chthonian cults to the fruitful earth that grows up along with man." Even after the advances in our understanding from paleoanthropology, there is much that argues in favor of this notion.[125] Although speculations about a primeval matriarchy have been discredited, it seems that there did exist in human history a long phase dominated largely by gathering and planting and hoe cultivation without the plow and large animals, a phase in which women were more clearly at the center of society than was the case later, and that this condition is reflected in cults and religion.

For the most part, however, it is difficult to perceive clearly what the veneration of "Mother Earth" was all about; and it is even more difficult to say whether and how it gave rise to behavioral norms. To be sure, one must not imagine the child–mother relationship along the lines of the bourgeois idyll of the same. Many mothers impart to their young children the experience that you can have your way and get your wishes met by bawling: dreams of power are born in the mother's lap. The mother image that is projected onto the earth does not necessarily protect against exploitation and violence: mothers are often exploited, and often without a sense that anything needs to be offered in return.

The metaphor of the mother does not always produce consequences beneficial to women. In popular belief in East Germany, the Rye Woman is bludgeoned to death during threshing. In the stories told by the Cherokee Indians, Selu, the Corn Mother, was once slain by her sons: where her blood seeped into the ground, corn grew. Cybele, the Great Mother of ancient Asia Minor "must be raped again and again to force her to be fertile" (Eduard Hahn). The cult of the mother is likely to have had the most advantageous effect where – as among the Mongols – it was combined with an appreciation of mother's milk and long lactation periods: since the likelihood of conception is small while the mother is nursing, this was one way of keeping the size of the population stable. However, sweeping statements about the practical significance of the belief in "Mother Earth" are not possible. Under the influence of Albrecht Dieterich's *Mutter Erde* (Mother Earth, 1905), generations of religious scholars have had much too uniform notions about primeval Mother Earth cults all over the world.

The counterpart to Mother Earth was often a male power that fertilized the earth and manifested itself in the sun and in rain. From that perspective, the notion that something had to be done to the earth for it to produce fruits for humans also has very old roots. "I am marked by the mighty heaven, by Mother Earth was I brought here," sings Temujin, the future Genghis Khan; he then goes on to exalt that he triumphed over his enemies: "I emptied their bosom, I tore their liver." "Heaven is my Father, the earth my mother" are the opening words of a text by the Chinese scholar Chang Tsai (eleventh century), which became "a kind of Neo-Confucian creed."[126] In the sixteenth century, Earth, like Heaven before it, was given a spacious temple complex in Beijing: the cult of the earth is not always an ancient one.

The belief in "Mother Earth" among the American Indians is particularly well known. However, the ethnologist Karl-Heinz Kohl believes there is irrefutable evidence that the "Mother Earth philosophy" of modern-day Indian tribes is European in origin. In the clash between Indians and European settlers, the purpose of this philosophy was above all to show the white man that he had no right to take the land of the Indians. Beyond that, did the profession of "Mother Earth" have significance for the Indian relationship to the earth? In a speech allegedly delivered at an Indian council in 1875, the famous Sioux chief Sitting Bull is said to have justified the rejection of the plow and evidently also of fertilizer by invoking the mother status of the earth: the whites "deface her with their buildings and their refuse. They compel her to produce out of season, and when sterile she is made to take medicine in order to produce again." This Indian testimony is not the only one of its kind.[127] But the belief in Mother Earth could take on this thrust only in the fight against the whites and their economic system, for the Indians were unfamiliar with the plow for lack of draft animals and therefore had no need to lay a religious taboo on it.

Were the religious ideas of the Indians *not* anthropocentric? One person who believes that this was the case is Eugen Drewermann, who regards the notion that God had given the entire world to humankind for its use as "originally Hebrew," just as he takes the forged speech of Chief Seattle ("The earth does not belong to man") at face value. In reality, anthropocentric thinking existed and exists throughout the world: we find it in ancient China and in ancient America. In 1805 the Iroquois chief Red Jacket told a U.S. official for Indian affairs: "The Great Spirit had made it [the land] for the use of Indians. He had created the buffalo, the deer and other animals for food. . . . He had caused the earth to produce corn for bread."[128]

In the picture of history that has become customary since the nineteenth century, religious history describes a great evolution since primeval times from the religion of the earth to the religion of heaven – or, in more general terms, from a worldly religion of nature to a transcendental religion of the hereafter. This used to be seen – though not entirely without a longing for the original state of nature – as progress toward the heights of spirituality. More recently, though, under the banner of the environmental movement, it has come to be regarded as a fall from nature, a path toward an increasing alienation from nature. Yet it is hard to imagine an evolution away from nature over the course of time. Since humans can never escape their bodies, it is doubtful whether they will ever be able to move very far from nature. Even the religion of the hereafter remains on some level very worldly; and, conversely: "Mother Earth" virtually demands as her corollary "Father Heaven." The Indians already venerated the rain god and the Great Spirit.

In all of this one must never forget that religions were always concerned primarily with humanity and not with nature.[129] References to nature appear within a context of human desires and fears, of magical and purifying rites and rituals. Since the relationship to nature is not the theme of Christianity, Christian teachings offer a contradictory overall picture on this issue, one that reflects the varied contexts of natural references. As God's creation, nature is good and the object of admiration and astonishment; but when it comes to moral theology and eschatology, sinful human nature is in need of redemption and mortification already in this life.

The standard argument of those who indict Christianity's antinature character, beginning with Lynn White, is the commandment that the Old Testament God gave to humans: "Be fruitful and increase, fill the earth and subdue it" (Gen. 1.28). But those whom one subdues one must care for. Earlier times derived from this commandment a human responsibility for nature; in eighteenth-century England, it was a weapon in the hands of those seeking to protect animals. In the next verse of the same passage (Gen. 1.29), God mentions only plants and the fruit of the trees as food for humans, but not animals. Noah saved not only the human race in his ark, but also the diversity of the animal world.

Saint Augustine, the greatest of the Church Fathers, while he did disdain the belief in a divine Mother Earth in his work *The City of God* and despised the eunuch priests of the Great Mother, was certainly familiar with the notion that one could find a reflection of God in living nature, and he knew the joy of gardening: "It is as though you could question the vital force in each root and bud on what it can do, and what it cannot, and why." In other words, this was not merely the joy of edification, but the joy of understanding. He was also aware of the cycle of matter, especially since it held profound importance for him: "Whereof does the earth grow fat, if not from the decay of earthly things?"[130] The core of the New Testament message – that death gives birth to new life – is intrinsically linked to basic agricultural experiences, as the parable of the mustard seed reveals. In the oldest pictorial representations of the Christmas story, the ox and the donkey are more important than Mary.[131]

In studying how Christianity affected the relationship of the common people to nature, one should look less at the history of theology, and more at the legends and cults of saints disparaged by modern theologians: here trees and animals play an important role, especially as the companions of hermits, and the boundaries to pre-Christian tree cults are fluid. Often saints' pictures that had been absorbed into trees over the course of time enjoyed special veneration. Francis of Assisi, with his brotherly and trusting relationship to nature, was not as unique within popular Christian beliefs as is often asserted today: many believed that animals, too, were receptive to God's message. Saint Augustine's demand that nonhuman creation be included in the commandment of love had its counterpart in a tradition of popular piety, even though the other tradition, that of the devaluing of the animal world was by no means absent. Incidentally, even Saint Francis was anthropocentric in his own way in his relationship to animals: for while he preached to the birds, he despised goats and mosquitoes as the embodiment of demonic powers.[132]

The modern environmental movement is probably more deeply rooted in Christian traditions than it suspects. The idea of a nature that has created and sustains us, and that establishes the highest norms whose violation it punishes, is an offshoot of the Christian conception of God. The expulsion from paradise as the result of sin contains the basic pattern of the sense of guilt that weighs on the environmental movement. The belief that the Fall of Man goes hand in hand with a decline of nature is part of ancient Christian tradition;[133] from there it was not far to the logical conclusion that sins against nature had caused the deterioration of nature. If it is often said in environmental circles today that Christianity, with its dualism between humans and nature, in contrast to Eastern religions promoted the destruction of nature, one must counter that it was possible only on the basis of this dualism to recognize a destruction of nature by man in the first place. After all, modern environmental awareness is *not* based on the assumption of a seamless unity of humanity and nature.

Far more so than Judaism and Christianity, Islam was a desert religion, not a farming and most definitely not a tree religion. In the 26th Sura of the Koran, the forest dwellers are enemies who vilify the messenger of God as a fraud. Was it a religion that not only came from the desert, but also produced deserts? The French Orientalist René Grousset lamented that all over Central Asia, the Muslims had "caused the water to dry up by deforesting the land; . . . even the soil they have destroyed." From the perspective of agriculture, Xavier de Planhol detects over the long run "a negative role of Islam everywhere," even if it initially helped some regions to attain agricultural prosperity. Islam, he argues, "led to an enormous reshaping of the cultivated land," and for the most part it was destructive in nature.

In response one must raise the fundamental question of whether it is realistic to make religion into an autonomous factor of economic and environmental history. Just as the cycle of the Christian year was shaped by the farming world of Central and Western Europe, Islam also entered into very diverse environmental constellations: Clifford Geertz demonstrated this impressively in his comparative study of Morocco and Indonesia, respectively the most western and most eastern Islamic polities. But while the sweeping thesis of the negative role of Islam in the history of the environment is open to challenge, even modern supporters of Islam find it difficult to offer a convincing demonstration that this religion has a close relationship to nature. The Egyptian Green Party, the first environmental party in the Arab World, even though it invoked Islam, had a difficult time gaining the backing of the imams in the mosques.[134]

The situation is very different today with Buddhism and Hinduism. Western animal lovers have long been impressed with the respect these religions accord animals, even if a Karl Marx or Heinrich Heine mocked the Indian veneration of the monkey. It was especially this respect for animals, but also the highly developed tree cult, that provided an opening through which one could invest these religions with a brotherly relationship to nonhuman nature. Gadgil and Guha, the authors of an environmental history of India, suspect that Buddhism and Jainism arose not least as a reaction to an excessive destruction of the forests and the overhunting of animals. If you see an isolated stand of trees on a mountain in a treeless Chinese landscape, it typically indicates the site of a Buddhist temple.[135]

However, one must never forget that Buddhism's goal is not to perfect the cycle of nutrients, but to release humans from the cycle of existence. There is some evidence that the Buddhist monasteries in Mongolia were ecologically destabilizing, since they led to population concentrations that were not adapted to the conditions of the steppe.[136] If the fearless encounter with tigers was for Thai monks proof of enlightenment, this was not motivated by a concern to protect the species. In 1990 Thai villagers under the leadership of Buddhist monks rose up to oppose the cutting down of their woods, but only after the forest in that country, 95 percent of whose population is Buddhist, had been largely destroyed.[137] To be sure, purity was a structurally formative element in the Indian caste system; but this kind of ritual cleanliness, which produced a revulsion against the "untouchables" and menstruating women, was not able to prevent the most noxious pollution of sacred rivers.

We should undoubtedly look for the broadest environmental effect of religions not so much in the "great" as in the "small traditions," less in theology and more in trivial and in part unintended areas: be it the constraint on population growth by Christian and Buddhist monasticism; underground traditions of contraception in the Islamic world; modern Catholicism's disparaging of contraceptive sexual practices; the elimination of an important protective element for the forest by the Jewish and Islamic rejection of the pig, even in regions where pig raising would have been advantageous; the tabooing of human excrement in the Islamic and Hindu cultural sphere; or the ritual consumption of horse meat and the exposure of children in the ancient Germanic religion. Religion is most likely to become a factor of environmental history in everyday culture.[138] But these everyday cultures are regionally circumscribed: it is hardly possible to erect an ecological contrast between the continents on them. The history of the world's religions is not, as so often assumed, a smooth and straightforward ideal path through global environmental history.

But this realization does not settle the issue of "religion" when it comes to the later periods of environmental history. As paradoxical as it may sound, especially in modern times, the need for an unselfish love of nature – and thus for a quasi-religious foundation to the affection for the natural world – is greater than ever before in history. In earlier times, the survival instinct of individuals and small groups was generally more or less sufficient as the driving force behind environmental protection. That is no longer true in an age when so many environmental problems go far beyond the local level and the individual no longer automatically feels the consequences of this actions.

There is thus a reason why new kinds of nature religions have been growing since the eighteenth century. Often they do not oppose the old religions, but pervade them – most of all Protestantism, the predominant religion in the countries that pioneered industrialization. To be sure, Puritanism was filled with a much stronger awareness of the sinfulness of human nature than Catholicism, but precisely a piece of this anxiety of sin entered into modern environmental awareness. A comparative study of environmental awareness in the various states of the United States showed a striking lead for the New England states, which were born of Puritan roots (along with California and Oregon).[139] It is enough to suggest the need for a new Max Weber who could analyze the relationship between the Protestant ethic and modern environmentalism.

3

Water, Forests, and Power

From a very early time, water and forests have been leitmotifs of environmental history. If we leave aside air, these are the two most important resources that were always used in tandem by many people, and here the characteristic problems of joint use appeared especially early and frequently. It is with water and forest usage, in particular, that environmental problems become a political issue early on. These problems were seized on by higher authorities, indeed, in some instances created by them in the first place. For it was here that environment first emerged as a common good that had to be defended against private interests. The fluid nature of water has always made it difficult to turn into private property.

Most early high cultures – from the Near East to China, from Egypt to Peru – were based on irrigated agriculture, while the supervision of the forests became a cornerstone of state formation in Central and Western Europe. Throughout the world, forest and water issues gave rise to regulatory forms that went beyond the house economy. Ecological necessities often go hand in hand with opportunities for the exercise of power. When it comes to hydraulic engineering, in many cases the one depends on the other, which is why it offers many opportunities for intervention from the top. When it comes to forests, the long growth period of trees is the standing argument for lordship, which sets the claim that it is protecting the interests of future generations against the narrow-mindedness of individual selfishness.

Water and forest policy came to be fused over the course of the modern period. Before the age of the railroad, large quantities of wood could be transported over longer distances only by water; this alone created a connection between forestry and river management. Moreover, in the eighteenth century, at the latest, it was discovered that a link existed between the forest and the water balance of the soil. In many regions, that discovery stands at the beginning of modern ecological awareness, whether in the Alps, in southern Europe, in India, or in the American West. When people looked on springs surrounded by forest in ancient times, they already suspected that it was not only the springs that nourished the trees, but the trees that also fed the springs. In Homer's *Odyssey*, Athena describes the land to Odysseus: "timber is there of all sorts, and watering places good through the season" (13.246 f.). Around 1300, a Dominican monk in Colmar wrote that before the forests were cut in the previous century, the brooks and streams had not been "as big as they are now, because the roots of the trees retained the moisture of snow and rain longer in the mountains." He did believe, however, that forests had made the land infertile.[1] Exactly what the link between forest and water meant for humans was often controversial.

The politicization of environmental problems led to the accumulation of ecological knowledge. However, bureaucratic administrations rarely looked after the environment in an entirely disinterested way. Usually their goal was to intensify its use, and in the process they often exacerbated environmental problems. The extent to which common goods required protection from above remained a contested question. In 1786 the parlément of Bordeaux, speaking on behalf of nature, sought to dissuade the central government in Paris from carrying out work to regulate the flow of the Dordogne River. The assembly argued that what the river lost in one part, it necessarily gained in another, hence the interest of the totality was never diminished and the result was "a perfect balance which commanded even reason to silence."

James C. Scott has described the rise of the modern state in the management of the environment since the eighteenth century as an essentially deleterious process, beginning with the afforestation of uniform forests by the state.[2] But we should be careful with sweeping judgments. We cannot determine a priori which kind of environmental management is good and which is bad. Max Weber's warnings against value judgments in science take on new relevance in environmental history.

I. HYDRAULIC ENGINEERING, POWER, AND ECOLOGICAL CHAIN REACTIONS

Water has been the leading environmental problem across wide areas of the world for millennia, and often in diametrically opposed ways: not infrequently the same regions suffer from too much water at certain times and from too little water at others. The water cycle shows extreme fluctuations especially in forest-poor areas. The ambiguous status of water as both a source of life and a threat to life pervades even religion and mythology. Myths from around the world show that since ancient times, the great flood has been *the* primeval trauma that nature has inflicted on humanity, and still today, floods account for about 40 percent of serious natural catastrophes.[3] On the flipside, the threat of stealthy death from natural events has always been worst in the form of the drought.

In many regions of the globe, the water supply is *the* environmental problem overshadowing all others. Water seems synonymous with fertility, even though it does not depend on water alone and can be ruined by excessive irrigation. Across millennia, humanity has learned above all that the yield of the soil can be boosted enormously by increasing the amount of water that is added to it: with rice the increase is more than tenfold, with sugarcane no less than thirtyfold. There was often a fluid transition between provisions against a water shortage and a multiplication of surplus product through intensified irrigation. From the time of the Sumerians, there was a potent incentive in many systems of political dominion to raise revenues and increase legitimacy through irrigation works. "When the Inca had conquered a new province he immediately sent engineers there, who were specialized in building canals for irrigation, in order to increase the corn acreage," wrote Garcilaso de la Vega.[4] Since the increase in the yield from artificial irrigation was so enormous over the short run, there has been a tendency, from the very beginning to this day, to pay little attention to the long-term pitfalls of irrigation. Even in modern Australia, little heed was paid to salinization for a long time, so entrancing was the vision of transforming sweeping deserts into blooming gardens.

What we today call "environmental awareness" probably developed earliest in connection with water; even during the initial phase of industrialization, that awareness still received its strongest impulses from the dangers of water pollution. As soon as people began to ponder water problems in a more considered way and in longer temporal rhythms, instead of acting simply out of a horror against either floods or droughts, they realized that the important thing was to develop a wise art of balance that took account of multiple considerations. In ancient China, some dam builders already had come to understand that it was not wise to resist water head-on; rather, dams had to be smoothly adapted to the force of the tide in order to direct it instead of being overwhelmed by it. People learned that one had to open paths for water to avoid bigger catastrophes.[5] It could be advantageous to leave certain areas to natural flooding: in this way they were fertilized and the force of the water diffused by being widely distributed. When it came to hydraulic engineering, the wisdom of adapting to nature was always very concrete.

Irrigated agriculture did not depend on the whims of the weather nearly as much as did rain-fed agriculture: people lived with the awareness that they were able to do something about the vicissitudes of climate. And if people suffered nonetheless, there was reason to assume that the cause – the neglect of the irrigation works – lay with humans. In this regard, as well, the environmental awareness was already a modern one. Still, humans were far from having control over all the problems consequent on hydraulic engineering. The list of typical pitfalls in irrigation and drainage technologies is fairly long, and the patterns of reaction to them are varied and not always easy to reconstruct. Among the standard problems that compelled routinized regulation, the distribution of water ranks at the very top. Often this proved to be a problem with no solution: for even when the allocation of water functioned peacefully within one social unit, it frequently came at the expense of those who lived further downstream, especially in drought regions, where a river is not replenished by tributaries. Difficult legal problems of regulation have always been inherent in the flowing nature of water. Our word "rival" is derived from Latin *rivalis*, meaning a person who shares the same brook or river. And even if these riverine neighbors reached an agreement, it did not mean that the water supply had been settled for those whose land did not directly abut the flowing water. In Australia the British colonists were forced to realize that the old English riparian law, which gave priority to owners of land adjacent to a flowing stream, was suitable only for land rich in water, while it obstructed development in Australia's dry regions.[6]

Tradition has it that the Buddha, as early as 523 B.C.E., mediated a quarrel over the allocation of dammed-up water that had brought two tribes in the Ganges plain to the brink of a bloody conflict. It may seem remarkable that while localized, armed clashes have not been uncommon through the course of human history, large-scale wars over water appear to have been very rare. Evidently water was an issue that gave rise early to habits of regulation without war. In fact, V. O. Kluchevsky believed that "rivers trained the dwellers on their banks to social life and the sociable habit."[7] Today, however, the quarrel over water in the Middle

East is exacerbating the hatred between Israelis and Arabs. But water is an object of dispute also among Islamic states. Whether these two potential sources of aggression will always neutralize each other is not clear. There is much to indicate that conflicts over water stand not only at the beginning of humankind's political history, but also at its end. The modern technical capacity to dam up enormous amounts of water and to redirect them over long distances creates potentials for conflicts that surpass in scale anything known in the past. Parched metropolises, from Mexico City to Beijing, can quench their thirst at the expense of other regions. The question of what can be ecologically justified is likely to become more explosive in the future.

In the hot regions of the world, extensive irrigation systems increase evaporation to an extreme degree and often lead to a salinization of the soil. This is how, from the Chinese perspective, the "yellow dragon" of desertification swallowed up many an old culture along the Silk Road. Peter Christensen believes that irrigation systems were never fully sustainable in the hot, semiarid regions of the Middle East, but were inherently limited in their life span.[8] There was a well-known and, in principle, simple method to drastically reduce the rate of evaporation: putting covers on irrigation ditches or constructing them underground. This method was already known in antiquity, was further disseminated by the Arabs, and was practiced from Valencia to China. But the construction and maintenance of covered canals and pipes was possible only under certain geographic conditions and was costly and time-consuming, and thus more feasible with intensive cultivation in a smaller area than with large and extensive irrigation systems. One famous example are the *Qanats* in Iran, the underground water tunnels fed by groundwater that date back to Assyrian times. They were excavated with the use of mining technology, and the work was so strenuous and dangerous that the builders sometimes called their *Qanats* "murderers." However, since these irrigation systems were usually operated by the villages, they were comparatively unaffected by changes at the center of power.[9]

The extent to which the danger of salinization was recognized early on and appropriate countermeasures were available is difficult to determine in many cases. The global dimensions of the salinization problem today seem to demonstrate that a sustained and effective response to this critical issue of artificial irrigation was not achieved in many regions. At least people learned to put soils with a low level of salinity, which would no longer support wheat, to use growing barley.[10]

In earlier times, as today, a typical mistake was that concern over irrigation, which seemed the most urgent problem, led people to neglect the necessary *drainage*, which would have prevented salinization and water logging. Even though the emergence of swamps was feared early on because of malaria, in areas that were threatened above all by a lack of water, the full importance of drainage was not as easy to grasp as that of irrigation, and many advances were not achieved here until modern times. Still today, one crux of irrigation projects in the Third World is often that too little attention is paid to drainage; much the same was once true for Central Europe. In 1836 the agrarian reformer Schwerz in the Paderborner Land lamented that people were ignorant of drainage ditches and that the "peasant rabble" would not be capable of such communal work on its own without "intervention" from the top.[11] The peasants who engaged in animal husbandry appreciated wet pastures. Moreover, drainage is often technically more difficult than irrigation, since in many cases there is only a minor natural gradient that can be used for that purpose; at the same time, its economic usefulness is not readily grasped everywhere, especially in arid regions requiring artificial irrigation.

Because drainage was not provided for in the same degree as irrigation in many arid regions, irrigation agriculture has often carried with it the threat of malaria, the plague of standing water. How severe the threat was depended on small and inconspicuous differences: whether the water was stagnant or in slight motion (which would limit the breeding ground of the Anopheles mosquito, the carrier of malaria), or whether fish – who would eat the mosquito larvae – were bred in the irrigated areas. Until the nineteenth century, people could only surmise such connections, even if swamps as such were feared. The technology for draining swamps generally lagged far behind irrigation technology. Until very recently, the readiness on the part of governments to take vigorous steps against the problems of salinization, water logging, and malaria by no means equalled the passion for large-scale dam, canal, and irrigation projects. The great canal construction by the British colonial government in India in the late nineteenth century revived the old dangers in dire ways; indeed, large-scale irrigation has led to salinization even in modern-day Australia. And the soil is salinifying in California's Silicon Valley, a supposed hotspot of the world's intelligence.[12]

Maintaining the fertility of fields depends crucially on the combination of agriculture and animal husbandry. In many cases, irrigation systems make this more difficult, especially when they are laid out in tightly knit networks, because the animals trample the dams and fall into the ditches.[13] That is not to say that traditions of an integration of irrigation agriculture and animal husbandry did not exist. Nonetheless, typical for many regions of the world is an alienated, if not hostile, coexistence of intensive irrigation agriculture and nomadic pastoralism. In those situations, the ecological fragility caused by the lack of fertilizer can be joined by a political fragility, a defenselessness against the warlike and, because of their mobility, superior nomads. It is not least this circumstance, and not necessarily the technical demands of irrigation, that gives rise to the dependence of farmers on a strong protective power.

Judgments about the stability and fragility of irrigation systems are often influenced by ideologies and political positions. Anyone who believes that salvation lies in the state pursuing water policy on a large scale will tend to construct historical shortcomings to show just that; by contrast, anyone who mistrusts centralized political power and favors village autonomy will pay closer attention to whether or not the great hydraulic achievements of state leaders in the past were mere façade.[14]

Since water is a liquid element, hydraulic systems must be as seamless as possible and try to follow the flowing water as best they can. Reasons for expanding systems of irrigation and water protection could always be found – which is why hydraulic engineering offered ambitious rulers the chance, very early in the history of state formation, to do something that would increase their power and revenues, while at the same time demonstrating their usefulness to their subjects. Water gave rise to the earliest technological networks on a large scale. Still, the complexity of human systems usually lags behind the complexity of nature, especially since the large water works, once they have been created, contain a considerable element of inertia. A complete history of hydraulic construction could be written from this perspective.

For half a century, the discussion about the great systems of hydraulic engineering has been dominated by a debate surrounding Karl August Wittfogel's (1896–1988) theory of "hydraulic society" or "Asiatic mode of production," whose later, anticommunist version bore the title "Oriental Despotism." When Wittfogel elaborated his theory in its original form around 1930 as an ardent communist – drawing on occasional remarks by Marx and Max Weber – he was driven by the passion to impart a global dimension to the Marxist worldview. Seeking to interpret advanced non-European civilizations – to which the feudalism concept did not apply – from the perspective of their forces of production, he discovered irrigation systems. He argued that wherever these systems grew to a large scale, they compelled a more highly developed social organization with central guidance, at a time when European rain-fed agriculture still favored decentralized, feudal conditions. This systemic compulsion could be interpreted as both an opportunity and a danger: a chance for a direct path to communism, and the threat of bureaucratic rule. When the communist Wittfogel was put to work in the National Socialist concentration camp of Esterwegen in 1933 draining moors, he experienced firsthand the despotic and murderous side of hydraulic engineering. The later anticommunist Wittfogel saw in "hydraulic society" the origin of totalitarian despotism, the curse of world history. The bureaucratic apparatus in these societies "obviously acted like a powerful hydraulic sponge" by absorbing an increasing number of economic functions beyond the sphere of water.[15]

In libertarian-Marxist circles, it became a kind of ritual to accept some of Wittfogel's ideas, but to condemn and never mention the man himself, since he had fallen into disrepute – probably unjustly so – as an informant in the service of McCarthy.[16] Still, his ideas have persisted to this day.[17] To be sure, there have been a series of weighty counterarguments: in many regions of the world – from Holland to Sri Lanka – hydraulic engineering has clearly not compelled the emergence of a centralistic despotism; and even in places where it was joined to a bureaucratic centralism, it is usually impossible to prove that it historically gave rise to the latter. Central governments generally do not work very effectively under premodern conditions of communication, as they are too far removed from the individuals on the ground. That holds true even for the great empires of India and China. Moreover, "irrigation system" can mean a lot of things in concrete terms: from the mere regulation of natural flooding in Egypt, to the construction of extensive reservoir lakes in China, which have to be maintained through constant, expensive labor. But such dammed-up lakes were rather the exception also in Asia, for technological reasons alone.

It is obviously important that we do not think about this question in a deterministic fashion, but in terms of possibilities. While irrigation does not *compel* a centralized bureaucracy, it contains for an ambitious government great temptation to expand the systems of artificial irrigation as far as possible as a way of stabilizing and expanding one's own power and increasing the tax revenue. And that precisely is what makes it ecologically risky.

In and of itself, irrigation possesses an element of self-regulation at the lowest level: the peasants maintain the system by shoveling the fertile mud deposited by the water onto their fields. Irrigation systems have presumably never functioned without this kind of initiative from below. One must bear in mind that before the age of cement, dams and irrigation canals required constant repairs. Still, there is no doubt about the links between hydraulic engineering and political power that have existed for thousands of years, even if these links were not a simple causality but a sequence of reciprocal interactions. Even today, people in the American West, much like in Australia, are making the experience that "small-scale irrigation" does not succeed without state intervention.

While an irrigation system may not originally require centralized rule, a central government can expand the irrigation network to such an extent that the latter can no longer be managed without a supralocal authority, at least in times of crisis. And even if irrigation itself continues to function without the centralized power, it does offer an ideal pretext for taxation. Wittfogel's theory remains valuable and stimulating as a heuristic device. It promises to offer a key to solving many exciting mysteries of history, perhaps concerning the decline of cultures as much as their rise. If the interest in Wittfogel experienced a first renaissance in the critical study of bureaucratic authority, more recently it has seen a revival under the banner of ecology: "It would appear," Mark Elvin wrote with a view to the environmental history of China, "that KAW's [Karl August Wittfogel's] ghost cannot be exorcized."[18]

There is a reason for that. The following assumption has some evidence in its favor: the most consequential effect that centralized power might have on hydraulic works (something Wittfogel hardly considered) is that the center expands the networks of irrigation and drainage to a size and complexity at which their vulnerability to crises – whether political or ecological in nature – increases to an alarming extent. The critical point is that a hydraulic society is *not* a technologically perfect system – quite the contrary! Canal networks are never completely stable and they never function perfectly: their builders are "locked in an eternal battle, a struggle against the problems created by solutions to previous problems." Modern-day findings in the area around the ruins of Angkor – that parts of the region became waterlogged and desertified – lend credence to the suspicion that the decline of the Khmer Empire went hand in hand with the siltification of its irrigation system. The striking importance of the Nagas (the snakelike goddesses of water) in Angkor, and of the rain god in the Mexican city of Teotihuacán, which may have been the largest pre-Columbian city in the Americas, indicate that these highly evolved "hydraulic" systems of political power were keenly aware of their vulnerability to the whims of water-nature. A famous painting in Teotihuacán depicts humans who have entered the paradise of the rain god, where they dance and swim and shed tears of joy over their good fortune.[19] Ecological vulnerability means at the same time social vulnerability, since the demands from the constant need to repair the hydraulic constructions often tax human energy to its limits. In the millennia before the age of fossil energy sources there were critical shortages in the energy of humans and animals.

Carl Schmitt taught that political power means making decisions in a state of emergency. It is probably primarily the *crises* in the human relationship to water that contribute to legitimizing central power. China's mythical first emperor saved his people from the great flood. Marvin Harris, who largely accepts Wittfogel's ideas, grounds the centralizing tendency of irrigation cultures especially in extreme conditions – threats of flooding or drought – and not in the demands of everyday life.[20] However, there is reason to doubt whether the way in which hydraulic rulers staged their role as saviors was a blessing in the long run. In that sense the history of irrigation systems contains a warning to those pioneering thinkers of the ecological movement who like to conceptualize environmental policy in global terms and to situate it at the highest possible level. Sometimes the problems become worse if one strives for a grand solution.

2. EGYPT AND MESOPOTAMIA: AN ARCHETYPAL CONTRAST

"Like Egypt, the whole country is intersected by dykes," Herodotus wrote about Assyria. And yet there was a major difference between the two countries in the technique of irrigation: in Egypt, the river was allowed to flood the fields, while in Babylonia, the water was poured onto the fields by manual labor using dipping devices. At the same time, our Greek observer noted that Assyria, though more fruitful by virtue of irrigation than any other country known to him, had no fruit-bearing trees, this symbol of generation-spanning stability. Herodotus's classic contrast still pervades some of the modern literature. On the one side there is Egypt, the "gift of the Nile" and model of a casual water economy in harmony with nature, the embodiment of eternity, of sustainability across many millennia until the construction of the modern Aswan dams. On the other side there is Mesopotamia, the archetype of a forced, labor-intensive, and costly irrigation in the teeth of the desert, as well as in its political conditions time and again a cauldron of war, chaos, and violence, all of which is already clearly reflected in the muscle-bound Assyrian kings depicted on monuments. The Nile was the model of the life-giving river that rises and falls in a regular cycle, whose gentle flood bestows abundant fertility on the land every year and was therefore accompanied by joyous festivals and cultic ceremonies along the entire length of the river. How very different from the Yellow River, the "sorrow of China," with its disastrous floods, and from the equally unpredictable Euphrates and Tigris rivers, which shifted their courses!

In Egypt, nature was from the beginning drawn with uniquely sharp contours: with the deeply cut, overwhelmingly fertile Nile valley flanked on both sides by the elevated deserts, whose irrigation was out of question. In Mesopotamia, by contrast, little was fixed and certain: the expansion of the cultivated land through irrigation had no distinct boundaries. Though the land was by nature disadvantaged compared to Egypt, it was possible to far exceed the riches of the Nile valley through the use of elaborate irrigation schemes. But the Euphrates and the Tigris carry five times the amount of sediment as the Nile, and along the lower reaches their slope was smaller than that of the Nile, as a result of which harbors became repeatedly clogged with silt and fields waterlogged. Instead of the villages that were nestled along the Nile valley, Mesopotamia had cities that sought – without success in the long run – to rule the land and fought over the water. From the very beginning, the gradual salinization of the soil was the price of artificial irrigation in Mesopotamia, unlike in Egypt, where the drainage that desalinates the soil occurred naturally. Waterlogged land brought the threat of malaria to Mesopotamia, the most famous victim of which was Alexander the Great, while Egypt was considered a healthy land as late as the nineteenth century. On closer inspection, however, the contrast is not quite so stark. Even Egypt was not entirely spared the scourges of malaria and salinization over the course of the millennia: around 1800, salt-tolerant barley became the chief grain also in this country.[21]

Karl W. Butzer, who has for decades worked to unite Egyptology and ecology, dismisses Wittfogel's theory: the notion that irrigation invariably gave rise to centralized authority along the Nile was fundamentally wrong. The first pharaohs had not found a swampy wilderness in the Nile valley that had to be made cultivable and liveable through an extensive network of canals, as Herodotus had been told. Instead, long before the period of the kings, the Nile valley had been farmland, and the Nile had created fertile agricultural land even without large-scale human technology. True, artificial irrigation did begin with the kings, but even during Pharaonic times, the regulation of irrigation works took place at the local level, not from a centralized location. Although Menes, according to Herodotus the oldest pharaoh, is said to have built a large dam to protect his capital from flooding, it would seem that this dam was destroyed during construction by a surging flood. Günther Garbrecht believes that, after this experience, Egyptian engineers did not venture to undertake large dam projects for several thousand years. Until 1843, there was no irrigation in the Nile valley that used dams and canal systems.[22]

And yet this is not the entire story. For the Nile, too, was not entirely reliable. Herodotus already knew that the Nile changed over the course of time: it cut more deeply into the valley and flooded the land only when it reached a certain height. That height, however, was not always reached: as the Biblical story of Joseph reminds us, there were years of drought. And even in good years the flood did not reach all parts of the valley without artificial irrigation. The French Egyptologist Jean Vercoutter even believes that "of ten floods, barely three are satisfactory, the other seven are either too weak or too strong."[23] At the end of the Old Kingdom, Egypt was afflicted by serious droughts, which went hand in hand with a "dark period" in politics that lasted for a century.

After 2000 B.C.E., in the Middle Kingdom, a few pharaohs emerged on the scene who fit the Wittfogel model well and who entered into history as saviors thanks to their irrigation works – some Egyptologists even speak of an "irrigation revolution." Herodotus writes that ever since the time of pharaoh Sesostris (Sesostris III, around 1850 B.C.E.) the Nile valley could no longer be traversed by land on account of the many artificial canals. The people sang of Amenemhet III: "He makes the Two Lands verdant more than a great Nile" – surely an enormous exaggeration, for even the Pharaonic irrigations systems were limited in their ability to control the whims of the Nile. It would appear that it was not until the New Kingdom, after the middle of the second millennium B.C.E., that the *shaduf* appears along the Nile, a lifting device that made possible the irrigation of the fields even when the waters of the Nile were low.[24] Originally it was operated by humans, later also by oxen and donkeys. However, a permanent, large-scale irrigation independent of the Nile flood could not be achieved with this simple technology. This modest level of hydraulic technology is one reason why the salinization of the Egyptian soil remained so low over millennia.

There is one exception to the restraint that ancient Egypt exercised toward large-scale hydraulic projects: this was the completion, under Amenemhet III, of the reclamation of the Fayum depression, which included the construction of an artificial lake that Herodotus still marveled at as one of the wonders of the world, and which was linked to the nearby Nile valley through an old side branch of the Nile. During high flood it was filled up with Nile water; during the dry summer it returned the water: in this way it made several harvests possible, though at the same time it increased the danger of salinization. But Ptolemy II (285–246 B.C.E.) drained the lake again to settle Greeks on its land.[25] Today we are not sure of the precise location of the lake, and some even doubt that it ever existed. In the end, the approach to year-round irrigation remained a local episode, even if modern hydraulic engineers elevated it into the great historical model.

The hydraulic builders of the modern era had their own kind of historical awareness, and their historical memory always began with ancient Egypt. At the same time, though, they already possessed certain ecological insights. From the very beginning, it went without saying that hydraulic engineering could not be undertaken without paying very close attention to natural conditions. William Willcox – whose plans were used around 1900 to construct the older Aswan dam, whose sluice gates still let through most of the Nile silt and continued to allow for the natural fertilization of the fields – always had the hydraulic engineering of the ancient Near East before his eyes, and he liked to hike along its remnants. But when he designed the dam, he was thinking not so much of providing fertilizer for the fields of the fellahin, but primarily of preventing the lake from silting up. "I was an irrigation enthusiast," he openly professed; and like other hydraulic engineers, he derived from history impulses for irrigation projects. At least he still had a much better historical awareness than the Soviet engineers who in the 1960s, with the construction of the new Aswan Dam, destroyed an irrigation culture that had ensured sustainable agriculture for five thousand years.[26]

While ancient Egypt has a good chance of becoming a model in the curriculum of historical ecology, Mesopotamia is in the process of turning into a warning example. It already begins with the oldest high culture, the Sumerians: in popular environmental history, we encounter them repeatedly as history's first ecological suicides, and thus as a fitting prelude to a pessimistic world history of the destruction of nature. The ruins of Ur and Uruk that rise forlornly from the desert gave reason to suspect that it was not only a culture that was destroyed, but also its environment – the only question that remained open was whether the decline of the culture brought that of nature in its wake, or whether the culture itself destroyed nature. Right up into twentieth century it seemed obvious that the decay of the irrigation systems had led to the victory of the desert, and that a new irrigation would once again turn Mesopotamia into a garden of Eden. Only when the state of Iraq put that notion to the test did the full extent of the salinization problem become apparent.[27] Now the suspicion grew that it might have been the irrigation itself, carried out for millennia, that turned the land into a desert, or more precisely: constant irrigation without a fallow period and without sufficient drainage, combined with the cutting down of the forests.

In fact, there is evidence for the salinization of the soil as far back as Sumerian times. What made this all the more irreversible was the fact that it reinforced a natural salinization process that had been going on even before human intervention. However, the Sumerians were not entirely helpless in the face of this fate: they responded by stepping up the cultivation of barley and brewed barley beer. One might say that the preference for beer counteracted the ecological suicide! Sumerian and ancient Babylonian sources allow us to trace, with remarkable precision, the decline in wheat yields and the transition from wheat to barley that was forced on the farmers by the salinization of the soil. At the same time, however, there was a growing incentive to open up new land to wheat cultivation by expanding the irrigation systems: signs of ecological crisis trigger a trend toward expansion, which creates new ecological risks.

The reliable sources that we have for the late Sumerian period, the time of the so-called Third Dynasty of Ur (ca. 2000 B.C.E.), offer us also a vivid picture of how the canals were regulated and how the erosion damage was repaired. The Law Code of Hammurabi (around 1800 B.C.E.) contains strict rules governing irrigation, though it posits individual responsibility: "If a man neglect to strengthen his dyke and do not strengthen it, and a break be made in his dyke and the water carry away the farm-land, the man in whose dyke the break has been made shall restore the grain which he has damaged."[28]

Ancient canal systems can be excavated only with great effort and expense, and are difficult to date precisely, especially since a good deal was usually buried in later periods. This leads to basic uncertainties about the early history of irrigation systems. Robert McC. Adams, studying the Mesopotamian heartland, came to a conclusion similar to Butzer's for Egypt, namely, that large-scale irrigation works had been the exception there in ancient times – a conclusion, to be sure, that did not go unchallenged. In Mesopotamia, as along the Nile, agriculture was possible even without extensive, centrally supervised irrigation networks. The explanation for the rise of centers of political power lies not in any economic-ecological inevitability, even if the written documents that praise the deeds of rulers suggest otherwise. On occasion large canals were in fact built, though they were in operation only briefly.[29] Thus, the contrast between the irrigation cultures of Egypt and Mesopotamia during the first millennia was not as extreme as was often believed. For Herodotus (I.193), who saw barren Greece in his mind's eye, the fertility of Babylonia was unbelievable and fabulous. Even the Hellenistic-Roman period could not have accelerated a fateful trend: otherwise it would be hard to explain that Baghdad was still able to flourish near the dual metropolis of Seleucia-Ctesiphon a thousand years later.

Strangely enough, it would appear that an overtaxing of Mesopotamia's ecological possibilities began only in late antiquity, under the Sassanids, and reached a fateful culmination in the early Islamic period under the Abbassids. A Babylonian textbook on agriculture, most likely composed during the Sassanid period, is pervaded by an agro-cultural spirit of conquest, a desire to make the land arable and to fight against the desert, and at the same time also by an awareness of the threat from the climate.[30] Back then, and in the subsequent Islamic period, the *noria*, a water-driven water-lifting contrivance, seems to have come into wider use. It was now possible to irrigate regions the water could not reach by mere gravity, and one could switch to year-round irrigation with multiple harvests, in the process of which the fallow period, which lowered the salinity of the soil, disappeared. One must assume that this seriously exacerbated the salinization problem over the long run. Moreover, the larger and more complex an irrigation system became, the more dependent it grew on the functioning of a higher administrative authority. As soon as that authority waned, parts of the irrigation would start to falter. The famines that resulted would in turn contribute to destabilize the system further, and this set in motion a vicious political-ecological cycle. This seems to have happened in the Abbassid period.[31] The more Mesopotamia approached Wittfogel's model, the more critical the situation became. The perfect "hydraulic" despotism was especially threatened in its ecological balance.

I will conclude with a brief look at Greece and Rome. What is striking in comparison with nearly all other high civilizations is something that escapes the inveterate classical philologists: how little we hear there of irrigated agriculture, even though the Mediterranean region lacks rain especially in the warm season, when the field crops could thrive. Not that irrigation ditches were unknown: Homer sang: "A farmer has dug an irrigation ditch / To lead the water from a dark spring / Into his garden plots." But this ditchdigger was not an archetype of Greek culture. A modern, demythologizing study of Greece has noted the lack of artificial irrigation and drainage as that country's great historical and contemporary shortcoming. However, if one follows Wittfogel, the freedom-loving Greeks had the right instincts in not emulating the canal building of the Chaldaeans, especially since it appears that, in general, they were able to manage more or less with the water that nature offered them. Greece, in fact, is not as arid as tourists who visit only in the dry season believe. Oliver Rackham concludes, on the basis of detailed studies, that the symbiosis between nature and humanity in Crete survived the millennia unscathed even without large-scale irrigation works, and has been disturbed only by the recent expansion of irrigation systems.[32]

More striking is the lack of irrigation on a grand scale among the Romans, who – as is still evident today in the mighty ruins of the baths and aqueducts – made hydraulic engineering into representational architecture of the first order. But that was hydraulic building in the service of urban consumers, not of producers in the countryside. The aqueducts show just how much the city-dwellers appreciated pure water from distant springs in the mountains. Vitruvius stated that you could tell a good spring by the fact that the people who dwelled around it had robust bodies, a fresh complexion, and clear eyes. The ancient Roman water awareness was the great model even for nineteenth-century urban reformers. Of all the administrative branches in imperial Rome, the cura aquarum had the most officials. However, the Curator aquarum Frontinus considered it scandalous to use the precious water brought in by the aqueducts to irrigate fields, even though artificial irrigation surely existed in Roman agriculture; in Cicero's eyes, in fact, it amounted to the creation of a "second nature." In spite of the great representative structures, it was private initiative that dominated hydraulic construction in the Roman Empire: here Wittfogel's theory does not fit. The usefulness of aqueducts was not evident to all: the philosopher Seneca mentions the building of water lines across difficult terrain as a typical way in which humans who suffered from inner restlessness wasted time.[33] The dynamism of Roman rule was obviously not hydraulic in origin, though its decline in North Africa was accompanied by the decay of irrigated agriculture there.[34]

3. THE IRRIGATED TERRACE: A SOCIOECOLOGICAL CELL CULTURE

A recent book on terraces in the Provence opens with this confession: "We scientists and artists passed through the terraced landscape without seeing it." European agrarian historians did not notice the terraces because for the longest time they were not a topic in the literature. The paucity of historical documentation is explained by the fact that terraces, at least in Europe, rarely called forth the need for regulation on higher levels: every farmer maintained his terraced fields and walls out of self-interest; only irrigation required an authority above the household economy. In southern France and elsewhere, terraces were a world of small farms, not of large landholdings. It was also a world of hoe and garden cultivation that resisted the agrarian progress tied to the heavy plough and teams of oxen: hence the silence of the otherwise so eloquent agrarian teachers about terraces.

Because terrace builders were so taciturn, speculation about the historical origins of terraces is endless, especially since they often cannot be dated by archaeological methods. Today terraces are a characteristic element of the Mediterranean landscape – but was that already the case in antiquity? Greek and Roman writers on agriculture are silent, and the classical languages did not even have a word for them, which is one indication that even if there were terraces, there was no highly developed terrace culture. In general, scholars have assumed that the construction and maintenance of terraces is so laborious that only an increase in population density – with the resulting need to make intensive use of the land even on mountain slopes – could prompt such exertions. However, simple terraces have been constructed for olive trees in the Mediterranean since antiquity. Still, even in more recent times, agriculture was practiced in parts of Tuscany without terracing and with furrows that ran from top to bottom, an arrangement that gave free rein to erosion.[35]

All in all, the picture we get in the Mediterranean is full of contradictions. Oliver Rackham and Jennifer Moody have emphasized that the appearance of terracing is the key to understanding the Greek landscape – but a key we unfortunately do not have. Most terraces can be documented only in recent centuries, but scattered finds can be dated back to the Bronze Age. However, it is a long way from primitive dry walls to the "state terraces" of the Incas and the elaborate wet rice terraces of Southeast Asia: "terrace" can refer to very different ecological and social systems. Highly developed, intricately irrigated systems of terraces seem to have spread in the Mediterranean region only long after the classical period, often not until the modern era.[36] Antiquity lacked the impetus from irrigation agriculture. In North Africa, the most numerous and most beautiful terraces are found in southwestern Morocco, that is, in the area furthest from Roman influence: this does not exactly indicate that the Romans were masters of terrace building.

In Languedoc, the construction of terraces seems to have spread for the first time deep into the mountains under the population pressure of the sixteenth century, but irrigation technology continued to lag behind for centuries. The picturesque *levadas* of Madeira, rediscovered in more recent times by tourist hikers, date for the most part from the last centuries; in some places on the island's steep mountains, the soil had to be brought in by baskets. The construction of irrigation canals in the mountains was also extremely laborious and did not make much progress until the nineteenth century. A tradition extending back thousands of years stands behind the irrigation terraces especially in the old rice regions of southern China and Southeast Asia. But even in southern China, wet rice cultivation received a further impetus in modern times, and on Java, rice terraces have more than tripled since the early nineteenth century.[37]

Clifford Geertz has written that the *subak* rice terraces in Bali represent "at once a technological . . . physical . . . social . . . [and] a religious unit." Irrigation systems sometimes gave rise to larger interconnections; typically, however, terraces are an agglomeration of small peasant cells that cultivate an intensive relationship to their soil. From a distance, terraces that climb entire mountainsides in many steps seem like a landscape pyramid conceived on a large scale, or, if one looks down into circular valleys, like an amphitheater. But if one tries to get through on foot away from the paths, one finds oneself unexpectedly in a labyrinth, and it is only with difficulty that one makes one's way out. These mazes were not a bad defense against military invaders coming from the plains. Here, small peasant cultures were able to hold out even in hard times; and since the construction and maintenance of terraces in the mountains required so much effort, this landscape architecture binds the farmer to the soil and forces him to pay the highest attention to every scrap of land.[38] In purely technical terms, terrace cultures promote the autonomy of small farmers of villages, at least in water-rich regions: not everything fits with Wittfogel's "hydraulic despotism."

Terraces, with their multitude of small, sharply demarcated fields, make it possible "to take the logic of a polyculture to the extreme." What made them into a complete and perfectly interwoven total system, however, was wet rice cultivation, with its abundant and yet precisely regulated irrigation. While the romanticism of the Mediterranean landscape includes above all the dry terraces with their vines and olive trees and wildflowers along the walls, from a global perspective, irrigation systems are the defining element of terraces, whether in East Asia, North Africa, or Latin America. They require the build-up of soil impervious to water, and for that reason alone they represent a more lasting intervention in the landscape than dry terraces. Especially when it comes to irrigation, the steplike construction, which makes many things so laborious, turns into an advantage, since irrigation and drainage can be regulated precisely and with relatively little effort, without lifting devices and drainage ditches. Drainage is particularly important in rice terraces, as rice is sensitive to salinization. To that extent, wet rice cultivation is a better teacher of soil conservation than other forms of irrigated cultivation.

However, the need for hydraulic regulation does not invariably give rise to a collectivist economy. Even with the *subak* terraces in Bali, where irrigation is perfectly and comprehensively organized, the small farmer remains his own master. In China, on the other hand, the government of Mao, as part of the Cultural Revolution of the 1960s and supposedly emulating the model of the People's Commune of Dazhai ("Learning from Dazhai!" became the slogan), launched a major terracing campaign. Here the terracing of mountain slopes became a model project intended to demonstrate the power of the collective. For the purpose of terrace construction, which happened under the pressure of a growing population, forests and pasture landscapes in the mountains were destroyed with no regard for geographic conditions; in many cases this promoted erosion, especially since the traditional village society, which was part of a good terracing culture, had been weakened by the communist dictatorship. There was a special fondness for terracing the tops of mountains, even though the water had to be pumped up. Terracing became an idée fixe: obsessed with the example of Dazhai, fanatical followers of Mao even built hills in plains in order to terrace them. One paradoxical element was the fact that this was a centralized campaign for decentralization, as every commune was supposed to use its own resources to accomplish the construction of terraces after the model of Dazhai (which was in reality subsidized from the top). In irrigation, too, local small-scale projects remained characteristic for Mao's China; in many instances they suffered from a lack of planning. Mao's terracing campaign is an especially striking example of how what is in principle a good idea ecologically can trigger an ecological disaster, if it is put into practice with the instruments of a totalitarian system without regard for local conditions. In environmental history, what is at least as important as the big ideas are the small details, the methods by which they are implemented.[39]

There are two very different sides to the environmental history of terraces. More vividly than all other economic forms, they reveal the deep ambiguity in the relationship between humans and the environment: the most radical reshaping of the landscape, which turns entire mountain slopes into steps, is combined with the utmost solicitude for the soil. But precisely this form of agriculture, grounded in an intensive environmental awareness, can quickly turn into rapid soil destruction once there is a dearth of people and concern for the land wanes.

Clifford Geertz has written that the "most striking feature of the terrace as an ecosystem . . . is its extraordinary stability or durability." This is the picture one gets gazing on the rice terraces of Southeast Asia, thousands of years old. Or do they appear stable only in a momentary snapshot and only in the dry period? After torrential tropical downpours and floods, they must be restored. Butzer believes that the dead appearance of the peripheries and highlands of the Levant, which were once filled with history, can be readily explained by the decay of terrace walls following the rapid erosion of the soil. Robert Netting has observed the degree to which the ecology of terraced landscape in Central Africa is threatened as soon as population pressure relaxes: once the people who renew the terraces disappear, erosion destroys them in a decade or two.

On Mallorca, each spring some of the terraces are destroyed by torrents. On the other hand, while erosion often proceeds unnoticed in the flatlands, every loss of soil is immediately apparent on terraces, and as long as this farming culture is intact, it is corrected. Along the slopes of the Cévennes Mountains around 1780, one could see locals of both genders carrying soil up the mountains on their backs – sometimes crawling on hands and knees – in all seasons of the year. In some places, the precious earth was even purchased in the nineteenth century! Needless to say, under those conditions, people pay scrupulous attention to the fertility of the soil. At the same time, more so than elsewhere, farmers were interested in intensive use of the land with the shortest possible fallow periods. In China one could observe as late as the twentieth century how peasants carried eroded soil back up in baskets, without lasting success, though: these peasants "must live with permanent erosion and a creeping transformation of the land."[40]

Even when the terraces were maintained intact, they possessed inherent draw-backs, as the soil heaped up behind walls on sloping terrain could easily suffer slumps and earth slides, and the earth newly brought in covered up the native soil. On the other hand, the dry wall technique developed with great skill in many regions of the world ensured that in case of downpours, the water flowed off through the wall as through a filter, as it were, without taking much of the soil with it. But it was the irrigated rice terrace, which requires waterproof dams, that seems most of all to have been an ecosystem that was stable across centuries, indeed, millennia, primarily because it needs little outside fertilization and self-generates many of the nutrients it requires, for example, through algae and the excreta of the small fish that multiply rapidly during the time of irrigation. While population pressure destabilizes "shifting cultivation" ecologically, it stabilizes the rice terraces, which call for intensive labor.

By contrast, in precolonial Mexico, terrace agriculture seems to have impoverished the soil, primarily, no doubt, because maize places a much greater strain on the soil than rice. The perfect and well-fertilized terraces of the Inca Empire, however, seem to have been a stable ecosystem, especially since they were constructed with artful drainage systems. Garcilaso de la Vega described the great care with which the inhabitants of the Inca Empire collected human manure as well as bird guano; killing a bird was prohibited on penalty of death, and the wasting of fertilizer was also punished severely.[41]

In the region of northern Ethiopia, where step terraces were constructed only after 1950, the people told the story that terrace agriculture had been invented by a crazy person (though in the end with surprising success), that is how stupid this labor seemed to a people who until then had known only shifting cultivation and seminomadic ways of life. Development workers in the Third World – whether in Central America or East Africa – repeatedly find that terrace agriculture fails without a corresponding mentality and work culture among the population: people simply watch as cattle damages the terraces, and cultivation on poorly maintained terraces merely accelerates erosion.[42] If the allocation of water and the cleaning of the ditches are not well regulated, the lowest-lying fields do not receive any water. In sub-Saharan Africa, agroforestry – which picks up on traditional forms of village economy – seems to offer better prospects for soil conservation than terrace cultivation.[43]

Irrigated terraces demand time discipline, as every farmer is allotted specific times during which he is allowed to open his sluice gates along the communal irrigation channels. On Madeira, a veritable trade was carried on with irrigation times, and because of it clock towers were erected at many sites on the island. On the rice terraces of southern China, writes an ethnologist of Southeast Asian rice cultures, life "is no longer a dance with frequent improvisations, but the timed moves of a courtly etiquette." Transitioning from shifting cultivation to rice terrace cultivation does not necessarily promote a more pleasant way of life, for the horizon becomes narrower and the menu less varied. Even "costumes have changed; austere black pyjamas have replaced garments decorated with seed necklaces and fur."

Gregory Bateson found the inhabitants of Bali nearly crushed by their many rituals; the Balinese, he writes, lives in constant fear of doing something wrong. When Esther Boserup highlights the advantages of small-scale, intensive forms of cultivation, which are capable of cushioning a considerable degree of population pressure, she, like so many other scientists, is so preoccupied with the question of progress that she overlooks the question of happiness. Is the reason why terracing fails so often especially in sub-Saharan Africa to be found in deeply rooted traditions of happiness in the moment? Even more so than elsewhere, population growth in that region regularly leads to accelerated soil erosion. But there are remarkable exceptions, for example, the tree gardens of the Chagga on the fertile volcanic soils on the slopes of the Kilimanjaro, where the cultivation of trees supports the protection of the soil from terracing. Once again, the ecology of the terraces is contingent on local conditions, cultural as well as natural.[44]

The cultivation of rice, which can produce multiple harvests through the addition of water, took terracing technology to its highest perfection: walls became small dykes, with which irrigation and drainage can be regulated precisely in accordance with the needs of the growth cycle of the rice plants. But does this culmination represent a high point of stability or ambivalence?

Geertz has described the irrigated terraces on Bali and in Morocco as a striking contrast: "Balinese irrigation is a huge, homogeneous, very precisely calibrated, multileveled, extraordinarily effective system. Moroccan irrigation . . . is a small-scale, quite heterogeneous, broadly at best, calibrated, single-level, but, at best, moderately effective system." The Javanese *sawah* rice terraces strike Geertz as nearly perfect – but are they really? If the monsoon rains arrive too late, the finely tuned water distribution system of the *subak* terraces in Bali is upset.[45] But that may be a kind of "stabilizing crisis" that activates the existing regulatory habits. Geertz, however, arrives at the conclusion that it is precisely the habit – established over many centuries – to respond to crises always with a further perfectioning of the traditional rice terraces that has led in modern times to a fateful inertia in pursuing innovations.

But what matters in the case of terraces is not only society, but also local nature. The effectiveness and sustainability of terrace cultivation on Java so admired by Geertz is the result not only of the diligence and collective disciplines of these farmers, but also of the constantly renewed fertilization of the soil with volcanic ash – something Geertz mentions only in passing. In Java, of all places, the amount of soil that is washed away by rivers is, according to one calculation, higher than anywhere else in the world – one indication that the protection of the soil through terracing is working very imperfectly even there. The geographer Herbert Wilhelmy reminds us, by way of warning, that the "rather uncritical transfer of Javanese conditions to other tropical regions has caused considerable confusion."[46] Terrace cultivation does not permit the general conclusion that small farmers, if only left to follow their traditions, are able to cushion all population growth.

In many cases, whether in the Po Valley or in East Asia, the ecology of the rice terrace includes the fish that are kept there at times of high water; the fish eat pests and turn them into fertilizer. When the water is drained in the Po valley, they end up in the local risotto. The mulberry/silk worm/dike/rice/fish pond ecosystem meets with the approval of researchers who take pleasure in discovering the environmental logic of traditional economic forms. Here everything seems to be part of a positive cycle, in which every link fertilizes the next link in the chain – provided the ideal type is real and there are no other problems.[47]

One can presume that the ecological stability of rice paddies is the natural foundation of the continuity of Chinese culture across millennia. But did the expansion of rice cultivation and the multiplication of harvests in the end turn into an element of destabilization? Does the ambiguous nature of the terrace in Chinese history assume a global-historical dimension? It is in thinking about these questions that we encounter contrary readings of China's environmental history.

4. CHINA AS A MODEL AND A TERRIFYING VISION

From the eighteenth century until today, from the time of the early Manchu emperors until the era of Mao and beyond, the Western images of China have repeatedly tended toward the extreme: on the one side, the horror image of Asiatic despotism ignorant of liberty and human rights; on the other side, the model of a polity ruled by philosophical mandarins. Ideas about the way in which the Chinese have related to their environment have been equally black and white. Alfred Weber, one of the early voices warning of a global destruction of the basis of life, believed that the "highest law" of Chinese culture was "integration into what was felt to be the magical order of nature." During his revolutionary phase, the writer Hans-Magnus Enzensberger reassured his readers (1973): "The best chances for the ecological survival of humanity is offered no doubt by Chinese society." But when more realistic information about the state of the environment in China began to reach the outside world, the country acquired the "reputation for being one of the most polluted in the world."[48] The suspicion lies at hand that all of this is Western projection. But the black-and-white picture corresponds in some regards with the way in which modern Chinese themselves see their own country.

In environmental history, the extremely contradictory image of China has special reasons and an empirical basis that are well worth analyzing. For there is no other large region of the world where environmental history − at least the history of agriculture and hydraulic engineering − can be traced across entire millennia on such a solid foundation and with such continuity; a comparable abundance of sources does not exist even in Europe for wide segments of Antiquity and the Middle Ages, to say nothing of India, Africa, or America.

"I shall show the teachers of agriculture another people, one that, without any science, . . . has found the philosophers' stone, which they in their blindness seek in vain": with this kind of missionary tone, Liebig began his 49th "Letter on Chemistry," written in praise of the Chinese. For Liebig, China was the land "whose fertility has been continually increasing for three thousand years, instead of decreasing," and this even though "more people live on a square mile there than in the Netherlands or England." Fertility increased: a miracle that actually goes against Liebig's theory. What was the cause of the Chinese miracle? The Chinese, so Liebig, knew and appreciated "no other dung than the excrement of humans." "The appreciation of this fertilizer goes so far that everyone knows what a person excretes in a day, a month, a year," and the Chinese considers it rather rude if a guest leaves his house without returning in the latrine the nutrients he has consumed. Praise for the utilization of "night soil" by the Chinese even reached the United States at the time: it was proclaimed by James Madison, and later by Horace Greeley.[49]

The Frankfurt municipal politician Georg Varrentrapp, the "Luther of sanitation in Germany" and a champion of the water closet and a combined sewer system, ranted at the time against the "fraud perpetrated with China." He did not dispute the excremental facts − only he saw in it a sign of foul-smelling barbarism, and what to Liebig was admirable continuity in the Chinese, to him was "3000 years of stagnation." To this day, some authors see the recycling of excrement as an exemplary cycle of nutrients, while others consider it a constant source of vile worm diseases. The strongest arguments are on the side of a positive assessment, since the careful preparation of excrement as fertilizer is likely to have destroyed most of the worm eggs as well as the harmful bacteria.

That the East Asians – including the Japanese and Vietnamese – paid great attention to the recycling of human excrement is a well-documented fact, which is explained by the density of the population and the lack of animal manure. In earlier times, Chinese tenant farmers were sometimes required to use the landlord's latrines, and human excreta – so-called night soil – was the object of an active trade. Land near the cities was said to be the most fertile, thanks to the abundant supply of night soil. As late as the early twentieth century, there are reports that the preparation of organic fertilizers – human manure chief among them – "took up to six months of the Chinese peasant's work year." European observers were astonished at the many procedures that were involved in this. The Communist People's Liberation Army sought to make itself popular among the peasants by collecting its excrement and making it available to them as fertilizer. When all human excrement was recycled into the soil, population growth did not lead to an overuse of the soil, at least not in theory. But is the cycle of nutrients that perfect in reality?[50]

Probably no other book did more to convey to a global readership the myth of the indestructibility of the Chinese soil than *The Good Earth* (1931) by Pearl S. Buck, who had excellent firsthand knowledge of Chinese peasants. Though drought and floods may kill many, the earth remains good: that is the message of the book, which eclipsed all of the German blood-and-soil literature of the time. Only laziness and immorality corrupted the earth. That is why Wang Lung, the hero of the novel, does not want to buy any land from his uncle: "He has been dragging a crop out of it in this way and that for twenty years and not a bit has he put back of manure or bean cake. The soil is like lime." By contrast, the soil and traditional peasant virtues in the end save everyone from misfortune. This view of the Chinese peasant was already traditional at that time. In his book *Farmer of Forty Centuries*, the American agronomist Franklin Hiram King (1848–1911), who traveled to East Asia around the turn of the century, praised the Chinese landscape as a model for the preservation of soil fertility indefinitely, in spite of dense settlement.[51]

To the supporters of the intensive economy of small-scale farmers, China is the best example of just how wrong Malthus was, and of the degree to which "smallholders" were able to absorb the greatest population growth in the world with their irrigated terraces. For many others, however, including many Chinese, China offers the worst example of how a country is constantly brought to the brink of catastrophe – economically and ecologically – from overpopulation. Here it is precisely the tendency of rice cultivation to promote procreation – as though more hands always create more food – that is China's downfall. Two leading members of the Chinese Ministry of Environmental Protection have described Chinese environmental history of the last four thousand years as purely a function of demographic development. Strong population growth always means a deterioration of environmental conditions: "History has taught us the high costs associated with population explosions and environmental degradation." Much of Chinese history unfolds against the backdrop of constantly recurring famines. That was already the view of Malthus, to whom China was a warning example, and that was also how more and more Chinese saw the situation at the time.[52] The periodic eruptions of floodwaters and nomads are joined by the tide of a swelling population as China's third great misfortune.

Some even accused the Chinese of an outright hostility to nature. From the perspective of Central Europeans, the deforestation of wide stretches of China, especially, was striking evidence of the disregard for nature. One principal witness of this attitude is Ferdinand Freiherr von Richthofen (1833–1905), the most eminent German traveler to China in the nineteenth century, whose influence came into play when the Germans took possession of Kiaochow (1898). He was familiar above all with northern China, and the loess with its gorges and earth labyrinth was his great theme. His writings give the impression that the Chinese owed their long survival chiefly to the natural fertility – indeed, the "self-fertilization" – of their loess soils, and not to their use of excrement as fertilizer, which he held in rather low regard. He mocked Western Sinologists who had been taken in by Chinese self-glorification, and he confessed that he had found nothing by which the Chinese distinguished themselves positively vis-à-vis the Europeans, though plenty of repulsive character traits. "The Chinese excel sadly in the destruction of vegetation," he wrote. "The ancestors of the present generation exterminated the forests; after that the last remnants of shrubs were also consumed." In some regions the people were already hoeing out grass, roots and all, to burn it: "This awful sin against the gifts of God, which have been bestowed overabundantly on the inhabitants of these regions, will yet avenge itself dearly." The old image of nature's revenge!

Strangely enough, Richthofen, for all that, arrived at this conclusion: "China is not overpopulated, as many believe." As he saw it, there were still vast stretches of unused ridges on which one could pasture sheep and thus feed additional masses. Utilization of the last open spaces, the pasturing of even barren ridges: as one can see, at times ecological crises are construed in such a way that the impulses for action they give rise to exacerbate the crises. The extent to which the destruction of the forests denounced by Richthofen actually occurred is not clear: some pollen analyses raise doubts as to whether the loess regions of northern China were ever covered in forests. Still, recent studies leave no doubt that the forest was originally far more extensive in that area than it is today. At any rate, in Richthofen's time the Chinese were engaged in the ruthless, destructive exploitation of the forests in Manchuria and Central Mongolia.[53]

Today the overall interpretation of the relationship between the Chinese and their environment is not usually discussed in Western scholarship as a question of forests or latrines, but on a more elevated level. The ancient Chinese school of Taoism, with its love of untamed nature, has come back into favor in the environmental movement, and discussions of Chinese environmental history show a penchant for focusing on the question of the real importance that attaches to the spiritual traditions. The Sinologist Herbert Franke has argued that a careful treatment of nature is already present in Confucianism, quoting from the sayings of Confucius: "The master caught fish with the rod, but never with the net; he hunted birds, but never when they were in their nests."[54] In this way he ensured that his quarry would replenish itself.

After this warm image of China, Gudula Linck's contrarian view is like a cold shower: "Yin and Yang – forget it!" To her the notion of an unbroken unity of man and nature that still existed in ancient China marks an "illusion," a "long tradition" of European misinterpretations. Western admirers of China took the longing for nature that pervades Chinese literature and art as a mirror of the real interaction with nature, failing to understand that this was a counterimage of actual conditions – the voice of the dropouts and hermits, an expression of "world weariness" and resignation.[55]

Other China scholars – like Mark Elvin and Vaclav Smil – who paint a gloomy picture of Chinese environmental history are also sharply critical of those who would confuse the history of religious–philosophical ideas of nature in China with the real history of human interaction with nature. On the whole, however, the problem of the connection between spiritual culture and agrarian economy is still largely unresolved, and the discussion often makes no headway; in part it is a fundamental quarrel between culturalists and materialists. Some of the arguments that are put forth are meaningless: for example, the fact that Chinese peasants – like all of the world's peasants – cut down forests, engaged in swidden agriculture, killed animals, and used the soil to produce their food goes without saying, and it proves neither the relevance nor the irrelevance of Confucian or Taoist ideas about nature. What matters is the development of a sense of sustainability, and here the discussion has often failed to reach Liebig's level. While culture is certainly not a negligible factor, it unfolds its effect chiefly in connection with practical rules and institutions capable of taking action.

Even Joseph Needham, the great encyclopaedist of the history of Chinese science and technology, believes – despite his, on the whole, materialistic view – that there certainly was practical significance to *wu wei*, the basic Chinese attitude of nonintervention toward nature and society. This was a kind of indolent laissez faire, which sometimes had a stabilizing, but sometimes also a destabilizing, effect on the relationship between humans and the environment. On occasion, the veneration of nature was combined with misanthropy already in ancient China. The Taoist rebel leader Chang Hsieng-chung (died 1649), who allegedly had thirty million inhabitants of Szechuan slaughtered, immortalized the essence of his teachings on a stone slab: "Heaven nourished the people with the Hundred Cereals, but the people do not do a single good deed to serve Heaven. Therefore kill, kill, kill, kill, kill, kill, kill."[56]

However, the veneration of nature at the expense of humans was certainly not the dominant Chinese tradition: "Probably no country in the world," Needham has said, "has so many legends about heroic engineers," especially when it came to the regulating of water. But even within hydraulic engineering one can at times detect a philosophy of *wu wei*: far better to leave openings for water than to confront it head-on. Chia Jan, a great Han engineer and a "Taoist in hydraulics," believed that the Yangtze "should be given plenty of room to take whatever course it wanted. Rivers, he said, were like the mouths of infants – if one tried to stop them up they only yelled the louder or else were suffocated." Evidently not everything in the Chinese harmony between man and nature was the impractical dreaming of poetic vagabonds and learned hermits. For example, the doctrine of feng shui, ancient

Chinese geomancy, certainly did have practical significance, though not always in the sense of modern ecology. Around 1760 broad resistance arose in the region of Hangchow against a quarry, on the grounds that it was upsetting the natural forces of the earth. Max Weber even believed that the dominance of geomancy in China had been "one of the most serious impediments to a rationalization of economic life."[57]

Chinese environmental history makes sense only if one pays attention to the fundamental difference between northern and southern China. In parts of the north, agriculture requires no artificial irrigation. The ox-drawn plow rules the deep loess soils. Well into the twentieth century, the chief food in many places was not rice, but the African millet-variety sorghum, which prefers dry soil. Wet rice cultivation on skillfully irrigated terraces characterizes above all central and southern China; here many peasants still work with hoe and spade and have no large animals. In northern and central China, the core agricultural regions are in the plains and the large river valleys; the people in the south had to rely more heavily on terracing of the mountains. In the plains of northern China, flooding and silting were for the longest time the most serious threats; in the hills of southern China it is the lack of water and erosion. Today, however, complaints about soil erosion and drought are also being heard all over northern China. In older times, the core regions of China lay more in the north, while in modern times the focus has shifted to the south: accordingly, the dominant problems also shifted over the course of time. The north-south contrast is joined by other regional differences, which make general statements about the development of the Chinese environment as well as a centrally guided environmental policy more difficult.

What, in all of this, constitutes a crisis? Chinese environmental history, too, has its problem with value judgments. As long as the focus of Chinese history lay in the valleys of the Yellow River and the Yangtze, the primeval catastrophes of Chinese history were the great floods; a constant burden was also the immense silt floods of these rivers, which raised the river bed, making it necessary to increase the height of the dykes, and from time to time caused river branches to shift their course. The Yellow River carries twenty-five times as much silt as the Nile, the Yangtze thirty-eight times. But catastrophes and dangers of this kind are not necessarily tantamount to ecological crises, since the effect was the same as with the beneficial Nile floods: masses of fertile soil particles reached the fields, and even new farmland could be created.[58] Not every form of erosion is disadvantageous to humans: one example is the kind that transports soil from difficult-to-cultivate mountain slopes into valley plains where it can be worked much more easily. And the raising of the riverbed, which increases the danger of flooding, at the same time makes irrigation easier, as lifting devices are no longer needed to move the water onto the fields. These stark contrasts in Chinese history are in part two different sides of the same coin. And the solution and trigger of environmental problems cannot always be clearly distinguished.

For Wittfogel, China was the archetype of the hydraulic society and the basis for his theory. Needham essentially agreed with Wittfogel, emphasizing that many Chinese scholars, too, confirmed the thesis that the origins of the bureaucracy lie in the hydraulic tasks.[59] A connection between hydraulics and political power in

China is beyond doubt; the question is only what kind of connection it was and with what sort of repercussions it was woven into the relationship between humans and their environment.

Much like in Egypt and Mesopotamia, agriculture is possible in the core regions of ancient China without irrigation, and when the latter was introduced, village authorities were for the most part enough to supervise and settle conflicts. It cannot be historically demonstrated that the Chinese state has its origins in irrigation, nor is it inherently plausible. An ancient popular song dating to before the founding of the empire in 221 B.C.E. declares: "We dig wells and drink, we plough the fields and eat; what do we care about the power of the ruler?"[60]

Even if irrigation did not require a higher power, that was not the case for drainage and protection against floods. It was precisely through these tasks that the Chinese emperors legitimated themselves first and foremost. The classic hydraulic founding myth, later embellished in superlative fashion by Chinese scholars, is the story of the legendary engineer-emperor Yu, who drained the floodwaters by opening up channels and deepening the river bed, thus saving the Chinese from turning into fish.[61] In Yu the Chinese possessed a much more energetic and popular model of the technician than the West did in Noah, who saved only himself and a few select others when the Great Flood came. But in recent times "Yu the Great," who gave the rivers their freedom and thereby saved mankind, has also been the mythological model of critics of the gargantuan dam projects. "Of all China's leaders, only Yu the Great managed the Yellow River well," declared the daughter of Huang Wanli, the brave campaigner against the Sanmexia Dam that was built across the Yellow River around 1960, and that became a fiasco as a result of the river's enormous silt load.[62]

For the longest time, most Chinese were aware that there was no final victory over water. Ssu-ma Ch'ien, the founding father of Chinese historiography (around 190–145 B.C.E.), recorded the lament of a despairing Han emperor in the face of a ruptured dyke: "The river broke through at Hu-tzu; / What could we do? / Beneath its rushing waves? Villages all became rivers / . . . / And there is no safety for the land." And on top of it all, there was not enough wood to repair the dykes.

Canal construction promised more lasting fame than dike building. For the most part its chief purpose was shipping, especially the provisioning of the capital with grain; the irrigation of the fields, the popular side of the canal, was secondary and could even by thwarted by the shipping channels. The purpose of the great canals was not above criticism. Ssu-ma Ch'ien reports for the time before the unification of the realm how the prince of Han sought to block the eastward expansion of Ch'in (Qin), which would later unite all of China under its rule, by tempting this project-happy state to overextend itself with the construction of a canal. To that end, the prince of Han dispatched the engineer Cheng Kuo, who persuaded the ruler of Ch'in to undertake the building of the later Cheng-Kuo canal: at the time a megalomaniacal project. Even after Ch'in had learned that the whole thing was a trick, construction was continued and eventually crowned with success, namely, the creation of a new, rich grain region. Needham assumes that the story contains a core of truth.[63]

But the usefulness of imperial canals to the people was by no means always so clear. Emperor Yang, who began the building of the Grand Canal around 600 C.E., was remembered by history as the example of a profligate and cruel ruler, though one with an enthusiastic love for nature. In fact, the primary purpose of this canal was to collect dues, and its dikes did more to cause flooding than to prevent it. This is true for dikes in general, and it is inherent in the thing itself: dikes merely divert the force of the water, and the diking of rivers also concentrates the water's power. Catastrophic floods knew no end during the course of Chinese history; at times they even seemed to be getting worse. Since the taming of the floodwaters was part of the imperial mythology, floods were seen as a sign that the government was corrupt. When the Yellow River burst over its banks destructively on several occasions around 1200, it prepared the way for the Mongol conquest by weakening the ruling dynasty; but the downfall of the Mongols, too, was preceded by the floodwaters of the Yellow River around 1350. At that time, the Mongol chancellor Togto, in a gargantuan project against the advice of his Chinese advisors, had the Yellow River diverted into a new bed south of the Shantung Peninsula. Not only the inundation itself, but also the corvée labor for the canal construction, stirred up unrest. As Klaus Flessel has shown, the Chinese administration of hydraulics in the Middle Ages was characterized not by centralization but by an impenetrable "thicket" of competencies; at that time, already, its effectiveness was the subject of critical discussions, especially since its failures were manifest.[64]

But none of this gave rise to calls for a better system, only for a better emperor and better officials. In modern times, the Chinese emperor had himself depicted inspecting flood-ravaged regions and supervising the construction of dykes. But as late as around 1854/55, the Yellow River shifted its mouth by nearly 500 kilometers to the north, killing millions of people in the process. It was the time of the Taiping Rebellion, and the floodwaters helped to undermine the authority of the government. No other river of the world has raged so destructively in historical times. Gigantic works to dam the river incessantly taxed the population, yet their efforts were puny compared to the might of the river. Before the era of concrete, the foundation of the dikes was clay and sand and was thus easily eroded by the constant onslaught of floodwaters. The dikes could be maintained only by the unceasing, organized labor of large masses of people. Everyone knew that: "Dikes are of no value without people to care for them," goes an old Chinese saying.

The greater the population pressure became, the closer the settlements crowded right up to the river banks, and the less one could afford to leave the river much freedom in keeping with the old Taoist philosophy of hydraulics. The "old method" of leaving "openings for water" became a nostalgic memory. But when the river spilled out of its constricted bed, the catastrophe was that much worse for humans. As late as 1947, the Guomindang and the Communists, otherwise already mortal enemies by this time, worked jointly on diverting the Yellow River, which was once again shifting to the south, northward. The hydraulic project gave rise to a moral impetus toward national unity.[65]

What has remained characteristic among Chinese water reservoirs to this day are not great artificial lakes, but – much like in India – village tanks, of which there are more than six million. The local water regime was the rule especially in the small-scale landscapes of the south.[66] But that does not mean that village society was able to cope with all water problems. Some authors, annoyed with Wittfogel, seem to downplay too much the need for regulation inherent in irrigation. One of the most fascinating regional studies of Chinese environmental history deals with the nearly 900-year history of Xiang Lake, an artificial lake constructed in 1112 southwest of Hangchow for irrigation purposes. Across many centuries, the leitmotif is the tug of war between private landowners, who want to drain parts of the lake and add it to their agricultural land, and the incorruptible officials (not that common, but for that reason all the more glorified) who preserve the lake in the interest of the common good. It was around such lakes that there took shape in China the notion of a common good that had to be defended against private self-interests, a notion that constitutes the modern environmental awareness. Political turmoil was regularly reflected in the siltification and shrinking of the lake. And this was not a unique case: elsewhere, too, with particularly good documentation for the nineteenth century, weakness and corruption within the administration manifested itself in the reclamation of agricultural land from irrigation lakes, even though they represented the common good in popular awareness. Xian Lake was completely drained only under the Communists, who destroyed the landowners but also believed that they no longer needed the lake for irrigation.[67]

During the Tang Period (the early Middle Ages in Europe), the water mill spread in China much as it did in Europe. But the boom in mills was only temporary in China, since water mills competed with the irrigation of the fields, and the agrarian interests were more powerful in the long run. By contrast, in Europe the operators of water mills, behind whom often stood the landowners, were usually able to assert themselves much more successfully against the peasants, who were concerned about the irrigation of their meadows. Since waterwheels are one of the most important historical origins of mechanization, water law offers one answer to the much-discussed puzzle why technological progress stagnated early on in China, in spite of some promising beginnings.[68]

Another kind of hydraulic problem, which also arose from private land reclamation interests, is attested along the middle reaches of the Yangtze between the sixteenth and the nineteenth centuries: landowners diked off some of the river meadows and in this way exacerbated the flooding catastrophes. Contemporaries already grasped the connection between the two. Here, too, the dilemma was often that the Chinese state was de facto not a real "hydraulic despotism," though it operated or let happen hydraulic projects that would have required a more effective centralized power in critical situations.[69] This happened especially in the wake of the increasingly dense settlement of ecologically fragile mountain regions and the expansion of rice cultivation requiring water.

Modern Communist China offers a prime example that a totalitarian, centralized state may well use hydraulic problems to legitimize itself, but that it cannot solve these problems satisfactorily with its top-down methods. Today the water resources in some regions of China are being overused to such a degree that wet rice farming around Beijing is declining as a result of dropping groundwater levels, and the Yellow River, whose waters were China's terror for thousands of years, barely reaches the sea in times of drought. It would appear that the spirit of cooperation that is necessary for successful water management can be effective, if at all, only on the local level, but not within the framework of a gigantic state.

Still, Mark Elvin's claim that all of Chinese environmental history is nothing more than "three thousand years of unsustainable growth" cannot be substantiated.

On the contrary, over long periods of time, Chinese agriculture must have possessed a high degree of inherent stability; in fact, it must have strengthened that stability even further with the spread of rice cultivation. It was presumably this fact that gave rise to a misleading sense of ecological security, which was still reflected in the delusion of Maoism that population growth was not a threat to China, but a source of strength. Much like Huang Wanli the dam critic, the economist Ma Yinchu (1882–1982), as president of Beijing University, warned repeatedly against continued population growth. Persecuted and denounced for decades as a "Malthusian," he was eventually rehabilitated in 1979 at the age of 98 and has become, with his fearless steadfastness, a hero of the Chinese environmental movement.

In the opinion of the vast majority of scholars, a large-scale ecological crisis developed in the eighteenth century and became acute and obvious in the nineteenth.[70] At that time the development in China showed in some respects a remarkable convergence with that in Europe, one of those astonishing parallels that give meaning to a *global* history of the environment. In China, as in Europe, one can detect in the eighteenth century a desire to use natural resources to their limits and to leave no more empty spaces, no quiet reserves. As in Europe, this was made easier by crops from the new world, especially the potato and maize. It was precisely the highest success of cultivation that led the country to its most severe ecological crisis: in this regard, China's fate is a warning to modern industrial society.

In the eighteenth century, European agrarian reformers, who were preaching the opening up of all wasteland, the elimination of the fallow, and unceasing industriousness, were carried away into raptures by the sight of Chinese rice terraces. Pierre Poivre assured his readers in 1768 that a "Chinese laborer could not but smile, if you informed him, that the earth has occasion for repose at a certain fixed period of time." Poivre did not recognize just how vulnerable China was becoming by colonizing its last reserves. As a result of an end to the great pandemics, the population began to increase steadily in the eighteenth century, both in China and Europe. Unlike Western and Central Europe, however, China achieved neither industrialization nor a modernization of the administration, which could have alleviated the consequences of the ecological crisis and absorbed the population pressure. Moreover, China did not have Europe's safety valve for a growing population pressure: emigration to America.

The Manchu Dynasty took the final step toward relieving the growing population pressure in 1859, following the Taiping Rebellion, when it opened Manchuria – where the Manchus had developed their nomadic basis and that had been closed to colonization – to settled farmers. The same thing happened in the early twentieth century in Inner Mongolia, which subsequently experienced an "explosive colonization." China still had widespread reserves of pastureland, but the only use it had for them was as agricultural land, which promoted erosion.[71]

The first signs of the danger of an overtaxing of China's natural resources began to emerge as early as the Middle Ages. In the eleventh and twelfth centuries, under pressure from the nomads pushing in from the north, and according to Herbert Franke also as a result of the exhaustion of the soil in northern China, a growing stream of settlers was already headed south, with the result that nine-tenths of the Chinese population supposedly lived in the south in the thirteenth century. This dramatic population shift was accompanied by an intensification of wet rice cultivation. Some scholars already speak of that period as an agrarian revolution or as a new model of agrarian energy flow. In one "Farmer's Lament" from the twelfth century we read the following: "If there's a mountain, we'll cover it with wheat. If there's water to be found, we'll use it all to plant rice. . . . With such labor we exhaust all our strength, all in the hope of enjoying a little peace."[72]

The conquest of China by the Mongols halted the southward shift of the Chinese centers of power. But from the fifteenth and sixteenth centuries on, the Ming Dynasty accelerated the agrarian development of the south. The yield of the rice fields was increased through improved fertilizer; rice varieties with a shorter ripening period and increased irrigation allowed for a second harvest each year. Beginning in the eighteenth century, cultivation in areas where rice could not be planted shifted to the sweet potato and maize, which allowed the rapid population growth to continue. As in Europe at that time, the Chinese governments pursued a successful policy of encouraging a growth in population; but when that policy encountered its limits, it was not possible to switch with the same success to a policy of population control. Senior officials understood the dangers of overpopulation and the overuse of resources. The thesis of the onset of the Chinese population and environmental crisis in the eighteenth century is based on contemporary documents. In this regard as well, premodern China offers analogies to modernity: insightful discourse certainly existed, though in many cases it floated high above the world of everyday practice.

By 1950 about half of China's mountainous and hilly land had been degraded by erosion. Loess especially, with its tiny soil particles, is extremely susceptible to erosion. The basic problem is readily apparent to anyone who ever picks up a handful of loess: at first it seems hard as rock, but this stability is deceptive – once the hard crust has been broken, the soil rapidly falls apart. Maintaining terraces was a part of the traditional peasant culture that had been deeply undermined by modern developments. According to current calculations, 1.6 billion tons of fertile loess is lost each year in northern China, partly as the result of the neglect of terraces.

What is regarded as the most critical aspect of the cultivation of mountainous regions – as of the Chinese interaction with the environment as a whole – is the decimation of the *forests* in mountain areas where they were needed as protection against erosion and for water. Those living in the loess regions could believe, in the face of what seemed inexhaustibly fertile soil as deep as a mountain, that one could dispense with forests altogether; but when this carelessness was transferred to the mountains of southern China, the results were disastrous. (By now, this carelessness is also affecting the north.) The cutting of broad expanses of forests in the south has been described as one of the greatest ecological mistakes in human history. The newer history of southern and western China has traits of a colonial history. Even where agriculture was otherwise laboriously maintained in an ecological balance, the lack of wood created a nutrient leakage, for it forced farmers to use the leftovers of the harvest as fuel, which meant that they were lost to the soil as fertilizer.[73]

Some contemporaries recognized, to a certain extent, the downsides of deforestation; complaints about the cutting of the forests are also part of Chinese tradition. Of course, Needham, who quotes a number of these laments, cautions us against "reading too much of our own ideas into their words." The Confucian Mencius (372–289 B.C.E.) even then bemoaned once beautiful mountain forests that had fallen victim to the axe. The powers of nature had allowed them to sprout again, "but then came cattle and goats to browse upon them." Thus the mountains were stripped bare, and the people believed that they had never been finely wooded. "But is this the nature of the mountain?" asked Mencius. Not unlike modern-day eco-idealists, he makes the cutting of trees into a moral defect: "The way in which a man loses his proper goodness of mind is like the way in which the mountain is denuded of trees by axes and hatches."[74] Forest cover as the nature of the mountains: this German notion was not wholly foreign to the Chinese, either, and they were also aware of the ruinous effects from the synergy of woodcutters and herders. One report from 1784 about a mountainous region in the province of Jiangxi laments: "The north-western countryside produced firs in abundance.... Recently the population has multiplied and the fertility of the soil has been exhausted . . . and the axes ring ding! ding!"

Did the Chinese recognize the danger to the soil and the water cycle? As evidence that they did many scholars point to the lament of a sixteenth-century scholar, Yen Shêng-Fang: even a generation ago, we are told, luxurious forests had covered the southeastern mountain slopes in Shangxi. They were not denuded because the people were gathering bundles of firewood. Under a new ruler they had begun to compete in the construction of houses, and they cut wood in the mountains without a yearly pause. Thereafter the treeless heights were turned into fields, and even the last bushes and shrubs were pulled out by their roots. Since that time, there was no longer anything to hold back the streams of water during heavy rains, and they caused serious destruction down in the valleys. In this way, the region had lost seven-tenths of its prosperity. This was a lament, then, that already noted the connection between deforestation and flooding. However, the fact that the same source is cited again and again would seem to reveal that there are not many passages of this kind for the older period. And here one must bear in mind that in the expansive regions of the Yellow River and the Yangtze, a causal connection between deforestation in the distant mountains and the terrible flooding was not immediately evident; even today, causalities of this kind cannot be established beyond a doubt in many cases. Where the protective function of a forest was directly apparent, for example, above irrigated terraces, the trees were sometimes left in place.[75]

As in many countries in the world, the picture becomes more favorable if one includes fruit-bearing trees, something that even the harshest critics of Chinese environmental behavior realize. In regions close to the shore, Richthofen often found "fruit-bearing trees planted" along the edges of terraces. Smil has emphasized that the "Chinese have traditionally been among the most proficient practitioners of agroforestry." And here one should recall the cultivation of mulberry trees, the basis of the Chinese silk industry, the symbol of China for more than four thousand years. Since the mulberry is slow-growing and long-lived, it promotes a long-term outlook.

The picture becomes more favorable still if one includes bamboo. Though biologists and forestry experts would point out that it is not actually a tree, but a grass, for the people of East and Southeast Asia it does possess in many respects the significance that the "real" forest has for Europeans: as the chief supplier of building materials as well as fuel. Love of bamboo pervades Chinese painting, poetry, and popular culture, and planting it is one of the traditional Chinese virtues. Though China may not look so good compared to Japan when it comes to forestry management, it does have twenty-five times as much acreage of bamboo. One environmental book celebrates the bamboo as a self-healing remedy for damaged nature: it flourishes even on slopes where the ecological devastation is at its worst. Wittfogel, however, had a suspicion that "perhaps this giant grass was one of the main culprits in the slaughter of China's forests."[76]

There is *one* dramatic reforestation period in Chinese history, one that occurred long before reforestation on a large scale began in Europe: in 1391 more than 50 million trees are said to have been planted in the area around Nanking to generate lumber for a future high sea fleet.[77] Here, as in Europe, naval construction was the impetus that for the first time elevated reforestation into a political matter of the first order. But when China abandoned its maritime ambitions, that impetus disappeared; a comparison with Europe allows us to measure how much political thrust Chinese forestry lost in this way. It would seem, however, that deforestation reached a critical stage in many Chinese regions only with the population growth and the mountain colonization of the eighteenth century.

China, too, had sustainable forestry management. Nicholas H. Menzies has provided a number of examples: an imperial hunting preserve, monastic, temple, and communal forests, and especially the planting of the China fir (Cunninghamia), apart from bamboo the most important Chinese timber tree, which the peasants cultivated not only for its wood, but also its leaf fodder. On the whole, however, all these examples of long-term forest cultivation seem to have been exceptions.[78] The small number of pertinent evidence from China's otherwise well-documented history speaks for itself. The geographer Yi-fu Tuan has commented: "The protected groves around the temples and monasteries bear melancholic witness to the probable forest wealth of the past."[79]

A comparison with Europe makes this deficit especially apparent, but it also explains it. All in all, in China dominion over the forest was not a basis for state power in even remotely the same degree that it was in Europe. The ruler made his presence felt not by protecting the forest, but by making it arable. The forest was notorious for being a refuge for bandits and rebels. Most of the time, naval construction was absent as an impetus toward the reforestation of high forests. Sovereign hunting as a factor in forest policy did not play remotely the role it did in wide regions of Europe from the Middle Ages until the Baroque and even later. To be sure, strict imperial hunting privileges had existed in ancient China, but their effect was not necessarily protective of the forests. "Entire forests are burned down for the sake of hunting," complained a prince in the second century b.c.e. With the growing power of Buddhism, hunting became suspect; it ceased to be a useful activity for imperial self-presentation.

Moreover, because of the small scale of animal husbandry in China, peasant interest in forest pasture was not nearly as important as in Europe. In China the steppe was the pastureland, not the forest. Fire-based industries were also not as dependent on forests as they were in the West, since pit coal was developed during the Chinese Middle Ages even for metal smelting. Salt works, the strongest industrial impetus toward sustainable forest management in Central Europe, do not seem to have played a comparable role in China.[80]

But there is probably another circumstance that is of importance: as a rule, forest protection can be successful only locally or within a region by taking the specific conditions into account. It is no accident that small, manageable territories often became pioneers of forest policy in Germany in the eighteenth and nineteenth centuries. The Chinese state was simply too vast for such achievements; the distance between the center and local problems was too great. This is the dilemma of Chinese environmental history as a whole: whenever environmental problems could be solved only with state means, the situation was usually bleak. The effectively functioning social entities to whom loyalty was given in everyday life were only the family unit and, at most, the local community.

Under Mao Zedong there was a strong state, and a forest consciousness was certainly present. It had long since been recognized that deforestation had deleterious consequences, and the project of the "great green wall" proclaimed in 1956 – a protective forest belt analogous to the Great Wall against the advancing steppe – was the greatest reforestation project of all times. Thereafter, a vigorous reforestation policy became in China as well a way to demonstrate the new, powerful state. What actually unfolded, however, was evidently the usual role play of forest policy: the protection of the forest became a not very popular matter for the central government, which clashed with the economic interests of the regions. Moreover, reforestation had to contend with the exacerbating conditions of a dry region. To this day it is difficult to assess to what extent the project is a success or a failure. In hilly regions the fertile land in the valley belongs to the collective, while the new land, which was cleared on the mountain slopes, could be privately worked. This created a strong incentive to clear land, even if this was probably not intended by the government.

To be sure, learning processes occurred over the course of time. For example, the government realized that it was necessary to decentralize the effort and activate the self-interest of the peasants, who were to be recruited for the reforestation work. In the early 1970s, the government issued the slogan of the "four arounds" when it came to the planting of trees: around houses, villages, roads, and canals. It would seem, however, that environmental policy was never able to hold its own against the economic and political priorities of Maoism. And while many ideological templates have disappeared in the post-Mao era, the dynamic of profit motive has given rise to new dangers for the environment. Forest-poor China has been particularly ruthless in its exploitation of the Tibetan forests as a wood resource, even though the forest regenerates itself only with great difficulty in the mountain conditions in that region. Today the best hope for a switch to a policy of protecting the forest lies probably in the concern on the part of the Chinese that the cutting of the Tibetan forests will exacerbate flooding in China.[81]

In spite of all the harassment of opposing environmentalists, an awareness of ecological crisis seems to have become quite strong even in informed, official circles in China, though it is undoubtedly more typical of educated elites than the common people. Today in China, environmental protection is the only sphere in which nongovernmental organizations are permitted, indeed, are promoted, by the state. In 1978 two influential experts went so far as to argue that an appreciable portion of the loess plateau around the Yellow River "should be reconverted to pastures and forests," for only this turnaround in a development that had been going on for thousands of years would prevent the erosion in the mountains and the eternally recurring flooding catastrophes in the valleys. They pointed out that great floods were quite rare prior to the first millennium c.e., before the agrarian colonization of the loess plateau. This is an example of a radical lesson from the environmental history across millennia, one that competes with the American prophets of wilderness. Others, however, saw the solution to these environmental problems in an intensification of agriculture. It is still popular in China to justify the dislike of nomads ecologically, and to equate nomadic grazing with overpasturing. In reality, Chinese settlement policy is today the primary culprit behind the acute overgrazing damage in Inner Mongolia, because it forces the nomads and their herds into the regions with the sparsest vegetation.[82]

I will conclude with a quick look at *Japan*. The image of Japan has fluctuated wildly within Western environmental circles since the 1970s: while there was initial talk of "Japan's ecological harakiri" and the country drew the ire of those opposed to whaling, Japan later emerged in many respects as a model. Japan, too, has a pronounced nature cult, though its practical consequences are doubtful. For centuries, the mayor of Nagasaki explained to a German interviewer in 1989, nature had assumed in Japan the place that religion and philosophy held in Europe; in the elementary schools of Nagasaki, "every school hymn begins with a verse about the mountains behind the school, about the bubbling brook in front, and the cherry trees next to it." It was never, asked, however, "who bore responsibility, who did what."[83]

If Japan nevertheless pursued a relatively successful land protection policy over the last centuries, that had to do more with practical common sense than with a love of nature. On the cramped Japanese island nation with its fragile mountain ecology, the limitations of early modern growth became apparent sooner than in China; in the early eighteenth century, severe famines already indicated that the outer limits of the food supply had been reached. By around 1800, however, when China's situation was becoming ever more desolate, Japan had once again come to a tolerable arrangement with its limited resources; the era of stagnation prior to the forced opening of Japan by Commodore Matthew Perry evidently had its ecological reasons. Population growth stopped on the island nation about 1720, while in China it accelerated precisely at this time.

Compared to China, Japan had one crucial advantage: it was smaller and more manageable, and within its circumscribed space a kind of national loyalty took shape earlier than it did in the enormous realm of China. Even reforestation was pursued with success from the end of the eighteenth century – in a remarkable chronological convergence with Central Europe. The Japanese seem to have recognized the regulating influence of the forest on the water carried by rivers. Reforestation took place early through planting, not – as was initially the case in Europe – through the mere regulation of the cutting of trees and natural rejuvenation; in the process – and this, too, was a stark difference to Europe – coniferous forests were turned into mixed deciduous forests. While in German regions at the time, the saw was in many cases virtually forced on woodcutters who were clinging to the axe, in some regions of Japan the saw was outlawed to protect the forest. Thanks to reforestation efforts, Japan – after a period of wood rationing – could afford to retain its traditional wood construction, which is best suited to the earthquake-prone country.[84]

Up until the 1950s, charcoal was a primary fuel of the Japanese. In 1949 Japan had a forest cover of no less than 68 percent, China, by contrast, a mere 8 percent – and this even though the Japanese, though creators of a "wood culture," traditionally do not have an especially close emotional relationship to the forest; they have a much stronger preference for spring water. But that, too, can give rise to a forest consciousness. One crucial reason for the high ratio of forest coverage is surely that a large part of Japan consists of steep mountains, which are unsuitable for agriculture. When Japan was in control of Korea, it exploited Korean forests ruthlessly; since the 1950s, however, South Korea has pursued a similarly vigorous forest policy as Japan. And since the 1960s, Japan, flush with foreign currencies, has had no difficulty meeting its demand for wood in New Guinea and other developing countries, where Japanese timber companies have become notorious for their ruthless clear-cutting.[85]

As the reasons behind the "Japanese environmental miracle" in recent years, John McNeill has emphasized the extreme environmental pollution that preceded it, but also the relative autonomy and greater responsiveness of local government and officials as one achievement of the constitution of 1947.[86] The example of Japan seems to demonstrate three things: (1) a relatively small geographical area and decentralization are advantageous for an effective environmental policy, (2) traumatic experiences are often necessary to produce a certain pressure to take action, and (3) in spite of all the situations of conflict between "ecology and economy," in the final analysis there is a connection between the energy behind economic policy and environmental policy. Moreover, when it came to dealing with its environment (and in other ways, as well), Japan had the advantage over China of a self-focused development, undisturbed by nomadic incursions and only temporarily disturbed by the European imperial powers. I will have more to say later about the ecological significance of imperialism.

5. WATER CIVILIZATIONS WITHIN CONSTRAINED SPACES: VENICE AND THE NETHERLANDS

Within a small geographical area, the complexity of the relationship between humans and water could be grasped early on, and it became the object of a skillfully balanced and comparatively effective policy. Prime examples in Europe are Venice, which coalesced from islands of the lagoon, and the Netherlands, much of which has been wrested from the sea. Both were unusual political entities, each in its way highly successful and at certain times a model admired throughout Europe. Both states were pioneers of maritime commerce as well as of hydraulic engineering and agrarian progress. Much as in the case of Japan, one gets the overall impression that economic and ecological energy is intimately connected, even if the two areas often encroach on each other. Were one to proceed from the ideal of "untouched nature," Venice and the Netherlands would appear in an environmental history only as negative examples of a highly artificial nature. But if one uses the prudent and forward-looking shaping of the natural environment as the yardstick, at least Venice in its heyday could be considered an exemplar.

From the very beginning, the Venetians were aware that they were living on unstable ground. All the later glorification of the *Serenissima* notwithstanding, the history of Venice is pervaded by a feeling of ecological uncertainty, which intensified at times into a pessimistic expectation of doom. Perhaps Venice attained its astonishing, thousand-year stability precisely because it never felt sure of its environment. Nature, wrote one Venetian chronicler, was continually waging an "exceedingly cruel war" against Venice. There is a story – which appears incredible to us – that in 1224, following a severe earthquake, there was a serious discussion in the Doge's palace whether the Venetians should resettle in Constantinople, which had been captured in 1204, and that this proposal, supported even by the Doge Ziani, failed by a single vote. If this story is true, it would indicate that it took many Venetians a very long time to identify with their precarious environment. But even during their city's heyday, they had a penchant for lamenting their imminent demise with tragic gestures: Piero Bevilacqua speaks of veritable *retorica delle fine, retorica dell'alarme* (which is regularly followed, however, much like today by a *retorica dell'incredulità*). The history of Venice could perhaps demonstrate that a certain purposeful, ecological pessimism has its advantages.[87]

The reason why the use of natural resources in Venice gave rise early on to an environmental policy in the modern sense is that the relationship to the water produced divergent impulses toward action, impulses that forced the Venetians to develop an increasingly diverse, "interconnected" way of thinking. As the Venetian economy developed, certain standard measures became increasingly inadequate for solving environmental problems, whether it was water protection or drainage; one had to be aware of chain reactions and balance various interests. The rivers that flowed into the lagoon were used as trading highways, but along with water they also carried silt into the lagoon: it was not easy to tell which effect was stronger, and whether it was advantageous or disastrous to divert rivers away from the lagoon. As late as the seventeenth century, one lagoon expert emphasized that when it came to making decisions in matters of water, it was "very easy to make the gravest mistakes."[88] In other words, one had to proceed with caution, avoid simple thought schemes, keep collecting new experiences, and engage in discussion: on this crucial issue of how to conduct an environmental policy, Venice was at times also exemplary.

To the Venetians, the environment in need of protection as a common good and an elixir of life already assumed concrete shape in the Middle Ages: this was the lagoon as it was, half sea and half inland lake, with all its islands and sand bars. And there were other powerful economic interests that factored into the equation and have nearly been forgotten today: salt works and fishing. "You have abundance only of fish," Cassiodorus wrote in the sixth century about the inhabitants of the Venetian lagoon. "All your emulation centers on the salt works . . . whence comes all your gain." Venice owed its rise to a trading metropolis in large measures to its sea salt works. Those salt works, however, were threatened by the inflow of fresh water and were destroyed over the course of time in the northern part of the lagoon: this, too, alongside siltification and malaria, was one impetus behind the rerouting of rivers that flowed into the lagoon. The lagoon did not possess the seeming endlessness of the sea, and the danger of wiping out the fish stocks through overfishing was clear early on. The Venetians took vigorous measures to head it off: the nets of the fishermen were rigorously controlled to ensure that they were wide enough to let the young fish pass through, and "diabolical inventions" – so a decree from 1599 – that threatened to exhaust the fish stocks were strictly prohibited.[89]

In the first few centuries, the chief goal of the Venetians was, understandably enough, protection against the water, draining of part of the lagoon, expansion of solid ground for the growing population, and the opening up of agricultural land and pastures. Gradually, however, there was a change in thinking. Beginning in the fifteenth century, draining ceased to be celebrated as a triumph over watery nature; instead, siltification and filling in by sedimentation, the interruption of the circulation of the water in the lagoon, was recognized as a deadly threat. From then on, every additional land reclamation was subject to rigorous and strict control by means of a land register. Environmental policy became Venetian power politics, not only toward the ecclesiastical orders located along the lagoon, but also toward the merchants, who were considered egotists and a threat to the common good even in a commercial city like Venice. Clashes between economic interests and the preservation of the environment do not date only to the time of the oil refineries of Porto Maghera, but are found back in the glory days of the *Serenissima*.

Torcello, whose two ancient churches sit forlornly surrounded by swamps and reeds, is for tourists today the embodiment of the lagoon dream. For the Venetians, it stood, together with the siltified *laguna morta* around it, as a warning example, even if the decline of this town founded back in Roman days was, strictly speaking, the work not only of nature, but also of a "deliberate strategy of economic and hydraulic neglect" (Christian Mathieu) by the overmighty neighbor Venice. Torcello, once an important trading city, not only lost its shipping through siltification, but was also overwhelmed by malaria, a fate similar to what probably befell the once mighty Aquileia much earlier. Looking at these towns, the Venetians acquired a new appreciation for their sea location and their salty water. Beginning in the fifteenth century, especially, the city's politics was dominated by a virtual horror at any sign of siltification. "In keeping with the saying 'palo fa palùo' (stake makes swamp), which means that a stake is sufficient to turn a piece of the lagoon into a swamp, the Serenissima declared war on stakes and pile construction, and nobody was spared. . . . Fines rained down on jetties, stakes, boat houses."[90]

The most forcible argument for the preservation of the lagoon was always the military one: one ritual mantra was that the lagoon was the wall of Venice, which was the only large medieval city without a wall following the dismantling of its fortifications in the twelfth century. The lagoon, it was further said, was a far better protection against attackers than the walls of other cities. Indeed, the Venetians simply had to pull up the stakes hidden below the surface of the water in the shipping lanes of the shallow lagoon and no foreign vessel would be able to enter. When it comes to implementing ecological concerns, it is especially advantageous if they converge with military interests.

Beginning in the middle of the fifteenth century, the Venetians diverted the two rivers Brenta and Piave as well as six other rivers that threatened to silt up the lagoon and made them flow around it: according to Philippe Braunstein and Robert Delort, these were the "most gigantic" landscape corrections in Europe's older history. In 1488 the project to divert the Brenta was emphatically justified in the Doge's palace, for it was completely obvious that this river was threatening Venice with "total destruction and devastation." More than three centuries earlier, Venice had tried in vain with military means to prevent Padua from diverting the water of the Brenta into the lagoon: an early ecological war! Later Venice sought to harm neighboring Ferrara by redirecting the Po River. The geography of the Po valley invites manipulation of the river.[91]

The hydraulic exertions of the *Serenissima* increased dramatically after 1500. In a situation when Venice's hegemony on sea and land was under threat, the Venetians addressed themselves with renewed energy to the task of living within their narrower environment with an eye toward the future. In 1501 the authority to deal with water issues was consolidated in the newly created Magistrato all'Aqua and the three *savi all'acque* (wise men of water). This move was justified first and foremost with concern for the city's *salubritas*, its health. A short time later, the city also established the Collegio Solenne all'Acque, the Grand Water College. It was a kind of "super commission" with concentrated authority, composed of the Doge, the three presiding magistrates of the Consiglio dei Dieci, and other top officials of the Doge's palace. The matter of water, it was said, was of such outstanding importance that the very cohesion of the entire state depended on it; and it was strongly emphasized that quick action was called for in this matter. This kind of urgency was highly unusual at the time. Evidently the Grand Water College proved too cumbersome, for in 1531 the Three Wise Men were joined by three *esecutori all'Acque* as an executive. The Council of Ten, which was involved in everything and became increasingly the control center of power, justified its special powers with the need for quick action in situations of crisis.[92]

Not only in China, but in Venice too, water and power were linked; and in both places that connection grew stronger over time, especially under pressure of crises. Venice, often lauded as Europe's oldest republic, appears at first glance as a striking refutation of Wittfogel's theory of the despotic tendency of hydraulics; even Wittfogel himself recognized Venice as a "nonhydraulic" polity. But the Venetian system had a totalitarian side that provided the stuff for black legends. The drinking water supply, however, was organized in a decentralized fashion: most of the over 6,000 *pozzi* (cisterns) were private or were under the control of the guilds of city quarters. The cisterns were not always adequate. Although surrounded by water, the Venetians "nearly died of thirst a few times in their history" and were forced to import Brenta water on boats.[93]

The city in the lagoon did not have a very salubrious climate. But far from accepting this natural disadvantage fatalistically, Venice (much like other northern Italian cities) was for a time far ahead of most of the rest of Europe in its public health policy. Today "environmental" policy is at its core to a high degree health policy, a configuration that extends far back historically. In Venice, especially, it was quite obvious. The city's water policies – whether draining swamps or stemming the inflow of fresh water into the lagoon – were also shaped by malaria prevention. Venice responded with measures of far-reaching impact on environmental policy also to the challenges of the plague epidemics, the worst catastrophes in the city's history. In contradiction to the prevailing medical doctrine of the humors, and without any of modern bacteriology, the Venetian authorities – like many laymen – suspected early on that the plague spread through contagion. Island-rich Venice gave birth to the concept of isolating the sick during an epidemic: "isolation" in the literal sense of the word by sending them to certain islands. Once again Venice benefited from its island location.

Beginning in the fifteenth century, when *bonifica* – reclamation – was stopped in the lagoon, it found a much greater field of action in the newly conquered terra firma. Here, too, there was a good deal of swampy land, and drainage was at the top of the agenda. While private initiative predominated on the ground, state dictates, river regulation, and canal construction were crucial preconditions. A first step was taken in 1463 with the draining of the province of Treviso. When it came to justifying the project, health interests were decisive alongside economic ones: "The death rate has once again been so high every year because humans and animals have hitherto been forced to drink water from murky and muddy ditches." The draining of the terra firma made substantial progress only in the sixteenth century when the state became more actively involved. But the involvement of the Venetian state was not free: toward the end of the sixteenth century, it laid claim to the control over all bodies of water in the terra firma, which were declared to be public goods.[94]

The year 1545 saw the establishment of the Magistrato dei beni inculti (Reclamation Commission), through which the drainage work on the terra ferma was given greater state backing. When the new agency sought to expand its zeal for drainage also to the lagoon, the result was a major and memorable conflict with the water authorities. The eloquence with which this controversy played out contrasts with the usual Venetian reticence. The quarrel took on a special intellectual caliber through the personalities of the two spokesmen of the opposing camps, Alvise Cornaro and Cristoforo Sabbadino. Both men were not only leading hydraulic engineers, but also visionaries about Venice's future.

Cornaro (1475–1566), still today known as the author of the tract *De vita sobria* (The Temperate Life, 1558), embodied in classical manner a combination of agrarian, environmental, and health ideology. Having moved from the city in the lagoon to Padua, he was proud of having recovered not only his material prosperity, but also his physical well-being in the new city, and of having found peace of mind. He was convinced that Venice would fare likewise if it turned away from the sea and to the land. With passionate enthusiasm he described smiling nature, the singing of the birds, and the Arcadian shepherd's idyll on the terra firma. He, too, opposed eliminating the lagoon, "the great and wonderful bulwark of my beloved fatherland," entirely. But he wanted to reclaim parts of it – as in the south near Chioggia – in order to gain farmland, as this would ensure that the Venetians would not suffer hunger even if their enemies prevented them from importing grain. Moreover, draining land meant to him not only bread, but also health and happiness. He gave his project the title "Previsione Saluberrima" – the "Most Prudent Foresight."

To supporters of the ideology of the lagoon state, this was heresy.[95] Cornaro's great antagonist, Sabbadino, hailed from Chioggia, and he was certainly provoked into action by the prospect of seeing his hometown transformed from a lagoon into a regular mainland city. He was afraid, to put it into modern language, that reclamation would cause the entire ecological system of the lagoon to collapse. "Three kinds of people destroy the lagoon: the landowners, the engineers, and private individuals." He turned the health argument around: fresh water and the stagnation of the water circulation would lead to the spread of reeds, from whose vapors malaria rises. Sabbadino held up to the Venetians the fate of deserted and desolate cities as warning examples. To be sure, although this whole quarrel was about economic interests and the authority of the different magistrates, it was also a clash of different mentalities and opposing visions of Venice. Sabbadino celebrated his Venice in poetic verses: "The rivers, the sea, and humans you have as your enemies," only the lagoon as certain protection. The modern-day tourist is happy that Sabbadino carried the day, and a Venetian historian has charged that Cornaro lost his "amphibian sensibility" in Padua.[96] For even if his plans had made sense in their own way, in the end Venice would have ceased to be Venice. The "nature" of a civilization is also a product of its history.

One political issue of the highest order was the *wood supply*. Venice needed not only firewood but also vast quantities of valuable timber for the foundations of its houses and for its fleet, yet it had no large forests nearby. Ancient Venice was built on stakes: the foundations of the Salute, the largest Baroque church, alone consumed 1,150,657 wood pilings. The question of wood was first and foremost a question of transportation, and great quantities of wood could be transported over long distances only on water. The rivers were needed as transportation lanes for this purpose, in particular, and this was another reason to worry about siltification. This situation created strong motivations for a farsighted forestry policy, since the cutting of nearby forests not only made the transportation routes longer, it also increased the siltification of the rivers and the lagoon through erosion. Interconnections between the forest economy and the water economy: this, too, made Venice into a pioneer of environmental policy. As early as 1530, the Consiglio dei Dieci mentioned the link between deforestation and the increasing silt load of the rivers as a well-known fact, especially since this offered the powerful Council a reason to expand its water authority to the forest. As one can see, those in the Doge's palace also understood the power-political potential of environmental regulation earlier than elsewhere.[97]

As elsewhere, it was primarily the needs of the fleet that made the wood supply into a highly important matter of state. The wood supply for the arsenal stood at the top of the list. Nearby forests that had a certain quality of oak trees were set aside exclusively for specific uses in the arsenal: the forest of Montello for keels, that of Cansiglio for rudders. But the supply of firewood also became a government task at that time; in 1531 the Council of Ten complained about the shortage of firewood, and, not content merely with regulating the cutting of wood, it took the step – highly unusual at the time – of ordering reforestation on the mainland.[98]

Was Venetian forest policy effective? This question is controversial to this day. Forest maps create the impression that the protected forests were in fact preserved for centuries at least in Venetia, where effective control was possible, even if they surely could not compete with the vast quantities of wood in Northern and Western Europe that were available to the newly emerging sea powers. The oak forests enjoyed protection to the very end of the Serenissima. As late as the nineteenth century, the former Venetian state forests in the Alps were among the favorite destinations of forestry expeditions. Robert P. Harrison believes that the rise of Venice into a sea power was a "disaster" for the forests, but he is obviously unaware that Montello, which he praises repeatedly as a prime example of a beautiful old-growth forest, was a Venetian state forest.[99]

Goethe, who was well informed about the flow of currents in the lagoon, noted in 1786, during his stay in Venice, that the city need not worry about its future: "The slowness with which the sea is receding leaves it thousands of years of room, and they will undoubtedly know how to retain possession of the water by skillfully helping the canals." Indeed, Venice experienced no water catastrophes on a Chinese scale; when it came to hydraulic engineering, there was time for a careful, well-considered approach. Goethe was quite right in seeing the resolution of environmental problems as a question of pace. The chief danger in his eyes was a drop in the water level. In 1783, as protection against surging floodwaters, the city had completed – on the lidi, the outlying sand banks – "massive sea walls called the Murazzi . . . built from huge blocks of Istrian stone"; it was the large-scale hydraulic project of the declining *Serenissima*.

Goethe, however, did complain vociferously about the lack of cleanliness among the Venetians, and many later tourists joined in that complaint. When Goethe asked for a lavatory, he was told that he could relieve himself anywhere he wanted. The *città pulita* had turned into a malodorous city. Did the interest of the Venetian ruling class in maintaining the health of the city wane the more it sought its future on the mainland? Vanzan Marchini believes that the political decline was accompanied by the decline of the Venetian environmental awareness. It seems, however, that the disposal of sewage was always a sore point in the city. In the fifteenth century, the humanist Enea Silvio de Piccolomini, the future Pope Pius II, was already complaining about what was at times an "unbearable stench in the canals."[100]

As late as the nineteenth century, Italy was considered in Europe the "classic land of irrigation," where irrigation technology had been elevated into a science. "The architecture of water was born in Italy, and it was almost entirely here that it developed to perfection," wrote an Italian hydraulic engineer in 1768. Beginning in the sixteenth century, the advance of rice cultivation in the Po valley had led in some areas to a reshaping of the landscape in an almost Chinese manner. However, the lagoonal water wisdom of Venice remained the exception in Italy. The model country of *drainage* in the early modern period was the Netherlands. In the seventeenth century, Dutch canal builders could be found at work from the Pontine marshes to Göteborg, from the Vistula to the Garonne.[101]

The hydraulic career of the coastal dwellers of western Frisia had already begun in the high Middle Ages, long before the Dutch existed as a nation. As early as the twelfth century we find Dutch master dike builders at the estuaries of the Elbe and Weser: starting from Holland, a spirit of resistance to the sea spread early along the entire coast of the North Sea. While the merchants of Bruges stood by and let their harbor silt up – much the same way in which they, instead of taking to the sea themselves, had their foreign customers come to them – the Dutch took an active stance toward the sea early on, even if they were continuously thrown on the defensive by the power of the water: the catastrophic floods would not end, and the Dutch lost far more land in the Middle Ages than they gained. But the political, economic, and ecological energies seemed to coalesce at the time of the long Dutch war of independence against the Spaniards. The Dutch were well aware that they lived in an artificial environment of their own creation. As one saying put it: "God created the world, but the Dutchman made Holland."[102]

The most crucial matter was the building of dikes, and here – as in ancient China – we find the philosophy that the surge of the flood must not be confronted head on, it had to be calmed and tamed through streamlined constructions. But one hydraulic engineer wrote that those floods that remained recalcitrant had to be "strangled" to death. The scenery involving humans and water was much simpler and starker in Holland than in Venice: the stormy North Sea was the great enemy, often mentioned as analogous to the Spaniards. Terrible floods, especially since they were a constant threat, persisted as traumatic experiences in the collective memory. Dike building and drainage canals would save the Dutch. The kind of careful, considered thinking in terms of balance that existed in the Venetian lagoon could hardly arise under these conditions. The Dutch were so specialized in drainage that they had to import French Huguenots for irrigation works in the Cape colony.

To be sure, dike building along the sea would have demanded a well-considered balance, since it made the drainage of water from the mainland more difficult. Builders sought to escape the problem with sluice gates; however, for technical reasons that approach was only imperfectly successful until the nineteenth century. That is why we find this resigned saying along the northern coast: "If we don't drown in salt water, we'll drown in fresh water." But let there be no doubt that priority belonged to the battle against the sea.

While it became an ecological raison d'état in Venice to put strict limits on private land reclamation in the lagoon, in Holland it was always seen as meritorious to wrest land from the sea; and the driving force behind the creation of polders was a private profit motive that was given free rein as never before in history. It was not until 1789 that a central office for water management was established, the Rijkswaterstaat. In Holland water policy was not connected with any forest policy. Peat was available as heating fuel, and once Holland had become the richest nation of Europe, it could import huge quantities of wood from Scandinavia and the entire catchment basin of the Rhine. Still in the eighteenth century, when Holland had long since gone into decline, the "Hollanders" wood trade on the Rhine, with its gigantic floats of up to 300 meters long, which had to be preceded by warning boats, was by far the largest German wood business at the time. Amsterdam, similar to Venice, required enormous amounts of wood for its foundations and for shipbuilding, but it did not need nearby forests. Holland, by its name actually a "wood land," a forest land, became, next to Denmark, the Central European country with the smallest forest cover, especially since it had no mountains that were difficult to cultivate and on which forests would thus have had the advantage of location.[103]

Holland was the land of dikes, canals, and lock gates, and at the same time the birthplace of liberty, both political and intellectual: Wittfogel himself admitted that the Netherlands, much like Venice, proved that the political culture of a country was, after all, not merely a function of hydraulics. For Huizinga, the water was even the basis for the democratic-cooperative structures of the country: "A country divided by watercourses such as ours must needs have a considerable measure of regional autonomy"; only the combined energies on the ground can maintain the dykes and canals. Traditionally, the maintenance was a matter for the village *Waterschappen*, the dike associations which profited from the dikes. However, they had to cooperate under the supervision of the authorities. Thanks to the natural conditions, the draining of the moors in western Frisia was also easier to undertake than in neighboring German regions through local initiatives, without the state to build a centralized drainage canal. Charles V had attempted, in Chinese fashion, to strengthen imperial power in the Netherlands through hydraulic means; but the communities responded that the central office of water works created in 1544 was not familiar with the local conditions.[104]

And yet, one should not form an exaggerated picture of the effectiveness of Dutch hydraulics; one expert of the matter has assured us that the dike masters were usually "boors and blockheads." Since the building of dikes often diverted the force of the North Sea onto neighboring coastlines, and since the sinking of the ground caused by the drainage of the hinterland exacerbated the danger of flooding, a need for more centralized guidance certainly existed. In Holland, too, hydraulics established authority; as some derisive English verses put it: "Who best could know to pump an earth so leak / Him they their Lord and Country's Father speak." Incidentally, the Dutch development also shows clearly the limitations of waterworks driven essentially by a private profit motive. For in comparison with commerce, the creation of polders remained an uncertain and murky business, and it virtually ground to a halt during the agrarian depression of the seventeenth century. One project that would have made a lot of sense, the draining of the Haarlemmermeer, which would have created 18,000 hectares in the Dutch central region between Amsterdam, Haarlem, and The Hague, though planned since the seventeenth century, could not be accomplished until the nineteenth century with the use of steam power. In the seventeenth century, the mill engineer Jan Leeghwater, who had the nickname "Jan Wind," drew up plans to use a battery of 500 windmills to drain the lake. Under preindustrial conditions, Leeghwater's scheme, as Simon Schama has said, "was positively Egyptian in scale."

That was even truer for the plan – first conceived in 1667 – to drain the Zuiderzee, more than ten times the size of Haarlemmermeer. This project, tailor-made for a megalomaniac hydraulic ruler, could be only partially carried out as late as the twentieth century. A national actor equipped with more modern technique was also required for the "Delta Plan," which received the decisive impetus from the catastrophic flooding in 1953: it called for a dyke connection between the islands in the Rhine-Maas delta to drastically reduce the overall length of the dykes. This high point of Dutch hydraulic engineering came under fire with the rise of the modern environmental movement.[105]

The cultivation of moorland was a questionable undertaking not only economically, but also ecologically. Here short-term profits were purchased at the price of long-term soil exhaustion. Drainage and peat cutting set a vicious cycle in motion: as the sinking ground approached the groundwater level, "agriculture became difficult, and the grassland became swampy. It was thus therefore necessary to lower the water table once again by deepening the drainage ditches and canals." But then the shrinking process would begin again. It was presumably in this way that the Zuiderzee was created in the Middle Ages, and the Haarlemmermeer since the sixteenth century. A good many of the water problems that the Dutch wrestle with were, in the end, home made! In this regard, Holland is an especially good example of what the future might hold.

And yet, we should beware of turning the environmental history of the Netherlands too much into a moral tale, after the motto "Nature punishes the sins of humankind." It would appear that the Netherlands, unlike many other regions, were among the winners of the "Little Ice Age" and the losers when the climate grew warmer: the melting of the polar ice masses caused a rise in sea level and increased the pressure on the dikes, while at the same time – and more ominously – the pile-worm spread southward as far as Holland and caused serious damage to the coastal fortifications.[106]

Peat was the energy source that fueled the Dutch Golden Age, and the profits were accordingly high. The fact that peat cutting was pursued with a true "gold digger mentality" after the motto "après nous le deluge" made the situation worse over the long run. This problem was recognized as far back as the sixteenth century, but a prohibitive tariff on the export of peat did not have the desired effect. In fact, complaints that the draining of the marshland promoted the drying up and erosion of the already sandy *geest* were voiced as early as the fifteenth century. The effort to wrest farmland from the sea can be explained as the result of an early ecological crisis of moor cultivation.[107]

None of this is an exclusively Dutch problem. Among the residents of the wet Blockland along the Wümme River near Bremen, the diking and poldering of land in the Dutch fashion caused constant grumbling: they were used to an amphibian life with fishing, duck hunting, and pasturing, they appreciated the fertilizing effect of inundations and despised the never-ending dike work as slave labor forced on them.[108] Similar scenes took place when the Oderbruch was drained under Frederick II of Prussia. It went so far that Frederick II threatened the death penalty for residents who, during the night, damaged the newly constructed dikes. Where great floods had not triggered a collective trauma as in Holland, dike building was usually a controversial project. Even Bismarck, who had been a dike captain (*Deichhauptmann*) as a young man, was throughout his life vividly aware of how the interests of agriculture and pasture collided over the dikes: to him it was a reminder of the need for strong leadership.[109]

Around 1800 a farmer in the province of Groningen rediscovered peat burning (*Rasenbrennen*) as a method for the short-term enrichment of the soil of the moor with nutrients. But this practice, which spread rapidly, was a dubious kind of progress. When the method started to take hold in the northwestern part of Germany and the acrid smoke became a nuisance for broad regions of Central Europe, virtual associations against peat burning were formed; the practice was eventually outlawed in Germany in 1923. After six to eight years, moor soil had been "burned to death."

In the late nineteenth century, however, it was said that "Holland's moor regions, once desolated by the practice of burning," had by now been "transformed into rich, flourishing landscapes," especially through "city fertilizer" – sewage mixed with ash and street sweepings. In fact, Chinese virtues were often attributed to the Dutch and the Flemish in matters of fertilization: in the eighteenth century, Flanders and Holland became model countries for agrarian reformers, places where everything useful – including human excrement – was used as fertilizer, where a trade in fertilizers existed, and where the soil was cultivated as intensively as possible.[110] Later, Holland became the classic land of greenhouses and chemical fertilization, that is, of a highly artificial agriculture.

During the ecological era, Holland was at times considered, from one perspective, as the "dirtiest country in Europe," if not the world, a country which, as a result of an agrarian economy that paid no heed whatsoever to ecology, was in danger of drowning in liquid manure.[111] Here were the beginnings of a reevaluation of the history of this country: Holland as a warning example of what will happen if a country, confident of its capital power, places too much hope on the creation of a thoroughly artificial environment. But the prominent profile of the environmental problems also contained a chance for vigorous countermeasures. The action plan *Sustainable Netherlands*, published in 1992 by the Dutch environmental group Milieudefensie-Friends of the Earth Netherlands, became a model also for the German environmental movement.

6. MALARIA, IRRIGATION, DEFORESTATION: ENDEMIC DISEASE AS NATURE'S AVENGER AND THE PROTECTOR OF ECOLOGICAL RESERVES

What we think of today when we speak of "environmental awareness" contains at its core an element of health consciousness, namely, the sense that health is influenced by the environment and is threatened by certain environmental conditions. This kind of consciousness has existed for thousands of years, especially in connection with malaria, of which one knew or suspected that it was somehow connected with the nature of certain landscapes. From antiquity until today, it has been and is the most serious and widespread endemic disease in human history. Long before ecology became fashionable, a connection between medicine, ecology, and history developed in malaria research.[112]

Since ancient times, malaria confronted humanity with a dilemma reminiscent of the alternative "economy or ecology?" that is presented so often today: to achieve abundant harvests, it was advisable to settle in wet areas and, if possible, to increase the moisture through irrigation systems; for health reasons, however, it was advisable to live in a dry climate. Malaria forced people to locate settlements and fields on mountains, even though the lowlands possessed soil that was better and easier to cultivate. As late as 1900, the German Social Democratic leader August Bebel, who had boundless confidence in science, was looking forward to a better future, when food would be produced by chemistry, and "deserts may then become the favorite homes of man, being healthier than the damp valleys and the swamp-infected plains" where agriculture had long been pursued.[113]

Anyone who studies the historical importance of malaria can get the feeling of having found one of the keys to world history, especially to the decline of civilizations and the failure of imperial ambitions. Whether it is the campaigns of Alexander the Great or nineteenth-century colonial imperialism: time and again we encounter the fever that rises from the swamps, assaults armies worse than the enemy, and gives history a new and unexpected twist. To be sure, it is difficult to reduce the historical importance of malaria to a common denominator; it is not easy to decide whom this disease weakened more, the Italians or the northern

Europeans who invaded Italy. Still, Angelo Celli, author of a classic Italian work on malaria, formulated this thesis: "[T]he history of malaria is to a large extent the history of those nations afflicted by it." Even the nomadism in dry regions has been explained as the result of efforts to avoid the swamp fever.[114]

The question to what extent malaria has always been endemic in the plains of the Mediterranean or grew worse only at certain times has not been satisfactorily resolved to this day. Cicero wrote that Romulus had chosen "a salubrious spot in a pestilential region" (*in regione pestilenti salubrem*). As early as 1900, when Italy and Greece were still suffering severely from malaria, observers suspected that the classical past of these countries had been marked by the disease. Celli believed that at the height of its power, Rome had pushed back – but by no means eradicated – the advancing malaria by means of drainage. In the late Middle Ages and again in the seventeenth century, however, this disease, according to Celli, ravished the population of the Roman environs more than ever before. The literature gives the overwhelming impression that this region experienced its worst malarial phase between the seventeenth and the nineteenth centuries. In 1709 the Italian physician Torti coined the misleading term "mal-aria" ("bad air"). It is possible that the impression of an increase in modern times results from the fact that there now existed a term and a medical policy dedicated to it, that a remedy was at hand in the form of quinine, and that hydraulic engineers were looking for work. At that time, malaria became the most dangerous enemy for colonial conquerors as well as for agrarian politicians eager to open up fertile plains to agriculture. In the nineteenth century, eucalyptus forests were sometimes planted to dry up the malarial swamps through their prodigious water consumption. Still, progress in fighting the disease remained spotty until the twentieth century.[115]

Cultural optimists among historians, like Toynbee and Braudel, mention malaria as the result of the decline of civilizations, the clogging up and siltification of irrigation networks: "Malaria progresses when man relaxes his efforts," wrote Braudel. But there are many indications that it is not the *decay* of irrigation systems, but the systems themselves that are one chief cause of malaria around the world. Even when they work, irrigations systems do not always function so perfectly that there are no backups and pools, especially since water reservoirs are often needed and drainage is frequently neglected. Even in the American state of Georgia, which did not offer especially favorable conditions for mosquitoes, malaria arrived in the eighteenth century with rice cultivation. George P. Marsh, the voice of warning against deforestation, believed that rice cultivation everywhere was so deleterious to health that only strong population pressure could justify this human sacrifice. Even in modern times one can still observe how the construction of dams and irrigation canals leads to new outbreaks of malaria.[116]

Moreover, as Celli already noted, the deforestation that accompanies the advance of civilization, and that often brings erosion, the siltification of rivers, and the marshification of plains in its wake, is presumably a chief cause of malaria. In that case malaria would be a nemesis after all, and even nature's self-protection, one might say, for thanks to malaria, the world preserved in its warm and moist regions an infinite store of ecological reserves that remained beyond human reach until the twentieth century. It was only to the degree that the Chinese acclimatized themselves to the local malaria that they were able to claim southern China for rice cultivation. One Portuguese seafarer of the sixteenth century described the swamp fever as the sword of Cherub that prevented the Europeans from entering the paradise of the tropics. On the whole, malaria was probably one of the most potent brakes in history; it wore down invading armies, reduced population growth, and spread indolence and lethargy.[117]

That irrigation brought the threat of swamp fever was already well known in earlier times, and where irrigation systems were newly constructed, the locals sometimes fought back in spite of the prospects of more abundant harvests. When wet rice cultivation was introduced in the Po valley in the early sixteenth century, it gave rise to an opposition movement that was fueled by the fear of malaria and persisted for centuries. The governments initially issued prohibitions against irrigated rice cultivation, but as time passed these were upheld only in the vicinity of the large cities. Johann Peter Frank, the hygienist of enlightened absolutism, still considered it a "fortunate privilege" of Milan that nobody was allowed to grow rice within miles of the city; and he advised other regions "to sacrifice unhealthful rice cultivation to the good health of the subjects." And this was his recommendation even though rice quadrupled the yield of the fields! The defenders of rice pointed out that in well-tended rice fields the water was in constant motion, and this counteracted the swamp fever. But there was still no understanding why that was so.

Even in the late nineteenth century, the large-scale construction of irrigation canals by the British colonial government in northern India sparked vehement complaints by the population about the increase in malaria, and not least about the impotence the disease caused in men. As Elizabeth Whitcombe has demonstrated in a pioneering study, these complaints were perfectly justified. Even an author who tends to be skeptical of canal critics has noted that in the wake of canal building, the ratio of malaria among total deaths in affected regions had risen to over 90 percent! Though observers were beginning to understand the etiology of malaria ever more clearly at that time, drainage continued to be neglected.[118]

Was the crucial information about the causes and prevention already known in antiquity, without the benefit of modern bacteriology? The Hippocratic text dealing with environmental influences highlights the great importance of water for good health and warns especially against swampy water; even greater importance seems to have attached to air and wind. Varro even anticipated microbacteriology: "Note also if there be any swampy ground... because certain minute animals, invisible to the eye, breed there, and, borne by the air, reach the inside of the body by way of the mouth and nose, and cause disease which are difficult to be rid of." In ancient China, as well, the connection between fever and stagnant bodies of water was well understood. Should humanity not have simply followed its experience and sound instincts to protect itself against swamp fever? As early as the sixth century B.C.E., the physician and philosopher Empedocles is said to have freed the citizens of the Sicilian city of Selinus from fever by diverting two fresh mountain streams through a putrid swamp.[119]

Was it not merely a question of will and energy to rid oneself of malaria? Indeed, the history of this disease offers warning examples of human indifference toward fateful environmental changes. However, the problem and its solution were by no means entirely obvious. Until the nineteenth century, it was not possible to distinguish malaria in all its forms clearly from other feverish illnesses. And while mosquitoes had been suspected as the transmitters since antiquity, there was no absolute certainty; even the African explorer Stanley thought nothing of mosquito nets. Mosquitoes do not pose a threat of malaria everywhere, and the disease does not always rise from swamps: sometimes it is endemic in other regions, as well, and not all marshlands are malaria infected.[120] The situation was much like environmental policy today: the person who was waiting for absolute certainty always found a reason to do nothing.

But even when people quite correctly recognized swamps as the cause, this insight often did not help much. In previous centuries, before the time of river regulation and sewer systems, there were far too many wet places in the landscape to drain them all; apart from the fact that draining created legal problems, since it could damage neighboring agricultural fields and pastures. As the modern age unfolded, quinine promised a way out of this dilemma, even if it was an expensive and makeshift solution.

Wherever malaria had gained the upper hand, it established a kind of self-replicating system: it created lethargy and a shortage of people; the dense population that was necessary for the construction of drainage networks did not exist; and if workers were brought in from the outside, they soon succumbed en masse to the disease. To that extent malaria possesses the characteristics of a historical subject. For the locals who – if they survived – had a certain immunity, malaria was both fate and protection against invaders; unlike the plague it did not trigger a shock effect that could have set large-scale countermeasures in motion.

The shining counterexamples to this lethargy are Venice and Amsterdam, which kept themselves fairly free of malaria by ensuring the free flow and circulation of seawater in their canals. But in these instances, malaria prevention was not an isolated issue but converged with the demands of shipping, the overarching economic interest. This was a very different situation from the wet rice regions, where the hygienic interest threatened to collide with the economic interest, even if the two were not invariably contradictory. Holland and Venice were rich hydraulic societies in which the regulation of water was part of the routine of daily life. At that time it was already apparent that the ability of environmental health concerns to gain a footing depended on their ability to link themselves to established interests and patterns of behavior. But it also depended on favorable natural conditions: in general Amsterdam and Venice had to deal not with the *malaria perniciosa* of southern regions, but with less serious types of disease, and Holland did not offer a particularly favorable breeding ground to the malaria transmitter. But when the Dutch began to construct canals in Batavia (Jakarta) modeled on Amsterdam, malaria began to ravage the city with such deadly effect that the Dutch were forced, around 1800, to abandon Batavia as the capital for a while, and the rich metropolis offered the sight of a desolate wreck. The cutting of the forests around the city seems to have been the chief cause for the silting up of the canals, an effect that even the Dutch, with all their hydraulic experience, had not foreseen, since Holland was a forest-poor country with no science of forestry.[121]

A gloomy contrast to Amsterdam and Venice is also offered by Rome, whose environs had been infested and depopulated by "*malaria perniciosa*" since the Middle Ages, or even longer. For Rome this ring of malaria around the city provided a certain protection against invading armies, but the disease also posed a constant threat to the city itself. Why did this Western metropolis, of all places, fail to pursue any vigorous countermeasures? The problem and its possible solution were certainly recognized: papal plans to drain the Pontine marshes reach back into the Middle Ages. In the late eighteenth century, Pope Pius VI, in an effort to keep up with the agrarian and hygienic advances of his day, finally tried to implement these plans – but the *bonifica* (reclamation) of the marshes, showered with advanced praise, turned into an ignominious fiasco. It became clear that neither the large Roman landowners, whose sheep herds could range freely in the infested Campagna, nor the sparse local population, some of whom lived off the abundance of fish in the water, were seriously interested in the success of the *"bonifica."*[122] And the combined energy of all those involved would have been required, for the draining of land that had been swampy and infested for a long time was a far more difficult task than the preservation of an existing lagoon. It was achieved only under the Fascist dictatorship: the ending to this story is not a bad fit with Wittfogel's theory.

The degree to which malaria marked a major epoch in environmental history is something that can be understood far better today than in earlier times. After the Second World War, DDT won a victory over malaria within a very short period in countries like Italy and Greece, a victory quinine had not been able to achieve in centuries. But it was precisely the excessive use of DDT that provoked Rachel Carson to sound the alarm in her book *Silent Spring* (1962), which provided the impetus for the American and eventually the global environmental movement. At the beginning of modern environmental awareness stands the redefinition of millennia-old environmental problems. The declining fear of malaria opened up a new vista on nature. "Vive le désert! Vive le dépeuplement! Vivent les moustiques!" (Long live the wasteland! Long live depopulation! Long live the mosquitoes!): these slogans were used by environmentalists in Limousine, who wanted to save river floodplains, in their opposition to Electricité de France, which was trying to make its hydraulic power projects in the region attractive by arguing that they would bring not only economic but also health benefits.[123] At the height of malaria, when it was still posing a threat to Europe, such slogans would have been pure cynicism. Today, though, many nature lovers find swamps even more delightful than forests. But in this day and age, as well, the provocative confrontation of nature's interests and humanity's interests should be seen as a false dichotomy: in truth, the connection between environmental concerns and health concerns is stronger than ever before.

7. DEFORESTATION AND "ECOLOGICAL SUICIDE" IN THE MEDITERRANEAN
REGION: A FICTITIOUS PROBLEM? EROSION IN HARMONY
WITH NATURE AND MISLEADING HISTORICIZATION

Since the nineteenth century, some have seen the shores of the Mediterranean, which are the delight of tourists, as ruined landscapes, victims of a millennia-old culture that, along with the forests, destroyed the soil and the water balance. The desertification researcher Horst Mensching mentions, as a well-known fact, that the influence of man had turned "the pre-classical forest landscape into an erosion landscape that is virtually without parallel in the world"; one could all but speak of an "eco-catastrophe" in "Mediterranean antiquity." Jared Diamond has claimed that at least the eastern Mediterranean societies had, like the "Fertile Crescent" of the Near East, committed "ecological suicide."[124] In the nineteenth century, the agronomist Carl Fraas (1810–75) – a disenchanted Philhellenist with practical experience in recultivating karst regions in Greece – had already made the thesis of the decline of the soil and of vegetation since ancient times the prevailing doctrine. It was a doctrine that appealed to forest-loving German patriots: the Romance countries, we read in a popular account (1885), had "dried up and the peoples with them," "but before that the forests were destroyed, these last places where the force of nature was freely at work! We in Germany still see a lot of green around us." The Greek-German Gaitanides, too, sees Greece as a "textbook example for the disastrous effects of deforestation."[125]

Italian environmental historians presented the history of their country in similar terms. One almost forgets that from antiquity to the eighteenth century, from Virgil to Goethe, writers were enthralled by the Italian landscape: all of Italy one big garden, filled not only with fertile fields, but also with fruit-bearing tress, and ahead of all other landscapes not least because of its rich diversity. In the nineteenth century, Victor Hehn – who glorified the ecology of the cultivated Mediterranean landscapes, this marriage of the vine and the olive tree – attacked what he regarded as the "mystical" and "anticivilization" notion that the Mediterranean landscape was destroyed.[126] Was it not so much the landscape itself, but rather the *view* of the Italian landscape that changed at that time, namely, in the same degree to which the Nordic forests and wild nature replaced the garden as the ideal of nature lovers? It is astonishing how difficult it is to clarify such central questions in environmental history.

In his *History of the Kingdom of Naples*, Benedetto Croce, a native of Naples and in his day one of the leading minds of the Italian intelligentsia, polemicized vigorously against the common notion that the decline of the Italian *mezzogiorno* was caused by the decline of the soil: for him the root of the evil was not the decline of the fertility of the land, but moral corruption. This position, however, was grounded more in Croce's idealistic worldview than in field research. Still, the ecological counterargument must also be critically examined.

One source that is cited to excess in eco-historical literature is the complaint about deforestation in Plato's *Critias*. There we hear about the good old days, which were already 9,000 years in the past, when there had still been much fertile soil and "abundant timber" on the mountains of Attica, "of which traces may still be seen." How the forest disappeared Plato does not tell us; does he assume as common knowledge that it was the work of man? The words of the text do not yield that interpretation. We hear of "formidable deluges in the course of the nine thousand years," which carried off the soil – and the forest? – and "what is left now is, so to say, the skeleton of a body wasted by disease."[127]

But the reason why this passage from Plato is repeatedly cited is that we have, in the extant classical literature, no comparably striking complaint linking defor-estation and karstification. Very much in contrast to the vast number of mod-ern lamentations about the forests, we find nowhere in the ancient writings a widespread alarm over the threat of a progressive deforestation, and that even though the ancients most certainly did appreciate trees. One of the few references to the large-scale cutting of forests comes from Eratosthenes as quoted by Strabo. It refers to the plains of Cyprus, which was once covered with rich forests, but now trees were being cut down to feed the smelting plants and the needs of ship-building. But that was not the point of his observation, for he concluded by saying that "although an incredible amount of wood was here consumed, still in no way and by no human device could the wood be exhausted." Even in late antiquity, Ammianus Marcellinus wrote that "Cyprus abounds in such fertility and plenty of all things that, with native labour and resource and without outside help, it can build a merchant ship from the very base of the keel to the tips of the sails," some-thing many Greek islands were at the time presumably no longer able to do: a sign of good high forest coverage.[128] Russell Meiggs, who wrote the most thorough study of trees and timber in the ancient Mediterranean, arrives at the conclusion that, even if precise statements about ancient forest cover are impossible, measured by the needs of humans there must have been sufficient woodlands until the end of antiquity. He believes that we must imagine the scenes of classical history as much more extensively wooded than they are today.[129] That would shift the problem of deforestation to a later period.

Or is there not really a problem? Braudel, by his own admission deeply moved by the "majestic immovability" of the Mediterranean, so much so that the *longe durée* of the Mediterranean way of life he describes becomes almost timeless, has a tendency to see between the lines of his sources a Mediterranean landscape that is eternally unchanged, or at least little changed, the yield of whose soil, compared to the more fertile northern regions, has always been more or less meager.[130]

Oliver Rackham, the English forest historian who did his work on Crete, has been much more radical in his attack on the "ruined landscape theory." He ques-tions all conventional wisdom. The Mediterranean landscape was, in fact, not everywhere as fragile as was long claimed; Crete's landscape, for one, proved to be rather robust overall. The tourist was right to take delight in this scenery: apart from alterations in most recent times, it was in fact not a ruined landscape, but the way it has always been. When the classical writers speak of "forests," so Rackham, we should not think of the high forests in the Northern European sense. *Maquis* can also be seen as a kind of forest, and it holds the soil better than many a high forest. In fact, Rackham maintains, the cutting of forest does not automatically mean erosion and desolation, for many plants grow back on the thinned slopes. Moreover, sheep and goats do not always destroy the forest; if there was the will, animals could very well be prevented from doing so. In Greece, at any rate, sheep and goats were traditionally watched over. And we should not forget: when the animals were not yet under human supervision, they ate their way through the landscape driven by their own instinct and reproduced to the limits of their food supply. "Crete has been 'overpastured' for two million years" – with this biting remark, Rackham mocks the theories of Mediterranean overpasturing. It was not the goat, according to Rackham, but the bulldozer that became the true agent of erosion. And he scoffs at the fact that the FAO, the UN's Food and Agricultural Organization, in its "bureaucratic obsession" with modern forestry and a false picture of history, called on the Mediterranean countries in 1948 to restore their forests.[131]

Soil archaeology and pollen analysis have produced *one* clear and surprising finding, at least for the Greek regions: a first and striking burst of deforestation and
erosion occurred there as far back as prehistoric times, namely, in the period of
early agriculture. It has a certain logic that the earliest farmers, who did not yet
have the experience of many generations, were especially prone to falling into ecological traps. And after that as well, erosion did not progress continuously, but came
in bursts with long interruptions, with another burst occurring in the postclassical
period.[132] This would mean that an intensification of cultivation was not always
accompanied by increased erosion; rather, it was precisely the shrinking of population, the decay of the terraces, and the advance of an unregulated pasture economy
that also caused the soil in the mountains to erode at times.

It is evident, however, that in many Mediterranean regions, especially mountainous ones, deforestation and erosion progressed rapidly in the nineteenth and
twentieth centuries, and that the deepest rupture in their environmental history
is to be found here rather than in the distant past. That would mean that modern population growth, coupled with the economic and technological dynamic, is
after all the greatest destabilizer of the historical relationship between humans and
their environment. John R. McNeill has substantiated the modern dating with
particular thoroughness for five widely separated mountain regions: the Taurus
range of southern Anatolia, the Pindus range in northern Greece, the Lucanian
Apennines in southern Italy, the Spanish Sierra Nevada, and the Riff Mountains
of northern Morocco. To be sure, his thesis applies only to higher elevations, and
he leaves open the question of how representative his regions are. Still, whether it
is in Syria or Cyprus, Anatolia or the Ticino, northern Africa or Sicily – deforestation on a large scale can be documented only since the nineteenth century, and it
would appear that extensive forests still existed until that time. Braudel described
the painstaking detective work that led him to realize that the conventional notion
(which he had initially accepted) that the decay of Sicily, once the "grain store"
of the Mediterranean, was already in full swing in the sixteenth century had to be
wrong, and that its economic and ecological decline entered into an acute stage
only centuries later. The Greeks liked to blame the barrenness of many of their
mountains on Turkish rule; but even Koloktronis, one of the heroes of Greek
independence, complained that mountains in the Peloponnesus, which had still
been forested during the Turkish period, were turned into barren slopes soon after
the liberation of Greece. More recent studies have shown that since independence,
the forest coverage of Greece has declined from 40 to 14 percent. Travel guides
confidently state that the forests of the Mediterranean were destroyed a long time
ago through the building of ships – whether it was by the Athenians, the Romans,
or the Venetians. But it often pays to take a look at islands, where forests were
preserved, and to ask why that was so. For example, the geographer Alfred Philippson (1864–1953), the leading scholar of Greece in his day, reported that until the
middle of the nineteenth century, the island of Skopelos "was covered by magnificent pine forests," since they furnished the wood for naval construction. The
logic was thus exactly the opposite of what is usually asserted! Only when the
great steamships dealt a death blow to the local building of sailing ships did goats
invade the forests.[133] Yet in spite of the goats, Skopelos, as any hiker will discover,
is still rich in lovely forests. What appeared to many travelers of the nineteenth and

twentieth centuries as a problem of the distant past was in reality a problem of the present.

In fertile plains and hilly countrysides, however, deforestation had been advancing since ancient times. What ecological consequences it had is a question that can be answered only from region to region. Anyone who looks for a grand theory in the small Mediterranean region will find it difficult to find one. High-quality timber had already become scarce in the Mediterranean region in antiquity, and even more so in the Middle Ages, as revealed by references to wood importation. Main trading centers like Egypt, Attica, and Rome had to procure their shipbuilding timber from the outside, but such metropolises had the money to do so, which explains the paucity of complaints in ancient sources about wood shortages.

By contrast, the shortage of timber seems to have become a sensitive handicap for the medieval Islamic world, especially since Christian powers repeatedly imposed a wood embargo. There are reports from medieval Arab cities that property managers had to make sure that tenants did not take the doors with them when they moved out, so precious was wood. Wood resources were surely a factor of no small importance why Western and Northwestern Europe left the East far behind on the seas.

But a lack of high forest is not tantamount to an ecological or energy crisis. A shortage of high-quality timber does not invariably entail a shortage of wood for fuel. Brushwood and shrubs are also suitable as soil protection and fuel. In Mesopotamia many things that were made of wood elsewhere were made of reed. In Constantinople, however, even firewood was very expensive as early as the sixteenth century, and necessity gave rise to wood-saving innovations. The Ottoman rulers evidently did not discover forest protection as an instrument of power. When the Ottoman Empire created state forest administrations in the nineteenth century, the consequences were "catastrophic": whereas use of the forests had until then be permitted only to adjacent residents, outside entrepreneurs were now able to procure charcoal for a small fee. Even Oliver Rackham limited his polemic against the "ruined-landscape theory" to European Mediterranean lands. In wide sections of the Islamic world, a scarcity of forests was and is the obvious reality.[134]

The question to what extent erosion processes in the Mediterranean mountains are natural or anthropogenic processes has been controversial for some time.[135] In many instances this dispute cannot be resolved unambiguously. But that, precisely, is the crucial point: the environmental changes promoted by humans coincided in many places with natural trends. When, after the waning of the last ice age, the climate conditions changed from being cooler and wetter to today's Mediterranean weather pattern, the forests corresponding to the moister climate presumably continued at first. The human impact must have accelerated the adaptation to the new climate conditions and intensified the erosion to which many Mediterranean mountain slopes were already susceptible. Unlike what is often believed today, human behavior often entails particularly heavy consequences when it occurs "in harmony with nature," with natural trends. If Madagascar appears to have offered extreme examples of anthropogenic erosion for centuries, the reason is that strong natural erosion processes have been occurring across wide areas of the island.[136]

Another point deserves to be mentioned: in the Mediterranean region, unlike in Central and Western Europe, the forest seems to have been a foundation of power only in exceptional cases, for example, for the Venetian imperium, and in the early eighteenth century in the Kingdom of Naples.[137] Although Aristotle knew of forest wardens, he did not consider it important to dwell on them. As far as we know today, early clues to the comprehensive importance of the forest, especially to its value for the water balance, are found chiefly where such an understanding formed the basis of political authority, as in Venice and in early modern Provence.[138] It is possible that Mediterranean archives still contain many undiscovered sources about forests. For now, however, the predominant impression is that of a telling silence of the sources across wide stretches of Mediterranean forest history – a silence that attests that there was an absence of relevant authorities who could have used complaints about the forest to justify the right of intervention.

The absence of such authorities, however, is not necessarily a tragedy for the forest. In the natural conditions of Central Europe, woodlands recover even without a forester. That was probably the reason why forest policy was not as attractive in terms of power politics in the Mediterranean as it was in the north. On Mediterranean mountain slopes it could not show success as easily as it could in those regions of abundant rain, where forest policy had to be merely a question of power and keeping other users out of the woods to allow the forest to regenerate. However, the combination of forest policy and power politics is also found in the European Mediterranean, not only in Venice. Especially in the eighteenth century, the Kingdom of Naples gave rise to a rhetoric of reforestation that praised the forest above all as a "gigantic water producer"; and Naples, of all places, the horror of Italian supporters of liberal progress, took the lead in Italy when it came to forest awareness.[139] In fact, the Mediterranean environmental awareness was even a step ahead of its northern counterpart when it came to the connection between woodlands and water.

8. FOREST AND POWER IN EUROPE: FROM THE FOREST-CLEARANCE MOVEMENT TO THE ERA OF FOREST REGULATIONS

Did our culture begin with the struggle against the forest? Walther von der Vogelweide, a medieval German *Minnesinger*, saw the forest cut down in his lifetime and felt the passage of his own years: "die mîne gespilen waren / die sint traege und alt. / bereitet ist das velt, / verhouwen ist der walt" (My childhood friends / are indifferent and old / the world is tilled / the forest cut down"). The forest clearing of the high Middle Ages is considered, if not the greatest, then certainly the most extensive landscape alteration in the history of Central and Western Europe from the ice age until today. Recent research, however, has taken away some of its dynamism: for example, we know from pollen analysis that the forest clearance movement of the high Middle Ages represented merely the highpoint and endpoint of clearing processes that had been going on for thousands of years, and that had begun with the early stages of agriculture. However, as long as humans were practicing shifting cultivation, the cutting of trees did not necessarily destroy the forest permanently; instead, in many cases it actually promoted the spread of the birch. Even in the postclassical period, Germania experienced an extensive reforestation, which reached its height in the seventh century.[140] Permanent agriculture began only when humans became sedentary and practiced multicourse rotation.

A large portion of the land cleared for that purpose was presumably areas which had long since been thinned out by shifting cultivation and had been found to be suitable for agriculture.

This is nothing special or unusual, since farmers around the world proceeded in much the same way. However, in contrast to other regions of the world, we encounter the very unusual situation that forest clearing, at its height, became a legalized, regulated, and broadly documented process. The contrast to the paucity of sources for the vast majority of other regions in the world is extreme. Clearing created freedom – to be more precise, specific, usually temporary exemptions from dues for the settler; however, these liberties presupposed that the clearing required permission and that the forest had become a legal sphere. To be sure, there was "unauthorized" clearing – there was no forest register and no extensive supervision that could have prevented it. As always, our written sources by no means tell the whole story. But the historical study of settlements has also noted that many clearing settlements were laid out in a planned fashion on the basis of a few, basic patterns. Where clearing was a method for expanding spheres of power into the forests, in which the ownership situation had been unclear until then, there was at times a "virtual race" in forest clearing between the territorial lords.[141]

Did the people at that time – as we are so often told – regard the forest as an enemy? One should not picture many of the woodlands at the time as primeval forests hostile to humans, but as thinned-out forest pastures that were exceedingly useful to farmers in raising pigs. The section on clearing in Charlemagne's *Capitulare de villis* (795) already comes with the qualification that "where woods ought to be" (*ubi silvae debent esse*), they must not be excessively cut and damaged. No doubt by way of explaining what makes forests necessary, the section goes on to mention hunting and the fattening of pigs. The capitulary presupposes that its recipients would know where the forest had to be left standing. And, in fact, the *Hagenhufendörfer*, the village settlements on cleared land in southern Lower Saxony, were limited to fertile loess soil. The clearing rights granted by the French kings to the monasteries of the Isle-de-France in the high Middle Ages contain stipulations about protected forests and tree hedges. As early as the twelfth century, landgrave Ludwig of Thuringia threatened the leader of an illegal clearing enterprise (*silvanorum exstirpatorum preposito*), telling him he should leave the forest promptly, otherwise he, the prince, would have everything that belonged to the forest colonists "laid waste with fire and plundering and danger to your own lives."[142]

The forest was needed above all as the supplier of firewood. Sainct-Yon, the author of the French Forest Code of 1610, believed that the people in the Mediterranean region, because of the warmer climate, were not as concerned as those in the north, where "wood was, as it were, half of life."[143] Indeed, the fear of the cold of winter as soon as the wood began to grow scarce in many areas was a primal fear of the northerners, and the pleasure of a crackling fire when the icy wind howled outside was the very embodiment of comfort. The yearly frost of winter gave rise, almost invariably, to a mentality of making provisions ahead of time, to which people in warmer regions were not compelled by nature in the same degree. This is presumably the explanation, not least, of why a planning- and future-oriented environmental consciousness is chiefly a product of the north.

In many regions, the clearing movement ended sometime around 1300, though in any case before the plague and the population collapse in its wake. Were the forest soils, still passably tillable, more or less exhausted? Some presumably were, but Marc Bloch believed that people had also come to realize that it was better, in the interest of one's own needs, to preserve the remaining forest. The forest protection regulations already began at the height of – and, as it were, as a response to – the clearing movement; subsequently, the declining population and clearing pressure as a result of the plague epidemics made forest protection less urgent for a century. The abandonment of settlements, a process that culminated in the late Middle Ages, affected especially the settlements carved out of the forests, up to 70 percent of which were given up in mountain regions like the Solling or the Rhön; for a long time afterward, ruined churches stood as desolate reminders to these abandoned communities. In the Reinhardswald, where twenty-five abandoned villages have been reclaimed by the forest, grouped rows of pasture oaks (*Hudeeichen*) reveal that they were systematically planted for forest pasture.[144]

Hans-Rudolf Bork, who studied the loess soil of southern Lower Saxony, found a "catastrophic," "almost breathtaking" erosion in the 1340s, such as had not occurred since the ice age. As the direct cause he identified a period of extreme rainfall in 1342. However, it is reasonable to assume that the forest clearance on sloping land created the conditions for it. Thereafter, according to Bork, things were more or less quiet for four centuries, up to the time of agrarian reform. The forest pasturage that advanced along the mountain slopes as settlements were abandoned presumably held the soil better than the plow did.[145]

A profound change occurred in the late Middle Ages: it was not forest clearance, but the forest itself that became the foundation of political power – of the rising royal house in France, and of the emerging territorial princes in Germany. Territorial lords manifested their claim to dominion in the forest no longer by clearing the forest, but by protecting it. That is the reason why from this time on, the availability of sources on the forest history of these lands is so uniquely good. Beginning in the sixteenth century, the territorial lords and their lawyers presented the dominion over the great forests as though it were unquestionably an ancient prerogative, even though in reality it was newly constructed on a very brittle foundation of tradition.[146] To be sure, a royal hunting privilege extending to the forests existed since the early Middle Ages; in that sense the link between forest and power was exceedingly old in Germano-Celtic Europe. However, originally this privilege did not include any supervision of forest use, which was not of interest to the ruler until the late Middle Ages. A large role in making it interesting in Germany was played by the rise of the mining industry: since it had an enormous appetite for wood, it was possible to derive access to these forests from the mining prerogative that Barbarossa proclaimed for the first time in the Constitution of Ronçales in 1158.

It was probably the Norman conquerors of England, who, beginning in 1066, were the first who consistently linked forest policy and power politics, and they did so in brutal fashion: "The royal forest provoked more negative comments from chroniclers than any of their other acts."[147] In many regions of continental Europe, an alliance of forest and power was forged only in the late Middle Ages. Right around 1500, the German territorial lords began, one after another, to pass forest regulations, which often applied not only to the demesne forest, but to all woodlands; the result was persistent conflicts with the estates of the land. There are many chronological parallels between Germany and France when it comes to forest policy. The late fourteenth century marked a first high point in royal forest legislation, when steps were taken to ensure the natural rejuvenation of the woods.[148] In 1516, under Francis I, there began a series of forest ordinances that signal a new era of vigorous royal forest policy. An "enormous number of forest regulations" have survived from the German Empire beginning in the sixteenth century: "Issuing forest regulations as often as possible was practically the fashionable thing to do."

Without question, the princes discovered forest protection as a first-rate instrument of political power. Their lawyers legitimated the contested claim to overlordship over all woods of the land on the grounds of the traditional hunting and mining prerogative as well as the territorial lord's supreme oversight of all peasant border forests (*Markwälder*), but even more by invoking what they asserted was a shortage of wood that was getting worse and threatening the entire populace. Only the latter justification was popular; princely hunting was detested by the peasants. At a time when public opinion became a force through printing, the Reformation, and the communication networks of the humanists, it was necessary to justify princely interventions with the common good.

And the threatening wood shortage was surely not a pure phantom. The growth of the population and of the "fire industries" – metal, glass, salt works, and brickyards – did in fact lead to local shortages. To be sure, the shortage was not absolute; all in all, there was still enough forest in Germany, and the wood supply was a question of distribution and transportation. Rafting and log driving began to surge as more and more rivers and streams were made accessible to timber rafts and log driving through the elimination of natural impediments. Around 1580 Duke Julius of Brunswick, who had made the Oker River raftable, boasted to the recalcitrant city of Brunswick that he was now able to build more with *one* gulden than his father could with 24. In return, large-scale timber rafting exacerbated the wood supply in many places from which timber was exported. The danger of a wood shortage seemed all the more threatening as the easily accessible forests visible to the cities were most quickly cleared out. For that very reason, the impending wood shortage became an increasingly effective instrument of politics, not only in Germany, but also in wide areas of Europe. Not only was this specter used to solidify territorial dominion and to open up fines for forestry violations as a source of revenue; the precarious wood supply was also a tool for the governments to turn the mining privileges (*Bergregal*) into money and to get greater control of the mining industry. The princes invoked the wood shortage, but by placing restrictions on the use of the forests they played a vigorous part in *making* wood scarcer, which was in their own monetary interests. In France Colbert, Louis XIV's powerful minister, warned: "La France perira faute du bois" – France will perish from lack of wood. His forest protection policy was aimed first and foremost at ensuring the availability of timber for naval construction.[149]

What effects did this early modern forestry policy have on the woodlands? This question is not easy to answer, and it has remained controversial to this day. In France the great works of Maurice Devèze and Andrée Corvol have staked out different positions: for Devèze, the French kings are the saviors – if only partially successful – from the timber shortage that was already widespread in the sixteenth century; for Corvol, the "tabooing" of the high forest was a highly symbolic demonstration of power on the part of the ancien régime and deforestation was a "myth."[150]

For England, Rackham believes – all complaints about the modern decline of the forests to the contrary – that "[w]oods were among the most enduring and successful of all medieval institutions." And that even though the royal dominion over the forests was especially hated in England. It dated to the period of William the Conqueror, that is, to a time when a timber shortage provided no basis for politics, and it contained a basic aspect of usurpationist brutality. Royal dominion was infamous for threats of gruesome punishments like blinding and castration, and it functioned as an expression of a tyrannical royal passion for hunting that did not yet hide behind any claim of the common good. There is good reason why Robin Hood, the rebel against the forest wardens of the Norman kings, became an English national hero – but he too, and especially he, needed the protection of the forest. The restrictions on royal power since the Magna Carta (1215) also affected the royal forests, where it brought other interests to bear. But did this necessarily ruin the forests? Rackham is right when he says that the verdict about the development of the English forests in older times is much more favorable if one includes the coppices, which reflected the interests of the peasants and the fire trades. Nevertheless, the forest never became as popular in England as it did in Germany, and this also had an effect on the landscape.[151]

Today, tourists notice the bare mountains: the sense that mountains are the natural location for forests is not part of the British tradition. While the high forest was the symbol of monarchy in England and in France, in Germany – right around the time of the French Revolution – it became the embodiment of the common good that had to be protected against self-interest. When the philosopher Hegel legitimated the state as the trustee of the common good, Heinrich Cotta (1763–1844), one of the founding fathers of modern German forest science, taught: "Only the state manages for eternity."[152] In England the thinking was rather the reverse, namely, that politicians are guided by short-term considerations in their actions, and only the private individual plans for his children and grandchildren. It would seem that the question of who is right has no general answer, only answers that vary according to time and place.

The history of forest regulations can be written as the history of their violations. New regulations were often justified on the grounds that the existing ones were no longer being observed. Many forest officials had no interest in seeing the prohibitions respected, since they lived from the fines. When the city of Böblingen resisted the Württemberg Forest Code of 1532, it explained that it did not need any seigneurial forest wardens to look after their city forest, because "the thing matters somewhat more to us and our descendants than to others." All one had to do was compare its forests with those of the territorial lord and one would see which needed more "care."[153] When Francis I asked the Carthusian monks why the forests of the Carthusian order were so nicely preserved and the royal forests were so damaged, they responded that it was because they had no forest officials. As it was, no precise forest maps and comprehensive surveys existed in the sixteenth century, which meant the princely forest wardens did not know many of the forests they were claiming to be protecting. On the other hand, conditions in Central and Western Europe were such that the mere restriction on use was enough to allow the forest to regenerate. The hunting interests that determined the princely forest policy in part – unless the "mining devil," the lust for precious metals, was stronger than the "hunting devil" – gave rise to severe restrictions on the economic use of many woodlands so as not to interfere with the game. In the eighteenth century, reforestation provisions appear with increasing frequency in the forest regulations.

European woodlands regenerated themselves not only through forest regulations, but sometimes also through violations of the regulations and through forest conflicts. When the peasants ignored the directive of the forest warden and did not clean out the "dead wood," arguing that it was fertilizing the forest soil, they were, ecologically speaking, right. When they clung to their *Plenterwirtschaft*, which involved the extraction of single trees as needed, instead of clear-cutting the forest, this "unsystematic" use of the forest, disparaged by foresters as a "plunder economy," promoted the natural rejuvenation of the forest. Poachers made possible the growth of a mixed deciduous forest by reducing the stock of game, kept at an excessive level by the hunting wardens.

Compared to other regions of the world, one can see quite clearly how in Central Europe, in spite of all the exploitive practices, a forest awareness developed that was effective in practice, and it did so not least by way of controversies that were fought out with legal instruments and forestry tools. Under these circumstances, a tacit, careless destruction of extensive woodlands across the centuries could not be so easily accomplished. Crucial to this was that a forest awareness from above merged with a different forest awareness from below – the cities and the peasant forest cooperatives. Conflicts over the forest can, under certain circumstances, have a destructive effect on woodlands, namely, when all sides, in an effort to assert their traditional rights, compete in exploiting the forest. But if these conflicts are put on a legal footing and are carried out in an institutionalized way, which was usually the case in Central Europe, they can sharpen forest consciousness and give rise to a competition as to who is the best protector of the forest. The peasants, often and rightly so, threw the accusations that they cut too many trees and wasted timber right back at the princes. They were by no means "woodworms" and "forest leeches," insulting names given to them by the princely forest wardens. In the Twelve Articles issued in 1525 during the Peasants' War, the cause of which should be sought not least in conflicts over woodlands, the rebellious peasants declared that the return of the forests to the communities as they demanded would not result in them being cleared, since "deputies" elected by the community would watch over the cutting of wood (Article 5). As late as the eighteenth century, the inhabitants of the *Mark* in the Solling mountains could rightfully respond to their territorial lord, who was accusing them of despoiling the forest as justification for his own intervention, that they had their own timber regulations and that their forest was in good condition.[154]

We have evidence for peasant forest cooperatives in many regions especially from the late Middle Ages on, when the conflicts of the woodlands reduced by clearance intensified. The basic norm of these cooperatives was in line with the subsistence economy and the principle that "forest should remain forest"; clearing forestland

and selling wood to outsiders was prohibited. Village hierarchies played a role in determining need: beginning in the fifteenth century, new settlers often no longer received a regular share of the forest land, even if they de facto shared in using it. This cooperative supervision of the forest usually took place in agreement with the territorial lords, whose early forest regulations adopted most of the legal principles of the *Markgenossenschaften* (forest communities). For all the struggles over the forest, lords and peasants did have common interests, and until the sharp separation of agriculture and forestry in the nineteenth century, the radical expulsion of peasants from the forests was unthinkable. Although the German Peasants' War ended with a bloody victory for the princes, the shock of the uprising traumatized the latter for a long time, and henceforth they were in general rather cautious about appropriating forest rights arbitrarily. The Tyrol *Markgenossenschaft*, after a five-hundred-year legal battle against the counts of Tyrol and later the Habsburg emperors, won a victory in 1847 and with it possession of their forests! The prospects for peasants were for the most part worse in French courts of the ancien régime; but Alain Rocquelet, who has studied the history of the forests in Normandy, believes he can state, "without exaggeration," that "the ancien régime was the era of the peasant forest." On this point, however, opinions are divided.[155]

What effect did the peasant economy have on the forest? The peasants needed grazed woodland for their animals, coppice for firewood, and the *Plenterwald* (selectively cut forest) for timber. From the aspect of "biodiversity," the peasant forests were quite respectable: they had far more diversity than the monocultural high forests cultivated by modern forestry. In general, the grazed woodland was probably the most extensive type. The question of how to assess the influence of pasturing on forests and the environment has long been controversial around the world and fraught with clashing interests. But the open forest with a lot of undergrowth, the type most preferred for providing fodder, can hardly be seen as ecologically ruinous. From an ecological perspective there are reasons to reassess the role of the peasants in the history of the forest. Modern ecologists have, for example, applauded the peasants of Lippe who, in the years around 1800, defended the mixed deciduous forest that met their needs against the afforestation of coniferous forests.[156] When the peasants of Westphalia, around 1800, acquired private ownership of the forest when the commons were divided up, they repeatedly inflicted bloody lynch law on wood thieves, which contrasted with the generally rather mild treatment they had previously received at the hands of the government.[157] That is not to say that the peasants, instead of the foresters of the territorial princes, should now be seen as the best protectors of the forest. Rather, history shows us that it is impossible to determine once and for all which institution or social class offers the best guarantee for the protection of the forest.

9. FOCAL POINTS OF AN EARLY CONSCIOUSNESS OF CRISIS: CITIES AND MINING

For cities and mining regions, the most critical issues were the supply of wood and the shortage of water; but it was also here that the problems of emission and waste – so rampant in the industrial age – first became acute. Likewise, it was above all in cities and mining towns that people began relatively early to make vigorous efforts at finding solutions to life-threatening environmental problems, especially where cities and the mining industry were joined and a high degree of autonomy existed. Max Weber saw the autonomous city as the most important source for the unique development of the West in economics, politics, and culture,[158] and that certainly also applies to a high degree to the engagement with environmental problems: until the twentieth century, the city was everywhere the most important arena for environmental policy.

Emission problems received relatively little attention in preindustrial times. Since smoke was used to drive out vermin, it could even be seen as salutary. But the harmfulness of arsenic-containing smoke from smelting works was undeniable, even if it was believed in Alpine smelting regions that low doses of arsenic enhanced male potency. Mercury was a similar extreme case that was impossible to ignore; in the sixteenth century Paracelsus had observed how mercury vapors made the smelting workers in Idria (modern Slovenia) sickly and shaky. Another well-known mining poison was lead. When the citizens of Cologne demanded in 1765 that a nearby lead foundry be shut down, "so that they should not be driven from their homes or poisoned in them," it would appear that they prevailed.[159] Even in the industrial age, environmental complaints were most likely to be successful when they involved the "classic" and highly toxic poisons.

When it came to pit coal smoke, it was its sulphur content that raised objections early on (which was not true of wood smoke). It was in London that it first became a public scandal. Between 1580 and 1680, the city's pit coal imports rose from 20,000 to 360,000 tons, the kind of explosive growth that we otherwise find only in the industrial age.[160] John Evelyn, in his treatise *Fumifugium* (1661), which was reprinted repeatedly for a century, railed against "that infernal Smoake," which he claimed was the source of all disease in London – this city with its incessant "Coughing and Snuffing . . . Barking and . . . Spitting," whose dense smoke reminded Evelyn of Mount Aetna or the vestibules of Hell. This place, he thundered, "because it kills not all at once, but always, since still to languish, is worse than even Death itself." He identified the trades and pit coal as the primary culprits, not the fires in the kitchen stoves; he pleaded for a return to wood and penned the most famous call for reforestation in English history, *Sylva*.[161] Evelyn's writings were rhetorical outbursts with little practical impact, especially since he was unable to back up his claim about the deadly effect of smoke with medical science. But London was at that time a unique situation, not an exemplary case, and Evelyn attacked it as such. He even held up Paris as a model for the Londoners.

Among the environmental problems of both early modern and early industrial cities, water problems typically headed the list. In that regard Venice is not entirely atypical. Many cities had their "little Venice," a partly artificial network of brooks and small canals that powered the mills, supplied the washhouses, and filled the city moat. In the case of Bologna, it was the rise of the silk industry in the early modern period that was the driving force behind the network of canals that was cut through the city and powered the mills. At times of low water, there were conflicts between the silk and the flour mills. A steady water supply for mills usually required the construction of mill ponds, and with them came the fear of swamp fever. Water reservoirs throughout the city were also needed to fight fires, the greatest threat to the old cities. To that extent, many cities had to find a balance between competing interests in their hydraulic engineering. In many instances that was surely not done prudently. The paucity of relevant sources for the premodern period already reveals that there was usually no such thing as systematic planning on a large scale; instead, these irrigation and drainage networks developed gradually, often without guidance from the city council.[162]

For a long time, it was usual for citizens to obtain their drinking water from private or neighborhood wells. Toward the end of the Middle Ages, however, there was a noticeable increase in public wells, as there was in the hydraulic activities of the communities generally. City fountains, whose enclosures were often elaborated into works of art, became a concrete symbol of the common good that was to be protected by the city authorities. The fourteenth century sees the beginning in German cities of an "age of water arts": a centralized supply system with pumping stations, water towers, and water pipes.[163]

It is easy to forget today that not only Venice but many other cities as well used to suffer from frequent flooding. On the one hand, the cities needed the rivers as traffic arteries, which is why most old cities are situated along rivers, if they are not located at the sea. On the other hand, the river became a danger during the snowmelt and continuous rainfall. Some water problems pushed beyond the level of communal regulation in those days. Commercial polluters – chief among them tanners and dyers – had to locate themselves downstream, below the city; but with continued economic growth, this externalization of the effluent would eventually collide with the interests of other water users.

In terms of sanitation, the situation in the densely constructed old cities can only be described as a permanent crisis, since there was no clean solution to the disposal of sewage. After the introduction of modern sanitation, the filth and stench of the old cities was always considered striking evidence for the lack of culture and the dullness of the senses in those days. In this regard, however, the picture of the premodern mind-set has changed most recently. Back then, as well, noses responded not so very different from today – stench is by no means merely a modern cultural construct. In fact, "bad air" played an incomparably greater role in the older etiology of diseases than it did in modern medicine. Ruins reveal that the desire for a lavatory with running water, which eliminated the bad smell, existed as far back as antiquity and in the Middle Ages. Those who could afford it and had a suitable course of water available sometimes built a "water closet." We learn this from the great mishap in the Episcopal palace of Erfurt in 1184: when a floor collapsed under the weight of the throngs assembled for a royal visit, the people plunged into the cloaca in the basement, and some drowned in the river running beneath it.[164]

"Stadtluft macht frei," as the medieval saying went – city air made you free, but it was neither pleasant smelling nor wholesome: people were only too aware of this. Anyone who had a country estate escaped there from the cities during epidemics. The death rate in the cities often exceeded the birth rate, and cities survived only through the constant influx of people from the countryside. Johann Peter Süßmilch, the founder of German demography in the eighteenth century, called the cities "a real nuisance to the state," not only because of the immorality emanating from them, but also because of the bad health effects caused by the environment. Worst of all were the large cities, which the physician Christoph Wilhelm Hufeland condemned in 1796 as the "open graves of mankind."[165]

In principle, it was always obvious that the waste problem of the cities and the lack of fertilizer in the countryside could be resolved in *a single* stroke: simply by transporting the waste to the countryside and turning it into fertilizer and compost. Even technocratic urban planners of the modern period were still fascinated by visions of such a cycle. A massive, 700-page German handbook from 1896 entitled *Die Verwertung der städtischen Abfallstoffe* (The Use of Urban Waste Material) reveals that there was a Europe-wide discussion about this "foul" topic, with a wealth of practical experiments. At the same time, it becomes clear that it was not possible to simply pick up on preindustrial traditions, but that this cycle of matter was not complete even in the old days of latrines.[166] In nineteenth-century Paris, the *poudrette* industry processed human excrement into fertilizer. Still, a large portion of human excreta reached the Seine, as Sabine Barles has recently shown in a quantifying analysis that is still without parallel.[167]

In the nineteenth and even still in the early twentieth century, it looked in some urban regions as though the restoration of the cycle of matter between city and countryside would receive another chance especially from industrialization. The chief problem in moving urban waste to the country was cheap transportation, and this problem could be solved better than ever before with modern transportation technology as soon as recycling was undertaken on a large scale. Modern technology also offered new options for processing waste into fertilizer. From the East Coast of the United States to Berlin, there were attempts at turning this kind of recycling into big business.[168] But success did not last, since chemical fertilizers were cheaper and their content could be more precisely calculated. In that sense, the best chance for an urban-agrarian cycle existed in preindustrial times, when the distance from the city to the country was not yet very great, when urban refuse contained hardly any industrial waste and no synthetic materials, and when agriculture's need for fertilizer was not yet satisfied by the chemical industry. To a certain degree this cycle of matter did in fact exist – to what extent and how it was blocked is one of the most fascinating questions of environmental history, one that can be answered only on a case-by-case basis.

It is certainly an open question why urbanites did not make efforts to sanitize their cities in earlier times, especially since city life was, after all, subject to an abundance of regulations in other ways. A fundamental dilemma was undoubtedly the fact that greater cleanliness would have involved greater water consumption, and that water was – naturally enough – used sparingly as long as one had to fetch it from a well with a pitcher. If all citizens had followed the example of the archbishop of Trier and run their latrines into the town's stream, it would have turned the latter into one large sewer. But there was surely another factor: the excreta generated in the house, with their value as fertilizer, were a possession that many house owners were reluctant to cart away without a compelling reason. As long as one still owned a piece of land or possessed some of the peasant mentality, one wanted to have one's own dung heap. Or one simply dug the latrine deeper. Eventually, however, one would hit groundwater and contaminate the wells; but in those days, people at most had a hunch about these complex underground streams.

Ulf Dirlmeier's conclusion has at least some partial truth to it: "It was not sloppiness and indifference that harmed groundwater and surface waters close to the cities, but precisely the deliberate use of methods for a more efficient disposal

of waste without damage to one's living environment." The initial tendency was
to keep disposal within the sphere of the house and the neighborhood; generally
speaking it became a municipal task only in the course of the modern period. In
medieval Basel, where sewer ditches were called *Dolen*, neighbors formed *Dolen*
communities. By contrast, the man-high *Dolen* of early modern Stuttgart were
maintained by the city.[169] The sewer projects of the industrial age followed a line
of preindustrial continuity stretching back all the way to the cloaca maxima of
ancient Rome.

It is evident that the disposal of waste has been torn between two mutually
contradictory goals from ancient times until today: the wish to practice recycling,
on the one hand, and what Joel Tarr has called "the search for the ultimate sink,"
on the other. This began with medieval latrines. If one wanted to process the
excreta into good fertilizer and add it to the fields in a timely manner, latrines
could not be too deep; but if one wanted to get rid of their stench, one had to
dig them deeper – which, as latrine archaeology has shown, was often done with
too much zeal. This clash of goals has culminated most recently in the field of
nuclear technology, where the search for the ultimate sink sparks efforts to seal up
nuclear waste as perfectly as possible and to store it out of reach, while the goal of
reprocessing – for a long time the magical attraction of nuclear energy – points in
the opposite direction.

What role did the old cities play in the history of the *forest?* A city's wood
supply depended in large measure on whether the city was situated along a river
on which large amounts of woods could be brought in by timber rafting and log
driving. Timber transport on water could easily fall under city oversight. But here
the city competed with others living along the banks of the river. On the water,
wood became a commodity that was more or less subject to the free market. It was
therefore advantageous to procure the timber from nearby forests over which one
had traditional rights and no major competitors. On land, however, wood transport
was very laborious and economical only over short distances. Many German and
Italian cities within the Holy Roman Empire owned or acquired their own forests.
However, these were used as much as pasture areas as they were as suppliers of wood
and timber. High-quality timber could be transported over greater distances. This
explains why the forests in the immediate vicinity of old cities often seem rather
puny by modern standards.

The historian Heinrich Tribbe from Minden, who as a member of the Cathedral
Chapter was not very favorably disposed toward the city's autonomy, described the
wood wardens who were supposed to protect the city's forest as corrupt drunks:
"They used all their brains for drinking."[170] Drawing on complaints like these,
the literature on forest history has usually painted a disdainful picture of the forest
economy of the cities.[171] But this verdict came from a biased camp: it sprang from
the perspective of the territorial lords who wished to curtail the autonomy of the
cities, and of their forest administrations, which measured the value of the forest
increasingly by its commercial yield and timber production. The city forests were
managed overwhelmingly on the principle of subsistence, with the needs of the
citizens taking precedence over the export trades. That is true even for a city like
Nuremberg, one of the leading commercial and trading cities of the old empire.
It had no river that was accessible to ships or rafts – which was highly unusual for
a trading city – and depended for its wood supply entirely on two nearby imperial

forests, in which it acquired extensive rights of use and oversight. This city, too, did not use its resources of wood to pursue a deliberate policy of promoting the trades, as one might expect from a modern perspective; on the contrary, beginning in the fourteenth century it pushed large-scale commercial wood users out of the forests. Although the city was a center of metalworking, after 1460 it moved its segregation furnaces (*Seigerhütten*) for the extraction of silver and copper to the Thuringian forest to spare the imperial forests near the city. In 1544 it prohibited the brass and wire hammer mills, the smelting works, and those "who otherwise make large fires," from procuring wood from the imperial forests, and it kept renewing the prohibition into the eighteenth century.

Royal prohibitions against forest clearance at the beginning of the fourteenth century came in response to pressure from the cities and were a means of "winning back the larger cities as partners for the monarchy against the rising territorial lords." French regents, too, at times showed so much consideration for the subsistence economy of the cities in their forest policy that they moved against the trades: in 1339 the Dauphin ordered the destruction of forges and smelting ovens in a valley of the Dauphiné to secure the wood supply for the city of Grenoble. On the whole, the sources about forest protection by the cities, much like water protection, become much more numerous in the late Middle Ages. The explanation lies not only in the fact that the problem became more acute, but also in that the regulatory zeal of the city fathers was generally on the rise at that time.[172]

The relationship between the city and its environs certainly had its elements of crisis. However, one must bear in mind that, as a rule, Europe's premodern cities, unlike the great Asian metropolises, were by their very structure aimed not at gigantic growth, but at self-containment. Max Weber repeatedly pointed to the special character of the Western city as a self-organizing association of citizens. A tendency toward self-containment lay not only in the city walls, but also in the old city's basic character as an association of people, which pursued expansion only under certain circumstances and for a limited time, since it developed a pronounced penchant for eliminating competition. Under these kinds of circumstances, scarcity of resources was in principle not an element of crisis, but one that stabilized existing structures. Therein lies, in spite of everything else, a basic, environmentally compatible quality of these cities.

Truly large cities were often the seat of a court; their driving engine of growth was primarily political, not economic. "Proto-industrial" economic growth took place more in the countryside than in the cities, which reflected the decentralized distribution of the natural resources. Cities in preindustrial Central and Western Europe generally did not lord it over the countryside as oppressively as they did in the high civilizations of Asia. The problems of the wood supply had a balancing effect structurally, for they affected the large cities most of all and favored peripheral regions that were densely forested. The growth of energy-intensive trades regularly conjured up the fear of a wood shortage. It would have struck most city authorities of the "age of wood" as absurd to seek their city's fortune in the unchecked growth of the "fire trades."

Central Europe, in particular, had a large number of mining and salt towns. In most cases, though, their growth remained within narrow boundaries. The city-creating power of the salt, mining, and smelting industries simultaneously helped to embed these sectors into social structures. Even Schwaz in Tyrol, around

1500 the "mother of all mines" and for a while a mining center with "explosive" expansionary dynamism, became no more than a middling – and in the end once again a small – city.[173] Since the fate of all such cities hinged on the supply of massive quantities of wood, they virtually specialized in the procurement of this crucial raw material. The salt town of Schwäbisch Hall obtained its boiling wood (*Sudholz*) from logs that were drifted down the Kocher from the forests of the neighboring county of Limpurg. The arrival of the driftwood was a major event in the life of the town, and the landing occurred with the boisterous participation of the entire population. When the city council in 1738, invoking an imminent shortage of wood, sought to push through a costly evaporation house, which promised to save boiling wood by enriching the brine, the *Haalhautpmann* rejected the "wood shortage" argument with these memorable words: the "complaints about the wood shortage" are "ancient," "a tune that is more than two hundred years old" and "hurts one's ears." "The Limpurgian forests stands, and the wood god is still alive." It was, as always, merely a question of coming to an arrangement with the Limpurgers for the "wood to be present again in abundance."[174] Still today, the picturesque evaporation houses are the landmarks of many old salt towns, especially those that have turned themselves into spa towns. Whether these elaborate installations, which functioned only when the sun was out and could be damaged easily by storms, were in fact economical is questionable. They offer a historical example that one must take a critical look even at subsidized energy-saving technologies.

The wood supply was a question of external politics also in other salt cities (like Lüneburg) that did not possess forests of their own. Lüneburg could let its deforested environs turn to heathland, since it received plenty of wood from the northeast by the water route; because of the high salt content of its brine, the expenses for wood in any event were not as critical as in other places. Salt cities that owned forests and were dependent on them practiced a comparatively prudent forest economy early on. The Bavarian salt town of Reichenhall even seems to have the distinction of being the first place to formulate the emphatic commandment of sustainable forest economy. The *Ratskanzler* of Reichenhall gave a classic expression of this norm to the *Obmann* of the salt industry in 1661: "God has created the forests for the salt spring, that they might exist forever, like He / hence man should do thus: before the old (forest) runs out, the young one has already grown up for chopping down." Sustainability as secularized eternity! Whether Reichenhall back then did indeed practice a sustainable forest economy is still controversial, but there is some evidence that "wood shortage" in that city resulted merely from conflicts with neighboring Salzburg. The Alpine salt town defended the principle "forest must remain forest" chiefly against the expanding Alpine pasture economy of the mountain farmers. They battled against the birch tree, which could not be floated, and promoted the dominance of coniferous forests. But it is open to debate whether the latter were ecologically more stable than the Alpine pastures of the mountain farmers.

On the whole, a planned, "sustainable" economic mind-set is most likely to be found in the salt towns, which, in keeping with the flow of brine and the demand for salt, were focused on continuity across generations, and less so in the mining cities, which were often subject to pronounced ups and downs.[175]

Did metal extraction in the "age of wood" lead invariably to the destruction of forests, and was it in turn undermined by the self-inflicted devastation of the woodlands? This question has been hotly debated. The wood problem became particularly acute in iron production, since the melting point of iron (1,528° C) is much higher than in most other metals, and since the trend was toward mass production. The concern that iron works were overtaxing the forests was widespread in the eighteenth century, at the latest. In France at the time, many communities were fighting against the iron works and denouncing them as insatiable wood devourers. This was connected with a general fear of a wood shortage that was spreading across all of Europe, and that rose to a "fever" pitch in pre-Revolutionary France, but not only there. "Wood shortage! Rising wood prices! is the general complaint in nearly all large and small states of Germany," asserted Laurop, a writer on forest matters, in 1798. In early industrial England, the following verses of praise were sung about John Wilkinson, a pioneer of coke steel: "That the wood of old England would fail, did appear, / And tough iron was scarce because charcoal was dear, / by puddling and stamping he cured that evil, / So the Swedes and Russians may go to the devil." The Swedes and the Russians – they were the wood suppliers. The threat of a wood catastrophe is part of the founding myth of the age of coal.[176]

Oliver Rackham has dismissed this historical picture, repeatedly adopted without examination, with scorn and derision, arguing that historians who assume that the owners of smelting works destroyed the basis of their own livelihood along with the forests have forgotten that they were not suicidal and "that trees grow again." It is precisely when the forest is needed that it is preserved. Moreover, the iron industry was not dependent on the high forest; best suited for coking was the coppice with a cutting cycle of 10–20 years, which could be quickly grown and regenerated easily. If you cut a branch from a well-sprouting tree, several branches will often grow back. In fact, if one includes the coppice, England was, even in the eighteenth century, not as poor in woodlands as is often asserted; pit coal only gradually acquired a price advantage over charcoal. The best-known example of a well thought-out and sustained coppice economy, which combined the supply of charcoal to the regional iron industry with agriculture and the supply of (oak) tanbark to the tanners, is the oak coppice economy (*Haubergwirtschaft*) of the Siegerland, which was put on a legal footing by the Nassau Forest Regulations of 1562.[177]

How well or poorly the wood supply functioned depended essentially on how much financial interest the peasant population of the surrounding regions had in carting the wood and how dependent they were on this source of income. Especially in mountainous regions with meager agriculture there were plenty of people who needed these cartloads of wood to make a living; it was here, however, that irreversible damage to the forests was most likely, since the forest administrations that were beholden to the mining industry often prescribed clear-cutting as a way of procuring most easily the required quantities of wood, which were transported to the valleys via wooden chutes and streams that had been made floatable. Many such clear-cut areas remained bare for centuries on steep Alpine slopes.[178] *Plenterwirtschaft*, the selective extraction of trees, was actually punished with fines.

What about the sustainability of mining itself, and how did contemporaries see the matter? From antiquity until far into the early modern period, it was widely believed that metals, like plants, grew – especially if one thought of the depth of the earth as a womb – and were regenerated if one granted them periods of rest during mining operations. It seemed as though many metals were putting forth sprouts into the rock. Pit coal showed even more signs of organic life. In 1691 Johann Philipp Bünting lauded pit coal as *sylva subterranea*, a "subterranean forest" and gift from "all-powerful mother nature" to shivering humanity. Alchemists did not recognize a sharp separation between the organic and the inorganic world, in any case. But Georgius Agricola, the author of the most famous early modern book on mining (1556), was not one of them, and he noted soberly what was only too well known from the history of mining: "After all, the tunnels eventually cease to give metals, while the fields always yield crops."[179] The realization that the transition from agriculture to mining meant the transition to nonregenerating resources was already possible at that time. The kind of sustainability that was important also to Agricola lay merely in extending the period of extraction by making use of lower-quality ores, instead of throwing them onto the waste dumps to allow for a more rapid exploitation of high-quality ore veins.

A sense that mining amounted to the crossing of a dangerous threshold is evidently old and found around the world. Pliny the Elder wrote about Spanish miners who destroyed entire mountains and redirected rivers: "The miners gaze as conquerors upon the collapse of Nature." He was especially passionate in his moral condemnation of the lust for gold and all the evil it spawned as well as of iron, which brought death on mankind in the form of weapons: "How innocent, how blissful, nay even how luxurious life might be, if it coveted nothing from any source but the surface of the earth." This verdict remained the basic motif of his condemnation of mining, combined with the charge that it inflicted injuries on Nature. For Pliny, earthquakes were "an expression of the indignation of our holy parent."[180]

Following classical tradition, Paulus Niavis (Paul Schneevogel) has Mother Nature appear around 1490 in green garb to complain, tearfully and bloodied, to Father Jove about mining, which was desecrating her. The naiads, too, joined in the complaint: the miners, in their impertinence, had disturbed and cut off the springs. Fortuna, who had the last word, did not deny the damage inflicted on Nature, but she noted that humans had no other choice but to dig through the mountains, though at least they were not faring well as they were doing it.[181] Agricola began his book about the mining and metal industry, for two centuries the standard work on the subject, with an elaborate defense of mining against its – equally eloquent – enemies, as though there had been a great debate for-and-against at the time. To a large extent the basic tenor of this imaginary debate remains within the classical tradition; Agricola tends to divert our attention from the forest problem of his day.

The two most important types of mining – the extraction of iron ore and pit coal – were usually not done in deep mines, but in open pits not much deeper than a man as a side activity by peasants. "Bog iron ore" (*Raseneisenerz*) and "swampy meadow ore" (*Sumpfwiesenerz*) were extracted from weathered stone right below the surface. Deep mining of coal was found in only a few regions of Europe in the late Middle Ages, for example, near London and Liège. That is why the profound turning point in environmental history represented by the massive transition to nonregenerating resources was by no means experienced that way everywhere. Even in the Ruhr region as late as 1827, two *Bergmeister* (master miners) warned in a memorandum against a strong increase in coal production by using the classic justification – which reflected the premodern mind-set – that this kind of massive extraction could not last, "since everything has its limits."[182] At that time, still, the "limits to growth" were a banal and well-known fact, not the topic for a bestseller.

Or was gold mining already the mental turning point, the emergence of a ruthless and boundless greed, and did the classical authors sense this quite rightly? Pliny reported that the Roman Senate prohibited the prospecting for gold in Italy – for what reason is not clear to this day. The lust for precious metals raged especially in the conquered territories, chiefly in Spain. Early modern mining regions also experienced waves of "mountain fever"; it too was most violent in some colonies at that time – another argument for the epochal importance of colonialism in environmental history, since mining in the colonies had to pay much less attention to the environment than was necessary in Europe.

But it was only in the nineteenth century that the dynamism of unlimited needs became the chief driving force behind all of life. In the "age of wood," the mining industry in general did not yet develop a growth dynamic disconnected from the social environment – it did so in Potosí but not in Goslar. Human life was simply not yet based on metals; even plows were for a long time made out of wood. Iron was long associated more with death than with life: hence this "hatred of iron" that, according to Mircea Eliade, can be found even in India, an old iron country.[183] In Central Europe it was still the norm in the eighteenth century – indeed, especially in the eighteenth century – to keep the ironworks "in proportion to the woodland," though one could surely disagree what that meant concretely in individual cases.

Looking at the final result, however, one could make the point differently: precisely because the wood supply for the mining and metal industry in Central and Western Europe was relatively well regulated over centuries and environmental problems were more or less solved, this sector of the economy was able to generate a dynamic that, in synergy with other dynamic forces, eventually overpowered everything. This is the insidiousness of the partial resolution of environmental problems: partial success all too easily masks creeping crises, thus shutting off traditional braking forces that until then kept the relationship between humans and their environment more or less in balance. Precisely the daily experience that human existence is ecologically unstable amounted, in aggregate, to an element of ecological stability inherent in the human way of life.

4

Colonialism as a Watershed in Environmental History

There are different kinds of colonialism that give rise to different problems for the environment: there is commercial colonialism, which establishes a foothold only in coastal ports, and there is settlement colonialism, which penetrates deeply into the land. The chief problem of commercial colonialism is that it subjects the colonized countries to foreign control and destroys the self-regulating elements of the subsistence economy. Settlement colonialism does not necessarily entail the same danger. Settlers often – and with success – seek their independence from the motherland. But in many cases they displace the local population along with its economy and way of life much more brutally than do those colonizers who are interested only in trade and in siphoning off wealth. The invasion of foreign settlers interrupts a tradition of local knowledge handed down over many generations. From the perspective of environmental history, however, colonialism and imperialism are important as much for their unintended as for their intended consequences. I am referring to the "biological invasions," the spread of many species far beyond their original regions. The victorious expansion of human empires was also a victory for rats, insects, and microbes. These spread overseas far more rapidly than European humans, whose numbers abroad barely exceeded one million until the eighteenth century.

Whether colonialism already amounted to an "ecological revolution" in the early modern period is debatable. Its swiftest and most terrible effects occurred undoubtedly in the Americas with the diseases introduced by the colonizers, which decimated the native populations. But this did not necessarily revolutionize the entire ecosystem. Even in a collective work on Latin American environmental initiatives that looks for indigenous environmental awareness, we come across the cynical-sounding thesis that several ancient American civilizations were on the verge of destroying their own environments in 1492, and only the "demographic collapse" from diseases "safeguarded the ecosystems of the New World for centuries." The great book by David Watts on environmental change in the West Indies after 1492 devotes a lot of space to the sugarcane plantations of Barbados, which clearly changed the ecosystems of this island radically. But the island of Barbados with its 430 square kilometers is one hundred thousand times smaller than America!

A travel guidebook that noted, on crossing the border between Haiti and the Dominican Republic, "dusty-gray, barren karst landscapes on this side, green mountains, forests, and fields on the other," concluded that Haiti had paid for the sugarcane cultivation of the colonizers with an "ecological catastrophe." But the Dominican Republic was a colony for a century longer than Haiti; and when the botanist Karl Ritter visited Haiti in 1820, some time after the end of colonial rule, he still found jungles of "indescribable beauty" and "vegetation of extraordinary vigor and lushness." Even a volume on Haiti's agriculture, published for the 160th anniversary of the country's independence, spoke appreciatively of the colonial period as the good old days, when Haiti was the "pearl of the West Indies." Paradoxically, the environmental situation is especially depressing in a number of Third World countries that were never colonies or were only briefly, as, for example, Ethiopia, Madagascar, or Nepal. These countries were even more poorly equipped for the challenges of modern civilization than many a former colony.

The chief problem of colonialism frequently seems to have been not so much its immediate ecological consequences as its long-term impact, the full extent of which became apparent only centuries later, in the era of modern technology, and many times only after the colonial states had acquired independence. In environmental history as well, the epochal turning points arise from a change in human institutions, systems of communication, and structures of power, and from the alterations this brings about in everyday habits.

The crucial point is presumably the emergence of a colonial attitude toward the environment: a ruthless exploitation of natural resources and the arbitrary transformation of the environment with no regard for regional traditions and experiences. What probably made this colonial attitude so attractive was, not least, the fact that it represented a regression into primeval human behavior that dated back to prehistoric times when the earth was still thinly settled. As the modern age unfolded, the colonial attitude shaped the treatment of the environment not only in the colonies but sometimes also in the colonial motherlands.

Even where the immediate ecological impact of colonialism is slight, in the long run it does weaken the indigenous traditions and installs outside control, though the latter may not take effect fully until the era of modern means of communication. Let us take India as an example. During the period of British colonial rule, Indian population growth, compared with today, remained for the longest time within such limits that the traditional Indian landscape was not fundamentally altered. However, since the British colonial administration long regarded India as underpopulated, it had no interest in strengthening those social institutions that helped to restrain population numbers. In a number of cases, colonial government over the course of time arrived at a more or less effective policy of forest protection. However, this policy regularly clashed with indigenous uses of the forest and burdened forest protection with the stigma of colonialism: this was a bad omen for the period of decolonization. Often the worst long-term ecological effects of colonialism occurred in the postcolonial era. Clearly an environmental historian should not think so much in terms of ecological revolutions as in terms of the interactions between institutional change and ecological processes.[1]

If one looks at imperialism from a world historical perspective, there is reason to follow it back to the Roman Empire, the archetype of all Western empires. As early as the nineteenth century, ancient Rome came under suspicion of having accelerated its own demise through environmental destruction. For George P. Marsh, who published his *Man and Nature* while in Florence as the American ambassador and who drew inspiration from his impressions of deforestation in both America and Italy, it was clear that the "brutal and exhausting despotism" of the Roman Empire was the *causa causarum* of Mediterranean desolation. More recently Horst G. Mensching, a student of desertification, believed the evidence was clear that Rome had promoted erosion and desert formation by pushing grain cultivation in semiarid regions of northern Africa; he draws this evidence from Roman ruins located in what are deserts today, and from reasoning by analogy from modern experiences.[2]

Latifundia perdidere Italiam: the latifundia have destroyed Italy – this was the famous lament of Pliny the Elder. He was referring to the displacement of the old Roman farming class by large landowners as a result of Rome's constant wars. This process did not necessarily amount to ecological collapse. Nevertheless, one can assume that the sound insights of the agricultural writers were of no use if the soil was being worked by slaves and tenants, who had no interest in preserving it for future generations. The Roman agrarian writers were already familiar with the benefits of crop rotation, but such insights seem to have had little effect on agricultural practice. Moreover, along with the latifundia there also spread a form of transhumance that presumably paid little heed to agriculture and deprived the fields of fertilizer. Max Weber, who had a keen eye for the agrarian foundation of history, found it noteworthy that "while Cato still treats animal husbandry as organically connected with agriculture, in Varro the *rex pecuaria* (animal husbandry) already assumes an independent place."

Beginning around 200 C.E., the *agri deserti* – abandoned fields – became a permanent problem of the Roman Empire. One main cause may have been escape from a growing tax burden. Still, this flight from the land is hard to explain without a decline in the yield of the soil; after all, it is unlikely that the city – especially in late antiquity – was becoming more attractive. There is plenty of documentation that the decline of the Roman Empire went hand in hand with signs of decay in agriculture, and the once well-regarded theory of climate change, with which Ellsworth Huntington triggered a discussion about ecological causes of decline in 1917, did not hold up as an explanation. When Max Weber saw in the decay of classical culture a process of recovery by which the culture adapted to its natural economic basis, and was reminded of the giant Antaeus from Greek mythology, "who gained new strength when he rested in the bosom of Mother Earth," this interpretation attests his ecological perspicacity.

In all of this, however, one should never forget one thing: what needs explaining above all is the long duration of the Roman Empire, not its eventual demise. The Roman agrarian writers were models even to the agrarian reformers of the eighteenth century. At the height of the Roman Empire, manifestations of crisis in agriculture sharpened the awareness that the fertility of the soil needed to be preserved.[3]

1. THE MONGOL EMPIRE AND THE "MICROBIAL UNIFICATION OF THE WORLD"

An unambiguously crisis-prone imperialism begins in environmental history with the Mongol Empire of the high Middle Ages. The Mongols were nomadic horsemen who were accompanied by herds of sheep and goats – in this regard the danger of overgrazing pastureland was greater than among the Arab camel nomads. Since Mongol rule never acquired an institutional framework in Central Asia, there was no higher authority that could have regulated the interaction with the environment. In China the Mongol conquerors allowed themselves to be converted to Chinese administrative methods, though not to be completely absorbed by Chinese culture. They transformed extensive agricultural fields to pastureland. But when Genghis Khan, shortly after penetrating into China, entertained the idea of exterminating the Chinese and transforming all of China into a playground for nomadic horsemen (so we are told by a fourteenth-century Chinese historian), he let a clever Chinese advisor, who calculated for him the tax revenue of an intact China, talk him out of this terrible plan.[4]

The greatest catastrophe that the Mongols inflicted on the Chinese was presumably unintentional, when the creation of their empire cleared the way for the advance of the plague from Central Asia into China. The plague is probably the primary reason for the sharp decline of the Chinese population under the Mongols from approximately 123 to 65 million (though this did relieve the already palpable population pressure for several centuries). And when the plague reached Caffa in the Crimea in 1346, the first European city, from where it went on to devastate all of Europe within a few short years, the immediate human transmitter was the Tartar Golden Horde, which had emerged from sections of Genghis Khan's troops; in a broader sense the transmission vector was no doubt also trade along the Silk Road, which flourished under Mongol rule.[5]

The spread of the plague as well as of other epidemic diseases is a consequence of the growing interconnection of the world, the disappearance of boundaries between traditional spheres of life. This allows microbes to penetrate into ecosystems that were not able to develop an immunity to them. Given the preindustrial means of transportation, trade could use the newly opened, global connections only with difficulty and to a limited extent. Meanwhile, microorganisms were much quicker at spreading and multiplying across the globe. Emmanuel Le Roy Ladurie has suggested the "microbial unification of the world" as a macrohistorical concept to grasp the role of the epidemics in the Old and New Worlds since the fourteenth century in world history.[6] At a time when the life of most people still took place within a narrow geographical area and the crossing of boundaries was slow and difficult, the great epidemics were a type of catastrophe pointing toward the future, based on the rapid and global diffusion of the causes behind them.

In the history of the globalization of environmental problems, the plague is a precursor and a bad omen. One could conclude, however, that as the world becomes increasingly interrelated, the danger that invaders will take ecosystems by surprise declines after a while, since there are no longer any large areas that have been isolated from the rest of the world for millennia. And in fact, the great epidemic diseases have been on the wane since the eighteenth century. It is still not entirely clear why that is so, and whether this retreat is permanent. The flipside of this retreat has been an almost uninterrupted population growth all over the world.

Somewhat confusing is the fact that the Mediterranean regions were evidently already being visited by disastrous plagues between the sixth and the eighth centuries, the so-called Justinian plague, which first appeared in Constantinople in 542. Unlike the late medieval plague epidemics, it did not become a collective memory; even modern historians often forget about it. And this in spite of the fact that its consequences may have been even more profound than the Black Death of the fourteenth century. There is much to indicate that it played an even greater part than the tribal migrations in the weakening of the Mediterranean region and the shift in the centers of power. As William McNeill has remarked, wide areas of the Roman Empire were devastated by a succession of epidemics as early as the second century C.E.[7] This would mean that the expansion of the world, the gift of the Pax Romana, exacted its epidemiological price in the long run.

Is the assumption that the waves of plagues more or less followed the expansion of the routes of human power and trade epidemiological plausible? Or can the plague pathogen spread into unprotected ecosystems by accident, through individual carrier organisms? Several considerations support the first assumption: the most important host of the plague bacillus was evidently the house rat, which spread only along the vector of human habitations, including ships. Since the rat itself dies from the plague, a certain concentration of rats and their habitats is necessary to keep the plague from rapidly extinguishing with the death of its carriers. But the plague pathogen can also be transmitted directly from person to person. As the plague reached the densely settled and interconnected regions of Europe, the rate at which it spread seems to have accelerated. In other diseases like typhus or dysentery, the concentration of humans and pathogenic environments as the precondition for their spread is even clearer than in the case of the plague.[8]

One exciting question concerns the possibility of whether there is another, and more intimate, way in which the plague is related to environmental history. It is striking that the plague fell on Europe about the same time that wide regions of Europe had reached the limits of their food supply, evidenced by famines, a general deterioration in dietary conditions, and the clearance movement that was pushing onto soil that was difficult to cultivate. Even before ecological explanations became fashionable, the medievalist Michael M. Postan advanced the thesis that British agriculture – like its counterparts in other regions of Europe – was sliding increasingly into an ecological trap in the high Middle Ages: not only through the expansion onto marginal soils, but also by the fact that the advance of grain cultivation at the expense of forest and forest pasture led to a shortage of fertilizer as long as the peasants did not learn to open up new, rich pasture areas by irrigating the meadows. The degree to which the "Postan thesis" can be generalized to wide areas of Europe is still controversial. It does, however, possess an inherent logic. And, in fact, contracts of lease in Central Europe also reveal that manuring became a critical area in need of regulation when land was rented out. In premodern agriculture it was only crises that triggered learning processes leading to a more sustainable management of the soil. Between 1315 and 1322, wide areas of Western, Central, and Northern Europe experienced a terrible famine, the full magnitude of which was rediscovered only by modern historians. The English agrarian historians J. D. Chambers and G. E. Mingay came to the terse conclusion: "Only catastrophe could rescue the medieval peasantry, and it came in the form of a drastic pruning of peasant households as a result of the Black Death."[9]

Even if the causal link between famine and plague is controversial, the drastic reduction in population by the plague significantly improved the balance between humans and the natural resources for more than a century. The plague epidemics have struck some historians as self-regulating mechanisms of large-scale ecosystems. Initially the plague ravaged the poor and the rich without distinction; as the centuries passed, however, it became a "social epidemic" that affected the lower classes most severely, especially since they could not escape to their country estates. Defoe called the plague that hit London in 1665 a "deliverance," because it "carried off in that time thirty or forty thousands of these very people, which, had they been left behind, would certainly have been an insufferable burden by their poverty." In the sixteenth and seventeenth centuries, when the plague had become endemic in Constantinople, plague epidemics were more common in Europe than they had been in the Middle Ages. The connection between these epidemics and the main currents of long-distance trade and troop movements becomes still clearer.[10]

It is the human reaction to the plague at least as much as its causes that makes it into an elemental event in environmental history. To be sure, initially the plague revealed the impotence of medicine; but the process that made Western civilization more hygienic and politicized the issue of hygiene, a process that runs through all of the modern period and is probably the most important source of an environmental awareness that was effective in practice, was to a large extent born from the traumatic experience with epidemics. That "civilizing process" with its elevation of the barriers of shame and disgust, which Norbert Elias explained in a rather complicated manner, can be derived most easily from the fear of contagion and "bad air," which was widespread long before the discovery of bacteria.[11] The sense that it is most salutary to live a solitary life in nature finds here a quite trivial-rational reason.

When it comes to the response to the plague in terms of medical policy, Europe was different from the Islamic world. Is the reason behind this difference that Islam accepted the plague fatalistically as kismet, a fate sent by God? In the Middle Ages, however, medicine was more advanced in some Islamic countries than it was in Europe. The crucial factor was probably that Islam lacked the autonomous city, which in the West took the initiative on medical policy. That Europe was taking different paths in environmental consciousness manifested itself – apart from the forest regulations – earliest in the reaction to the great epidemics. To be sure, for centuries the countermeasures were not very successful. As long as the trading cities were the primary actors, rigid quarantine measures could be enforced only to a limited extent. Progress became evident only when the territorial lords assumed the initiative, and the Habsburg monarchy, beginning in 1728, set up a wide plague cordon on the Balkans (whereby the organized defense against the plague coincided with military interests). Some medical historians believe, however, that the peculiarly rapid disappearance of the plague in Europe in the eighteenth century resulted not from human measures but from the displacement of the house rat by the brown rat. In modern times, as well, the history of epidemics retains an eerie and unpredictable quality.[12]

2. ECOLOGICAL DYNAMICS IN OVERSEAS COLONIALIZATION

Today, it is frequently claimed that globalization already began back in the sixteenth century. However, the effect that early modern colonialism had on the global economy is often overestimated. On the whole, the quantity of people and goods that crossed the world's seas remained so marginal until the eighteenth century that it seems questionable whether the economy did in fact assume global dimensions with the discovery of America. However, some plants and weeds, microbes and rats, rabbits and sheep, cattle and horses were able, much more swiftly than European humans, to expand widely in new worlds where the food supply was initially unlimited and natural enemies were absent. If the epochal character of early modern colonialism becomes doubtful when measured by the criteria of conventional history, it assumes new meaning in environmental history.

One such meaning has been offered by Alfred W. Crosby in his book *Ecological Imperialism* (1986), in which he laid out a grand concept of environmental history that has had a global impact like few others.[13] Its success was based, not least, on the fact that Crosby managed the feat of turning the conquest of the Americas by the Europeans into the consummation of ecological laws, while at the same time satisfying to a high degree a widespread need in the Third World to blame the First World for its misery.

Crosby draws a grand arch across a thousand years of global history, from 900 to 1900, from the settlement of Iceland to the heyday of imperialism. He analyzes the reasons why the European efforts at expansion led to a series of failures in the first 500 years, and thereafter to a chain of unparalleled successes. The contrast is especially striking between the crusades and the conquest of America, if one compares the effort and the outcome: on the one side two hundred years of mad battles by the crusaders, with virtually nothing to show for it in the end; on the other side the rapid victories of the conquistadores, which led to the subjugation of the vast New World without anything more than episodic rollbacks by the natives. The solution to this riddle is simple in principle: in the first case the Europeans had nature working against them, in the second case for them. And not only the nature they found in the distant land, but also the nature they brought with them, some of it intentionally, some unintentionally: useful plants and animals, but also the seeds of weeds, pests, and bacteria. In fact, the unintended baggage proved especially effective.

For Crosby, the reasons for the ecological weakness of the New World – which struck many Europeans as the very embodiment of untamed wilderness – are to be found in the history of the earth. Ever since America had split off from the Eurasian-African landmass, it had fallen behind the Old World in species diversity and in the selection processes that promoted immunity. Colonization restored the primeval ecological unity of the continent of Pangaea, and it thus took place in a certain sense in harmony with nature. For that reason it became a success story of the grandest kind, even if it exacted a terrible price and in the end made the world poorer in biological diversity.

Crosby is able to prove the transfer of many individual species and the part this played in the displacement of autochthonous species. But when he describes the victory and defeat of ecosystems, what he presents is a substantially constructed history, one which assumes that the Old World and the New World exist as more or less compact, large-scale ecosystems above all ecotopes and ecological niches. However, if one imagines the world as composed of many ecological microcosms, it is not necessary to assume a general ecological inferiority of the New World.

And indeed, in reading Crosby one almost forgets that many American species showed great resilience in Eurasia and upset ecosystems of the Old World. At the top of the list is the potato, followed by maize, tobacco, beans, tomatoes, the Australian eucalyptus – and lest we forget, the syphilis bacillus, phylloxera, the pest that destroyed most of the European vineyards in the nineteenth century, and in the twentieth century the potato beetle, which Nazi and Soviet propaganda turned into a secret weapon of the Americans'. Incidentally, most of Europe's useful plants and animals originated in Asia, and yet their adoption by no means promoted Asia's rule over Europe; in fact, the Europeans benefited more from many species than the Asians themselves. The Native Americans, too, were perfectly capable of making use of European species: the most famous example is the symbiosis – for a while highly successful – of some Indian tribes and the horse, whose acquisition by the Indios the Spaniards had tried to prevent in vain. In the seventeenth century, the Indios also integrated the sheep and the pig successfully into their economy. In fact, the manure of sheep was even better than that of the lamas.[14] Newer field research has tended to better place the Andean peasant as an active participant in the process of transformation and to liberate him from the position of a mere victim. In Crosby, political and ecological history run all too smoothly on parallel tracks.

Crosby likes to spend time on islands: Madeira, the Azores, New Zealand. In these small, isolated places, European flora and fauna were able to assert themselves completely within a short period. The situation on the large continents is different – they were not so easily Europeanized. Three centuries after Columbus, Alexander von Humboldt did not get the sense that he found a foreignized and destroyed nature in America. If Crosby's book contains a practical lesson, it is, in the final analysis, this: globalization, while it may be fateful to many segments of humanity, is an ecologically unavoidable, inevitable, and irreversible process, and one would do well to be on the side of the winners, even if one is incensed at its injustice. Fortunately, however, ecology is not as tightly interconnected as the ideal global market in the age of electronics.

Crosby's background is in the historical study of infectious diseases, and on the epidemiological level his concept is surely most applicable, although that is where the notion of "imperialism" makes the least sense. There is no question that the colonizers influenced the natural history of the New World most rapidly and profoundly through the infectious agents they introduced, which triggered disastrous epidemics among the Indios who had no immunity, thereby creating – unintentionally – the vacuums and zones of weakness in which they could establish themselves and their large herds of sheep and cattle. The size of the indigenous population on the arrival of the European has been the subject of endless speculation, with estimates ranging from below 10 million in the 1930s to more than 100 million in the 1960s. The trend has been toward the confirmation of the pronouncement by Las Casas that the regions into which the Spaniards penetrated in the first fifty years after 1492 were crowded with people "like in a beehive." If Columbus felt he had arrived in "paradise," William M. Denevan has observed, he was talking about a "humanized paradise," not the paradise of the modern lovers of wilderness. The reason why the conquistadores were so much more successful than the crusaders is not that they – unlike the latter – encountered a sparsely settled wilderness; rather, much of the American wilderness that delighted the romantics of the nineteenth century must have been created only as a result of the depopulation from imported epidemics. Numerous indications – whether a shortage of fire wood among the Indians of the Northeast or the irrigation terraces in Mexico and Peru – suggest that broad regions must have already been settled to the outer limits of their food supply.[15]

Among the biological baggage that the Europeans carried into the New World intentionally, large domestic animals were the most important. The military superiority of the Spaniards was based to a large extent on the horse. Along with horses and oxen came the plow, which the ancient Americans did not possess for lack of draft animals. Cattle and sheep turned wide areas into pastureland. In the first century after Columbus, pasturing was pursued with the same ruthlessness as the conquest itself, without the restrictions that herders were subjected to in European farming countries. The result was the destruction of vegetation and soil, followed by erosion. But that is not the end of the story, for there were also reactions against this development. On the Caribbean plantations in the eighteenth century, the plow was soon replaced again by the hoe, after it was discovered that plowing promoted erosion. In any case, the traditionally labor-intensive methods of working the soil were here more in tune than the plow with the existing system of slavery.[16]

Events in Mexico have been studied in the greatest detail. Elinor G. K. Melville has gathered a wealth of indications for the ruthless overgrazing of the Valle del Mezquital north of the valley of Mexico in the sixteenth century; her work is the most important study to date on the basis of the Crosby thesis. But the consequences of overgrazing were painfully evident to the herd owners the late sixteenth century, when the size of the herds declined abruptly. Overgrazing is not the type of environmental damage that occurs slowly over a long period of time and without harmful consequences to those responsible. As soon as the herders are no longer able to move onto new land, they are forced, sooner or later, to limit their herds in line with the carrying capacity of the pastureland. The policy of protecting the Indios that was pursued by the Spanish crown and the church, who consistently defended the common land of the Indians and the water rights that went with it against the greed of the Spanish haciendneros, helped to ensure the survival of many Indian villages and agricultural cultures that were destroyed or threatened only much later, in postcolonial times. In many areas of the land, the traditional maize-bean-squash economy of the Indios survived into the twentieth century and came under pressure only from the "Green Revolution."[17]

In Mexico colonization brought tremendous processes of deforestation in its wake, especially through the creation of extensive pasturelands and the prodigious quantities of wood consumed by the sugar refineries. Still, it is doubtful whether the early colonial period constituted a profound change from pre-Columbian deforestation processes. The first Mexican viceroy was already well aware of the danger that deforestation posed to his capital. The exploitation of precious metals, the greatest riches of the colonies for Spain, in particular depended heavily on wood. The most ominous waves of deforestation probably occurred in postcolonial Mexico; at the same time, they reveal the kind of rich forest cover that must have still existed. In 1899 the French consul in Mexico believed that the trade in tropical woods was "the best business in the world." In the 1990s, according to the head of Mexico's Environment Ministry, the country had the highest deforestation rate in Latin America. Rigorous efforts to protect nature by trying to ban any human use from primeval forests are now colliding with the Indian resistance movement of the Zapatistas.

For those northern Mexican areas that became part of the United States in 1848, the invasion of U.S.-American civilization brought by far the most profound environmental changes, compared to which the Spanish era would almost appear to be part of ancient America. Recently scholars have begun to rediscover that Spain's colonial policy was fairly reasonable. We are now told that the Castilians, who came from dry regions in Spain, found in Mexico a landscape they understood – at least they understood it better than the Yankees, who were intent on transforming the steppes into farmland no matter the cost.[18]

Apart from animal pasture, it was above all the plantation economy of the colonizers that altered the nature of the New World on a large scale. The oldest and most widespread type of colonial economic unit, which offers the worst combination of harmful social and ecological effects, is the sugarcane plantation. Sugarcane had no equal among cultivated plants in the colonies in the way it promoted large capitalist landholding and slavery as well as deforestation: not only through the insatiable consumption of good soil, but also through the need for firewood by the refineries, which was one reason why the production of sugar was profitable only in large enterprises with plenty of capital. Prior to the rise of the sugarcane plantation in Madeira in the fifteenth and sixteenth centuries, Cyprus had been Europe's sugar island; the fact that a Cypriot refinery foreman sought to conserve wood by using eggs reveals how hopeless the wood problem was becoming for large-scale wood users in the forest-poor Mediterranean. The island of Madeira, whose name means "wood," and which was originally famed for its abundance of woodlands, lost the majority of its forests to sugarcane. Since harvesting of the cane leaves behind a stump in the ground from which a new plant will grow, crop rotation, which regenerates the soil and broadens the dietary basis, is impossible. Except for the need for wood, this was presumably the most important reason for shifting the cultivation of sugarcane from the Mediterranean to sunny colonies: "Apart from the single bonus of the inherent fertility of forest land, there was no apparent reason in the early sixteenth century for growing sugar 4,000 miles and three months away from the market in Europe."[19]

On the sugarcane island of Barbados, soil exhaustion reached a critical level as early as around 1700. Pressured by the acute crisis, however, the planters were capable of taking countermeasures: to generate manure they kept livestock that was fed with sugarcane waste; to retain the soil they built walls, and they had the black slaves carry the earth that had slid down the slopes back up again: "Our negroes work at it like ants and bees," remarked a contemporary account. In the enormous territory of Brazil, however, which became one of the world's leading sugar producers, the sugarcane plantation economy was pursued into modern times as mere shifting cultivation, in which the exhausted soil was abandoned and new land was cleared. But it was probably not until the industrial age, when sugar changed from a luxury article into an item of mass consumption, that sugarcane cultivation attained a scale at which it not only destroyed the nature of islands, but completely transformed landscapes even on continents. As one of the most common addictive substances of the modern world, sugar became a kind of historical actor. Like never before, the dynamic of consumption influenced world and environmental history: in tandem with a way of life that was in constant pursuit of stimuli, an entire configuration of luxury goods like sugar, rum, tea, coffee, cacao, and tobacco drove colonization and its plantation system.[20]

For one historian of Brazil, it is a well-known fact in the nineteenth century that sugarcane promoted the rule of the aristocracy, while the coffee bush was "a democratic plant, as it were," which could be successfully cultivated also on a small scale. It used to be advantageous to grow coffee shrubs in conjunction with other plants – in Brazil with maize and beans – that protected the young coffee seedlings. In this way, coffee plantations were compatible with the subsistence economy and a certain degree of biological diversity. But as soon as the coffee bush grew in size, other plants would no longer grow in its dense shade. As a result of the "superstitious belief" that "the coffee bush would grow only on virgin forest soil," a lot of jungle was cleared unnecessarily for coffee plantations in Brazil. By contrast, the cacao tree has a forest-preserving effect, since it needs the protection of large trees. In Ghana an important motivation for forest protection disappeared with the decline of cacao production.[21]

Colonialism developed a global impact that spanned entire continents only from the nineteenth century on, in conjunction with industrialization, the steam ship, and the railroad. Only the mass export of meat to Europe turned the Argentinian ranch into a gigantic enterprise. In fact, the full dynamic of the industrialized age did not take hold of many Third World countries until postcolonial times. Colonial governments were wont to preserve existing social structures, provided they were useful or at least not dangerous to them. Although some proponents of progress have criticized them for this, the verdict of ecologists is likely to be different in some cases. During colonial times, the Indios of the La Plata region successfully clung to maize and the digging stick and resisted wheat cultivation and the hoe. It was only in independent Argentina that the gauchos waged an unchecked war of annihilation against the Indios and practiced ruthless overgrazing over wide areas. Not until the second half of the twentieth century did the destruction of tropical forests reach the catastrophic scale of today – a time of the postwar economy and decolonization, of the truck and the chainsaw, of mass exports for the cellulose industry and a population explosion. Albert Schweitzer vividly recounted how, still in his day, cutting and transporting trees along the Ogowe was very laborious; all the wood that was more than a kilometer from the road or the river was essentially untransportable.[22]

Extreme examples of deforestation in Asia are Thailand and Nepal, which were never colonial countries, and in America Haiti, where, uniquely in history, black slaves fought for and won their independence in the wake of the French Revolution. After this victory, the mass of the population moved from the plantations in the plains to the mountains, but they failed to establish a stable terracing culture. Once the richest colony in the world, Haiti turned into an extreme case of erosion.[23] Ethiopia, only briefly a colony and as late as the 1950s considered an especially fertile and promising land (a "land without hunger"), has become, since the famine of 1982–4 and those in subsequent years, the embodiment of economic and ecological impoverishment: evidently as the result of the spread of the "oxen-plow system" into ecologically fragile regions, but also as the result of an instrumentalization of environmental protection by a brutal dictatorship. With the argument that the high plains were overpopulated and the soil "completely spent," the Mengistu dictatorship in 1984–5 justified its resettlement of more than a million peasants, which, according to the philosopher André Glucksmann, was the main reason for the catastrophic famine that followed. This, too, is part of the theme "nature and power": the marriage of environmental policies and power politics in such a way that existing problems are exacerbated and new ones are created.[24]

In some central African regions (like Rhodesia) the colonial powers created the worst disaster at the end of the nineteenth century when, under the influence of big-game hunters, they forbade the indigenous peoples from hunting large animals, thus promoting the advance of the tsetse fly, which lives in a symbiosis with large game and infects humans and cattle with the sleeping sickness. The connection was well known to contemporaries knowledgeable about bacteriology; intense controversies raged over the question of whether the hunting of large game should be permitted once again. When the colonial power willingly-unwillingly promoted the spread of the symbiotic relationship between big game and the tsetse fly, it was not invading a foreign nature, but merely allowing an already endemic nature to expand.

In Africa, as in America, colonialism had particularly rapid and for humans disastrous consequences in the realm of the microbes. But not all of these effects can be subsumed under the rubric "destruction of nature." As a case study of Tanganyika has shown, the precolonial economy of the indigenous peoples contained an "agro-horticultural prophylaxis" against the tsetse fly, while the colonial policy of protecting game led to the "loss of control over the environment" and gave "nature an advantage over humans." The history of political power is not in every respect a history of growing mastery over nature! The tsetse fly, which kept human settlements away from large animals, enjoyed the sympathy of big-game hunters and of the animal conservationist Bernhard Grzimek. Even those who considered the cutting of the forest and the spread of cattle herds in Africa an ecological calamity saw the tsetse fly secretly as a blessing for Africa; long before the environmental era there was a saying that the tsetse fly deserved to have a monument erected in its honor. For those who did not love the fly, insecticides became the alternative to the extermination of large game.

As long as blacks were still regarded as part of nature and not as fully human, whites did not see them as foreign bodies in the nature reserves. That changed, however, as Europeans began to recognize that the Africans, too, interfered with nature in their own way. The resulting confrontation between nature parks and the indigenous population, which continued after decolonization, was not favorable to the development of an African environmental awareness. To this day, the relationship of many Africans to environmental protection is burdened by the tsetse fly.

The situation is similar with the largest of the land animals, the elephant. From early on it held the greatest fascination for tourists, and European animal conservationists in Africa were already worrying about the decimation of the elephant in the nineteenth century. In the 1980s "the elephant emerged as conservation's central figure, the embodiment of everything worth saving in Africa." Even exaggerated claims about the extent of the threat to the African elephant were believed. Pictures showing natives killing elephants always aroused loud cries of indignation in the West. This led to real excesses in elephant protection, which played a part in Uganda's being virtually overrun by elephants in 1936.[25] This kind of environmental protection had to spark outrage among the natives, since the African elephant, unlike its Indian counterpart, cannot be tamed and often wreaks havoc in planted areas. Even Albert Schweizer, who preached "reverence for life," considered the fight against the elephant necessary. As paradoxical as it may seem, in some respects, colonialism was harmful in the long run not only through the environmental changes it brought about, but possibly – and more disastrously – by some types of environmental protection it initiated. When the central authority collapses in an African state, the usual response of the population is to hunt down all the animals in the national parks – a process that reminds one of the open season on game during the European revolutions between 1789 and 1848. The conflict over large animals can block the realization that the preservation of a diverse nature is in fact perfectly compatible with the vital interests of the natives.

3. THE BIRTH OF THE GLOBAL PERSPECTIVE: COLONIAL AND INSULAR ORIGINS
OF MODERN ENVIRONMENTAL AWARENESS

Richard H. Grove's *Green Imperialism*, which traces the genesis of modern environmental awareness back to colonialism, reads like an answer to Crosby's *Ecological Imperialism*. One admirer has noted that "Grove's scholarly travels made Marco Polo look like a layabout."[26] In this far-ranging study, Grove presents a delightful and surprising story: our environmental awareness did not arise – as is so often assumed – in the odorous atmosphere of the London sewers, but under far distant palm trees, on exotic islands, out of an awareness of threatened dreams of paradise. It was there that people first experienced – or believed they were experiencing – the connection between rapid deforestation, the drying up of springs, the desiccation of the soil, and a change in climate. From St. Helena, St. Vincent, and, above all, Mauritius, this new awareness spread onto the British-Indian subcontinent around 1800. There, Grove maintains, it moved beyond good intentions, as ecology became an influential "lobby," an "establishment" of scientific expertise for politics.[27] It was especially in forest protection policy that it had far-reaching effects. And here the issue was not primarily wood, but the ecological, and especially the climatic, importance of the forest. Physicians and botanists took the initiative, and the Botanical Gardens evolved into seedbeds of political ecology. The power of this eco-lobby evidently rested on the colonizers' fear of tropical diseases and on its dominance over the political discourse with the help of a global intellectual network, which reached from Darjeeling to Göttingen, from the Botanical Gardens of the colonies into the studies of German scholars.

Grove's well-documented study is persuasive up to a point. The Europeans' encounter with tropical forests and tropical forest peoples, the naked "savages," imparted a magical attractive power to the ideal of paradisiacal nature and of the unspoiled, natural human being; the nature enthusiasm of a Rousseau would have been unthinkable without this experience. "An exotic excitement seized the imagination" – an excitement that radiated all the way into philosophy, as the philosopher Wilhelm Windelband has observed about that time. Biology and the "desire of tree cultivation" received very powerful impulses from the exotic vegetation.

At the same time, however, in some colonial regions – earliest of all on the islands – Europeans confronted nature-destroying chain reactions far more starkly than in Central and Western Europe. In part this was the result of the natural conditions of these regions, but in part also of the fact that the colonizers often engaged in a much more rapid and ruthless exploitation of the forest, the wildlife, and the soil than they did in their own homelands. In most Central and Western European regions, erosion progresses for a long time unnoticed, and the cutting of forest is not followed by an immediate and irreversible loss of soil. Where rainfall is distributed across the entire year, the connection between the forest and the water cycle of the soil is not so readily seen as problematic. The study of erosion and desertification received its impulses from North America and the subtropical and tropical regions; only in the course of the twentieth century did it become clear that these phenomena existed also in Central Europe.[28]

Especially in the colonies, Europeans worried constantly about the climate and its consequences for their health. Since antiquity, from the time of Herodotus and Hippocrates, encounters with foreign environments had stimulated the thinking about the influence of the environment on humans, and the overseas discoveries and conquest in the modern era gave such ideas a tremendous boost. Some ruminations followed the classical thought patterns. But when Europeans invaded foreign worlds as conquerors, this raised the reverse question with greater urgency than ever before: namely, that about human impact on the environment. Experiments with the introduction of European species into the colonies and of exotic species into Europe created a kind of practical environmental knowledge. New Zealanders discovered in the nineteenth century that bumblebees had to be introduced for pollination in order to make the cultivation of clover a success.[29]

In all of this, *islands* became the exemplary cases: these small, isolated worlds created virtual laboratory conditions for the study of ecological interrelationships. Colonized islands are the prime examples for both Crosby and Grove. On small islands it was possible for the forest to be completely destroyed within a short period of time; no wind-born seed from neighboring regions was able to regenerate it. Animal species, too, could be quickly and completely eradicated: one example of early fame was the dodo, the giant, flightless bird of Mauritius, which became extinct in the seventeenth century. As early as the beginning of the eighteenth century, observers on this island noted that the cutting of the forest was a calamitous mistake where the lush vegetation gave a misleading impression about the fragility of the topsoil.[30]

The fate of a large Nordic island like Iceland, which was settled by Vikings around 900, was discovered in the nineteenth century as a didactic example of environmental destruction. Roscher counted Iceland "among the most splendid examples of nature made worse through the destruction of the forest." For centuries, Iceland, it would seem, has offered a prime example of the ecological vicious cycle that leads from deforestation to overgrazing to soil destruction, with the last made worse in the case of Iceland by wind and water erosion. A cooling of the climate here, at the edge of the Arctic, appears to have further exacerbated the misery of the inhabitants, whose number dropped from around 80,000 in the twelfth century to below 30,000 in the eighteenth century. The original motivation behind forest protection, which was targeted at fruit-bearing and pasture trees (*Maastbaum*), did not protect the sparse birch forest of ancient Iceland. Although England and Ireland teach us that deforestation and sheep pasturing do not always lead invariably to soil destruction, the vegetation of ancient Iceland could not tolerate pasturing. The settlers of Iceland had experience only with different ecosystems, which is why they failed to adjust quickly enough to a nature they were unable to adapt to their own economic forms. But political circumstances also appear to have played a part in why the Icelanders acted as though paralyzed in the face of the decline of their environment: they lost their autonomy first to the Norwegians, and then to the Danes. By around 1700, 94 percent of them had sunk to the status of poor tenant farmers with very few options, who, if they wanted to produce enough to pay the rent, could not afford to keep land fallow, which would have regenerated the soil. To that extent, Iceland's fate also falls into the category of "colonialism."[31]

From Iceland a leap to the other side of the world: Easter Island, that desolate isle with the giant statues, witnesses to past and perhaps fateful ambitions. This, the remotest of all civilization-bearing islands, is today regarded as a prime example of ecological suicide through deforestation: the fate of Easter Island as a warning for "spaceship Earth"! The inhabitants must have destroyed the forests knowing full well what they were doing, for the island is small enough that one would have known that one was cutting down the last tree. Or is the true story of Easter Island not one of suicide but of murder? According to the pollen evidence, it would appear that the island was nearly treeless already more than a thousand years ago; but the Dutch admiral Roggeveen, who discovered the island in 1722, still found there a flourishing agriculture with a rich variety of fruit. Here, too, deforestation was not tantamount to inevitable desolation, especially since there were still palm trees. The downfall seems to have come only subsequently in a cruel civil war, completed in 1862 when the majority of the population was dragged off by Peruvian slave traders and the island was transformed into a large sheep ranch.[32] Ecological models are highly susceptible to human projections.

Striking examples for some elements of Grove's theory can be found outside the time period and geographic area he examined: for instance, the wildlife preserves set up in Africa from the end of the nineteenth century under pressure from the big-game hunting lobby, which was supported by conservationists, and the cries of alarm prompted by the destructive exploitation of forests and fields in North America. Even modern imperialism, which pushed ahead with steamships and the railroad, had a kind of environmental awareness: it was an awareness of the limited nature of global resources, which intensified as the more unknown portions of the globe were filled in and stimulated the competition over raw materials. In 1913 Walther Rathenau warned that the shortage of raw materials was foreseeable; the world had been divided up: "Woe to us that we gave and received virtually nothing." The forestry scientist Franz Heske, the leading German strategist for a future imperial forestry during the Second World War, prophesied the downfall of humanity as the result of the worsening "disturbance of the organic harmony of the balance of nature." In the late eighteenth century, fear of a timber shortage was already one driving force behind Britain's India policy, and restrictions on the cutting of wood in the New England states, intended to secure the timber supply for British naval construction, had embittered the settlers there and encouraged the independence movement.[33] Does this kind of concern over resources have anything to do with contemporary environmental awareness? The answer is not entirely clear. The ecological justification of power politics is likely to increase in the future.

Like many good stories, Grove's account of the colonial genesis of "environmentalism" offers only the partial truth. All told, the evidence for the practical effect of early colonial concerns for nature is rather sparse and unclear. Even Pierre Poivre, Grove's crown witness for an ecologically motivated forest protection policy radiating from Mauritius, governed the island for only nine months and with no lasting impact; moreover, Poivre was, above all else, a physiocrat intent on boosting agricultural production. Grove offers the Dutch colonies and the Dutch environmental awareness that supposedly emerged there as a prime example for his thesis, but it is precisely the Dutch case that does not hold up well to closer scrutiny. To be sure, superb botanical studies were done at the request of the Dutch East India Company (VOC), but from an ecological point of view, the VOC's approach was at times almost grotesquely shortsighted. On the island of Ambon, it forced the natives to plant clove trees and then to cut them down, depending on the ebb and flow of the economy. This back-and-forth demoralized the natives and ran counter to a sustained tree cultivation.[34] The low average life expectancy of Europeans in the tropics at that time favored a shortsighted, mercenary mind-set, not a spirit of permanence and sustainability.

British forestry policy in India in the nineteenth century revolved largely around teak, not around the preservation of the ecological and climatic functions of the forest. To preserve their health, British colonial officials in tropical India took refuge in the "hill stations"; that was not the reason they engaged in forestry policy. Here as elsewhere, the decisive impulse for reforestation came from Germany, not from the Botanical Gardens in the colonies. Germany's pioneering role in forestry science can be explained by the fact that it had *no* colonies and was forced to make do with its native woodland resources. Much of Grove's evidence seems "ecological" in the modern sense only if one takes it out of its context. Even if some observers then recognized ecological interconnections, the primary goal was to boost the yields from agriculture and forestry, often also to "acclimatize" certain useful plants to a new terrain, but not to preserve existing ecosystems.[35]

Among Grove's primary witnesses are the world travelers Forster (father and son), Alexander von Humboldt, and Charles Darwin. They form a line of tradition: Humboldt's enthusiasm for the tropics was kindled by Georg Forster, Darwin's by Humboldt. All offer fascinating examples of how – under the impact of exotic worlds – a holistic vision of nature, of the limitless interdependencies of man and animals, vegetation and the morphology of the earth, becomes a passion and the driving force behind an impetuous curiosity. They all opposed slavery and colonial exploitation, but their travels would not have been possible without colonialism. Grove believes that the "Humboldtian environmental ideology," in particular his ideas about the value of the forest in preserving atmospheric and soil humidity, had a significant influence on the scientists of the British East India Company. In all of this, however, one must not forget that the basic tenor in Humboldt is dominated through and through by a boundless enthusiasm for the endless diversity of nature in the tropics; concern over the preservation of nature in the wake of human colonization is only an occasional theme. Since nature in Latin America struck him as inexhaustible, he did not understand the sense behind the birth control practiced by the natives.[36]

Anxiety about the depletion of resources in Forster and Humboldt was German in origin, and it was typical for a country that could not protect itself against shortages with colonial imports. The wood-saving mentality had become second nature to many Germans around 1800, so much so that they retained their wood-saving stoves even after emigrating to the United States, where hardly anyone else at that time was thrifty with wood. In New Zealand, however, Johann Forster thought it was unpleasant to see "nothing but forest," and he gazed with great satisfaction on a piece of land the sailors had cleared. By contrast, during a journey along the lower Rhine, which he undertook in 1790 with Humboldt, he was overcome by a gloomy premonition that the wintry and cold regions would become uninhabitable because of a shortage of wood sometime in the future, and that the cold would drive the European peoples southward. In the revolutionary year of 1789, when warning cries about a great impending wood famine were heard everywhere, Humboldt perceived a "shortage that is spreading on all sides." As he saw it, the practical value of his world travels lay in opening up new sources of food for humanity through knowledge of the infinite variety of vegetation. To be sure, he was entranced by wild nature, but at the same time he was driven by the thought that nature could be made even much more useful to humanity. The same is true for Forster, who chided the Europeans for scorning dog meat, seeing as nature had evidently created the dog – which propagated readily and ran after humans – as food for man![37]

At the beginning of his book *Ecological Imperialism*, Crosby places an observation from Darwin, which he was prompted to make by the decline of the aborigines of Australia: "Wherever the European had trod, death seems to pursue the aboriginal. We may look to the wide extent of the Americas, Polynesia, the Cape of Good Hope, and Australia, and we find the same result." Yet another piece of evidence for the colonial origins of the modern environmental awareness? Perhaps, but it if one puts this remark into its context, it becomes clear that Darwin registered this decimation of the natives with human regret, to be sure, but at the same time also with grim satisfaction. In his eyes, the process was in no way testimony to a decline, but rather to the creative ability of nature, which ensured the survival of the fittest species. This is the Darwinian law of the "survival of the fittest," which supposedly worked in favor of the Europeans – and especially the British – throughout the world. The chief thrust of Darwin's message was that man, too, is an integral part of nature, which is why he made no fundamental distinction between the extermination of species by humans and by natural enemies. Both processes were necessary for nature, not destructive. In Darwin's logic, species preservation made no sense.[38]

Like the physico-theologists of the eighteenth century, Darwin, too, took pleasure in ecological causal chains. Darwin's most popular ecological witticism is probably his observation "that the ascendancy of the British Empire was determined by its spinsters: spinsters kept cats, which kept down populations of mice, which were therefore unable to destroy the nests of bumblebees, which could then pollinate red clover, which could be used to feed cattle, which provided beef to the armed forces which defended and maintained the Empire."[39] That, however, was not modern political ecology, because it did not concern nature but the British Empire, and Darwin, moreover, did not advocate an increase in spinsters.

To be sure, vital components of what we think of today as environmental awareness come from the colonial world. We can still see this in the passions aroused in the environmental movement by the destruction of tropical rainforests, while extensive deforestations in dry and northern coniferous forests, which give no less cause for ecological concerns, hardly ever trigger strong emotions.[40] The Amazonian rain forest has become the symbol of nature under threat – to the industrialized nations of the north, who see their dream of paradise disappearing there. But tradition, originating in colonialism though often linked with an anticolonial sentiment, has a fundamental problem: this is an environmental consciousness from above and from afar, the consciousness of the scientist, the traveler, or the colonial expert. As soon as it becomes a power on the ground, it runs the danger of clashing with the perceived interests of the locals. Since environmental protection is difficult to enforce over the long run *against* the locals – one cannot put a policeman next to every tree – this trend poses a danger to environmental policy. Colonial history does not lack examples of how a passionate enthusiasm for nature and profound insights into natural history went hand in hand with a treatment of the environment that was in fact careless and ruthless.

The vast new insights that spring from an expanded look at the world are beyond question. There are, indeed, many things that are best seen from a distance and by way of comparison. The expansion of the horizon through colonial conquests did much, directly and indirectly, to make the science of nature into a force with international networks and a growing institutional foundation. In this way there arose a new kind of knowledge, which left classical tradition far behind and could no longer be matched by mere local experience. But, intentionally or not, this knowledge was perfectly in tune with the interests of power-conscious administrations and with a scientific world that ignored the "tacit knowledge" of local populations.

4. COLONIAL AND POSTCOLONIAL TURNING POINTS IN INDIA'S ENVIRONMENTAL HISTORY

In India, as in so many other countries, woods and water offer themselves as leitmotifs for environmental history. However, judging from our current state of scholarship, sources for studying these topics are available, at the earliest, for the Mughal period (sixteenth and seventeenth centuries), and continuously only from the period of British colonial rule. Questions about environmental history concern chiefly the effects of this foreign rule, which is why it makes the most sense to look at India within the context of colonialism.

The existing sources and the state of scholarship about the premodern period are incomparably poorer than in the case of China. That makes it all the more tempting to reconstruct the older history of India's environment on the basis of ideological preconceptions. The only large-scale survey of the "ecological history of India" to date conceives of the precolonial period – with a few caveats – as a harmonious era between humankind and the environment, and of the period after that as an era of a deeply disturbed relationship; Mughal rule, however, did *not* represent a turning point. By contrast, a history of agriculture in Mughal India, written before the ecological age, interprets India's history as a "stubborn struggle against nature . . . carried on for thousands of years." Even Jawaharlal Nehru, the future prime minister of India, wrote to his daughter Indira from jail in 1932 that the real history of humankind, behind all the confusion of political history, was "the story of man's struggle through the ages against Nature and the elements."[41]

Until the early twentieth century, India was a magical land for Europeans; today, however, it has changed from the very embodiment of wealth into the symbol of poverty. The old image was linked with the idea of a paradisiacal nature, the new one is linked with that of a destroyed nature. Is this radical turnaround merely a change in European perspective, or is India's modern environmental history in fact the history of a dramatic collapse? The French traveler Bernier, who regarded Bengal as the most fertile land in the world in the seventeenth century, even then described the poor peasants as a miserable lot squeezed to the bone by the local governors, people who could not possible develop a relationship to the soil and take an interest in preserving its fertility. In Mughal India, unlike in China, tax was levied on the harvest, not the land itself: this destroyed any incentive to intensify cultivation, but it also put a brake on population growth. For Malthus, China – but not India – was a warning example about overpopulation. In fact, the British in the nineteenth century even regarded India as underpopulated, a view that was based, however, not on actual but potential food resources.[42]

For a long time, both imperialists and anti-imperialists took the British Empire as *the* great turning point of Indian history. In the early years of British rule, its passionate opponent Edmund Burke thundered that England had become more ruinous to India than the Mongols had been and had transformed the country from a "paradise" into "a howling desert." More recent research, by contrast, has revealed that "British rule was ephemeral both in terms of its time span and of the intensity of its impact." The English presence in this enormous country remained scattered; the empire worked chiefly through the way in which local, native rulers and tax collectors used the foreign power for their own ends. To be sure, the British weakened the Indian subsistence economy by promoting the cultivation of cotton, sugarcane, and indigo in the interest of exports. Still, the difference to the colonization of America is profound: a plantation economy was not introduced into India by force, and the traditional structure of the Indian village was preserved. Even the growing of tea took place until the second half of the nineteenth century in tea gardens, and only later on plantations.[43] It was quite impossible to impose a large-scale, European ecosystem on the Indian subcontinent. Moreover, the microbes in India were definitely not on the side of the Europeans, threatening them constantly with disease and death.

Other peculiarities of Indian environmental history emerge from the comparison with China, especially so in the area of irrigation. It is here that the fundamental difference of Indian to Chinese history is most clearly evident: the lack of state unity and continuity and the absence of a highly developed bureaucratic tradition in the precolonial period. Only under British rule did the Indians begin to feel like Indians.

In some respects the plains of the Indus and the Ganges offered ideal opportunities for large irrigation systems similar to those of the valleys of the Nile, the Euphrates, and the Huang-ho. Sir Proby Thomas Cautley, the architect of the Ganges Canal in the 1830s, described the northern plains of India as a "region designed by nature as a great field for artificial irrigation." In fact, the natural predestination for irrigation was not quite that self-evident. In Bengal agriculture was possible even without large hydraulic systems: the villages had their wells, and the summer monsoon brought rain at the most favorable growing period. The rain, however, was not reliable, and there were terrible years of drought. From that perspective, the Indians would have had an even greater incentive than the Chinese to construct large water reservoirs.[44]

One modern hydraulic engineer was driven to raptures by India and called it the "fairy tale land of irrigation": "This land vastly surpasses even China in the diversity of its irrigation methods." Nevertheless, until the nineteenth century, the continuity that extended across centuries lay in southern India chiefly in the village ponds, the "tanks," and in the wells from which the water was diverted onto the fields by means of a scooping mechanism operated by two men. No state power was required for this kind of irrigation.[45] The collapse of the Mughal Empire, often seen as the beginning of the Indian tragedy, was not necessarily a disadvantage to the village economy and ecology.

Friedrich Engels believed that every Indian despotism "was fully aware that its first duty was the general maintenance of irrigation throughout the valleys, without which no agriculture was possible. It was reserved for the enlightened English to lose sight of this in India; they let the irrigation canals and sluices fall into decay."[46] In reality, though, a large segment of the India of old was *not* a "hydraulic" society. Until the British period, water and power in India were not nearly as intimately related as they were in China and Egypt.

It is revealing that the highly developed irrigation systems of the ancient Indus civilization of Mohenjo-Daro found no successors. No dike builder or tamer of waters stands at the center of Indian mythology; instead, the god Indra is celebrated as the liberator of the streams. In the Rig Veda, however, we read that the Indo-Aryan immigrants diverted the rivers to irrigate the fields. The Arthashastra, a treatise on the art of government that dates presumably from the third century B.C.E., encourages the ruler to levy a higher tax on artificially irrigated land, and this advice was often followed in Indian history. To that extent the rulers certainly had an incentive to expand the irrigation systems, but the tax did not make such projects popular with the subjects. To be sure, some Indian rulers made a name for themselves with ambitious irrigation projects, but in Indian history such power strategies do not have even remotely the importance they do in Chinese history. Looking at India from China, where the emperors linked the Huang-ho and the Yangtze, there would have been reason to expect that Indian kings would develop a similar ambition to link up the watersheds of the Ganges and the Indus rivers, but the organization to accomplish such a feat did not exist. The literary sources convey a strangely hazy picture even of the canals built by the Mughal emperors, traces of which the British canal builders encountered everywhere. In many cases, upkeep of the canals depended on the peasants. Bernier noted as early as around 1660 that the irrigation works were decaying, since nobody was willing to put in the necessary work. Nevertheless, in its early stages British canal construction was able to build on Indian experiences.[47]

For Toynbee, the silting up of India's canals was a sign of cultural decline. But from an ecological perspective, it is quite possible to put the accents differently, and here the traditional well irrigation has much in its favor. Evaporation remained minimal, and a salinization of the soil was largely avoided. As early as the Mughal period, those areas where agriculture depended entirely on artificial irrigation were especially prone to crisis. The great canal projects undertaken by the British Empire beginning in the nineteenth century had a high price: considerable loss of water, salinization, and malaria. The flipside of large-scale hydraulic works was quickly understood, not only by individual experts, but also by the affected population.

For the British colonial government, these projects were evidently a method, beyond all cost-benefit calculations, to present themselves as a regime based on science and progress. The colonial rulers asserted that it merely took a canal to turn a semi-nomad from a cattle thief into a model farmer. In Europe the colonial lords were criticized for still doing too little for irrigation in India, thereby causing the famines in that country. In fact, the Mughal rulers were repeatedly held up as hydraulic exemplars! The distribution of water to the end user was largely beyond the reach of British regulation – this is where the local rulers held sway. The large-scale hydraulic systems weakened the self-regulation of the villages. This was an unintended effect, since the British government needed the villages as sources of local authority.[48]

Much more distinctive than India's older hydraulic history is that of Ceylon (Sri Lanka). It was here, not in India, that the premodern hydraulic technology of southern Asia reached its highpoint. The central region of the Anuradhapura Kingdom, whose beginnings reach back into the fifth century B.C.E., lay in the island's northern dry zone, where rice cultivation was not possible without artificial irrigation, some of which came from extensive reservoirs. Needham believed that the most elaborate of these dam systems was the largest water reservoir in the world for more than a thousand years. As late as the twelfth century C.E., this hydraulic civilization reached a final climax, but in the thirteenth century it collapsed. Subsequently, the political centers of Ceylon moved away from the dry zone. Since then, the irrigation on this island has followed the Indian type of local tanks that collect the monsoon rain.[49]

Alongside water, the *forest* is the other great leitmotif of environmental history; in India it is a more distinctive element than in China. At the beginning of history in India we find, as in so many regions, an era of slash-and-burn cultivation, which destroyed large sections of the forest in the plain of the Ganges. The Indo-Aryan myths glorified the burning down of the forest and its wild animals by Agni, the fire god, though at times they reveal the experience that the disappearance of the forest already caused the rivers to dry out or to swell into raging torrents during the rainy period. India's legendary first king, Manu, cleared the forests; the tenth king had to save himself from a great flood. It was said that after the death of the Buddha, his followers found it difficult to procure the necessary wood to cremate his body.[50]

One could see the rejection of the killing of animals in Buddhism and Jainism as a reflection of this experience with the harm that came from an unbridled assault on forest and wildlife. An edict by Emperor Ashoka, a convert to Buddhism, forbade the needless burning of forests or the killing of animals. But the ancient Indian traditions of forest protection are not very distinct. All we know for sure is that here, as everywhere, fruit-bearing trees – in particular, mango trees and coconut palms on the coast – were held in especially high regard. Because of the curative properties of its bark, leaves, seeds, and oil, the Niem tree has been revered in Indian villages since ancient times as the "healer of all ills" and is planted along the edges of fields. The peasants spread the oil cakes left after pressing onto their fields, since they reduce plant pests and roundworm. In the 1990s, an Indian environmental initiative, with participation by Vandana Shiva, fought successfully against a patent granted to the U.S. Department of Agriculture and to an American chemical company for the use of the Niem tree.

But was there already an ancient Indian connection between forest and power? The Arthashastra was well aware of the value of the forest and suggests that forests could be planted in many regions. Since the elephant was the embodiment of the power of the Indian ruler, the elephant forest enjoyed special protection. According to the Arthashastra, anyone who set fire to an elephant forest or a useful forest should himself be burned. The ancient Indian law code Dharmashastra, however, contains this stipulation: "The first person to clear a piece of land shall own it." Here it is land clearing that bestows power and property! In all of this one must bear in mind that the great forests of India were, right into the modern period, not only the realm of wild animals but also home to autonomous forest and mountain peoples, that is to say, a world that was beyond the reach of state power, though it did influence Indian culture subterraneously. The close connection between agriculture and the forest in India was similar to what existed in Central and Western Europe. Animals were pastured in the forest, and the leaf fall of the woodlands served as fertilizer. To the poor the forests offered a last refuge in times of famine. To premodern rulers, however, they were a resource that could be regulated and exploited only to a limited extent. One of the few forest protection edicts from precolonial times that have survived comes from the Maratha king Shivaji (ca. 1670), the leader of the Hindustani rebellion against the Mughal Empire. But a tradition of institutionalized forest protection is not evident in this. The German-British forest inspector Brandis (see below) found native traditions protective of the forest only in sacred groves and princely game preserves.[51]

It is only with British rule that the connection between woodlands and power was put on an institutional footing. From the very beginning, a deep ambivalence pervaded forestry policy in British India: the commercial exploitation of the forests was pursued more systematically than before, but at the same time the understanding of the disastrous consequences of destructive exploitation was present early on, in some respect even earlier than in the British homeland. At first, in the period of the Napoleonic wars, the primary concern revolved around teak lumber for naval construction. Oak wood of the requisite quality had become rare in Europe. In this situation, against the resistance of the London shipyards, the construction of some battleships was successfully moved to Bombay, which already had a native ship-building tradition. However, since the shipyards could use only a particular quality of lumber, this kind of demand did not lead to large-scale forest destruction. That occurred only from the middle of the nineteenth century, spurred by the enormous demand for lumber for railway sleepers, the preferred wood which came from the sal and deodar forests of northern India. In 1861 none other than Hugh Cleghorn, one of the founding fathers of forestry administration in British India, sharply criticized the way his countrymen were treating the forests: of all European nations, the English, he maintained, had the lowest understanding of the value of woodlands, and this carelessness was carried on also in the United States, where the emigrants had ruthlessly destroyed the forests. For the physician Hugh Cleghorn (1820–95), from 1858 the first Conservator of the Forests in Madras, the value of the forest lay not only in its timber yield, but at least as much in its influence on climate and human well-being.[52]

Time and again throughout history, the timber needs of the navy provided the earliest and strongest impulse for reforestation. That was also the case in British India, thanks chiefly to the warnings from a German, Baron Franz von Wrede; in 1806 the East India Company appointed the first Conservator of the Forests. After the Napoleonic wars, however, this initial forest protection initiative petered out. What Adam Smith had observed about the Dutch East India company proved true also in this case: namely, that a "company of merchants" like the East India Company "almost necessarily" prefers "the little and transitory profit of the monopolist to the great and permanent revenue of the sovereign."

The situation changed only when the British crown, following the Sepoy revolt in 1858, took control of the holdings of the East India Company. The year 1860 saw the establishment of the Indian Forest Department, "the colonial world's first and ultimately most sophisticated Forest Department." In 1862 Dietrich Brandis, who had habilitated at the University of Bonn in botany and was head of the forestry administration of British Burma, was appointed advisor to the British central government; in 1864 he was named General Forest Inspector. For decades he was the leading mind of the Indian forestry system. Rudyard Kipling still celebrated him as the "giant German," "Terror personified, feared by all official agencies," the "Lord and Master of all the forests and woodlands of India" who had no peer as a forester. Under his supervision as well, teak was the chief goal of forestry, from an economic point of view even to an excessive degree: political practice always tends toward simple goals. However, the importance of Brandis, which extends to this day, lay in the fact that as early as his first years in Burma he recognized the necessity and possibility of combining the cultivation of teak trees with the swidden agriculture of the natives into a kind of "agroforestry," the so-called Taungya system. Brandis learned this method from Thai peasants. Under his direction there was, for at time, at least the beginning of a social and ecological balance between the subsistence economy of the natives and the commercial interests of the British. But this harmony, which depended on the overall political climate, would not last. What remained of his policies were the reserved forests, in which the colonial lords, not the natives, had the say, and in which teak wood was the highest priority. Even if ideas are multifaceted, in the end practice is often primitive.

Brandis, who was aware that successful forest protection over the long run was possible only in cooperation with the locals, and who had the German communal forests of his Rhenish homeland in mind as a model, sought to give the village forests official status, but on this issue he did not get his way. He was also more far-sighted than some of his successors in that he made bamboo, which was highly important to the natives but was seen by other foresters not as a tree but a weed, a component of forest cultivation. Initially he fought against the swidden cultivation of the natives, but then he learned that teak was adapted to fire and that suppressing forest fires too zealously actually caused its numbers to decline. His successors Wilhelm Schlich and Berthold Ribbentrop, who also came out of German forestry, sought to continue the tradition he had established. John M. MacKenzie has said about them: "However tempting it would be to see these German foresters as the heralds of a less liberal forest policy, in fact Brandis was keener on finding a reconciliation between imperial forestry needs and the rights of forest dwellers than his British counterparts."[53]

Forest policy created problems not only where it failed, but also where it was successful for a while: by enforcing forest protection in conflict with the traditional woodland uses of the locals, it turned the latter into enemies of the forest. The tension between the subsistence economy of local inhabitants and the focus on the commercial use of wood on the part of forestry was and is a global phenomenon, one also encountered in Central Europe. But in the colonies it was exacerbated and politically charged by the fact that the forest overseers embodied foreign rule. Setting fires in the forests became a method of resistance; these political forest fires, which were apparently directed chiefly against the pine forests, reached a disastrous climax in India in 1921.[54]

After India attained independence, the unpopular forest protection was neglected for three decades, even though the colonial forest administration continued; corrupt foresters acted as accomplices to an unrestrained exploitation of the woodlands. Since the state sought to make wood cheap for industry, there was a strong incentive to be wasteful with wood and a weak incentive to practice reforestation. The 1960s saw the introduction of clear-cutting, which is especially disastrous under tropical conditions. The first decades of Indian independence were – also as a result of the population explosion – evidently a worse phase for the environment than the late colonial period.

All the more epochal is a change in sentiment among segments of the rural population, especially that at the southern edge of the Himalayas: since the 1970s there have been no rebellions *against* forest protection, but there have been some *for* forest protection. One movement that has achieved global fame is the *Chipko* ("hug the trees") movement, which is largely women-based and opposes commercial logging. Of course, the struggle was not over ecology for its own sake, but over the traditional forest uses of the villagers. Beyond that, however, another impetus came from an understanding of the connection between the forest and the water cycle. To quote the words of an old man from the Munda tribe: "The forests are like your eyes. You recognize their importance only after you have lost them." At the edge of the Himalayas, the protective function of the forest was especially striking.

The Chipko movement became a model for other local resistance initiatives, particularly against dam projects that entailed the resettlement of numerous villages. These movements faced a more difficult struggle, though, since they collided with the main goals of India's energy and agrarian policies. Jawaharlal Nehru referred to dams as the "temples of modern India," at a time when they promised not only irrigation for agricultural fields and the regulation of the rivers, but also an inexhaustible energy source. Vandana Shiva has lamented that after independence, especially, "dam-building took the form of an epidemic"; at the same time, proponents liked to depict it as good old Indian tradition, even though – as a study by the Club of Rome determined – most irrigation programs do not even cover their own costs and, moreover, are biased in favor of large landowners. While the Chipko movement soon enjoyed widespread support, even Tirunellai N. Seshan, for a time State Secretary for Environmental Questions, who has described the Indian environmental crisis unsparingly and knows the ecological pitfalls of irrigation, told the opponents of hydraulic projects in no uncertain terms: "Anyone who opposes irrigation is a national enemy."[55]

Those within the Indian independence movement who were firm believers in progress used to charge that the British had obstructed and undermined India's industrialization. But that was precisely not one of the accusations that Gandhi, who described European civilization as "satanic," leveled at the colonial rulers. In his idealization of the Indian village community he was essentially not all that far removed from British social romanticism. By contrast, an Indian historian in the progressive camp believes that the unchanging nature of the Indian village had consequences for the country "far deadlier than any invasion." Be that as it may, colonial rule cannot be blamed for a deliberate destruction of traditional village culture.

Does ecology lead to a partial rehabilitation of enlightened colonialism, namely, where it promoted village traditions? It may do so in a few instances, though it is doubtful whether the traditional economy of the villages in general possessed the sustainability that ecological nostalgists ascribe to it. To be sure, Sir Albert Howard, one of the early British opponents of the massive application of chemical fertilizers, praised Indian agriculture in his *Agricultural Testament* (1940) as a model for a perfect recycling of organic matter into the soil. But that was by no means true of all regions of India. On the whole, it appears that the art of nutrient recycling was far less developed in Indian agriculture than in its Chinese counterpart. Human excrement was often taboo, and cow dung was needed for fuel. This circumstance alone explains why the ability of Indian agriculture to cushion a growth in population by intensifying cultivation was inadequate with traditional methods. As early as the nineteenth century, British officials in Bengal saw signs of catastrophic soil exhaustion, especially since cotton, a crop that was promoted under colonial rule, was very hard on the soil. The German forester Franz Heske, who traveled through northern India in 1928 as the forest organizer of the Maharadja of Tehri-Garwhal, found indications of a rapidly progressing soil impoverishment and completely inadequate fertilization wherever he went.

The greatest leap in the intensification of Indian agriculture occurred with the "Green Revolution" of the 1970s, with its high-yielding strains, artificial fertilizer, and motor pumps. The boost in yields was purchased, however, at the price of a substantially higher consumption of water and an overuse of groundwater, as a result of which wells dried up and villages had to be abandoned. Indian institutions were also not prepared for the wastewater problems of an industrialized society. The Mughal emperor, who took a special interest in good water, preferred to drink Ganges water – inconceivable today; in our own time, most Indian rivers have been turned into sewers.[56]

What seems to have been most successful in modern India is a not very human-friendly type of environmental protection, which is pursued largely in the interest of tourism: the protection of tigers and their jungle habitats. Although protection of the big cat is an inheritance of colonial big-game hunting, the tiger conservationist Kailash Sankhala has proclaimed an Indian tiger nationalism: "The tiger is the soul of India, our national inheritance from nature." He goes so far as to praise his initiative behind the establishment of tiger preserves as "the most successful protection project in the world." The contrast to other areas of Indian environmental protection could not be greater. Members of forest tribes were expelled in large numbers from the national parks and tiger preserves in Madhya Pradesh. As Richard Grove has noted with concern, "the continuing human cost of wildlife conservation in India" is high.[57]

5. YANKEE AND *MUSHIK* ECOLOGY

More so even than India or Latin America, the United States became a warning example for the ruthless exploitation of forest, wildlife, and soil as early as the late eighteenth century. An anonymous book entitled *American Husbandry*, published in London in 1775, one year before the Declaration of Independence, contains a general attack on the New England farmer: "The American planters and farmers," the unnamed English author claimed, "are in general the greatest slovens in Christianity," who ruined landscape after landscape in every possible way. It was the same old story over and over again: these colonists had allowed the overabundance of land and the initial fertility of the freshly cleared forest soil to seduce them into forgetting all good farming rules and to practice an "absurd" husbandry. They allowed their cattle to roam freely in the woods without collecting the manure. They paid no attention to crop rotation but were constantly growing maize, the "great exhauster." Instead of restoring the fertility of the soil, they simply ploughed new land if the old was exhausted, thereby destroying more and more forests without making any provisions for the future wood supply. It was not only European travelers to America who came to this conclusion. Benjamin Franklin admitted: "We are bad farmers, because we have so much land." The Virginian John Taylor, one of the Founding Fathers, denounced the usual Yankee husbandry – much like Liebig did later – as "murder of the soil." George Washington, as experienced a farmer as he was a statesman, lamented: "We ruin the lands that are already cleared and either cut down more wood, if we have it, or emigrate to the western country." Unfortunately this destructive behavior possessed a kind of rationality: "Here it is more profitable to cultivate a lot of land poorly than a little land well." He and many other contemporaries already had experience of how the continuous cultivation of tobacco, by far the most lucrative export product of the southern colonies in the eighteenth century, exhausted the soil. Washington and Jefferson experimented with crop rotation systems on their own land, but they found few imitators.

It was not only the ecology of the soil that dictated what was grown in the fields: the market did so as well. In John Steinbeck's *Grapes of Wrath* (1939), everyone knew what cotton cultivated without crop rotation "does to the land; robs it, sucks all the blood out of it." If "King Cotton" created the unity of the Southern states in the nineteenth century, it did so not only by its dominance, but also by its ecological fragility. Not least because of the progressive soil exhaustion, made worse by the growing monoculture, it was a question of survival for the Southern states to keep the road to the West open to cotton along with slavery – and that triggered the Civil War.[58]

In 1926 the agrarian historian Avery Craven, on the basis of thorough research, introduced soil exhaustion as a chief factor in the history of Virginia and Maryland, indeed, of wide stretches of American history. While his teacher Frederick Jackson Turner, with his famous "frontier" thesis, elevated the pioneer life at the boundary of the Wild West into America's fountain of youth, Craven made the misery of the depleted hinterland the driving force behind expansion: the great westward migration as flight from an ecological crisis! At times his arguments are based more on ideal types than empirical facts: "Frontier communities," he argued, "are, by their very nature, notorious exhausters of their soils." At the frontier there was no husbandry aimed at the long run; and this frontier mentality persisted even when the frontier had moved farther west, just as it also generated the insatiable land hunger that constantly exerted pressure on the frontier.

Craven's thesis is undoubtedly most applicable to regions and periods with a continuous cultivation of tobacco, maize, and cotton. However, a precise empirical verification of the thesis is difficult, especially since "soil exhaustion" – as Craven himself admitted – is not an exact concept. To be sure, one must distinguish various regions: the intensive agriculture of the East was a different world from the farms of the Midwest. Craven's thesis, however, was not merely a retrospective construction, but was based on a wealth of contemporary testimonials. One memorandum from the Society of Virginia for Promoting Agriculture (1818) noted: "Our woods have disappeared, and are succeeded, too generally, by exhausted fields and gullied hills."[59]

In America's early years, when the road to the West was not yet open, the settlers of necessity adopted many practices of Indian agriculture: "Abandoning most European agricultural practices, planters adopted girdling and slash-and-burn clearing, long fallows, and hoe culture from Native Americans, as well as embracing maize and tobacco." European agriculture did not establish itself as easily in the New World as one might have expected from the Crosby thesis; nature was by no means on the side of the Yankees in every regard.[60] Even the constant move to and clearance of new land corresponded essentially to the sort of shifting cultivation the settlers encountered among the Iroquois. This kind of agriculture without animal fertilizer is not necessarily ecologically ruinous, at least not as long as settlement is sparse and land abundant.

From the perspective of European peasants, American farmers were already extremely market-oriented in the nineteenth century. In Johannes Gillhoff's novel *Jürnjakob Swehn der Amerikafahrer* (1917), which is based on letters of German emigrants, the son of a German peasant who emigrates to the United States from Mecklenburg recounts how on his farm, depending on rapidly changing market conditions, he would feed eggs to the piglets, the piglets to the chickens, the eggs to the calves, and the calves to the pigs, while his wife was horrified at this "round-trip from one end of the farm to the other"; "It's against God's order for chickens to eat pigs."[61] Of course, this was a caricature. Large segments of American agriculture were dominated for a long time by a subsistence economy, not different from Europe's, especially in those regions where urban markets were far away. One constant complaint from farmers were the steep railroad rates, whereas the bond that tied German peasants to the market was promoted by railway rates kept low by the state. As long as farmers were left to their own devices, their economic practices invariably contained an element of ecological self-regulation.

Things began to change when this partly seminomadic economy was combined with a capitalist pursuit of profit, a market orientation, monocultures, and population pressure. This created a synergy between the ecologically fragile elements of agriculture and the American dynamic of expansion. Later, in the era of commercial fertilizer, the entire problem was redefined from an ecological to an economic one: the issue was no longer the restoration of the natural fertility, but the creation of the fertility needed for specific crops, and that was a question of money and artificial fertilizer.

Of course, the farmers were not crazy and tried, in their way, to counteract the exhaustion of their soils. Precisely because the decline of the land was in many cases not insidious and imperceptible, but occurred at a frightening pace, it provoked responses, all the more so in an active population much given to experimentation and not inclined to accept impoverishment fatalistically. The option of switching to virginal soil was by no means open to everyone. And especially in the early nineteenth century, there were heated public debates whether it was wiser to go west or to restore the fertility of the depleted soil.[62]

If the United States as a whole was seen as a land of inexhaustible resources, that does not mean, of course, that every individual farmer lived with the consciousness of having inexhaustible resources. Agrarian magazines in the United States eagerly disseminated the teachings of the English agrarian reformers on how to increase soil fertility through better fertilization and crop rotation. In fact, one gets the sense that especially in American agriculture, because it had less tacit knowledge and fewer self-evident customs than Europe when it came to fertilization, public discussions of optimal fertilization were all the more lively, especially since fertilizer became a commercial object earlier than it did in most parts of Europe; indeed, it turned into big business with competing products. The more the commercial spirit penetrated into agriculture, the more intensive became the efforts to boost yields, as a consequence of which the demand for fertilizer also increased. In the environs of the large cities along the East Coast there was for a time a flourishing business with the processing of urban waste into fertilizer. But in the end this large-scale commercialization of the fertilizer economy opened the way for chemical fertilizers, especially since the recycling of urban wastes was limited in its profitability. Today recycling and chemical fertilization present themselves as alternatives; historically, however, there was a fluid transition from one to the other.[63]

Since the advantages of a fertilizer depended critically on the cost of transporting it, the recycling systems of the nineteenth century seem to have been important to agriculture only in proximity to the East Coast, but not in the West and the South. Instead, sewage farms, where urban waste was directly diverted onto the fields, were set up in the nineteenth century in a number of Western cities, but only there.[64]

The dynamic cycle of soil exhaustion and expansion entered an especially critical phase when the settlers crossed the Appalachian Mountains and the Mississippi and penetrated into the ecologically fragile landscape of the Great Plains. It was only then that the immense vastness of the West opened up to them – but behind that there was no more expanses that one could settle after the previously occupied land had been used up.

Initially it was not the farmers but the ranchers who spread all over the Great Plains with their rapidly growing herds, and they experienced their ecological disaster in fairly short order once the expansion had reached its natural limits. The cowboy mentality and the atmosphere of violence that characterized the West in those days had no room for concern over sustainability. Animal husbandry was already experiencing a serious collapse as a result of ruthless overgrazing in the 1880s – only a decade or two after the conquest of the Great Plains by the cowboys. After a succession of cold winters, the land was covered with the corpses of thousands of starved and frozen cattle. Since overgrazing led to the spread of flora the cattle disdained, the destruction of the grazing land was in part irreversible, at least for an extended period of time.

It was possible to blame the disaster on a deficit of property rights and to explain the lack of foresight by noting that many ranchers had no formal rights to their grazing land. Such an explanation was in keeping with the traditional American ideology, which expects all good things to come from individual freedom and private property. Nevertheless, it became clear that in spite of the heroic sheriffs and vigilantes of Western mythology, self-regulation in the West was functioning poorly. Added to this was the growing realization that, in large sections of the West, agriculture was impossible without large-scale artificial irrigation. Years of abundant rainfall had for a time conveyed a deceptive picture of the agrarian possibilities of the West, a picture that was destroyed in years of drought. On their own, at least away from the rivers, it was mostly large landowners with plenty of capital who could construct irrigation systems; the American ideal of an abundance of medium-size farms required the intervention of the state.

As early as 1878, the geographer John Wesley Powell (1834–1902), in his famous *Report on the Lands of the Arid Regions of the United States*, called for an irrigation-based common economy for the arid regions of the West, in the tradition of the old European commons and under state supervision. Although he became the head of the U.S. Geological Survey in 1881, which made him "perhaps the most powerful bureaucrat in Washington," he was unable to get anywhere with his demands, which ran counter to the liberal spirit of the times. But his opponents, who advocated the privatization of all of the federal lands, were equally unsuccessful. The need for artificial irrigation upset liberal ideology. In times of drought it was the farmers and ranchers themselves who called for the state to help. As Richard White has noted: "The dependence on the federal government has been the central reality of western politics." The notion that the Great Plains were a public good that required state oversight carried the day completely under the New Deal. In 1934 Congress established the National Grazing Service in an effort to prevent overgrazing and the destruction of the soil.[65]

An even more serious crisis was created that same year as a result of the transformation of the Great Plains into an agricultural region: 1934 saw the beginning of the Dust Bowl. The streams of outmigrants called "Okies" or "Exodusters" – farmers who had lost their land – have become a fixture in American literature and films. The Dust Bowl was a traumatic experience that deeply influenced an era of American environmental awareness. Although the issue of erosion was later overshadowed by discussion of other environmental problems, the Dust Bowl stimulated erosion research around the world during the 1930s. "Soil Conservation" became a political task of the highest order under the New Deal. The Tennessee Valley Authority (TVA), the most famous of the New Deal agencies, which developed a special esprit de corps and missionary zeal, not only built dams and power plants, but also propagated the construction of agricultural terraces with an enthusiasm reminiscent of China. *Fortune* magazine declared at the time that the Dust Bowl catastrophe was the culmination "of the whole tragic history of American agriculture, dating from the earliest misuse of the soil." It is evident how a new vision of history emerged from the Dust Bowl, one that clashed with the traditional picture of progress. In Nazi Germany, as well, the notion gained ground at that time that, for thousands of years, the presumed progress had come at the price of the advancing desert.[66]

When the grain regions of the Midwest later, in wetter years and with the use of artificial irrigation, once again produced rich harvests – though only with the growing application of chemical fertilizer – it seemed there was reason to be hopeful that the Dust Bowl had not irreversibly destroyed the fertility of the soil. Were the "Exodusters" in fact the victims of an ecological crisis, or of an economic and social catastrophe? John Steinbeck, whose *Grapes of Wrath* is the classic novel about the Dust Bowl refugees, turned precisely the small and medium farmers who were displaced from their land into good, soil-conscious farmers who could save themselves and America through solidarity, while he assigned the blame for the misery to the great agro-capitalists and the banks allied with them. Many others believed, however, that the Dust Bowl victims were responsible for their own misfortune. Henry L. Mencken, who had the Pennsylvania Dutch in mind as the model of solid farming communities, disparaged the Exodusters as "bogus farmers" who, after they had plundered the soil, wanted to plunder the taxpayer as well.[67]

As we can see, the Dust Bowl is not one story, but a whole series of possible stories: one can interpret the Dust Bowl as punishment for the cardinal sin of the Yankee economy, the obsession with short-term profit, or as punishment for a failure to keep pace with modernization. For parts of the Great Plains the recommendation could be irrigation projects, for other regions the return to a pasture economy – now under government oversight; but some questioned whether it made any sense at all to turn the Dust Bowl, in the spirit of the New Deal, into the justification for wide-ranging state interventionism. The agrarian historian James C. Malin – the very rare case of a historian who influenced ecological theory – sought to demonstrate in detail that dust storms in the plains were entirely normal natural events that had occurred for ages, and that merely shifted the soil, and did not destroy it. He complained that this kind of understanding was being impeded because "public attention is being bombarded by propaganda to authorize gigantic programs dealing with natural resources." He and others argued that invoking a presumed natural, ecological optimum of the Great Plains made no sense, since its original state had long since been altered by the fire-burning cultivation of the

Native Americans. Hence there was no fundamental reason why the whites should not use the plains for their needs like the Indians had done before them.[68]

But this deflection of an ecological fundamentalism did not mean in any way that the economic methods in the American West promised lasting success. From our perspective today, the technocratic New Deal optimism, with its pride in dams, also led the emerging environmental awareness astray on numerous occasions. The New Deal offers a prime example that precisely the attempt at large technological solutions to environmental problems creates new problems. More recently there has been a growing perception that the greatest environmental dilemma of the West is not drought and dust storms, but the large projects that were conjured up to prevent those things from happening: the large artificial lakes and irrigation works, which are economically as well as ecologically highly dubious and threaten to exhaust the groundwater resources. Once, in the nineteenth century, the large railroad companies and their supporters in the publishing industry had conducted a virtual propaganda campaign against the notion – widely held until then – that the treeless expanses of the West were a desert. They were nothing of the sort; they were in fact the granaries of the future and the future heartland of the nation. Today, by contrast, there is a serious discussion over whether it might not be better to accept this landscape as a desert. According to one calculation, irrigation in hot desert regions, because of the extremely high evaporation rate, requires ten thousand times as much water as wet regions![69]

A counterexample to the pure soil exploiters were sects like the Amish and the Hutterites, who clung to the agrarian traditions of the Old World for religious reasons (and thus suddenly became fashionable in the environmental age), and groups of German immigrants who preserved the principles of Central European farming under American conditions (in very diverse regions from Pennsylvania to Texas), complete with its sedentary mentality. They paid attention to good fertilization and crop rotation as well as a careful treatment of the forest, and even maintained German wood-saving practices in wood-rich America. American agrarian teachers, too, had the European ideal of a balance of field, forest, and pasture in mind. The pride of the American farmer, however, was and remained the fence, not the dung heap.[70] And, unlike old European farmhouses, typical American farmhouses are not built to last for generations.

But a metaphysically transfigured nature romanticism is found in American culture no less so than in the Old World. The American passion for wilderness, however, often bypassed efforts aimed at sustainable husbandry. The enthusiasm for (seemingly) untouched wilderness took little interest in the reforestation of logged woodlands or the regulation of logging. Henry David Thoreau, the hermit and forest dweller, was a preacher of unrestrained individualism, not of regulation. In the United States, forest romanticism and forest cutting on a large scale existed side by side, much like the romanticization and genocide of the Native Americans. Tocqueville believed the romantic effect of the American forests stemmed from the knowledge that they would soon fall to the axe.[71]

Over the long term, nature romanticism was not without effect. The national parks movement, which spread from the United States to the rest of the world, is the practical consequence of the glorification of the wilderness. In many instances, however, it amounts to the colonial type of conservation enforced by the metropolises against the wishes of the locals. Not only the Yankee economy, the American type of environmental awareness also follows in many respects in the footsteps of colonial traditions.

In *Russia*, where land existed in similar abundance to North America, and the *mushik*, the serf, had little interest in land cultivation to begin with, we find a treatment of the soil that was in many respects comparable (partly archaic, partly colonial): across wide – especially newly settled – regions, fertilization and crop rotation were neglected into the twentieth century. Once the soil was exhausted, it was abandoned and new land was brought under the plow. With the exception of sheep rearing, animal husbandry was generally little developed. V. O. Kluchevsky, once the dean of Russian historiography, spoke of "the old Russian peasants' unique talent for ravaging the land." The British historian Harry Willetts noted that where land was abundant, the Russian peasants left one part fallow and worked the other part "until it was completely exhausted"; in times of rapid population growth and an increasing scarcity of land, this habit amounted to "suicide." Max Weber, who during the Russian Revolution of 1905, influenced by the loudly articulated "land hunger" of the peasants, studied Russian agrarian conditions in detail, noted that in the regions of land shortage there was found "extensive fallow and yet soil exhaustion" as a result of "entirely inadequate fertilization."

Or was the fallow period – which often lasted ten years or more – enough to regenerate the fertility of the soil? If the general sluggishness of conditions was scandalous from a modern economic perspective, it was not necessarily ecologically ruinous. What is clear, however, is the serious ecological damage that was wrought by the clearance of the steppe belt in southern Russia since the seventeenth century. At that time it was newly conquered territory, and the Russian treatment of the new, enormous agricultural resources has colonial traits. Extensive regions that were once fertile have now lost their value to agriculture through erosion. In the especially fertile region of *chernozem* soil, the land was – with rare exceptions – never fertilized; instead, animal dung served as fuel, as it did in India and Central Asia. The practice of slash-and-burn cultivation was particularly excessive and uncontrolled in Siberia.[72] In its own way, the Russian Empire – much like North America – passed on basic patterns of nonsustainability. In spite of their pioneering work in soil research, the two superpowers of the twentieth century lacked a tradition of practical soil awareness.

Russian environmental history is still largely unexplored. This is paradoxical, since Russian science was a global leader in soil research far into the Soviet period, indeed, it was virtually the "birthplace of modern soil study" and a center of erosion research. Soil research led early on into soil history: for example, there were long controversies in the nineteenth and early twentieth centuries over whether the steppes of southern Russia had originally been forested or not. This was a question of immediate practical significance, especially in the face of poor harvests and famines, since it revolved simultaneously around the issue of whether reforestation projects in the steppe made sense or not. At the beginning stood the thesis of an original forest cover that was propounded by the orthodox clergyman, Slavophile, and amateur scientist Ivan Palimpsestov (1846–1901). This was opposed by Vasily Dokuchaev (1846–1903), the founder of modern Russian soil science. It is ironic that later paleobotanical studies have proven the amateur Palimpsestov right, to a certain extent. But Dokuchaev, too, advocated protective strips of forest in the steppe. Others claimed, however, that the forest was destroying the valuable *chernozem* soil. Soil research often did not provide clear signals to the politicians. Moreover, accurate insights into soil protection were useless if the Soviet government, by eliminating the kulaks, was destroying the most active segment of the peasantry, potential pioneers of soil conservation.

In 1936, at the time of the Dust Bowl, the Soviet government called for the first pan-Soviet conference in Moscow to fight soil erosion. Douglas Weiner, the historian of Soviet environmental protection, has characterized Stalin as "forest-obsessed," and on his orders a gigantic project was launched to establish protective forests in the steppe of southern Russia. But a sustainable forestry has been the exception in Russia to this day; moreover, the many regions in the south have remained susceptible to erosion, in fact they have been made even more vulnerable by the expansion of agriculture.

The colonial-style treatment of the environment reached its high point in the Khrushchev era with the monomaniacal fixation on maize and the gigantic project of opening up wide areas of Central Asia to cotton cultivation through irrigation. Khrushchev had much more of a relationship to agriculture than Stalin, and in all likelihood it was especially disastrous that he considered himself an expert on agriculture. The rise and fall of Khrushchev was based on good fortune and bad luck in an ecological gamble, which was initially favored by years of abundant rainfall. But time and again, soil degradation became the number one environmental problem of the Soviet Union, even after Chernobyl.

Similar to the American West, irrigation was long considered the best soil protection. The plan to redirect large rivers from Siberia to the south for this purpose and to save the Aral Sea – a project with immense and incalculable ecological consequences – is the extreme of an environmental policy that is creating environmental problems of an entirely new dimension.[73] Not infrequently there arose an unholy alliance between environmental protection and a mania for planning. In history, an understanding of nature and its manipulation often lie cheek to jowl.

6. THE QUESTION OF EUROPEAN EXCEPTIONALISM IN ENVIRONMENTAL HISTORY: THE EFFECT OF COLONIALISM ON THE COLONIAL POWERS

Historians have puzzled over the premodern roots of Europe's superiority in modern times, without arriving at universally accepted answers. At first, scholars looked for an early head start in economic life and science, in industry and technology. But in many of these areas, China was far ahead until the early modern period. Max Weber and his successors, all the way to Lynn White, the founding father of American environmental history, believed they had found in religion the source of a striking contrast between Western culture and the rest of the world. As I have already shown, however, this view, too, does not stand up to closer scrutiny.

During the Cold War, when, under the leadership of the United States, the ideology of the "free world" was the reigning doctrine, observers used to see in freedom – both political and spiritual – the special quality of the West. But the tradition of freedom as we understand it today does not reach back very far historically. A more recent trend looks for Europe's uniqueness more in the area of social ties, of institutions and legal systems. Here we are on more solid ground. Under the polycratic conditions that prevailed in Europe, the law became more so than elsewhere an autonomous power, one that was – at least to a certain extent – independent of political power. The law of private property and inheritance has premodern roots that reach back into classical antiquity. But durable usage rights existed also in non-Western civilizations – if not de jure, at least de facto. What matters for the human interaction with the environment is not only written law, but also informal institutions, unwritten law, and collective patterns of behavior established by long-standing custom.

Environmental history casts a new light on many things. Ethnologists like Marvin Harris and Jared Diamond, similar to Alfred Crosby and Eric L. Jones, have pointed to a very crucial natural advantage that Eurasia had over America, Africa, and Australia: the diversity of domesticable plants and, especially, animals.[74] It was not indolence that deprived the others of this advantage, for the vast majority of animals cannot be domesticated in a way that is useful to humankind. Long before the industrial age, its large mass of domesticated animals gave Europe a lead over the cultures of ancient America – and to a certain extent over China and India – in putting energy and calories to work for its own benefit. Europe's relative abundance of forest almost meant a relative wealth of pastureland. That, however, did not automatically bestow an ecological advantage. The heavy plow pulled by oxen is harder on the soil than agriculture done with hoe and spade, and pasture animals can damage the forest and the vegetation cover. Moreover, when it comes to useful plants, Asia was initially ahead of the West.

Still, it is not difficult to explain why Europe, over time, acquired a growing lead over the Near East, where agriculture originated. The ecology of large parts of Europe is much more robust than that of the Near East. The dangers of soil exhaustion, erosion, desertification, and salinization are all incomparably less in Europe. Where rainfall is distributed across the entire year, there is no need for the kind of fragile irrigation systems that plunged Near Eastern agriculture into crisis precisely at the height of its development. Europe's abundance of streams and rivers that carry water all year round already made possible in medieval times a much denser diffusion of the water mill than in almost any other region of the world. Looking back we can see that this was of the utmost importance, for the waterwheel was the most important historical source of mechanization. Mill ponds became a characteristic element of the European landscape, one that counteracted an excessive desiccation of the soil through the drainage practiced by the peasants.

Importance attaches to yet another factor in which natural and social conditions interacted: over large parts of Europe, an ecologically advantageous combination of agriculture and animal husbandry developed far better than in many non-European regions. Wherever we find the nomadic lifestyle, there is a social watershed between field and pasture. It is not the peasants that profit from the successful domestication of the camel, with its myriad benefits. Nomadic incursion often weakened sedentary farming communities. In areas with scanty forest cover, animal dung is needed as fuel. In hot regions, the keeping of dung heaps is presumably also impeded by fear of disease. Where the soil does not tolerate the heavy plow, farmers lack the chief impulse behind the keeping of large animals. And another point is important: the pastoral element of European agriculture ensured – far more so than the intensive rice cultivation of East Asia – the continued existence of extensive ecological reserves. On the other hand, one must not imagine the balance between field, forest, and pasture as too perfect even in European history. But over the course of the modern period that balance was improved – until the technological revolution in agriculture overturned this tradition in the twentieth century.

The combination of agriculture and pasture is a question not only of the natural, but also of the social and legal frameworks, of formal and informal institutions, from three-field rotation to feudal dues. This brings us to the question of whether European exceptionalism in the interaction with the environment exists also on an institutional level. There is, in fact, a good deal of evidence that the answer is yes. The fundamental condition of European history is evident also here, namely, the much vaunted "unity in diversity": a multitude of sources of power and law, an increasingly broad and dense network of communication, and the desire, above all feuds and wars, to make conflict resolution a legal process. Max Weber's thesis holds true to this day: "Only the occident knows rational law, made by jurists and rationally interpreted and applied."

To be sure, one must not overlook the fact that across broad stretches of time, the history of the struggle over law is a painful one, the history of a much pointless escalation and waste of human energy and time. It always saved a lot of effort if the treatment of resources could be regulated without legal conflict. Moreover, the European legal traditions were not ecologically advantageous in every respect. From an African perspective, the criticism is heard today that the high respect for "property rights" that is enshrined in the European, and especially the English, legal tradition protects individual liberties far better against the state than it does public goods against private encroachments.[75] Wherever environmental protection does not overlap completely with the preservation – driven by private interests – of the small environments of individual households, but requires also the protection of public goods against private selfishness, the excessive protection of private freedom of action has a deleterious effect.

But Europe developed a lead over many other regions of the world also when it came to the creation of supralocal, territorial, and national institutions and loyalties. A comparative constitutional history of Europe begins with the terse statement "Europe invented the state."[76] The process by which the law pervaded all aspects of life in Europe affected not only the private but also the public sphere. Whether it was the *salus publica* in ancient Rome, the *bonum commune* in medieval scholasticism, or the *gemeine Beste* ("common good") of Germanic law: the protection of public goods had a long tradition in European legal thought, even if the precise definition of the "public interest" has proved an extraordinarily difficult challenge. Yet the fact that the public interest was never fixed once and for all, but always remained the subject of negotiation, was not necessarily a disadvantage.

The poorly developed right of private property in many regions of the world did not promote environmental protection, either. With regard to the way in which the Syrians deal with agrarian and environmental problems, one scholar has observed that those "tasks which a single person or family can manage on their own," like caring for a grove of trees or sinking a well, are "for the most part done extremely well. . . . Organized community actions, on the other hand, usually do not get a friendly reception from the Syrian." Much the same holds true for a good many regions of he world. The individualistic legal thinking in Nepal is so extreme that when an inheritance is divided up, valuable carved wooden windows are sometimes sawed into pieces to satisfy the various heirs. The popular notion that individualism is a typically modern and Western phenomenon and that the typical non-Western person thinks of himself as one link in a large community is evidently wrong. As late as the 1930s, Lin Yutang noted in the case of the Chinese, with their continuous tradition of the state stretching back thousands of years, that their loyalty belonged de facto exclusively to the family and reached its limit at the boundary of the neighborhood. The Chinese kept his own house clean, but he swept his garbage to the front of this neighbor's house.[77]

In early modern Europe, as well, loyalty to the state was initially an ideal more than a reality; it succeeded in asserting itself effectively only in the wake of nationalism and the growth of bureaucracy. This process, as well, is not in and of itself an advantage for the environment. Even in modern times, environmental problems were very often solved best on the local level; what higher authorities did was frequently no more than symbolic problem solving. "A well-organized village community was often better able to preserve and maintain its forest to meet its needs than was a capital-weak lordship with large needs and too little territory." But such village-based regulatory traditions did, in fact, exist in many European regions; the diffusion of law occurred on several levels, oral as well as written. In any case, Europe was on the whole better equipped than most other parts of the world to deal with situations in which the solution to environmental problems called for authorities and loyalties outside of the house.[78]

The history of the forest offers the best example for what I have been talking about. The fact that precolonial sources from the vast majority of non-European regions are silent about forest damage is revealing. It shows the absence of authorities that legitimated themselves by punishing transgressions against the woodlands. The link between forest and power appears to be largely a phenomenon of Central and Western Europe, and a global survey provides striking confirmation of this. It is here that one finds, more prominently than almost anywhere else, a European (or at least Central and Western European) exceptionalism. To be sure, one must not exaggerate the ecological achievement of the linkage of forest and power. In not a few cases it was precisely the authorities that claimed to be protecting the forest that were by far the largest consumer of wood. But it was not the authorities alone who benefited from the juridification of forest usages; other forest users were able to ward off encroachments from higher up. And that, precisely, is the crucial point: various users were able to struggle over forest rights by legal means. The back and forth of charges and countercharges gave rise to a keener perception of what was happening in the woodlands, and the forest awareness to which this gave rise had practical consequences. One can trace this process vividly in the increasing precision of the forest maps that were originally created for the most part in connection with legal quarrels.

In some respects it was presumably the Chinese who, for many centuries, developed the art of a nearly sustainable agriculture to its highest level; but that was not the case for forest protection and for the combination of agriculture and animal husbandry. Moreover, it would appear that the European regions had another advantage over East Asia and other densely populated riverine civilizations on a more informal and hidden level of self-regulation, one that had great significance for the ecological balance: the limitation of population growth through late marriage and constraints on marriage following the medieval dictum "no land – no marriage," through discrimination against illegitimate children, through contraceptive sexual practices, and probably also through clandestine infanticide, especially of baby girls. In the seventeenth century we encounter for the first time the "West European pattern of late marriage and a relatively high ratio of unmarried"; in the eighteenth century, France, at the time Europe's leading power, became the classic land of contraception. The limitation on the number of children was no longer merely a reaction to oppressive misery, but increasingly also a concern to secure the standard of living. Malthus had such an enormous impact because he articulated anxieties that had been worrying many people for a long time, even if they were politically incorrect at a time when the absolutist states were advocating a policy of population growth. To what extent Europe had a lead over the Islamic world when it came to methods of birth control is not clear; scholars note that the erotic literature in the Islamic world handed down contraceptive practices. Moreover, in the hot, humid, and densely settled regions of the world, epidemics kept population growth contained in the premodern period. Under such conditions, it was not necessary to establish informal traditions of birth control.[79]

Beginning in the eighteenth century, the overseas territories acquired by the colonial powers offered a safety valve for the population pressure at home – earliest of all in England, which, more so than its colonial rivals, possessed not only trading colonies but also settlement colonies. Here, and in other areas, the question arises what feedback effects colonialism had on the colonial countries. Was the traditional awareness of the tight limits to growth weakened? Or was the environmental awareness described by Grove, which developed in certain circles of the colonial administration, important also back at home? I will look first at Spain, Europe's first colonial power, and then at England, the leading power of the late imperialist phase.

In *Spain* transhumance experienced an enormous boost in the immediate aftermath of colonial expansion; at that time it was unfettered and freed from all previous restrictions. Colonialism caused Spanish economic policy to become export rather than subsistence oriented, to such an extent that it undermined the basis of Spanish subsistence. Export of the much sought-after merino wool brought the greatest profit to the crown: as a result, the Mesta, the syndicate of owners of sheep herds first chartered in 1273, was henceforth systematically favored by the kings at the expense of agriculture. Like the nobility, breeders of merino sheep paid attention to "purity of blood." "The local communities fenced in their fields in vain. The wandering herds of sheep were accompanied by judges who, by virtue of the Mesta privileges, decided disagreements in favor of the transhumance."[80]

In the sixteenth century, the privileges of the Mesta were already encountering opposition from the Cortes, the Spanish estates. In the eighteenth century it drew criticism from the physiocrats, who eventually pushed through the prohibition of the Mesta. Since that time, the Mesta has been seen as Spain's curse, a "monstrous usurpation" and the "greatest scourge to which agriculture has ever been subjected anywhere," responsible for the decay of the Spanish economy and the desolation of the landscape. In recent times, the three million sheep that "ravage" Castile every year have also been mentioned as an example of the ecological "suicide" of a region from overgrazing.[81] But is this historical picture of the environment plausible?

For Douglass C. North, the leader of the institutional school of economics, the Mesta is the very embodiment of a disastrous institution – negative confirmation of the doctrine that everything depends on institutions. But that judgment is based on the criteria of economic growth. From an ecological perspective, the assessment is more difficult: in fact, transhumance is almost a perfect exemplar of the problem of value judgments in environmental history. Pastureland is not in itself any worse than fields or forests; when it comes to species diversity and soil protection, it can even have advantages. Many pasture areas are in fact not as barren as they appear from a distance. Seen over the long term, it would not appear as though Spanish transhumance committed ecological suicide: it survived much too long for that, even after the end of the Mesta.

The number of sheep was already in decline in the sixteenth century, one sign that sheepherders were adapting to the carrying capacity of the pastureland. If the Mesta insisted that fallow land be retained undiminished, thereby impeding the intensification of agriculture, it drew condemnation from agrarian reformers, but not necessarily from ecologists. Moreover, it would appear that Spanish transhumance was able to reach a better accommodation with farming interests after the loss of the Mesta privileges, and especially after a majority of the sheep were slaughtered by French troops during the Napoleonic wars.

Today the historian is amazed to see how the preservation of the remaining transhumance regions in Spain is popular not only with environmentalists but also with farmers. Since the 1990s, environmentalists have celebrated transhumance as the "great treck for nature" and "most environmentally compatible form of animal husbandry," and they are discovering the *caminadas*, the old transhumance routes, as a connected biotope. Farmers, meanwhile, prepare a festive reception for a herd of sheep that has set out again along an ancient route! By contrast, at the height of Spanish colonialism, when the power of the Mesta also reached its zenith, the pasture economy surely altered the landscape to the disadvantage of the peasants.[82]

If Spanish environmental history – from the reconquista on, at the latest – is today often seen as a tragedy, even though Spanish vegetation with its biodiversity ranks first in Europe, one chief reason for this is the deforestation of large areas of the land. It is said that in the old days, in the Middle Ages or even earlier, the Iberian peninsula was largely covered with woodlands; today large stretches of the interior strike a traveler coming from the North as almost desertlike. The notion that this represents an all but unique historical environmental disaster forces itself on the observer, and with it the suspicion that Spanish colonialism, which led to the neglect of the Spanish economy, also entailed the neglect of the environment. And in fact, Ferdinand and Isabelle confirmed the privilege of the Mesta to cut "smaller trees" for use as animal fodder. In the nineteenth century, the time of the great reforestation movement, the Spaniards were considered the worst enemies of woodlands. The director of the Tharandt Forestry School, Carl von Berg, detected especially in Castile a "hatred of trees inherent in the people" that was the product of a narrow-minded interest in pasturing and agriculture, and that allowed a "terrible chewing-up of the forests" from thousands of goats. George P. Marsh found the "Spaniard's proverbial hatred of trees" attested as early as the sixteenth century, and he believed that Spain was the only European country that practiced neither forest protection nor reforestation, and instead carried out "a systematic war against the Garden of Eden."[83]

The destruction of many forests was clearly not intentional on the part of the higher authorities. Royal forest protection ordinances are found in Spanish history. As in Central Europe, they began in the fourteenth century and reached a first highpoint in the sixteenth century under Charles V and Philip II. Henry Kamen, the biographer of Philip, has even styled this Spanish monarch, a lover of hunting woods and Flemish gardens, "as one of the first ecological rulers."[84] Still, it would appear that even at the height of Spanish royal power, forest policy had little practical effect.

It was probably not only the power of the Mesta but colonialism as well that weakened the appreciation for the value of domestic wood resources in Spain. Beginning in the sixteenth century, Spain procured shipbuilding timber from Central America, especially Cuba. Not until 1748, when Spanish naval power was lost beyond recovery, was an "Ordinance for the Protection and Promotion of Naval Forests" passed, with detailed stipulations about afforestation; it met with resistance in parts of Castile. The nineteenth century saw a reforestation policy on the German model; but precisely at that time, the liberalization of forestry led to what was presumably the greatest wave of deforestation in Spain's modern history.[85]

The history of Spanish forestry in modern times is not merely one of decline. With the victory in the *reconquista*, the pig, despised in Islamic culture, returned to many Spanish regions; here, as elsewhere, the pasturing of pigs was the strongest impulse behind the cultivation of oak groves. Another motivation on the Iberian Peninsula was the harvesting of cork from the cork oak. These open oak groves (*dehesas*) are a different world from the sheep pastures, for here we find no trace of a Spanish hostility against trees. It is here that ecologists have recorded the greatest species diversity in Western Europe. Moreover, when foresters drew up their reports on the state of the woodlands, they tended to overlook the *matorral*, the maquis-like Spanish brush forest. By the criteria of forestry, it is not a forest, but ecologists today appreciate it more than many newly forested woods. In 1985 Spanish environmentalists chained themselves to excavators that were supposed to dig up land grown with *mattoral* to prepare it for afforestation.[86]

Today, a special forest awareness is often attributed to the Germanic regions of Europe. It is all the more striking that in Northwestern Europe it was precisely the Netherlands and England, the two colonial powers, that paid the least heed to forest protection from the early modern period, when efforts at forest protection intensified in Central Europe. Holland, by its very name a "land of wood," became a land impoverished in woodlands; instead, wood trade with the Dutch became the greatest timber business in Germany in the eighteenth century. The colonial powers had the wherewithal to import wood from Central Europe, Scandinavia, the Baltics, and from overseas. Custom registers reveal that the volume of lumber transported westward through the Danish Straits increased eighty-fold between the sixteenth and the eighteenth centuries. Denmark too, as long as it controlled Norway (until 1814), was able to import its wood from there: as a result

Denmark became a forest-poor land exposed to wind erosion. The agronomist J. D. W. Westenholz complained in 1772: "Everything is being exterminated in Denmark that stands in the way of the plough, all forests, bushes, undergrowth, all streams, rivers and bogs." Thorkild Kjaergaard, who has identified an "ecological revolution" at that time in Denmark, remarked sarcastically: "Oak timbers were seen in Jutland only when there had been a shipwreck."[87]

In *England* John Evelyn wrote the most famous appeal for afforestation in the seventeenth century with *Sylva* (1664), which was quoted and plagiarized for more than a century; still, on the British island, "plantations were mainly a gentleman's hobby rather than a serious business." Beginning in the eighteenth century, English poets and landscape painters glorified the forest no less so than German romantics, but this pleasure in woodlands benefited the parks more than the great forests. However, the coppice forest, which was used to provide firewood, seems to have still been widespread in England in the eighteenth century. Inherent sustainability is ensured in the coppice by a type of woodcutting that leaves behind a stool capable of resprouting. It was only pit coal that removed the incentive behind the preservation of the coppice.[88]

Among the ecological reverberations of colonialism we must also reckon the importation of guano from Peru that began in England around 1840. The discovery of guano, which the Incas had used as a fertilizer, had been a side effect of Alexander von Humboldt's travels in Latin America around 1800, a discovery he himself ignored. In the 1840s, however, as the demand for fertilizer grew, a veritable "guano mania" spread from England, which, by commercializing fertilizer, prepared the subsequent rise of chemical fertilizer. Some reckoned guano as thirty times more effective than farmyard manure. Henceforth it no longer seemed so important in agriculture to pay attention to a balance of field and pasture, since a deficit in fertilizers, that is, a lack of inherent sustainability, could now be remedied with guano. This opened the door to the triumphant advance of the water closet, which robbed agriculture of human excrement.

The miraculous effect of guano on the fields lasted for only a limited time, however. Moreover, guano was a resource that regenerated itself at a vastly slower pace than that at which it was being harvested at the time. In the beginning, people did not worry about it very much. Joseph Victor von Scheffel, the most popular composer of German student songs, in whose Swabian homeland guano was being eagerly spread onto the fields, composed his "Guano song" in 1854 to the melody of Heine's "Lorelei." The last verse says about the guano birds: "Sie sehen im rosigsten Lichte / die Zukunft und sprechen in Ruh: / Wir bauen im Lauf der Geschichte / noch den ganzen Ozean zu" (The future they see in the rosiest light, and calmly they speak: in the course of history we shall fill the entire ocean). His contemporary Liebig saw the matter very differently. In his eyes, British agriculture was now the pinnacle of destructive agrarian exploitation, and guano covered up the ecological crisis that had long since begun. Peru, whose state budget in the period of the guano mania depended entirely on guano exports, had to look around for a replacement for guano as early as the 1870s. At the time it believed it had found it in the nitrates of the Tarapacá Desert, which are also suitable as fertilizer, but this embroiled it in the unfortunate "Nitrate War" with Chile.[89]

I will now move on to look at "enclosures," the fencing in of once open fields to raise sheep, engage in more intensive agriculture, and free private initiative from any encumbrances. This process began in the sixteenth century and peaked in the second half of the eighteenth. It is at least among the indirect reverberations of colonialism and the greater focus on external trade that it brought about. Beginning around 1750, the enclosures, previously undertaken mostly through private agreements and for a long time opposed by the crown, were promoted by Parliament in such a systematic manner that the English landscape was transformed at a "revolutionary pace." The enormous profits from the wool trade gave sheep raising an enormous boost in England, as it had in Spain. And the social costs of the expanding sheep herds were highly controversial in England, as well; in Thomas Moore's *Utopia* (1516) we already hear the lament that sheep were driving out people. The concept of the "common weal" arose in England as a slogan in opposition to the enclosures. Arthur Young, though in principle a supporter of enclosures who condemned the open fields, remarked nevertheless: "I know of no country where the people are not against enclosures." The ecological effects in England were, however, quite different from those in Spain: under the conditions of the emerging law of private property, the boom in wool did not lead to the expansion of collective pastureland at the expense of agriculture, but, quite the reverse, to a typical combination of sheep raising and agriculture within a limited area and with the landowner's full freedom to do as he pleased.

The English agrarian historian Joan Thirsk believes that in England, more so than anywhere else, the enclosures had brought about a revolution on the mental level: "After enclosure, when everyman could fence his own piece of territory and warn his neighbours off, the discipline of sharing things fairly with one's neighbour was relaxed, and every household became an island to itself. This was the great revolution in men's lives, greater than all the economic changes following enclosure."[90] In examining the ecological consequences of enclosures, one must take this psychological change into account: the decline of the sense of community that was necessarily connected with the old commons, regardless of the fact that there had always been many quarrels over the use of the common resources.

Enclosures certainly did not cause sheep to displace humans everywhere. It happened most radically in the Scottish highlands, where the natural conditions offered the landowners a strong incentive to raise sheep, while agriculture hardly got beyond the subsistence level. The romanticism of the Scottish highlands, with their treeless expanse and solitude, which nature lovers are today defending against afforestation, was created after 1750 through "highland clearances." The Scottish highlands had just recently been settled as densely as never before on the basis of the cultivation of the potato; now the landowners drove the tenants ruthlessly from house and land en masse, under the progressive slogan of "improvement." Scotland's fate reminds us of that of the Spanish highland regions dominated by the Mesta. Within the administration of the British Empire, it was above all Scotsmen who developed an early environmental awareness, perhaps because their perception had been sharpened by the destruction of the forests in their own country. However, the question of whether – and if so, how – sheep pasture in the Scottish highlands led to degeneration of soil and vegetation is controversial to this day. A development that is socially scandalous is not necessarily ecologically ruinous.

In parts of Scotland, in any case, the "sheep bonanza" was short-lived, at least on its original scale: overgrazing caused the pastures to be overgrown by the kind of vegetation the sheep could not eat. The ecologist need not regret this as much as the sheep did.[91]

The erstwhile "common fields," with their compulsory tillage and a wide pasture radius, were presumably not as bad at preserving the fertility of the soil as agrarian reformers claimed. Still, one can assume that enclosures, on the whole, improved the ecological balance. It was easier to collect the valuable sheep dung on the enclosed land, and the hedges, which became more than ever a characteristic element of the English landscape, delight nature lovers to this day and provided wood. The German encyclopedist Johann Georg Krünitz wrote in 1789 that the English, even though they had cleared nearly all their forests, suffered no shortage of wood, since they surrounded all fields with "living fences and trees." After 1750 deforested Denmark was also covered by a network of hedges on royal orders, and they were later seen as a characteristic element of the Danish landscape. Among German peasants and agrarian reformers, on the other hand, especially where hedges were not needed as wind breaks and wood suppliers, it was always controversial whether hedges served as a shelter to useful or harmful birds and insects.[92]

Some contemporaries already noted that the intensification of agriculture increased the danger of an overuse of the soil in some places, a danger that had been less in the old way focused largely on subsistence rather than growth. Moreover, the commercialization of English agriculture led to an increasing specialization and thus to a division between "arables" and "pasturables." As the German agrarian reformer Albrecht Thaer noted critically, under this arrangement a lot of fertilizer was lost to the "arables." The ecological potential of the enclosures was undermined by the trend toward a compartmentalized agriculture.[93]

A European exceptionalism in forestry in the direction of sustainability is found less in Spain, the Netherlands, and England than in France and most strongly in Central Europe. Germany, in part because it had *no* colonies for the longest time and therefore depended on its domestic wood resources, became the classic land of high forest afforestation. The European advantage of decentralization was more pronounced in particularist Germany than in the older national states. These circumstances allowed the development of a large number of forestry doctrines and practices that were more or less adapted to regional conditions, whereas in France, the attempt toward a centrally directed forestry policy that was begun under Colbert did not have much of a future. Germany did not see the kind of sharp dichotomy between "scientific" forestry and local, practical experience that emerged in many other countries of the world. This explains how it was possible that the forester, who, as the overseer of the territorial rulers, was traditionally held in low esteem by peasants around the world, became the most popular profession among Germans in the nineteenth century.

When all is said and done, the peculiarities of Europe's development contained considerable advantages not only in economic, but also in ecological respects. However, those advantages were to some extent impaired by colonialism, which removed the barriers to resources. But these advantages also contained an inherent danger when combined with Europe's economic dynamism: because they enabled

Europe to cushion economic growth better than other civilizations, they helped to fully unleash this dynamic. Only an agriculture that was ecologically fairly robust could develop the ambitions to boost yields beyond anything that had ever been seen. Only heavy and wet soils, little threatened by erosion, could tolerate deeper and deeper ploughing over long periods of time. Only a region of the world with an abundance of woodlands and a more or less sustainable forestry could place metal smelting onto a growth path that eventually developed pit coal – until then merely a local wood replacement – as a new resource for even stronger growth. Water-rich regions alone could give rise to a type of industrial civilization that entailed a gigantic demand for water, and whose transfer to drier regions of the world drove them into difficult shortages. Only countries with functional local and territorial institutions that were able to at least ameliorate the worst industrial damage to the environment, or remove it from sight, were in a position to push an industrialization that not only did not smother itself in short order, but enjoyed growing popularity. In this way, the environmental limitations of economic growth were not eliminated, but merely postponed and concealed. The feeling of relative security that European institutions were able to create in conjunction with a relatively robust ecology is correspondingly treacherous. Equally treacherous is the allure that the "European model" exerts on the rest of the world. As long as one thinks strictly in economic terms, it is possible to look on Europe as an exemplar that can be generalized at will. From an ecological perspective, however, it becomes clear that much of the European path to success was exceptional and becomes a dead end for other regions of the world.

5

At the Limits of Nature

I. TOWARD THE LAST RESERVES

It would appear that humanity entered into a new era in the eighteenth century in the history not only of ideas but also of the environment. But how are we to define this period in the relationship between humankind and the environment? "Age of Enlightenment," "Industrial Revolution": Do these labels also make sense with respect to the environment? Did the "Industrial Revolution" amount to an "ecological revolution," and if so, what was it?

One definition of what was new at that time has already established itself in environmental history: the shift from a solar to a fossil energy system as the essence of this transformation. In hindsight, this is, in fact, the crux. However, coal was not from the outset the driving force behind industrialization. The steam engine, an energy source fueled by coal, has often been overrated as the motor of the Industrial Revolution, and its suggestive impact has led to a false notion of how the development unfolded. Its applicability was limited to specific sectors of the economy, and its effectiveness was not yet all pervasive. It was only through electrification and the gasoline engine that industrial technology penetrated into every corner of the world.

What stands at the beginning of industrialization is *not* the new energy source; the environmental historian should not reinforce the picture of energy history that led people to place false hope in nuclear energy in the 1950s. Even in England, and more so still in continental Europe, the early phases of industrialization were based largely on wood and on water, on animal and human power – indeed, they were often accompanied by efforts to harness these regenerative resources completely. This, not least, is what imparts to that era its fundamental character. E. A. Wrighley has characterized even England of the Industrial Revolution as an "advanced organic economy" – especially with a view toward agriculture – and has noted that the number of horses in England rose from 1.29 million in 1811 to 3.28 million by 1901.[1]

The origin of the "Industrial Revolution" was described as a great ecological drama long before the "ecological age": a catastrophic shortage of wood resources, first in England and then in other parts of Europe, supposedly forced people to transition to pit coal. Environmental historians, too, ever fascinated by "ecological crises," have adopted this version of history, even though it coincides with the version of their opponents, the advocates of nuclear energy: progress toward more powerful and concentrated energy sources as the crux of history. But as we have seen, the thesis that the preindustrial world came to an end through ecological suicide rests on fragile ground.

Should we assume that the dynamism of capitalism was at the heart of all of this? In part, no doubt, but by itself this explanation is inadequate. As Carville Earle has shown, "capitalism" in no way always meant the same thing to the environment, not even within the same family in the eighteenth century in the Chesapeake Bay.[2] Capitalism as such, namely, the striving by individuals to maximize profit, does not constitute a society or a culture; inherently it is virtually antisocial and it has often enough demonstrated this fundamental character. For capitalism to become part of a system that shapes a geographic space, it needs social and political elements that complement it. Nobody showed this better than Max Weber in his book *The Protestant Ethic and the Spirit of Capitalism*. Throughout history, these complementary elements have been very different in kind, and consequently their effects on the environment have also varied profoundly.

Over many centuries, European capitalism developed even in cities closely allied to feudal structures; rich entrepreneurs typically sought security and peace in landholdings and became indolent on their landed estates. Until the eighteenth century, private capitalists were generally not obsessed with costly technological innovations. For a long time, they were not fond of tying up their capital in expensive factories, preferring to keep their fixed capital as limited as possible. The construction of large manufactures and spectacular machinery was more the style of ambitious territorial rulers who did not draw up detailed cost-benefit analyses. And the ambition to put the entire territory to use also originated with these rulers. The development of the territorial states and their bureaucracies – which made all-encompassing control possible – advanced by leaps and bounds in the eighteenth century, though the state apparatus – even of absolutism – may seem modest by the standards of modern bureaucracies.

Characteristic of the "proto-industrialization" of the eighteenth and early nineteenth centuries was the trend away from the cities, which contrasts sharply with the later agglomerations of high industrialization. This trend corresponded above all to the decentralization of natural resources. As soon as quantitative growth in premodern times crossed certain thresholds, it invariably acquired a decentralized quality, but it was precisely in this way that people reached into the depths of the forest, to the limits of nature. The unfettered advance of proto-industrialization depended on the backing of territorial lords, since many cities sought to suppress rural trades in their environs. The growth of subpeasant classes who could not live off the land alone was promoted by the governments' population policy, which opposed traditional peasant marriage prohibitions, infanticide, smallpox, and discrimination against illegitimate children. Most especially, though, the end of the great plagues initiated a continuous rise in population, slowly at first, then at an accelerating pace in the nineteenth century. It is important to see environmental history time and again in connection with the great epidemics and with fears of disease. The end of the plague pandemics in the eighteenth century was one condition for the optimism of the Enlightenment and for the new quest for sustainability, for an eternity in this life. At the same time, the continual growth of the population forced people to think more intensively than before about sustainable development.

Nature became a challenge in the eighteenth century. In 1773 the English agrarian reformer Arthur Young denounced the "monstrous proportion" of British soil that was wasteland, which he regarded as a "scandal to the national policy." As the forest historian Adam Schwappach has noted, Germany in the eighteenth century still had "enormous stretches of wasteland" that belonged to the territorial lords.[3] Wolves were found in Central Europe until the eighteenth century, and tigers in southern China. Until then, the terrible conditions of travel alone ensured that large segments of the world were left undisturbed and were only marginally touched by the dynamism of transregional trade. All that began to change at that time: again, slowly at first, then at an accelerating pace.

The expansion and growing density of traffic networks imparted an all-pervasive character to economic developments once linked to specific cities and trade routes. Significantly enough, the eighteenth century saw – in part prompted by military interests – the beginning of the era of exact cartography on a large scale. This was an innovation of the greatest importance for the way in which the environment was perceived. Henceforth, the state and the public directed a keen gaze at what had been until then little-noticed marginal areas. Economic and technological processes that were at first separated were now increasingly interrelated and generated synergistic effects. A first highpoint in this process of an all-pervasive interconnectedness – both in reality and in contemporaries' outlook on the future – came with the railroad. Its psychological effect was at least as powerful as its material one: no new technology conveyed to contemporaries the overwhelming feeling of having entered a new era of global history as powerfully as the locomotive did. The railroad created a new horizon for the future, a new style of planning across large expanses. Whether Germany, France, or the United States, many nations were forged into a cohesive entity only by the railroad.

A basic characteristic of that time that was especially significant for environmental history was the universal push to make optimal use of the last reserves of nature. Until the middle of the eighteenth century, authors who wrote about the *Oderbruch* (a large enclosed river polder in the eastern state of Brandenburg) delighted in the abundance of fish in this wetlands area; now Prussian hydraulic engineers suddenly saw in these natural conditions a challenge to dike building. The reclamation of moors, swamps, and river plains was a typical goal of the eighteenth century, from the Oder to the Campagna. Propagandists of moor cultivation spoke enthusiastically of using drainage to turn desolate wasteland into paradise. In some sense the recourse to the last reserves became – if one thinks of China – a global trend at the time. Several global studies date the ecological problems resulting from the systematic reclamation of once empty spaces in the agrarian landscape to the period around 1700.[4]

This urge to exploit the last reserves possesses an epochal character in environmental history. It led to a fundamental shift in strategies of sustainability. Until then, the sustainability of agriculture was in many cases guaranteed not only by fertilizer and fallow, but also by the fact that one could make use, as needed, of semiwild outlying areas: commons, forests, heaths, moors, and swamps. The more these areas receded – and until the twentieth century that was a slow process – the more agriculture became dependent on an inherent, precisely calculated sustainability. Only now was it compelled to clarify exactly what sustainability meant. The peasants were well aware of the threat to their traditional system of sustainability.

Agrarian reformers who advocated making wasteland arable always posed as friends
of the peasants; and yet, as Rita Gudermann has noted, the officials who carried
out the improvement projects always "confronted a determined opposition on the
ground.... As moor and heath, which had always been very important for ame-
liorating grave social hardships especially in times of crisis, were eliminated from
the landscape, their social buffer function also disappeared."[5] With the end of the
age of the commons there began the age of revolution.

As the world became increasingly interconnected, concurrences in environmental history were also on the rise. Maize and the potato, America's most important
agrarian exports, became an epochal innovation in many regions of Eurasia, which
led to an intensive utilization of land previously worked extensively. Both crops
initially served the subsistence economy of small farmers more so than trade.
Sometimes the landlords were the first to point out to their tenants that maize
was exhausting the land. The lopsided cultivation of maize harmed people even
more than it did the soil: among the peasants of Romania, long the leading maize
country of Europe, pellagra, which drove many of those it afflicted into suicide
by damaging their nervous system, became a national disease and one factor that
triggered the Romanian peasant uprising of 1907, the last great peasant rebellion
in European history.

These kinds of health risks were not associated with the potato, even if the
effect of a predominantly potato-based diet on people remained a debated issue.
Around 1800 a controversy erupted between the pessimist Thomas Malthus and
the optimistic agrarian reformer Arthur Young over the potato monoculture of the
Irish peasants: for Young it was the optimal use of the land, for Malthus it entailed
a high risk. The potato in particular aroused the enthusiasm of many friends of
progress in those days: "The potato gives us courage and hope to survive bad years,"
cheered the Transylvanian agrarian reformer Stephan Ludwig Roth; "its gypsy
nature and domicile below the earth promises us help." Unlike grain, it could not
be destroyed by hail. But the great Irish famine, which was triggered by a potato
blight, showed that it harbored other risks instead. In the Pyrenees and the Alps,
and later even in the Himalayas, it promoted population densities that led to the
overuse of forests and pastures.[6]

The heavy plow with the iron moldboard, for Lynn White the source of an
agrarian revolution in the early Middle Ages, does not seem to have become
widely used in Europe until the eighteenth century. It could be one reason why
a wave of erosion can be observed at that time. Soil nutrients that had previously
been beyond reach were now mobilized for agriculture. The summer use of the
fallow in the wake of the agrarian reforms eliminated the wilderness that had been
systemically inherent in the old agriculture; the eighteenth century is a watershed
also for the history of the weed.[7]

One consistent basic trait of this new reach into nature was intensified hydraulic
activities in irrigation, drainage, and canal construction. Prussia sought to open
up new agricultural land through large-scale drainage projects. Irrigation initiated
an era of increasingly intensive agriculture in England, southern France, and the
Schweizer Mittelland. It allowed the yield of meadows to be boosted five, indeed,
eightfold. Water meadows made it possible to keep more animals in a small area,
and this made more fertilizer available to agriculture.

In rain-rich Central Europe, the peasants – as even the agrarian reformers acknowledged – were perfectly capable of constructing the necessary ditch systems on their own, even if it pulled them into numerous conflicts over water and into a "vicious circle of a constant burden of maintenance." But there were also larger projects that demanded the participation of the state. Whereas Venice and the Netherlands had once been the chief pioneers of political hydraulics in Europe, beginning in the eighteenth century, European politics in general acquired a hydraulic dimension. From the time of Louis XIV, French governments undertook canal building as large-scale prestige projects. Their time frame far exceeded what was possible for private entrepreneurs: "Three centuries of projects, to which is added half a century for the implementation, that is almost the normal time for the construction of a canal," remarked a French canal historian in reference to the history of the Canal de Bourgogne. Before it suffered a railway fever, early industrial England witnessed a "canal mania," though in this case the construction of the canals, which were no more elaborate than was necessary, was done by private companies. Adam Smith believed that the construction and operation of canals could be managed by joint stock companies, though he otherwise didn't have much confidence in their abilities.[8] Below ground, canal construction went through another boom in the age of the railroad in the form of urban sewer systems, which in the end concentrated the urban problems of waste management in an entirely new way.

To this we must add the construction projects to protect against water. In 1711 the Great Council in Bern, following a disastrous flood, decided to redirect the Kander, which until then had been flowing into the Aare, into Lake Thun. During construction work, the builders had dramatic experiences with the mountain river's willfulness; and once it discharged into Lake Thun, it increased the danger of flooding there. This was the first European venture on this scale since the Venetians had redirected the Brenta. Compared to today, hydraulic engineers in those days still had, of necessity, tremendous respect for the power of the rivers.

The largest German hydraulic project after 1800 was the correction to the course of the Upper Rhine, under the supervision of Johann Gottfried Tulla (1770–1828), who had been trained at the Ecole Polytechnique in Paris. This was a project that was Napoleonic in spirit, and it was begun by the Magistrat du Rhin whom Napoleon had installed in Strasbourg. The Europeanization of Rhine River traffic and its regulation decreed by Napoleon was maintained also by the Congress of Vienna, even though the Rhine became at that very time the "German river" for nationalistic romantics in Germany. Rhine romanticism was a different world from the technological interaction with the river. Johann Gottfried Tulla established a grand tradition of hydraulic engineering at the new School of Engineering in Karlsruhe. The "rectification" of the Rhine was for Tulla a matter for the state, one that required a "consideration of the totality" beyond particular interests. The primary concern was protection against flooding and the reclamation of agricultural land in the Rhine meadows. Just as a person needs only one bed, declared Tulla, the Rhine, too, like any other river, needs no more than one bed.

For all that, the chief danger was clear from the outset, namely, that the accelerated flow of the water through the straightened course of the upper Rhine would exacerbate the threat of flooding downstream. Between 1826 and 1834, Prussia,

Hesse, and the Netherlands protested against the construction, which was delayed by these objections. The author of one tract opposing the project prophesied "terrible consequences" to the "residents along the middle and lower Rhine" from the rectification of the upper Rhine. His arguments are still valid today: the twists and bends of rivers must be seen "as a very beneficial arrangement of nature, which, by means of frequent damming up, substantially guides the acceleration in the speed of the rivers and their becoming too shallow at low water levels, thereby ensuring and preserving better shipping." Moreover, fishing would be "extraordinarily impaired" by the straightening of the river. "The more calmly a river flows, the more meanders and thus significant deep spots it has, the richer in fish we find it to be."

In fact, the correction of the Rhine led to the decline of fishing as a way of life, without fulfilling the expectations of shipping. At that time, however, following the dissolution of their gilds, the fishermen do not seem to have had an institution that could fight back. The situation was different in 1750 when it came to the regulation of the Oder; in that case, the justly alarmed fishermen submitted their petitions to the king. There the "pike catchers" (*Hechtreißer*), who had established their own guild in 1692, now saw their existence threatened.[9] But it, too, could not prevent the Oderbruch from being turned into arable land. But the correction of the Oder neither made this river more navigable nor prevented future flooding.

When Prussia and Lippe jointly began to channel the small Werre River in 1772, the vast majority of the peasants living along the river around Herford objected on the grounds "that the spring floods, like the beneficial overflows of the Nile, fertilize their land with flowers and tasty herbs." The meadows situated along the Werre were the "most valuable and productive properties" in the entire area of the town of Herford. The city physician Georg Wilhelm Consbruch, who pondered the connection between the environment and human health, was concerned that a river "locked into tight barriers" might make "room for itself" in floods that were even more devastating– which is precisely what happened.[10] Along the Werre we thus find, on a much smaller scale, the same problem that existed along the Yellow River.

In the eyes of the Prussian *Baurat* Johann Christoph Schloenbach, who was pushing the canalization of the Werre, these objections betrayed merely stubbornness and stupidity. But not all contemporary experts thought so. One leading Prussian hydraulic engineer, Johann Esaias Silberschlag (1721–91), argued that all parties concerned should be heard in river regulation projects, and he noted that rivers, "like willful friends . . . are eager to serve only as long as one treats them politely; if one comes even a little too close to their streambed, their revenge does not easily find an end." Silberschlag's riverine diplomacy is reminiscent of the riverine pedagogy of the ancient Chinese hydraulic engineers, who saw the rivers as children whose mouths should not be stopped up. In Silberschlag's eyes, the true expert distinguished himself by the careful way in which he dealt with the rivers.

With this opinion he was not alone among the hydraulic engineers of his day. In 1781, following a catastrophic flood along the Danube, Viennese public opinion was convinced that the recent work to shore up the banks had constrained the river too much, and Emperor Joseph II agreed. Tulla, who had to undertake the Rhine correction without steam shovels, proceeded on the principle that the regulated river will dig its own course; even by the standards of modern environmentalists, this was gentle river correction. An "increasingly menacing desertification of large segments of the plain of the Upper Rhine" did not begin until the 1920s, when France – on the basis of the Versailles Treaty – built the Rhine Lateral Canal, which deprived the rest of the Rhine of much of its water. The French could point out that the Germans themselves had been planning such a canal prior to 1918. A polemical tract of 1879 against the "nature-averse water economy of modern times" contrasted the older type of river regulation, which still had considered all the interests of those living along a river, with the river canalization of its day, which was pursued from a lopsided perspective.[11]

The sort of environmental protection that people need can emerge not only from fending off human interests, but also from the very interaction of a multitude of interests. The old fisherman and water millers, as well as the brewers and the peasants concerned about the irrigation of their meadows: they all – in their own way – had a more or less pronounced sense that river beds should be preserved in their existing form. If someone dammed up the river without permission or diverted it with groynes, militant protests followed. Günter Bayerl is no doubt right when he says that the water interests of "fishermen, millers, farmers, bargemen, brewers, and so on" constituted a "mutual corrective" in premodern times, even if the farmers often complained that the courts were on the side of the millers.[12] There is reason to doubt that this plurality of interests always functioned reliably on behalf of sustainability; still, the difference to the industrial age, when many streams degenerated into mere "outfalls" for sewers, is striking.

The basic thrust of agrarian and forest reforms in Central and Western Europe in the eighteenth and early nineteenth centuries was to push an economic model based on regenerative resources to its highest perfection – and that often meant also to improve its sustainability. This is true first and foremost for agriculture, but in Central Europe also increasingly so for the forest; it was not unusual, though, for the boost in agricultural production to come at the expense of the woodlands. Still, beginning in the eighteenth century, efforts to protect forests and promote afforestation intensified throughout the German lands, and the concern to be sparing in the use of lumber (*Menage des Holzes* – wood economizing) runs like a red thread through the history of technology at that time. Some of these projects existed only on paper, but under the pressure of rising prices, wood economizing did become part of everyday life.

Never before had society been so aware of the wooden foundations of its existence as it was at that time, when it systematically probed the limits of its woodland resources; in that regard Werner Sombart's notion of the "wooden age" makes sense. Occasionally there appeared the utopia of the total wood state: an all-encompassing control of wood use and a regulation of all of life in the interests of the forests! To be sure, one can describe that period as the prehistory of industrialization, as the unleashing of seemingly unbounded growth. But if one takes a close look, one is repeatedly struck by how self-evidently people lived with the notion that there were limits to growth, and how quickly any growth that put a strain on the forest raised the fear of wood scarcity. Even pit coal revolutionized the basic attitude only after some time. As the extraction of coal penetrated into the depths of the earth, the drudgery required to do so far surpassed what was involved in cutting trees in the forest. Woodcutters were often seen as cheerful fellows and the best dancers at village feasts; the realm of coal, on the other hand, was the embodiment of a dark and gloomy world. A memorandum by two mining foremen (*Bergmeister*) from Essen in 1827 warned against a quantum leap in coal production, "since everything has its limits."[13]

Barrington Moore has rightly said that "there is no evidence that the mass of the population anywhere has wanted an industrial society, and plenty of evidence that they did not." Similarly, Karl Polanyi believes that "eighteenth century society unconsciously resisted any attempt at making it a mere appendage of the market." That was true for large sections of the upper classes as well as for the common people. Many artisans and merchants would have evidently preferred to maintain their oligopolistic position within a protected market, even if that meant they had no prospects of amassing great riches.

Even in the absence of a modern environmental awareness, a policy of carefully maintaining the balance between the human economy and natural resources had many allies at that time, and one must ask why no stable alliance of this kind was able to hold its own in Europe. One answer is that ecological motivations were spread out over various groups and authorities, some of which had clashing interests. The belief in nature's capacity of self-regulation was widespread especially among liberals and critics of the old order. They were opposed by forces that defended a relative autonomy of circumscribed spaces and thus had a framework in which the balance between man and nature could have been enforced.[14] Enthusiasm for nature usually went hand in hand with a call for "freedom," for deregulation, while the alarm about wood scarcity was generally heard in combination with efforts to regulate the forests. The main thrust of the Enlightenment was to explain natural processes in natural ways. In that situation, the search for human fault could seem like a relic of the belief in witches.

In the files of state-supervised consumers of large quantities of wood, like the iron industry, we find the statement that production must be kept "in proportion to the woodlands." However, one must not be too quick to infer from this a stable harmony between forests and the economy. To be sure, people were concerned to achieve the exact balance. Erich Jantsch has reminded us, however, that situations of balance are, contrary to a popular belief, unstable: a minor push is all it takes to upset a careful balance.[15] Stability can be envisaged merely in the form of a "steady state" that reestablishes itself after turbulences. The capacity to do that requires security reserves. Where an exact balance between woodlands and the economy was achieved in the eighteenth century, those reserves no longer existed. Unforeseen events like the Napoleonic wars, which consumed prodigious amounts of lumber, upset everything. The decline of China that set in at that time shows the fate of a civilization that has few ecological reserves left. Still, the ideal of a balance between forests and economic life functioned for a long time as a brake in the transition to energy-intensive sectors of the economy.

The more the state arrogated authority in forestry matters, the greater was its interest in protecting woodlands. However, the role of the state in forestry is often a dubious one. It pushed the peasants out of the forest so that it could cut much larger areas of the forests itself. It was not least these timber sales that paid off state debts that exploded in the eighteenth century, debts that eventually triggered the French Revolution. While the traditional economy of the cities put increasing restrictions on large commercial consumers of wood, in many states the mining and smelting industry was privileged for reasons of fiscal policy and power politics.

In prerevolutionary France, the fear of a timber scarcity intensified – much as it did in Germany – into a virtual "fever" that erupted in many places in attacks on "wood-devouring" iron-smelting works. Evidence of this comes from the *cahiers de doléances*, letters of complaint to the government that document the mood that culminated in the Revolution. Had the French Revolution followed its original impulses, it would have put the brakes on energy-intensive paths toward industrialization. But the change toward a warlike imperialism made the growth of the iron industry a question of national greatness, and in the engineering elite of the Corps de Mines, the iron industry acquired a powerful institutional lobby for its efforts to lay hands on the forests. In a similar manner, Heynitz, the head of Prussia's Department of Mining and Smelting, expressed his hope in 1786 that the king would never allow one of his smelting works to be "deprived of the necessary charcoal," since the smelting works were indispensable "for a war-state."[16]

The way in which the category of "nature" appeared in the political and economic doctrines of that time by no means always contained a reminder of the limits to growth. Quite the opposite: nature, venerated by the nature enthusiasts of the day, was characterized by inexhaustible fertility. It was not rare for nature to be invoked in conjunction with growth strategies, as, for example, in the notion of a country's "natural riches" that still waited to be tapped. But it was also the claim of an environmental crisis advanced especially by many reformers – the allegedly dismal state of the forests and the declining fertility of the soils – that served as an argument in favor of a systematically organized use of nature.

And lest we forget: the nature that the dynamic forces of that time sought to pervade and use to its limits was not least humanity's internal nature. But how did this new, "natural" human fit into ordained limits to growth? "Natural" was the spirit of freedom that rose up against seigneurial prohibitions of marriage as much as against gild limitations on commercial activity and the customs barriers that interrupted the natural flow of the rivers. "Unnatural" was not only the suppression of sexuality, but also contraceptive sexual practices. The eighteenth century witnessed the beginning of a hysterical campaign against onanism, culminating with Rousseau, of all people; it was said that these kinds of practices "cheat nature." In the light of the new enthusiasm for nature, old methods of regulating demography in the relationship between humans and their environment seemed repulsive and unnatural. To speak in the spirit of Gregory Bateson's "Ecology of the Mind": the traditional mentality that was part of an economy based on limited, regenerative resources, this "homeostasis" that did not always strive for new stimuli and climaxes, was in retreat in the age of revolution and musical crescendos. It still existed, it was even very common, but it was losing attractiveness.

There is a thesis that industrialization won because it offered a way out of an acute ecological crisis by providing relief to the overused forests in the form of pit coal as the new fuel, and restoring the fertility of overused fields through artificial fertilizers. Sombart presented industrialization as the savior from an imminent catastrophe of wood scarcity, Liebig proffered his chemical fertilizer as the savior from a catastrophic famine caused by the exhaustions of agricultural fields; for both men, the very survival of European civilization was at stake.

This thesis cannot be dismissed lightly, for a good deal of contemporary testimony seems to confirm it. The fact is that pessimistic verdicts about the state and future of the forests and the peasant commons abounded in the eighteenth century in Western and Central Europe. Ricardo, little impressed by the successes of the agrarian reformers of that time, formulated the law of declining crop yields with growing labor input, and this pessimism quickly became the common property of economics.[17]

And yet, seen from a distance, the limits of the "solar energy system" had by no means been reached in the eighteenth century; even on the basis of regenerative resources there was still considerable leeway. The situation was precarious only if one assumed an inexorable, continuous growth of population and commercial activity. *One* development at the time was aimed at perfecting, in a planned way, the sustainability of an economy (both agriculture and forestry) that was based, in the final analysis, on solar energy. In this regard, industrialization upset promising trends: guano and artificial fertilizer made the perfectioning of crop rotation and the balance of agriculture and animal husbandry obsolete over the long run. Pit coal devalued the birch forests, appreciated above all for their firewood and charcoal; in Central Europe it paved the way for coniferous monocultures, in other regions for the neglect of woodlands.

One crucial issue was surely that the use of regenerative resources driven to the extreme entailed growing regulatory problems. When many streams were crowded with mills and hammer works, and every foot – indeed, very inch – of the water's fall was spoken for, it was necessary to deal with a growing number of existing water rights if one wanted to redirect or dam up the flow of water, unless one could circumvent them altogether with support from the state. In this situation the steam engine, in spite of its technical complexity, seemed like progress toward greater simplicity. It was much the same with pit coal at the time, as many smelting works saw their old forest privileges threatened by new wood interests. The presumed ecological crisis of premodern civilization was at its core often a regulatory crisis. A global comparison reveals clearly that industrialization did not begin in regions with a particularly crisis-ridden ecology, but in regions with an especially stable – indeed, increasingly stabilized – ecology.

If we go by the perceptions of many contemporaries, industrialization presented itself in two phases: a first phase in which it improved the environment, and a second phase in which it made the world an increasingly ugly place. Travel accounts about early industrial landscapes often lapse into a basic tenor of enthusiasm: the traveler, who still remembers the area from the time before the division of the commons, beholds in utter delight wasteland transformed into swaying fields of grain, mills crowded along streams, and everywhere the pulse of bustling commercial zeal and animated life. George Forster, the enemy of the old feudalism, beheld the cloth manufactures of Aachen "with an indescribable pleasure."[18] All that changed in the age of coal. Now forests of smoke-belching chimneys sprouted above the new industrial landscapes; around them proliferated soot-blackened workers' settlements, whose social and hygienic problems boded ill for the future. With coal and carbon chemistry, the emissions of industry into the air and the water became the most incendiary environmental problem; that had not been the case in the "age of wood."

One must picture the novelty of the situation: the common good that needed protection was no longer the commons or the communal forest, where the challenge was to accommodate the interests of a more or less manageable circle of users. Instead, it was air and flowing streams, where the circle of those affected was beyond conception, and the environment had to be increasingly protected against all interests. Unfortunately this great change in the nature of environmental problems occurred at a time in world history when economic liberalism was becoming the dominant doctrine, and with it a notion of common good that established itself by allowing the market to sort out the various interests. To this day, humanity has been struggling with the practical consequences of the novelty of its environmental situation, and given what we know about the preceding millennia, this sluggish response is not really surprising.

Since industry in the age of coal congregated initially in conurbations, its environmental problems were chiefly municipal tasks, much more so than was the case with preindustrial forest and agricultural problems. A widespread awareness of problems existed from the very beginning, but the urban and state supervisory authorities usually reacted only with ad hoc regulations. Whether the modern historian can condemn them for doing so is doubtful: especially from a modern-day perspective, it is evident that, up until the nineteenth century, industrialization generally did not destroy nature irreversibly. Not a few sites of early industrialization in England have been transformed into natural idylls. Compared to the asphalt wastelands created by motorization in the twentieth century, the railroad over long stretches integrated itself more or less harmoniously into the landscape, and the amount of land it used relative to its transportation capacity was fairly small. Modern ecologists are astonished at the species diversity on railway land.[19]

Environmental historians have all too often created the impression that the environmental problems of early industrialization were so terrible and society's lackluster response to them so scandalous that things couldn't get any worse. The present then seems idyllic against this gloomy backdrop. This version of history is open to challenge, however.

What provides the environmental history of the industrial age its structure is not only the economic growth spurts it experienced, but also the period-specific limits to growth and society's diverse responses. Epoch-making in environmental history are not only the factories, but also the great longing for nature that emerged in the eighteenth century and the hygienic movement that spread widely in the immediate wake of industrialization. Of epochal importance is also the nationalism that sought to establish the state on nature.

2. "WO MISTUS, DA CHRISTUS" (WHERE THERE IS DUNG, THERE IS CHRIST):
FROM THE FALLOW TO THE "CULT OF DUNG" AND
THE POLITICIZATION OF AGRICULTURE

The basic thrust of the agrarian reform doctrines of the eighteenth and early nineteenth centuries was to maximize the use of arable land and, above all, to eliminate the fallow period with the help of crop rotation, the cultivation of fodder plants, and barn feeding of animals. At least in theory, many of the innovations were a well-thought-out, perfectly interconnected system: the common pasture on the fallow was abolished, and in its place fodder plants were grown on the fallow land – clover became one symbol of agrarian reform. The fodder plants allowed barn feeding of animals year round. In the barn, unlike on the pasture, manure could be completely collected. The much larger amount of available manure multiplied the yield of the fields.

The new system was fascinating as an idea, but reality was often not nearly as perfect. The reason for this was not least the weak link – human beings. After all, the agrarian reformers at that time had no new energy source at their disposal. Instead, they raised the demands on human energy, not least on the work output of women. The old communal pastures turned into the embodiment of outdated "slovenliness." As the agrarian reformer Johann von Schwerz wrote: "Never and nowhere have I found anything that fosters indolence more, is a greater impediment to agriculture, is more detrimental to the owner, and in and of itself less productive than great, expansive communal meadows and forest pastures." This was an example of the "nomadic economy" that he found so repellent.[20] His damning judgment sprang from considerations of work ethic, but also from agrarian ecology, for a good deal of manure was in danger of getting lost on the expansive pastures, especially its liquid part. At any rate, under the conditions of the pasturing economy, animal manure could not be optimally prepared and used in a targeted manner; and that is what was to be done now.

In many cases, the agrarian innovations occurred not as sudden upheavals guided by new theories, but as a gradual process groping its way forward by experience. The agrarian reformers at the time also drew on peasant experiences; until the nineteenth century, they did not possess a science, a source of knowledge superior to the peasants, and the peasants were well aware of that. In general, the reformers still thought, much like the peasants, in terms of a balance of agriculture and animal husbandry. Crop rotation was not sufficient to regenerate soil fertility; animal manure had to be added. An intensification of agriculture without animal husbandry, using only plant, human, and mineral fertilizer, was in general beyond the mental world of Europe at the time, even if Europeans admired Chinese agriculture. The humus theory of Albrecht Thaer (1752–1828), the founder of German agrarian science, placed the emphasis more strongly than ever before on organic fertilizer. Until the middle of the nineteenth century, many peasants in Germany kept animals "only for the sake of manure"; meat could not be sold at prices that made animal husbandry profitable. "Agriculture is a machine in which one wheel is continuously interacting with the other," Schwerz taught. "But the main spring driving this machine will always be the stock of animals, in other words, fodder." "The meadow is the mother of agriculture," went a saying: part of the wisdom of the agrarian reformers entered into the proverbial sayings of the peasants.[21]

Though the agrarian reformers might proclaim a lot of paper doctrines and mock the practitioners, when it came to the question of fertilizer they saw eye to eye with peasant thinking. "The peasant will do everything to get a lot of manure," declared the pastor Johann Friedrich Mayer (1774) of Hohenlohe, whom Schwerz gave the title "the gypsum apostle." He described as an aside how inventive his peasants could be with their fertilizers, after the motto "Every creature, when it is dissolved, fertilizes the other." In a travel account of 1794 we read that "farmers in Scotland removed their hats as a mark of respect before a well-made midden." The Swiss model farmer Kleinjogg (1716–85), who became famous throughout Europe as the "farmer-philosopher" thanks to the Zurich city physician Hans Kaspar Hirzel, sought "to make everything suitable into manure"; to create an abundance of fertilizer, he gave his animals so much straw as bedding "that one sank down to the knees on the soft bed in his barn." He placed particular store on the collecting of liquid manure, calling it "the most delicious material." Liquid manure became the proverbial "gold of agriculture"; the gold metaphor became popular from Europe to America. "His manure is his gold dust," proclaimed a letter published in *American Farmer* in 1828; another letter put it even more simply: "manure is money." Some even turned their latrines into "gold mines"; others made fun of them.[22]

"Wo Mistus, da Christus" (Where there is manure, there is Christ) became a saying, and it did not sound blasphemous to the ears of the farmers at the time to rhyme "Christ" and "Mist." In 1848, the year of revolution in Europe, one farmer in Paderborn carved these words into the beam of his door: "Willst Du sein ein frommer Christ / Bauer, bleib auf Deinem Mist; / laß die Narren Freiheit singen, / düngen geht vor allen Dingen" (If you want to be a pious Christian / farmer, stick with your manure; / let the fools sing of freedom / manuring goes before everything). Arthur Young, who said that French agriculture was in many places on no higher level than that of the Hurons, fell into raptures at the sight of an Alsatian dung heap; these heaps, carefully piled up with bundles of straw and covered with leaves, were "the most beautiful spectacle I have ever seen. . . . Admirable! Deserves world-wide emulation!" For Young, however, the greatest exemplar in matters of fertilizer was Flanders, where systematic use was made also of urban waste, not least human excreta. There Schwerz saw prettily dressed women collecting horse droppings to sell, an activity that also did much for the cleanliness of the streets.[23]

What was new about this consciousness of fertilizer? After all, the Romans had already been well aware of the value of fertilizer, and in that civilization the wise men could also learn from the farmers: Seneca noted that the farmers themselves were "discovering a thousand new devices to increase the yield" without the help of philosophers. Pliny the Elder had already pointed out the beneficial effect of the lupine that was praised in the eighteenth century. Liebig, however, believed that the Roman "manure cult" returned to glory only in the eighteenth century, after a hiatus of two thousand years. The *Amtmann* Tiemann in Brackwede near Bielefeld, who on Christmas in 1784 was rubbing the latest teachings of the agrarian reformers in the face of the residents of his district, accused the farmers of being "enemies of fertilizer," since they refused to convert to barn feeding and instead "drove" their animals "out of the barn."

At that time, Mayer in Hohenlohe already knew farmers who were exceedingly conscious of fertilizers; but the situation was probably that much of the fertilizer problem more or less resolved itself where animals were driven onto the fallow and no record yields were expected from the soil. The valuable manure of the sheep who eliminated in the pen could be collected without barn feeding. From early modern England came a number of reports about a multitude of fertilizers; in that country we find a perfect witch's brew of experimentation, though it also becomes apparent that manuring represented in many places a problem that was never entirely solved, especially since the soil processes caused by fertilizing were not understood. Moreover, in England, as well, the model country of the agrarian reformers, an appreciation of fertilizer was not found everywhere; as late as the eighteenth century, we are told that cow pats were used as fuel, as in Asia.[24]

At the time when some were rhyming *Mist* and *Christ*, others were denouncing the "manure economy" as a bad practice. The main reason was that, on an open pasture, urine was lost as fertilizer. This was, indeed, the chief ecological leak in the old agriculture, where even under conditions of autonomy, the cycle was not complete. It was only barn feeding and the underpinning of barns with masonry that solved this problem. Although the value of liquid manure as a fertilizer was known to farmers before then, especially in the gardens, in this respect the agrarian cycle of nutrients was substantially closed in the eighteenth and nineteenth centuries.

The overall picture is more contradictory when it comes to the utilization of human excreta. Latrine archaeology has shown that it must have been less than complete in older times. In this regard, John Evelyn – unlike Columella – warned against the use of human waste. The example of Flanders was not emulated everywhere. Johan Georg Krünitz devoted a long article to "The use of human excrement as fertilizer" in his *Ökonomisch-technologische Enzyklopädie* (1798) and polemicized vigorously against the prejudice that this malodorous substance imparted a bad smell to plants. In the end he got carried away to a veritable Gaia rhetoric: "The Earth, our kind Mother, gives us everything and we give nothing back, we hide the nutrients that are good for her ... in secret places, where they cannot be put to use."

While the outhouses on German farms were often directly on the dung heap, French agriculture did not use human excrement or did so only hesitantly. Popular medicine attributed healing powers to excrement; revulsion against one's own excrement is not a phenomenon of modernity, however, but has long been found among many animals. Nineteenth-century natural sciences, on the other hand, were not disgusted and set out eagerly to calculate the fertilizing value not only of animal but also of human waste. In Liebig's day, an experiment was run with the soldiers of the garrison in Rastatt to test whether their excrement would supply enough fertilizer to grow the grain necessary to feed them. The American press also conducted campaigns in the nineteenth century to promote the use of "night soil," and the Sanitary Commissioner of Massachusetts, Lemuel Shattock, saw it as a "law of nature" in 1850 that these substances had to be returned to the soil as fertilizer.[25] As the demand for fertilizer grew, human excrement seemed to become a sought-after trading commodity in the environs of many urban regions – but then the water toilet, combined sewer systems, and artificial fertilizer thwarted this perfecting of the cycle of nutrients. The discoveries of bacteriology and the modern sensitivity of civilized noses made the threshold of disgust over excrement lower than ever before.

While a lack of fertilizer had no doubt been a chronic shortcoming of agriculture in many regions, it became *the* great bottleneck chiefly through the growing push to increase agrarian output that began in the eighteenth century. The wave of innovation it sparked led in the long run to economic forms that abandoned the strategies of ecological balance on the basis of regional, regenerative resources. Still, it would be wrong to draw a straight line from the agrarian reforms of the eighteenth century to the present. Well into the nineteenth century, the basic trait of the innovations lay in improving the sustainability of traditional agriculture. In fact, the agrarian expert Hermann Priebe, who was transformed from a European Union advisor into a sharp critic of the agrarian policy of Brussels, sees the development of German agriculture up to the Second World War as an "exemplar of an organic development"; it was only then that the grand agrarian epoch that was based on a consciously sustainable treatment of regenerative resources came to an end.[26]

In regions with long agrarian experience, the peasants had a traditional fear of exhausting their soil, a fear that agrarian reformers had to overcome with a philosophy that emphasized the activation of the soil. Many farmers saw the soil as a living being, often hungry and exhausted like they themselves, in need of nourishment and rest when it was tired. Giving away fertilizer for money – said the peasants of Hohenlohe – was "just as despicable as it is to deprive a newborn child of her mother's breasts." Long before Liebig, farmers knew full well that different plants taxed the soil in different ways. "The farmer from Brabant treats his land like a horse," wrote Schwerz: "From both he demands constant labor, but in return he also feeds and cares for them in the same way." Schwerz – like Young and other reformers of that time, who were not yet focused on the use of machinery – had a special fondness for the small farmer who knows his land through and through and seeks to improve it "with an admirable indefatigability." "Wherever he can dig a ditch to capture the mud brought by the rain, he does it."

Although zealous farmers were intent on using every inch of their soil, the battle against "weeds" was not nearly as radical as it would become in the twentieth century – after all, these were plants that agriculture had lived with for many centuries, and some of them were highly valued as popular remedies. The destruction of weeds was largely limited to plowing; "now grow yourself," the farmers used to say after sowing. Only the Flemish weeded so zealously that in all of Flanders Schwerz did not see as many cornflowers as he did back home on a few acres. After Thaer had taken a tour of inspection through fields blooming red, yellow, and blue, he scolded the farmers: "Gentlemen, if you are harvesting ten centners of charlock and cornflowers from a *Morgen*, you can demand another fifteen centners of wheat!" Evidently the farmers at the time had nothing against the cornflower, and it did not occur to them that it was depriving the grain of nutrients. As late as the nineteenth century, the cornflower was the favorite wild flower of the Germans; it was the favorite flower of Queen Louise, the "Prussian Madonna," at whose grave her son, Wilhelm I, placed a bouquet of cornflowers following the victory over France in 1870. It was only the herbicides since the 1950s that did the cornflower in – though not, it would seem, forever.[27]

Rolf Peter Sieferle believes that from earliest times to the present, agrarian societies have always been under ecological stress, since a "constant, evolutionary 'arms race' between farmers and parasites" takes place within them: a race "between the genetic mutation of the pests and the technological innovations responding to it." If he is right, "harmony with nature" would have been a picture that was wrong even for premodern times. But the metaphor of an "arms race" draws a picture of the old days that is too dramatic. Many farmers do not seem to have seen their own situation that way. For certain kinds of pests, the old polycultures were not as attractive a prey as modern monocultures are, especially if semiwild areas still existed in the neighborhood as feeding grounds. The old, spelted strains of wheat were far better protected against birds than are the modern ones, where the grains are openly exposed: this, too, is one of those minor differences that are epoch-making not only in social but also in environmental history.

Moreover, farmers had known since ancient times that birds ate harmful insects, though with some kinds of birds it was debatable whether they did more good than harm. The idea of "biological pest control" is anything but new. As early as 1335, the Council in Zurich prohibited the catching of birds – especially quails – for that very reason. Martin Luther, in a short work that shows the reformer's humorous side, has "honorable birds" lament bitterly that Luther's servant, Wolfgang Siberger, was hunting them. They threatened that if it continued, they would no longer stop over in Wittenberg, and then God would send mice and pests as punishment. Needless to say, the "honorable birds" distanced themselves from harmful birds like sparrows and magpies. But even the latter do not seem to have worried many farmers very much. In the early nineteenth century, it was the Prussian government that urged the farmers to hunt sparrows, demanding that each farmer deliver a certain number of sparrow heads. In the late nineteenth century, the bird protection movement was able to ally itself to a certain extent with the farmers, who appreciated at least some of the bird species as pest fighters, even if passionate bird protectors fundamentally did not like these kinds of utilitarian arguments.[28]

Still, reformed agriculture was not a pure ecotopia. Liebig was probably not entirely wrong when he charged that many reformers often masked the basic problem – that in the long run one could take from the soil only as much as one returned to it – and thus ran the risk of exacerbating the overuse of the soil over the long term. The manure pantheism that "everything fertilizes everything" – which in reality does not work, after all – was suited to promoting the illusions of unlimited growth. While many reformers certainly had an understanding of the diversity of soil conditions and of the complexity of the interactions in the soil, for reasons of quick practical results they tended to embrace certain patent remedies with a single effect, whether it was clover, gypsum, or marl. Liebig was right when he pointed out "that every specialized fertilizer will invariably exhaust the field." Even the cultivation of clover could be overdone if it was pursued too single-mindedly. That is what happened in Denmark, which experienced its "Dust Bowl" in the eighteenth century and went overbord with clover as a reaction to the devastation of the deforested land by wind-borne sand.[29]

Above all, however, the insatiable hunger for fertilizer often came at the expense of the forest, whose fate was a matter of complete indifference to most panegyrists of agriculture. Barn feeding considerably increased the demand for leaf fodder, and the use of leaves presented a greater threat to the ecology of the forest than did clear-cutting. The "gypsum apostle" Mayer noted that his farmers would – if they could – surely "strip all pines and firs of their branches and spread them in the barn."[30]

The carefully calibrated crop rotation of the reformers was upset by the currents of the market. The period of proto- and early industrialization saw a growing demand for flax; where farmers did not have previous experience, they had to learn that "flax was incompatible with itself as a preceding crop" and generally could be planted on the same field only every seven years. Still, flax did promote crop rotation and polyculture. The sugar beet, which had the most explosive career on German fields in the nineteenth century, could also be integrated into crop rotation; but with permanent cultivation it became the classic field of experimentation with artificial fertilizer, from super phosphate to potassium. The most strikingly successful innovation at the time in many regions of Europe was the potato. Although it boosted the caloric content in the diet of the poor, it also spurred population growth, promoted a monoculture that was susceptible to pests, and encouraged the use of the last land reserves, contributing in this way to the ecological destabilization of the landscape. Potatoes and flax, however, made for a good crop succession.[31]

In today's ecological agriculture, the old fallow – even of the multiple-year variety – has returned to favor. In a regular rotation, the fallow abandoned the land to whatever grew wild, and it was able to regenerate the fertility of the soil at least as effectively as the cultivation of certain fodder crops. Even Schwerz occasionally admitted that not all traditional laxity was completely absurd: "Tolerating the shortcomings in a world where everything is so imperfect sometimes has its usefulness." He already had negative experiences with excessively one-sided and schematic agrarian reforms and impressed on his students: "All shrewd and clever schemes, all hypotheses and systems avail nothing if they do not coincide with the whole of nature." As late as 1872, a popular agricultural handbook noted that year-round barn feeding was "really somewhat cruel" toward the animals" and highly contrary to nature, and that in the long run a "sensible combination of barn feeding with exercise in the open air" was no doubt better for the health of the animals.[32]

However, as early as the late eighteenth century, this kind of careful, nature-oriented good sense competed to some extent with a different rationality. One must look not only at the direct effect of the agrarian reforms on the soil, but also at the type of person they produced. Economics becomes an obsession that expels all comfortable enjoyment of living and closeness to nature from farming life already in the "philosopher-farmer" Kleinjogg; in some contemporary sources, Kleinjogg appears as a miserly and greedy know-it-all, intent on depriving his housemates of all enjoyment of feasts, leisure, and generosity.[33]

Over the course of the nineteenth century, Western and Central European agriculture, in its insatiable hunger for fertilizer, moved beyond the limits of its regenerative resources: initially, beginning around 1840, through the mass importation of Chilean guano, later through the large-scale application of potash and phosphates. In the history of German agriculture, the "period of mineral fertilizer" is dated from around 1880.[34] At that time, the German Reich had become the world leader in potash extraction. These new substances also possessed all the known disadvantages of one-sided fertilizers. After initial successes, they invariably impoverished the soil, unless the newly created nutrient shortages were offset by new chemical fertilizers: this was the case beginning in the early twentieth century with the synthetically produced nitrogen fertilizer in particular, whose necessity Liebig had still denied for a long time in his battle against the "nitrogeners."

In all of this, however, the problem of soil structure was ignored. Instead, the trend toward deeper plowing was tremendously accelerated by the emergence of steam power. The steam-plow pioneer Max Eyth became the leading mind of German agricultural technology, even though the steam plow was much more difficult to use in small German landscapes than in the United States or Egypt, settings for steam plow adventures that Eyth recounted with a Wild West romanticism. The consequences of ever deeper plowing for soil ecology were only partly understood.[35] At the same time, spurred by industrial technology, the trend toward the consolidation of fields that had been broken up and scattered during the period of the open-field system continued under the slogan "land consolidation." As early as the end of the nineteenth century, nature lovers found the increasing monotony of the agrarian landscape, the disappearance of hedges and ponds a depressing sight.[36] As the open pasture vanished, enclosures and drinking holes were no longer needed.

The long-term history of the agrarian reforms confirms – like many a story of long-term effects in the relationship between humans and their environment – that the solutions to environmental problems at times become more dangerous than the problems themselves. The agrarian reforms with their mania for fertilizer and the creation of full private ownership of land were, to a certain extent, a response to ecological weaknesses in premodern agriculture, and in some respect they did in fact make agrarian ecology more stable. However, the economic-psychological dynamic that accompanied them had destabilizing side effects in the long run. One chief factor was surely the unleashing of the private profit motive, though the ambitions of the states also came into play. Under the influence of the physiocrats, agriculture became a political matter of the highest order in Europe. Never before had the creative power of nature become the starting point of an economic doctrine, as it did with the physiocrats; likewise, never before had the state been so encouraged to lend this creative power a helping hand. Frederick II of Prussia acted entirely from an awareness that the issue in his sandy realm was not to preserve good nature, but to improve a miserable nature.

Ever since, agriculture has remained a political issue; paradoxically enough, as its economic importance has declined, its political importance has grown. Many parts of the world are ruled by the dogma that agriculture must be subsidized even though farmers make up only a minute share of voters in the industrialized countries. In many countries of the world, uneasiness over the explosive growth of industrialization favored the influence of the agrarians and their call for the protection of agriculture. But precisely the resulting system of agrarian protectionism in Europe and America in the long run drove the outside control of the farming economy and its alienation from nature to new heights, so much so that even the new organic agriculture can barely manage without government support.

3. ALARM OVER WOOD FAMINE, THE AFFORESTATION MOVEMENT, AND THE RISE OF AN ECOLOGICAL FOREST APOLOGETICS

Like water, the forest runs like a leitmotif through all of global environmental history that one encounters even in many unexpected places, and there is an abundance of sources on the history of European woodlands in the modern period. And yet, for many historians the forest has remained impenetrable. Forestry sources require their own methods of source analysis. Without an elementary knowledge of the forestry and ecology of a woodland, there is much one simply cannot understand. Moreover, a whole host of questions often needs to be examined: What is meant by "woods" and "forest"? What are we to make of complaints by foresters about "sad forest conditions"? How seriously is one to take warnings of an impending, catastrophic shortage of wood? What interests stand behind the romanticism of the high forest? What is pretext and what are real motivations in the human interaction with the forest? What is good, what is bad?

When the Grand Duke of Tuscany traveled through the Apennines on a visitation, a delegation of mountain dwellers came to him and complained that their poverty was the result of the very forest protection laws that had made Tuscany a model in northern Italy. What is true? What was behind it all? At that time, forest protection in fact often came at the expense of the poor. In this case, however, the mountain farmers had been sent by rich speculators.[37] One has to look very closely and take the context into account to detect the reality behind the sources in forest history, and to get a sense of what certain measures meant for the forest.

We have already discovered that across large regions of Europe (from France to Russia and especially in Germany), particularly in the late eighteenth century, a chorus of shrill alarms was heard, warning against a catastrophic deforestation that would cast humanity into misery. In the process, the prophets of doom often extrapolated a present trend of rising wood prices into the distant future. The inventor of a wood-saving oven proclaimed in 1797: "If the shortage of wood increases over the next twenty years the same way it has over the past twenty years, so help us God!" Most people would have to spend the better part of their income for wood, and no tree or fence would be safe from wood thieves.

Some environmental historians have eagerly embraced this genre of sources and see dying forests everywhere! But usually there was a specific intent behind the complaints, and the extent to which they were valid is often questionable. For a while there was a real backlash against the alarmist proclamations: the "terrible noise about a wood scarcity that was setting in" was a way for "forest charlatans to impress the government and the public," critics exclaimed, "and "the approaching monster of terrible wood misery" was a "picture of horror with which many foresters and other writers are trying to intimidate us in the same way that Africans intimidate their women with their mumbo jumbo." The "bad forester" who participated in this hysteria was an enemy of the people: "Locked in eternal battle with agriculture, hating every useful domestic animal more than the most raging wild animal, and the plow more than the plague," he was unfortunately battling with success, "because he makes the specter of wood scarcity into his ally against the timid people." These outbursts are all the more remarkable considering that the forestry administration benefited from this alarmism.[38]

More so than anything else, the forest in Central and Western Europe – and later also in the United States – became, in popular consciousness, the embodiment of the natural world in need of protection against exploitive private interests on behalf of the common interest in the future. Here, even more so than in agriculture, the state steps onto the stage as one of the main actors; in many territories a state forestry policy begins as far back as the sixteenth century. Replacing the previous exploitation with a sustainable silviculture that guaranteed the balance between woodcutting and regrowth became the motto in the eighteenth and nineteenth centuries. Where policy had been dominated by the mere regulation of cutting through concessions and prohibitions, there now began an active afforestation policy, which often went hand in hand with a reforestation of woodlands with higher-yielding tree species. However, one must not confuse the history of forestry regulations with the true history of the forest: high forests were not created only at that time, but had long since emerged "in a thousand transitions from the practice of selective cutting [*Plenterwirtschaft*]."[39]

State intervention is usually justified with an acute crisis of the forests, indeed, with an impending catastrophe in the wood supply. To this day, the historical self-image of institutionalized forestry is grounded in the belief that it once acted as the savior in the face of the imminent ruin of the forests. In reality, afforestation was often more like a *re*-forestation of woodlands with higher-yielding tree species. The premodern landscape had been dominated by the coppice and the forest pasture, since woodlands were needed above all as pasture and as a supplier of fuel and leaf fodder. In the eyes of many forest reformers, who were interested in high-quality timber, these were sad and pitiful forest conditions, hardly deserving of the name "forest." By contrast, many ecologists today would have been delighted by the species diversity of these landscapes. In Central Europe, the nineteenth century is considered the great age of afforestation, even if the acreage of woodlands actually declined a little in some German regions when the commons were divided up and common forests were cut down. In the Mediterranean region, though, and even more so from a global perspective, the nineteenth century was much more an era of deforestation.

German governments used to justify afforestation and enhanced supervision of woodlands by invoking an imminent, catastrophic scarcity of wood. However, claims of wood scarcity and accusations of woodland devastation brought by state authorities or privileged forest users against other forest users should always be taken with a grain of salt: for as Krünitz's *Ökonomische Enzyklopädie* noted in 1789, "if the highest policing and finance office determines that the woodlands in the land are not in proper proportion, and that more wood is consumed every year than grows back," the state, according to the prevailing notions, had the right to intervene also on private land. Commercial sectors with traditional forest rights used warning cries about a wood shortage to keep new wood users out of the forests. The impending ruin of the woodlands provided a good argument for strengthening the forces of order. A complaint about wood scarcity that was published in the *Westfälischer Anzeiger* in 1801 culminated in a general attack on the effeminate "philanthropists" who could no longer bring themselves to whip thieves and hang them from the gallows.[40]

Now, the state is not absolutely necessary to protect the forest; private owners of woodlands were often better able to do so. In some areas of the Paderborn region the farmers got into a veritable tree-planting "mania," which the agrarian reformer Schwerz believed went too far. When the farmers in Westphalia took private ownership of their forests following the division of the commons, they sometimes – as in Vermold in 1806 – took the law into their own hands to punish wood thieves, as a result of which "people were lying around like stuck pigs." There was no logical inexorability by which complaints about the decline of the forests led to a call for the state. Johann Jakob Trunk, as Professor of Forestry in Freiburg one of the German pioneers in making forestry into an academic discipline, denounced the state's forestry officers in 1802 as a "corrupt, deceitful race," who were at the very top among the forest criminals they pretended to pursue. When the new foresters elevated woodcutting into the "chief use" of the forest and demoted the traditional woodland uses of peasants and subpeasant classes – whether pasturing or resin tapping – to "secondary uses," this sharp reduction in the diversity of uses did not necessarily benefit the ecology of the forest, since most "secondary" uses had been forest-preserving, more so than clear-cutting and coniferous monoculture.[41]

Contrary to what is often claimed today, however, ecological principles are by no means new in forest science: in principle, people were always more or less aware that one had to pay heed to the natural conditions of a given stand, and that these conditions were often quite complicated and could be ascertained only through the patient observation of nature.[42] But it was one thing to proclaim the "iron law of the habitat" (*eisernes Gesetz des Standortes*) – as the Prussian forestry teacher Wilhelm Pfeil did – and quite another to practice a forest science whose final results did, in fact, do justice to local conditions, especially since a scientific study of forest soils was barely in its infancy at the time.

The Hannover forester guardian knew as early as 1833 from bad experiences with coniferous forests in northern Germany that pure stands of fir trees provided a feast for an "army of insects." The trend toward the coniferous forest often won out behind the back of forest science, spurred by the incentive of short- and medium-term financial interests, especially since the afforestation of coniferous woods was the best way of making it impossible for farmers to use the forest as pasture. The small region of Lippe owes what is still today a high proportion of deciduous woodlands not least to the effective resistance of the rural population to the afforestation with coniferous trees imposed from above.[43]

All told, one can detect the following basic pattern, which can also be applied to other episodes of environmental history: as the starting point there are traditional economic ways that have their own kind of sustainability but also certain ecologically fragile sides, which – if one extrapolates specific trends into the future in a linear fashion – can have worrisome consequences. There are various strategies for dealing with these problems: some are unspectacular, everyday, decentralized ones, others are more suited to large, state-run reform projects and to the development of institutions. The latter strategies emerge not merely as responses to acute problems, but also take advantage of and exaggerate them. It is similar to the situation today with certain large-scale projects of development aid that are justified on the grounds of environmental protection.

That does not mean that these strategies fail completely in dealing with the real problems. The standard argument is that silviculture, because of the long growth period of trees, cannot regulate itself – via the market and the interests of private owners of woodlands – and requires intervention from the top. This argument has some truth to it in some situations. And yet, the forestry reforms that were justified by invoking an impending wood crisis exacerbated the dire situation of the poor with respect to wood, as they lost their traditional rights in the forest.

Moreover, afforestation is an ambiguous process not only from a social but also from an ecological perspective. Enhancing and endangering sustainability sometimes lie cheek to cheek. After all, one could argue that in order to ensure sustainability, it was necessary first of all to make the forest and silviculture predictable: to do that, one had to divide the forest into equal stands and then reforest and cut stand by stand. In this way, the precept of sustainability led to clear-cutting and monocultures. One forester in the Harz complained in 1863: "In a similar sense that Linné called the dog the sacrificial victim of anatomy, one could call the forest the sacrificial victim of the forest appraisers. . . . The beautiful old stands with their impressive giant trees have largely disappeared." And the yields of the high forest had not improved across the board; in fact, "in many instances they have declined."[44]

The sustainability concept of the Prussian forestry reformer Georg Ludwig Hartig (1764–1837) presupposed – in spite of the revolutionary times in which he lived – an eternally static world, in which every year across generations about the same amount of wood was used and the same price achieved for it. Hartig, believed, for example, that he could determine the yearly felling for a century and even more, down to our own time. In the guiding idea of "sustainability," economic and ecological interests initially ran on parallel tracks: by limiting cutting in line with regrowth, one not only maintained the substance of the woodlands but also kept the price of wood at a high level – provided the market for wood was regionally limited. As soon as timber was imported from a distance, however, and could be exported to faraway places, economics and ecology tended to diverge. The principle of sustainability, although it spread across the globe beginning in the nineteenth century, was in danger of being undercut by large-scale log driving and timber rafting, and even more so by the railroad, the steamship, and trucks. Still, around the middle of the nineteenth century, not even the social romantic Wilhelm Heinrich Riehl understood the wisdom of the old peasant subsistence economy when he made fun of the fact that Rhenish farmers thwarted the state-imposed auction to sell their wood: when "outside bidders came, they chased them out of the forest with flails and pitchforks to prevent a high bid, and then proceeded to auction off their own wood to each other at ridiculously low prices."[45]

The German afforestation movement, whose beginnings reach back to the early eighteenth century if not before, expanded in the early nineteenth century into a pan-German, and subsequently a global, trend. At first, the systematically practiced afforestation of high forest was a German *Sonderweg*. This same period also saw the emergence and popularization of a forest romanticism that has been considered typically German ever since. It seems logical to draw a connection between these two valorizations of the forest. But what kind of connection? Factually the link is not as evident as one might expect; in fact, some evidence suggests a contrapuntal relationship. After all, popular forest romanticism often did not cultivate the kind of forest that foresters intent on achieving the highest wood yield had in mind. The favorite tree of national forest romanticism was the oak, specifically the ancient, gnarled, free-standing oak whose branches spread widely on all sides. That, however, was the aesthetic of the old grazed woodland of the peasants, not that of the new cultivated woodlands of the forester.

One moonlight night in 1772, a group of students from the university in Göttingen met in an old oak grove to swear eternal friendship as they held garlands of oak leaves in their hands; they had been inspired by a scene from Klopstock's Hermann trilogy, in which a druid invoked the oaks as the seat of the Germanic gods prior to a battle. This was one of the beginnings of forest romanticism and of the German nationalism that was taking hold in student fraternities. Ernst Moritz

Arndt, one of the prophets of German nationalism during the Wars of Liberation, fought throughout his life for "the two primeval pillars of the state": "the forests and the peasants." He fought for the forests not only because of the wood, but also because of their importance to climate, the fertility of the soil, and the "health and strength" of people. In 1820, in an appeal for a national cultivation of the forests, he had warned that the axe that was put to the tree was in danger of becoming an axe that was "put to the entire nation." Foresters should have been horrified by his words; after all, they lived from wood cutting and worked on its behalf. But when Arndt derived from his national-economic appreciation of the forest the demand that woodlands being offered for sale should be turned into state forests "at any price," foresters could be pleased. The same was true when Arndt called for the expulsion of commercial interests from the forest: "Away, then, with the forest-destroying factory owners! Away with them from the heights and mountain tops!"

The romantic ideal of woodland solitude overlapped with the forester's goal of having the sole authority in the forest, and not being bothered by the customary rights of charcoal burners, glass makers, or pitch distillers. Riehl, another of the great ideologues of German forest romanticism, also had mixed feelings about the new forestry zeal: Germany, he complained around 1850, had, "in recent times," lost at least as much of its peculiar forest character from the "artificial transformation of the proud deciduous high forest into short-lived coniferous forests as it had from the complete clearance of immense tracts of woodlands." He wanted the forest as wilderness and a realm of liberty, where the German was allowed to cast off the constraints of civilization and the adult could revert to being a child.[46] And yet, Riehl's influence was felt when the first chairs of forestry were created at the University of Munich, outposts of a strictly rational treatment of the forests.

At the beginning of German forest doctrines in the eighteenth century stood the desire to extract the maximum yield from princely forests in order to restore the often highly indebted state budgets to financial soundness. Forestry practice, however, was in its origins an entirely different world, arising typically from princely hunting. That provided a better bridge to forest romanticism, for hunting is a primeval source of passionate delight in the forest. The hunter does not like the thick coniferous forest, but the mixed deciduous forest with a lot of undergrowth and punctuated by clearings, which offers plenty of food and hiding places for wildlife. The social prestige of forestry was originally derived from seigneurial hunting. By contrast, the "wood-proper" (*holzgerechte*) forester, who was called for beginning in the Reformation in opposition to the old "stag-proper" (*hirschgerechte*) forester, stood – even if he would not admit it – within the professional tradition of the wood cutters, who were usually far better than the professional forester at assessing a forest's lumber value. A leading forester in the nineteenth century observed with a sense of unease that the district forester was now to be "trained" to serve as a "living axe."[47]

Incidentally, the battle of the forest reformers against wood pasture and litter raking sparked serious social conflicts. As late as the 1860s, poor farmers in southern Germany asserted that litter raking was "the pivot around which our entire economy revolves." "Better to have no bread on the table, we say, than no forest litter in the barn. If the latter is now taken away by the foresters, we will have to sell our only cow, our source of food and fertilizer." Litter raking was, in fact, the worst that could happen to the forest from an ecological point of view. One popular tract in 1885 called on "the entire nation" to stand up against litter raking and "for the preservation of the natural forest fertilizer."[48]

If foresters followed regulations to the letter, they often clashed with the poor. For that reason, forestry was for a long time an especially hated profession in Germany and elsewhere. It was truly a phenomenal turnaround when forest service became the dream job of Germans in the nineteenth century – the embodiment of a vigorous, nature-bound life in service to the nation's future. Forest romanticism surely played a crucial role in this radical change in image. It is evident, especially in comparison with other countries and regions of the world, to what extent a successful afforestation policy depends on a broad consensus within the population, precisely because it usually involves intense conflicts with local population groups in its initial phase, and because it is not possible to put a policeman next to every tree. It would appear that this broad consensus emerged in Germany around 1800 in a relatively short period of time, even if it was in part based on romantic illusions about forestry.

In France forest protection and afforestation seem to have become popular only from the late nineteenth century on; for too long, forestry had been an area of tension between the central authority and local communities. Andrée Corvol has written that the "cult of the high forest" had been a "state religion" under the ancien régime; the old high forest, the embodiment of the social hierarchy, had stood under a quasi-sacral "taboo." In 1731 one Claude Rondeau was burned alive like a heretic in a valley of the Vosgues Mountains because he had set fire to the forest; here, as elsewhere, burning was the way in which land-hungry farmers obtained new arable land. Under these circumstances, the protection of the high forest carried a very heavy political burden at the time of the Revolution; as Marsh has written, there now began a "general crusade against the forests." Back then – as still today in many parts of the Third World – a social forest policy meant providing the common people with woodlands for grazing and firewood, indeed, allowing goats into the forest, to the horror of foresters. The counterreaction was not long in coming: the protection of the high forest became a strategy that the political restoration shrouded in an idealized mist of nature romanticism.[49]

Peasant rebellions aimed at defending old customary rights in the forest were a tradition in France and Germany, as well as elsewhere. Since the gathering of firewood and litter raking was women's work in many regions, women often took violent action during such unrest: indeed, they were sent out by the men to take the lead. Beginning in the eighteenth century, there were repeated cases in some areas of France – the first time apparently in 1765 in the Forêt de Chaux near the royal salt works of Salins – where men who attacked forest overseers disguised themselves as women. The *demoiselle* revolts became a French type of forest rebellion that continued into the nineteenth century, especially since the forest rights of the peasants were in some places in a far worse state than they had been before the Revolution.[50] When it came to the forest question, however, rebellious villages found less and less support among the bourgeois–urban left in the nineteenth century. The notion that state protection of the forests was a precept of reason spread at that time in France as well. A reforestation policy on a large scale began under Napoleon III. Coal was already on the rise by that time, and so the argument of wood scarcity did not carry as much weight as it once had. Instead, the importance of the forest to the hydrological balance assumed prime importance – a change that was crucial to the genesis of modern environmental awareness.

In premodern times there was already an appreciation of the forest that put its economic utility second: "Le principal plaisir qui vient du bois sauvage est / Que par la verdure il délecte merveilleusement" (The principal pleasure from the wild forest / is the marvelous delight in its greenery), we read in a didactic poem published in Paris in 1583: "Le bois vou défend de l'injustice du soleil et de la grande chaleur" (The forest protects you from the mercilessness of the sun and the great heat). This was a sylvan pleasure that was felt most strongly in the south.

In Restoration France, studies were done to determine how the destruction of forests during the revolutionary period had altered the climate. Toward the middle of the nineteenth century, quasi-ecological arguments for forest protection attained priority in forestry policy for the first time in many parts of Europe. Greater emphasis than ever before was placed on the value of woodlands to the hydrological balance, the soil, and climate, and thus to human health. At that time the theory that deforestation is responsible for flooding, or, even more, for the succession of drought and flooding became the dominant doctrine. It spread from France in the early nineteenth century and dominated the debates on forest policy also in Italy. At a time when German forest policy was still operating primarily with the wood-scarcity argument, in France – according to Andrée Corvol – the "ultras of the Restoration" blamed the deforestation in the wake of the Revolution for the catastrophic flooding that occurred.[51]

In the German-speaking lands, the idea that flooding was caused by deforestation appeared first in the Alps, where the protective function of the forests against avalanches was obvious, anyhow. Around the middle of the nineteenth century, the prevention of flooding became the leitmotif of Swiss forest policy. When the Economic Society of Saxony in 1856 held an essay contest about the "disadvantages" that had emerged "from the devastation of private woodlands," first prize went to a submission that highlighted the importance of the forest in the "balance [*Haushalt*] of nature." Once the alarm over wood scarcity fell silent, the question of water and climate became the decisive argument that state supervision was indispensable: "Which private person will plant his arable with firs and oaks merely to regulate the precipitation of the land?"

For the American George Marsh, "perhaps no one point" in the forest discussions in 1864 was of greater importance than the water question, even though opinions about it were still divided. *Forest and Stream* became the most popular American forest magazine. Toward the end of the nineteenth century, the position that emphasized the moisture-enhancing value of the forest carried the day in the United States. The interest in irrigation became a powerful driving force behind the emerging American forest policy. Marsh found an enthusiastic audience also in Australia, which was threatened by droughts. In India the catastrophic floods in 1970, although their immediate cause was an unusually heavy monsoon, triggered the protests against forest cutting that gave rise to the Chipko movement.[52]

If one surveys these developments from a distance, it becomes fairly obvious that the ecological argument for forest protection initially owed its rise in large measure to the strategic and tactical interests of state forestry administrations. It had to take over when the alarm about wood scarcity no longer worked. Moreover, it built an ideological bridge to the popular forest romanticism of that time. In Germany it was also the challenge from the doctrine of net soil yield (*Bodenreinertragslehre*), which sought to focus forest science with ruthless consistency on cost-benefit analysis and to purge it of all hidden sentimentality, that caused ecological positions to be more sharply articulated within forest science.[53]

In all these debates and controversies, forest scientists were well aware that a good deal about the claims concerning the ecological significance of the forest was more or less speculative. This was most true of the connection between forest and climate, but it applied also to the link between deforestation and flooding. Contemporaries already knew that this was a political controversy. Today we have a sense of how complicated and varied the interactions are between the forest cover and the soil's water balance; but it was possible in the nineteenth century to already recognize that there was no simple and universally valid causality. In theory, two scenarios were equally possible: trees could store water and gradually release it again, or they could extract water from the soil through evaporation. In some species (eucalyptus, birch), the dewatering effect is stronger. Water is bound and soil retained not only by the forest, but also by grass and shrubbery. Major catastrophic floods are usually not a direct result of deforestation, but of periods of heavy rain. The consequences of shrinking woodlands are largely slow and insidious, not acute. Still, the fact remains that the expansive forest, by virtue of its deep root system, on the whole regulates the water balance in the mountains better than low vegetation does.[54]

In Switzerland, which has no tradition of absolutist forest policy, it was the catastrophic flood of 1868 that led the Confederation to intervene in forestry matters. Long before that, the forest reformer Xavier Marchand (1799–1859) had already emphasized the "higher purposes" of the forests in the "balance [*Haushalt*] of nature"; but only the floods were able to overcome the resistance of the cantons to a forest policy run from Bern. The inundated lowlands blamed the mountain farmers for the "Alpine plague," which to Marchand was Nature's punishment for past sins against it. Yet experts knew even then that the guilt of the mountain dwellers was by no means proved. Series of floods had occurred also in times when there were no large-scale clearances in the high mountains.[55] An old clash between the highlands and the lowlands was being fought out within forest policy. Still, no one would deny today that afforestation in the interest of water, soil, and avalanche protection was, on the whole, reasonable. Even if weather was the primary factor in floods, and the state of the forest at best a secondary factor, there was something one could do about this secondary factor. To this day, environmental policy finds itself reduced to this logic whenever it is proceeding in part on the basis of hypothesis and cannot deal with all the causes of a problem.

Today many complaints about deforestation in the Third World pose similar problems of source criticism as the European forest laments of the eighteenth and nineteenth centuries. In both cases, the environmental historian must engage in an exercise of constructivism: he or she must examine what is real and what is con-structed in the complaints about deforestation. Colonial governments used to assert a threat of deforestation so they could push back the forest rights of the indigenous population. Many governments of former colonies continued this tradition after independence, since it strengthened the central government's right of intervention in areas that were at risk of eluding its control. Moreover, in most recent times an ecologically ruinous deforestation is often an effective way of procuring developmental aid for reforestation. The book *Misreading the African Landscape by* James Fairhead and Melissa Leach deals with alleged forest destruction by the indigenous population in Guinea, which quite possibly never happened.[56] Nevertheless, it would be wrong to end with a complete deconstruction of deforestation: not every destruction of woodlands is imaginary. Only those complaints that rest on a solid foundation will be credible, in environmental history as elsewhere.

4. "SWEET, HOLY NATURE": THE AMBIGUOUS DEVELOPMENT OF THE MODERN RELIGION OF NATURE

"Süße, heilige Natur / Laß mich gehen auf deiner Spur, / Leite mich an deiner Hand, / Wie ein Kind am Gängelband" (Sweet, holy nature / let me wander on your path, / guide me by your hand / like a child on leading-strings). Thus begins the poem "To Nature" (1775) by the young Count Friedrich Leopold zu Stolberg, a member of the Göttingen Grove who swam in the nude in a Swiss lake with the young Goethe. The eighteenth century was in Europe the first great age of nature enthusiasm. Humanity's relationship to nature is shaped not only by pragmatic, but also by emotional and spiritual, motives, and that is true for ancient as well as modern times. These motives, however, do not all run on a *single* track. What they mean and effected in practice is not always evident, and can be ascertained only through close examination. Since meditations on nature are already inherently joyful, they often provide no urgent incentive for practical action!

In her book *The Death of Nature*, Carolyn Merchant tries to show that the notion of Nature as a female power – Nature as nourishing mother – fell victim to modern, patriarchal rationalization processes. But studies by Keith Thomas and Simon Schama reveal that it is just as easy to arrive at the opposite conclusion: namely, that the wild proliferation of ideas and ideals about nature reaches its highpoint precisely as modernity unfolds.[57] To be sure: Descartes, Merchant's most widely quoted witness, described animals as soulless automatons whose cries of pain were like the squeaking of a machine; but that was not the last word of modernity. "When I play with my cat," Montaigne asked himself," who knows if I am not a pastime to her more than she is to me?" Thomas discerns in early modern England a "tendency . . . to break down the rigid boundaries between animals and men," a tendency that had its vital undercurrent in the growing love of pets. Cats were burned alive at many church feasts until the seventeenth century – here the cat is a symbol of diabolical witchcraft and falseness. Beginning in the eighteenth century, the cat became a cuddly pet showered with loving affection. Unlike love for a dog, human love for a cat is the love for an animal that is affectionate but will not be tamed.

The slaughterhouses and animal factories of the twentieth century are not the logical endpoint of the modern relationship between humans and animals, but unintended consequences of the dynamic of mass consumption and not least of modern norms of hygiene. Yet their existence demonstrates that for a long time many nature enthusiasts took no interest in guiding economic and technological developments. In the beginning, the new hygiene in the barns offered a picture that seemed kind to the animals. One textbook of agriculture proclaimed triumphantly in 1872 that people had finally understood that even the pig, traditionally considered dirty, needs "healthful, spacious, and clean living space."[58]

Is modernity marked by the secularization and scientification of nature? This is a prevalent thesis, and there is a good deal of evidence that fits this scheme. At the same time, however, a core element of the divine lives on – indeed, has experienced a resurrection – in nature. The faith in the goddess Natura, for many centuries a secret religion dressed up in Christian garb, is now becoming for an ever growing public the only solid ground of thought and faith. No less a figure than Francis Bacon (1561–1626), who describes the experiment he demands as a rape of nature, could also plead for an erotically tinged cult of nature: "'This strange and prodigous story seems to bear this meaning: that Art – when it endeavours by much vexing of bodies to force Nature to its will and conquer and subdue her . . . rarely attains the particular end it aims at; . . . because men . . . rather struggle with Nature than woo her embraces with due observances and attention." So close do the love of nature and the manipulation of nature lie side by side – in all of history, not only in Bacon.

Over the course of the eighteenth century, the embrace of nature developed "into a kind of religious act." Even a sober and practically minded man like Krünitz pleaded in his encyclopedia for a new nature religion to clean up the rivers. Emilie Fallenstein, Max Weber's grandmother, still enthused in old age: "The rapture of spring is the first revelation of eternal love to us . . . ; such nature religion seems to me the foundation of all religiosity!" And Weber himself, who initially presented religion in his *Protestant Ethic* as antinature, later drew close to his grandmother's faith.[59] Romantic painting and poetry imparted to natural landscapes a glow that points toward a beckoning hereafter and fills the viewer with a sense of awe. Even the new natural sciences participated. Alchemy had conceived of nature as anthropomorphic and had blurred the boundary between organic and inorganic nature; it was only afterward that people learned to think in terms of nature having its own laws and the organic being unique. In the "natural laws," nature is present as the highest lawgiver.

Is all of this, then, a history of wordplays, fantasies, painting, and, at best, gardening? I think not, for in the background one does discern many vital driving forces, old and modern experiences of pleasure and pain. From antiquity right into modern times, erotic dreams of desire have been concealed within the love of nature, of the garden and grotto idyll. The continuously reprinted *Hypnoerotomachia Poliphili* by Francesco Colonna, a love novel first published in Venice in 1499, is a treasure trove of the Renaissance's fantasies of eros and at the same time of nature. The young Goethe, who himself often deified nature, also parodied the nature cult of his day in his dramatic sketch "Satyros," in which a nature preacher who was captivating the people is unmasked in the end as a lecherous, goat-footed faun who mounts a girl in the inner sanctum of the new nature religion.

But the suffering caused by the stress of advancing industrialization and urbanization is reflected in the longing for nature. There is good reason why modern nature romanticism first flourished in early industrial England: it accompanied industrialization from the very beginning and echoed its pains. The early phase of the nature cult saw the discovery of nerves and irritability. "The tradesman, the attorney comes out of the din and craft of the street, and sees the sky and the woods, and is a man again," wrote Emerson. Later, John Muir, the American prophet of national parks, found in the nervous his allies in the struggle against woodcutters and hydraulic engineers.[60] Biographies, whether of Rousseau or Hermann Löns, supply plenty of evidence for the connection between nature cult and psychic suffering in individual lives. The culture of the industrial age included early on also antitheses to the industrial world; it would be a mistake to think of these reactions against industrialization as archaic relics.

The wild romanticism of rocky landscapes can be explained least of all in utilitarian terms. It is, as such, a phenomenon of modernity, though it reminds us of the old belief in sacred mountains as the seat of higher powers. Especially in its beginnings, this romanticism contained an element of fear. Heine's "Lorelei," the most famous poem of German romanticism, tells of the fisherman's mortal fear of the rocky cliffs. The gorges of the Yangtze, whose flooding is today opposed by a broad protest movement, were still called the "gateway to hell" a generation earlier.

The more one discovered that nature is inherently full of order, the more plausible was the idea that nature was superior to human orders, whose shortcomings were obvious. This led people to an appreciation of "wild" nature that was not ordered by human hand. Rousseau, too, loved nature not as chaos, but as the founder of new order; he thought highly of Linné, who introduced categories and system into the animal and plant worlds. And yet: nature enthusiasm, like nature itself, developed an uncontainable dynamic of its own already in the eighteenth century. In garden design, in the English "garden revolution," in the opening of the old hortus conclusus into a "landscape garden," one can follow how people grew weary of ordered nature and sought out unbounded, surprising nature. "No one deems himself at ease in a garden that does not resemble open land; nothing shall remind him of art, of coercion," Goethe wrote in *Elective Affinities*. The eternal dilemma of the "nature garden" was that the supposed wilderness still always remained planned, arranged nature, and even the meandering lines of paths and ponds soon became a cliché. The productive and genuine aspect of the feeling for nature expressed itself in the fact that garden design has remained fluid since the eighteenth century.

The rise of the modern nature cult did not follow a linear progression, nor was it always an edifying history. Adam Smith complained that piece-workers were ruining their health by suppressing the natural need for relaxation: "It is the call of nature, which requires to be relieved by some indulgence, sometimes of ease only, but sometimes too of dissipation and diversion." Yet it was precisely the liberal doctrine, which sought to let the economy take its natural course, that paved the way for the transgressions against human nature Smith lamented. The aristocratic tree cult flourished in eighteenth- and nineteenth-century England, and trees became "an indispensable part of the scenery of upper-class life"; forestry, however, decayed. The famous parks of Prince Hermann Pückler-Muskau were financed by the "total devastation of the Muskau forests": thus the one nature triumphed at the expense of the other.[61]

When Bartolomé de Las Casas pleaded passionately for a more humane treatment of the Indios to Charles V, he invoked natural law: these people, he argued, were "by nature free." Natural law, whose roots reach back to the classical Stoa, experienced its golden age in the eighteenth century, and – as Franz Wieacker has emphasized – it established a respect for the human body: under its "influence, the stakes slowly begin to burn out from the beginning of the eighteenth century, the groans of the tortured or those executed in excruciating ways fall silent." But nature was soon exhausted as the leading legal authority; victory belonged to countertrends that made law the product of the state and history.

The French Revolution adorned itself with nature symbolism: when the cathedral in Strasbourg was consecrated as the Temple of Nature in 1794, a mountain of craggy rocks was erected in the choir. Many Liberty Trees of the Revolution were – unlike conventional May Trees – dug up with their roots and replanted, though no small number of trees died this way.[62] This was arboreal theater, which contrasts with the massive damage inflicted on the forests during the time of the Revolution. The protection of woodland nature and the notion of the state as an organism that does not tolerate any sharp cuts became weapons in the hands of the Restoration. Certain kinds of political subservience were not good for nature in the end – though in the long run, the idea of nature always managed to escape such subservience.

The "landscape gardens" in which the ideal of nature assumed natural shape were inspired by landscape painting. The notion of "landscape," which influenced geography and ecology in the nineteenth and twentieth centuries, is derived from painting. The technique of perspective invented by Renaissance painters – a characteristic element of European exceptionalism – trained the eyes to perceive simultaneously foreground and background, micro- and macrostructures. Since thoughts are carried by feelings and interact reciprocally with sensory perception, this sharpening of the gaze is not without significance to the development of environmental awareness. The blue hills on the horizon created a sense of pleasure in the infinitude of nature. Idyllic and wild nature, flower-carpeted meadows and jagged rock panoramas are combined in landscape painting. In the knowledge that pleasure in the one and the other is related, painting is ahead of modern conservationists, who quarrel over whether national parks should cultivate the traditional pasture landscape or should be consigned to wilderness in its pure form.

Of importance are not only the new ways of perception, but also the new bodily experiences linked with the new gardens and parks. The stroll is invented in the late eighteenth century, and its history, as Gudrun König has written, is a part not only of the history of mentalities and the body, but also of the "history of the feeling for nature." By promoting digestion, the stroll eliminates a major source of physical discomfort in members of the sedentary classes. The fluid sociability along the tree-lined avenues broke open the domestic sociability that was fixed in seating arrangements and closed off by social class. The hidden corners of landscape parks were an ideal place for lovers, and courtly society of the Rococo in fact wished them to be just that. The "Wörlitzer Garden Realm" near Dessau was full of erotic depictions with which its creator, Prince Leopold Friedrich Franz von Anhalt-Dessau, tried in vain to stimulate the sensuality of his beautiful young wife.[63] For others, the love of nature replaced the love of women. Beginning in the nineteenth century, vacation trips and weekend outings into the country made the contrast between industrial society and nature into the ritualized experience for an ever-expanding mass of people.

Was the modern science of nature a completely different world, with its cool, analytical concept of nature? In fact, there was a network of cross-connections between it and the cult of nature, beginning with the physico-theology of the seventeenth and eighteenth centuries. And the links were no doubt not merely intellectual but also emotional: the natural sciences, too, for a long time possessed a libidinous substratum of joy in nature and an insatiable curiosity about it. Natural scientists found their inspiration not only in the laboratory, but also on walks. "Amusements" were a popular part of titles about nature.

Belief in the healing power of nature had a physical immediacy especially in the healing arts. That is true not only of romantic-holistic medicine, but also of its counterpart developed by analytical natural science: precisely because the latter led initially to a "therapeutic nihilism," to the realization that a therapy founded on exact science did not exist, the physician found that he had to rely all the more on the *vis medicatrix naturae*, the healing power of nature. One leading mind of romantic medicine, Andreas Röschlaub, warned as early as 1800 against the harmfulness of coal smoke, which some physicians would not accept even around 1900, under the influence of bacteriology. One student of Röschlaub's, Johann Nepomuk Ringeis, fulminated against the emerging use of instruments in medicine.

The forceps had been particularly controversial for some time. In the seventeenth century, William Harvey, the discoverer of the circulation of the blood, already had opposed all unnecessary interventions that disturbed "nature's calm work" during birth; in fact, for a long time British doctors made only very sparing use of the forceps. In Paris, by contrast, doctors in the eighteenth century were increasingly quick to use this instrument. Johann Lucas Boer, one of the great authorities of Viennese medicine, experienced the trauma of his life in 1790, when Archduchess Elisabeth died after he had used the forceps to help her give birth more quickly. Henceforth, Boer was very cautious with this instrument, and he became a "pioneer of natural midwifery." He said he had "learned in France what art can accomplish, in England what nature can."[64]

The most famous nineteenth-century naturalist, Charles Darwin, acquired his knowledge about the origins of the species through travel and observation, not through analysis in the laboratory. Did his thesis of the murderous "battle for survival" introduce a deep rupture in the idyllic image of nature, as Donald Worster believes? Not quite: people have always known that death is part of nature, even if many like to suppress that thought; at the same time, loveable nature was by no means lost through Darwin. The quasi-religious fascination of Darwinism is based on the new feelings of a oneness between humans and nature: "Among the scenes which are deeply impressed on my mind, none exceed in sublimity the primeval forests undefaced by the hand of man; whether those of Brazil . . . or those of Tierra del Fuego. . . . Both are temples filled with the varied productions of the God of Nature: – no one can stand in these solitudes unmoved, and not feel that there is more in man than the mere breath of his body."

Leading German Darwinists like Ernst Haeckel and Wilhelm Bölsche did not emphasize struggle, but created a seductive picture of the unity of humanity and nature. In Bölsche, man's naturalness manifested itself above all in love, specifically, in the many varieties of sexuality. Social Darwinism was by no means mere proto-fascism, as was so often claimed after 1945. Even Walther Schoenichen, the chief conservationist in the Third Reich, emphasized in a "Darwinian lecture" in 1903 how "tremendously important apparent death," and not least intentional invisibility, was to the survival of all living forms: a rather antiheroic Darwinism! The philosopher Ludwig Klages, in his fiery message "Man and Nature," addressed in 1913 to the German youth movement assembled on the Hohe Meißner, denounced "the erroneous doctrine" that "always reads only one thing into nature, the unrestrained 'struggle for existence.'" And he, the lover of the wild Countess Franziska zu Reventlow, closed with the vision that a reawakening of the "all-uniting love in mankind" would heal the "matricidal" wounds inflicted on the earth.[65]

The cult of nature could induce an exaggerated confidence in the indestructibility of nature, thus opening the way for the exploitation of the last remaining natural resources. For Immanuel Kant, the presumed fact that regions poor in wood were supplied with driftwood in a way that was difficult to explain offered one clue to the working of "a wisdom ruling over nature." Yet at that very time, cries of alarm about the imminent wood famine went up everywhere. The concern about the overuse of nature arose not so much from natural philosophy, as from the practical interest in nature. But even forest and nature protection was based in its own way on the idea that nature could be planned, finding it difficult to accept its unpredictability. Engineers spoke more frequently about this unpredictability than scientists – by necessity, for nature repeatedly upset the calculations of the technicians. There was a respect for nature that grew out of the practical application of technology.[66]

The flipside of the modern nature cult was the neglect of the city. Under the spell of the fantasies of wilderness, the interest in shaping urban landscapes in a way that was close to nature and life-affirming often atrophied. In this way the horror of the industrial cities became a self-fulfilling prophecy, as their explosive, chaotic growth confirmed the worst fears. And the guiding image of "nature" does not appear to have played a large role in subsequent attempts at sanitizing the cities. Thus the nature cult initially skirted the problems of industrial civilization.

5. NATURE AND NATION: MAKING CONCRETE THE NATURE IN NEED OF PROTECTION

Modern Europeans are all too familiar with the *dangers* of nationalism, but the spell it once cast and still possesses for many peoples today is hard to conjure up after two world wars. What was the basis of this fascination? There were the attractions of power politics and economics, to be sure, but that was not all. Nationalism gave every member of a nation, beyond the small piece of land he could call his own (if that much), an enormous land as his imagined property and grounded participation in it on nature. In this it resembled the family, whose special sense of belonging comes from the fact that one belongs to it by birth or marriage, without any other conditions or requirements. One did not have to profess certain religious doctrines, did not have to believe something that went against one's own experience of reality – you belonged to your own nation "just like that," by virtue of your own corporeal nature, which is conceived as part of a collective nature. In this, nationalism, for all its idealistic pathos, did possess a sensual substructure, thus creating a unity between internal and external nature.

That requires certain ideas about national nature, about the "nature" in landscape and in humans. "Das ist des Teutschen Vaterland, / Wo Eide schwört der Druck der Hand, / Wo Treue hell vom Auge blitzt, / Und Liebe warm im Herzen sitzt – / Das soll es sein!" (This is the German's fatherland / Where hand in hand the oath does swear / Where loyalty gleams brightly in the eye / And love resides warmly in the heart – / This it shall be!) wrote Ernst Moritz Arndt: "German" was heartfelt, tender, unmannered, and uncalculating love – a naturalness that was not far from Rousseau's ideal of nature and, in the final analysis, supranational in character. When Johann Gottfried Herder witnessed a sun festival in Latvia in 1765, at which Latvian women and girls performed wild dances and songs beneath burning tar-barrels, "the singing and dancing of primitive man," as Friedrich Meinecke wrote, became an embodied notion and the model of natural national character.[67]

Nature was ambiguous when it came to nation. One way of looking at it was that, on some level, humans were all the same by nature, and even beneath an exotic shell one found the same primal phenomena of love and pain. On the other side, nature had equipped individual humans and peoples with striking differences. The variety among peoples and races engendered by climate, landscape, and way of life has been an inexhaustible topic of travel accounts from antiquity to this day, a topic that saw its first period of explosive popularity in the early modern period with a growing number of journeys of discovery, exploration, and edification. Those years gave birth to the genre of "natural history" and the description of the flora and fauna of a given region: "What incredible delite is taken in beholding the diversities of people, beastis, foules, fishes, trees, frutes and herbes," wrote Thomas Elyot in 1531, "to knowe the sondry names and conditions of people and the varietie of their natures."[68] It was not easy, however, to derive a nature of the German from the German landscape, let alone in contrast to France: after all, the German landscape is not sharply distinct from that in northern and central France.

A people like the Norwegians had it easier in this regard. When they broke away from Denmark in 1814 and created their national identity virtually ex nihilo, they were able to constitute themselves as a Nordic people of the forest and the mountain as distinct from the Danes, the people of the treeless flatland. Here the national nature landscape was almost ready-made, and through Norwegian "outdoor culture," cross-country skiing during the long winters, it became a lived experience. The Nordic element was here a much stronger reality and less of an ideology than in Germany.

Eighteenth-century England, meanwhile, saw the creation of a vision that sought to transform the entire land into a magnificent garden, of course, a natural garden in the English style in contrast to the mannered parks of French absolutism: here national nature was something that had to be practically created. Alexander Pope, in his poem "Epistle to Burlington" (1731), praised the early landscape garden of his friend Lord Temple in Stowe as a countermodel to Versailles, as the expression of an inborn British thirst for freedom, the opposite of the French nation born to servitude. But even in France, the new dream of free nature flourished. In both countries, the "Arcadian" idyll was inspired by the pasture landscape. In

1804, however, William Blake saw "England's pleasant pastures," once home to "the holy Lamb of God," disfigured by "dark Satanic Mills."[69]

A "German garden" was designed by Christian Hirschfeld, the leading German garden theorist of Goethe's day, though he did it only in theory, not in practice. He was one of the first to call for parks open to the public. There a "certain overgrown" quality should exist; the garden ideal thus did not entirely exclude the wilderness ideal. These gardens became places for the soul's recuperation, where "all passions rest." And Hirschfeld ranted against the "crawling scum among the French" intent on stimulating lasciviousness. But Ludwig Tieck, a romantic, already found Hirschfeld's garden ideology comical. In 1808 the Fuldau garden architect Gustav Vorherr, in his tract *On the Beautification of Germany*, coined the slogan "Germany, all of Germany a great garden!" His final goal was to beautify the "great construction that was earth" and in this way refine humanity.

One unacknowledged source of modern environmental policy is to be sought in these garden-building projects that expanded into the landscape. Rita Gudermann has reminded us that from the end of the eighteenth to the middle of the nineteenth century there existed a "land beautification movement," which picked up the slogan "all of Germany a great garden" and sought to combine the aesthetically beautiful with the economically and sociopolitically useful, all of this under the banner of patriotism. Ian Tyrrell has discovered similar movements in California and Australia as forgotten precursors to the modern environmental movement.

Yet even at the height of German national nature romanticism, it always proved difficult to determine what exactly German nature was. Was it a variation of the new English garden nature? Beginning in 1804, Friedrich Ludwig von Sckell oversaw the construction of the English Garden in the Isar meadows in Munich. Some praised it as the "expression of the German spirit"; others thought it was dull. Riehl spoke disparagingly of the "shackled," fenced-in English parks that the hiker was not allowed to enter, and he glorified the "free forest" as the natural foundation of German liberty.[70] But which forest?

The difficulties that arise in the attempt to uncover and invent national nature can be productive. After all, nature is always a totality of infinite complexity, and that is why it was positive that observers were compelled early on to conceive of German nature as a multilayered thing. For Wilhelm Heinrich Riehl, German nature carries traces of history, and it is by no means elevating in every respect: although the Mittelgebirge, where Riehl himself came from, is the old German heartland, he saw it as an area enfeebled by fragmentation and overcultivation, while resources of strength could be found only in northern Germany and in the large region of southern Germany and Austria.[71] The natural tripartite division of Germany, however, was by no means destined by nature to form a trinity.

By contrast, the popular and edifying national nature presented itself in pictures that stylized real nature and picked out only individual elements from it. A pictorial quality was often attached also to the nature invoked by nature and landscape conservationists in an effort to justify the preservation of certain landscape scenarios. The invention of national natures can be traced earliest and most clearly in landscape painting, which reflected the taste of a wide range of consumers. At the beginning we find the Dutch depiction of their country, reclaimed from the sea and always threatened by water. When Old Dutch landscape painting broke with its Italian models and dispensed with the picturesque romanticism of mountains and valleys, it indulged in expansive space, in water and clouds, and in the charms of winter. All this possessed the appearance of wild nature, even though Holland was more intensely cultivated than Italy. In Germany, Russia, and Scandinavia, as well, there was a penchant for creating national landscapes as a Nordic contrast to the Italian idylls, much of which had sprung from the imagination of northern painters in the first place.[72]

The question of how one should conceive of national nature in concrete terms became a controversial one, especially with respect to the forest. The answer still seemed fairly straightforward in France, which has remained to this day far more a country of deciduous forests than Germany. Around the middle of the nineteenth century, the painting school of Barbizon at the edge of the forest of Fontainebleau fought an organized and effective battle against coniferous afforestation in what was a mixed deciduous forest region broken up by a traditional pasture economy. This school stands at the beginning of impressionist plein air painting, which is why it needed the forest more so than did studio painters; in fact, in 1860 it pushed through the establishment of a nature preserve expressly for artistic purposes. This was the first action on behalf of landscape protection in France. In contrast to France, German forestry, as Wilhelm Pfeil emphasized, was "solely the product of Germany's division into various states," which is why it did not know a "German" forest – at least not for the time being.[73]

In his painting "Hunter in the Forest," created under the influence of the Wars of Liberation, Caspar David Friedrich depicted a dense coniferous high forest, reminiscent of a Gothic cathedral; as the embodiment of the German forest, it devours the French intruder. The fir became popular as the German Christmas tree in the nineteenth century. In summer, though, most Germans preferred the mixed deciduous forest; and in the twentieth century, pollen scientists confirmed that this type of woodland was the natural vegetation in most regions of Germany. Incidentally, palynology provided the evidence for expanding the range of species that constituted the "natural" forest: it discovered that prior to the last ice age, many species had been native in Germany that were later pushed south by the ice. The most famous controversy after 1800 in Germany and France revolved around the introduction of the North American Douglas fir, which gave rise to veritable factions among foresters. Pollen analysis revealed, however, that ancestors of the Douglas had existed in Europe and had disappeared only during the ice age.

Some conservationists lauded the mixed forest of deciduous and coniferous trees as "German to the core" (*urdeutsch*). Yet it was precisely in the core regions of Prussia as well as Alpine Austria that the coniferous forest predominated. During the Nazi period, a committee to save the deciduous forest was formed within the Deutsche Heimatbund, and in 1941 it went public with a memorandum. One versifier complained: "O deutscher Wald, o Buchengrün / Und Kraft der starken Eichen / O deutscher Wald, du sinkst dahin / Von deines Würgers Streichen!" (O German forest, O birchy green / and the power of the strong oaks / O German forest, you're laid low / by your strangler's blows!). The committee invoked statements by Hitler that "the German landscape" must be "preserved at any cost as the source of the power and strength of our people." But the activists were honest enough to admit that before a "genuine German landscape" could be restored, it was necessary first to "ascertain the erstwhile forest" and to reconcile it with current interests. It is noticeable that in the mass of statements supporting the memorandum the national motive recedes completely behind ecological and hydrological arguments – and this in 1941! And for all that, if there was a forest that was especially "German," it was in fact the birch forest.[74]

The forest romanticism of German popular literature – whether Ludwig Ganghofer's *Schweigen im Walde* (Silence in the Forest), Peter Rosegger's *Waldbauernbub* (The Forest Farmer's Son), or Heinrich Hansjakob's *Waldleute* (Forest People) – has a predominantly regional, not national, character: it is the *Heimat* literature of the Alps and the Black Forest. In northern Germany, the most passionate nature romanticism focused on the Lüneburg Heath, which was the product of anthropogenic deforestation, but which became for Hermann Löns and his admirers the symbol of magnificent wilderness.

For Riehl, German nature, the forest wilderness, was a landscape that still existed in his day and was widely found, though threatened by many forces "hostile to nature." In the late nineteenth century, however, a growing number of pessimists believed that the gap between present reality and primordial German nature was growing ever wider. In 1913 Ludwig Klages found "Germania's fauna" nearly completely destroyed. Even the songbirds were becoming rarer "from year to year." "Only a human lifetime ago," he noted, "the blue air was full of the whirring of swallows in the summer even in the cities"; now it had grown "eerily quiet even in the countryside." Here we already find Rachel Carson's horror vision of a "silent spring" – and with a global perspective, no less – that so alarmed the public in the United States in the 1960s. Against this gloomy scenario, the "nature protection" that began to emerge at that time became the protection of small remaining preserves. Did it have to be that way? Especially the most passionate conservationists often failed to see that there was much that was worthy of protection outside of (supposedly) untouched nature, indeed, that new things were arising. For example, in the nineteenth century, the crested lark, a native of the steppe, made its way into Germany, where it found a habitat in the growing "cultivated steppes."[75]

Beginning at the end of the nineteenth century, nature protection and *Heimat* protection – the latter understood as the preservation of traditional rural architecture and villagescapes – were closely allied in Germany, similarly also in France. It is possible to construe a tension between the two endeavors: *Heimat* reflected a longing for the safety of home, while "nature" reflected the longing for freedom. But this was not necessarily a contradiction. Under European conditions, it makes sense to combine the two, for even the presumed wilderness areas are usually old pasture zones. Both yearnings had regional landscape images in mind: although people spoke of "German *Heimat*," they were usually talking about the *Heimat* of their most immediate, familiar environment. The strength of the German movement of nature and *Heimat* protection lay substantially in its regional associations.

The relationship between these movements and the political elites of Imperial Germany was mixed. Often they complained bitterly that their demands were being ignored by officials and industry. On the other hand, there was no lack of connections to the highest circles. And in principle there was a broad consensus that the desire to protect nature and *Heimat* was honorable and worthy of support. In 1906 the State Office for the Preservation of Natural Monuments (Staatliche Stelle für Naturdenkmalpflege) was set up in the Prussian Ministry of Culture under Hugo Conwentz; this seems to have been the first time in history that a separate office for the protection of nature was created. It was given a decentralized substructure through provincial branch offices. Conwentz avoided the public limelight, but he was well versed in the workings of the bureaucracy, and he won international renown. *Heimat* protection advanced rapidly after 1907 by means of the "despoliation laws" that were passed in rapid succession in the German states, and that established a shared code and routine of cooperation between the state and those in the movement. From the outset, nature protection was close to the bureaucracy, even if its energy came mostly from supporters who volunteered their time.[76]

Heimat and nature protection achieved its primary successes in the preservation of individual buildings and noteworthy trees, while the core areas of agrarian, forestry, and economic policy remained closed to it. In the popular imagination, however, the incarnation of nature was not only trees, but animals as well. Where was "German" nature when it came to animals? Wild megafauna with a national-German symbolism no longer existed. Germany had no counterpart to the American buffalo; the "German shepherd" was a new breed from around 1900. In the 1930s, the Nazi government tried in vain to naturalize the European bison on the Darß peninsula. The only reintroduced animal that survived the Nazi period was the beaver – more suitable as the symbol of Canada, though, than of Germany.

Instead, in Germany, as in many other countries, it was birds that enjoyed the greatest affection from nature lovers. The bird protection movement, much of which was borne by women, was among the pioneering groups of nature conservation, and it, especially, introduced an element of fanaticism into the love of nature. To this day, conservationists like to justify the need to protect certain areas by arguing that they are breeding or resting grounds of endangered birds. Bird protection met with a positive response from governments, all the way up to the Reich level. A Reich Bird Protection Law was passed in 1888, after twelve years of deliberation, though to the chagrin of many bird conservationists it continued to distinguish between useful birds (those that ate the right kind of insects) and useless birds. At the same time, the English bird protection movement, also carried on the shoulders of women, fought against bird hunting by trying to change consumer behavior with a vigorous campaign against plumed hats. The issue of bird protection opened up a split at that time between Northern and Southern Europe, where bird catching, under the banner of free hunting, became a popular sport. At one time it had also been popular in German-speaking lands, as we learn from Papageno's bird-catcher aria in Mozart's *Die Zauberflöte*. Henceforth, however, bird hunting revealed what was in the eyes of the Germanic nations the disturbed relationship of the Southern Europeans to nature. A sharp and widely noted response came from the Italian clergyman Giovanni Salvadori, a representative of Trent in the Austrian National Council, himself both a bird hunter and ornithologist. At the International Congress of Ornithologists in Vienna in 1884, he pleaded, on behalf of the insects threatened by birds, for a lifting of all restrictions on bird catching! In so doing he touched on a basic problem of conservation, namely that the protection of some species often occurs at the expense of others.

Presumably the strongest impulse behind German bird protection legislation at that time came not from nature romanticism, but from agriculture, which had discovered the extent to which the unrestricted hunting of birds exacerbated cater-pillar and insect infestations. An ecological approach to the question of birds and insects emerged above all from the pragmatic interests of farmers. Long before the DDT controversy, it was these interests that gave rise to a tradition of "biological pest control." And since migrating birds were indifferent to borders, an interna-tional convention for the protection of birds beneficial to agriculture came into effect as early as 1902.[77]

Looking back, one would have expected to find "national" motives especially when it came to protecting the Rhine against pollution. In the late nineteenth century, however, that became a hopeless endeavor, as far too many streams of waste collected in the "German river." In 1899 a high-ranking state official complained at the West German Fishery Meeting: "In 1870 we fought for the German Rhine River – in a new war our sons will be fighting for the German Rhine sewer!"[78]

Conceptions about a national nature were more sharply focused in the United States than in Germany. Since that country lacked a visible historical identity in the form of old cities and architectural monuments, Americans were even more deliberate in seeking out a national identity in nature. But what identity and in what nature? Thomas Jefferson thought the Potomac valley was unique, though European travelers felt reminded of the Rhine valley. Most impressive were the enormous forests with their gigantic trees, though they were threatened by an army of loggers: the axe was as American as the giant trees. Thomas Cole (1801–48) painted his great romantic forest panoramas already painfully aware that this nature was under threat. His poem "The Lament of the Forest" (1841) closes with a look ahead at the immediate future, when denuded mountains were baked by the sun, springs dried up, animals died, and "our old race" was scattered among the nations like the Israelites.[79]

It was only in the far West that the Americans discovered grandiose nature that could be said to surpass the Alps. Here the Yankees, who had long fought against wilderness, discovered their new ideal of wilderness. Yet they found it at precisely the time when this wilderness was under threat. American nature, too, was a nature in need of protection. This gave rise in the 1860s to the American national parks movement, which led to similar initiatives all over the world in the twentieth century. Yellowstone National Park was established in 1872, Yosemite National Park followed in 1890; a California state park had already existed in the Yosemite valley since 1864. These wildly romantic mountain landscapes have always remained the guiding images of the national parks idea – as one observer put it, "the best idea America ever had." This wild and gigantic mountain world offered a kind of nature identity in keeping with America's rise to a world power. Not until the 1930s and 1940s, when efforts were made to establish a national park in the Everglades in Florida, did the aspect of ecological "biodiversity" take precedence over the search for picturesque scenery. But the nationalist motive continued to be present in American conservation. When Rachel Carson, the future author of *Silent Spring*, participated in a contest for young people for the best "Conservation Pledge," she won second prize with the following entry: "I pledge myself to preserve and protect America's fertile soils, her mighty forest and rivers, her wildlife and minerals, for on these her greatness was established and her strength depends." But when her group "threatened to memorize and repeat the pledge unison every morning, Rachel had a sudden lapse of memory and never provided them the text."[80]

The national parks movement found a leader in John Muir, a man of the wilderness of prophetic stature who elevated the battle for the forests into "part of the eternal conflict between right and wrong," and who created the impression that this movement came out of the forests. In reality, though, the national parks idea sprang from the yearnings of city-dwellers and often collided with the interests of ranchers and loggers on the ground. For that reason the proponents of the national parks sought backing from the federal government, and since there was still a good deal of "public domain" in the West, federal intervention had a legal basis.[81]

At the same time, there were growing economic concerns about the logging of America's forests. As early as 1876, *Scientific American* published an editorial titled "Timber Waste a National Suicide" that saw the existence of the American nation acutely imperiled as a result of uncontrolled logging. In the 1880s Chicago's lumber market, until then the largest in the world, hit a crisis because the forest within its reach had been largely cut down. Much like Europe a century earlier, the United States now witnessed a wave of deforestation phobias with an exaggerated pessimism.[82]

The American president Theodore Roosevelt (in office 1901–9), a hyperactive reformer and imperialist of boundless energy, found in the protection of national resources against the greed of speculators and land robbers an activity he pursued with vigor and enthusiasm, and that attracted other men of action. In Gifford Pinchot, who was the head of the forestry division within the Department of Agriculture since 1900 and who saw himself as the leader of a great forestry renewal movement, Roosevelt found a congenial ally in the struggle for forest protection and afforestation: "There was something pantherlike about the Chief Forester, with his long, lean walk and hypnotic stare" (Edmund Morris). The protection of natural resources was a Herculean task for charismatic personalities.

As in Europe, the forest became a locus of power. After the United States had engaged for over a century in the greatest destructive exploitation of forests in the history of the world, forest and nature protection now became, as never before, a national task of the highest order and an ideal area in which to demonstrate statesmanlike energy. Nature protection, water protection, forestry policy, economic planning for the future, greater efficiency, strengthening of the nation: Theodore Roosevelt (and, in the 1930s, Franklin D. Roosevelt) united all these objectives, which in Europe often led a disparate existence, into a potent – though not harmonious – combination. The tension between "conservation" and "preservation," between sustainable resource use and protection of wild nature, remained obscured for a time. In the eyes of the forestry administration established by Pinchot, however, the gigantic ancient trees, the kings of the American forest, were merely a sign of ineffective forestry management.

Politically the strongest driving force behind forestry policy were the interests of the water economy; after all, it was believed that trees held the water. When it turned out that the irrigation of desert-like areas was not economical, it became a national task, though without being truly removed from the power play of special interests. Plans by the growing city of San Francisco to bring in water from the Hetch-Hetchy valley in Yosemite National Park led to a clash between "conservation" and "preservation," which the supporters of wilderness lost. This was at the same time the first great clash between conservationists and dam builders. "Remember Hetch-Hetchy" would become a battle cry of the Sierra Club throughout the twentieth century. From an ecological perspective today, the era of Theodore Roosevelt as well as Franklin D. Roosevelt's New Deal mark not only a turning point in environmental history, but also stages in a lasting disruption of the natural water balance.[83]

Even ardent conservationists usually did not have their eye on the totality of nature, but had certain preferences. For Theodore Roosevelt, the great hunter, nature consisted chiefly of animals, and he was surprised that John Muir, in whose company he visited Yosemite, "cared little for birds or bird songs, and knew little about them. The hermit thrushes meant nothing to him, the trees and the flowers and the cliffs everything." The problem of the selective love of nature became acute in the Kaibab controversy of the 1920s. At the time, the National Park Service had been so successful in decimating the predators in the Kaibab National Forest that the deer population rose from 4,000 to nearly 100,000 and devastated the forest. The power struggle between game wardens and the forestry administration turned into a clash between the state of Arizona and the federal government; eventually the Supreme Court weighed in and handed down a decision in favor of the federal government in 1928. The controversy became a transformative experience for Aldo Leopold, the new guiding intellect of American nature protection: though previously a hunter of predators, the affair taught him that it could be wise to leave nature to its own devices, which also meant leaving the predators to increase at their natural rate.[84] Since this respect for wilderness was in the end beneficial to the forest, it was also clear that the contradiction between "conservation" and "preservation" did have a solution. The later success of the environmental movement was based on the fact that it knew how to combine both traditions effectively.

More so than anywhere else in the world, the protection of nature and resources became in the United State a prime matter of national politics as early as the turn of the century; however, whether one can infer from this a broad and sustained effect remains an open question. A sustainable silviculture began to establish itself only in the 1920s, when limits on logging were in line with the interests of the oligopolistic lumber trade.[85] The waves of spectacular activism that were linked to a politicization at the highest levels remained invariably one-dimensional in their thrust, and they did not prevent the United States from becoming by far the greatest resource consumer in the world and an obstructionist on international agreements to reduce emissions. It would seem that the nature ideal of wilderness diverts attention away from guiding industrial civilization in a way that is more compatible with the environment.

What conclusion can we draw – also with a view toward the United States – about the history of nature and *Heimat* protection in Germany? "The nature protection we have is trivial nonsense [*Pritzelkram*]," scoffed Hermann Löns in 1911: "By contrast, one cannot deny that nature spoliation has a certain brilliant generosity. Nature spoliation works *en gros*, nature protection *en detail*. Teeth-gnashing wrath seizes one at the sight of the horrible despoiling of the German landscape." Indeed, from a distance many successes of nature protection seem rather trivial, and often enough, the movement to protect nature and *Heimat* dissipated its energies in petty and dreary political infighting. Ernst Rudorff warned in 1911 that the members of the executive would organize the Bund für Heimatschutz (League for *Heimat* Protection) "to death."[86] Still, these sarcastic comments are not the final word. One should not become too fixated on individual groups and episodes when drawing an overall historical conclusion. In the end, what matters is this: What kind of dynamic did these movements generate over the long term? What networks and interconnections to other currents of the time did they create? What was their part in providing environmental protection with institutional anchors, with a sustained long-term effect?

Although the Bund für Heimatschutz was opposed by manufacturers of lime and tar paper, it received financial backing from Krupp. The creation of the nature preserve at the Lüneburg Heath in 1911–12 even received massive support from Emperor Wilhelm II. Hugo Conwentz, the leading man of Prussian nature protection, enjoyed the protection of the powerful ministerial director Althoff. While many individual conservationists might have been powerless and inexperienced in the ways of the world, that is not true of nature protection as a whole. To be sure, in the struggle over the Laufenburg rapids, which were flooded by the damming of the Rhine to generate electricity, the *Heimat* protectors suffered a heavy defeat, even though many prominent intellectuals of the empire were on their side. Soon thereafter, though, a nature and *Heimat* protection initiative was partially successful when it came to the canalization of the Isar. Friedemann Schmoll, the most thorough student of the conservation movement during the empire, arrived at this surprising conclusion: "Contrary to the self-image often cultivated by conservationists, this was an exceedingly successful social movement. Within a very short period, their concerns were recognized also by the state as question of the common good and the public interest."[87]

Of course, there was and is no nature that is "only German." Still, it was a step forward scientifically and practically to think of nature not merely as something philosophical and general, but also as something regional and special, something that evolved in a reciprocal relationship with certain cultures. It is only within circumscribed spaces that one can get a concrete sense of the dynamic whole of nature. The possibilities of this intellectual approach were by no means exhausted in the age of nationalism, especially since it was ahead of the science of ecology.

Did the combining of nature and nation promote nationalistic illusions? At times it no doubt did; in some cases, though, it was precisely the national nature ideals that in the end led to the kind of disillusionment that gave rise to a critical environmental awareness. Rudorff admonished his countrymen as early as 1880 that in some respects the English and the French were far ahead of the Germans when it came to *Heimat* and landscape protection. Even in 1936, in the middle of the Nazi period, *Urdeutschland*, a representational volume of German nature protection, praised the conservation of the old forest of Bialowice by the Polish state as exemplary: nothing of the kind existed in Germany at the time. German nature offered no basis for nationalistic megalomania. It was self-evident even to the likes of Walther Schoenichen that many "natural wonders of foreign countries surpass in size and enormity the revelations of nature's powers that can be found in our homeland."[88]

Ulrich Beck's thesis that the older nature protection was never able to "shake off the nimbus of hostility to progress and backwardness that surrounded it" is not true; in fact, nature protection had good relations with science, economics, and technology. And it had an affinity with many reform movements of the time: the *Wandervogel* movement, educational reform, and the broad spectrum of reformers of sanitation, health, and life, who all had dynamic connections with each other. Here "nature" was not only something to be preserved, but also something to be newly created: for example, beginning in 1900, the "vegetarian fruit-growing colony Eden" created its fruit and garden paradise near Berlin, on sandy soil of the Brandenburg March using horse manure collected in the streets of Berlin. *Heimat* protectors fought not only to preserve old half-timbered houses, but also against water pollution and industrial emissions.[89] To be sure, the initiatives to protect nature and the environment were at that time still more scattered and less inter-connected than they were after 1970; but there is good reason to believe that over time, something like the later environmental movement would have arisen, had not the world wars destroyed so many nascent developments. From a modern perspec-tive, however, it is noticeable how few crosslinks existed a century ago between nature protection and environmental protection. What we today call "environ-mental protection" was found back then largely within the frameworks of "urban sanitation" and "urban renewal" and was beyond the mental horizon of nature protectors.

That there was something constructive and forward-looking about the love for one's native land is clear when we see the extent to which flight from the land and the chaotic growth of megacities is the bane of many countries around the world. In fact, one could see it as a weakness on the part of the contemporary environmental movement that it no longer has, to the same degree as the old nature protection movement, a foundation in love for *Heimat* and in the attachment to a familiar image of one's native land. For it is only such a guiding image that can be infused with popular support and desire – a threshold value for emissions that is negotiated among experts is not the kind of goal that inspires people.

The nationalization of *Heimat* and nature protection had the purpose, not least, of mobilizing state support at the highest levels. The assumption that the goal of these movements could be achieved only with strong state backing was fully justified – after all, any efforts along these lines would eventually bring you face to face with the entire industrialization process. At that time, however, the immediate environmental damage from industrialization was addressed almost entirely on the municipal, not the national, level. This was a time when the old city still existed on the outside more or less as a separate world marked off from its environs. It was above all in the cities that the downsides of industrialization attained a powerful sen-sory obtrusiveness, and for a long time the technical networks of supply and waste removal needed to remedy these situations were possible only within the urban framework. Far into the twentieth century, the city remained the most impor-tant arena of environmental policy; the nationalization of the human interaction with nature was more program than reality.

As it had been in preindustrial times, London, since 1810 the first city of the Western world with a million inhabitants, was in the nineteenth century the lead-ing metropolis of environmental complaints and renewal projects. An important innovation occurred in England in 1848 with the Public Health Act, which authorized local authorities to take over water companies, though only with their consent. Toward the end of the nineteenth century, however, Germany moved ahead of England, thanks to its tradition of urban self-government. Edwin Chadwick (1800–90), who was accused of wanting to turn himself into the British "health dictator," saw local governments as the enemy and fought for the establishment of a centralized, state health office; but in spite of its public impact, this centralized path threatened to turn into a dead end in the nineteenth century. The alliance between the sanitation movement and the cities that took shape in Germany in the late nineteenth century was more effective at the time. In the gloomy picture that Hans-Ulrich Wehler paints of Imperial Germany there is virtually only a single ray of hope: compared to other countries, Wehler argues, the German cities had the most modern and effective technical administration at the time, which responded in an "amazingly productive" way to many challenges posed by urbanization.

For a long time, the city was also the most important stage of environmental policy in the United States, where the local "Smoke Inspector" became a hero in the battle against the plague of smoke. Around 1940 all of America was transfixed by the battle that Raymond Tucker, the "Commissioner of Smoke Regulation" in St. Louis, was waging against the coal barons, a battle he won. "Never before," Frank Uekötter has written, "did a single engineer have similar power within American air quality control. And – as it would turn out – never again." In the 1950s, the fight against smoke began to shift to the national level.[90]

In England, the motherland of the Industrial Revolution, if we leave aside the conurbations around London and Manchester, it was much easier than in other countries to get rid of smoke and effluent: the constant westerly winds usually carried the smoke away from the British island fairly quickly, and most rivers dumped sewage and waste swiftly into the sea. It is no surprise that the head start that England attained in environmental policy in the nineteenth century was subsequently lost, and that later it was more likely to be one of those countries in the European Union that put the brakes on environmental policies.

Urban "sanitation" became the symbol of a great era of municipal politics and "urban technology," though it was also a period when cities became accustomed to a growing burden of debt. This happened even though municipal policy concerning utilities was profit-oriented, wherever possible, and for a while this policy was in fact successful. Accordingly, the building of sewage treatment plants was far less popular than the construction of water pipes, gas lines, electrical lines, and sewers. In 1877 the Prussian state made a determined attempt to stop the discharge of all untreated sewage into the rivers, but the cities, led by Frankfurt, were successful in softening the prohibition by invoking the theory of the "self-cleaning power of the rivers." For many cities this proved to be a Pyrrhic victory, since they themselves were suffering from discharges further upstream. Hamburg, which had taken the lead among German cities by constructing a sewer system on the English model and had thereafter enjoyed the reputation as an especially clean city, was thoroughly disgraced by the cholera epidemic in 1892, which cast a light on the absence of water treatment facilities and dismal hygienic conditions. Meanwhile, the Prussian-German public health policy, spearheaded by Robert Koch, emerged as the winner from the disaster. Altona, which was located downstream along the

Elbe and had long ago built a treatment plant since it was the recipient of Hamburg's effluent, was spared by the cholera; the lesson could not have been more
striking. At that time, state pressure was often necessary to get the cities to do
something about wastewater treatment. But the cities did learn from this terrible
experience: elsewhere it did not take a cholera epidemic for treatment facilities to
be built.[91]

Until the end of the nineteenth century, the situation was complicated by the
fact that while public health advocates everywhere fought for centralization of
the water supply, they were divided in matters relating to waste water disposal.
For decades, the schools of the miasmatists and contagionists were locked in battle.
Miasmatists directed their main attention to the pollution of the soil, and as a result
efforts to fight epidemics remained a largely local problem. While they possessed a
more varied environmental awareness than the contagionists, they had few objections to the discharge of waste into the rivers. It is no surprise that the miasma
theory was long popular with local municipalities, in Europe as well as the United
States. Bacteriologists, however, found that water was transporting pathogens over
long distances, and this discovery gave rise to calls for treatment plants and state
intervention. It was no coincidence that in Germany the chief miasmatist was a
Bavarian, Max von Pettenkofer, and the leader of the contagionists was a Prussian, Robert Koch; nor was it a coincidence that Pettenkofer taught in Munich,
whose river (the Isar) quickly carried away the city's effluent, and Koch in Berlin,
a city located in a plain. Pettenkofer publicly drank a sample of cholera bacteria
from Koch's laboratory to ridicule his opponent, and he was lucky to survive this
stunt without harm. But the Hamburg catastrophe of 1892 was his great defeat;
he shot himself in 1901.

The epidemics created pressure for a centralization of public health policy. The
1870s saw the establishment of the National Board of Health in the United States,
and of the Reichsgesundheitsamt (Reich Health Office) in Germany. Once the
bacteriologists had proved that water was an important transmitter of pathogens,
it would have been logical to elevate the concern for water purity into a national
task, but any effort in that direction encountered a multitude of obstacles. "Heaven
protect us . . . from a Reich waste water law," proclaimed Carl Duisberg, the head
of Bayer-Leverkusen, in 1912 at a meeting of the chemical industry. At that time it
could thus be foreseen that regulatory laws on a national level would be stricter than
the regulations of the cities, at least of those cities in which industry was dominant.

In the twentieth century, local control over waste disposal often acted as a drag
on environmental policy. The more expansive the "ecological footprint" of the
large cities became, and the wider the network of water supply and waste disposal
pushed into the surrounding areas, the greater was the temptation for a city to
clean itself up at the expense not only of its neighbors, but also of more distant
regions. In the United States, Chicago is an especially infamous example: to keep
Lake Michigan clean, it began to discharge its sewage into the Mississippi river
system through a Sanitary and Ship Canal beginning in 1900. St. Louis filed a
petition with the Supreme Court to stop Chicago from doing this, but the case was
dismissed.[92]

The new dimensions of the environmental problems demanded supraregional
authorities and loyalties, and to that extent the connection between nature and

nation makes sense. Still, even in modern environmental policy there is a logic that does not lead only to centralization. Wherever the strongest impulses came not from the discussions of the scientists, but from the sensory perceptions of those immediately affected – as was the case with smoke and noise pollution – more was often done on the local than the supraregional level.[93] The nature that needed protection was always most concretely present to the senses locally.

Within the modern environmental movement, globalization – not nationalization – was the slogan of environmental protection. Yet even in the late twentieth century, the story of the alliance between nature protection and nationalism was not over yet: the motif of nature and environmental protection played an important role in the nationalism of several of the new states that emerged from the breakup of the Soviet Union. So far, however, it is not possible to say what this new national nature rhetoric will mean in practice. To date, nature has usually resisted being instrumentalized by nationalism, even if the alliance between nature and nation was productive for a while. In Germany today, nature protection has become a way of coming to terms with the scars of the divided Germany and the loss of territory after World War II. Ecologists have discovered the prohibited zone along the former East German border as a refuge of rare species and would like to preserve it as a "green belt" straight across Germany. The Unteres Odertal National Park is in the process of expanding into an international park, since a national park has now been set up on the Polish side as well. After German refugees lamented for decades that the formerly German territories in the east were being sorely neglected, nature lovers are now discovering the pockets of wilderness there with great enthusiasm. The former GDR, much less densely settled than West Germany and until 1990 far behind in the push toward modernization, also presents itself as a realm of nature in tourism advertising. It is doubtful, though, whether this nature identity reflects the consciousness of the majority of the people living there.

Modern Israel offers a particularly striking example of the relationship between ecology and nationalism. Originally Israeli national pride was grounded in the belief that the country had restored, through irrigation and reforestation, the fertility of a land that had been nearly turned into a desert by many centuries of nomadic life. The American soil expert Walter Clay Lowdermilk had proclaimed this environmental interpretation as early as 1944 in his book *Palestine – Land of Promise* (a characteristic product of the Dust Bowl era and the New Deal), and it was eagerly picked up by the Zionists. However, the extremely high water consumption of the orange groves and eucalyptus forests – two showpieces of Zionist colonization – pushed Israel's water economy into an increasingly precarious situation. That prompted a leading Israeli journalist to write in 1997 of the danger that Zionist colonization could create an "ecological catastrophe" for the "small and fragile country." In contrast to the earlier ecological nationalism, environmental awareness today tends to promote an understanding between Israelis and Arabs.[94]

6. THE FIRST INDUSTRIAL ENVIRONMENTAL CRISIS AND THE GENESIS OF BASIC PATTERNS OF MODERN CRISIS MANAGEMENT

Contrary to what is often said, it is simply not true that humanity stumbled into industrialization unaware of its undesirable side effects. A blind faith in the blessings of technological progress never existed all by itself. The steam engine with its danger of explosion and its noise and smoke signaled early on that something disquieting of an entirely new kind was heading toward humanity, something that required a new vigilance. Complaints and anxieties accompanied industrialization from the very beginning. Perhaps the greatest achievement of environmental history to date has been the rediscovery of what was once a flood of complaints. There are often two different ways to read these sources: on the one hand, they throw light on deplorable conditions; on the other, they also demonstrate that people did not accept them passively.

Back then, the principle (derived from Roman law) that nobody has the right to impair his neighbor's full enjoyment of his property was more firmly entrenched than it was in some later periods. The right of private ownership, which was strengthened in the course of the modern period, was inherently well suited to consolidate this legal principle. In Paris around 1800, according to a contemporary account, a "constant battle" was raging "between factories and neighbors."[95] Although the ruthlessness with which expanding industry damaged its environment through emissions has always been lamented, and rightly so, one should also pay attention to the limits that were placed on this ruthlessness – especially in the leading industrial countries, and as early as the nineteenth century.

In the wealth of complaints we find the outlines of a general awareness of crisis, in particular once industry began to concentrate in large cities and conurbations. Here the deplorable downsides of industrial growth could be seen, heard, and smelled to a degree that is hard to imagine for residents of large, cleaned-up Western cities today, where one is no longer confronted by thick black smoke, roaring jackhammers, and discolored rivers. A broad consensus emerged in the nineteenth century that something had to be done. In 1901, at the general meeting of the Association of German Chemists, Hans Wislicenus, a chemist at the Tharandt Forestry College who had been battling the emissions of the smelting district in neighboring Freiberg since the 1850s, described "the plague of dust, the nuisance of soot, the question of sewage, the smoke damage" as the "problem children [*Schmerzenskinder*] of our industry" that challenged the "paternal care of the state [*Staatsgemeinschaft*]."[96]

More so even than today, urban environmental concerns in the nineteenth century were part of contexts that seemed to pose an immediate threat. The dirt and stench of industrial cities formed a continuum with the danger of epidemics and socially explosive problems. In miasma theory, which dominated thinking until the late nineteenth century, pollution of the soil was the worst source of disease. Bad odors were thus not only unpleasant but also the sign of a deadly threat. People back then had environmental concerns that today are forgotten. The cleanup of the cities began under the banner of miasma theory; the triumph of bacteriology toward the end of the nineteenth century, by contrast, allayed some early environmental fears. As Huber Hill noted in his essay *New Public Health* (1916): "The old public health was concerned with the environment; the new is concerned with the individual."

Yet the reign of bacteriology was not absolute around 1900. In fact, the belief in the healing power of fresh air and of sunlight that was not blocked by clouds of smoke was more popular than ever within the circles of the growing natural healing movement. "Where there is sun, there will be no doctor," was the credo of many mountain health resorts. But urban reformers, too, believed in the blessings of "light and air." In the health resorts lies one of the historical sources of the modern environmental awareness, and it has a certain logic that with the growing orientation of people toward recreation, this consciousness spread from vacation spots into everyday life.[97]

Today's ecological fundamentalists, who accept only respect for nature for its own sake, tend not to take the old environmental awareness that was intertwined with "sanitation" and "social questions" all that seriously. Yet it was precisely the close link to public health and social policy that could lend a special potency to environmental concerns. To be sure, the experiences of the nineteenth century in this regard are ambiguous. If the "social question" was defined chiefly as a problem of water pipes and ventilation for tenements, it was easy to divert attention away from conflicts over the distribution of wealth. Edwin Chadwick, the champion of "public health" and sewerage in England, was a hardliner on social policy, a proponent of the workhouse and enemy of bleeding-heart philanthropists. At the same time, though, attention to living conditions, water supply, and environmental conditions did bring home some very essential aspects of the disadvantages suffered by certain social groups, aspects that were overlooked if the focus was solely on wages and working hours. In the nineteenth century, "environmental justice" – a goal that the modern environmental movement was late in discovering – was a firm part of the environmental awareness.

In his book *The Condition of the Working Class in England* (1845), which became a Bible of the workers' movement, Friedrich Engels drew extensively on the report of the physician James Kay, a colleague of Chadwick's, titled *The Moral and Physical Condition of the Working Classes Employed in the Cotton Manufacture in Manchester* (1832). Then, as now, quality of life was as much a question of the environment as of wages. That was something that leading Social Democrats of Imperial Germany already understood. Philipp Scheidemann, as a representative of Solingen in the Reichstag, declared that the sight of the Müngsten Bridge, where technology corrected "apparent inconveniences of nature," made your "heart open up with joy; but then it is immediately painful to see the ink-black Wupper flowing beneath this marvel of technology."[98]

For a long time, the chief concern was directed at the contamination of soil and water with sewage. This concern had a long history, especially in the large cities. In Paris complaints about the Seine turning into a latrine reach back to the Middle Ages, especially since Parisians derived their drinking water from the Seine until the 1860s. Louis-Sébastion Mercier, who painted an exciting picture of Paris before 1788, was overcome with disgust when describing the hygienic conditions, and he listed the cemeteries in a litany of scandals along with the latrines. In Paris, as in many old cities, the complaint was voiced that the content of latrines was leaching into nearby wells: as long as the water supply and the disposal of sewage was a matter, not of the municipality, but of individual houses and neighborhoods, this was a nuisance whose cause was structural.

To a certain degree, however, this problem was in principle solvable, since excrement provided valuable fertilizer; the problem of industrial waste that was not readily recyclable appeared initially only peripherally. A *poudrette* industry that processed urban excrement into fertilizer established itself in and around Paris in the nineteenth century, and American cities emulated this example. Up to about 1890, Berlin acquired an area more than twice the size of the city itself to lay out sewage fields. The Berlin sewage fields, initially detested by the city's residents as a source of epidemics, were lauded at the time as a "first-rate accomplishment of civilization," even though their operation always required subsidies and Berlin's housewives – unless they were poor – turned up their noses at the vegetables grown there. After 1923 Cairo operated sewage fields with good success in the desert near Heliopolis, where nobody was bothered by the stench. Even street waste was valued as fertilizer because of the high ratio of horse manure it contained. Horse manure seems to have become an urban scandal most of all in the United States, which was less concerned with fertilization than the Old World.[99]

Among industrial waste and emissions, attention for a long time was given to those substances whose dangerous nature was already known from preindustrial times: arsenic, lead, mercury, sulphur, and hydrochloric acid. In late-nineteenth-century Prussia, it was the leach (waste with a high concentration of salt) of the rapidly growing potash production that drew a special storm of criticism; the unpleasant effect of saliferous effluents on drinking water and watered meadows in the environs of salt works was a well-known nuisance. Incidentally, the primary emission problem of the chemical industry in the nineteenth century consisted of sulphuric and hydrochloric acids; as such it seemed manageable in principle, since these harmful substances could be transformed into valuable products. When it came to coal smoke, the chief danger was seen to lie in its sulphur content; smoke from wood fires, which contained no sulphur, was considered harmless.[100]

Chemical plants had a bad name as "poison factories" and aroused special suspicion, for good reason. At the same time, the chemical industry, which transformed the pit coal tar generated in gasworks into glowing colors, was able to create an image for itself as the great future recycler of residual materials. Earlier than other industrial sectors, it built up a scientifically trained staff of experts that sought – with some success – to monopolize the discussion of the risks of the chemical industry. The new risks posed by this industry were far murkier than the well-known dangers of the old. That is no doubt a general dilemma in all discussions about the environment.

The main topic of environmental concerns in the nineteenth century was very old: *water!* In the nineteenth century, the fear of epidemics was focused above all on polluted water, so much so that other environmental problems initially receded into the background. Pressure to take action was much more acute with water pollution than with air pollution. For a long time, sanitizing the cities meant sewer systems, the disposal of wastewater, and the supply of controlled, clean drinking water. To this was added the many spas and hydrotherapy; the desire for recreation and recuperation revolved around water, even though it went against the insights of scientific medicine.

When it came to the supply of drinking water, the trend was initially from ground to river water; urban wells were generally suspected of being unclean, and the amount of water that was now required – not least for water closets – could be obtained at first only from rivers. However, this made the contamination of the rivers, terrifyingly exacerbated by the new sewer systems, into that much more of a threat. In light of bacteriology, the rivers – as Heinrich Zellner, a state chemist from Prussia warned in 1914 – were "highly suspect from a sanitary point of view." In 1912 the Rhenisch-Westphalian Committee to Keep Lakes and Rivers Clean lamented, in a submission to the Landtag, that "many rivers" could be "referred to only as fecal rivers." Filtration plants were built to clean river water, but given the state of purification technology at the time, this was, according to Zellner, "a very bad makeshift solution" and a "hygienically worrisome, aesthetically reprehensible business."[101]

In this situation, progress lay in opening up new groundwater resources through deep-well drilling. One expert described this groundwater as a "treasure in the womb of the earth," like "the loveliest spring water," "most excellently preserved from pathogens and often stored in immense quantities. . . . It is merely a question of lifting this treasure." Others, however, were already warning that the notion of the inexhaustibility of groundwater was a great fallacy.[102] And how could one be so certain that groundwater was hermetically sealed off from the dirt of the world above? Deep-will drilling took one into the realm of unpredictable and insidious risks. Had the cities stuck with their urban wells from the outset and taken steps to ensure their purity, this would have created a powerful impulse toward fighting contamination of the groundwater right where it occurred. Overuse of groundwater would have been evident from the need to dig the wells deeper. The large-scale use of groundwater and the application of motor pumps became the weakest point in the water supply systems in the twentieth century, especially in the world's arid zones. In many regions around the world this represents an especially dangerous ecological time bomb. Unlike with the forest, when it comes to the use of groundwater, what is missing is a sense of sustainability based on visual evidence and centuries of traditions.

In some respects, water protection was legal in a fairly favorable position. Abuses in water usage could be penalized much more easily than nuisances from smoke and noise, since the regulation of water use had a legal tradition stretching back into antiquity. Back then – much like today – some water protectors emphasized that the laws and regulations needed to keep water clean already existed, they merely had to be enforced.[103] Still, the liquid element did not make the work of lawyers easy. Moreover, the discharge of wastewater into the rivers was regarded as a customary right. Since the contamination of rivers was visibly manifest in dead fish, fishermen would have been in the best position to insist on traditional usage rights against polluters – but a right of fishermen to a precisely calibrated and actionable level of water purity was not stipulated anywhere in the law. This kind of specific stipulation would have been asking too much from the legal system at the time; moreover, up to a certain level, the discharge of sewage into water bodies actually boosted fish stocks. It is no surprise that the legal system was not prepared for the new situation; it was much more geared toward mediating between rafters, water millers, and farmers concerned about the irrigation of their meadows. And since drinking water had been obtained mostly from wells until then, any need for regulation had remained within the framework of neighbor law.

Quantitatively the largest single wastewater problem of Imperial Germany – the leachate of the potash industry, in which Germany held a global monopoly – was eventually regulated through a cartel system: through leachate concessions, production shares were distributed among the potash companies. In other words, a combination of economics and ecology, of limits on production and wastewater. Pressure to do something was created by the fact that the leachate of the potash industry in central Germany flowed into agricultural regions where – unlike in the Rhine-Ruhr area – it could not hide behind "local custom," and that it encountered not only influential large-scale agrarian entrepreneurs, but also assertive large cities like Magdeburg and Bremen, who invoked the needs of urban water sanitation. The years before 1914 saw public controversies whose rhetoric is reminiscent of the later ecological era. However, the regulation arrived at with the leachate cartel represented a dubious kind of trickery: although it contained an impetus to reduce the ratio of leach in order to increase production, it also established a right to pollute rivers, and it gave it mostly to those who had already been creating most of the river pollution. Although it kept the pollution load of the rivers within limits for a while, it was far from representing a solution to the problem.[104]

At a time when forests of belching chimneys towered over the industrial cities, *smoke* was an even more all-pervasive nuisance than water pollution. But the "plague of smoke" did not trigger a fear of epidemics. On the contrary, smoke had a long history as a disinfecting agent. The physician Samuel Hahnemann (1755–1843), who later founded homeopathy, published a polemic in 1787 to refute the "Prejudices against coal burning" and the fear that coal smoke caused lung diseases. While there had been a suspicion for a time that coal smoke was partly responsible for causing tuberculosis, the greatest plague of the nineteenth century, bacteriologists proved that this was not the case. True, the feeling that smoke was unhealthful was still widespread, but this was no more than a vague unease. Around 1900 it was chiefly cleanliness, not so much health, that was the slogan of those fighting smoke pollution, whether in Germany or the United States. The suspicion that smoke caused cancer did not begin to mount until the 1950s.[105]

The most plausible harmful effect was the impaired growth of vegetation from the reduction in sunlight. In Germany, as in other countries, it became customary to resolve this problem legally through compensation, which made some "smoke farmers" (*Rauchbauern*) into veritable beneficiaries of the smoke nuisance.[106] Incidentally, smoke was not only a problem of industry; a substantial proportion of the smoke hanging over the cities came from the chimneys of houses. Right up into the twentieth century, the "smoke plague" hardly ever became a political issue; instead, in continental Europe it was dealt with through the bureaucracy, in the United States through local citizen initiatives.

From the period of early industrialization, there was a standard remedy to reduce the nuisance that smoke caused to the immediate neighborhood: increasing the height of the chimneys. This was a one-time step, in keeping with the spirit of good neighborliness and the tradition of neighbor law. Moreover, high chimneys became a widely visible representational architecture of powerful factory owners. In many places the policy of tall chimneys continued into the 1970s; it shows the attractiveness of simple technical solutions that could be readily presented to the outside world.

As early as the seventeenth century, however, physicists had concluded from air pressure measurements that the atmosphere around the earth had to be limited. Moreover, earth's gravity, which – as air pressure revealed – reached high into the air, led to the conclusion that the smoke from chimneys did not dissipate into the infinity of space. Hence it was already understood in the nineteenth century – if one *wanted* to understand it – that tall chimneys were in many cases (for example, with "large quantities of acidic gases") no real solution at all. Although some occasionally reassured the public that the "mass of burned coal" disappeared "without a trace in the enormous sea of air," even Hans Wislicenus, who had reaffirmed that belief as late as 1901, described the 114-meter-high "Halsbrücker Esse," at the time the largest chimney in the world, in 1933 as a "giant cannon for the long-distance shelling of larger areas of woodland."[107] In the case of sulphur dioxide, scientists were able to prove that, even with tall chimneys, it did not vanish into thin air. Little attention was paid to carbon dioxide, however, and that indifference continued until the 1960s.

In the nineteenth century, it was already a well-known fact that at least the visible smoke could be drastically reduced through improved burning. And in this case – unlike with the costly tall chimneys – environmental protection and greater efficiency went hand in hand. In 1880 the English socioromantic and proto-ecologist William Morris held up the textile entrepreneur Titus Salt as a model: his factory chimneys in the model settlement of Saltaire near Bradford were "as guiltless of smoke as an ordinary kitchen chimney." So why were many entrepreneurs so hesitant to respond? Presumably not least because the boiler room was a "black box" to them, which they did not like to enter. It was a dark world inhabited by grim-looking characters, which was long beyond the reach of the engineers and for which lawyers could not come up with any legal norms. Regulatory authority and practical competence lay with completely different groups of people. But there was no fundamental conflict that would have blocked efforts to fight the "smoke plague." In principle, there was a broad consensus at the end of the nineteenth century from Germany to the United States that a good deal had to be done in this area and could be done. Here, as with so many environmental problems, the dilemma did not lie in a basic contradiction between society and nature, but rather in human inertia and the lack of effective coalitions of actors.[108]

The largest German debate over smoke damage in the nineteenth century, a debate that marks the beginning of the scientific study of smoke damage beyond Germany, as well, was carried on not in the large coal mining districts but in Saxony. The primary reason was that powerful state interests weighed in on both sides: opposed to the mining industry was the agricultural and forestry industry, which also had institutional representation within the state apparatus. In addition, two world-famous and neighboring institutions of higher learning clashed in the controversy over damage from the smoke of smelting works: the Freiburg *Bergakademie* (Mining Academy) and the Tharandt *Forsthochschule* (College of Forestry). On both sides there were eminent scientists who saw the smoke problem as a chance to demonstrate their expertise. In this way the smoke debate turned into a long-running controversy that did yield new scientific insights amid the clash of competing interests. And the insight into ecological interconnections can be found not only among those who placed the greatest emphasis on smoke damage: after all, such a monocausal argument diverted attention from forestry's responsibility for damage to woodlands.[109]

In the efforts to combat smoke damage, a significant difference emerged between American and German cities beginning in the late nineteenth century, a difference that mirrors the "civil society" in the United States and the bureaucratic traditions of continental Europe, the repercussions of which reverberate down to this day. Frank Uekötter has examined this contrast by studying numerous German and American cities. A hundred years ago, the smoke nuisance in large American cities was presumably even worse than in their German counterparts, since coal was cheaper in the United States than in Germany, which made small steam engines economical. Moreover, it was far more rare in American cities for residential and industrial zones to be separated, a separation that prevented at least the upper classes from being bothered by industrial emissions in German cities. The Englishman Arthur Shadwell remarked around 1900 – undoubtedly exaggerating – that "compared with the inferno of Pittsburgh," Essen, the German steel metropolis, "was a pleasure resort."[110]

In return, though, the smoke problem was tackled with a lot more vigor in American cities. Here there was no state policy one could rely on in such cases; instead, private initiative was called for. The organizations dedicated to fighting smoke pollution sought out an alliance with industry, and in many cases they were remarkably successful in doing so, at least as long as the issue revolved around visible smoke, which threatened a company's image in the neighborhood. "Smoke means waste!" was their slogan – a reduction in smoke emissions meant at the same time higher economic efficiency. While this idea was not unknown in Germany, it never became the slogan of large public campaigns. In Germany greater reliance was placed on the judicial system and the bureaucracy, but as a rule they did not have contacts with technology. Since the fight against smoke could be implemented in practice only in alliance with technicians, the American way often seems to have been more successful than the German one. That was less and less the case, however, when the problem of emissions could no longer be directly perceived by the senses and thus ceased to pose an immediate threat to a company's image. This was the situation in which the modern environmental movement arose, and which explains its tendency to be critical of industry. [111]

The most potent single factor behind the efforts to deal with environmental damage in the nineteenth and early twentieth centuries, in Germany as well as in Western Europe, was the *sanitation movement*. It is no exaggeration to speak of "movement" in this context: under the banner of hygiene, there arose a European-wide network comprising municipal politicians, physicians, and engineers, driven by an ethos and an enthusiasm that rose to the level of fanaticism. Sanitary rhetoric, with its central concern of the supply of clean water, focused especially on saving innocent children threatened by epidemics, which meant that its opponents did not fare much better than the Biblical Herod, the murderer of innocent children.

An international scientific community of urban sanitationists arose especially after the first International Sanitation Congress in 1852. This was a great period of "public health," when medicine seemed to be turning into social policy. The movement derived its potency from concrete, practical goals, but once these were reached, it found new ones, since the concept of health was broad and became broader still after 1900. The concern was not only individual cleanliness, but the health of society. More recently scholars have shown a predilection for interpreting the struggle over sanitation as a bourgeois strategy of social disciplining; it is more likely, though, that we are dealing with an elementary phenomenon, one that was by no means limited to the bourgeois elites, and that in fact created some discomfort to the latter. There was not only sanitation propaganda from the top, but also a sanitation movement from below with its own inherent dynamic.[112]

Unlike nature protectors, many sanitationists were filled with a sense of pride at the turn of the century. In 1911 the Cologne politician Peter Krautwig, who had turned the once noxious city of Cologne into a model of urban sanitation, could look back on half a century of splendid success. Since 1888 the mortality in German cities had for the first time dropped below that of the countryside: contemporaries saw this as a triumph of sanitation, even though it has not been demonstrated to what extent it was an achievement of the latter. Sanitationists had a much more enthusiastic relationship to modern technology than did nature protectors: after all, the networks of modern urban technology were at the very center of sanitation. This casts a light on what was at that time still a wide gap that separated nature protection and environmental protection as we think of it today.

From our current perspective, the sanitation movement was at the same time a solution to problems and the source of new problems. Leading sanitationists propagated first and foremost the water closet and sewer systems. Soon it reached the point that refined noses could no longer bear the smell of the "outhouse." The physician Georg Bonne, who was concerned about water pollution, complained in 1907 that it was "as though a frenzy seizes the population when they hear others raving about the water closet, and as though their magistrates and city councillors are hypnotized."[113] After all, like no other innovation, the water closet played a role in exacerbating the problem of river pollution to the point of crisis. Different ideals of cleanliness and sanitation worked at cross-purposes.

This drama was repeated in the 1950s, when the new chemical detergents covered entire rivers with a layer of foam. If one looks for the great historical driving forces of environmental protection, one encounters not least the human longing for cleanliness with all its ancient religious, moral, and sanitary motivations. But here, too, more than once the unintended consequences of solutions to problems were what created new problems.

The discharge of wastewater was also justified with a kind of faith in nature, namely the "self-cleaning power of rivers." Around 1900, however, it was obvious that nature's ability to help itself was no match for the sewers of the large cities. The debate over combined sewage systems was undoubtedly the greatest technological controversy of the nineteenth century that was relevant to the environment. At times Liebig condemned the "mixed sewage system" (*Schwemmkanalisation*), which carried off solid excrement together with liquid and other domestic wastes, as the downfall of civilization, because it deprived the already impoverished soils completely of nutrients. That this kind of sewage system did win out in the end was by no means a foregone conclusion: in the beginning, it was opposed by a broad coalition of established interests – from farmers to homeowners – and it forced municipalities to go into debt and raise taxes. As a result, in the vast majority of cities, the completion of the sewage system dragged on well into the twentieth century. However, unlike other alternatives, *Schwemmkanalisation* had the advantage that it was a compact, grand solution, around which interests could crystalize and which increasingly had the revulsion over foul odors as the "clinching argument" on its side. Within the mixed sewage system there are to this day various options, sometimes even within the same city, depending on whether rain water is carried away together with household wastes or separately. In many places, the controversy between supporters of a mixed and a separated system has continued.

Conceptually, treatment plants or sewage fields were part of the sewage system early on. James Hobrecht, the chief planner of the Berlin sewage system, pointed out that the small Silesian town of Bunzlau (modern Boleslawiec), which had constructed a sewer as early as 1559, had put sewage irrigation in place. For Chadwick, too, sewage fields were part of sewerage; only these fields made the system perfect. With sewage irrigation, as he put it, "we complete the circle, and realize the Egyptian type of eternity by bringing as it were the serpent's tail into the serpent's mouth."[114] Still, sewage fields did not manage to become common practice, and if they were laid out, they usually did not last long.

As a rule, the building of treatment plants also lagged far behind the construction of sewage systems. Although there were many opinions on this issue, there was no major discussion, and even less so a compact and definitive solution. When the cholera outbreak in Hamburg stopped at the borders of Altona in 1892, the treatment plant seemed like the "happy end" to the catastrophe; in reality, though, the search for the perfect water treatment method continues to this day. True, a growing number of treatment facilities were built around 1900, mechanical and even chemical and biological ones; but as the physician Bonne put it, "the waters into which these 'treatment plants' discharge their yellowish-brown, murky tides" were "a foul-smelling warning sign." In the course of the twentieth century, treatment plants grew into a large-scale technology and a mirror of scientific disciplines by splitting into mechanical, chemical, and biological divisions. Still, expensive water treatment technology remained, on a global level, a specialty of the leading industrial countries, and not even there did it become standard in all cities. And the sewage fields, which returned urban excreta to agriculture and which the sanitationist Alfred Grotjahn as late as 1902 saw as the source of "abundant fertility" for Berlin's sandy environs, were an utter abomination in the eyes of the landscape protector Alwin Seifert and a mockery of any notion of sanitation.[115]

In the late nineteenth century in the leading industrial states, a whole host of basic patterns for dealing with industrial environmental problems – patterns that are still in effect today – were laid down and anchored with tenacious inertia within technological systems: from sewerage to the "end-of-the-pipe" technologies like treatment plants and chimneys, from the negotiated setting of emission thresholds to the partial separation of residential and industrial zones. It is not all that easy to assess these strategies as a whole. Technical "sanitation" in the factories usually meant improved ventilation and the transportation of harmful substances from working areas into the environment; this could create a clash between protection of the workplace and protection of the environment, with the result that the cadre of physicians, often the only usable experts on environmental dangers in court, was split on this issue.

"Nothing would be easier," Frank Uekötter has said, "than to write a satire about threshold values" – whether we are talking about the effluent from early chemical factories or radioactive emissions from nuclear power plants. In the beginning the politics of threshold values often had more symbolic than practical significance, since the threshold values could be neither scientifically justified nor enforced. But what was the alternative? In hindsight, the strategy of setting limits to what was acceptable is an encouraging example of how an environmental policy that was at first merely symbolic acquired real substance over time. For James Lovelock, the creator of the Gaia hypothesis, nineteenth-century urban water policies are a good example of how a practically minded generation can manage its worst environmental problems even without an adequate scientific basis.[116] To be sure, from our perspective today, many of the measures taken back then were not real solutions, since the worst abuses were merely removed from the sight of the middle class and demonstrated to the outside world that action was being taken. Still, measured against the emission levels at the time, and what was known back then about their harmful effects, the large projects of "urban sanitation" were more than a farce.

And yet, a look back at the long history of waste management reminds us that there is no definitive solution and no end to the story, at least not under the conditions of modern industrial civilization. The systems of centralized water supply and wastewater removal that were put in place at the end of the nineteenth century were impressive accomplishments for their time, but they left urban water sanitation with the typical problem of large technical systems: a lack of flexibility. Martin Melosi's summary assessment at the end of his comprehensive study of urban sanitation in the United States applies to the entire world: "The commitment to permanent, centralized technical systems to resolve sanitary problems in fact left little room for adapting those systems to meet new and serious challenges."[117] And there has been no lack of such challenges.

It was not only the authorities that became active; the private sector also got involved. As Ulrike Gilhaus has written, around 1914 there already existed "such a wealth of environmental technologies" that a "guide to the smoke and soot issue" declared that it was impossible to discuss them all.[118] At that time, electricity and "white coal" (hydropower) seemed to permanently resolve many of the environmental dangers and threats to public health that had been created by the first, dark phase of industrialization. Advances in chemistry also seduced many into the optimistic belief that technology would solve its own problems by moving forward. Strictly speaking, however, many of the advances in safety and "sanitation" were merely a by-product of a development that was focused primarily on private profit. A reorientation of technology toward collective environmental interests did not take place.

6

In the Labyrinth of Globalization

Today, historical consciousness as it relates to environmental issues means realizing, above all else, that the current economic system is utterly unlike anything that has ever existed before in history: in a *single* year, this economy burns and vents into the atmosphere fossil fuels that took a million years to create, without comprehending – let alone managing – the full consequences of these processes. The origin of this great turning point is already found in the transition to the age of coal. Yet the full unleashing of the nonsustainable economy did not occur until the twentieth century; in fact, much of it has taken place so recently that this period has yet to take on clear contours in historical scholarship.

The new element is less the exploitation of nonrenewable resources as such than the rapidly accelerating pace and the all-pervasive and global dimension of this process. Because in the age of electrification, motorization, and mass media, individual occurrences do not remain confined to specific regions and sectors of the economy as much as they used to, there are an ever growing number of unintended synergistic effects. Roads cut into remote areas and population growth made possible by modern medicine thwart the official forest protection policies in many parts of the world. It was not only spectacular, cutting-edge advances like nuclear and genetic technology and the new chemistry that established a new era in the history of the environment – inconspicuous, mundane technologies like the motorized pump and the chainsaw did the same.

The first two decades after 1945 in West Germany have often been described as an "era of restoration." In reality, the backward-looking models of the Adenauer era were overpowered by the dynamic of mass consumption and the interaction of many technological developments. The acceleration of a multitude of processes, for Arnold Toynbee the most unsettling aspect of the modern development, reduces the ability of society to create institutions to monitor and control them. While train crashes were major events that called for action and consequences, society's capacity to react could no longer keep up with the growing avalanche of automobile accidents in the twentieth century. Unlike coal smoke, car emissions were a new kind of environmental problem, in the face of which the institutions of the state failed for a long time. Motorization acquired the irresistibility of a natural process. In the nineteenth century, that great era of the railroad, the increase in tempo still took place in a linear and more or less comprehensible fashion: in the twentieth century, by contrast, acceleration impulses of the most diverse kind intersected and interacted.

Of epochal significance for environmental history is the fundamental change in the nature of the environmental problems, especially in the industrialized state. The Club of Rome study *Limits to Growth* – which was published on March 6, 1972, was translated into thirty-seven languages and sold twelve million copies worldwide – still appealed to the old fear of the exhaustion of resources, and this accounts for its immediate and immense impact.[1] Subsequently, however, it turned out, unexpectedly, that the problem of resource depletion was not acute. Instead, the pollution of the "global commons," the atmosphere and the seas, emerged as a growing threat. The environment was not threatened by a scarcity of energy, as still seemed the case in the "oil crisis" of 1973, but by the abundance of cheap sources of energy – at least in the leading industrial states. In agriculture, the ecological problem is no longer a shortage of fertilizer, but overfertilization; no longer weeds and pests but the excessive use of herbicides and pesticides.

The new situation has been created precisely by the radical solution to problems that were thousands of years old. Some historians emphasize that the destruction of the environment today springs from roots that have always been present in human beings, but that is at best a partial truth: human beings had customary ways of dealing with the age-old environmental problems. From a historical perspective it is not surprising, however, that human norms and institutions are not adapted to most of the contemporary ecological risks, and that the countries of the Third World, which were overrun by modern technology much more rapidly than the old industrial nations were, are in a particularly bad situation in this regard.

Traditional environmental woes in many cases still have priority in the Third World: declining soil fertility, erosion as a result of deforestation, salinization as a consequence of irrigation. In many cases, however, these have been greatly exacerbated by the new economic dynamic, which is especially destructive where it reinforces traditional ecological instabilities. Only since the 1950s has the destruction of tropical forests in parts of Africa become a large-scale disaster – no less a man than Albert Schweitzer had still proclaimed: "What a joy it was to win fields from the jungle!"[2] In the industrialized countries, the ecological destabilization of the agricultural economy is concealed by the energy expenditure on chemical fertilizer and by the importation of animal feed, partly from the Third World. Whereas traditional erosion often merely transported soil from the mountain slopes to the valleys and thus did not remove it permanently from human use, the rapidly spreading sealing of the soil through construction and asphalt amounts to an irreversible loss of land over the medium term. Much of this is a direct or indirect effect of mass motorization, which has advanced unabated even in the ecological era.

To all appearances, the *automobile* has been the largest single factor in environmental history since the middle of the twentieth century. Not only did it generate a new kind of emission problem and lead to a paving of the landscape on a large scale, but it also created a new mentality, a new way of life, which has most likely become so irresistible around the world because it stimulates in humanity an ancient

yearning for mobility. To what extent the automobile responded to an already existing need or created this need in the first place is open to debate. In the expansive
United States, the mobile mentality was surely more pronounced earlier on than
in much less expansive Europe. There, too, the automobile aroused enthusiasm
already at the beginning of the twentieth century. Resistance to unchecked automobilism, however, was for a long time just as passionate and widespread, even
though it was not as well organized as were the car enthusiasts, which is why it
has been forgotten today.[3]

The Swiss environmental historian Christian Pfister has contributed the term
"50s syndrome" to the debate and has identified the 1950s as the most profound
turning point in the history of the environment, as the time when the era of the
global threat truly begins. For him, the decisive criterion is the greenhouse gases
emitted into the atmosphere: these emissions began to accelerate so sharply in the
1950s that everything that came before seems harmless by comparison. To Pfister,
the good old days extend into the 1940s – a view that is perhaps easier to arrive
at from a Swiss perspective than in countries affected by the Second World War!
One can debate whether – from a global perspective – the turning point is marked
best by the 1950s, the 1960s, or the 1970s; but the fact *that* a great turning point
occurred is confirmed by a wealth of indicators. Since the most recent past lies
within the blind spot of the historian's perspective, this epochal watershed has so far
been hardly conceptualized, even though it is in all likelihood far more important
than the Industrial Revolution of the eighteenth century.[4]

As the term "syndrome" already indicates, several developments of differing
origins came together in the turning point of the 1950s; still, Pfister assigns crucial
responsibility to *one* cause: declining oil prices. From the perspective of the age
of oil, the age of coal seems in many respects a continuation of the age of wood:
the extraction of coal was a laborious process, and it still required a lot of human
labor to provide this energy source. Under these circumstances, industrialization
remained strongly tied to places where coal was found. Only oil launched an almost
effortless exploitation of the earth's fossil resources, which could be intensified at
will in a short time, and which made possible a wasteful mentality that is without
parallel in human history.

The term "recycling" took on its current meaning around 1960: at precisely
the time when the reuse of disposed items ceased to be an everyday habit and
the utilization of the growing quantities of garbage spawned new industries and
technologies. The advance of synthetic products was making reuse by the consumer
more difficult, in any case. The avalanche of plastic, which created an entirely new
kind of waste problem, is also a result of cheap oil. The effect has been all-pervasive:
nothing enrages the hiker across the globe more than the plastic trash that mars even
the loveliest landscapes. Garbage archaeologists believe they can show, however,
that some conventional garbage alters the subsoil more strongly than plastic trash,
which gets compressed and is inactive.[5]

There are a number of obvious objections to the thesis of the "50s syndrome."
To begin with, the monocausal emphasis on the oil factor is open to debate. One
counterexample is the former German Democratic Republic, which received little
from the abundance of cheap oil, but whose per capita energy use and associated
emissions surpassed even Western countries: a careless relationship to energy and

the environment could develop just as easily on the basis of brown coal. The example of Japan also shows that low oil prices do not have the importance for an explosive economic dynamism that is often attributed to them in the West.

There are also fundamental reasons why it is unsatisfactory to image a new source of energy as a first cause. After all, the cheap oil did not flow by itself: feverish prospecting and a global race between large corporations was the precondition, which means that in the final analysis the reason was the justified expectation of an enormous business opportunity. Incidentally the 1950s as the turning point is open to challenge. Even in a "car country" of today like the Federal Republic of Germany, the automobile began to dominate urban and land planning on a large scale only after 1960. The change in lifestyle that caused the environmental burdens to surge occurred substantially only in the 1960s and 1970s. As late as 1967, consultants who were supposed to persuade housewives to buy new electric appliances were heard to complain: "Inside all of us there is still the fear of throwing things away."[6] The fixation on the "50s syndrome" could divert our attention away from new, environmentally harmful developments even more recently than that, for example, mass tourism and air travel. No small number of environmental burdens did not peak until the age of the "ecological revolution"!

This entire process was not merely an accidental concurrence of diverse circumstances. Instead, it also contains a strong intentional aspect: around the world, the United States was seen as utopia realized – the "land of unlimited opportunities," which had long been accustomed to a wasteful relationship to space and resources, and whose expansiveness became a trump card like never before in the age of motorization and mobility. Although the gasoline engine, the greatest single factor behind the new assault on the environment, was developed in Europe, the dynamism of an economy founded on fossil energy sources was in many ways still being obstructed and slowed down in the Old World through cartels, artificially high energy prices, political boundaries, and traditions of thrift. This dynamism was fully unleashed only in the United States. The world wars destroyed not only Europe's political but also its cultural hegemony. And communism, as we now know, had nothing comparable to challenge the attractiveness of U.S. civilization.

Since the 1950s, the technological revolutions in agriculture have been at least as important to the environment as the innovations in industry. While the agrarian reforms of the eighteenth and nineteenth centuries had still been generally aimed at perfecting the traditional cycle of matter – improving the crop rotation and combining agriculture and stockraising, that goal became obsolete with the massive application of chemical fertilizers: it meant the end of an agricultural era that was thousands of years old. As a cynical witticism put it, the best crop rotation was "wheat – maize – building land."

Even a geographer who is otherwise not given to ecological pessimism concluded: "With the second agrarian and technological revolution since the 1950s, the degradation, erosion, and poisoning of the soil caused by humans has intensified to an almost exponential degree."[7] At the same time, the remnants of the subsistence economy that had persisted into the twentieth century rapidly came under pressure: with it dwindled an element that had not only offered the last hope in desperate times, but that had, all in all, contributed to the ecological stability of human existence. Like never before, economic growth began to shape ways of thinking as well as the outlook on the future. In the 1950s, people were initially unsure whether they could trust the new prosperity; in the end, though, the economic thinking that declared growth the normal state of affairs triumphed. The presence of cheap oil was joined by the belief in a future of even cheaper nuclear power. And within the field of nuclear technology, the reactors of the present were joined by visions of fast breeder reactors and fusion power plants, which promised to provide any amount of energy that was needed for all times. Especially in the 1950s, when civilian nuclear power was still more fantasy than reality, the fast breeder and fusion reactors were seen as the final goal of nuclear technology. Today, what was once the future of nuclear power has been nearly forgotten.[8]

In Europe, the 1950s seemed a strikingly new era against the background of recent war and misery. This turning point was one that transcended individual nations and became a global phenomenon, not only with mass prosperity created by a booming economy, but even more so with the consequences for the environment. In Germany, France, and Italy, the development was largely parallel, at least in its basic traits. Vito Fumagalli even went so far as to use the term "final solution" for the elimination of the last woodlands, gardens, and hedges in the Po valley at that time. According to one French environmental study in 1990, the French landscape has been changed more profoundly since 1950 than in the previous thousand years.[9]

Confronted by the American way of life, Soviet Communism never developed its own concept of technological progress, conceiving instead the hopeless ambition of overtaking the West. Although defenders of nature were not absent in the original cadre of Russian revolutionaries, communism's disdain for peasant traditions led to a ruthlessness in the treatment of the soil that surpassed even that of Western capitalism. Moreover, a system in which the state professed to solve all problems arising from the narrow-mindedness of self-interest lacked any counterweight to the state.

As late as the 1930s, the Soviet Union was a leader in erosion research. Khrushchev, however, who pursued a boost in agricultural production much more single-mindedly than Stalin had, caused an ecological disaster on an enormous scale in regions of Central Asia prone to desertification by pushing maize and cotton campaigns that paid little heed to regional soil and water conditions. In the 1960s, the Aral Sea began to dry up as a result of the Karakum Canal, and the large-scale pollution of Lake Baikal by the cellulose industry became a scandal. In 1985 the Russian writer Valentin Rasputin remarked that it "took very little" to become a convert to the Soviet environmental movement: "One simply has to remember and compare what our earth looked like twenty, or even ten years ago and what has become of it."[10]

At the beginning of the 1970s, at the time of the UN's Stockholm Environmental Conference (1972), the ecology movement was still widely seen as a phenomenon of rich industrial states that no longer knew hunger and could thus pursue "postmaterialist" values. Representatives of the "Third World" initially reacted indignantly to the "Limits of Growth," as though this was an evil trick of the First World to deny the rest of the world the growth it had successfully achieved. Since then, however, it has turned out that wide regions of the Third World are affected much worse and more directly by environmental problems than the First World, though in many cases it is traditional problems that dominate, which are not so interesting to modern ecology. However, once the "Green Revolution" began advancing in the Third World, traditional problems there were joined by new problems created by solutions to old ones.

Although the "Green Revolution" began in Mexico as early as the 1950s with "Mexican Wheat" or "Miracle Wheat," its breakthrough on a large scale did not occur until the 1970s, that is, almost contemporaneously with the environmental movement, and on some issues – such as replacing the massive application of DDT with more gentle methods of pest control – it certainly learned from ecological criticism. Nevertheless, like the second agrarian revolution in the industrialized countries, it has led to a massive use of chemical fertilizers all over the world, often to much more intensive irrigation together with its resulting problems, and always to the breakup of the small-scale cycles of nutrients that formed the basis of the ecological stability of agriculture across millennia. Mexican farmers, who had initially been given the chemical fertilizers free of charge, found themselves caught in a vicious cycle of debt when they could no longer manage without the purchase of fertilizer and had to buy pesticides as well: their fate has long since become emblematic of small farmers in the Third World. Even Asian rice cultivation, which in its traditional method got by almost without fertilizer, is being invaded by highly bred Japanese varieties that are dependent on chemical fertilizers and destroy the old, inherent ecological stability of rice cultivation.[11]

From a historical perspective, one thing becomes especially clear in all of this: the older, sustainable type of agrarian reform, which sought to optimize the balance between agriculture and pasture, possessed an inherent affinity for the small and medium-sized farmer, who on his manageable piece of land had his eyes everywhere and did what he had to in his own interest. Here the ecological problems of intensive agriculture were compensated by the farmer's intensive relationship to his land. By contrast, modern-day technologized and chemicalized agriculture has an affinity to large-scale operations; an intensification of the highest degree is now possible over large areas. In that regard, social power structures can reverberate into daily agrarian life more so than before and destroy the peasant subsistence economy in a way that would have been impossible before the twentieth century.

Rural flight and the cancer-like growth of large cities and their slums have become the most depressing markers of the Third World – this, too, has happened only in the decades after 1945. Until the 1940s, Mexico City was famous for being one of the most beautiful cities of the world, an idyllic place of canals, gardens, and bowers; in fact, as late as the 1960s, people spoke of the "champagne air" of the Mexican capital. More recently, however, Mexico City has been called "the antechamber to an ecological Hiroshima," where smog levels in 1988 exceeded the limits of the World Health Organization on 312 days, and where in 1991 oxygen booths were set up for residents.[12] This city, which had about 200,000 inhabitants around 1850, had reached the twenty million mark by the end of the twentieth century and had grown into the largest metropolis in the world. In a great many large cities around the world, we can discern today an inability on the part of existing institutions to cope with the ecological as well as social problems of rapid urban growth. In hindsight it is apparent how right the critics of megacities were, who watched the rise of the metropolises with grave suspicion, and what kind of horror scenarios were avoided in the old industrialized states in spite of the many deplorable conditions that did exist. However, since the urban way of life usually lowers the birth rate, it may also have ecologically stabilizing effects. "Harmony with nature" does not always go hand in hand with an aesthetic idyll!

During the second half of the twentieth century, hydropower megaprojects and nuclear power plants have become environmental risks of the highest order. Both technologies were born of the awareness that fossil fuel resources are finite – that is to say, in their origin they were aimed at solving environmental problems. The UN's First Geneva Atomic Conference in August of 1955 triggered a global wave of enthusiasm for nuclear power. In retrospect that seems paradoxical, since not a single civilian nuclear power plant existed anywhere in the world at that time. Stranger still is the fact that the greatest sensation at Geneva was the reference to the prospect of fusion energy by Homi Bhabha, the Indian conference chairman. Journalists did not understand that the idea of a fusion reactor was pure fantasy. With complex technologies, the very complexity itself becomes a factor. As late as 1952, Bhabha had been an advocate of solar energy – a sensible goal in a tropical country! It is evident how in 1955 the established vision of a high-tech utilization of solar energy was absorbed by the phantom of fusion, which was supposed to generate energy after the model of the sun, though in reality the model was the hydrogen bomb.

As strange as it may sound, psychologically speaking, the atomic euphoria at that time was not all that dissimilar from the later environmental movement that fought against nuclear technology. Messianic hopes were generated at the Geneva Conference not least by the fact that against the backdrop of the "thaw" in the Soviet Union following Stalin's death, the fear of nuclear war was submerged by the hopes placed in the "peaceful atom." A nightmare of humankind was being transformed into a beautiful dream. All this explains the enthusiasm that was directed at civilian nuclear technology around the world at the time, and that sustained the international nuclear community.

Prior to that, engineers all over the globe had been convinced that *hydropower* was the way of the future, a seemingly clean and inexhaustible source of energy. The future seemed to belong to the alliance of electricity and hydropower, even though electricity was being generated largely by steam. In his early, optimistic phase, Lewis Mumford believed that electricity ushered in a new era of environmentally friendly "neotechnics" that would replace the dark "paleotechnics." The great era of the gigantic dams began around 1900 in Germany, France, and the United States. In densely settled regions of Europe, where the collapse of a dam would be catastrophic, the awareness of the risk was high, and the construction of many early dams was preceded by heated debates. In Germany, the so-called cyclopean masonry construction was initially given preference over concrete. The effects that the artificial lakes had on a region's natural water cycle were unclear to the public at the time; in fact, questions about regional water cycles were studied only in the wake of the creation of lakes for hydropower. In Germany the initial impulse for the construction of dams came from the immense growth in the demand for water in the Ruhr region (the country's industrial heartland); the drinking water quality of the artificial lakes was at times the topic of heated controversies.[13]

Around the world, however, the strongest new impulse for the construction of dams in the twentieth century came from the generation of electricity. Dams became the preferred national prestige projects, whether in the United States during the New Deal, in Stalinist Russia, in Nasser's Egypt, or in Nehru's India. To an entire class of engineers, dams became the fascinating mega-project par excellence, which fulfilled several functions all in one: generating power without smoke-belching chimneys, regulating the water level in the interest of shipping, preventing flooding, and in some cases also supplying drinking water and irrigating agricultural land. In general, though, *one* function had priority and often clashed with other water interests.

In Germany dam construction collided with the *Heimatschutz* movement, but this opposition usually did not have any lasting impact. Some members of the movement were, in fact, not sure of where they stood: Did artificial lakes not contribute to beautifying the *Heimat?* Were they not the alternative to smoke-spewing coal plants? Did not nature herself collect water in lakes? In Germany's water-rich Mittelgebirge region, the ecological effects of artificial lakes were not all that dramatic. But in the Alps, Europe's "mountains of power" in the eyes of the prophets of hydropower, the situation was more worrisome: as a result of the lakes created by dams, idyllic Alpine valleys dried up and turned into gravel-covered slopes. Resistance to a further expansion of hydropower usage grew in the course of the twentieth century, and in the 1960s it even merged with an enthusiasm for nuclear energy as the new alternative to hydropower.[14]

In the Third World, the great era of gigantic dams began in the 1950s, when Egypt laid out plans for the new Aswan Dam. At that time, the twenty-one dams of the TVA (Tennessee Valley Authority), the most famous organization of the New Deal, were the shining model. The World Bank, which funded many dam projects in the Third World, stood in the TVA tradition. More so than ever before, it was above all the fascination with the generation of power that crushed all concerns and overpowered the traditional, diverse perception of water. As we now know, in southern countries the large artificial lakes often brought an ecological fiasco in their wake, whether through the enormous silt deposits, the increased evaporation, or the breeding grounds of epidemic diseases provided by the standing bodies of water. Dams, and chief among them the Aswan Dam, have become the prototypes of ecologically disastrous mega-technology. However, some of the alternatives also have their pitfalls, for example, the more intensive utilization of groundwater, which leads to a lowering of groundwater levels. That is why a principled ecological opposition to every kind of dam project is not justified. It is not possible to make sweeping statements about the ecological effects of artificial lakes: if the rate of evaporation is not excessive, these lakes can counteract the decline in groundwater levels caused by river regulation. Here, as with many measures of environmental policy, there are no absolute truths that apply independent of space and time.[15]

Even in the second half of the twentieth and at the beginning of the twenty-first centuries, the changes that humans are making to nature have not become completely unrestrained. Perhaps a hundred years from now people will look on our world as one that was comparatively close to nature. And one must never forget that there still is a lot of nature to be lost. To be sure, in Europe wilderness has long since become an artefact of the imagination, but as late as 2002, according to one calculation by a committee of international experts, nearly half of the world's landmass was still covered by wilderness. In the face of all the nature-destroying mega-projects that became reality, one should occasionally recall those even larger and more far-reaching projects that were *not* carried out: the diversion of the rivers of Siberia southward to irrigate the desert ("Davidov Plan"), the draining of the Mediterranean by means of a gigantic dam at Gibraltar (Hermann Sörgel's "Atlantropa" project), the plans that floated around during the period of atomic euphoria to melt the polar ice with nuclear heat, or the plans to use nuclear bombs to blast a mega–Panama Canal through the Panama straits at sea level ("Panatomic Canal").[16] So far, megalomania, too, has had its limits.

Epochal in a promising way has been the development of effective contraceptives that, unlike previous methods, do not reduce sexual pleasure. In fact, this is quite possibly the most valuable achievement in the most recent history of the environment, since the symbiosis of humankind and nature cannot be harmonized over the long term without birth control. Previously this always demanded that humans violate their inner nature, whether through abstinence from sexual intercourse, coitus interruptus, abortion, or infanticide. There was something utterly pitiless about the Malthusianism in older times. In this case, modern contraceptives have resolved a millennia-long contradiction in the relationship between humans and nature.

Initially it seemed as though the modern methods of birth control were useless in particular in poor Third World countries suffering from the pressure of explosive population growth. However, since the 1970s, a decline in the rate of population growth has been apparent even there, presumably as a result of urbanization and the growing autonomy of women.[17] The thesis that was heard often and for a long time – that birth control presupposes a certain level of prosperity, which is essentially a discouraging thesis, since high birth rates prevent that very prosperity – does not have the inevitability of a law. This is something one could have learned from looking at history, for often it is precisely the poor who seek to keep the number of children low. In many cases it was the ambitions of governments that promoted population growth. But with modern weapons technology, military strength is no longer a question of how many soldiers one has: this, too, is a significant change.

As environmental problems became more pervasive and widespread, there were growing interactions between the various problematic areas, and this gave rise to a new awareness in the second half of the twentieth century. Many older problems – for example, preserving the fertility of agricultural fields – were transformed into a problem of energy, and the energy problem in turn became an environmental problem. To a greater degree than ever before, the multitude of problems were perceived as aspects of *one* great and global problem, and in this way the term "environment" acquired the meaning it has today. If one recalls the more or less separate existence of the older approaches of conservation and "urban sanitation," one can appreciate the power behind this new, global context. Saving a single stream is no longer a trivial matter, but part of a task for all of humanity. This new outlook has not been without impact, for it alone has made environmental protection into a political issue of the highest priority – at least at times. Still, the term "environment" can divert our attention from the fact that if environmental initiatives wish to accomplish anything, they must address specific areas of human activities and pay attention to their rules. Regardless of its holistic pretensions, environmental policy, which arose as a fusion of many older policies (from forest policies to water protection), still consists, once it becomes concrete, of such localized and specific policies, and at present, since the experience of great ecological enlightenment is everywhere on the wane, it runs the risk of fracturing once again into scattered and individual initiatives.

Is it in fact possible to have an environmental policy that lives up to its holistic and global claims? Protection of the old village commons required nothing more than an agreement among the various interested parties. Protection of the global commons, however, of the seas and the atmosphere, is dependent on powerful authorities *above* all interested parties. Given our historical experience to date, it is difficult to imagine effective powers and institutions of that kind.

One source of skepticism is the fact that the new global environmental risks are largely *hypothetical* in nature. This holds true for the risks associated with nuclear technology, genetic engineering, the chemical industry, the threat of a dangerous warming of climate through human emissions into the atmosphere, and the consequences of the pollution of deep groundwater and the world's oceans. History seems to show – and logic itself would suggest – that humans respond most effectively to well-known risks that are plainly visible and with which humanity has already had traumatic experiences. However, since humans are beings with a good deal of imagination, they are up to a certain degree capable of worrying about hypothetical risks and letting them influence their behavior.

The controversy over nuclear technology has been the most bitter dispute in the history of technology to date, because here the contrast between the actual harm suffered and the hypothetical harm that was possible was more extreme than ever before. Proponents of nuclear technology could point out that the victims of this technology – at least before Chernobyl – were a mere fraction of the victims of mining and automobilism. Opponents could argue that the nuclear material in a single reactor could contaminate an entire nation.[18] To what extent hypothetical risks are real enough for politics to respond is often not easy to judge, and it is more difficult still to say what an appropriate response would be. When it comes to hypothetical risks, we are for the most part not dealing with clear causalities, but with probabilities and complex interrelationships.[19]

Environmental changes in earlier times contained an element of inherent stability in that the perpetrators and those affected could often be readily identified and knew each other; indeed, these two groups were identical. In more recent times that is less and less the case. Another consideration also provides cause for concern: the simple law of inertia was once the chief factor in the preservation of the environment. It was laborious and dangerous to cut and transport trees, to extract ores from the depths of the earth and process them, to catch fish in the deep oceans; simple inertia, life's most powerful force, helped to keep the exploitation of nature within limits. Today, however, the working of the law of inertia has been turned upside down, as it were: simply allowing things to keep going will tend rather toward destabilizing the relationship between humanity and the environment. What this means is that an inconspicuous element of inherent stability in the humanity-environment relationship, one that has been active throughout all of prior history, has been lost. Only a small portion of humanity has exchanged this old kind of stability for a wonderful new world. Juan Martínez Alier admonishes us that a good historian must never forget that "the majority of humankind lives almost exclusively from the annual revenue of solar energy." Americanization has not been successful on a global scale – nor could it be, for ecological reasons alone. Global disparities have become greater than ever before, and it appears that the gap has widened precisely as a result of the increasing interconnectedness of the world.[20]

2. BLOOD AND SOIL: SELF–SUFFICIENCY GONE MAD

A historical antithesis to U.S. civilization from an ecological perspective was not so much Soviet Communism, but rather German National Socialism, which placed humankind's ties to nature and the soil at the center of its ideology.[21] The horrendous disaster of the Nazi regime contributed substantially to the global hegemony of American civilization. As long as one conceives of Nazism as the incarnation of evil, its fate invites little reflection. Only if one recognizes the elements of ecological insight within the Nazi movement, does the Nazi catastrophe become fully a thorn in the side of historical reflection. But in what way?

If one regards the "50s syndrome" as *the* fateful turning point in humankind's relationship to the environment, the rise and fall of Nazism occurred at five minutes to twelve, as it were; the blood-and-soil ideology, for all its craziness, did possess a kind of ecological presence of mind. At that time there was indeed a traditional agrarian culture to be saved at the last minute, a culture that contained the experiences of many centuries. At the same time, the Nazi dictatorship provides the most extreme example to date of how quasi-ecological ideas can become the mark of a political system obsessed with power.

Twelve years are not long by ecological standards, and yet National Socialism is not a meaningless episode in the history of the environment. The blood-and-soil rhetoric was no mere concoction of slogans, but borne by strong emotions as well as rational motivations. Even David Schoenbaum, who was the first to emphasize what was in the end a modernizing effect of Nazi politics, goes so far as to assert that the grounding in the native soil was the only true goal of Nazism – so much so that he speaks of "SS chieftains whose eyes brightened and voices caught as they contemplated a life on the land." Max Horkheimer, who fled Nazism to the United States, saw National Socialism as the "rebellion of nature against civilization" and as the revenge of nature: the Nazi movement possessed for him a kind of historical logic.[22]

In fact, compared to both communists as well as liberals of the day, many Nazi ideologues had a much better feeling for the frustrations that the loss of the familiar *Heimat* and of the relationship to nature produced in many people. And that, not least, explains why the Nazi movement, for all its violence, did convey to many a sense of security. However, one must also take rational motivations into consideration. During the food shortages of the First World War, the Germans had learned what it meant if a country could no longer feed itself with its own resources. That experience provided the impetus for the development of a sustainable, national subsistence economy with agriculture the top priority, especially since the Germans after 1918 repeatedly experienced, to their misfortune, that one could not rely on global trade. A partial re-agrarianization of Germany involving the dissolution of industrial conurbations seemed far more realistic back then; even area planners in the Ruhr region were guided by these kinds of models.[23] Verdicts on what the Nazi period looks like from an environmental perspective are still uncertain. Making some headway requires that one distinguish a number of separate areas that were, for the most part, but weakly interconnected:

(1) *Nature protection.* On a legislative level, the Nazi era was epochal in this area: already in the first two years after seizing power, the regime had – with striking speed – pushed through comprehensive new regulations in the areas of animal protection, hunting, and nature protection. Animal protection possessed an anti-Semitic component in its opposition to kosher butchering in accordance with Jewish religious law. As early as August 1933 Göring, in his capacity as the minister president of Prussia, outlawed vivisection, which had already drawn public outrage from Richard Wagner, and he threatened to send violators to a concentration camp; the medical lobby, however, was able to have the prohibition modified. The Reich Nature Protection Law of June 26, 1935, was based on preliminary work during the Weimar period, and it contained so little Nazi jargon that it was able to remain in force for decades without objections after 1945. While nature protection had previously been in the hands of the *Länder*, in the wake of the *Gleichschaltung* of the states it became a matter for the Reich, and it was given a corresponding institutional basis in the Reich Office for Nature Protection. De facto this was the Prussian Office for the Preservation of Natural Monuments that had been in existence since 1906; new offices or positions were not set up at the time. Together with the accompanying rules and regulations, the law was an exemplary regulatory instrument in its day, one that went beyond the protection of natural wonders and preserves and involved nature protection in all planning that altered the landscape. However, one landscape conservationist noted in retrospect that there were "probably few legal regulations that were violated as often" as the one concerning the participation of nature protection. In the following years, the law led to a boom in the establishment of new nature reserves. It allowed for the possibility to expropriate property without compensation in the interest of nature protection. Even if this option was used only in exceptional cases, the mere threat was enough to make property owners compliant.

Nevertheless, Edeltraut Klueting has concluded that the initial nature protection activism of the Nazi regime seems in hindsight like a "flash in the pan," since this "legislative offensive collapsed as quickly as it had begun." Göring himself offers a prime example for the connection between love of nature and a passion for hunting, which we have already encountered so often in history. He wanted to turn the Schorfheide, his favorite hunting grounds, into Germany's first national park, but not even Göring could prevail against competing interests.[24]

(2) *Agrarian policies.* Here it is important to look at the historical background. Germany already had become a pioneer in the application of chemical fertilizers in the late nineteenth century – initially thanks to the German global monopoly on potash, joined in the First World War by the synthesis of ammonia that was invented in Germany. At that time, the chemical industry was considered a "German" industry. After 1918 the gunpowder industry retooled to produce fertilizers. But precisely for that reason, German agriculture early on discovered the harmful

effects of excessive fertilization, which is more damaging in the case of nitrogen than with potash. The National Socialist era coincided with a phase of reaction to these experiences. Nazi Reich Agricultural Minister Walter Darré picked up on these trends. He sought to stabilize the medium-size farmers, replaced the dominance of the market and profit maximization in agriculture with the principle of meeting basic needs, railed against "capitalism's diabolical grin," and strove to slow down currents in agrarian modernization that harmed the soil. Darré, who had some of the personality traits of a drop-out from society and had dreams early in life of becoming a gaucho in Argentina, seemed like an odd bird within the Nazi leadership and was the butt of derogatory jokes (epitaph of a pig: "Auch ich erlitt den Heldentod / ich starb an Darrés Gerstenschrot!" – I, too, died a hero's death / I died of Darré's barley groats). He lacked the strength to assert himself successfully, and during the war he lost all influence and authority. Precedence belonged to what the Nazis called the *Erzeugungschlacht* (battle for food). The chemical industry was one of the favorites of the Nazi regime. However, in order to save foreign currencies to pay for the importation of feed, the farms had to boost production with their own resources to whatever extent possible, for example, by improving crop rotation. That is why the Nazi policy of self-sufficiency represented the final culmination of the old agriculture.[25]

(3) *Forestry policies.* In 1934 Walter von Keudell, a landowner east of the Elbe and ardent advocate of the mixed deciduous forest and opponent of clear-cutting, assumed – under Göring's protectorate – the position as head of the newly created Reich Forestry Office. In this capacity he tried to implement his model of the "permanent forest" (*Dauerwald*) in a rigid way and – as his enemies complained – with no regard for regional conditions. This led to a rebellious mood within forestry circles; many foresters saw red when faced with Keudell's *dirigisme*. Moreover, the single-tree extraction method put in place by Keudell clashed with the heightened demands that the Nazi policy of self-sufficiency placed on the forest. Keudell was replaced in 1937, and his successors issued a compromise slogan about the "natural economic forest" (*naturgemäßer Wirtschaftswald*). The overcutting ordered by the Nazi regime, which violated the principle of sustainability, was allegedly blocked in part by officials of the Reich Forestry Office. What is interesting is that "ecology" – previously a marginal field of biology filled with a rather contemplative spirit – became for the first time a battle cry in German forestry. The supporters of the permanent forest claimed that their position was based on the insights of ecology; but the forestry scientist Alfred Dengler – a neighbor of Göring's and Keudell's in the Eberswald who defended clear-cutting – also presented his views as "silviculture on an ecological foundation."[26]

(4) *Landscape protection.* In this area there was a prominent fighter: Alwin Seifert, the "Reich landscape advocate" during the construction of the Autobahn and a warning voice against the "suicidal desertification of Germany" from excessive draining and river regulation. A German biographical lexicon in 1937 described Seifert as a passionate gardener, and now "all of Germany has become his garden." As a collaborator of Fritz Todt, who oversaw the construction of the Autobahn, Seifert fought to have the roadways adapted to the terrain in a sinuous line and to have them bordered not by ditches, but by planted slopes. Yet Seifert also used his prominent position to launch fundamental attacks on methods of hydraulic

engineering that were contrary to nature and on the consolidation of arable land. This was a peculiar spectacle: the most militant protector of nature arm in arm with the highest-ranking technician of the Third Reich, indeed, of all of German history up to that time, collaborating on a project that, more than anything else, set the process of motorization in motion! For Seifert and other nature protectors at the time, the great enemy was not the automobile and road construction, but the railroad along with its administrative apparatus. From their perspective, the railroad cut up the landscape more sharply than the road, which nestled into the terrain much better with its curves. Heated public discussions about questions of landscape protection and a technology that was compatible with nature were possible even in the totalitarian Nazi state. These kinds of topics were in the air at the time, and there was no obligatory party line.

Seifert made use of the new science of ecology while at the same time professing a spiritual veneration of nature. Yet he had no scruples about forging an alliance with modern technology: as Thomas Zeller has said, he was "opportunistic, eccentric, pragmatic, principled, and flexible all at once," on top of which he was also filled by a strong craving for recognition. Todt was surprised at how much public approval Seifert received from very diverse circles when he attacked hydraulic projects; he called on the engineers to find a "total solution for the long term." On the outside, Seifert propounded a philosophy of the great synthesis: the best technology was simultaneously the most nature-friendly technology, and the best protection of the landscape was simultaneously the best protection of agriculture. In 1942 he wrote that all technology was a "child of fire" and thus a gift from both Prometheus *and* Lucifer; in 1949, however, he lamented that industry and technology were "Luciferian." His motivation, however, was not only pragmatic, but in the final analysis metaphysical: water was for him a living thing, and he believed that the person who was close to nature could sense it. Seifert, whose background was in gardening, was remembered longest as the founding father of the "eco-garden," whereby he regarded the garden as the field of experimentation for the reform of agriculture as a whole.

Seifert was an unusual figure and anticipated the later motifs of the environmental movement. Since he had a talent for self-promotion, his actual importance has often been overestimated. Only one-one-thousandth of the costs for building the Autobahn went into landscape protection. Added to this was the fact that Seifert had his own ideas about landscape protection: since he wanted motorists to experience as much beautiful nature as possible, he proposed that the Autobahnen traverse especially beautiful landscapes, and he stabbed those nature protectors who were trying to protect the romantic Siebengebirge on the Rhine against an Autobahn in the back.[27]

(5) *Recycling.* The National Socialist policy of self-sufficiency was a heyday for projects on reusing waste and recovering raw materials, though they often had – as they did in the First World War – the sour taste of the stopgap measure. Sewage fields, before 1933 the targets of growing popular opposition as sources of foul odors and nurseries of bacteria, now turned into models of sewage reuse, though to the disgust of Alwin Seifert and without much practical effect. Government decrees in 1935 and 1936 stipulated that any treatment of sewage first had to examine the possibility of agricultural reuse and that the construction of treatment plants could

be considered only if such reuse was demonstrably unfeasible. Still, the great days of the sewage fields were already over by then.[28]

All in all, the Nazi period was epochal in the history of nature and environmental protection above all in words and less so in deeds. Little was done to combat water and air pollution. On the contrary, the situation grew worse, and industrial interests were able to thwart a Reich Water Law, as they already had done during the empire. The environmental balance sheet of the Nazi policy of self-sufficiency is also hardly positive; one need only think of the large-scale projects for the hydrogenation of coal. The sudden transition to an intensified exploitation of domestic resources without a more efficient use and without structural changes within industry, and instead with an accelerated military rearmament, led invariably to overuse, especially of the forest, a situation that eventually provided one justification for the conquest of new "living space."

Worst of all in the eyes of many nature protectors was the cultivation of "wasteland" undertaken by the Labor Service, of small scraps of wilderness in heaths and on stony soils that farmers had hitherto ignored completely. This activity drew irate protests already during the Nazi period. Hitler decreed in 1941 that the cultivation of moorland was to stop, since the Germans were about to acquire plenty of land. In the later memoirs of Hans Klose, who – though not a member of the Nazi Party – headed the Reich Nature Protection Office from 1938 to 1945, the Nazi era presents itself in an extremely ambiguous light: on the one hand as a great time of nature protection, on the other hand as a period in which the "nature-destroying powers were immensely intensified."[29]

The crucial point in all of this is no doubt that in spite of the duo of Todt and Seifert, there was no potent alliance of environmental protection and power interests in Nazi Germany. A hostile relationship developed between Seifert and Darré, of all people, and there was also rivalry between Seifert and Klose, the top-ranking nature protector. A strong if diffuse yearning for closeness to nature was in the air at the time, but it belonged more to Nazism's sentimental side than to its tough, activist one. Where power was at stake, Hitler was, by his own admission, "crazy about technology," especially American technology, though he displayed sympathy for a decentralized use of regenerative energy sources and occasionally even indulged in Gaia-like ideas about the total interconnectedness of the earth.[30] The National Socialist policy of autarky did not spring from a spirit of self-sufficiency, but was a means of preparing for war under conditions in which foreign currency was scarce. In its concrete reality, National Socialism was not a consistent reaction against "Americanism," but rather a desperate imitation of the great empires under the cramped conditions of Central Europe.

In *Mein Kampf*, Hitler spoke of nature as the all-powerful goddess: but this was the Darwinian nature of the eternal struggle, not the conservationists' nature in need of protection. During the Nazi period, many conservationists embraced the *völkisch* jargon, if they had not already done so long before 1933, but they always had problems with the Darwinian picture of nature. Hitler, on the other hand, had so little interest in nature protection that he did not even invoke it where he could have made good use of it as an argument: namely, in the polemic against the concept of an internal colonization as a peaceful alternative to external expansion.

Had National Socialism in fact taken its blood-and-soil ideology seriously and genuinely believed that German nature was rooted in German soil, it would not have pursued the conquest of new settlement space in the east for fear that, in the long run, German settlers would assimilate to the native population in the monotonous expanses of the east. Some landscape planners offered a way out, though: they discovered the conquered east as a golden opportunity to reshape nature, promising to refashion the landscape there in such a way that German farmers would feel at home. Since these plans presupposed the expulsion of the native population, this is where nature protection was most likely complicit with the criminal sides of the Nazi regime. However, the concrete plans that were made – protection against erosion through hedges and rows of trees – were largely in line with the demands of soil conservationists all over the world.[31]

When it came to actual practice in nature protection, the Nazi regime largely carried on traditions from the Weimar Republic. Still, after 1945 the nature protection movement was, to its chagrin, widely regarded as compromised by its association with Nazism. There was a whole grandfather generation of the German environmental movement – men like Klages, Seifert, Grzimek, Günther Schwab, Konrad Lorenz, the brothers Ernst and Friedrich Georg Jünger, and the philosopher Heidegger[32] – who were later spurned because they showed an affinity for Nazism at one time or another. Because of this truncated past, it appeared as though the German environmental movement was lagging behind its American counterpart by at least a decade, and much of the long prehistory of environmental protection in Germany was forgotten. While the American environmental movement looks with pride at its long line of ancestors, from Henry Thoreau, John Muir, and Aldo Leopold to Rachel Carson, many like-minded Germans recoil from their history.

To be sure, the Nazi experience is not proof that nature protection possesses an inherent tendency toward fascism. The history of nature protection outside of Germany argues against this view. On the other hand, it gives us pause that – as far as we know today – nobody protested against Nazi crimes in the name of nature. This sheds light on just how far the idea of nature at the time had moved away from the idea of human rights, once the connection between the two via natural law had disappeared and the philosophy of natural law had been replaced by legal positivism. The idea that nature needed protection from humans ruptured the old bond between love for nature and love for humanity, and the challenge for us is to think about how that bond can be restored in the future. This is one answer to the question I posed at the beginning of this chapter, namely, in what sense the Nazi catastrophe can prompt us to reflect on the history of the human relationship to nature.

3. SUBSTRATA OF ENVIRONMENTAL CONCERNS: THE NUCLEAR APOCALYPSE AND CANCER FEARS

The strongest human impulses grow out of an interaction of love and fear. Environmental awareness, too, becomes an urgent passion when the love of nature – sensory and suprasensory love – is united with fear. Anxiety about nature is most acute when it is also anxiety about one's own welfare, and it becomes a public force when the objects of individual concern can be melded credibly into a great threat to the nation and humanity. This kind of interconnection of anxieties stands at the beginning of the modern environmental movement.

Donald Worster has asserted that the "Age of Ecology began on the desert outside Alamogordo, New Mexico on July 16, 1945, with a dazzling fireball of light and a swelling mushroom cloud of radioactive gases" when the first atomic bomb was detonated. But for the global public it was only a decade or more later that Alamogordo and Hiroshima became the signal of a new era, and initially this was not the era of ecology. In 1945, the Europeans were facing their own mountains of rubble, and the nuclear devastation of Hiroshima and Nagasaki was still far from their minds. Anton Metternich, whose book *Die Wüste droht* ("The Threat of the Desert," 1947) was the first postwar German environmental apocalypse, was still influenced by the Dust Bowl and Seifert's warnings and called soil erosion "the most terrible spectre of the modern age."[33] Until well into the 1950s, the inferno of Hiroshima was not very concrete in public awareness, since Japan was subject to U.S. military censorship until 1952. It was only during the 1950s that people started to get a sense of the enormity of long-term nuclear effects. Until then, the public had paid little attention to the threats posed by radioactivity, especially since radon spas were using the healing properties of radioactive substances in their advertising. Moreover, to many Americans the nuclear bomb provided a feeling of reassurance, as long as the United States possessed a nuclear monopoly.

The situation changed once the West came under threat from Soviet nuclear missiles. An even more radical shift in public perception took place, however, when alarming information about the dangers from the radioactive fallout of atomic tests became known. The disaster of the Japanese fishing vessel *Lucky Dragon*, which was hit by the fallout cloud from an American hydrogen bomb in 1954, signaled the change in the world's perception even more than Hiroshima.[34] It was now recognized that the atomic disaster was not a one-time and locally contained event, but a lasting danger that threatened everyone, even future generations. And here the fear of nuclear arms combined with a great new fear: that of cancer. In this way, the fear of atomic weapons was able to link up with a host of anxieties about civilization in a way that proved important for the future.

This brings us into contact with another fundamental level of events: the history of the fear of disease. The history of medicine provides the key to no small number of mysteries in a history of the environment that also incorporates the change in human mentalities. Medical sociologists Claudine Herzlich and Janine Pierret have pinpointed a secular turning point in France right around 1960: the fear of epidemics and other infectious diseases, which had dominated medical anxieties for at least six centuries (since the first great plague), now receded into the background rather quickly – and with it also the fear of feverish swamps and human germ carriers. Instead, fears about illnesses induced by civilization moved to the top. The findings for France can be generalized to other countries.

To be sure, as such this phobia is nothing new, but it now included also the worst of all fears: the fear of cancer. Many have such a panicky fear about it that they would rather not even utter the very word. In this situation, concern for the environment can become a cipher for the fear of cancer. And cancer became in turn a metaphor for environmental problems: "Growth for the sake of growth is the ideology of the cancer cell" was one slogan in the American environmental scene. Even older people who had always kept a distance from the environmental movement became receptive to ecological anxieties through the fear of cancer.

In the 1950s, the cancerous effect of environmental damage was a new theme; the alarm over nuclear fallout catapulted it into the headlines like never before. "Was it fear of cancer, that great standby of all environmentalist demagogues, that stirred our worries about the earth?" asks Lovelock. The American Environmental Protection Agency devoted itself for years chiefly to the fight against cancer, even though it had little to contribute. Around 1970 the public discovered that automobile exhaust could cause cancer. The environmental movement that spread worldwide at the time differed from the nature romanticism of earlier periods not least in the great importance that attached to health arguments. "Environment" and "nature" were not infrequently code words for "health" – to be sure, this too is part of a tradition reaching back into antiquity.[35]

As early as the late nineteenth century, the industrialized states were seized by a wave of fear concerning environmentally caused diseases, and at that time this fear was already able to mobilize considerable resources. However, the triumph of bacteriology diverted attention away from the factor "environment." There was no synergy between the great fears such as occurred in the 1950s and 1960s. The fear back then of the civilization illness "nervousness" led into a different direction than the fears about cholera and tuberculosis. Cancer was not yet a major theme: even the health apostles at the time did not know what do about it, though they suspected that the culprit was the increasing consumption of meat and tobacco.[36] What is new in the vegetarianism that began to grow rapidly in the late twentieth century is not its ethical fundamentalism, which has long existed, but its health argument, which is more solidly supported than before.

If the environmental movement was able to draw support from a far more impressive medical foundation than its precursors were able to, the chief credit for this goes to modern occupational medicine, the study of illnesses caused by different kinds of work and working conditions. After the triumph of bacteriology in the late nineteenth century, it was above all occupational health and safety that reintroduced the "environment" factor into the etiology of diseases. At a time when bacteriology was dominant, it was astonishingly difficult even in a case seemingly as clear-cut as that of silicosis, a lung disease of miners and stone polishers, for dust to be recognized as the cause – that is how all lung diseases were initially seen within the bacteriological paradigm. And the radiation damage that became known almost immediately after the invention of X-ray technology around 1900 was trivialized for decades in a way that seems incredible in retrospect. The breakthrough in the recognition of these ailments was achieved chiefly in the field of occupational medicine; in the process, a new environmental paradigm emerged in the field of medicine. In the United States, occupational medicine advanced more steadily in the twentieth century than it did in Europe, where the development was interrupted by two world wars. Rachel Carson drew her alarming information about the cancer risks to humans from DDT from the field of occupational medicine, especially from Wilhelm Hueper, the head of the Environmental Cancer Section of the North American National Cancer Institute.

Nonetheless, on the whole the relationship of occupational medicine to the environmental movement was rather distant. The interests of the two sides were very different, in fact, under certain circumstances even opposed: occupational doctors wanted to prove harm to an individual through local environmental conditions to obtain individual compensation; environmentalists, by contrast, usually emphasized the threats to the population of an entire region – or even all of mankind – that emanate from sources of danger with far-reaching effects. While this alarm about the environment was politically effective, it was useless – if not actually disadvantageous – in legal trials involving individuals. The relationship between occupational medicine and the environmental movement has been little studied to date. On the whole, it would appear that, all the tension and distance notwithstanding, the two currents more often than not reinforced each other. The 1960s, when *Silent Spring* became a best-seller, was also the time "when occupational health would be placed back on the national agenda" in the United States. All in all, the reputation of occupational medicine rose in the wake of the rise of ecology. In West Germany it was the radiation protection regulations of 1960, triggered by nuclear technology, that put an end to the silliness of x-ray machines in shoe shops.[37]

One interesting case is the microbiologist René Dubos (1901–81): the leading historian of tuberculosis, who made personal contributions to the study of the disease, he became internationally an intellectual pioneer of the environmental movement and its apocalyptic mood. His book *Only One Earth*, written in collaboration with Barbara Ward, became the Bible of the Stockholm Environmental Conference in 1972. This would appear to contradict the thesis that there is a connection between the genesis of environmental awareness and the change in what diseases were feared. But Dubos attacked the dominance of bacteriology in his work on tuberculosis: he emphasized environment as a factor and polemicized ardently against what he regarded as the absurd and ecologically disastrous goal of eliminating all pathogens with antibiotics. He recognized in that endeavor the spirit of total war. His own thinking was shaped by fear of nuclear war, later also of the "population bomb."[38]

Rachel Carson (1907–64) is regarded as the founder of the American environmental movement, although the immediate and stunning success of her book *Silent Spring* (1962), which was soon mentioned in the same breath with *Uncle Tom's Cabin*, clearly shows that the public was ready for her message. When the book was published, Carson was already suffering from terminal cancer, and her life had long been overshadowed by the fear of this dreaded disease. The reason why *Silent Spring* had a far greater impact in the United States than all environmental books that preceded it was not least that Carson, although she pointed to a broad spectrum of environmental toxins, set her sights on a *single* target: the insecticide DDT, which had been widely and liberally sprayed since the Second World War. And for many readers the critical point was surely that DDT had fallen under suspicion of causing cancer in humans. Carson argued that humans were in fact especially threatened, since DDT accumulated in the food chains and humans stood at the top of most of them.[39] At that time, it didn't help DDT very much that only a decade earlier it had still been seen as the great savior against malaria, for the old fear of malaria was no longer shaping public consciousness.

The food chain argument played a role also in the early criticism of nuclear technology, namely as a warning against the accumulation of radioactive substances in organisms that served as food for humans. In the United States, far more so than in West Germany, there was a direct transition from protest against nuclear weapons to criticism of civilian nuclear technology, transmitted by way of opposition to atomic tests, whose after-effects lead directly into the environmental problem. The horror vision of the "population bomb," which became – with Paul Ehrlich's book of the same title (1968) – a leitmotif of the American environmental movement, was modeled after the atomic bomb.

In 1964, when news about the first Chinese nuclear weapons tests became known and there was a brief threat of a nuclear war between China and India, initiatives began on an international level to promote "nonproliferation," to prevent the further spread of nuclear weapons and of fissile material that could be used in weapons. Thereafter these initiatives dominated the nuclear discussions in the 1960s. The United States and the Soviet Union assumed the leadership in the global implementation of nonproliferation. For the nuclear powers this way of securing peace and environmental protection was advantageous, since it allowed them to maintain their own nuclear oligopoly. The same was true in the 1970s for American efforts to prevent the spread of breeder and reprocessing technology, since both contained a proliferation risk. In the United States, a policy that was critical of nuclear power went hand in hand with the preservation of national power. That is why the protest movement against nuclear technology, which originated in the United States in the early 1960s, lost its character as a protest against the power elites relatively early in that country, whereas that aspect was much stronger in Central Europe.[40]

In many countries, including Germany, fear of the nuclear bomb was joined in the 1950s, thanks to a nimble publicity apparatus, by exalted hopes for the "peaceful atom," as though the latter promised salvation from the former, its evil twin. The German antinuclear power protest in the 1970s, which became the catalyst of the entire environmental movement, initially regarded the theme "nuclear bomb" as more of a distraction. Only around 1980, in the wake of the protest movement against the resumption of the nuclear arms race, did the linkage between civilian and military nuclear technology become the target of German opposition. It is no coincidence that West Germany, where the antinuclear power movement was stronger than anywhere else, saw the emergence of the largest and best-financed Green party in Europe. German supporters of nuclear technology liked to attribute opposition to an irrational-romantic German tradition of hostility to technology, but that tradition is largely a myth invented and disseminated by proponents of technology. It was, in principle, quite rational that nuclear technology would receive a particularly critical reception in a country as densely settled as Germany, since the reactor technology adopted at that time from the United States was intended for thinly settled regions and included "distance" as one factor in its safety calculations. The nuclear power plants that were erected in West Germany in the 1960s looked exactly like their American counterparts; ten years later, as a result of German safety requirements, they looked quite different.[41]

The experiences undergone in the struggle against nuclear technology were of great importance to the controversy over genetic engineering, which peaked for the first time in the United States in the 1970s. "I started thinking in terms of the atomic bomb and similar things," remembered Janet Mertz, one of the originators of the controversy. One standard argument was that both genetic and nuclear technology altered the basic building blocks of nature and could therefore trigger unpredictable and irreversible consequences that were potentially disastrous. To be sure, genetic engineering was not burdened by a Hiroshima, but Anglo-American plans for the use of germs in the Second World War, which became public after the fact, revealed that a biotechnological super-Hiroshima was certainly conceivable. It was not moral scruples, but the lack of military predictability, that had prevented the use of biological weapons at the time. Genetic engineering promised, however, to render biological weapons calculable.[42]

Nuclear weapons made it a very real and conceivable possibility that humanity could exterminate itself – not through archaic instincts, but through its unstoppable inventiveness. This basic conceptual idea promoted similar concepts in other problematic areas. Today it is sometimes asserted that what is new about the modern environmental movement is the respect for nature for its own sake. But that was already an element of nature protection and nature romanticism; what *was* new was the concern that in the long run the destruction of nature would threaten the physical existence of humankind. It was this, above all else, that created an urgency to take action, an urgency that was also felt by politicians.

Hiroshima was surely not the only source of apocalyptic visions about the environment; a good deal followed in the footsteps of older traditions, whether their background lay in religion, pessimism about civilization, or Malthusianism. Contrary to what is often asserted today, eras of an overpowering and blind faith in progress have been rare even in the past; for the most part, modernization was accompanied by anxieties, not least about the disruption of the relationship between humans and the environment. As early as 1900 there emerged science fiction literature that entertained its readers with horror visions of the future. As a literary motif, the notion that humanity would destroy itself through its own creations has a history that stretches back at least to Mary Shelley's *Frankenstein* (1818).[43]

Still, in the most recent environmental apocalypticism one can discern not only the old traditions, but also what is new and part of the mental climate of our times. This apocalypticism is pervaded by a profound pessimism, while at the same time also containing practical impulses, though with the awareness that there is no simple recipe on how to solve the problems. Its literature achieved a new level of quality through its thematic breadth and the fullness and precision of its data. The catastrophes were as much intellectually deduced as they were emotionally suggested. Apocalypticists have grasped a wider spectrum of partly new environmental damage more keenly than the nature protectors of the old school, who are less interested in the latest developments of industrial society and more in the perpetuation of nature preserves.[44]

Günther Schwab (born 1904) probably had the widest impact among the early environmental apocalypticists in the German-speaking lands. His book *Der Tanz mit dem Teufel* (Dance with the Devil, 1958) led to the founding, in 1960, of the "World League for the Defense of Life," the germ cell of the movement against nuclear power. His book *Morgen holt dich der Teufel* (Tomorrow the Devil Will Get You, 1968) was the best handbook of arguments against nuclear power at the time. The devil became Schwab's trademark, as it were: he appeared in the titles of all his books, and time and again Schwab presented the destruction of nature as the devil's clever ruse aimed at the destruction of humankind. In literary terms this was the invocation of ancient fears of hell, but at their core his books were based on solid research. Rachel Carson's warning against DDT can be found in Schwab years earlier.[45] And yet, what a difference in the style of these two authors and in the presentation of their message! Carson always assumed the demeanor of a scientist, even in her visions; Schwab, by contrast, the Styrian forester with a Nazi past, presented even his scientific findings in demonological terms. His books sold in large numbers, but the author himself never became a public figure.

To what extent was apocalypticism supported by science? Dating back to the nineteenth century, "catastrophism" was a "highly loaded word" in natural history. The early nineteenth century had witnessed great controversies between catastrophe theorists and evolutionists, and the latter had won. They believed in gradual development over long periods of time, and catastrophe theories struck them as a reincarnation of the old belief in the Biblical Flood.[46] Darwinists, too, knew the extinction of entire species, but only as the result of the triumph of more highly evolved rivals; the issue was never a decline of nature as a whole.

But in the final analysis, evolutionism, too, was a faith and not a firmly secured doctrine. In more recent times it has lost its dominance, and catastrophe theories have experienced a revival. When it comes to ecological catastrophism the influence of the mass media is evident, since pronouncements about the end of the world have the best chances of garnering headlines.[47]

This circumstance does not necessarily reflect on the truthfulness of the cries of alarm. One cannot rule out the possibility that the imagination of the popular journalists has discovered something that has escaped the restrained scientists. In his book *The Fate of the Revolution: Interpretations of Soviet History*, Walter Lacqueur devotes one section to the "Pitfalls of Academe." He notes that those who drew their information about the Soviet Union in the 1930s and 1940s from scholarly literature would have had no inkling of the Stalinist Terror, but readers of trashy stories like "I Was a Prisoner of the Red Terror" most certainly did.[48] And the readers of horror fiction could most readily foresee Chernobyl and September 11, 2001. Since the greatest environmental threats of recent times are hypothetical in nature, it takes imagination to create a mental picture of what they might entail, and in this regard the apocalyptic literature deserves credit. The person who knows only secure facts cannot join the conversation about modern risks. While it is useful to look at the heuristic value of the prophecies of doom, one must also subject them to the necessary epistemological critique.

It would be completely rash to conclude, on the basis of the experiences of a few decades, that alarmist predictions of catastrophe are simply part of the psychological history of our fears and not part of the history of the real dangers humankind is confronting. Cassandra speaks the truth not only in Greek mythology. Even Malthus, whose gloomy prediction was long regarded as having been refuted by actual developments, could be right if we take centuries as our framework. Critics of nuclear energy focused initially on the insidious dangers: nuclear waste and the low radioactive emissions that are part of the normal operation of reactors. Then they discovered the "total meltdown" as the maximum risk of a catastrophe, and this marked the high point of the controversy.[49] Subsequently, the discussion of the most catastrophic reactor failure fell silent for years – until Chernobyl taught us that this scenario was by no means merely a phantom!

Though the inertia of politics in the face of these warnings has often been criticized, one must admit that this slow response has its reasons. Often it takes some time before one understands which is the truly important problem and what is the effective solution. Confronted with these uncertainties, it would appear that environmental policy has embraced the maxim – either explicitly or tacitly – that one should proactively take those measures that are reasonable to begin with and whose sense is not based solely on certain hypothetical assumptions. In and of itself, dealing with undefined risks and uncertain solutions should call for an experimental political style that is always open to new experiences. However, it is evidently very difficult to create such a style without sliding into merely muddling through. Especially if the environmental movement wants to become a power to be reckoned with, it must have solid and secure positions.

Certain catastrophic scenarios are initially not badly suited to establishing such positions. But if the prophesied catastrophes do not materialize, this method fails in its purpose. One problem also lies in the fact that the fear of catastrophes, once it is actually felt, fixates one's thinking and commits it to the kind of large-scale, global solutions that do not exist. Historical experience suggests that precisely the dangers that few think about might be the most insidious. They include above all the risks that arise from slow environmental changes that never appear alarming. The importance of the alarm bells about catastrophes is a negative illustration of how difficult it is for society to respond appropriately to dangers that are chronic and rarely acute. And this difficulty has presumably been exacerbated by the mass media and the fact that we have grown accustomed to sensationalism. Christian Pfister, speaking of Switzerland, has lamented how difficult it is to persuade a "population which can be reached only with sensational news" that the alarm signal of human-induced climate change "is not so much an accumulation of natural catastrophes that play well in the media, but rather insidious processes like the disappearance of the snow from the lowlands."[50]

When a new kind of damage to the forests was noted on a large scale around 1980, the catchy word *Waldsterben* (forest death), combined with the alarmist pronouncement "First the trees die, then people," created the misleading picture of an imminent catastrophe. Since that time, this has been used to ridicule ecological alarmism – while the evidence for the slow decline of many forests remains worrisome. Does the environmental movement really need the fear of the end of the world? Religious history could teach us that practical ethics do not need the belief in hell, and that such a belief is not necessarily a wellspring of reason and humanity.

4. SCIENTIFIC, SPIRITUAL, AND ECONOMIC ORIGINS OF THE ENVIRONMENTAL MOVEMENT

If there is anything one can learn from the history of the environmental movement, then it is surely first and foremost that the movement did not emerge out of nowhere: it did not arise from a sudden enlightenment, or from an abrupt transformation of a naive faith in technology into pessimism about progress. Rather, it provided an outlet to a feeling of discomfort that had been building for more than a century. A "50s syndrome" is discernible not only when it comes to environmental problems, but also when it comes to an environmental awareness. In the United States, as well as in parts of Europe, complaints about water and air pollution – sometimes also about the despoiling of the landscape and noise nuisance – took on a new, challenging tone in the 1950s, one that demanded fundamental solutions. Moreover, the issue of the environment clearly acquired greater political priority.[51] That is the only reason why Rachel Carson's *Silent Spring* was able to have such an immediate impact in 1962.

At first glance, the United States, which had not been set back by war-related destruction and rebuilding, seems to have been the pioneer of the new environmental awareness. One can see the same basic pattern that was already in place in the early twentieth century: at first, the Americans sin against nature to excess, but then they stage countercampaigns that are more spectacular than what we find in countries of the Old World, where people had for a long time been concerned to a degree with the protection of the forest and the soil, where even in the 1950s DDT was not sprayed from airplanes by the ton, and where the authorities already became active on their own initiative. Nineteenth-century America tolerated far more train wrecks than Europe did; as late as 1913, the risk of getting hurt in a train crash was eighteen times higher in the United States than in Imperial Germany. In the twentieth century, however, the American "safety first" movement became a model for Europeans, as did the "health engineer" and the American-style national park. What people in smaller Europe had long since known, American conservationists discovered in spectacular fashion in the 1920s in the "Kaibab affair": namely, that the unrestrained increase in certain kinds of wildlife destroys the landscape.

In the United States, the soil was treated far more ruthlessly than in the Old World. But in the wake of the Dust Bowl, Americans experienced, under the banner of "conservation tillage," a large-scale attack on the plow, such as had not been seen in Europe until then: a polemic that declared the "plowman" to be crazy.

Pittsburgh, around 1900 an industrial inferno and the "smoky city" par excellence, became in the twentieth century the exemplar of urban environmental renewal: "Everyone is a smoke inspector" rejoiced the Pittsburgh Bureau of Smoke Prevention in the early 1950s. When the initially mysterious photochemical smog in Los Angeles – until then famed for its salubrious air and the center of the American "sanatorium belt" – reached shocking levels beginning in 1943, and Los Angeles became the "Smog Metropolis of the World," California took the lead in environmental awareness and L.A. became the global pioneer in the fight against smog and the metropolis of environmental anxieties. As early as 1952 it was said in the United States that the concern over air pollution was growing week by week and turning into hysteria. It is clear that America was becoming ripe for Rachel Carson's message.[52]

There was no Rachel Carson in Germany, but a close look reveals that environmental awareness had also been growing in that country since the late 1950s, though in an inconspicuous manner. Compared to the preceding decades, the complaints take on a new tone: more urgent, fundamental, and demanding. In the Saarland, the community of Kleinblittersdorf sounded the alarm in 1957 that the ash from the burning of coal dust in a neighboring mine – which is indeed one of the worst sources of emissions there is – was turning the town "into a Pompeii and all human and plant life is suffocating in the dust." One water conservationist detected as early as 1958 a "widespread fear psychosis," especially since one did not have to be an expert at the time to be horrified at the water pollution caused by cities and industry.[53]

When it came to keeping the air clean, West German legislation, as Frank Uekötter has discovered, was more productive in the late 1950s than around 1970. Compared to later, however, what was missing at the time was an alliance between environmental protection and general ideas of political reform. Typically, environmental protection tended to have a conservative cast to it. As so often in history, it was not so much the awareness that was lacking, but an effective coalition of actors. When it came to the mobilization of science, as well, there was not much going on in the first few decades after the war. By far the most popular German advocate for nature in 1960s was Bernhard Grzimek: although he unquestionably had a broad knowledge of biology, he appealed to sentimental emotions and saw his allies far more among the man on the street than the intellectuals.

The environmental movement has often been accused of being hostile to technology. From a historical point of view, however, what is remarkable about this milieu is not its discomfort with but its interest in technology. The chances of bridging what Charles P. Snow ruefully referred to as the gap between the "two cultures" – the culture of the humanities and social sciences, and the culture of natural and technical sciences – was never as favorable as they were at the highpoints of the environmental movements. To a considerable extent, the way out of the ecological crisis is sought in technological solutions, in "gentle energy" and an increase in energy efficiency; the guiding figure is not someone like Hermann Löns, but Amory Lovins. The 1960s, when the environmental movement started to take shape, was internationally a time of planning euphoria. While the pioneers of environmental protection criticized a technocratic megalomania, they were confident in their own way that it was possible to guide and direct the development of the world.

Although critics tend to accuse supporters of the environmental movement of emotionalism, from a historical perspective it is the exact opposite that stands out in comparison with the nature romanticism of earlier times: namely, the degree to which this movement presents itself as applied science, as "ecology," and its success in seeking to make a connection with science. Rachel Carson was already a pioneer in this regard. To be sure, she opened her book with a vision of death that appealed to the emotions: the dying of the birds, the silent spring without bird songs. Nonetheless, a new characteristic of the environmental awareness of the last few decades is that its primary focus is on invisible dangers that cannot initially be perceived with the senses, and of whose existence only science can convince us: radioactivity, the risks of genetic engineering, climate change through CO_2 emissions. But even the environmental movement cannot dispense with the sensory perception. The risk of nuclear energy was driven home most profoundly by the catastrophe of Chernobyl, which had a very visible and sensory side. And the public is most likely to believe in the seriousness of global warming during unusually hot summers.[54]

The rise of the environmental movement cannot be explained through the history of science. To be sure, Ernst Haeckel coined the term "ecology" (*Ökologie*) in 1866 by way of analogy to "economy" and with great expectations, and his book *Welträtsel* (Riddles of the World, 1899) – a global best-seller at the time – became the Bible of the "monists," who founded an entire worldview on the basis of the unity of humankind and nature. But Haeckel's "ecology" was a mere program without practical scientific research behind it, let alone practical political endeavors. There was no direct path from there to the "ecology" of the environmental movement. What existed in science as "ecology" between the time of Haeckel and Carson was for the most part a side branch of biology remote from politics and public attention, which long led an inconspicuous niche existence and would never have been able to conquer public opinion on its own. Although conservationists sought scientific legitimation from the beginning, for a long time they could not find the kind of science they needed: the ecology of the old school was, generally, remote from politics. The scientific basis of nature protection has remained uncertain to this day.

It was only in forestry that ecology was occasionally political. But if the environmental movement did not grow directly out of modern, specialized science, it did develop in proximity to science and in a close reciprocal relationship to it. Up to a point, the environmental movement supports the thesis about modern "scientific society," except that one must take a very close look in each case at what exactly is meant by "science" and what effect it has.

It is a peculiar historical paradox that at the very time when the environmental movement was taking shape, scientific ecology developed in a direction that took it away from what was now the popular notion of "ecology." Arthur G. Tansley's concept of the "ecosystem," first articulated in 1935, meant a departure from the older ecological ideas about a community of life and reduced the world to flows of matter and energy. This turned ecology into a "hard," precisely quantifying, but at the same time entirely unromantic and value-neutral science, in which the human being as a creature sui generis did not appear at all. In the wake of the subsequent development of ecology, the old ideal of "virgin nature" was also dismantled and ecosystems entered into a state of flux: an ideal state of equilibrium no longer existed. The environmental movement had originally embraced the outdated concept of this idealized, primeval biocenosis of humans and nature – which is not to say that it could not also keep in touch with the new developments in the science of ecology. But when Hubert Weinzierl, the chairman of BUND (Bund für Natur- und Umweltschutz Deutschland, German League for the Protection of Nature and the Environment), proclaimed as late as 1980 that nature protection was based on "unalterable basic ecological laws," it had long since become questionable whether ecology actually provided such laws. In 1999 Weinzierl admitted: "Nature protection is in the final analysis a question of love." This sounds like an echo of the words of John Muir: "Every wild lesson is a love lesson."[55]

The Soviet Union was – surprisingly enough – the first country where nature protection sought to avail itself of the authority of science. Russia had few of those "picturesque" sceneries like Yellowstone or Yosemite of which aesthetic nature protection is so enamored. Instead, under communism, which styled itself a "scientific socialism," science became an authority more so than elsewhere. The nature preserves (*zapovedniki*) that were set up in the 1920s were justified – and this was unique at the time – with their usefulness to the science of ecology, which was in turn presented as the most basic of the sciences of society. The dubious theory of "biogeocenosis" was developed specifically for the *zapovedniki*: it maintained that in large territories where nature was left to itself a harmonious ecological balance was created, which seemed suitable as the model of the human society of the future. This theory did not hold up to serious testing, and it was not able to protect the *zapovedniki* against economic interests in cases of conflict. "When Stalin realized that the zapovedniki contained wood," Douglas Weiner remarked, large areas of them were subjected to logging without further ado. Later Soviet nature protectors like Vera A. Varsonefeva professed their spiritual motivation more openly than the ecologists of the 1920s had dared to do. Weiner believes that in the final analysis it was a symbol of freedom that fascinated the supporters of the *zapovedniki*: nature preserves as areas of freedom within the totalitarian state! Needless to say, though, this motif can be found at best between the lines of the sources.[56]

Today, as in the eighteenth and nineteenth centuries, the study of anthropogenic environmental damage received its strongest impulses not from trends within certain scientific disciplines, but primarily from outside, from practical experiences and the interests developed in areas of practical application. This circumstance, far from indicating that these concerns are not well founded, suggests, on the contrary, that in fact they *are*. Nevertheless, it is remarkable how much the environmental movement, in which much fundamental criticism of modern science was heard in the beginning, has come to be pervaded by science. That scientific pervasion has had its price, and it is not always clear whether the price has been worth it. The process of setting environmentalism on a scientific foundation creates hierarchies, with laypeople at the very bottom, even though the original impulse and initiative came from them. The knowledge of laypeople is devalued, even if it is at least as useful to the practice of environmental protection as the knowledge of experts. When experts talk shop about threshold values, the layperson can hardly participate, even though these values are in the final analysis negotiated rather than deduced in laboratory experiments. Since the study of many environmental problems never ends, it has long been a delaying tactic in politics to refer questions to the scientific community.[57] Defining environmental problems as "ecological" conceals the fact that decisions are usually also questions of interests.

Moreover, experts have a tendency to complicate problems and their solutions to keep them within the domain of their own expertise. They also like to deflect problems that are not of interest to their own discipline. Simple conventional themes like soil erosion or noise, which are of the utmost importance for the life and welfare of a great many people and were high up on the list in the proto-environmental debate only a few decades ago, have generally sailed far below the radar over the last few decades: they offer little material for attractive research projects. Airplanes and trucks also do not receive nearly the attention they deserve as serious destroyers of the environment. Hermann Scheer, a German champion of solar energy, is probably right with his thesis that the exemption of fuel taxes for international aviation and shipping is the worst and at the same time least-noticed environmental scandal. Trucks, too, largely escape serious environmental regulation everywhere. In West Germany, the government of Konrad Adenauer took on the truck lobby much more vigorously than the later governments of the "environmental age."[58]

The point is that the environmental movement is not always rational in the choice of its goals, and it would not even be fair to subject it to fundamental criticism because of that. Like many other movements of history, it would sever its own roots if it devalued sensory experience and no doubt also if it denied its spiritual foundation. No matter how often ecosystem contexts are invoked, the nature that the environmental movement is concerned about contains at its core a good deal of the old goddess Natura, whom one can love and with whom one can have imaginary dialogues: this is evident from slogans such as "Peace with Nature!" Especially today, when the greatest environmental problems can no longer be perceived with the senses in everyday life, a purely pragmatic foundation is not enough for the environmental movement.

If one applies the basic ideas behind Max Weber's famous treatise on the Protestant ethic and the spirit of capitalism to an analysis of the environmental movement, two questions arise: (1) Does this movement possess a quasi-religious passion that gives rise to a practice, a way of life, and a willingness to engage in selfless action? (2) Is there a convergence between this movement and powerful material interests, even if it is inherently as remote from these interests as Puritanism once was from the capitalist quest for profit? Both questions are important if one wishes to take the environmental rhetoric and the multitude of environmental initiatives seriously as a real *movement* of historical significance, and if one sees in popular ecology not only a trendy topic of conversation and a label for a hodgepodge of heterogeneous efforts. Given the current state of scholarship, definitive answers are not possible. But at least there is some indication that the answer would be affirmative for both questions.

The spiritual element of environmental awareness varies depending on a country's cultural tradition. The spiritual roots of the new environmental movement are especially evident in the United States, where a "transcendentalist" tradition runs from Emerson and Thoreau, via John Muir and Aldo Leopold, to Rachel Carson. Carson revered Albert Schweitzer and embraced his awe for all of life, including animals. She made friends with a spider and was deeply moved by the sight of salmon leaping upstream, drawn back to their place of origin even though they could have remained in the sea. The medievalist Lynn White argued in his famous essay about the "historical roots of our ecological crisis" that the final cause of this crisis lay in Judeo-Christian religion, which is why, in the final analysis, it could only be overcome spiritually. He recommended the ecologist Francis of Assisi as the patron saint and praised the Beatniks, the precursors of the Hippies, with their "affinity to Zen Buddhism" as the true revolutionaries of our time. The Hippies, initially influenced by Thoreau, made no small contribution, at least atmospherically, to the new model of the "gentle" relationship with nature – including human nature – provided they did not become addicted to hard drugs. Later observers liked to date the beginning of the American environmental movement to "Earth Day" in 1970: this version of history also emphasizes the spiritual element.[59] Of course, it neglects the institutional level – for example, the establishment of the EPA (Environmental Protection Agency), also in 1970 – and ignores the much older traditions of urban sanitation and forestry. And perhaps the great Hippie meeting in Woodstock in August 1969 should also be remembered as an event in the founding period of environmentalism.

Among American pioneers of the environmental movement, like Fritjof Capra, the "German model" as it presents itself in the German Green Party is seen to contrast with the "spiritual insights of deep ecology." Still, in 1984 the American eco-feminist Charlene Spretnak wrote that she could detect a source of spiritual warmth in the German Greens, one that was, however, embarrassing to many Greens, who preferred to deny it. In fact, in professionally written analyses of the Greens by German authors, whether by Hubert Kleinert or Joachim Raschke, we find virtually none of it – it is as though we are dealing with a completely different party from that of Spretnak. Her star witness is Petra Kelly, who was strongly influenced by the time she spent studying in Washington, where her spiritual openness was reinforced. Yet mysticism of any kind made many German leftists think immediately of Nazism, especially in the first decades after 1968.[60]

By contrast, for the broader environmental milieu in Germany, from which the Greens draw their voters and whose emotional impulse is often derived from natural healing, nature esotericism, and Eastern religions, the spiritual dimension is presumably of great importance. Perhaps this is even the inner cohesion of this milieu, which social scientists have been looking for in vain so far. In fact, people in this milieu liked to tell stories of ecological enlightenment. But as Max Weber had already realized, in the long run the enthusiastic phase of religiously tinged movements will invariably become mundane and be followed by a feeling of disenchantment. That phase has, in fact, long since begun, and it makes no sense to criticize this process.

Religious traits were already found in the "ecology" of Ernst Haeckel, the professed enemy of the Christian churches. The "goddess of truth," Haeckel declared, "dwells in the temple of nature, in the green woods, on the blue sea, and on the snowy summits of the hills." Jacob von Uexküll, the creator of the modern concept of "environment," wrote in a very similar vein: "The realm of nature are the environments from which it builds its temples." The nature cult was by no means merely a matter for writers and aesthetes. Even down-to-earth champions of a more nature-friendly water-economy like Alwin Seifert felt a need to justify their work spiritually. In a 1958 publication by the Vereinigung Deutscher Gewässerschutz (Association of Water Protection) we read that "a tabooed kind of basic 'romantic' attitude," a feeling for the "age-old pagan relationships to the clear water of the streams" was "indispensable" for a consistent "fight against effluent."

During the 1970s, the element of nature romanticism intensified also within the German antinuclear power movement, especially when it was defending the archaic, remote Wendland against the reprocessing project near Gorleben. Under the slogan "Gorleben shall live" it became a broad collective movement, where previously it had been in danger of fragmenting into moderates and radicals. This religion of life, however, had no need for martyrs, at least not for voluntary ones: the teacher Hartmut Gründler, a speaker of one of the antinuclear power groups who immolated himself on the steps of the Petri Church in Hamburg on the Day of Prayer and Repentance in November 1977, did not became part of the collective memory of this protest movement and was soon forgotten; very unlike

Pastor Oskar Brüsewitz, who immolated himself in August 1976 in Zeitz (GDR) to protest the harassment of the Church by the East German dictatorship.

The new German environmental movement achieved its greatest popularity through the alarm over *Waldsterben* it sounded in the early 1980s, when it was able to mobilize the old German forest romanticism for its cause. In Switzerland, too, the environmental movement attained political force only through *Waldsterben*. The cry of alarm at that time, however, diverted attention away from the sins of forestry, namely the spruce monocultures. It was only hurricane Wiebke in the spring of 1990 – with the disastrous damage it caused to woodlands – that led to a change toward a more nature-oriented forest in wide circles of German forestry.[61]

Clearer even than the environmental movement's spiritual roots is its institutional basis. For if one takes a long-term perspective, this movement certainly did not break into the political sphere from the outside. Under the immediate impact of the dramatic scenes when protestors opposing nuclear power in Germany and France became the target of police water cannons, it would be easy to forget that protection of nature and of the environment by and large developed in cooperation with state authorities, and that it would be completely unrealistic to write a history of environmental awareness without this background. Whether in Europe or in the United States, this was inherently most definitely not a movement that was hostile to the state, but rather an integrative movement, the many collisions with state authority in concrete cases notwithstanding. The state educational systems, the research institutions, the forestry administrations, the health offices, the supervision of trades, and not least the municipal administrations: without them the modern development of environmental awareness and of the response to environmental problems is entirely inconceivable.

Rachel Carson acquired her ecological competence as an employee of the U.S. Fish and Wildlife Service (FWS); when she wrote *Silent Spring*, however, she had left the Service and was researching on her own. Her fame came from the resonance she found in the public and the media, as well as from her appearances before a Senate committee and the president's scientific advisory council. The government of John F. Kennedy quickly realized that environmental protection was a suitable theme for asserting itself politically. That was even more true for Kennedy's successor, Lyndon B. Johnson, who in his "Great Society" speech of 1964 for the first time placed the environmental problem in the larger context of a vision of what American society could be in the future. At that time it was a far more attractive problem than the Vietnam War, and it also seemed suitable for reuniting a divided American society.

The situation was no different in Germany during the time of the protest movement of 1968. In 1966 the Deutsche Naturschutzring published a documentation titled *Natur in Not* (Nature in Trouble), which it embellished with appreciative letters from Chancellor Konrad Adenauer, Franz Josef Strauß, and President Heinrich Lübke – no indication here that the conservative power cartel was being set up as the enemy! The editor of the volume, Hubert Weinzierl, later chairman of the BUND, was at the time a State Commissioner for Nature Protection in Lower Bavaria; in those days he was still seeking to form an alliance with the influential hunting lobby. "Environmental policy" as a new, comprehensive field of politics was invented in 1970 by the new social-liberal government in search of a popular area of activity, based on the U.S. model; in fact, environmental initiatives by citizens initially even received government support. That same year, French president Georges Pompidou called for a *morale de l'environnement*.[62]

As is true of the opposition between environmental protection and the state, one should also not exaggerate the opposition between ecology and economics. Of course, if one takes the nonanthropocentric self-conception of some segments of the environmental movement seriously, the contradiction seems fundamental and irresolvable. In historical reality, though, no such fundamental conflict exists, and it is doubtful whether it was wise to assert that it did, since environmental protection, if it wants to be successful, is dependent on cooperation with economic forces, especially in times of high unemployment. Aurelio Peccei, who initiated the study *Limits of Growth* in his capacity as president of the Club of Rome, had been a successful head of the Fiat dealerships in Latin America for twenty years, and the study was partially funded by the German Volkswagen Foundation and carried out using computers at the Massachusetts Institute of Technology (MIT).

On the whole and from a long-term perspective, there was usually a good deal of convergence between economic and ecological interests. That is true even for the controversy over nuclear energy: by stopping the gigantic nuclear power plants of the early 1970s, with their breeder reactors and reprocessing facilities, the protest movement saved the energy economy from the greatest investment blunder in its history; within circles of the German energy sector, it was said that one really owed the protestors a debt of gratitude. A clear convergence exists also between the environmental movement and the declining importance of industry vis-à-vis the tertiary sector and the declining importance of energy in the "electronic age." As a result of excess production in agriculture, taking land out of cultivation, reforestation, and the creation of new wildernesses have become rational choices. And in some sectors of agrarian technology there has even been a turning away – for purely practical reasons – from the age-old tradition of plowing and an embrace of soil-preserving techniques. Some nature preserves are backed by forces interested in protecting water. In forestry, rising wage costs and declining yields have promoted a tendency to simply leave the forest to fend for itself.

I have repeatedly spoken about the "environmental movement." However, the question of whether all the ecological initiatives and networks added up to a coherent "movement" in the sense of earlier historical movements still needs to be investigated, and the answers are likely to vary from country to country. Is this movement still part of the present, or is it already history? There are times when one might doubt whether this movement still exists as a separate entity, whether its motivations, so far as they have practical significance, have not long since been absorbed by political and economic forces. This process of absorption, which is sometimes identified most clearly by disgruntled outsiders, can create new problems for which a critical public does not yet exist.

5. NEPAL, BHUTAN, AND OTHER SUMMIT PERSPECTIVES: ENVIRONMENTAL
PROBLEMS IN TOURISM, DEVELOPMENT AID, AND SPACE FLIGHT

In the fall of 1966 the slogan "Christmas in Kathmandu" made the rounds in the Hippie scene, and hundreds of "flower children" did in fact flock to the capital of

Nepal at Christmas time – at the same time that Lynn White was lauding them as the heralds of a new ecological era. This Himalayan kingdom became the magical destination of an eager and curious long-distance tourism. Beginning in 1969, the gentle Hippies were followed by the robust trekking tourists, whose number had grown nearly one hundred–fold by 1979. After the establishment of the Nepalese National Park, they were joined by a growing number of eco-tourists, who discovered not only the high mountains but also the jungle regions of the south. Royal Nepal Airlines created the advertising slogan that, alongside Hinduism and Buddhism, Nepal now had a third religion: tourism. At the same time, the country became the preferred destination for ethnologists and development workers. Today Nepal is one of the best-studied countries of the Third World and one of the countries with the highest development aid per capita.

Nepal, which initially presented itself as an Eldorado with a lavish ancient culture and grandiose nature, was simultaneously seen, from the late 1970s, as a paradigm for the worst kind of natural and cultural destruction. The new leitmotif was provided in 1975 by an article by Erik P. Eckholm, who argued that in no other mountainous region of the world were the forces of "ecological degradation" as rapidly and visibly at work as in Nepal. In the 1980s, Nepal was seen as the country with by far the highest rate of deforestation in southern Asia: it became an exemplar of the vicious cycle of overpopulation, deforestation, erosion, and even greater population pressure. Strictly speaking, though, it could just as easily become an exemplar of the problem of an outside environmental perception, the construction of environmental problems according to specific schemes, the influence of forces interested in certain projects on the definition of environmental crises, and in general the dilemma environmental policy finds itself in in large parts of the world.[63]

True, the rapid development of Nepal tourism has broadened and sharpened the perception of the environment there, and it did so also in a critical sense, not only at the level of travel brochures. Euphoria and disenchantment are often close companions on vacation travels. Here, as in other respects as well, the environmental perception of tourists tends toward an extreme of black-and-white: there are few intermediary stages between heaven and hell. In the national parks, Nepal presented itself more so than ever before as a paradise of "biodiversity." At the same time, however, the valley of Kathmandu – which had seemed like a fairy tale out of the *Thousand and One Nights* as late as the 1970s – is being suffocated by exhaust, smog, noise, and garbage. A diagnosis of ecological catastrophe seems only too plausible in the inferno that is Kathmandu. Trekkers in the Himalayas saw the damage wrought by other trekkers, as well as the fragility of terraced fields in the highest elevations. From an airplane one can already detect landslides everywhere, though without being able to judge whether they are natural or caused by humans. Hardly any tourists are found in the agrarian lands of the middle regions and the lowlands, and these areas are also of little interest to researchers. Eco-tourists are looking for the "jungle" and pay little attention to the countless small bamboo groves in the midst of agricultural regions. Then there is also a foreshortening of the temporal perspective: since Nepal was a closed country until 1950, foreigners have a tendency to date the processes of change to the time after that.

Convergences and interactions have developed between the environmental perception of tourists, the developmental aid organizations, Nepalese authorities as well as public opinion in India. This is typical for many parts of the Third World. One reason why the global environmental conference in Rio in 1992 was of such epochal importance is not least that environmental protection was linked with development aid and thus handed over to the established apparatuses of development aid, which were partly responsible for a good deal of environmental damage. Since then, "sustainable development" has become such a self-evident conceptual amalgam that one hardly notices its inherent tension. Since the 1970s when the development model along the lines of the conventional idea of progress came under question, the field of development aid has been searching for a new ecological legitimation. It therefore needs these definitions of environmental crisis, because it provides the basis for development projects. If one defines the heart of the crisis as "deforestation," one can use it to justify large-scale reforestation projects even if they do not accord with local needs and fail to provide relief where the cutting of trees is having a deleterious effect. If one defines the heart of the crisis as an energy shortage and a result of the overuse of firewood, hydroelectric dams promise a way out, even if they simultaneously flood valuable agricultural land in the valleys. The incentive to build hydro-electrical power plants in the Himalayas is extremely high: in theory, the water forces there contain as much potential energy as all the rivers of North America combined; so far, such projects have been blocked primarily by political tensions between the Himalayan countries and by technical difficulties.

A report by the World Bank in 1978 prophesied that, within twenty years, Nepal would have no accessible forests left. Here, as in other countries of the Third World, environmental protection and especially reforestation projects became a proven way to obtain funds from the World Bank and other development organizations. It did not take long for the Nepalese state to adjust to the new situation in its language. The diagnosis of an ecological catastrophe became official doctrine. To implement government forest protection programs, forestry officials declared at village meetings that, without these projects, the agricultural soil would be washed into the Bay of Bengal. In India, too, the theory of catastrophe was picked up, since it could be used to blame Nepal for the floods in Bengal. One Indian anthology spoke of an "Environmental Holocaust" (1989), though the evidence it presented did not sustain this stark pronouncement.[64]

If one examines the background to the alarm over deforestation in Nepal, it is reminiscent in some respects of the deforestation alarms in Central Europe in the late eighteenth century. A certain kind of crisis is defined into existence to justify intervention from the top. In both cases, the complaint about "deforestation" is based on a definition of forest that excluded wood pastures and scattered peasants' forests. In many mountainous regions of Nepal, the forest can be identified only through aerial photography: statements about the extent of forest coverage vary, depending on the crown density that one defines as "forest." There is one difference, though: in Germany, reforestation actually happened; in Nepal, it is all too often done merely on paper.

What can we determine about the real environmental situation in Nepal and its causes? Global pronouncements are always open to challenge, since the regional differences in a country like Nepal are extremely pronounced: simply by virtue of geography, but also as a result of the differences among the cultures there. In all likelihood the sweeping blame that is assigned to the mountain farmers, and that follows a pattern common around the world, is wrong. In the mountains it is often not overpopulation but the exodus of people that leads to the deterioration of terraces. While it is often said that mountain farmers turned even the last tree into firewood, anyone who hikes through Nepal will quickly discover that this is not true. Since many farmers need the leaves of trees as animal feed, a peasant silviculture is widespread. A scarcity of firewood is often noted in the countryside. One must consider, though, that the gathering of firewood in Nepal, as in many countries of the world, is traditionally women's work: men are not affected if procuring wood requires covering ever longer distances. Often they don't even seem to be aware of what is happening!

There is clear evidence that large-scale deforestation took place above all in the lowlands, the Terai, after malaria was eliminated there through the use of DDT beginning in 1957, thus opening the way for settlers from outside to make the land arable. Once again, the end of malaria and the large-scale application of DDT mark an epochal shift. But this wave of deforestation was historically rather a unique event, which has by now been halted through the establishment of national parks. Until 1982 Nepal was an important wood exporter. And until recently the Nepalese lived with a sense that they had an abundance of woodland, which also explains why older traditions of forest protection are often nonexistent.[65]

On the whole, the environmental damage from tourism does not seem to have nearly the importance that critical tourists often attribute to it. Most strongly affected by tourism are the sherpas, the guides and darlings of trekkers in the high mountains. But contrary to earlier claims, it would appear that tourism actually strengthened their culture. The most profound turning point in sherpa ecology was presumably the introduction of the potato, which began as early as the end of the nineteenth century. However, since the sherpas used part of this new caloric surplus to found monasteries, in this case the potato indirectly promoted birth control. Yet the Tibetan-Buddhist sherpas, among whom we can also find evidence of certain forest-protection traditions, are by no means typical for the Nepalese population as a whole. It would be wrong to counter the sweeping condemnation of the mountain dwellers with an ecological apotheosis of mountain farmers. There certainly are processes of soil degradation that the latter cannot manage, let alone grasp.[66]

It would be quite rash to allow the insight that much in claims of environmental catastrophes is deliberately constructed to mislead one into making the sweeping judgment that *all* environmental crises are merely intellectual constructs. The fact that the empirical evidence of the pessimists has gaps most certainly does not mean that the contrary position of the optimists is firmly substantiated. Nepal in particular offers little cause for ecological optimism. Even critics of the catastrophe theory are watching the changes to the Nepalese environment with great concern. To be sure, one must remember that the vicious cycle "overpopulation – deforestation – erosion" is an ideal-typical scheme, one that usually applies to reality only in part and under certain conditions. Yet the contrary ideal type, in which population growth leads to an improved use of the soil, applies even less to Nepalese conditions. The growing population density is accompanied not by rising but in part by declining yields per area unit. Although many sherpas are as conscious of fertilizer as the German model peasants were in the eighteenth and nineteenth centuries, there are numerous indications of inadequate fertilization, a lack of soil protection, and declining soil fertility.

While the Nepalese agricultural terraces may seem very picturesque, they generally are not very stable structures. Most have no supporting wall; instead, the embankments are cut and reshaped every winter. On steep slopes, however, every heavy monsoon downpour can cause this entire system to slide away – and with growing population pressure, the terraces are marching up the mountains ever more steeply. In Nepal, as elsewhere, the old, labor-intensive tradition of terrace management along with its attendant culture of cooperation is in decline. As it is, Nepal, with its heterogeneous cultures, is not a tightly organized hydraulic society like Java or Bali; instead, it is quite common that the farmers divert the water from each other at night. Agriculture in Nepal is based on animal fertilizer, that is, on extensive pasture areas, but the latter are being squeezed by the growing population density. Even if it has not been possible to identify an acute environmental catastrophe, numerous indications point to a slow and insidious crisis.

Presumably, however, that crisis is not of the kind that could be effectively addressed by development projects and outside experts. And while declarations about the "participation" of the mountain farmers have long been part of development aid jargon, even a publication by ICIMOD (International Centre for Integrated Mountain Development) in Nepal has confessed: "Mountain people are invisible to policy-makers, even in a predominantly mountain country like Nepal." Large-scale development projects usually do not concern themselves with bamboo groves and terrace embankments. The entire style of a policy conceived from a distance fits poorly with the problems of mountain farming. Here, as elsewhere, it has been precisely the state's claim to the forest, a claim that has never been accompanied by an effective forestry management, that has played its part in stirring up the anger of the local population against forest protection from the top.

The ecological literature on Nepal is imposing; equally impressive and revealing, however, is the fact that there is no connection between the ecological discourse and what is happening in the country. Even more so than in Europe, in a country like Nepal the historian must be vigilant not to confuse discourse with real history. Environmental publications require their own kind of source criticism. In Nepal, as in many other Third World countries, the most calamitous issue seems to be that a majority of the rural population no longer believes that its way of life has a future, and that especially the most active among the younger generation want to go to the city – and if possible, straight to the United States – even though they often suffer from homesickness once they are there. As a social and mental basis, sustainability requires a population that is at home not only outwardly but inwardly and that believes in a future for its homeland – just like the farmers at the time of the old agrarian reform, whose confidence in the future expressed itself in splendid farmhouses. This mind-set, however, is in danger of eroding in the age of universal mobility, and this process may well be even more disastrous than soil erosion.[67] Many development workers unwittingly promote the "Let's get out of here!" mentality by their mere presence – by their enviable lifestyle and salaries, exorbitant by Third World standards.

When the valley of Kathmandu was drowning in a sea of smog, some tourists discovered the existence nearby of another, truly archaic and untouched Himalayan paradise: *Bhutan*. This remote and until then little-known Buddhist kingdom, so similar to Nepal in its natural conditions, has presented itself since the 1980s as the opposite extreme: as a country that has consistently avoided Nepal's mistakes. Like virtually no other attractive country in the world, Bhutan has so far closed its doors stubbornly to mass tourism and to large-scale development projects. A report on *Biodiversity and Tourism* (1997), written at the behest of the German Federal Office for Nature Protection (Bundesamt für Naturschutz), praised Bhutan's tourism planning as "one of the most exemplary in the world." In 1990 Bhutan had nearly twelve times as much forest per capita as Nepal. It is one of the very few Third World countries that is pursuing an effective forest protection not only in nature preserves, and it is doing so within the framework of an overall policy that protects the traditional wood and textile trades and keeps the import of industrial mass goods low.

To those who came to know and love it, Bhutan was a new Shangri-la, a Buddhist dream country that could take the place of Tibet, which has been occupied and rudely deforested by the Chinese. Travelers believe that they are ascending through misty forests into a fairy tale land, where time has stood still and nature is still unharmed. But even in Bhutan there was a time of ruthless exploitation of the forests. It was only after 1980, in the wake of the global ecological era, that the government switched to a vigorous policy of forest protection and reforestation. On the whole that policy seems to be working, even though the prohibition against slash-and-burn agriculture could not be enforced everywhere. The chief reason for the good condition of the forests is surely the very low population density. Bhutan has no broad valleys in which an agrarian growth dynamic was able to unfold. Moreover, the practice of polyandry, the high proportion of monks, and perhaps also the relative independence of women has kept population numbers stable in the past. The remote location of the country and the absence, for the most part, of conspicuous consumption by the upper classes favors an atmosphere of modesty and few wants. There are no larger cities and barely the beginnings of a "dual economy," that is, the jarring existence side-by-side of modern and traditional economic sectors. All this has meant the absence of major problems of the Third World that make effective environmental protection difficult. In 1960 the forests of Bhutan were nationalized; but this move, which in Nepal and in many other countries alienated the forest dwellers, does not seem to have had the same negative effect in Bhutan.[68] This is the advantage of a small country, in which the capital is hardly more than a large village, and where, in spite of the authoritarian system of government, the rulers and the subjects are within sight of each other, as it were.

Since 1990 the Bhutanese ecotopia has had one dark side, and it, too, could take on exemplary significance: the expulsion of more than 100,000, mostly Nepalese, immigrants. The refugees make up about one-sixth of Bhutan's population. The immediate cause was unrest triggered by the policy of "Bhutanization" that the government pursued in the 1980s. Its outward sign was the general enforcement of a national dress as well as the creation of a "green belt," an uninhabited stretch of forest on the border with India. That is precisely where the Nepalese population was concentrated. The government justified the expulsions by arguing that the immigrants lacked loyalty, and by invoking quasi-ecological arguments: the

Nepalese reproduced more rapidly than the native population and destroyed the forest with their slash-and-burn agriculture; the natives, along with their culture and nature, were becoming an "endangered species."[69] This is in line with the usual sweeping picture of the Nepalese environmental crisis, though closer examination reveals that it is only partially true.

It is clear how closely in Bhutan ecology is intertwined with the preservation of the political system. One warning was the fate of neighboring Sikkim, which lost its independence when Nepalese immigrants had grown into the majority among the population. The supposed threat to Bhutanese culture and nature was hardly mere fabrication. An environmental dilemma that has so far barely registered in the Western environmental discourses became acute in Bhutan: in this regard the ancient mountain country could be a signpost to the future.[70] However, it is unclear whether or not Bhutanese exceptionalism is sustainable over the long run.

The Worldwatch Institute in Washington believes it is a general rule that a rise in population pressure and regional resource shortages lead people to fall back "on ethnic and religious commonalities for their protection."[71] And that behavior is not completely misguided, for a balance between people and nature can be imagined most readily in culturally homogeneous social microcosms. But what if there is no return to these small traditional worlds, or the way there involves terrible bloodbaths? The way out would be a nation-state that arises from a historically evolved symbiosis of neighboring cultures. But in many parts of the world, loyalty does not belong to the state but to family, clan, tribe, religion, party. The state is often – and not without reason – seen as corrupt and the mere tool of the ruling faction. Therein lies the dilemma not only of social but also environmental policy in much of the world today. It explains the emergence most recently of "nongovernmental organizations" (NGOs) in development aid and in international environmental policy. In Nepal even the king established a nature protection NGO in 1984! But the NGOs, initially surrounded by an aura of autonomy, suffer from the problems afflicting development aid in the form of projects financed and run from the outside. Historical experience gives reason for serious doubts whether "development" in a productive sense can ever happen this way.

The failure of many states could lead to the conclusion – as it often has – that environmental policy can be pursued effectively only on an international, and ideally a global, level. It is on that level, one might argue, that one finds the broadest perspective, the widest competency, and the greatest distance from the environmentally destructive short-sightedness of particular interests. As it is, the science of ecology knows no national boundaries, and many emissions also cut across borders. Precisely the dangers that conjure up apocalyptic scenarios – damage to the atmosphere and the world's oceans – can be tackled only globally. What is more: environmental standards for industry can be implemented best if they apply to *everyone* and do not put any national industry at a competitive disadvantage. Much of the rhetoric of "globalization" that dominates the economy today comes from the environmental movement. Frank Uekötter has remarked that if you listen to environmentalists, you could at times get the impression that "global" is a common synonym for "important."[72]

Since 1945 apocalyptic thinking – initially born of a fear of another world war – has led, time and again, to the conclusion that the goal of all reasonable people today must be a world government. Global environmental threats have reinforced the logic of this argumentation. However, since that goal is opposed by tremendous difficulties and countless interests, it is precisely the quest for universal solutions that could push humanity into the worst conflicts. In the end, the better part of ecological wisdom might be to recognize that this goal makes no sense, based on the insight that the concrete symbiosis of humanity and nature always occurs in smaller units, functions best through a careful interplay of regulation and self-regulation, and cannot, in principle, be organized from the top. Erich Jantsch, the theoretician of the "self-organization of the universe" wonders whether we should not "direct our attention at the symbiosis of sub-global, autopoietic systems . . . instead of a world government and world culture."[73]

This preference is supported not only by systems theory, but also – and emphatically – by historical experience. Crucial to an effective environmental policy is not abstract awareness, but organization, a coalition of actors, and a shared practical code. It is this, and not the basic awareness of environmental problems, that was often lacking, and these practical, organizational tasks are best managed in specific regions and situations. To be sure, many environmental problems are, in essence, more or less the same the world over, but strategies for solving them vary, depending on the region and the historical situation. At times they are even different from one valley of the Alps to the next. The majority of environmental problems that are relevant for the Third World are substantially local and regional in nature. Forest protection, reforestation, "agroforestry," "social forestry," and soil-preserving irrigation are impossible to organize in a global framework, but depend largely on local knowledge and a local arrangement between various interests. The delusion, which has become the global ideology, that essential outside help exists for these problems has itself become an environmental risk factor. In fact, the goal of "sustainability" remains an empty formula on a global level: it is only in much more narrowly circumscribed frameworks and with reference to concrete models that it can be given substance. And it is only within a regionally circumscribed framework that one can imagine a participation on the part of the population in question.

Even the report *GEO (Global Environmental Outlook) 2000* by UNEP (United Nations Environmental Programme) argues for regionally circumscribed MEAs (multilateral environmental agreements): "Regional MEAs in which countries share and manage common resources result in relatively high levels of public information and awareness; generally, the smaller the membership of the agreement, the wider the coverage in local mass media. For example, the Ganges Water Sharing Treaty is known even to poor farmers in the remotest parts of Bangladesh and West Bengal in India."[74] It would appear that a supranational environmental policy has the best chances of success in relatively contained natural areas with shared environmental problems that are clearly evident to all those concerned: examples would be the Alps, the Baltic Sea region, or the Sahel zone in North Africa.

In all of this, the historian will not neglect the question of power. Expert discussions that indulge in scenarios of how Germany will retool the Chinese energy economy in an environmentally friendly way through "joint implementation" move in a strangely unreal atmosphere, as though the power and individual will of states simply did not exist. And if loyalty to the state is often weak on environmental questions, loyalty toward international organizations and authorities is likely to be even weaker.

Effective environmental protection that mobilizes the masses cannot consist merely of prohibitions and threshold values, but must be built around positive models. This, too, is not conceivable on a global level. To prevent such models from being limited to empty formulas and to allow them to take on concrete shape, they must be designed within much smaller frameworks. One need only recall the treatment of waste: here a good deal depends on national culture and regional conditions, and creative politics is possible only on this level. One of the worst environmental problems, noise, is inherently local and is always ignored in a globalization of environmental policy.

This does *not* mean that it would be sensible to fall into the opposite extreme and dismiss international environmental policy as pointless. Environmental history surely does not suggest that "local knowledge" solves all problems, especially if the local experiential traditions have been ruptured – as is so often the case today – as a result of a rural exodus and migration.[75] In the search for historical analogies, one should also ponder whether it would be possible for certain environmental norms to become "second nature" for the decision makers of the world much the same way in which the norms of hygiene more or less are. *One* path to a solution presumably points in this direction. The institutional current within contemporary economics has rightly emphasized that there is not only a "government" through bureaucratic institutions, but also a "government" through generally accepted rules. It is only in this sense that a global "government" in the interest of environmental protection is conceivable. Still, given our past experiences, it is ill-considered to focus as one-sidedly on global solutions as segments of the German environmental scene, with their horror of the nation-state, tend to do. It is peculiar how unaware many "green" policy drafts often are that they presuppose a functioning nation-state.

The UN is the test case for the opportunities and pitfalls of the global approach. The Stockholm Environmental Conference of 1972 deserves a lot of credit for making "environment" into a global theme. The supranational boom in environmental policy that began around 1970 can be explained in part as a run-up effect to the conference. The UN Conference on Environment and Development in Rio in 1992 also became an epochal event in the international environmental discourse by elevating "sustainability" into the goal of policy. Yet these kinds of environmental initiatives always ran the risk of being nothing more than words and symbolic gestures that diverted attention from the fact that in reality no great change occurred. In some respects, UN conferences are even counterproductive, because at these meetings the "environment" becomes the plaything of existing power blocs and alliances. In this game there is usually a tendency for the preservation of the environment to be seen as a concern of the highly industrialized states, while in the Third World the idée fixe prevails that its own interests are not at stake in all of this, and that one should take action only if the First World gives something in return. Since many poor Third World countries cannot pay for the costly international conference diplomacy, they need the financial help of the oil-producing countries, whose interests they have to represent in return: this, too, makes them into a brake on environmental protection. But it is precisely in many Third World countries, as Dieter Oberndörfer has noted, that there is "no contradiction between ecology and economy" in the short or medium term; the role playing that is developing between the First and Third Worlds distracts from countries' vital self-interest.[76] Effective environmental protection, however, can succeed only if it is based on such self-interest.

The best model of international eco-diplomacy to date came at the conference in Montreal (1987), which resulted in the banning of the production of certain aerosols to protect the ozone layer. In this case there was a global problem, and countermeasures were called for. It was almost entirely the industrialized countries that were affected, and they did not find giving up the production of harmful aerosols to be onerous. The negotiations were advanced in crucial ways by the initiative of individual states, sometimes the United States, sometimes Germany: even the global level needs national actors.

Even in matters of solar energy, Hermann Scheer, since 1988 the president of Eurosolar (the European Association for Renewable Energies), puts little hope in the European Union as a whole, especially since the breakthrough into solar energy will take place not in the energy sector, but in solar construction and in agriculture: "Not the global but the regional framework of action is called for." In France, 80 percent of whose supply of electricity depends on nuclear energy, solar energy is not a major theme, even though in the 1970s the country had undertaken a visually impressive – though in reality a merely symbolic – leap by erecting giant mirrors near Odeillo in the Pyrenees.[77]

The European Union, established in 1957 as an economic community, acquired responsibility for environmental policy only in 1987. The EU is politically much more effective and capable than the UN. Central and Western Europe have much in common culturally and economically, and they are drawing closer in their environmental awareness. Since environmental policy is in the final analysis a question of industrial standards, one key in this area lies in the equalization of standards within Europe. With respect to the policy of environmentally friendly products, however, the EU has lagged behind. In 1983 the Federal Republic surged ahead by enacting regulations for large furnaces for the reduction of sulphur dioxide, but as a country of automobiles it acted much less exemplarily when it came to nitrogen oxides. Today, France leads Germany in some areas of environmental policy: it would appear that there is not such a thing as a constant leadership position in environmental protection.

At times a noble competition has developed – at least verbally – among the EU countries over who is the better protector of the environment. Yet national animosities also erupt: they are difficult to discuss in depth since different philosophies of environmental protection clash here, each of which has its own inherent logic from the perspective of the country in question. England, on its island swept by the west wind, prefers – unlike the conurbations in continental Europe – to set air quality without establishing a specific threshold to emissions. On the other hand, the British are much more sensitive than continental Europeans to the damage to the world of the birds from EU agrarian policies. Since public pressure on a European-wide level is difficult to generate, Brussels lacks a crucial impetus toward taking the initiative in environmental policy, an impetus that exists only within the nation-states. The publics in the EU states have been and remain national, not

European. For the vast majority of Europeans, the EU apparatus is completely impenetrable, which is why few know how to exert pressure on it. During the negotiations on the ozone layer, the EU as a whole did *not* play an active role.

The EU, which in its origins was closely linked with nuclear energy, was at first not popular in environmental circles. There were jokes that the bureaucrats in Brussels were settings standards even for bananas. Carl Amery, a German writer active in the environmental movement, used to argue – very much in the spirit of the slogan "small is beautiful" – that the bigger organizations are, the dumber they are; hence the EU was much dumber than his family.

After 1990, however, the EU bureaucracy increasingly discovered environmental policy and the environment as a field of action that was far less colonized by national traditions than other areas of politics. In terms of nature protection, the EU led the way in the 1990s with the FFH (flora, fauna, habitat) guidelines. Many nature protectors who were originally skeptical about the EU have since transformed themselves into supports of a European nature protection policy. Environmental protection organizations have Europeanized themselves; some ended up financially dependent on the EU and turned into its advisory bodies. But the EU is not able to solve the problem of how to impart the necessary popularity to nature protection. Even in villages that are to some extent supportive of organic agriculture, hostile opposition is aroused when nature protection is imposed from the top. Members of the private organization EURONATUR who were trying to protect the Mediterranean and were negotiating the establishment of the Northern Sporades National Park with the local fishermen felt that the EU's nature protection policy, which does not care about local interests, was an obstacle, indeed, a kind of "megalomania." Moreover, they were outraged that EU agrarian policy was at the same time subsidizing the keeping of goats in the Greek mountains![78]

It also makes one uneasy to see how utterly impenetrable environmental law has become in the wake of Europeanization, a situation that has transformed environmental protection completely into the exclusive purview of experts. More disastrous still is probably the generally higher mobility produced by the growing integration of the EU, since traffic is today in many respects the leading cause of environmental damage. On the other hand, the environmental policy of Denmark and the Netherlands, which has now become a model, shows the advantage of small and manageable countries, where a praxis-relevant consensus can be established fairly easily and where the problems are tackled in a comparatively concrete and uncomplicated manner. This is another indication that it is unwise to strip functioning nation-states of authority in environmental matters without a compelling reason, and to shift it to higher levels. The Australian ecologist Timothy F. Flannery even believes that countries with a growing environmental awareness are fracturing internally, a process that has its own inherent logic. If he is right, the growing internationalization of environmental policy would make no sense. Such a policy presumably has its strongest foothold in the realm of natural areas that cut across national borders, are not excessively large, and have shared environmental problems – examples might be the Alps and the Baltic Sea.[79]

The fundamental question at which level environmental policy should be primarily located is not simply discussed rationally (if it is discussed at all), but also involves strong emotions. Emotions are linked to the nation-state, but also to the dissolution of boundaries. The feeling that today one must think mostly in global terms when it comes to the environment was given a strong and suggestive boost by space travel and satellite images. They are the source of the rhetoric of "spaceship earth" that needs to be seen and guided in its vulnerability as a single entity, and that compels its inhabitants to act in solidarity. "We travel together, passengers on a little spaceship," declared the American ambassador to the UN, Adlai Stevenson," in 1965, a few days before his death, "preserved from annihilation only by the care, the work, and I will say, the love we give our fragile craft."

The spaceship metaphor quickly became popular. The paradox of space travel was that it destroyed its own magic and made humans aware of how empty and lifeless the universe is. As Wolfgang Sachs has written, "the rediscovery of the earth became the real revelation of space travel." While in the 1950s many still believed in Martians and that humans would emigrate to other planets if their own became too crowded, the absurdity of such fantasies has now become clear, and people understood that humans have only this one earth. In a certain sense, the "Copernican revolution" was undone: earth, ever since Copernicus simply one planet among many, became once again something unique in space. Seen from space, it seemed small, lonely, and fragile, and its atmosphere – in the words of the German astronaut Ulrich Walter – like a "razor thin layer of morning frost."[80]

Thereafter, the global perspective seemed like the marker of ecological enlightenment. To be sure, rational insights and organizational interests were also involved. Study of the threatened ozone layer offered NASA a perfect opportunity to distinguish itself as an ecological pioneer and to make people forget its links with former plans for a world war in space. NASA, according to James Lovelock, presented itself as the "Prince" that would redeem the earth from its "Cinderella" existence. Satellite images offered a comprehensive picture such as had never existed before of the state of tropical forests and desertification. One desertification researcher, however, has argued that the satellite photos ushered in an era of fallacies, in which desertification was erroneously believed to be a uniform problem around the world.[81] The implied idea that desertification could be combated at the highest level with global projects is quite unrealistic: "Of all the major international action programmes connected with water and land degradation, the most conspicuous failure has probably been the UN plan to halt desertification" – so the verdict of Robin Clarke, a former member of UNESCO. Erosion, too, is usually a process that is triggered by specific local conditions. Like every piece of soil, every erosion gully has its own special history: a global soil protection policy would be an absurd enterprise.[82]

Tourism is today presumably the most widespread emotional foundation for a broad perspective on nature. Beginning in the eighteenth century, traveling for its own sake – initially more to cultural than natural sites – became the fashion among the upper classes. Modern mass and long-distance tourism, however, has its own "50s syndrome." It experienced a powerful surge especially with the charter-flight tourism that began in the late 1950s, particularly among the Germans, who had had to suppress their wanderlust for a long time. It would seem that many people in the industrialized nations – and not least also many members of the elite – see the chief meaning of their lives in travel. In contrast to traditional educational trips, the dominant impulse in tourism has become the quest for the experience of nature – be it as simple as swimming and sunbathing. For decades, tourism has been the greatest growth sector around the world, and most recently, "eco-tourism," the yearning for luxurious nature, has posted the strongest growth within this sector, whether in Carinthia or in Indonesia.[83]

It would appear that travel looms very large in the history of feelings for and ideals about nature, but also in the frustrations about despoiled nature.[84] Alongside anxiety over health, it is probably the most commonly denied origin of what is today regarded as "environmental awareness": for travel leads not only to emotional experiences, but also to the acquisition of knowledge about the environment – of whatever quality – on a mass scale. Algal blooms (commonly referred to as "red tides") and dying coral reefs sensitize seaside vacationers to the pollution and warming of the world's oceans. Travel guides and brochures, overflowing with glossy and sophisticated visuals, offer a wealth of environmental information about the entire world in a highly suggestive manner and are constantly in search of new nature-culture charms, from the irrigation canals on Madeira to the mangrove swamps of Malaysia. Contrary to what Max Weber diagnosed as a modern "disen-chantment of the world," this is a constant attempt at enchanting the world – an attempt, however, that is tripped up by realities that do not fit the magical images.

The age of the railroad quickly gave rise to a tense relationship between nature protection and tourism. As early as 1880, Ernst Rudorff complained that tourists were despoiling the nature they were seeking out. In the Alps, the movement for homeland and nature protection was triggered around the turn of the century by the struggle against the project of building a railway to the Matterhorn and against plans for other mountain railroad lines. One Alpine conservationist saw the tourists as the "locusts" of the mountains. In 1925 a nature protector in Bohemia professed his lifelong, "passionate hatred of the tourism industry."[85] The horror back then had its reasons, and today the environmental damage from industrialized tourism has become a fully global phenomenon. The most disastrous effect of long-distance tourism is presumably that it contributes to elevating the water- and energy-intensive Western way of life into the model all over the world – even in regions where water and energy are scarce.

The roots of some criticism of tourism are more ideological than ecological. Lovers of the wilderness pure and simple despise the mere nature parks with their benches and kiosks, even though these are indispensable for popularizing nature protection. In time-tested centers of Alpine tourism like Grindelwald and Davos, where the local communities have taken control of tourism, the latter has helped to preserve Alpine farming.[86] It is always necessary to evaluate tourism's effect on the environment against the economic alternatives that are available to a given region and that in many cases would pose a far greater burden on the environment.

In Costa Rica, which had the highest rates of deforestation in Latin America as late as the 1980s, tourism, especially eco-tourism, has helped to achieve an ecological turnaround, in the wake of which a quarter of the country's land was placed under nature protection and Costa Rica emerged as the global model of sustainable development. By the 1990s, eco-tourism had become the country's largest single source of revenue. However, some nature preserves still exist only on paper, and others had to be imposed over the vigorous opposition of the local population.[87] Moreover, the nature preserves divert attention from the fact that outside – on the plantations and pastures – little consideration is given to the environment. Still, Costa Rica remains an exemplar, compared, for example, to neighboring El Salvador, which for a long time has had the worst erosion damage in Latin America next to Haiti, even though it was once considered the most progressive state in Central America thanks to its road and bridge building. El Salvador and Haiti reveal that under modern conditions, where the state is needed as the protector of the environment, there is a connection between political and ecological stability. Haiti holds the Latin American record not only for bloody revolutions, but also for soil erosion.[88]

Today "wild nature" presents itself to the travel-happy nature lover primarily in a multitude of fascinating coffee-table books and illustrated brochures of national parks. All over the world, the establishment of national parks is driven not by a feeling of awe for nature, but by tourism interests. Without the latter, as one expert on species protection from the WWF has said, "many nature areas of the world would be worse off."[89] If the preservation of the tropical rain forest has become the paradigm for nature protection in the Western world, the influence of the tourist's gaze is unmistakable, combined with the old dream of the "last paradise." When French president Francois Mitterand suggested in 1988 that large areas of the Amazon region should be placed under the oversight of the UN in order to protect the rain forest, this caused a storm of outrage in Brazil. And the boycott of tropical woods called for at that time by environmental organizations, which was very popular in Germany for many years, does not seem to have boosted forest awareness in the affected countries; instead, it appears to have triggered a response of defiance, especially since those countries could point out that the industrialized countries had long since cleared their own ancient woodlands or had reforested them into useful forests. As a result, the boycott was called off in the 1990s. There is no dearth of examples that the forests fare worst where wood has the least value. It is not the virgin jungle untouched by humans that is useful as a popular ecological model for the Third World, but "agroforestry," the combination of agriculture and silviculture.

As we learn on a stroll through the centuries, there are two opposing poles to the love of nature: one close by and one far away – in one's own garden and in an exotic Arcadia. Often the two kinds of longing and pleasure combine in the same person. The environmental movement in Germany and elsewhere sought to reconcile this dichotomy with the slogan "think globally – act locally"; but if one took this too literally, one would end up in a state of schizophrenia. It is often quite useful to think locally. Today it is frequently implied that the global perspective is morally superior, and the focus on the protection of one's own immediate environment is ridiculed as a short-sighted NIMBY ("Not in My Backyard") syndrome. From a historical perspective there is no reason to do so: one need only recall the colonial origins of the long-distance view of nature! Everything depends on effective coalitions of actors, and such coalitions will not come about if environmentalists are more interested in an imaginary solidarity with Indian tribes in the Amazon than in cooperation with local foresters. Effective opposition to nuclear power projects arose only when the debate over the risks of nuclear energy ceased to be abstract and involved concrete threats in one's own neighborhood. Vandana Shiva has complained that the concentration on "global environmental problems, instead of expanding the perspective, has in fact narrowed the radius of activism."[90]

6. THE PROBLEMS OF POWER AND UNCERTAINTY IN ENVIRONMENTAL POLICY

The rise of the environmental movement is phenomenal, from a historical perspective as well. The labor movement in the nineteenth century had to struggle for generations to escape the stigma of criminalization and become a negotiating partner to the powerful: it is striking, then, how rapid the process has been with the environmental movement, almost as though politics had been waiting for it to arrive on the scene. And how rapidly it has conquered the jargon of politics around the world, in the remotest corners of the globe. If one believes that discourse constitutes our reality, there is every reason for ecological optimism. Ecological themes offer plenty of topics for conversation, even in the day-to-day life of nonintellectuals: one hears it in schools, on the subway, in the health club. And this is by no means only a typically German or Western phenomenon. Even in Russia, a rather hopeless country from the perspective of the Western environmental scene, "eco-lyceums" are being set up as experimental institutions, "sustainability" is becoming a magic word, and ecology is turning into the new religion for some circles. In Tuva in Central Asia, environmental education became an important subject in schools, and it culminated in the participation in rituals at sacred springs and trees.[91] Ecological fascination arises from the global gaze, but also from the new regionalism, the return to tradition.

If one looks at the media landscape, one could actually believe that we have been living in the age of ecology since 1970. Greenpeace, the most famous and financially most powerful environmental organization, founded in 1971, is an acknowledged master at dealing with the media. Nobody was better suited to freeing environmentalists from the image of being timid hypochondriacs than these "Rainbow Warriors," who created a model of modern heroism and at the same time knew how to combine idealism with sober and precise political calculation. Greenpeace's fame attained a first peak in 1975, when members of the organization in rubber boats maneuvered themselves between a Soviet whaler and the whales it was hunting and filmed themselves in front of the harpoons. On their return to San Francisco, they discovered that they had become national heroes. In response to U.S. pressure, an international ban on whaling was issued in 1986 – even Japan had to yield to protect itself from losing face. As Richard Ellis has written, the stop to commercial whaling was "the greatest single victory in the history of the environmental community. Consolidating all of its various species into a single symbol, we have elevated one animal to near-divine status" – and a symbol of threatened nature.

Large animals possess this symbolic power to a special degree. This is clear from the enormous popularity of Bernhard Grzimek's campaign on behalf of the elephants of the Serengeti, and Dian Fossey's fatal struggle to save the mountain gorillas of Rwanda, even though it was doubtful whether these species were especially threatened, and even though the methods employed by these wildlife protectors were well suited to make conservation hateful to the indigenous peoples. In 1988 seals, with their beseeching eyes, became another moving symbol of threatened creation when they were dying off en masse in the North Sea – even though the environmental causes were controversial. The same is true for the cute panda, which China chose as its national animal, though it is also claimed by the Tibetans, who complain about the destruction of their nature by the Chinese.[92]

As one can see, "panda politics" can be used to divert attention from other kinds of environmental destruction. At its core, environmental politics has often remained the politics of *symbolism*, even if it accomplishes something real now and then. Yet it is not necessary to dismiss it for that reason as pseudo-politics. Symbols are of great importance in providing orientation for humans, and over the long term they may very well acquire real relevance. Nowhere does the situation of environmental politics present itself more ambiguously than it does in this situation, and nowhere else is the need for long-term analyses as clearly evident. In all likelihood, only the future will show whether a genuine "ecological revolution" took place in the world after 1970, or whether this picture, conveyed by the media, is deceiving.[93]

Optimists will point chiefly to the flood of environmental laws that were passed in the last thirty years in the United States, Germany, and many other countries. Environmental law, once an addendum to other legal fields such as commercial, water, or forestry law, has become its own legal discipline – from a legal point of view an important development. In part, we may be dealing merely with a new title above already existing branches of the law; still, over the course of time, at least the beginning of new and seminal principles have also come to the fore in environmental law: preventive protection instead of post facto compensation, prevention of the production of environmentally harmful substances instead of filtration after the fact, shifting the burden of proof in cases of environmental damage from the victim to the perpetrator, and so on. Impressive successes were achieved – at least in the leading industrialized states – especially with a series of "classic" environmental damages: water pollution and the "plague of smoke," at least with the visible smoke and the long-infamous sulphur dioxide.[94]

Unfortunately, that is not the whole story. The list of counterarguments by the pessimists is also long. Environmental policies have not been nearly as successful in dealing with new and vague risks, and that is not surprising. While DDT was outlawed, at least in the United States and the EU, according to the American organization National Coalition Against the Misuse of Pesticides, the United States in the 1990s was producing pesticides "at a rate thirteen thousand times faster than . . . when *Silent Spring* was published." The initiative continues to lie with industry, not with environmentalists, who see themselves in a hopeless race with the substances continually introduced into the market by the chemical industry, which have numbered into the millions over the course of the last few decades.[95]

From the very beginning to this day, it has been a truism that a good deal in environmental law exists more or less on paper only, and that sensible principles are not implemented in practice, indeed, *cannot* be implemented because of a lack of effective tools and mechanisms. Rivers became cleaner in the leading industrialized countries, but the pollution of groundwater with nitrites by a chemicalized agriculture and the pollution of the world's oceans continue apace, as does the emission of CO_2 into the atmosphere. In most of the world's large cities, sewage still flows into rivers and seas untreated. Eco-optimists tend not to talk much about the Third World. In Africa, which as late as 1960 was exporting more food than it was importing, environmental destruction and the overuse of resources have grown worse since the 1970s, that is, during the supposed "ecological age."[96]

In a perfectly understandable tactical move, environmental policy – much like environmental history – began by seeking out niches in the existing political landscape (from wastewater to species conservation) where it would not collide head-on with powerful, established interests. However, to get at the heart of the matter, it would also have to become part of the politics of energy, town planning, agriculture, transportation, and taxes. But as soon as it enters core areas of power, it usually encounters a granite wall of opposition – today sometimes even more so than in the first great phase of environmental awareness, for counterforces have long since organized themselves (whether openly or secretly), even though hardly anyone attacks environmental protection openly. A growing chorus of voices is declaring that the ecological era is already over.[97] Although climate change is still generating reams of paper, the torrent of words can make one forget that many politicians no longer consider it an urgent problem, and that many speeches about an "agenda" cover up a lack of willingness to take real action. Secretly, many regions, especially in the northern hemisphere, are counting on being among the "winners" of global warming. "Hot air" is the usual term for negotiated pseudo-reductions in emissions, as when Russia, for example, sells to the United States a right to emissions that it is not even generating.[98]

Ecological themes lend themselves to a lot of empty talk: public ecological discourse often serves merely the rhetorical posturing of those involved, as a result of which positions with the greatest rhetorical effect often trump others with a more practical orientation. A speaker will do better with grandiose words about how humanity must develop a new awareness and learn to think of itself as part of nature than with a concrete plan for even the most modest energy tax.

The sociologist Niklas Luhmann has pointed with biting sarcasm to what is often a complete disconnect between "ecological communication" and what is actually going on. He argues that pompous ecological proclamations aimed at action for a totality ignore the fact that modern society is differentiated into subsystems, each of which has its own code and logic of action and does not respond to a different language. From his perspective, the environmental movement seems like a big baby that is prattling pointlessly on its computer about "society" and bawling out commands that the former cannot understand. One should bear in mind, though, that Luhmann had the sociological environmental discourse of the early 1980s in mind: grandiose words that lacked a practical connection. His ridicule was aimed only at idealized, not real environmental politics, which has always known how to work the social subsystems; after all, historically it grew out of various specialized areas of politics and is still today largely made up of these various branches: nature protection, water protection, clean air, forestry policies, technological safety, and so on.[99]

Embittered radicals in the environmental movement are outraged at the growing number of environmentalists who enter into consensus-seeking talks with the established powers in politics and the economy. What is even more surprising, though, is how little use governments have made of this new opportunity to legitimize power. For in and of itself, the "environment" offers an ideal justification for tax increases of various kinds and for a comprehensive – even military – interventionism, whether domestically or around the world.[100] In point of fact, the state can be justified better ecologically than on the grounds of economics and social policy: what is at stake in ecology, as we understand it today, is the long-term needs of *all* humans, not merely the material interests of certain groups. Ecology brings out what a society has in common, not what separates it. Moreover, the *abilities* of state bureaucracies seem to accord far better with environmental protection, with its basic tendency to be controlling and retarding, than with policies on economics and technology, which require an entrepreneurial talent. As the history of forestry and hydraulic engineering shows, certain kinds of environmental policies have been highly attractive to systems of power for centuries.

As humans confront the new global environmental problems, one aspect that is often missing – compared to earlier problems – is a directly discernible political benefit. But there is more: the ecological era coincides with the breakdown of ideologies of state interventionism and a centralized, planned economy. The alliance between ecology and socialism once hoped for on the left, which certainly had its own logic in theory, was discredited by the ecological and economic disaster of the Eastern bloc. Nationalism, too, in some respects a suitable ally of nature protection, has fallen into serious disrepute in Germany and elsewhere, especially in the eyes of reformers, as a result of two world wars and Nazi crimes. When it comes to the possibilities of suitable political alliances, the environmental movement has, in some respects, arrived too late. At another time, when the vast majority of people even in the Western world did not own a car, when many municipalities would have happily closed most of their roads to automobile traffic, and when the slogan "public need before private greed" (*Gemeinnutz geht vor Eigennutz*) had not been worn out by overuse, the environmental movement would have had an easier time on critical issues: the alternatives it seeks would have been *more realistic.* The history of the German Greens shows that while it is easy to win votes with ecological slogans, it is much more difficult to be an ecological party in everyday politics. In fact, environmental protection is only one topic among many others with the Greens, and often not even the most important one.[101]

One of the most brilliant and fascinating environmental manifestos of the 1990s was *Earth in the Balance* (1992) by Al Gore, who was elected Bill Clinton's vice president that same year.[102] In this book, Gore lays out, in a compelling and suggestive way, a global environmental policy as American power politics in an explicit analogy to the Cold War, from which the United States emerged the winner. At the time one could believe that the alliance of passion for the environment and power at the highest level had become a reality. A few years later, however, the book was instead a striking example for the disconnect between ecological pathos and real politics even in the same person. Effective global environmental politics cannot be pursued in the style of the Cold War after all, for the greatest adversary in this case was Gore's own country – the "American way of life."

So far, it would appear that environmental protection satisfies the ambitions of states and industries only to a limited extent. To be sure, some ecological criteria, like those concerned with improving energy efficiency, go hand in hand with efforts to perfect economic and technological processes; moreover, the recycling of residual material fits into the traditional strategy of the chemical industry, to a certain point. Less attractive, however, is the decentralization of the energy economy and the reduction of pollutants. The biggest sacred cow of all is the biggest problem of all: the automobile. And this is the case even though the Adenauer

Foundation, which is friendly toward industry, has declared that all climate experts agree that the ecosystem earth would not be able to survive a motorization of the entire planet along the Western model.[103]

From a long-term perspective, the vital question concerns progress in the utilization of regenerative resources. It seems logically compelling to conclude that humanity must return at some point to solar energy – the only question is, when. In the final analysis, only this change in the energy economy would confirm that an ecological turnaround is in fact taking place. But what is the imperative for our time: Is it a massive entry into solar technology? Or is it too soon for that, and would such a premature step merely lead to horrendous miscalculations that would discredit solar energy? Will it turn out in the end that plants are, after all, the most effective and environmentally friendly solar collectors? Situating the present within historical time is not easy. During the 1980s, oil became unexpectedly cheap, and since the 1960s, natural gas has – again unexpectedly – emerged as a major factor in the energy economy. In the eyes of many energy experts today, history teaches us that fear of an acute "energy shortage" is wrong and that the earth's energy resources are regularly found to be larger than previously believed. Beginning with the First World War, people have repeatedly constructed future projects on the assumption that global oil resources would soon be exhausted: to this day none of them have had any success. Still, it is clear that the oil reserves are finite, but the time factor remains the biggest unknown in all calculations.

When it came to the implementation of previous energy technologies – steam, electricity, the combustion engine, and especially nuclear energy – political background conditions always played a key role: the great advances in energy were not brought about by market mechanisms alone. But how is the requisite political will generated? All of these older energy technologies possessed early on the fascination of power. It was readily apparent that they would bestow superiority in the global dynamics of power – both military and economic. The situation is very different with solar energy. Its promise of power comes, at best, in the form of solar collectors in space that send the energy of the sun down to earth in the form of laser beams; but these kinds of plans are even more spine-chilling than the futuristic projects of the nuclear industry. Sensible solutions are usually decentralized and consist of combinations with other regenerative energy sources. In all of this, however, the problem of a sustainable coalition of actors is more critical than ever, and that is probably the real reason why solar technology is making such slow headway. Klaus Traube has pointed out that in order to push through nuclear energy, one only had to persuade small elites, but with solar energy the enormous number of end users has to go along.[104] A successful environmental policy therefore requires new kinds of government.

The experiences of the past can hardly be used to argue that it is best for politics to leave the regulation of the relationship between humans and their environment to take its own course. We no longer live in the era of the subsistence economy and local microcosms, where the balance between humanity and environment virtually regulates itself, namely, at the level of single households and neighborhoods. And the always nice-sounding rhetorical flourish that what matters is not so much politics, but a new consciousness, must also be taken with a large grain of salt. An awareness of damage to the environment has often existed, but awareness alone can do little in the absence of effective authorities and instruments. Moreover, public concern has its short-lived ups and downs: it is often superseded at an astonishing pace by other themes and emotions. In this respect, too, the history of just the last few decades is highly instructive. Only institutions possess the long duration that matches the chronic character of many environmental problems. As a rule, however, public pressure is needed for institutions to take action that goes beyond their accustomed routine.

The more state interventionism has fallen into discredit in the prevailing economic doctrine, the louder the call for market-based measures in environmental policies has grown. And in fact there are cogent reasons for such an approach: industry insiders usually know far better than the state's supervisory authorities what energy-saving potential is still hidden in the production processes and how the generation of pollutants can be prevented during production. The imaginativeness of the economy often contrasts in history with politics' lack of imagination. For the most part, the most effective action comes from what the economy does out of its own interest and not in response to decrees and regulations.

The fact is that long before the ecological era, useful forms of amicable cooperation had already developed between industry and the public authorities on environmental questions, whether in Central Europe or in the Anglo-American world. However, experience also shows that in matters of environmental protection, economic forces will take action only when confronted by the threat of state mandates if they do not. Left to its devices, industry often would not even undertake the kind of smoke-reducing measures that improved the burning of fuel but were initially simply tedious. And the "environmental technology" of which Germany has by now become the world's leading exporter, all this filtration, wastewater treatment, and recycling technology, is frequently introduced only under pressure from the state. Incidentally, much of the environmental technology one can make money on is "end-of-the-pipe" technology, which merely shifts the pollutants and removes them from sight, while at the same time creating new problems. With many materials, recycling is even more harmful to the environment than disposal.[105]

Some kinds of market-based environmental policies tend to increase social inequalities. There is generally little discussion of winners and losers in the ecological discourse. Plans for environmental taxes casually override a century of efforts in social policy to shift the fiscal emphasis from the consumption tax to income and corporate taxes. Taken to its logical extreme, the trade with emission quotas hands most of the right of disposing over the atmosphere to the financially strongest companies: given the continuing concentration of capital in the world, this is a deeply demoralizing prospect.

After the collapse of socialism, environmentalism is left as the only ideological alternative to the absolute hegemony of the quest for private profit and consumption. It cannot be said that the environmental movement has so far used this opportunity in a very conscious or effective manner. If it maintains that it is not concerned with human happiness but with nature for its own sake, it remains aloof from all social policy debates and undercuts the argument that legitimizes environmental protection by invoking the social obligations of property. Often it also deprives itself of the ability to offer resistance by attaching itself to the rhetoric

of globalization, drawing from the notion that "emissions know no borders" the –
not exactly logical – conclusion that environmentalists must actively participate in
creating a world without borders. The environmental movement takes this position
even though it has long since become obvious that unfettered global competition
undermines every social as well as environmental policy. The preservation of the
beauty of the world and of human happiness is not conceivable under conditions
of unrestrained global competition, but only on the basis of an infinite diversity of
social and ecological niches, the individual environments that Jacob von Uexküll
was talking about, which every life form needs for its well-being.

In the end, the apparatus of the state remains the only – at least potential –
counterweight to the omnipotence of private capital interests. But the historian
must admit at the same time that states often enough do not perform this function
or do not do so intelligently. Experience has shown that ecological reason does
not thrive in the omnipotence of the state, but rather in the conflict between
state authority and public criticism. And yet: on questions that do not overlap
with entrepreneurial self-interest, environmental policies do not stand much of a
chance without binding legal norms and instruments for their implementation.
It is especially from a world historical perspective that one learns to appreciate
the Western tradition of placing everything on a legal footing. Not infrequently
that tradition has a high price, as for example the grueling expenditures of legal
quarrels; on the other hand, we know that when the negotiating of environmental
norms is left informally to the chief parties concerned, the result is insider dealings
that disregard the interests of third parties.

Within jurisprudence there is a tendency, in the wake of "deregulation," to
turn away from pursuing regulatory paths of environmental policy. The primary
argument is backed by historical experience: in the face of technology that is constantly changing, regulatory law finds itself in a hopeless "hare-and-tortoise-race" –
it always lags behind the environmental problems created by technological innovations and is often impossible to apply in practice. The past offers a wealth of
experiences with the pitfalls of the process of bureaucratization. Environmental
problems can have a fatal attraction for bureaucrats, for they create nearly inexhaustible material for a proliferating jungle of authorities and laws, which are seen
as pure harassment by those affected and bring everything having to do with "environment" into disrepute. Under these circumstances there is a tendency to avoid,
whenever possible, core areas of environmental protection where one encounters
powerful opposition, and instead to regulate third-rate issues with excessive petti-
ness, for example, whether farmers are allowed to mow their meadows in nature
preserves, or whether fruit trees are properly situated along the banks of brooks.[106]
When that happens, acts of defiance by those affected should not surprise us. Today,
nature protection, one source of ecological thinking and, thanks to the aesthetic
charms of nature, the pretty side of environmental policy, unfortunately plays a
big part around the world in making ecology unpopular and misconstruing the
symbiotic relationship between humans and nature.

Still, one must not take every lament about "bureaucratism" at face value, since
it is the standard complaint of those who do not *want* state regulation on principle. When it comes to safety regulations in nuclear technology, for example, the
reason they have become so complicated is not least because the nuclear industry

abandoned the philosophy of inherent safety and shifted instead entirely to external safety precautions. The precondition for such a move – in both the United States and Germany – was the assumption of risk by the state: this rendered inoperable the risk containment usually created within the economy by insurance costs. It is doubtful that the private sector would ever have built nuclear power plants if it had been required to shoulder all the costs of insuring against their enormous potential risk.

From the history of pandemics, the medical historian Alfons Labisch has drawn the conclusion that while society most certainly responds to threats to its health, it responds "not to all risks, but only to certain ones." Much the same applies to how society deals with environmental damage. As a rule, the more precisely laws are focused on specific goals that are at the center of public attention, the more effective they are; by contrast, one can render laws ineffective by packing too much into them. This may present the greatest problem of environmental protection over the long run. For the more environmental protection takes on institutional form, the stronger its tendency to fixate on certain risks that seemed primary until then, while newly arising risks, or those that attracted little attention previously, are neglected. Daniel Fiorino, an American expert on environmental protection, has called this the "trap" of environmental policy.[107]

One lesson from environmental history is especially striking: it is that precisely the large *solutions* to certain environmental problems always *create* new and very complex environmental problems. Let us recall the great dams, which were supposed to regulate the water levels of the rivers once and for all and secure a smokeless energy supply; the irrigation systems meant to prevent drought and wind erosion; chemical fertilizer, which was supposed to solve the ancient problem of declining soil fertility; chlorine chemistry, which would use the chlorine generated by electrolysis; nuclear power, which would overcome our dependence on fossil fuels; the reprocessing of spent fuel, which would close the cycle of nuclear power; biotechnology, which is supposed to replace chemical processes that are a burden on the environment, and so on. Ernest Callenbach's *Ökotopia* (1975) had an energy-saving magnetic train, but when it became reality, it ran into opposition from the environmental camp. The lesson of environmental history indicates that environmental politics must not only fight against the undesirable consequences of industrialization to date, but that it must also pay attention to potential unintended consequences of its own making.

This story of changing problems and horizons is presumably not over. As soon as ecological taxes make up a substantial part of a government's budget, an especially insidious problem arises: namely, that the state profits from transgressions against the environment, indeed, lives from them, much like early modern foresters lived off the fines of those who violated forest law. And if fuel is produced from energy plants, it can easily happen that the energy supply of the First World competes for soil with the food supply of the Third World: a truly dreadful scenario. Brazil's Proalcool program, launched in 1975 to produce fuel from sugarcane, gives us a foretaste that the path of regenerative resources is by no means fundamentally clean and benign. Some ecological successes can exacerbate social problems. The greatest obstacle to environmental politics of tomorrow could be the environmental institutions of yesterday. History can teach us how important it is to analyze the organizational side in all environmental policy projects. Such an analysis can reveal a lack of effective organization as well as an excess of bureaucratization. Environmental protection is rife with temptations for bureaucracies eager to expand, and it is therefore subject to the danger of bureaucratic ossification. Max Weber was prophetic in recognizing the danger that socialism would be suffocated by bureaucratization. Environmental protection by the state is also subject to this danger, and "learning from history" means addressing this danger early on.

The more institutional power the environmental movement attains, the more sharply internal tensions will invariably come to the surface. Professionalization and cooperation with industry and politics have already brought factionalism and alienation in their wake. By now, conservationists are fighting with promoters of wind power, lovers of "wilderness" with the traditional cultural landscapes, and champions of "virgin" nature with the managers of eco-tourism. "Nature" as a guiding model has multiple meanings and can never be completely attached to a single conception or a specific technology. A historical perspective reveals the mischief of an intolerant "nature" dogmatism and the need to continuously renegotiate concrete nature models between those involved and affected. If "green" politicians are sometimes less successful on environmental issues than politicians of the old school, the explanation is in part that the environmental movement often conceived of its visions of the future too much as imperatives of nature and not as political goals, which can only be attained by overcoming resistance and winning allies. Moreover, many ecological blueprints present their goals with an utterly inadequate time frame, and they hardly contain any thoughts about which priorities map onto the current situation.[108]

Because there is no prospect for effective global guidance of the relationship between humans and the environment, and because politics, with all its institutions, can cope with the complexity and changeability of environmental problems only to a very limited degree, it is likely that humanity, as always in history, will have to depend in the future in essential ways on nature's self-healing powers. For that reason we are usually on safest ground where we leave reserves for nature, instead of pushing an intensive use into the last and most remote corners of the world. The model of "sustainability" will become a dangerous mirage if it is used to legitimize ecologically the total utilization of the last reserves. The sustainability of traditional agriculture was also in part due to the "untapped reserves" that existed.[109] From that perspective, the opposition between those environmentalists who want a sustainable economy and those who want wilderness is not irreconcilable.

In essence, environmental protection today means providing for the future – but the future is uncertain, and therein lies the dilemma. A striving for sustainability that postulates the unending continuation of one's own world as one imagines it, and pursues that goal with rigid monomania, suffers from a dangerous delusion. We must be prepared for the unexpected. This, too, is one argument for a basic stance that is concerned and not excessively optimistic: optimism favors a linear prognosis and a false sense of security, and it easily makes one forget the negative experiences of the past. A "Quality Assurance" review of the World Bank in 1997 concluded "that institutional amnesia is the inevitable consequence of institutional optimism."[110] The many partial successes that environmental policy has achieved reinforce the illusion of security. In reality, even today, the history of the environment is not completely congruent with a history of environmental policy, that is, with a history deliberately and consciously created by humanity. Instead, at its core it remains a history of the unplanned and unexpected, of the always unstable symbiosis between humans and nature. This is the fundamental problem of an environmental protection that is firmly rooted in fixed institutions.[111] The "wandering gaze,"[112] whether of the historian or amateur ecologist, is presumably still best prepared for surprises. For while it may have a certain logic to believe in the "End of History" from an economic point of view – from an ecological perspective, such an end is nowhere in sight.

Epilogue: How to Argue with Environmental History in Politics

Revelation on Monte Verità. Some years ago I took part in an international conference on technological safety. The conference was held on Monte Verità at Lago Maggiore, the same "Mountain of Truth" on which a hundred years ago – in the words of Max Weber, who was vacationing there – "nature people" and "magical women" gathered: followers of natural healing doctrines, Eastern religions, anarchism, vegetarianism, nudism, and free love.[1] As on several previous occasions, I had been invited as a historian and critic of nuclear technology; not only because a critic should be present, but evidently also because it was thought that the stories historians can tell are well suited to create a friendly atmosphere.

Late one evening I set out on a walk with one of my "adversaries," a representative of the nuclear industry. I asked him to give me some idea of how the industrial circles in which he moved imagined that the environmental problems connected with energy production could be solved in the long run. For a while he said nothing. Then he stopped and answered in a bitter tone: "How can you think that an industry that does not even care about retirement provisions for its own employees will be concerned about the future of humankind?" The Mountain of Truth was living up to its name.

The question of what one can expect from industry on behalf of environmental protection is perhaps the most pressing issue today, for after the collapse of communism, economical liberalism is dominating the world. Many old hopes that were placed in the state and in imagined large communities have been dashed. Any thinking about environmental politics today must start from this realization. We now find frequent articles in the press about the accomplishments of industry in environmental protection, in recycling, and in the utilization of regenerative energy.[2] BP, British Petroleum, is now supposed to mean "Beyond Petrol." How much of this is merely public relations, and how much is genuinely important? The question therefore arises: Are there "lessons of history" about what private business can contribute to the solutions to environmental problems?

For many environmentalists, the answer seems to be clear and simple: the contribution has been far too little, since private business is motivated not by the protection of the environment, but by the desire to achieve the greatest possible profit. Many environmental historians around the world would answer likewise, because the first generation of environmental historians usually emerged out of a milieu that was critical of capitalism. For some historians who came to the subject from Marxism, the environment took the place of the proletariat as the object of exploitation. Yet even the response by the representative of industry in the darkness of Monte Verità provides startling confirmation of this skepticism.

But the matter is not that simple. Environmental history allows for no sweeping verdict about capitalism as such. From the perspective of the treatment of the environment, there are many and very different variants of capitalism, and this book offers numerous examples. "Capitalism" is not the same in fifteenth-century Venice as in the United States in the twenty-first century – neither for the economy nor for the environment.

Legally secured private property, combined with the right of inheritance, contained in and of itself a strong incentive for sustainable economic behavior to ensure that one's children and grandchildren would also be able to live a good life. Trade made it possible for each region to specialize in those sectors of the economy for which it was suited by nature. For example, the peasants of the Alps could shift entirely to pasturing and Mediterranean peasants entirely to viticulture, without the need any longer to engage in agriculture on fragile mountain slopes. The tradition of neighbor law made sure that anyone who interfered with a neighbor's enjoyment of his property had to expect tough opposition.

The drawing of the battle lines "ecology vs. economy," a popular viewpoint today, is absurd from a historical perspective, since in history economic interest was in many cases identical with interest in protecting the environment. And there are plenty of examples of this in the present. Today, as well, it is imperative to examine case by case whether state-sponsored environmental protection is truly necessary, or whether the self-interest of those affected is not sufficient to ensure some kind of protection for the environment. Unnecessary activism in environmental policy can accomplish the opposite of what is desired.

Up into the nineteenth century, it was usually the combined interests of the traditional water users that protected the rivers against drastic alterations. That changed in the wake of industrialization. Still, there was in principle always a broad consensus in the industrial age that something had to be done to combat the pollution of air and water. To be sure, environmental historians were the first to uncover the great conflicts that aroused public attention and in which industrial enterprises resisted the demands of environmental protection. But they often failed to recognize that away from these conflicts, on the local level – whether in Europe or the United States – and especially from the late nineteenth century on, when the slogan "sanitation" took on the same importance that "environment" would have a hundred years later, there was a good deal of inconspicuous and often successful cooperation between industry and the authorities on questions of environmental protection.[3]

This raises the question of whether we can draw any conclusions from this about the present, and if so, what they are. After all, a historian should be an expert not merely for the past that lives on in the present, but also for those processes of transformation leading up to the present that one can discern when surveying a longer period of time. And this perspective raises some concerns. The great companies of today are usually no longer family enterprises – the Buddenbrooks are part of history. Managers today usually think about their shareholders, not their grandchildren – at least when they are making business decisions. And especially during the last few decades, all the talk of "environment" and "sustainability" notwithstanding, the time horizon for actions taken in business and the economy has clearly shrunk.

Today, the global trend seems to be, more so than ever before, toward giving priority to maximizing profits over the short term – which does not rule out the possibility that some managers also ponder longer time perspectives. Scanning many corporate PR publications, one could get the impression that industry today is concerned largely with environmental protection. Nor do I want to rule out that many managers are thinking about it seriously. However, the crucial question is what will determine the action of large companies when push comes to shove.

This trend toward short-term profits coincides with other developments that are noticeable especially to the historian whose gaze encompasses larger periods of time. Traditionally, industrial enterprises were rooted in a particular place and were eager for that place to identify itself with it. A policy of good neighborliness was in accord with their own business rationality. Of course, one must not exaggerate the environmental protection that resulted from this. Many places were proud of their smoke-belching chimneys, because they were evidence of a flourishing industry. But that pride stopped when the chimneys emitted too much black smoke with soot particles and yellow sulphurous vapor. There is no doubt that industrialists often behaved with frightening ruthlessness toward the environment. Still, the policy of good neighborliness set certain boundaries and limits.

Such conditions have not entirely disappeared today, which is something the environmental historian, especially, should bear in mind. And yet there is no denying that the chief trend in the economy of the powerful nations around the world is heading in a different direction: in the direction of growing mobility. Companies are rooted in a particular place and integrated into a local society to an ever lessening degree. And there is another factor we must add: the chief problem is increasingly those industrial emissions that escape sensory detection, and whose harmful effects are no longer so readily discernible in the immediate neighborhood. The transition from visible to invisible damage to the environment is an anthropological threshold in environmental history. Logic and historical empiricism lead to the same conclusion: the more this trend continues, the less one can rely on industry to keep its emission within acceptable limits out of self-interest and in amicable cooperation with local authorities. Industry already put up much greater resistance to the reduction in car emissions from the middle of the twentieth century than it had done to the reduction of sulphurous vapors in the nineteenth century. A look at history, especially, leaves no doubt that there is a need for environmental policy today. The ignominious end of the totalitarian systems is no proof that the exact opposite is the right approach and that humanity can place all its confidence and trust in the free market.

Environmental protection as a bureaucratic dream? If one recognizes that environmental protection cannot do without the state, what lessons does history offer us in this regard? One lesson, most definitely, is that the environmentalist has no cause to embrace state interventions with unqualified enthusiasm. The traditional Prussian-German Hegelian ideology, that the state by its very nature embodies the common good and higher reason above all human selfishness, was wrecked by National Socialism. If Saint Augustine once taught that great empires were merely great gangs of criminals (*latrocinia*), simply successful ones that did not end up on the gallows, the historian can come up with many examples of this, from the past and the present.

Max Weber proved to be a prophet when he accused the socialists of his day of being blind to the fact that their socialism – regardless of what their personal dreams might be – would promote an unfettered bureaucratization that would, in the end, destroy human freedom. In fact, socialism has proved to have a disastrous attractiveness for bureaucracies, and wherever socialism triumphed, they distorted it beyond recognition from the visions of its founders. The environmentalist should learn not only from environmental history, but also from the history of socialism. For ecologism, too, has an attraction for bureaucracy. It is surprising how few bureaucracies around the world have so far seized on this opportunity.

Environmental concerns can be used to justify all kinds of interventions and taxes. For five thousand years, since the time of the pharaohs, water policy has been a foundation of political power; the same is true for forestry policy over the last five hundred years. But one should not make this, in the manner of the old Lewis Mumford (*The Myth of the Machine*), into a crime story from beginning to end, a story of the murderous "megamachine." On the contrary, and this precisely is the point: in history, a realm of good and a realm of evil can rarely be separated clearly one from the other. To some extent the Prussian bureaucracy did indeed embody Hegelian reason, not least in forest protection. There were often sensible reasons for state intervention. Today, those reasons exist more so than ever before – of that, there can be little doubt.

But that makes it all the more imperative that we remind ourselves of historical experience with the mechanisms of power. Time and again throughout history, it was precisely the state's protection of the forest that turned locals into enemies of the woodlands, especially when they felt – and rightly so – that the state was not really interested in the forest, but in expanding its power and its sources of revenue. Examples of that can be found in European history and today in parts of the Third World. The more environmentalism becomes a force, the more it is subject to the temptations of power. Drawing on the experiences of the past, the historian must ponder the problems ahead of time.

And those problems have long since become apparent on the horizon. It has been said that environmental protection in Germany has already changed "from a movement into a bureaucracy" (*von der Bewegung zur Verwaltung*). Not only in Germany: in the 1980s even the Mexican Party of the Institutionalized Revolution (PRI) – what a contradiction in terms! – created an environmental movement that was interwoven with the party and the state in an effort to preserve its own power.[4] As early as 1972, immediately after the beginning of the international ecological era, the Nigerian government – picking up on colonial traditions – outlawed traditional fire-clearance agriculture on pain of death.[5] In Europe, farmers who were sympathetic to nature protection as long as it was combined with protection of the local *Heimat*, turn into enemies of nature protection as soon as it is imposed from above with EU regulations in the name of ecology.[6] On a hike through a national park in the United States, the German biologist Gerhard Trommer met a farmer who was beside himself with rage over the fact that the national park rangers would not allow him to mow his meadows twice, as a result of which they were increasing the danger of a range fire: "The rangers are all liars!"

The environmental historian must be sensitive to such situations – in that way he would also be rendering a good service to environmental policy. In the history of the love for nature there is a tradition of love for humanity, but also one of contempt. Not in every situation are the nature protectors the "good guys" and their adversaries the "bad guys." That is especially true of parts of the Third World, where nature protection stands in the traditions of colonialism and, today, in tourism. Even if nature in many cases must be protected against certain human interventions, when all is said and done, nature protection springs from human needs: nobody who knows history can doubt this even for a moment. And under the conditions of democracy, nature and environmental protection has a chance in the long run only if it is popular.

Some environmentalists may secretly dream of an ecological dictatorship. But if that came to pass, the problems of the connection between nature protection and power would only multiply. The totalitarian systems of the twentieth century possessed a good deal of ecological knowledge, and yet the environmental balance sheet of these systems is disastrous. In this regard the lesson of history is unambiguous: effective environmental protection requires a spirited civil society, the courage of one's convictions, citizen initiatives, and a critical public. The Nazi dictatorship, which initiated, at least in part, a relatively effective environmental policy during its few peaceful years, only appears to contradict what I have said: for even under this dictatorship, there were – unlike in most communist dictatorships – free debates and citizen initiatives on questions of nature and environmental protection. In this area, the situation under the Nazi regime was not totalitarian, but polycratic; there was no ideological doctrine.[7]

In environmental policy, historical consciousness means accepting state interventions where they are necessary, while at the same time making sure that such interventions are done in the true interest of the environment and not chiefly to expand the power of the state and to boost tax revenues, that they are not seized by the bureaucratic dynamic of Parkinson's Law, do not assume an unnecessary scale, do not end up in excessive confrontations with those affected by them, and do not give birth to a monstrous tangle of regulations that end up becoming virtually unmanageable. Anyone familiar with forest history knows full well that the old question of whether the state or the private owner is the best protector of the forest has no final answer that applies to all situations. There is no truth here that is valid independent of place and time. One must always take a close look and analyze the specific circumstances.[8]

An adversarial environmental policy? What is better, to pursue a tough strategy based on state laws, or to seek informal consensus? Here, too, history offers no general lesson. Instead, historical experience instructs us to think in terms of long-term development. From that perspective, a harsh conflict and vigorous intervention by the state may be useful at certain times, but an informal consensus at others. On the whole, it is probably better for the environment if the consensual approach dominates and conflict remains rather the exception. The environmentalist would do well not to follow too closely in the footsteps of the political theorist Carl Schmitt, who saw politics only as a struggle and looked at the world through the categories of "friend" and "foe" – which is what happened in Germany during the time of the great nuclear controversy.

The costs of conflict are generally high. In the long run, environmental protection has a chance only if local practitioners actively participate. An old saying in forestry policy has it that you cannot post a policeman next to every tree: without a certain consensus, forest protection has little chance in the long term. Frank Uekötter, in his thorough study of the hundred years' war against air pollution in American and German cities, arrives at the conclusion that while the public protest movement against polluters had become necessary in the 1960s, since the traditional consensus approaches were no longer working adequately, the confrontation also destroyed a good deal of useful, cooperative tradition. His verdict: legal proceedings as such, where expert witnesses on both sides engage in endless battles, are usually "highly counterproductive"; however, the *fear* of legal proceedings that leads to a peaceful settlement has often proven to be very productive.[9]

The problem of power becomes much bigger still as soon as one moves onto the international level, and many environmental problems cross national boundaries. In those cases the application of bureaucratic coercion gets to be very difficult. Nobody who is intimately familiar with the history of supranational bureaucracies will place great hopes in them as far as environmental policies are concerned. It can be fatal to the environment if it becomes the instrument of existing national conflicts. Nor will the environment benefit if, at the UN level, it turns into a bargaining chip between the leading industrialized nations and the Third World, and when developing countries do not pursue environmental protection in their own interest, but as a quid pro quo for the very "development aid" that often ended up promoting the destruction of the environment in the first place.

"Government" without bureaucratic apparatus. A worldwide environmental government that is truly effective cannot assume the form of a gigantic global bureaucracy. Rather, one should imagine it more like a "government" in the sense of the institutional economy: as a group of the simplest possible rules whose rationale every intelligent person in the world can understand. Is the hope for this kind of "government" realistic? No one can say for sure. But it is not entirely absurd, even from the perspective of the skeptical historian. Let us look back at the history of nuclear weapons: in the 1950s and 1960s, many in Europe, for whom the reality of war was still fresh in memory, were expecting a nuclear war. Past experience seemed to show that a cold war always turns into a hot war and that it will be fought with the most modern weapons available. The atomic Armageddon has not come – not yet. To whom does humanity owe this fortunate circumstance? Simply to nuclear deterrence? It is strange that there has been no major debate among historians about this existential question for humanity. Evidently the shock of Hiroshima was deep and has had an effect. The environmental movement, too, is partly based on this traumatic experience. We can conclude from this that the chance for a global environmental government does exist, at least on issues that clearly touch on questions of human survival.

Traumatic experiences, however, do not last forever; with the coming of new generations they lose their potency. The historian is a specialist for collective memory, which is why one of his tasks is to make sure that Hiroshima and Chernobyl, Seveso and Bhopal are never forgotten. Yet warnings alone do little if they are not accompanied by practical perspectives. A global history of the environment would render the greatest service to the world if it made a contribution – however modest – to deriving that set of simple rules on which a global environmental government could be based, one that would be in accord with the experiences of humanity around the world.

Demands such as "protection of tropical jungles," foregoing the use of natural resources, and costly technologies for the reduction of emissions are suitable for provoking poor countries, but little else. By contrast, soil protection, the expansion of public transportation, birth control, and the promotion of local cycles would presumably represent far more acceptable goals – especially if they are not derived from an imaginary ecological imperative, but from the historical experiences of a given country. Even China, where birth control was denounced as reactionary Malthusianism in the Mao era, has made a radical turnaround in this regard since 1980 and has combined it with a reinterpretation of its own history.

The priority that population pressure has assumed among environmental problems is also not necessarily an eternal verity: there are some indications that the theory of the "demographic transition," the dramatic decline of birth rates in modern industrial society, applies not only to the Western world but also to large parts of the Third World. Population growth has been in decline worldwide since around 1970. However, global averages conceal the fact that the population not infrequently grows most strongly where the danger of an overuse of the environment is greatest. It is difficult to believe in an inherent reason of world history. The environmental historian, especially, should beware of historical pictures that – explicitly or implicitly – contain a teleological element. Whether today's environmental movement marks the height of wisdom in world history is not certain.

The complexity of many environmental analyses should never make us forget that on the most fundamental level, environmental protection is something very simply that springs from the basic needs of all humans: the need for clean air and good water. If these needs were consistently implemented in practice, many other environmental problems would be solved at the same time. Environmental history, as well as one's own sensory perception, shows us just how powerful these needs are. It is a great pleasure to breathe clean air if one has been breathing bad air for a long time, and to drink clean, fresh water after having to drink dirty water. All humans on earth share these experiences, and they are presumably the best basis for an environmental ethics on a global scale: a government without a state.

The affinity between history and modern ecology. Theoreticians would prefer to have a solution for the entire world and for all times. The historian knows that such a quest is pointless. Especially in environmental protection, solutions exist generally only for circumscribed areas and for specific historical situations. One must analyze a situation and its prehistory to gain some clues as to what options for action there are and how broad or how narrow the political arena needs to be. An inner connection exists between historical thinking and modern ecological thinking, although it seems that so far neither historians nor ecologists have appreciated this. Both disciplines see the world in a process of constant change. Both pay attention to space and time and focus not on a single aspect, but study the interplay of a multitude of aspects. Both deal with the unintended side effects and consequences of human actions. Those who have an aesthetic love for nature may be perturbed that modern ecology does not have a static picture of nature, only one of nature undergoing continual change: the historian does not find this unsettling – at least he shouldn't.

Supranational environmental policy has the best chance for success where, as a result of natural conditions, a certain common environmental problem exists, along with traditions of supranational cooperation. The Rhine is a good example in more recent times: even in periods of German-French enmity, when the Rhine became a national symbol for the Germans, there was a good deal of cooperation in solving common problems arising from the use of the Rhine. Might it be possible to apply this model also to the Mekong?[10] History shows that rivers often spawn forms of cooperation, especially since conflicts over water are very old but always need to be resolved somehow out of the sheer necessity of survival. However, the modern technological capacity to divert water over long distances could trigger conflicts for which history offers hardly any precedents. Sometimes the "lessons of history" are that history provides us with no models.

Environmental history: shifting environmental problems forward and back in time. The newest insights from the historical study of the environment over the last decades have moved – to put it in strongly simplified terms – in two seemingly contrary directions: one current is shifting the origins of humanity's problems with the environment back further and further into prehistory; the other, however, maintains that the modern, global dimensions of the environmental problem are, in their magnitude, of fairly recent date and hardly go back much beyond the 1950s and 1960s, indeed – *horribile dictu* – that they have achieved their highpoint only in what is supposedly the "ecological era."

Palynology and paleobotany have revealed that large-scale forest clearing did not begin in the high Middle Ages, but started already in prehistoric times as the result of fire-clearance agriculture and a pasturing economy. If human beings in prehistoric times shifted their domicile frequently, the modern globetrotter likes to explain this by saying that mobility is part of human nature. Traveling, however, was not much fun in prehistoric times: people usually changed location only out of necessity. That is why a good deal of evidence suggests that human beings, especially in prehistoric times, often overused their environment – whether through hunting or agriculture – and were then forced to leave their homeland; it was only unpleasant experiences that moved them closer to a sustainable way of life.

And even then, they generally did not attain perfect sustainability: ecological crises and subsequent learning processes – or destruction – seem to have occurred repeatedly in the history of the relationship between humans and nature. No doubt a temporary harmony, though hardly ever an absolute one, existed in this relationship. Still, one can impart a positive spin to this historical balance sheet: human experiences with environmental problems are very old, and corresponding learning processes have also been around for thousands of years. The goal of "sustainable development" was not invented by the Brundtland Commission: wherever humans settled down and could not plunder neighboring regions at will, they were forced to orient their behavior toward this goal. The reason why there was no counterpart to the Rio conference in the old days is that "sustainable development" used to be more or less self-evident. In the Old World, it was an integral element of the peasant economy and did not require a separate state sector labeled "environmental policy."

Historians intent on irritating environmentalists have always been fond of countering environmental alarmism by noting that none of these horrors were anything new: thousands of years ago people were already cutting trees, killing animals, and polluting the rivers, and fires were causing smoke already way back in antiquity. However, John R. McNeill, in his "Environmental History of the 20th-Century World," entitled *Something New under the Sun*, has rightly pointed out that this is only half the truth, indeed, perhaps less than half. For today it is impossible to overlook the fact that environmental change by human hand has assumed entirely new dimensions in the last fifty years. Let us be a little cautious: already *before* the middle of the twentieth century, many critical contemporaries believed they could discern much the same – one thinks of Ludwig Klages and his message *Mensch und Erde* in 1913 – and it cannot be ruled out that to those living a hundred years from now, even our own time will have become the "good old days," when there was still great biodiversity and much intact nature. And truth be told, we still have much to lose – we should never forget that in the face of all the pessimism about the environment. Be that as it may, from our perspective today, a profound – perhaps *the* most profound – turning point in global environmental history has taken place over the last fifty years.

What is new about the situation is not only the risks as such, but also the circumstance that cause and effect are increasingly difficult to localize, that polluters and the victims of pollution are increasingly separated, and that the connection between cause and effect is increasingly less obvious. When I gave a critical talk on nuclear technology years ago and saw a banner in the back with the words: "*Fällt der Bauer tot vom Traktor / brennt schon wieder ein Reaktor* (If the farmer falls dead off his tractor / We have another burning reactor), I could barely suppress my laughter, in spite of the seriousness of the topic. Because that is precisely the point: with a whole range of new technologies, the connection between cause and harmful effect is *not* that evident. Radioactive emissions do not register with the senses; except in the immediate environs of serious accidents, their effects do not become apparent right away. Experts can debate endlessly why people in certain regions die of cancer at a greater rate. Nobody can say with certainty how safe or unsafe nuclear technology is – for the simple reason, already, that here, as with all technology, humans are a major risk factor, and human errors cannot be exactly predicted. The methodologies of probability, as well, encounter their limitations when it comes to complex new technologies.[11]

The hypothetical dimension of the risk applies also to large areas of genetic engineering, chemistry, and pharmacology. It is likewise true of the most sinister and most global of all risks: the effect of emissions on our planet's climate. Both logic and historical experience show that human societies are most likely to respond to well-known risks when the connection between cause and effect is clear and both are within a regionally circumscribed framework. Under those circumstances, a society has a chance to establish habits and institutions to ward off the threat, and to create a consensus that guarantees that corresponding rules are actually observed in daily life. Everything is more difficult with the second, new type of risk.

Historical perception and political style. In discussions about the question of style in environmental policy, two positions typically clash. One side emphasizes that it has been more or less clear for a long time what needs to be done. The important thing is not to keep researching and discussing, but to take action and to fight. When Jens Scheer – a professor of physics at the University of Bremen who belonged to a Maoist group – gave a sober and factual lecture in the 1980s at a German university about the risks of nuclear technology, he raised his voice at the very end and asked: "And what do we conclude from this?" Whereupon he closed with the loud exhortation: "To battle, then!" It was an abrupt change of scene: from the formulas of physics to an impassioned battle cry.

Not so quick, the other side responds, it is not quite that easy. If one is honest, we don't know the precise nature of the risk, and we know even less about which is the optimal counterstrategy and what are the best instruments for achieving it. If you raise an alarm but no catastrophe occurs, you are publicly embarrassed. This creates the "cry wolf" effect, and soon nobody will be listening when the wolf is really coming. And even if the risk is real, we are still left with the question about the best strategies to counter it. If you put ineffective strategies and ineffective institutions in place preemptively, you will block future strategies that are more effective. If you draw up the battle lines too soon, you will wreck your chances of cooperation with industry, and without such cooperation there is no prospect for effective action. If demonstrators battle the police, you are not doing anything to promote harmony between humans and the environment. The old romanticism of the struggle is completely out of place in environmental policy. Moreover, with many environmental risks there is nothing concrete to demonstrate about, as for example when it comes to the pollution of the atmosphere through carbon dioxide: here you would have to demonstrate in front of your own chimney!

Does the historian have anything to contribute to this controversy? Up to a certain extent, these two positions can be assigned to certain pictures of environmental history. Anyone who believes that the environmental problems along with their causes and solutions are well known by now, has every reason to maintain that the important thing is not to engage in a lot of discussion, but to take action and to implement the right steps as vigorously as possible. By contrast, anyone who believes that there is much about today's environmental problems that is new, and that we understand only in part which risks pose a real danger and how one can counteract it, will take the second position.

This connection between historical perception and political style is not entirely inevitable, however. One can also imagine other kinds of historical argumentation. If one assumes that humanity has essentially been wrestling with the same environmental problems since time immemorial, problems that are in the final analysis based on humanity's short-sighted selfishness, one could arrive at the resigned conclusion that all environmental policy is really quite pointless, since it runs counter to human nature. But anyone who believes that the truly important problems are relatively recent could take the position that a good deal could be changed. In that case, reestablishing the harmony between humans and the environment would not be tantamount to a "return to the stone age."

However, neither of these versions of history is inherently credible. All simple pictures of environmental history are open to challenge. Accounts of environmental history that follow a known pattern a priori, and where one knows at the very beginning what will happen at the end, are not only boring, but also dubious from a scholarly point of view.[12] The simple pictures are mere ideal types in the Weberian sense; one must not confuse them with reality. Of course, environmental history needs such models, otherwise it would turn into an unthinking accumulation of facts. But it must not forget that these are *models*. At the same time, real historians will never forget that they are called to be discoverers of new realities. While they will never be content with theoretical constructions alone, they must not look down on them. Especially the environmental historian usually will not find in the sources what he is looking for; instead, he needs models to interpret these sources.

A historian must test these models not only by holding them up to empirical findings, but also by trying out alternative ones. *Both* versions of environmental history mentioned above contain a piece of historical reality. One must examine case by case which picture captures reality better – or whether neither of the two quite fits and a very different model is called for. The same holds for the alternative discussed at the outset: on the one hand, the environmental protection that is in the interest of the actors who are immediately involved, on the other hand, the environmental protection that requires state intervention. On the whole, over the course of the twentieth century the necessity for intervention by the state has increased; there is a reason why environmental protection in many countries of the world spawned opposition movements that demanded a new kind of politics. But one must always assess case by case to what extent this is true. Especially in agriculture, although it appears as the opponent of nature and environmental protection in many situations, we continue to find a good deal of convergence between economy and ecology around the globe; the only problem is that farmers often need to rediscover the ecological conditions of their work.

In many instances one cannot recognize at first glance what is well known about certain environmental problems, and what is novel and partly hypotheti-cal. The problem of salinization with irrigation has been known for a long time and reaches back to the beginnings of recorded history; the agriculture of the Sumerians already suffered from a build-up of salt in the soil. It is all the more curious that this problem was still found in the twentieth century as a result of irrigation even in such advanced countries as the United States and Australia. To what extent was salinization predictable in those countries, or so strongly influ-enced by special geographic circumstances that only practical experience brought clarification? Evidently this question still needs to be studied.[13] There is a good deal of evidence, though, that the basic problem is very ancient and very simple: the short-term benefits of irrigation seem so enormous that people ignore the long-term risks. A forward-looking policy would be possible in principle – there merely needs to be the *will* for it.

What is the situation with nuclear technology? For a long time it was the very embodiment of new technology with novel risks. But even with nuclear power plants, not everything was new, and one has to take a close look to distinguish the known from the hypothetical risks. The nuclear industry always sought to use, as much as possible, construction elements from conventional power plants when building nuclear ones. That is why nuclear reactors were also affected by the risks of conventional power plants. This was anything but comforting. Every expert knew that great explosions occur in power plants that concentrate enormous energy, that human error could have disastrous consequences in nuclear power plants, and that they would provide a prime target for hostile air attacks in case of war.

In some passages, the book on nuclear power plants by the nuclear power plant engineer Friedrich Münzinger, the standard work in Germany in the 1950s, reads like a tract from opponents of nuclear energy![14] For it was known that a nuclear power plant contained as much fissile material as many Hiroshima bombs, and Hiroshima was reality, not science fiction. Leading German experts on nuclear energy, led by Carl Friedrich von Weizsäcker, repeatedly advocated that in a densely settled country like the Federal Republic, nuclear power plants should be built underground. How this demand was quashed again and again has the makings of a crime story.[15]

In the case of nuclear power, there is another issue that applies also to other new technologies: even if a risk is merely hypothetical for lack of historical experiences, it must be taken seriously if the worst-case scenario would produce a national catastrophe. In the mathematics of insurance companies, risk is the product of the extent of the damage and the likelihood that it will happen. Even with an extremely high level of damage, the calculations can come up with a low risk if one regards the probability that such a circumstance will happen as very low. However, with complex new technologies, the probability calculations are not reliable.

The logical conclusion is that extreme harm from a failure must be taken seriously as such – even at the risk that the future might prove such concerns to have been exaggerated. This has been emphasized even by Wolf Häfele, who was long regarded as the "pope of the fast breeder" in Germany; and he has demanded that the discussion about the nuclear risk should play a "pathfinder role" in how we deal with hypothetical risks.[16] The German Bundestag's Commission of Inquiry on "Future Nuclear Energy Policy" (1979/80), in which Häfele participated, cautiously picked up this idea in its final report, even if it did not draw any immediate, concrete consequences from it. At the time this was seen as a "historical compromise" between proponents and opponents of nuclear power.

The discursive style of politics in the light of environmental history. The Social Democratic politician Reinhard Ueberhorst, who chaired that commission, has since analyzed the experiences made at that time at length and has sought to apply them also to other areas of technology and environmental policy. In contrast to the prevailing "positional" style of politics, where the important thing is to take a firm position from the beginning and to fight for it, he calls for a "discursive style of politics," for it alone is adequate to many problematic areas in environmental policy.[17] For all that, it is clear that politics is not a university seminar, but has to do with power, interests, and decisions. Still, the history of nuclear technology shows that many of those involved never analyzed very clearly or even understood what their own interest was, which is why the issue triggered such an enormous controversy, which at times seemed to push the Federal Republic to the brink of civil war.

Rudolf Schulten, the inventor of the German high-temperature (pebble bed) reactor, a now-all-but-forgotten alternative *within* nuclear technology, once pointed to this paradoxical fact: to understand anything about the history of nuclear energy, one had to realize first of all that everything that happened in this field happened against the will of everyone.[18] Hardly anyone originally wanted the light water reactor, which is today the dominant type everywhere: it was the interplay between economics and politics that eventually produced this reactor type. RWE, Germany's largest producer of electricity, was a leader among the nuclear skeptics in the 1960s; in the 1970s, however, it found itself in the position of defending nuclear energy with a vengeance against its opponents. In the heat of the atomic conflict of the 1970s, the prior history was forgotten, and many came to believe that this was a fundamental conflict between two very different types of people. This irony of history is a good argument for a discursive political style. In retrospect, many managers in the energy sector are glad that the opponents stopped the construction of nuclear power plants.

The irony of environmental history as a political issue. This irony of history is nothing new to the environmental historian. No small part of the present book deals with it. Anyone who studies the history of the interrelationship between humanity and nature needs a sense of irony so as not to turn into a cynic in the process. Since nature always contains an element of unpredictability, human interventions in nature also have unpredictable consequences, even when they are undertaken with the good intention of improving the relationship between humans and nature. For millennia, the classic example of this has been hydraulic engineering. But the same can be said for forest protection: when it functioned as an instrument of state power, it often turned the locals into enemies of the forest. The fight against forest fires reduced species diversity and increased the danger of large conflagrations that damaged the humus layer of the soil. The protection of some animal species came at the expense of others.

The original motivations of the proponents of nuclear technology bear in part a striking similarity to the later motivations of the environmental movement: the search for a nearly emission-free and – through reprocessing and breeders – virtually regenerative energy source, which also eliminated the disadvantage of those countries that had neither coal nor oil. Once again it becomes apparent that it is misleading to write environmental history like a "Lord of the Rings" saga as a great battle between Good and Evil. And it can also be misleading if one uses history again and again to call for a struggle against the dangers of yesterday. The goal of historical learning should not be a fixation on the past, but an awareness of the present, and environmental historians, especially, should pay attention to the most recent processes of change.

All this makes a good argument for a discursive political style. When it comes to environmental policy, one must constantly ponder these questions anew: What has been our experience with politics to date? To what extent did the predictions come true? Are there new and relevant aspects in the relationship between humans and nature to which we have hitherto paid too little attention, and have existing themes lost some of their importance? What does the present call for? The theologian Paul Tillich coined the notion of *kairos*, what one might call "right timing." In politics, much depends in crucial ways on the right moment: in a particular situation, something that has long seemed impossible suddenly becomes possible. One task of the historian might be to provide a little help in recognizing this kairos.

During a discussion, moderated by Reinhard Ueberhorst, about the German edition of this book, several environmental politicians voiced the critique that my kind of environmental history failed to give politics any impulses for action, showing instead that environmental policy was meaningless. Ulrich Troitzsch, a historian of technology and one of the founding fathers of German environmental history, defended me: at least my book opened up *small* prospects for doing something positive, whereas they themselves often acted as though they were unable to do anything at all.

The fact is, a historian will be modest when it comes to practical prospects. The role of the prophet in the wilderness does not suit him or her. Grand pronouncement such as "Humanity has been alienating itself from nature for millennia – repent and return to nature!" are to him so much eco-blather. Every historian knows, if he is honest, that most of history unfolds unplanned. Political action never takes place on a tabula rasa, but always within historical and natural contexts, and these often ensure that the result of action in the end looks very different from what was intended. The historian who watches a few dozen intellectuals at conference engaging in planning games of how "global change" can be directed as though they were God almighty must smile to himself, even if he sometimes plays along to be a good sport.[19]

If one talks about environmental policy, one needs to clarify first of all where there is room for political action. Is it possible to influence the way people live, their patterns of consumption, their reproductive behavior? History provides little cause for optimism in this regard. On the other hand, historical scholarship shows that inconspicuous measures can sometimes have enormous consequences. Hans-Ulrich Wehler has spoken, especially with respect to the history of nuclear technology, of the "dictatorship of small decisions."[20]

When the German Bundestag decreed in 1960 that the income from the gas tax had to be used for road construction, this created – since the revenue from this tax grew sharply – an automatic drive toward the increasing paving over of the landscape.[21] On this level of small decisions with large consequences politics can certainly have an impact. One merely has to identify these small decisions and have the imagination to picture the possible effects. Perhaps the historian can offer a little help in this process. The "dictatorship of small decisions" is a kind of dictatorship that a democratic public can tackle.

The distinction between facts and hypotheses. The first commandment of historical scholarship is to separate facts and hypotheses as well as experiences and prognoses, and to have a keen perception when doing so. While this may seem self-evident to the historian, this distinction is anything but trivial in modern discussions about technology and the environment, where these distinctions are, in fact, systematically blurred. This is equally true for enthusiastic supporters of technology and for ecological apocalypticists. There is often a dialectical relationship between the two camps, without them being aware of it: each side reinforces the other.

This was especially extreme in the 1970s and 1980s during the global controversy over genetic engineering.[22] There was little experience with either the dangers or accomplishments of this technology; both sides dramatized it with extreme hypotheses, with some of the horror visions of the critiques merely the flipside of the paradise visions of the proponents. In this situation the historian can make a substantial contribution to making sure that the discussion is conducted in a reasonable way. Yet the historian, too, must never forget that when it comes to new developments, one must talk not only about facts, but also about hypotheses. But one can only talk about the latter if one seeks to determine their real substance by referring back to real experiences. Here, too, history provides arguments for Ueberhorst's "discursive political style."

Eco-bubble and parallax: misleading "lessons of history." Introducing historical arguments into the discussions about technology and environment is legitimate for the simple reason that these discussions, even in the absence of historians, incorporate certain ideas about history, which are often dubious. Karl Winnacker, the head of Farbwerke Hoechst and the most influential industrialist in the early stages of German nuclear politics, explained in 1955, in his report to the Geneva Atomic Conference, "that civilized peoples are in a situation similar to the moment when the steam engine or the electric generator was invented."[23] This was the traditional picture of the history of energy: progress through an increase in power. With this picture in one's head, one cannot but see nuclear technology as the embodiment of progress. And it seems petty and shortsighted to ruminate about the relationship of costs to benefits. "Rational choice" is usually much more difficult in historical reality than in theory.

Some environmentally aware historians also tend to structure history in accordance with "energy systems."[24] By contrast, anyone who approaches the issue from the perspective of the controversy over nuclear energy has a spontaneous aversion to this picture of history. After all, one advance in the discussion over energy was precisely the awareness that we do not need "energy" as such, but warmth and propulsive power of various degrees of intensity, and that all of this need not necessarily be generated through electricity.

Of course, this insight is nothing new in history. There are good reasons why the career of the modern concept of energy does not begin until the nineteenth century: a need for it arose only with the transformation of heat into motion by means of the steam engine, indeed, fully so only with the broad application of electricity.[25] "Energy" suggests a unity that did not and could not exist in preindustrial times. The forest was, after all, not merely a source of energy, but even more so an area of pasturage. The most important source of energy was people.

Did humanity live in a "solar energy system" prior to the era of coal? But the solar age stretches from the Paleolithic to beyond the French Revolution. Evidently, it contained a wide range of options. If the term "system" is to have any kind of precise meaning, it makes no sense to speak of a "solar energy system" and to use this notion to structure history: solar energy was not a structure that determined history. Of course, it imposed limitations and made airplanes and rockets impossible; but even in the nineteenth century, humanity had by no means reached the limits in the use of solar energy.

One of the most striking early Germany eco-apocalypses was the book *Die Wüste droht* (The Threat of the Desert, 1947) by the journalist Anton Metternich. It was written during the Second World War and resembles those American apocalyptic visions that were created under the impact of the Dust Bowl of the 1930s. Here one already finds many motifs of the later environmental movement, and an admirable breadth of knowledge about the ecological downside of what was alleged to be progress. Modern, scientific environmental history has nonscientific precursors that are today forgotten. But what, in the end, was the point of the book? A hymn of praise to synthetic chemistry! Since the desert was advancing like an all-devouring monster and destroying the vegetation, Metternich argued, humanity was dependent more and more on the arts of chemistry. And that is why he devoted an entire chapter to synthetic liverwurst. Chemistry, too, had its own version of history, and it, too, could use environmental risks to present herself as the savior, similar to the way in which the coal industry claimed that it had saved humanity from a catastrophic wood famine.

Among the various sectors of politics and technology that are of central importance to environmental policy, *forestry* and *hydraulic engineering* possess a historical consciousness that reaches far back into the past. One key event in the historical consciousness of foresters is the supposed great crisis of wood scarcity in the eighteenth century, from which modern forestry, so the legend goes, saved first the Central Europeans and then large portions of the rest of humankind. The present book has repeatedly taken a critical look at this thesis.

The historical picture of hydraulic engineers extends back not only two hundred or three hundred years, but five millennia, all the way to ancient Egypt and the oldest cultures of Mesopotamia. That is the source of the confidence that hydraulic engineering is an essential foundation of human culture, which leads to the conclusion that there is no such thing as too much hydraulic engineering, since every expansion in this regard represents a progress of culture. At the same time, one can repeatedly detect a startling schizophrenia in the hydraulic literature: on the one hand, a blind fascination with gigantic water projects; on the other hand, and long before the ecological era, a pronounced environmental awareness, especially an awareness of the importance of the forest to the water cycle.

Reimar Gilsenbach, once a popular science writer in the German Democratic Republic, described, in his 1961 book *The Earth Is Thirsty*, six thousand years of world history as the story of the struggle for water. He glorified the Soviet irrigation projects at the Amu-Darja and the Syr-Darja, which led to the drying up of the Aral Sea, as exemplars of what humans had learned from thousands of years of hydraulic engineering: that irrigation had always been the foundation of flourishing cultures in Central Asia, and that the destruction of these systems was the reason why these cultures were being swallowed up by the desert. At the same time, though, the book is replete with ecological insights that anticipate much of what we find in the subsequent environmental movement. Later Gilsenbach himself became the central figure in a semi-illegal communication network about environmental problems in the GDR; because of his earlier book, he was given the nickname "water man."[26]

One learns little from environmental history if one presumes that people were all blind in the past and that we today possess the monopoly on ecological wisdom. Modern historical scholarship arose at the moment when historians ceased to look down on earlier times, and instead sought to *understand* their otherness. Environmental history, too, will only rise to the level of real scholarship if it makes an effort to understand, even if that is surely not its only goal.

Those Soviet hydraulic engineers who caused the drying out of the Aral Sea certainly appear to have had history in mind. Great irrigation systems had existed in that region already many centuries earlier, though not nearly as large as those planned under Khrushchev, and they had given birth to legendary cultures. The rivers in this flatland had been repeatedly redirected centuries earlier, and the

Aral Sea, too, has been larger at some times, and smaller at others. Unlike Lake Baikal, whose pollution outraged the Russian soul, the Aral Sea had never been a great attraction for tourists and romantics; it was hardly taken note of. It was predictable that the Aral Sea would shrink considerably, but was that so bad? Some, however, foresaw the dangers of disastrous, salt-containing sandstorms and recommended that Siberian rivers be redirected toward the Aral region. This would have been a classic case where the solution to one environmental problem entails other problems whose impact is more difficult to gauge.[27] Under those circumstances, the alternative of accepting the shrinking of the Aral Sea may have been the lesser evil.

And yet – there is a good deal of evidence that a lot of shortsightedness, irresponsibility, and dispersion of bureaucratic competency played a part in the processes within the Soviet administration. The UN report Geo-2000 comes to the conclusion: "A classic example of an environmental disaster caused by lack of action is the fate of the Aral Sea. Policy makers were well aware that continued and uncontrolled water abstraction for irrigation would lead to the death of the Aral Sea. They could, however, find no other way of meeting the economic imperatives of the time than through ignoring the problem."[28]

Far from being unique in environmental history, this tale has typical traits. To what extent environmental damage was caused also in other cases against participants' better knowledge and even though other alternatives existed is something the historian must examine on a case by case basis. He or she will often find that while alternatives had theoretically existed, they had no practical significance. People who deal with practical matters are usually not vacillating Hamlet-like figures: they prefer to picture a situation in such simple terms that one, and only one, way stands out.

This truncated perception, however, is not necessarily in the interest of society. This, too, is an argument for a discursive political style and for including historians in it. This does not mean that the historian has perfect "lessons of history" to offer. Time and again we have seen that the historian must look as closely as possible at the past in order to learn from it. Superficial historical analogies are misleading if the important fact, on closer inspection, is the existence of significant differences between past and present. If irrigation in Central Asia in the Middle Ages produced the fabulous gardens of Samarkand, described in glowing terms in old travel accounts, this does not mean that the new irrigation projects for cotton cultivation created an even greater paradise. The projects that were pursued under Khrushchev were, strictly speaking, very different from the irrigation systems of the Middle Ages.

Gary Paul Nabhan coined the term *parallax* for meaningless historical parallels. The most striking and terrifying example in his view was this argument: because "the" Indians, according to Paul Martin's hypothesis, drove the American megafauna to extinction ten thousand years ago, they pose a threat to nature and must be removed from the national parks.[29] The term *parallax* is indeed a useful coinage: argumentation on the basis of history is replete with examples of this kind. Unfortunately, historians sometimes participate in this game themselves.

While I was writing this conclusion, a friend returned from the Sahara, where she had ridden with the Bedouins through the desert on a camel for several weeks.

She was overwhelmed by the gentle way these nomads treated people, animals, and plants: this had been the most profound travel experience of her life. When Ibn Khaldun wrote around 1400 that it was in the nature of nomads to plunder and destroy, and that they were like wild animals, he was evidently describing a historical and not an inherent and permanent nature of these desert dwellers. Drawing a line straight from Genghis Khan to the nomads of today would be an example of a historical parallax.

Unfit for sustainability? It is quite remarkable to think of all the things history is supposed to prove. Again and again one can hear the opinion that history unfortunately makes it abundantly clear that the lovely goal of "sustainability" is hopeless, since in the evolutionary process of natural selection, *non*sustainable strategies generally came out on top.[30] The emergence of the United States as the world's superpower is often seen as striking proof. This thesis calls for a careful examination, however. So many historical controversies are carried on about unimportant themes: why is there no major controversy about this theme?

The triumph of sedentary agriculture over shifting agriculture was – although one often reads the opposite – the victory of relative, though not absolute, sustainability. The same is true, at least up to a certain degree, for the rise of Europe against the Asian and African civilizations.[31] Economic and ecological energy often went hand in hand in history, whether in Venice or Japan. And the cultural continuity in Egypt and China that stretched over thousands of years was – as this book has shown – also possible only on the basis of relatively sustainable forms of agriculture. John McNeill is surely correct in his observation that "human history since the dawn of agriculture is replete with unsustainable societies."[32] Yet a striving for sustainability was often present, even if it never had perfect success for all times, and it is probably here that we can find stories from which we can learn the most.

But here there is much to be rediscovered even by historians. Many German environmentalists still believe "sustainability" is a new Americanism and know nothing about the three-hundred-year-old tradition of "sustainability" in German forestry history.[33] And this goal is in fact older still in gardening and agriculture: except that in those areas it was so self-evident that people did not need a word or theory for it.

There are many today who believe that the "lessons of history" are largely negative, examples of what did not work and what went wrong; I am not convinced that is true. The kind of learning that consists merely in repeating monotonously, like an ancient Greek chorus, "How terrible everything was back then, today we must do everything very differently," is tiring in the long run, and I am not even sure that one learns much with this approach.

There is an inherent connection between the striving for power and the striving for sustainability: both contain a desire to immortalize one's own world. But it is this, precisely, that turns "sustainability" into a concept of power and infuses it with all the problems that come with the quest for power. To be sure, it is not an innocuous term; but in the history of forestry it is not a term devoid of content, unlike so many discussions in the wake of Rio. Originally, "sustainability" was not an ecological but an economic term – but in the connection between economy and ecology lies one source of strength. It is not a clearly circumscribed term: Wiebke

Peters came up with more than a dozen different definitions for sustainability in recent German forestry alone.[34] Yet it is a term that has made history. If more than a decade after Rio, "sustainability" is already the subject of jokes, a look at history could help to bring some substance back into the discussion.

The environmental movement in environmental history. The public expects to be enlightened about the environmental movement by the environmental historian. Are we dealing with a "movement" in the conventional sense, or rather with a network of communication – or better yet: a networking of networks, that is, a typical phenomenon of our age of new information and communication technologies? Is it truly international, or is it a conglomeration of national and regional initiatives that are sometimes very different in nature and have little to do with each other? And most of all: Has it been successful on the whole, and did a new era in environmental history begin around 1970? Is this movement itself already history, does it still exist today – or has it long since transformed itself "from a movement to a bureaucracy"? Let no one expect definitive answers to these questions. They offer a wealth of material for discussions by future generations of historians. Still, I will venture to make a small beginning.

Anyone who has previously known the environmental movement only from a distance and then takes a closer look with an innocent naiveté will be, first of all, irritated that in everyday practice it does not constitute the kind of large unified entity it presents itself as to the public. In actuality it is made up of a whole series of sectors that lead a more or less separate existence: air quality, water protection, forestry policy, technical safety, consumer protection, occupational medicine, and – last but not least – nature protection. Behind the scenes there is often tension between nature protectors and those who are active in other sectors. Environmentalists often think it ludicrous that nature protectors are more interested in ensuring an undisturbed incubation period for certain bird species than in saving humanity. For many nature protectors, environmentalists are cold technocrats who have no heart for nature, but are more interested in improving the thermal coefficient. Nature protectors often feel run over and taken advantage of by the environmental movement.

None of this comes as a surprise to the environmental historians. The environmental movement has a long prehistory – yet over long stretches that history consists precisely of the history of these individual sectors. What was new around 1970 was not the themes and motifs as such, but the way in which they were bundled and interlinked. Has this interlinking had a practical effect, and have all those involved benefited from it? Or should we learn from the past that the great environmental movement is merely appearance, and that behind the façade is in fact a conglomeration of heterogeneous spheres of activity, each with its own rationale? And is it necessary to specialize in one of these areas if one seeks to pursue effective environmental policy?

A conclusive answer to all these questions is not possible. Yet one is forced to admit that much points to an affirmative answer. Environmental policy surely has no great prospects for success if it intends to do everything all at once. There seems to be a good deal of truth in Niklas Luhmann's contention that in our modern, highly differentiated society, one can operate only through subsystems and must acquire their code in order to do so. Some ecologists who emphasize the totality of nature celebrated the road from Montreal 1987 to Rio 1991 as progress from *single issue* to *holistic approach*. But Montreal at least had a concrete result: a halt to the production of CFCs (chlorofluorcarbons) in the leading industrial states, while the same, unfortunately, cannot be said about Rio more than fifteen years later. It would be unrealistic to dismiss single issue initiatives in environmental policy, no matter if one knows that they are of limited value even if successful. This is another argument that one must think of environmental policy as a discursive policy without end, regardless of the fact that it must make decisions time and again.

In Germany, nature protection and the sectors of environmental protection had different traditions; much the same is true of the traditions of conservation and preservation in the United States. Still, it was the close connection between conservation and preservation that once made Theodore Roosevelt's efforts in both areas so effective in public and invested them with political power; and this connection was renewed by Rachel Carson. The success of *Silent Spring* was hardly conceivable without this link. In Europe, too, it would appear that the great alliance represented by the environmental movement more or less benefited all those involved, even if it did so in varying degrees. Environmental protection, which was concerned with the welfare of humanity, created pressure for political action; nature protection, by contrast, offered the chance of wonderful experiences that were capable of inspiring people.

A philosopher might juxtapose the "biocentric" interest in nature to "anthropocentric" self-interest; but the historian, who looks back deeper into the past, knows full well that the selfless love for nature was often inseparable from a utilitarian interest – as Rousseau, Goethe, and Emerson were well aware.[35] Nor will it come as a surprise to the historian that the Chipko movement in India and Chico Mendes in Brazil were guided by a utilitarian interest in nature. Individuals may act selflessly; larger movements never act entirely selflessly. It is perfectly normal, indeed "natural," that the love of nature is always combined with other motivations.[36] In Germany, as in other countries, nature protection developed in close alliance with *Heimatschutz*, the protection of traditional houses and villages. Many ecologists do not like this alliance, but it makes nature protection popular.

To be sure, environmental protection usually focuses on certain issues and not on the totality of nature. But even earlier it was often the perception of the whole that gave the individual goals their meaning. Ideas about the interconnectedness of forest, water, soil, climate, and health have existed for centuries, even if some of the earlier assumptions were, from a modern perspective, deficient. In southern Europe, the United States, and India, it was concern for a steady water level in rivers and streams that gave essential impulses to forestry policy. The nature cult of the eighteenth century was based on "physico-theology": the belief that all of nature was pervaded by divine wisdom, which meant that all elements of nature had a function. The individual actions of nature and environmental protection drew vigor from the fact that they saw themselves as parts of a larger task, that of reestablishing the harmony between humanity and nature. If the only thing at stake in an effort to rescue a small brook were the brook itself, the action would hold no interest for the larger public.

It would appear that today there is a danger in many regions that the environmental movement will fracture again into its component parts and lose a good deal of its energy in the process. The study of history can confirm that a concentration on individual issues is necessary for practical reasons, but it reminds us also of the larger contexts. This memory has a very practical value in certain situations. The more influential environmental protection becomes, the more different currents clash – bird protectors fight against wind farms. Since all camps have their own nature dogmatism, they do not know how to discuss the conflicts rationally. One German environmental politician groaned that nature protection was wasting most of its energy on infighting. This is a situation that the environmental historian could see as a challenge.

John Stuart Mill (1806–73), the theorist of classical liberalism, expressed the firm belief that the discomfort that every sensitive person felt about a world in which every scrap of land was cultivated and nothing was left to the spontaneity of nature, could in the end have a rational reason even from an economic point of view, for it was dangerous to live without reserves.[37] This comment reminds us that there is no inevitable contradiction between the ideal of wilderness and that of sustainability, and that nature protection and environmental protection are not necessarily separated by an ideological divide. In human history, sustainability was usually guaranteed by the existence of expansive spaces that were used only extensively. The generation of John Stuart Mill still remembered this well. Mill's words point out that nature protection and environmental protection stand within the tradition of intelligent and thoughtful classic economics to a far greater degree than many today would believe. Perhaps it is more important to understand our own traditions better than to learn from imagined Indians.

What matters in environmental policy in the end is not details, but the possibility of politics as such: the chance to enforce the long-term demands of the common good against shortsighted, selfish interests. When the environmental historian does intellectual history, he or she should examine not only the history of ideas about nature, but also the history of conceptions of the common good and of the legal and political protection of the community's concerns. Vilém Flusser, the pioneer of communication studies who came to São Paulo in 1940 as an immigrant and lived there thirty-two years, writes about the inhabitants of that city: "The Paulista has no 'political' (in the true sense of the word) feeling whatsoever. The public matter is for him not a matter for all, but a no man's land that must be appropriated: parks are despoiled, flowers and plants are dug up, lawns are destroyed, benches are stolen." For him this is proof that it is only with "great reservations" that one can consider this Brazilian city part of Western civilization, of the classic Western tradition of "politics" as the pursuit of a common interest.[38] Environmental politics is, in the final analysis, precisely about this tradition. It is not concerned with discrete and marginal issues, and the historian should remind us of that.

New awareness or better organization? Any discussion of environmental policy in Germany eventually reaches the point where one of the participants declares, in a weighty tone: "What we need most of all is not new laws, new measures, new research. *What we need most urgently is a new awareness.*" What is meant is an awareness that we are part of nature and should feel and act like such a part; that we have respect for nature, make our peace with it, and live in fraternal harmony with it. If a speaker concludes his remarks in this way he can always count on applause. But what are we to make of such words of wisdom?

Once again, one should not think that there is a simple and definitive answer. But the environmental historian does have a few stories to offer on this topic. First, it must be emphasized that the awareness that we are part of nature is nothing new. All different kinds of humans – whether Goethe, Darwin, or Hitler – lived in that awareness, and they drew quite distinct conclusions from it. And the realization that industrialization, in combination with population growth, threatens the natural foundations of humanity is anything but new – John Stuart Mill is the best evidence of that. The same is true of the feeling that something has to be done to guard against this threat. What was lacking in many instances was not so much the awareness itself, but rather the practical implementation of that awareness and the organization and coalition of actors this would have required. In many cases it was simply not clear what practical consequences flowed from the awareness: what the existing options for action were, where one should be looking for allies, and how these allies together could come up with a practical code. Lawyers were often unable to formulate environmental regulations in such a way that the technicians knew what to do with them.

Frank Uekötter, in his study of the fight against smoke in American and German cities, concludes: "In many cases, the fundamental awareness of the value of keeping the air clean was the least of the problems in the past. Nobody had to convince the housewives in Pittsburgh and Essen that smoke constituted a massive problem to cleanliness. Much more important was the question of how effective countermeasures should be organized and implemented – but on this point there was often times merely awkward silence."[39] Again and again, he was surprised by the willingness on the part of industry from early on to do something about the nuisances caused by smoke.

But perhaps that is not the whole story. "Good intentions" do not necessarily mean a determination to act. And when it came to matters of keeping the air clean, the latter was evidently often lacking. People did understand the problem, but they felt no acute pressure to act. On the issue of water purity, things changed in the nineteenth century as soon as people realized that polluted water posed the threat of typhus and cholera, and even members of the upper class faced a terrible death. A comparable situation involving air quality did not develop until the 1950s, when the link between air pollution and cancer was understood. Only then did air became an object of national politics.

When the pressure to act becomes enormous, a society that possesses an active energy is capable of solving the organizational problems of environmental protection. Today, however, the dilemma is that with many long-term environmental risks – chief among them climate change – there is no acute pressure. The fate of the Kyoto Protocol is the best illustration of this. A "New Age" awareness is evidently not enough; instead, one has to analyze in detail what chances for action exist under what conditions.

To make any headway in this regard, knowledge alone is not enough – a wealth of different experiences must come together. I myself, in working on this book, often enough felt the limits of my ability to process information, and time and again I had the feeling that buried in the mountain of facts were "lessons of history" that I myself could not recognize. The Internet has removed virtually all limitations to the possibilities of collecting information. I fully sympathize with Antoinette M. Mannion's confession that she undertook the revision of her book *Global Environmental Change* only "with fear and trepidation."[40] The longer and more intensively one immerses oneself in global environmental history, the more one realizes that the phenomena of our world are infinite: very different from those astronauts to whom our "blue planet" seemed very clear and self-contained.

The discussion about environmental history and environmental policy is a never-ending discussion. And it is not easy to convey complex messages in such a way that they are understood. "Are you still worried about our environment? Then you have not read the new book by Joachim Radkau": these were the opening lines to a radio show on the German edition of this book. I flinched: By God, that is not what I meant to say! To be sure, I believe that the historical study of the environment, in the face of the ecological apocalypses of the early years, can benefit from some critical revisionism. But if some alarms about impending catastrophes turned out to be unfounded, this does not mean by any stretch that ecological optimism is justified. A handful of newspaper articles do not amount to proof. Even if there is not a new Chernobyl every five years, a look back at environmental history offers reason enough to be concerned: reason enough, in any case, for the burden of proof to rest at least as much on the shoulders of the eco-optimists as it does on that of the eco-pessimists. And the question of the burden of proof is of immense importance in all environmental discussions: a majority of the controversies surrounding nuclear energy and genetic engineering hinges precisely on this question.

Earthly and heavenly love. Still, for all the justified skepticism about a New Age and about an exaggerated emphasis on the "awareness" factor, it would amount to intellectual narrow-mindedness for an environmental historian to disregard the emotional relationship to nature. History, especially, reveals that at the beginning of the modern ideal of reestablishing the harmony between humanity and nature we find strong emotions and revelatory experiences, which are hardly conveyed today by the "red lists" of threatened species that nature protection uses to legitimate itself. Modern neurophysiology has discovered what common sense has always known: thoughts and feelings are inseparably connected in the human brain. That gives cause for concern that conservation and environmental protection are destroying their emotional foundation through an excess of rationalization – an excess of scientification, bureaucratization, and professionalization.

Even if Lynn White's Christmas message in 1966 about the "historical roots of our ecological crisis" is outdated in many respects, his understanding of the Hippies, who otherwise hardly appear in the scholarly literature on modern environmentalism, deserves respect. Herbert Marcuse, the prophet of the 1968 movement, once complained that American teenagers had their first sexual experience no longer in nature, but in the back seat of a car. Anyone who knows the relationship between humanity and nature, the whole history, not only the philosophical history, should know how important the connection of nature and love is, and how important it is for the joy in nature to be constantly *experienced* anew.

All the talk about nature can mask an alienation from nature. Once I overheard a conversation between two witty German–Turkish women. One asked: "What do you think is typically German?" The other thought for a moment and then answered: "To make love for five minutes and talk about it for five months." To which the first replied: "I think the other way around is better." And both laughed. The love of nature is not so very different from sex. The environmental historian, too, should sometimes remember this. Donald Worster was right when he said that it was important "to get out of doors altogether, and to ramble into fields, woods, and the open air. It is time we bought a good set of walking shoes, and we cannot avoid getting some mud on them."[41] Through hiking, biking, and swimming, we refresh our emotional relationship to nature, become healthier, and even make surprising discoveries about environmental history. Environmental historians must never forget that much in the human relationship to the environment is not articulated, that one discovers it better on hikes than in books. Anyone who hikes through Greece will often be outraged at lovely landscapes spoiled by plastic garbage, but he will also be often delighted by the symbiosis of gardens and wild nature at Greek country houses. Neither the one nor the other is found in the literature on Greek environmental policies.

To be sure, environmental history presents itself to us largely as a discursive history. Still, we should not take words too seriously. The environmental historian must always attempt to read between the lines of his sources. What is often most important in environmental history is not the eloquent discourses, but what is little spoken of: the things of everyday life that are self-evident, especially what is "not quite clean" and burdened with taboos. And what applies to the human relationship to nature, applies also to politics. Anyone who looks at politics from the outside might be fascinated by the great speeches; in politics, however, the most important decisions are often made with few words. In his play *Soldaten*, the playwright Rolf Hochhuth has Winston Churchill say: "Politics is what one does not speak about." That is not exactly a pleasant realization, and it does not make it any easier to analyze politics. One difficulty in environmental history is likewise that much remains unspoken in the human relationship to nature. Talk about "nature" does not always have much to do with nature itself.

But is not the love of nature in fact a form of self-love, because nature is a construct of our mind? Since the 1990s, constructivism has been conquering environmental history. In Germany, the mammoth congress in Stuttgart in 1993, under the title "Natur im Kopf," was the first large offensive by constructivism.[42] The trend has been continuing ever since. Not only in Europe and the United States, but even in Russia and Australia, where the inherent power of nature is very palpable, we read papers today about the "social construction of nature."[43]

And now it is time for a mea culpa. One of the experiences that initiated me into environmental history around 1980 was the discovery that precious little can be found in the sources to support the notion of a catastrophic wood scarcity in the eighteenth century that is ubiquitous in the scholarly literature – that this catastrophe was evidently in large measure a construct. At the time I made a lot of enemies with that thesis and triggered a controversy that has continued for more than twenty years.[44] As time went by, some of my own supporters made me uncomfortable, since they tended toward the view that all deforestation was a construct, indeed, that the forest itself was a construct. Later, fascinated by the work of Michel Foucault, I turned to the history of nervousness: a classic case of medical history, in which real suffering blends with cultural construction, and where one discovers pathological substrata of the love for nature. "Thousands of tired, nerve-shaken, over-civilized people," wrote John Muir, "are beginning to find out that going to the mountains is going home."[45] ("Nature and neurosis" – is it possible that no one has yet discovered this topic?) But as one reads more and more works about the "social construction of illness" that hardly take an interest any more in the suffering of the sick, constructivism becomes suspect.

To be sure, one must not deny that contribution that Foucault's followers have made to environmental history. Constructivism and deconstructivism gave new impulses to source criticism and ended the deplorable habit of turning nature into a proclaimer of dogmas. Nature is not the "cruel queen of all wisdom," as Adolf Hitler described her in *Mein Kampf*, nor is it a harsh judge who punishes homosexuals and lesbians for their "unnatural" sexuality.[46] Nature commands nothing, and one cannot have a dialogue with it – unfortunately.

Where constructivism turns into an ideology, however, it often ceases to be a tool of research and becomes instead a convenient replacement for laborious field research; no longer an instrument for a keener analysis of reality, but a new subjectivism that denies reality. This constructivism cannot be taken seriously: "There is an armchair of coffeehouse smell about it," as Paul Shepard has aptly remarked.[47] Illness and health as a construct, life and death as a construct, gender and nature as a construct, only money is not a construct. Cut the salary of a constructivist and he will protest loudly – that, after all, is serious business! The terminally ill Foucault responded to a friend who wanted to turn AIDS into a construct that this disease really did exist: "This is no myth."[48] Nature the way it presents itself to our mind may well be a construct that is meaningless from the perspective of the universe, but it is not an *arbitrary* construct of our mind: *for us* it is a reality, an elementary condition of our life. This was already understood by Jacob von Uexküll, who coined the modern concept of "environment."[49]

Without a doubt, the nature we love and can fight for is a nature *for us*. But not for us alone, for we share this nature with many other people and life forms. It is not an eternal but a historical nature. Venice is the best historical paradigm for a culture that reached a clear awareness of its specific natural foundations. Nature as such would not have been impoverished if the lagoon had silted up, but Venice would have ceased to be Venice. But how the *Serenissima* preserved its lagoon was never clear once and for all, but a topic for endless discourse: in this regard, too, Venetian history is a paradigm for environmental policy. Desolate Torcello is a good place to meditate, not only for Hemingway, but also for an environmental historian!

When more and more clergymen participated in the demonstrations against nuclear power plants in West Germany in the 1970s, invoking the human responsibility for creation, I witnessed at a meeting of the energy industry how one manager remarked, to universal laughter, that if the clergymen continued what they were doing, he would hand the supplying of electricity over to the Protestant Church. Not only for businessmen, but for historians, too, it is easy to make fun of the eco-theologians. Although Christianity is not as hostile to nature as Lynn White made it out to be, the Bible is not a very useful handbook for environmental policy.

Nevertheless, it would be rash to ban religion from environmental history. There is no doubt: the connections between environmental history and the history of religion are far more complicated than White presented them, but they are presumably present, nonetheless. In fact, there are many indications that forms of natural religion – some of which do not even appear as religions – are on the rise as modernity unfolds. There is good reason for this development: never before was the need of human societies for a selfless love of nature greater than in the era of industrialization. Before that, an intelligent egotism of small groups was by and large enough to preserve the natural foundations of life, at least passably; most recently, that is less and less the case.

Perhaps we can learn once more from Max Weber. In his famous treatise *The Protestant Ethic and the Spirit of Capitalism* (1904/1905) he described how a new, dominant power of world history was arising through the combined interaction of economic and spiritual motivations. The two motivations are different in kind and origin, but they reinforced one another. One of the two motivations alone is not enough to make world history: what matters is the synergy of these heterogeneous motivations. In the process, the spiritual motivation exerts its effect not so much through its theological substance, but more through the quotidian way of life that it establishes. Paradoxically enough, the end result of this strict religiosity that merged with capitalism was the secularization of the world.

It is worthwhile to apply this model – which Weber considered an ideal type, not an exact reflection of empirical reality – to the environmental movement as well. It presents itself as an "ecological" movement, that is, as applied science; but anyone who is familiar with the history of scientific ecology knows that the "ecology movement" was much more than applied ecology. In spite of the frequently construed clash of "ecology vs. economics," one will find a good many convergences with economic trends, and at the same time also spiritual motivations, sometimes half hidden. Whoever approaches the subject from the ideas of Max Weber will take also this motivation seriously and not dismiss it as eco-blather.

Even if one believes that Weber's thesis about Protestantism is not adequately substantiated, many historical experiences suggest that powerful historical movements require both a solid foundation of material interests and a vision that transcends daily life, that inspires and arouses passionate emotions. The strongest impulses are often generated by a fusion of selfishness and selflessness. Anyone who recognizes this will not dismiss spiritual elements in the environmental movement as thoroughly unscientific and will understand why at the center of nature preserves there must be zones that are off limits to everyone: a religion needs sacred trees! However, it might be best if the zones from which humans are banished are not too big: in cathedrals, too, visitors can approach close enough to see the altar.

Does a quasi-religious movement need not only sacred spaces, but also dogmas, punishments, an apocalypse, Hell, and the Devil? Are there "lessons of history" in this regard? God forbid! Living religiosity has often clashed with an orthodoxy that is grounded in dogmas, for it is based more on love than on the fear of hell and the Devil. Real nature does not issue threatening orders, but leaves many options: a modern nature religion should also breathe the spirit of freedom that was often linked to the ideal of "nature" within history.

In the New Testament, the rise of Christianity into a world religion begins with the Pentecostal experience, when the Apostles began to speak in many tongues through divine inspiration. For Max Weber, the "conceptual moment" of western culture was the day in Antioch when Peter approved the community of the table between Jewish Christians and uncircumcised proselytes. This was the moment when Christianity moved beyond being a regional Jewish religion.[50] Has the environmental movement already had its Pentecost, its day of Antioch? It often thinks that it is an international movement, but in reality it is not. In fact, a certain degree of regional rootedness is part of its nature. A global environmental history that uses the global perspective to simultaneously sharpen our awareness for regional peculiarities might be able to play a small part in transforming environmentalism into a secular world religion. History shows that, contrary to the "parallax" that sees only the analogies between the past and the present, something new does appear from time to time. And a new kind of politics is what environmental protection urgently needs today.

Notes

PREFACE TO THE GERMAN EDITION

1. Anil Rawat, "Forests and Plant Sciences in Ancient India," in *History of Forestry in India*, ed. Ajay S. Rawat (New Delhi, 1991), p. 241 f.
2. Eric L. Jones, *The European Miracle* (Cambridge, 1981), viii.
3. Oliver Rackham, *The Illustrated History of the Countryside* (London, 1994), p. 6; Rackham, "The Countryside: History and Pseudohistory," *The Historian* 14 (1987): 13–17, also Chap. 3, note 132.
4. A strange contrast: while urban waste problems have been quite central to German environmental history, in the United States it was debated until recently whether cities were even part of environmental history! Donald Worster, the Nestor of American environmental history, takes a skeptical view of the goal of "sustainability"; see his essay "Auf schwankendem Boden: Zum Begriffswirrwarr um nachhaltige Entwicklung," in *Der Planet als Patient*, ed. Wolfgang Sachs (Berlin, 1994), pp. 95 ff. More recently, however, the situation within American environmental history has changed fundamentally; at times, one can even discern the pendulum swinging in the opposite direction. This is documented most impressively by the 700-page volume *The Great New Wilderness Debate*, ed. J. Baird Callicott and Michael P. Nelson (Athens, Ga., 1998). John R. McNeill remembers the "firestorm that followed when in 1995 William Cronon explained that there really isn't any wilderness in America": J. R. McNeill, "Observations on the Nature and Culture of Environmental History," *History and Theory, Theme Issue 42* (Dec. 2003): 5–43, quote on 34.
5. On his approach see Frank Uekötter, "Confronting the Pitfalls of Current Environmental History: An Argument for an Organisational Approach," *Environment and History* 4 (1998): 31–52.
6. Preliminary reflections on the book's concept: Joachim Radkau, "Wald- und Wasserzeiten, oder: Der Mensch als Makroparasit? Epochen und Handlungsimpulse einer humanen Umweltgeschichte," in *Mensch und Umwelt in der Geschichte*, ed. Jörg Calließ (Pfaffenweiler, 1989), pp. 139–74; Radkau, "Unausdiskutiertes in der Umweltgeschichte," in *Was ist Gesellschaftsgeschichte? (Festschrift für H.-U. Wehler)*, ed. Manfred Hettling et al. (Munich, 1991), pp. 44–57; Radkau, "Was ist Umweltgeschichte?" in *Umweltgeschichte*, ed. Werner Abelshauser (Göttingen, 1994) (Sonderheft von Geschichte und Gesellschaft), pp. 11–28; Radkau, "Beweist die Geschichte die Aussichtslosigkeit von Umweltpolitik?" in *Nachhaltige Entwicklung*, ed. Hans G. Kastenholz et al. (Berlin, 1996), pp. 23–44; Radkau, "Natur als Fata Morgana? Naturideale in der Technikgeschichte," in *Natur im Kopf*, ed. Kulturamt Stuttgart (Stuttgart, 1994), vol. II, pp. 281–310; Radkau, "Unbekannte Umwelt: Von der altklugen zur neugierigen Umweltgeschichte," *Praxis Geschichte* 11, no. 4 (1997): 4–10. I have discussed recent relevant literature in a review in *Geschichte in Wissenschaft und Unterricht* 48 (1997): 479–97; 50 (1999): 250–8, 356–84.

PREFACE TO THE ENGLISH EDITION

1. On this see Mark Stoll, "Rachel Carson's *Silent Spring* in Europe and America. A Comparative View of Its Reception and Impact," paper delivered at the Conference of the European Society for Environmental History (ESEH) in Prague, September 8, 2003: in Germany, Stoll points out, Rachel Carson's work was picked up chiefly by the bird protection movement. In most other European countries as well, the book had only a minor resonance, which was in no way comparable to its reception in the United States. One should bear in mind that DDT was not being used in Europe on nearly the scale it was in the United States.

2. As someone who has spent many years studying the controversy over nuclear technology, I was very surprised to discover that a collective work on the environmental history of St. Louis (Andrew Hurley, ed., *Common Fields* [St. Louis, 1997]) had not a single word on this topic: around 1960, St. Louis was the first focal point in the world for the criticism of nuclear technology, which at that time grew out of the protest against nuclear arms testing. The report by the Committee for Nuclear Information, *Nuclear War in St. Louis* (1959), is one of the most striking documents from the early period of the antinuclear movement: see Joachim Radkau, *Aufstieg und Krise der deutschen Atomwirtschaft* (Reinbek, 1983), p. 436.

3. Rainer Beck, *Ebersberg oder das Ende der Wildnis: Eine Landschaftsgeschichte* (Munich, 2003), p. 271.

4. An overview of the most important reviews can be found on my homepage: www.joachim-radkau.de.

I. THINKING ABOUT ENVIRONMENTAL HISTORY

1. On this point I would therefore place the emphasis differently than Donald Worster, who, in his essay "Doing Environmental History," sets environmental history in complete opposition to previous historiography: "In the old days, the discipline of history had an altogether easier task. Everyone knew that the only important subject was politics and the only important terrain was the nation-state." See his *The Ends of the Earth: Perspectives on Modern Environmental History* (Cambridge, 1988), p. 289. It was not quite like that, not even in Germany. In England great historians like Thomas Carlyle and G. M. Trevelyan were among the most enthusiastic supporters of conservation: see Merlin Waterson, *The National Trust: The First Hundred Years* (London, 1994), pp. 20, 31, 75 ff. Nature appeared especially at the beginning of historical accounts, much as it did at the beginning of love poems. But after that, historians often did not know what to do with nature.

2. See Joachim and Orlinde Radkau, "Geschichte als Magna Mater und ihre Ausstattung mit Attributen der Natur," in Joachim and Orlinde Radkau, *Praxis der Geschichtswissenschaft: Die Desorientiertheit des historischen Interesses* (Düsseldorf, 1972), pp. 149–57; Reinhart Koselleck, "Wozu noch Historie?" *Historische Zeitschrift* 212 (1971): 2.

3. Jürgen Mittelstrass, "Der idealistische Naturbegriff," in *Vom Wandel des neuzeitlichen Naturbegriffs*, ed. Heinz-Dieter Weber (Konstanz, 1989), p. 161. Immanuel Kant, *The Idea of a Universal History on a Cosmopolitan Plan*, trans. Thomas de Quincey (Hanover, N.H., 1927), p. 12.

4. Arnold Toynbee, *A Study of History*, abridged by D. C. Somvervell (Oxford, 1987), vol. I, p. 80; Othmar Anderle, *Das universalhistorische System Arnold J. Toynbee* (Frankfurt a. M., 1955), p. 196 f.

5. Fernand Braudel, *The Mediterranean and the Mediterranean World in the Age of Philip II*, trans. Sîan Reynolds (New York, 1972), vol. I, p. 17. Emmanuel Le Roy Ladurie, by contrast, described the periodic misery of overpopulation. Ladurie, however, dismissed the complaint that the distillers were driving up the price of wood and discharging foul water into the environment: "There was no standing in the way of progress" – progress from wine to liquor!" Emmanuel Le Roy Ladurie, *The Peasants of Languedoc*, trans. John Day (Urbana, Ill., 1974), p. 226.

6. Dorothee Ahrendt and Gertraud Aepfler, *Goethes Gärten in Weimar* (Leipzig, 1994), p. 56 f.
7. Jeffrey A. McNeely and Paul S. Sochaczewski, *Soul of the Tiger: Searching for Nature's Answers in Southeast Asia* (Honolulu, 1995), p. xv. John R. McNeill, *Something New under the Sun: An Environmental History of the 20th-Century World* (New York, 2000), pp. 279 ff. The Indonesia Transmigration Program, the "most ambitious settlement project of the world," which moved millions of poor Indonesians from the densely settled interior islands to the outer islands, left in its wake not only mass impoverishment, but also a large-scale ecological disaster: Bruce Rich, *Mortgaging the Earth: The World Bank, Environmental Impoverishment, and the Crisis of Development* (Boston, 1994), pp. 34–8.
8. Vandana Shiva in the introduction to John Vandermeer and Jvette Perfecto, *Breakfast of Biodiversity* (Oakland, Calif., 1995). Florence Shipek, "Kumeyaay Plant Husbandry: Fire, Water, and Erosion Management Systems," in *Before the Wilderness: Environmental Management by Native Californians*, ed. Thomas C. Blackburn and Kat Anderson (Menlo Park, Calif., 1993), p. 388.
9. William Beinart and Peter Coates, *Environment and History: The Taming of Nature in the USA and South Africa* (London, 1995), p. 10.
10. Wilhelm Heinrich Riehl, *Die Naturgeschichte des deutschen Volkes*, abbr. ed. G. Ipsen (Stuttgart, 1939), p. 76 (orig. 1853).
11. Especially important internationally have been Clifford Geertz, Garret Hardin, Marvin Harris, and Jared Diamond.
12. Ramachandra Guha, *The Unquiet Woods* (Delhi, 1989), p. xii.
13. Marcel Lachiver, "Eheliche Fruchtbarkeit und Geburtenbeschränkung in der Pariser Region," in *Biologie des Menschen in der Geschichte*, ed. Arthur E. Imhof (Stuttgart, 1978), p. 212.
14. Jared Diamond, "Ecological Collapses of Past Civilizations," *Proceedings of the American Philosophical Society* 138 (1994): 368.
15. Qu Geping and Li Jinchang, *Population and the Environment in China* (Boulder, Colo., 1994). Qu Geping was deputy chairman of the environmental protection office in the state council of the People's Republic of China; see Bernhard Glaeser, *Umweltpolitik in China* (Bochum, 1983), p. 15.
16. Robert Sallares, *The Ecology of the Ancient Greek World* (Ithaca, N.Y., 1991); Hesiod already advocated a 'K' strategy in his "Works and Days" (p. 376 f.): "Hope for an only son to nourish his father's house, for this is how wealth waxes in the halls": *Theogony and Work and Days*, trans. M. L. West (Oxford, 1988), p. 48. John R. McNeill, *The Mountains of the Mediterranean World: An Environmental History* (Cambridge, 1992), p. 356.
17. Rita Gudermann offers a vivid account of the drama of the drainage boom in nineteenth-century England, when pipes were mass produced, exempted from taxation, and subsidized with loans: *Morastwelt und Paradies* (Paderborn, 2000), pp. 393 ff.
18. Hubert Markl, "Die Dynamik des Lebens: Entfaltung und Begrenzung biologischer Populationen," in *Natur und Geschichte*, ed. H. Markl (Munich, 1983), p. 88. The question to what extent a deliberate adjustment of population size to the food supply can be found in traditional cultures is controversial among anthropologists to this day; on this see Steven Folmar, "Variation and Change in Fertility in West Central Nepal," *Human Ecology* 20 (1992): 226 f. The background to this debate is the fundamental problem of whether cultures can be explained in functionalist terms.
19. However, Esther Boserup was remarkably cautious in articulating the consequences of her theoretical approach: "Sustained demographic growth among primitive peoples does *not always* result in deterioration of the environment, because the *possibility* exists that the population, when it outgrows the carrying capacity of the land with the existing subsistence technology, *may* change to another subsistence system with a higher carrying capacity." Esther Boserup, "Environment, Population, and Technology in Primitive Societies," in *The Ends of the Earth*, ed. Donald Worster (Cambridge, 1988), p. 28. Her thinking also reveals the concern that population growth does not bring about such a change – or only in part or not always. Some of her students are more optimistic in this regard.

334   Notes to Pages 9–14

20. Joachim H. Schultze, "Das Wesen der Bodenerosion und ihre Problematik in Thüringen," in *Bodenerosion in Mitteleuropa*, ed. Gerold Richter (Darmstadt, 1976), p. 57.

21. John und Stamati Crook, "Explaining Tibetan Polyandry: Sociocultural, Demographic and Biological Perspectives," in *Himalayan Buddhist Villages*, ed. John Crook and Henry Osmaston (Bristol, 1994), pp. 765 ff. Noyan Dinckal and Shahrooz Mohajeri, eds., *Blickwechsel: Beiträge zur Geschichte der Wasserversorgung und Abwasserentsorgung in Berlin und Istanbul* (Berlin, 2001).

22. Alwin Seifert, "Die Versteppung Deutschlands," in *Die Versteppung Deutschlands, Sonderdruck aus der Zeitschrift "Deutsche Technik"* (1939), p. 7 f.; his explanation for this hydrophobia is that the climate in Central Europe was once wetter. In 1815 the preacher Friedrich Heusinger complained about the "single-minded zeal" to "rid oneself" of rainwater "as quickly as possible": Hans-Rudolf Bork et al., *Landschaftsentwicklung in Mitteleuropa* (Gotha, 1998), pp. 169, 263 f. On Pettenkofer: Jürgen Büschenfeld, "Vernetzung der Umweltmedien Boden und Wasser: Kaliindustrie und Umwelt in der Geschichte," in *Veränderung von Böden durch anthropogene Einflüsse* (Berlin, 1997), p. 167. Joel Simon, *Endangered Mexico: An Environment on the Edge* (San Francisco, 1997), pp. 60 ff. Ahistorical risk theories have so far failed to provide a convincing explanation why human beings respond to some risks far more vehemently than to others that pose a greater threat statistically. Virginia Stibbs Amandi, *Encounters with Ancient Beijing: Its Legacy in Trees, Stone, and Water* (Beijing, 2004), pp. 227, 253.

23. Friedrich Wilhelm Toussaint, *Die Bodenkultur und das Wasser, ein hydrotechnischer Leitfaden für Land- und Volkswirte* (Breslau, 1872), p. 133.

24. Joachim Radkau, *Technik in Deutschland* (Frankfurt a. M., 1989), pp. 21 ff.; Radkau, "Kontinuität und Wandel nach 1945 in West- und Ostdeutschland," in *Deutsches Museum Bonn: Forschung und Technik in Deutschland nach 1945*, ed. Peter Frieß and Peter Steiner (Munich, 1995), p. 57 f. Eduard Pfeiffer, *Technik der Stadt* (Stuttgart, 1937), p. 127: "Each individual organic decomposition area (*Faulraum*) displays unique features, one is almost tempted to say, it shows a will and mood of its own."

25. Clarence J. Glacken, *Traces on the Rhodian Shore: Nature and Culture in Western Thought from Ancient Times to the End of the 18th Century* (Berkeley, Calif., 1967), pp. 132 ff. Seneca, *Seneca's Letters to Lucilius*, trans. E. Phillips Barker (Oxford, 1932), letter 90.

26. Justus v. Liebig, *Die Chemie in ihrer Anwendung auf Agricultur und Physiologie*, 9th ed. (Braunschweig, 1876), vol. II, pp. 73, 86; Liebig, *Chemische Briefe* (Leipzig, 1865), p. 470.

27. Richard A. Wines, *Fertilizer in America* (Philadelphia, 1985), p. 72.

28. Wilhelm Henneberg, "Die agriculturchemischen Streitfragen der Gegenwart in ihren wesentlichsten Momenten," *Journal für Landwirtschaft* 6 (1858): 249, 254. J. Conrad, in *Liebig's Lehre von der Bodenerschöpfung und ihre geschichtliche, statistische und nationalökonomische Begründung* (Jena, 1864), p. 126 f., emphasizes that people had already been mindful of the utilization of human excreta in antiquity. However, in the European past the topic seems to have been controversial and sometimes taboo; see Donald Woodward, "'Gooding the Earth': Manuring Practices in Britain 1500–1800," in *The History of Soils and Field Systems*, ed. S. Foster and T. C. Smout (Aberdeen, 1994), pp. 100–10. In his *Oekonom. technolog. Encyklopädie*, Krünitz included a detailed discussion of the "Use and Usefulness of Human Excreta as Fertilizer" (see Günter Bayerl and Ulrich Troitzsch, eds., *Quellentexte zur Geschichte der Umwelt von der Antike bis Heute* [Göttingen, 1998], pp. 210 ff.): at that time (1789), too, it was a controversial topic, and Krünitz complained that human excreta was often being thrown into the rivers.

29. Wilhelm Roscher, *Nationalökonomik des Ackerbaues*, 13th ed. (Stuttgart, 1903), p. 102; Heinrich von Treitschke, *Treitschke's History of Germany in the Nineteenth Century*, trans. Eden and Cedar Paul (New York, 1968), vol. VI, pp. 104–5.

30. Wilhelm Abel, *Agricultural Fluctuations in Europe: From the Thirteenth to the Twentieth Centuries*, trans. Olive Ordish (London, 1980), e.g., pp. 263 ff.

31. David Pimentel et al., in *Bodenlos: Zum nachhaltigen Umgang mit Böden* (Munich, 1997 [= *Politische Ökologie*, Sonderheft 10]), p. 10.

32. Jean Vogt, "Aspects of Historical Soil Erosion in Western Europe," in *The Silent Countdown: Essays in European Environmental History*, ed. Peter Brimblecombe and Christian Pfister (Berlin, 1990), p. 86 and elsewhere; Vogt draws on decades of research on erosion history, especially in eastern France. Bork, *Landschaftsentwicklung* (note 14), pp. 31 ff. Jacks (1939), quoted in Monique Mainguet, *Desertification* (Berlin, 1991), p. 7.

33. Lynn White, Jr., "The Historical Roots of Our Ecological Crisis," *Science* 155 (1967): 1203–7.

34. Heinz Ellenberg, *Vegetation Mitteleuropas mit den Alpen*, 5th ed. (Stuttgart, 1996), p. 150, finds indications as early as the warm interglacial period 200,000 years ago that fires set by humans, together with grazing patterns of elephants and other large animals, changed the vegetation on a large scale. Karl W. Butzer, *Archaeology as Human Ecology: Method and Theory for a Contextual Approach* (Cambridge, 1982), p. 155; McNeill, *Mountains* (note 10), p. 353.

35. Franz M. Wuketits, *Evolution, Erkenntnis, Ethik: Folgerungen aus der modernen Biologie* (Darmstadt, 1984), pp. 67, 74.

36. Dieter Brosius et al., *Die Lüneburger Heide* (Hannover, 1984), p. 8; Arie J. Kalis, "Zur Umwelt des frühneolithischen Menschen: Ein Beitrag der Pollenanalyse," in *Der prähistorische Mensch und seine Umwelt*, ed. Hansjörg Küster (Stuttgart, 1988), pp. 128 f., 136.

37. Max Weber, *Jugendbriefe*, ed. Marianne Weber (Tübingen, 1936), p. 160 (June 16, 1885).

38. Ruth and Dieter Groh, "Von den schrecklichen zu den erhabenen Bergen: Zur Entstehung ästhetischer Naturerfahrung," in *Vom Wandel des neuzeitlichen Naturbegriffs*, ed. Heinz-Dieter Weber (Konstanz, 1989), p. 58; Heinrich Schipperges, *Der Garten der Gesundheit: Medizin im Mittelalter* (Munich, 1990), p. 16; Stephen R. Kellert and Edward O. Wilson, eds., *The Biophilia Hypothesis* (Washington, D.C., 1993); Ernst Schubert, *Alltag im Mittelalter: Natürliches Lebensumfeld und menschliches Miteinander* (Darmstadt, 2002), p. 135.

39. Glacken, *Traces* (note 16), p. 49 f.; Seneca, *Letters* (note 25), letter 89; Wolfgang Bauer, *China and the Search for Happiness: Recurring Themes in Four Thousand Years of Chinese Cultural History*, trans. Michael Shaw (New York, 1976), p. 39; Kenneth Ch'en, *Buddhism in China* (Princeton, N.J., 1964), p. 23 f. Klaus M. Meyer-Abich, *Aufstand für die Natur* (Munich, 1990), p. 89: "In fact we only experience the nature of the external world when we experience it as one with our own, inner nature.... This is the program of an alternative science."

40. Ernst Robert Curtius, *European Literature and the Latin Middle Ages*, trans. Willard R. Trask (Princeton, N.J., 1953), pp. 117–22 (Alan of Lille), 123; Schubert, *Alltag im Mittelalter* (note 38), p. 130; Hans-Liudger Dienel, "Homo Faber – der technische Zugang zur Natur," in *Technik und Kultur* (Düsseldorf, 1994), vol. VI, p. 48.

41. Joachim Radkau, "Warum wurde die Gefährdung der Natur durch den Menschen nicht rechtzeitig erkannt?" in *Ökologische Probleme im kulturellen Wandel*, ed. Hermann Lübbe and Elisabeth Ströker (Paderborn, 1986), pp. 47 ff.

42. Norbert Elias, "Über die Natur," *Merkur* 40 (1986): 471.

43. Robert Spaemann, *Rousseau – Bürger ohne Vaterland* (Munich, 1980), p. 57: "The unambiguousness of the concept of nature is guaranteed by the unambiguousness of its opposite."

44. Friedrich Albert Lange, *Geschichte des Materialismus*, Book 1 (Leipzig, 1873), p. 218.

45. Friedrich Tenbruck, *Das Werk Max Webers* (Tübingen, 1999), p. 53.

46. Rolf Peter Sieferle, "Aufgaben einer künftigen Umweltgeschichte," in *Umweltgeschichte heute*, ed. Christian Simon (Mannheim, 1993) (*Environmental History Newsletter*, Special Issue no. 1), p. 33.

47. The thesis comes from Michael Harner, "The Ecological Basis of Aztec Sacrifice," *American Ethnologist* 4 (1977): 117–35; spelled out at great length in Marvin Harris, *Cannibals and Kings: The Origins of Cultures* (New York, 1977), chap. 9: The Cannibal Kingdom. According to Aztec reports, the wars in the fifteenth century were conducted as "flower wars" in agreement with the enemy, so that both sides might get enough captives for the human sacrifice that was necessary to appease the gods after a great famine. See Hanns J. Prem and Ursula Dyckerhoff, *Das alte Mexiko* (Munich, 1986), p. 234 f. A similar thesis had been discussed earlier for New Guinea: Mark D. Dornstreich and George E. B. Morren, "Does

New Guinea Cannibalism Have Nutritional Value?" *Human Ecology* 2 (1974): 1–13. As far as the Aztecs are concerned, most scholars now reject this thesis: Lane Simonian, *Defending the Land of the Jaguar: A History of Conservation in Mexico* (Austin, Tex., 1995), p. 27.

48. Madhav Gadgil and Ramachandra Guha, *This Fissured Land: An Ecological History of India* (Oxford, 1992), pp. 93–110. Marvin Harris, *Cannibals* (note 47), p. 50, even toys with the ecological justification of warfare, which "tends to prevent population from growing to the point where it permanently depletes the environment."

49. Werner Franke et al., *Wald im Emsland* (Sögel, 1981).

50. Joachim Radkau and Ingrid Schäfer, *Holz: Ein Naturstoff in der Technikgeschichte* (Reinbek, 1987), p. 262 f.; Ian Tyrrell, *True Gardens of the Gods: Californian-Australian Environmental Reform, 1860–1930* (Berkeley, Calif., 1999), pp. 56 ff. and elsewhere; Beinart and Coates, *Environment and History* (note 9), p. 41; Valentin Thurn, "Die Wüste greift nach Europa. Die Zerstörung der Mittelmeerwälder," in *WüstenErde*, ed. Valentin Thurn and Peter E. Stüben (Gießen, 1991), p. 126 f.

51. Richard Pott and Joachim Hüppe, *Die Hudelandschaften Nordwestdeutschlands* (Münster, 1991), pp. 119–70, on the "Borken paradise" and the "Verden paradise" and why they deserve to be preserved, even though elsewhere (p. 23) they speak of the "disastrous effects" of grazing on the forest vegetation. Helmut Jäger, *Einführung in die Umweltgeschichte* (Darmstadt, 1994), p. 223; *Meyers Naturführer Harz* (Mannheim, 1992), p. 16; Josef H. Reichholf, *Comeback der Biber: Ökologische Überraschungen* (Munich, 1993), p. 20.

52. Ludwig Hempel, "Jungquartäre Klimaveränderungen im ostmediterranen Raum: Auswirkungen auf Reliefgestaltung und Pflanzendecke," in *Probleme der Umweltforschung in historischer Sicht* (Munich, 1993), p. 180.

53. Harris, *Cannibals and Kings* (note 47), p. 21; Fernand Braudel, *The Identity of France*, trans. Sîan Reynolds (New York, 1990), vol. II, p. 276; Jäger, *Einführung in die Umweltgeschichte* (note 51), p. 20. Helen Mayer Harrison and Newton Harrison, *Grüne Landschaften, Vision: Die Welt als Garten* (Frankfurt a. M., 1999), p. 68: "Thus the meadow is teacher, exemplar, and prophetess." Bernd Gerken and Martin Görner, eds., *Europäische Landschaftsentwicklung mit großen Weidetieren: Geschichte, Modelle und Perspektiven* (The Development of European Landscapes with Large Herbivores: History, Models and Perspectives) (Höxter and Jena, 1999).

54. Werner Bätzing, *Die Alpen: Naturbearbeitung und Umweltzerstörung* (Frankfurt a. M., 1984), p. 1.

55. J. V. Thirgood, *Cyprus: A Chronicle of Its Forests, Land and People* (Vancouver, 1987), p. 29; p. 346 has a review of the controversial literature on goat pasturing in Cyprus. Ralph-Raymond Braun, *Nordzypern* (Erlangen, 1996), p. 52. In general: Radkau and Schäfer, *Holz* (note 50), p. 63.

56. Colin Maher, "The Goat: Friend or Foe?" *East African Agricultural Journal* (Oct. 1945): 115. Marcus H. French, *Oberservations on the Goat* (Rome, 1970), p. 32 f.; David Mackenzie, *Goat Husbandry* (London, 1990), pp. 28, 66, 78; R. W. Dennell, "Archaeology and the Study of Desertification," in *Desertification and Development*, ed. Brian Spooner and H. S. Mann (London, 1982), p. 53; Bruce D. Smith, *The Emergence of Agriculture* (New York, 1995), pp. 57 ff.

57. Radkau, *Technik* (note 24), p. 83, Jäger, *Einführung in die Umweltgeschichte* (note 51), p. 126; Wilhelm Hamm, ed., *Das Ganze der Landwirtschaft in Bildern* (Leipzig, 1872), p. 266.

58. Alfred Runte, *National Parks: The American Experience*, 3rd ed. (Lincoln, Neb., 1997), p. 60. Gifford Pinchot, *Breaking New Ground* (Washington, D.C., 1998 [orig. 1947]), p. 181: at that time the sheep had been "ten times worse than the cattle." Pinchot even holds them primarily responsible for the dust storms of the 1930s. With appropriate controls, however, the damage that sheep pasture caused to the vegetation could be minimized.

59. Georg Sperber, "Der Umgang mit dem Wald – eine ethische Disziplin," in *Ökologische Waldwirtschaft*, ed. Hermann Graf Hatzfeld (Heidelberg, 1996), p. 51; Hartmut Boockmann, "Erfahrene Umwelt – Deutschland in einem Reisebericht aus dem 15. Jh.," in *Von der Angst*

zur Ausbeutung – Umwelterfahrung zwischen Mittelalter und Neuzeit, ed. Ernst Schubert and Bernd Herrmann (Frankfurt a. M., 1994), p. 110; Brosius et al., *Die Lüneburger Heide* (Anm. 25), p. 17; Walter Kremser, *Niedersächsische Forstgeschichte* (Rotenburg, 1990), p. 346; Dieter Haßler et al., eds., *Wässerwiesen* (Karlsruhe, 1995), pp. 32, 122; Robert Delort, *Der Elefant, die Biene und der heilige Wolf: Die wahre Geschichte der Tiere* (Munich, 1987), p. 265; S. N. Adams, "Sheep and Cattle Grazing in Forests: A Review," *Journal of Applied Ecology* 12 (1975): 147. Clifford Geertz, *Agricultural Involution: The Process of Ecological Change in Indonesia* (Berkeley, Calif., 1963), p. 4: "The sheep and the pasture form an integrated, equilibrated system"; to recognize this and to get beyond the immediate perception of the destructive effect of the sheep pasture characterizes the "ecological approach."

60. Wolfgang Jacubeit, *Schafhaltung und Schäfer in Zentraleuropa bis zum Beginn des 20. Jahrhunderts* (Berlin, 1987), pp. 36, 50, 92, 409, and elsewhere.

61. Radkau and Schäfer, *Holz* (note 50), p. 262 f.; Tyrrell, *True Gardens of the Gods* (note 50), pp. 56 ff. and elsewhere; Beinart and Coates, *Environment and History* (note 9), p. 41; Valentin Thurn, "Die Wüste greift nach Europa" (note 50), p. 126 f.

62. Michael Kienzle, *Natur-Schauspiele* (Tübingen, 1993), p. 10.

63. Colin M. Turnbull, *The Mountain People* (New York, 1972), chap. 10: "The Loveless People."

64. Riehl, *Naturgeschichte* (note 10), p. 76.

65. Jacob v. Uexküll, *Niegeschaute Welten: Die Umwelten meiner Freunde* (Berlin, 1936), p. 21.

66. Ellenberg, *Vegetation* (note 34), p. 52.

67. Edwin N. Wilmsen, "The Ecology of Illusion: Anthropological Foraging in the Kalahari," *Reviews in Anthropology* 10, no. 1 (1983): 15; Georges Bertrand, "Pour une histoire écologique de la France rurale," in *Histoire de la France rurale*, ed. George Duby and Armand Wallon, (Paris, 1975), vol. I, p. 44. For ecological determinism as fashion and episode in archaeology in the 1960s, see "Donald V. Kurtz, "The Economics of Urbanization and State Formation at Teotihuacan," *Current Anthropology* 28 (1987): 346; Erwin K. Scheuch, "Ökologischer Fehlschluß," in *Wörterbuch der Soziologie*, ed. W. Bernsdorf (Stuttgart, 1969), p. 757 f.

68. Anders Hjort, "A Critique of 'Ecological' Models of Pastoral Land Use," *Nomadic Peoples* 10 (1982): 23.

69. William S. Abruzzi, "Ecological Stability and Community Diversity during Mormon Colonization of the Little Colorado River Basin," *Human Ecology* 15 (1987): 317–38; Marc Reisner, *Cadillac Desert*, 2nd ed. (New York, 1993), pp. 53 f., 231.

70. Gordon R. Willey and Demitri B. Shimkin, "The Maya Collapse: A Summary View," in *The Classic Maya Collapse*, ed. T. Patrick Culbert (Albuquerque, N.M., 1973), pp. 487, 491; Joseph A. Tainter, *The Collapse of Complex Societies* (Cambridge, 1988), pp. 50 ff.; Robert Sharer, "Did the Maya Collapse? A New World Perspective on the Demise of the Harappan Civilization," in *Harappan Civilization*, ed. Gregory L. Possehl (Warminster, 1982), p. 376.

71. William T. Sanders, "The Cultural Ecology of the Lowland Maya: A Reevaluation," in Culbert, *Collapse* (note 70), p. 361 f.; Sharer, *Collapse* (note 70), pp. 373 ff.; Linda Schele and David Freidel, *A Forest of Kings: The Untold Story of the Ancient Maya* (New York, 1990), chap. 1, note 33, chap. 8, note 38. In one ancient Mayan book we read: "The forests burn for the planting of corn, and all burns, and the animals of the land die." Simonian, *Land of the Jaguar* (note 47), p. 23. Jeremy A. Sabloff, *Die Maya* (Heidelberg, 1991), pp. 188 ff. ("Lessons from the Collapse of the Maya").

72. Herbert Wilhelmy, *Welt und Umwelt der Maya: Aufstieg und Untergang einer Hochkultur* (Munich,1981), pp. 444, 533, 183 f., 405–8; David Webster, *The Fall of the Ancient Maya: Solving the Mystery of the Maya Collapse* (London, 2002), p. 255.

73. Joel Mokyr, *Why Ireland Starved: A Quantitative and Analytical History of the Irish Economy, 1800–1850* (London, 1985), pp. 276, 291 f. Cecil Woodham-Smith, *The Great Hunger* (London, 1987), p. 29; Redcliffe Salaman, *The History and Social Influence of the Potato* (Cambridge, 1985 [orig. 1949]), p. 339; Pier Paolo Viazzo, "An Anthropological Perspective of Environment, Population, and Social Structure in the Alps," in Brimblecombe and Pfister, *Silent Countdown* (note 32), p. 64.

74. Salaman, *Potato* (note 73), p. 515 f.; Karl-Heinz Ziessow and Helmut Ottenjohann, eds., *Die Kartoffel: Geschichte und Zukunft einer Kulturpflanze* (Cloppenburg, 1992), pp. 24 ff.

75. Liebig, *Chemie* (note 26), II, p. 64; Frank Mitchell, *Shell Guide to Reading the Irish Landscape* (London, 1986), pp. 149, 177, 181, 185, 190; Michael J. Conry and G. Frank Mitchell, "The Age of Irish Plaggen Soils," in *Paleopedology*, ed. Dan H. Yaalon (Jerusalem, 1971), pp. 129 ff.; Vernon G. Carter and Tom Dale, *Topsoil and Civilization* (Norman, Okla., 1974 [orig. 1955]), p. 183 f.; David Grigg, *Population Growth and Agrarian Change: An Historical Perspective* (Cambridge, 1980), p. 124.

76. Eileen McCracken, *The Irish Woods since Tudor Times: Distribution and Exploitation* (Newton Abbot, 1971), pp. 56, 68; Mitchell, *Irish Landscape* (note 75), pp. 181, 195.

77. Moses I. Finley, Denis Mack Smith, and Christopher Duggan, *A History of Sicily* (London, 1986), p. 101.

78. Jared Diamond, *Guns, Germs and Steel* (London, 1997), p. 412 f. A contrary view was taken by Peter C. Perdue, *Exhausting the Earth: State and Peasant in Hunan 1500–1850* (Cambridge, Mass., 1987), p. 22: "The limits to Chinese agricultural production lay not in the blindness to the threat of overpopulation or lack of interest in improving productivity . . . but in the ecology of rice production."

79. See note 33.

80. Rachel Carson, *Silent Spring* (New York, 1962), p. 54; Gerhard Eisenbeis and Michael Sturm, "Technik und Boden," in *Technik und Kultur*, (1994), vol. VI, p. 449. The study of the soil was long regarded as a fruitless and "dirty" field of research: Jill E. Cooper, "The Scientific Roots of Environmental Thought," paper delivered at the 1997 ASEH meeting in Baltimore, Md., p. 4. On the methodological problems of studying processes of soil degradation see Boris G. Rozanov et al., "Soils," in *The Earth as Transformed by Human Action: Global and Regional Changes in the Biosphere over the Past 300 Years*, ed. B. L. Turner (New York, 1990), p. 213; also the classic study by Avery Craven, *Soil Exhaustion as a Factor in the Agricultural History of Virginia and Maryland, 1606–1860* (Urbana, Ill., 1926), pp. 9 ff.; Mike Stocking, "Measuring Land Degradation," in *Land Degradation and Society*, eds. Piers Blaikie and Harold Brookfield (London, 1987), p. 61; Bork, *Landschaftsentwicklung* (note 22), p. 44 f. Klaus Kümmerer et al., eds., *Bodenlos: Zum nachhaltigen Umgang mit Böden* (= *Politische Ökologie*, Nov./Dec. 1997), pp. 33, 47, 75 (Martin Held, Karl Stahr, Christian Hiß).

81. August Bernhardt, *Geschichte des Waldeigentums, der Waldwirtschaft und Forstwissenschaft in Deutschland* (Aalen, 1966 [orig. 1875]), vol. III, p. 321; also vol. II, pp. 370 ff.

82. Michael Machatschek, *Laubgeschichten: Gebrauchswissen einer alten Baumwirtschaft, Speise- und Futterlaubkultur* (Vienna, 2002): the 540-page book is the work of a pruning enthusiast, who continually emphasizes that this was a form of sustainable cultivation. The aesthetic of pruned and pollarded trees also pervades the images in Oliver Rackham, *The Illustrated History of the Countryside* (London, 1994).

83. David S. G. Thomas and Nicholas J. Middleton, *Desertification: Exploding the Myth* (Chichester, 1994), p. 24; R. W. Dennell, "Archaeology and the Study of Desertification," in *Desertification and Development: Dryland Ecology in Social Perspective*, ed. Brian Spooner and H. S. Mann (London, 1982), pp. 48, 53; Monique Mainguet, *Desertification: Natural Background and Human Mismanagement* (Berlin, 1991); Horst G. Mensching, *Desertifikation* (Darmstadt, 1990), pp. 1 f., 11, 34, 69; Andrew B. Smith, "The Neolithic Tradition in the Sahara," in *The Sahara and the Nile: Quaternary Environments and Prehistoric Occupation in Northern Africa*, ed. Martin A. J. Williams and Hugues Faure (Rotterdam, 1980), p. 451 f.

84. David S. Landes, *The Wealth and Poverty of Nations* (New York, 1998), p. 3.

85. Christian Pfister, "Strategien zur Bewältigung von Naturkatastrophen seit 1500," in *Am Tag danach: Zur Bewältigung von Naturkatastrophen in der Schweiz 1500–2000*, ed. Christian Pfister (Bern, 2002), pp. 223, 227.

86. Christian Pfister, *Im Strom der Modernisierung: Bevölkerung, Wirtschaft und Umwelt im Kanton Bern, 1700–1914* (Bern, 1995), pp. 341, 448; Andreas Ineichen, *Innovative Bauern* (Lucerne,

1996), p. 185; H. H. Lamb, *Klima und Kulturgeschichte: Der Einfluß des Wetters auf den Gang der Geschichte* (Reinbek, 1989), p. 252; Christian Pfister, "Spatial patterns of climatic change in Europe A.D. 1675 to 1715," in *Climatic Trends and Anomalies in Europe 1675–1715*, ed. Christian Pfister and Birgit Glaeser (Stuttgart, 1994), p. 289. Environmental changes were repeatedly explained by the climate change hypothesis, but subsequent, detailed studies cast doubt on it. On this see in general Stefan Militzer, "Klima – Klimageschichte – Geschichte," *Geschichte in Wissenschaft und Unterricht* 47 (1996): esp. 82 ff.

87. Christian Pfister, "Strategien zur Bewältigung von Naturkatastrophen seit 1500," in *Am Tag danach: Zur Bewältigung von Naturkatastrophen in der Schweiz 1500–2000*, ed. Christian Pfister (Bern, 2002), pp. 223, 227.

88. Joachim Radkau, "Hiroshima und Asilomar," *Geschichte und Gesellschaft* 14 (1998): 356 f.

2. THE ECOLOGY OF SUBSISTENCE AND TACIT KNOWLEDGE: PRIMEVAL SYMBIOSES OF HUMANS AND NATURE

1. Max Weber, *Wirtschaft und Gesellschaft, Teilband 1: Gemeinschaften*, Max-Weber-Gesamtausgabe I/22–1 (Tübingen, 1984). English translation: *Economy and Society: An Outline of Interpretive Sociology*, ed. Günther Roth and Claus Wittich, trans. Ephraim Fischoff et al. (Berkeley, Calif., 1978).

2. Robert Boyd, ed., *Indians, Fire and the Land in the Pacific Northwest* (Corvallis, Ore., 1999), p. 20: "These environmental historians have adopted (consciously or intuitively) the anthropological concept of 'ecological transition,' an abrupt shift in systematic relations." However, we are talking here about a system change from a human perspective, not from the perspective of nonhuman nature.

3. The idea that the autonomous, self-sufficient existence of the polis was the perfect state of happiness formed one of the foundational axioms of Aristotelian political philosophy: see Friedrich Tomberg, *Polis und Nationalstaat* (Darmstadt, 1973), pp. 233 ff., 239. A feminist analysis of the subsistence economy can be found in Veronika Bennholdt-Thomsen and Maria Mies, *Eine Kuh für Hillary: Die Subsistenzperspektive* (Munich, 1997); Veronika Bennholdt-Thomsen et al., *Das Subsistenzhandbuch: Widerstandskulturen in Europa, Asien und Lateinamerika* (Vienna, 1999). I am grateful to Veronika Bennholdt-Thomsen for many pointers and stimulating suggestions.

4. Roscher, *Ackerbau* (Chap. 1, note 29), p. 105 f.; Abel, *Agricultural Fluctuations* (Chap. 1, note 30), p. 111.

5. Karl Polanyi, *The Great Transformation* (Boston, 1957 [orig. 1944]), pp. 163 ff.; Fernand Braudel, *The Mediterranean and the Mediterranean World in the Age of Philipp II*, translated by Siân Reynolds (London, 1975 [orig. 1949]), p. 152; Perdue, *Exhausting the Earth* (Chap. 1, note 78), p. 239; Stüben and Thurn, *WüstenErde* (Chap. 1, note 50), p. 24 f.; Jean Jacquart, "Immobilisme et catastrophes," in *Histoire de France rurale*, ed. G. Duby and A. Wallon (Paris, 1975), vol. II, pp. 259 ff. Among those authors who hail the reasonableness of the subsistence economy one sometimes finds the thesis that it behaved in keeping with the principle of "risk minimization instead of yield optimization" and therefore always preferred polyculture; see, e.g., Rainer Beck in Werner Konold, ed., *Naturlandschaft – Kulturlandschaft* (Landsberg, 1996), p. 42 f. However, I doubt that one can generally posit such a forward-looking risk calculation, since history has no lack of counterexamples.

6. Otto Brunner, *Adeliges Landleben und europäischer Geist: Leben und Werk Wolf Helmhard v. Hohbergs 1612–1688* (Salzburg, 1949), p. 245; Susan Reynolds, *Fiefs and Vassals: The Medieval Evidence Reinterpreted* (Oxford, 1994), pp. 59 ff. and elsewhere: in the Middle Ages, as well, "full ownership" by individuals was normal; the all-pervading feudal pyramid is a myth. Robert McC. Netting, *Smallholders, Householders: Farm Families and the Ecology of Intensive, Sustainable Agriculture* (Stanford, Calif., 1993), p. 168, note. Bruce Campbell and Ricardo A. Godoy, "Commonfield Agriculture: The Andes and Medieval England Compared," in *Proceedings of the Conference on Common Property Resource Management* (Washington, D.C.,

1986), p. 330: individually worked segments of land also within all forms of commonfields. Eric Kerridge, *The Common Fields of England* (Manchester, 1992), p. 112: there is no evidence for co-aration of the common fields.

7. Netting, *Smallholders* (note 6), p. 41 and elsewhere; Mariano Feio, *Le Bas Alentejo et l'Algarve* (Evora, 1983), pp. 75 ff. José Lutzenberger, a Brazilian of German descent, recipient of the Alternative Nobel Prize, and former Brazilian secretary of the environment once said: ignorance once led him to be angry at the small farmers "who were causing terrible erosion on the steep slopes, and who, once the soil was gone, continued to cut trees until no forest existed anymore, gigantic mud slides disfigured the mountain, and the rivers were dead and silted up. . . . Only later . . . did I realize what masters of survival they were, how interesting their culture was, and how aware they were of their own hopeless situation." In José Lutzenberger and Michael Schwartzkopf, *Giftige Ernte* (Greven, 1988), p. 26. He, too, does not deny the reality of the destruction of the soil caused by the impoverished small farmers.

8. E. P. Thompson, "The Moral Economy of the English Crowd in the 18th Century," *Past and Present* 50 (1971): 76–113; Joachim Radkau, *Das Zeitalter der Nervosität* (Munich, 1998), p. 254.

9. Joachim Radkau, "Das Rätsel der städtischen Brennholzversorgung im 'hölzernen Zeitalter,'" in *Energie und Stadt in Europa: Von der vorindustriellen 'Holznot' bis zur Ölkrise der 1970er Jahre*, ed. Dieter Schott (Stuttgart, 1997), p. 62. The pride that premodern regions took in their ability to supply their own needs is revealed in a passage from a statistical-topographical survey of the small territory of Hohenlohe in 1791: "The natural situation of this land is so outstandingly good that if, as in China, one were to surround it with a wall . . . , it could do without the rest of the world, such abundance does it posses." Werner Konold, "Liebliche Anmut und wechselnde Szenerie," *Hohenloher Freilandmuseum Mitteilungen* 17 (1996): 6.

10. Roscher, *Ackerbau* (Chap. 1, note 29), p. 195; Woodward, "Gooding" (Chap. 1, note 28), p. 107; Albert Wirz, *Sklaverei und kapitalistisches Weltsystem* (Frankfurt a. M., 1984), p. 204; Bennholdt-Thomsen, *Kuh* (note 3), pp. 22 ff.; Polanyi, *Great Transformation* (note 3), p. 43.

11. Hesiod, *Works and Days*, trans. H. G. Evelyn-White (London, 1977), 346; Columella (*De re rustica* I 3) gives lengthy advice that anyone buying a farm should pay attention to who the neighbors are.

12. Radkau and Schäfer, *Holz* (Chap. 1, note 50), p. 63 f.; Franz Hafner, *Steiermarks Wald in Geschichte und Gegenwart* (Vienna, 1979), p. 31; Engelbert Koller, *Forstgeschichte des Salzkammergutes* (Vienna, 1970), pp. 443 ff.; Arthur Young, *Travels in France*, ed. Constantia Maxwell (Cambridge, 1929), p. 289. Young's attitude toward slash-and-burn agriculture was ambivalent: in another passage he praised well-regulated burning, paraphrasing the peasant saying that fire is a good servant, but a poor master: Stephen J. Pyne, *Vestal Fire: An Environmental History, Told through Fire, of Europe and Europe's Encounter with the World* (Seattle, Wash., 1997), p. 249.

13. Shepard Krech III, *The Ecological Indian: Myth and History* (New York, 1999), p. 113.

14. Stephan J. Pyne, *Fire in America: A Cultural History of Wildland and Rural Fire* (Princeton, N.J., 1982), p. 302 f. My interest in the ecological history of fire was piqued by an excursion I undertook with Stephan Pyne into the Catalina Mountains (Arizona) in April 1999. Alfred Runte, *Yosemite: The Embattled Wilderness* (Lincoln, Neb., 1990), pp. 58 ff.

15. Bernard Campbell, *Human Ecology: The Story of Our Place in Nature from Prehistory to the Present*, 2nd ed. (New York, 1995), p. 83.

16. Bertrand, in Duby and Wallon, *France rurale* (Chap. 1, note 67), p. 92; Nancy M. Williams and Eugene S. Hunn, eds., *Resource Managers, North American and Australian Hunter-Gatherers* (Boulder, Colo., 1982), p. 10; François Sigaut, *L'agriculture et le feu: Rôle et place du feu dans les techniques de préparation du champ de l'ancienne agriculture européenne* (Paris, 1975), p. 14 and elsewhere.

17. Axel Steensberg, *Fire-Clearance Husbandry: Traditional Techniques throughout the World* (Herning, 1993), pp. 187 ff.; Virgil, *Georgics*, trans. H. Rushton Fairclough, rev. G. P. Goold (Cambridge, Mass., 1999), I, 84 f.: "Often, too, it has been useful to fire barren fields, and burn the light stubble in crackling flames." Hafner, *Wald* (note 12), p. 258.

18. Sigaut, *L'agriculture et le feu* (note 16), p. 194; Stephen J. Pyne, *Burning Bush: A Fire History of Australia* (New York, 1991), p. 161; Steensberg, *Fire-Clearance Husbandry* (note 17), p. 186; P. Rowley-Conwy, "Slash and Burn in the Temperate European Neolithic," in *Farming Practice in British Prehistory*, ed. Roger Mercer (Edinburgh, 1981), p. 95; Ellenberg, *Vegetation* (Chap. 1, note 34), p. 31.

19. A wealth of material in Stephen J. Pyne, *Vestal Fire* (note 12); Kunst- und Ausstellungshalle der Bundesrepublik Deutschland, ed., *Feuer* (Bonn, 2001).

20. Gordon G. Whitney, *From Coastal Wilderness to Fruited Plain: A History of Environmental Change in Temperate North America 1500 to the Present* (Cambridge, 1994), p. 109. "Indian summer" originally referred not only to the red foliage, but also to the glow of fires set by Native Americans. Ibid., p. 119: many scholars believe that the prairies of the Midwest were created by the fire husbandry of Native Americans. This is a favorite argument used to demythologize the notion that Native Americans lived in harmony with nature.

21. Steensberg, *Fire-Clearance Husbandry* (note 17), pp. 116, 216; Sanders, "Ecology" (Chap. 1, note 71), p. 344; Williams and Hunn, *Resource Managers* (note 16), p. 49; Peter Hennenigsen, "Das finstere Jütland. Eine dänische Landschaft im Umbruch," in *Dünger und Dynamit: Beiträge zur Umweltgeschichte Schleswig-Holsteins und Dänemarks*, eds. Manfred Jakubowski-Tiessen and Klaus-J. Lorenzen-Schmidt (Neumünster, 1999), p. 113; Mark Elvin, *The Retreat of the Elephants: An Environmental History of China* (New Haven, Conn., 2004), p. 105; Clara Sue Kidwell, "Systems of Knowledge," in *America in 1492: The World of the Indian Peoples Before the Arrival of Columbus*, ed. Alvin M. Josephy, Jr. (New York, 1992), p. 395; Susanna Hecht and Alexander Cockburn, *The Fate of the Forest: Developers, Destroyers and Defenders of the Amazon* (London, 1990), p. 44 f.; Pyne, *Fire in America* (note 14), p. 122; J. V. Thirgood, *Man and the Mediterranean Forest* (London, 1981), p. 67; Jorge Freitas Branco, *Bauernarbeit im mediterranen Alltag* (Berlin, 1984), p. 168; Pyne, *Vestal Fire* (note 12), p. 287.

22. Jussi Raumolin, *The Problem of Forest-Based Development as Illustrated by the Development Discussion, 1850–1918* (Helsinki, 1990) (Dept. of Social Policy, Research Reports 4), p. 124; Raumolin, ed., *Special Issue on Swidden Cultivation* (Helsinki, 1987) (*Suomen Antropologi* 4), and here especially Raumolin's Introduction (pp. 185 ff., 192) and Matti Sarmela, "Swidden Cultivation in Finland as a Cultural System" (pp. 241 ff., 259 f.). Fritz Schneiter (1879–1970), a longtime mountain pasture inspector (*Alminspektor*) in Styria, defended the traditional swidden cultivation in that region against the charge of destroying the humus, while at the same time praising this kind of subsistence economy for being resistant to the ups and downs of the market: *Agrargeschichte der Brandwirtschaft* (Graz, 1970), p. 89 f. A soil analysis in the Kondel Forest along the Mosel concluded, contrary to the common perception, that slash-and-burn cultivation had "undoubtedly led to some improvement in the soil": Christoph Ernst, "Den Wald entwickeln," dissertation, University of Trier, 1998, p. 177.

23. McNeill, *Mountains* (Chap. 1, note 16), p. 276 f.; Pyne, *Fire in America* (note 14), p. 415.

24. David G. McGrath, "The Role of Biomass in Shifting Cultivation," *Human Ecology* 15 (1987), p. 240; Harris, *Cannibals and Kings* (Chap. 1, note 47), pp. 90 ff.

25. Geertz, *Involution* (Chap. 1, note 59), p. 27; Pyne, *Fire in America* (note 14), p. 39.

26. Richard B. Lee and Irven DeVore, eds., *Man the Hunter*, 3rd ed. (Chicago, 1972), p. 3; a critical response by Bruce Bower, "A World That Never Existed," *Science News* 135 (1989): 264–6. For a detailed discussion on the long man-the-hunter discussion see Matt Cartmill, *A View to a Death in the Morning: Hunting and Nature Through History* (Cambridge, 1993). Cartmill concludes that the "hunting hypothesis originated as a myth, concocted out of antique preconceptions and wishful thinking" (p. 225). But he detects ideological preconceptions also among critics of hunting. The assumption that the male role over

tens of thousands of years was strongly shaped by the hunt still seems plausible. On this see Kim Hill, "Hunting and Human Evolution," *Journal of Human Evolution* 11 (1982): 521–44.

27. Robin Ridington, "Northern Hunters," in Josephy, *America in 1492* (note 21), p. 25; W. W. Hill, *The Agricultural and Hunting Methods of the Navaho Indians* (New Haven, Conn., 1938), p. 182; Liebig, *Briefe* (Chap. 1, note 26), p. 344.

28. Critique: see note 26. Also: Thomas N. Headland and Robert C. Bailey, "Have Hunter-Gatherers Ever Lived in Tropical Rain Forest Independently of Agriculture?" *Human Ecology* 19 (1991): 115–22; similarly Terese B. Hart and John A. Hart, "The Ecological Basis of Hunter-Gatherer Subsistence in African Rain Forests: The Mbuti of Eastern Zaire," *Human Ecology* 14 (1986): 29–55; Bruce D. Smith, *The Emergence of Agriculture* (New York, 1995), p. 81; Lévi-Strauss, in John Seymour and Herbert Girardet, *Far from Paradise: The Story of Man's Impact on the Environment* (London, 1986), p. 21.

29. For Midas Dekkers, such myths have a real basis in ancient and worldwide practices of sexual contacts between humans and animals: *Dearest Pet: On Bestiality*, trans. Paula Vincent (London, 1994).

30. Peter Iverson, "Taking Care of the Earth and Sky," in Josephy, *America in 1492* (note 21), p. 117.

31. Paul S. Martin and Richard G. Klein, *Quaternary Extinctions: A Prehistoric Revolution* (Tucson, Ariz., 1984), with a broad discussion. On the whole, the "overkill" hypothesis seems more convincing than the climate change counterhypothesis. Niles Eldredge, *Wendezeiten des Lebens: Katastrophen in Erdgeschichte und Evolution* (Frankfurt a. M., 1997), pp. 257 ff., 267 ff., with interesting findings from Madagascar; of special importance to environmental history is his idea it was not the killing of the animals that was crucial, but the destruction of their habitats.

32. Jens Lüning, "Leben in der Steinzeit," in Markl, *Natur* (Chap. 1, note 18), p. 136; Christian Goudineau and Jean Guilane, eds., *De Lascaux au Grand Louvre: Archéologie et histoire en France* (Paris, 1989), p. 264 f. (Catherine Farizy); Eldredge, *Wendezeiten des Lebens* (note 31), p. 259; Werner Müller, *Geliebte Erde: Naturfrömmigkeit und Naturhaß im indianischen und europäischen Nordamerika*, 4th ed. (Bonn, 1982), p. 52. Empirical findings against sustainability of the hunt among "natural peoples" include Michael S. Alvard, "Testing the 'Ecologically Noble Savage' Hypothesis: Interspecific Prey Choice by Piro Hunters of Amazonian Peru," *Human Ecology* 21 (1993): 355–87; Timothy F. Flannery, *The Future Eaters: An Ecological History of the Australasian Lands and People* (Chatsworth, N.S.W., 1994), pp. 180 ff. (changes to the Australian vegetation as the result of the extermination of the megafauna by the Aborigines).

33. Turnbull, *Mountain People* (Chap. 1, note 63), p. 21; Klaus Rösch, "Einfluß der Beweidung auf die Vegetation des Bergwaldes, Nationalpark Berchtesgaden," *Forschungsbericht* 26 (1992): 13; on the question of family hunting grounds among the Algonquin Indians see Rolf Knight, "A Re-examination of Hunting, Trapping, and Territoriality among the Northeastern Algonkin Indians," in *Man, Culture, and Animals: The Role of Animals in Human Ecological Adjustments*, eds. Anthony Leeds and Andrew P. Vayda (Washington, D.C., 1965), pp. 27 ff., 40 f. John F. Richards, *The Unending Frontier: An Environmental History of the Early Modern World* (Berkeley, Calif., 2001), p. 536.

34. Robert Krottenthaler, *Die Jagd im alten Indien* (Frankfurt a. M., 1996), p. 13 f.; *Kritische Blätter für Forst- und Jagdwissenschaft* 6 (1832, Leipzig): 226 f.

35. Tsui Yenhu, "A Comparative Study of the Attitudes of the Peoples of Pastoral Areas of Inner Asia towards Their Environments," in *Culture and Environment in Inner Asia*, eds. Caroline Humphrey and David Sneath (Cambridge, 1996), vol. II, pp. 14, 18 f.; Michael P. Hoffman, "Prehistoric Ecological Crises," in *Historical Ecology*, ed. Leser J. Bilsky (Port Washington, N.Y., 1980), p. 36; Roscher, *Ackerbau* (Chap. 1, note 29), p. 23.

36. J. Donald Hughes, *North America Indian Ecology* (El Paso, N.M., 1996 [orig. 1983]), pp. 25 ff.; Peter Gerlitz, "'Religionsökologie': Gibt es ein 'ökologisches Bewußtsein' unter den Pak Pak Nordwest-Sumatras?" in *Seelenfischer: Mission, Stammesvölker und Ökologie*, ed. Peter

E. Stüben (Gießen, 1994), p. 209 f.; David Watts, *The West Indies: Patterns of Development, Culture and Environmental Change since 1492* (Cambridge, 1987), pp. 53, 57, 60, 531; Karl Hasel, *Forstgeschichte* (Hamburg, 1985), p. 14.

37. Fernand Braudel, "Das Meer," in F. Braudel, G. Duby, and M. Aymard, *Die Welt des Mittelmeeres* (Frankfurt a. M., 1997), p. 40; Arthur F. McEvoy, *The Fisherman's Problem: Ecology and Law in the California Fisheries 1850–1980* (Cambridge, 1986), pp. 19, 29 ff., 271. Patrick W. Kirch, "The Ecology of Marine Exploitation in Prehistoric Hawaii," *Human Ecology* 10 (1982): 455–76 (partly empirical, partly hypothetical strategies of adaptation to the fish stocks). For the regulation of fishing in German lakes in the fifteenth century, see Ernst Schubert, *Einführung in die Grundprobleme der deutschen Geschichte im Spätmittelalter* (Darmstadt, 1992), p. 59.

38. Bauer, *China* (Chap. 1, note 39), p. 24; Anne-Marie Cocula-Vaillières, *Un fleuve et des hommes* (Paris, 1981), pp. 120 ff.; Richard Ellis, *Men and Whales* (New York, 1991), p. 265.

39. Landesamt für den Nationalpark Schleswig-Holsteinisches Wattenmeer, *Umweltatlas Wattenmeer* (Stuttgart, 1998), vol. I, p. 168; Victor S. Kennedy and Kent Mountford, "Human Influences on Aquatic Resources in the Chesapeake Bay Watershed," in *Discovering the Chesapeake: The History of an Ecosystem*, eds. Philip D. Curtin et al. (Baltimore, Md., 2001), pp. 196 ff., 209 ff.

40. K. N. Chaudhuri, *Asia before Europe: Economy and Civilization of the Indian Ocean from the Rise of Islam to 1750* (Cambridge, 1990). Similarly, with an even stronger emphasis on the role of the monsoon, Kenneth McPherson, *The Indian Ocean: A History of People and the Sea* (Oxford, 1993). The most comprehensive and ambitious recent attempt at a synopsis of Mediterranean history that includes environmental aspects is the 760-page opus of Peregrine Horden and Nicholas Purcell, *The Corrupting Sea: A Study of Mediterranean History* (Oxford, 2000). But their point is that the Mediterranean, upon close inspection, consists of a multitude of small spaces, which imparts to it a certain ecological stability. The title is meant to be ironic: shipping is *not* corrupting, as the moralists believed, but had something stabilizing about it by virtue of the connections it created.

41. Anna-Katharina Wöbse, "Grenzfälle – Internationaler Naturschutz im 20. Jahrhundert (1. Teil)," *Studienarchiv Umweltgeschichte* 8 (2003): 4–14.

42. James A. Powell, *The Liber Augustalis* (Syracuse, N.Y., 1971), p. 144; Gottfried Hösel, *Unser Abfall aller Zeiten* (Munich, 1987), p. 38; Rita Gudermann, *Morastwelt und Paradies* (Paderborn, 2000), p. 451 f.; Claus-Peter Hutter et al., eds., *Seen, Teiche, Tümpel und andere Stillgewässer* (Stuttgart, 1993), p. 20 f.; Horst Johannes Tümmers, *Der Rhein: Ein europäischer Fluß und seine Geschichte* (Munich, 1999), p. 67 f.

43. *Der Sachsenspiegel*, ed. Walter Koschorrek (Frankfurt a. M., 1976), p. 48 f.; Robert P. Harrison, *Forests: The Shadow of Civilization* (Chicago, 1992), pp. 69, 75; Karl Hasel, *Studien über Wilhelm Pfeil* (Hannover, 1982) (*Aus dem Walde*, no. 36), pp. 32 f., 167.

44. Josef H. Reichholf, *Comeback der Biber* (Munich, 1993), p. 113 f.; Beinart and Coates, *Environment and History* (Chap. 1, note 9), pp. 21, 24; Douglas R. Weiner, *Models of Nature: Ecology, Conservation and Cultural Revolution in Soviet Russia* (Pittsburgh, Pa., 1988), pp. 9 ff., 151 ff.

45. Jonathan S. Adams and Thomas O. McShane, *The Myth of Wild Africa: Conservation without Illusion* (Berkeley, Calif., 1996), p. 46. Joachim Radkau, *Mensch und Natur in der Geschichte* (Leipzig, 2002), p. 86.

46. John M. MacKienzie, *The Empire of Nature: Hunting, Conservation and British Imperialism* (Manchester, 1988), p. 262 and elsewhere; Radkau, "Nervosität" (note 6), p. 378 f.; Theodore Roosevelt, *An Autobiography* (New York, 1913), p. 347; Susan L. Flader, *Thinking like a Mountain: Aldo Leopold and the Evolution of an Ecological Attitude toward Deer, Wolves, and Forests* (Madison, Wisc., 1994), pp. 168 ff. Even Thoreau, though later in life a vegetarian, praised hunting and fishing as the best way of acquiring an intimate knowledge of nature: Henry D. Thoreau, *The Illustrated Walden* (Princeton, N.J., 1973), pp. 210 ff.

47. Thomas Dupke, *Hermann Löns* (Hildesheim, 1994), pp. 92 ff.; Hubert Weinzierl, "Jagd und Naturschutz," in *Natur in Not*, ed. H. Weinzierl (Munich, 1966), pp. 294 ff.; Grzimek:

Introduction to the same volume; Hans-Helmut Wüstenhagen, *Bürger gegen Kernkraftwerke* (Reinbek, 1975), p. 39; Brunner, *Landleben* (note 6), p. 292 f.

48. Harris, *Cannibals and Kings* (Chap. 1, note 47), p. 27.

49. Eduard Hahn, *Die Haustiere und ihre Beziehungen zur Wirtschaft des Menschen* (Leipzig, 1896), pp. 28 ff.; Homer Aschmann, "Comments on the Symposium 'Man, Culture, and Animals,'" in Leeds and Vayda, *Man, Culture, and Animals* (note 33), pp. 259 ff., 263 ff.; Keith Thomas, *Man and the Natural World: Changing Attitudes in England 1500–1800* (London, 1984), pp. 28, 108.

50. Lynn T. White, Jr., "History and Horseshoe Nails," in *The Historian's Workshop*, ed. L. P. Curis, Jr. (New York, 1970), pp. 47–64; Alfred Weber, *Das Tragische und die Geschichte* (Munich, 1959 [1943]), pp. 58 ff.; Karl Jaspers to Alfred Weber, November 14, 1951, in *Alfred Weber-Gesamtausgabe*, X/2 (Marburg, 2003), p. 493 f.; Marija Gimbutas, "Die Indoeuropäer: Archäologische Probleme," in *Die Urheimat der Indogermanen*, ed. Anton Scherer (Darmstadt, 1968), p. 546 f.

51. Udelgard Körber-Grohne, *Nutzpflanzen in Deutschland: Kulturgeschichte und Biologie* (Stuttgart, 1987), pp. 57, 67.

52. Glacken, *Traces* (Chap. 1, note 25), p. 186; Jutta Nowosadtko, "Zwischen Ausbeutung und Tabu: Nutztiere in der Frühen Neuzeit," in *Tiere und Menschen*, ed. Paul Münch (Paderborn, 1998), pp. 257 ff.; Thomas, *Man and the Natural World* (note 49), p. 35; Hahn, *Haustiere* (note 49), p. 50. Norbert Benecke, *Der Mensch und seine Haustiere: Die Geschichte einer jahrtausendealten Beziehung* (Stuttgart, 1994), p 43: "There is reason to believe that from the beginning of domestication, an unconscious selection took place in favor of animals that posed the fewest problems to humans in terms of continuous interaction."

53. Günther Franz et al., *Geschichte des deutschen Gartenbaues* (Stuttgart, 1984), pp. 20, 200, also for the discussion that follows.

54. Ian Tyrrell, *True Gardens of the Gods: Californian-Australien Environmental Reform 1860–1930* (Berkeley, Calif., 1999).

55. Francis Bacon, *The Essayes or Counsels, Civill and Morall*, ed. Michael Kiernan (Cambridge, Mass., 1985), p. 139 (essay "On Gardens"); Roscher, *Ackerbau* (Chap. 1, note 29), pp. 132, 190. One of the most famous testimonies in world history to a passionate love of gardening – combined with a precise knowledge of nature – is the autobiography of the Mogul ruler Babar. But he was also enthralled with wild nature, especially under the influence of alcohol: see Stanley Lane-Poole, *Babar* (Delhi, 1990 [1890]), pp. 27, 37 ff., 149. Babar's description of India gives the impression that he found the frogs of that country more remarkable than its people; Peter Brown, *Augustine of Hippo* (Berkeley, Calif. 1967), p. 143; Marianne Beuchert, *Die Gärten Chinas* (Frankfurt a. M., 1998), p. 137.

56. Wilhelm Hamm, ed., *Das Ganze der Landwirtschaft in Bildern*, 2nd ed. (Leipzig, 1872; reprint, Hannover, 1985), p. 52; Ramón Gutiérrez, "Pueblos and Spanish in the Southwest," in *Major Problems in American Environmental History*, ed. Carolyn Merchant (Lexington, Ky., 1993), p. 49 f.; George Ordish, *The Living Garden: The 400-Year History of an English Garden* (Boston, 1985), p. 46 f.; Heide Inhetveen, "Die Landfrau und ihr Garten: Zur Soziologie der Hortikultur," *Zeitschrift für Agrargeschichte und Agrarsoziologie* 42 (1994): 41–58; Inhetveen, "Farming Women, Time and the 'Re-agrarianization' of Consciousness," *Time & Society* 3 (1994): 259–76; Inhetveen, "'. . . ein Beet mit schönsten Rapunzeln bepflanzt': Frauen und Pflanzenzucht," manuscript (on Anna of Saxony). I am grateful to Heide Inhetveen for providing materials on the history of the garden. Elisabeth Meyer-Renschhausen, "Die Gärten der Frauen: Gärten als Anfang und Ende der Landwirtschaft?" in Bennholdt-Thomsen, *Subsistenzhandbuch* (note 3), pp. 120–36. In Germany, as well, not all regions had an old tradition of garden cultivation: see Rainer Beck, *Unterfinning* (Munich, 1993), p. 42.

57. Fernand Braudel, *Civilization and Capitalism 15th–18th Century*, vol. I: *The Structures of Everyday Life*, trans. Sîan Reynolds (New York, 1981), p. 337. He repeats the same quote in *The Identity of France*, trans. Sîan Reynolds (New York, 1990), vol. II, pp. 250–2, this time

without an expression of amazement. Ulrich Bentzien, *Bauernarbeit im Feudalismus* (Berlin, 1980), p. 112. The Mecklenburg agrarian reformer Andreas Christlieb Streubel (1698–1774) recommended giving up the plough and returning to the old "Mecklenburg hook" (*Mecklenburgischen Haken*): U. Bentzien in *Mecklenburg, Volkskunde*, ed. Karl Baumgarten et al. (Rostock, 1988), pp. 14 f., 128 f. Kerridge, *Common Fields* (note 6), p. 107.

58. Ordish, *Living Garden* (note 56), p. 226: it is said that during the time of George III, 7,000 (!) new plants were introduced to the country.

59. Victor Hehn, *Kulturpflanzen und Hausthiere*, 4. Aufl. (Berlin, 1883), p. 97 f. *Cultivated Plants and Domesticated Animals in their Migration from Asia to Europe*, ed. James P. Mallory (Amsterdam, 1976), p. 102 f.

60. Mary R. Berenbaum, *Bugs in the System: Insects and Their Impact on Human Affairs* (Reading, Mass., 1995), pp. 81–90.

61. Brown, *Augustine of Hippo* (note 55), p. 172; Günther Franz, ed., *Quellen zur Geschichte des deutschen Bauernstandes im Mittelalter* (Darmstadt, 1974), p. 491; August Bernhardt, *Geschichte des Waldeigentums* (Berlin, 1872), vol. I, pp. 118, 133. M. N. Srinivas, *The Remembered Village* (Delhi, 1976), p. 135 f.: in Indian villages, planting trees is seen not only as a commandment of utility, but of ethics, and the cutting down of a tree, especially a fruit tree, is regarded as especially heinous.

62. Franz, *Gartenbau* (note 53), pp. 143 ff.; Cervantes, *Don Quixote*, trans. Edith Grossmann (New York, 2003), Part 1, Chap. 11, para. 1; similarly Paulus Niavis, *Judicium Jovis* (Berlin, 1953) (*Freiberger Forschungshefte* D 3), p. 27, Ceres: "Indeed, when humans were still living on acorns, they honored all the gods." See also Virgil, *Georgics* (note 17), I, 147 ff.: "Ceres was the first to teach men to turn the earth with iron, when the acorns and the arbutes of the sacred wood began to fail." Tikal: Harris, *Cannibals* (Chap. 1, note 47), p. 91. Ibn al-Awan's "Book of Agriculture" (around 1300) was largely devoted to the cultivation of trees: Philipp Blanchemanche, *Bâtisseurs de paysages* (Paris, 1990), p. 183.

63. Thirgood, *Cyprus* (Chap. 1, note 55), pp. 60 f., 349, note 23; Atluri Murali, "Whose Trees? Forest Practices and Local Communities in Andhra, 1600–1922," in *Nature, Culture, Imperialism*, ed. David Arnold and Ramachandra Guha (Delhi, 1996), pp. 92, 97; Braudel, *Mediterranean* (note 5), I, p. 239; Ludwig Reinhardt, *Kulturgeschichte der Nutzpflanzen* (Munich, 1911), p. 195.

64. Hugh Johnson, *The International Book of Trees: A Guide and Tribute to the Trees of Our Forests and Gardens* (New York, 1973), p. 240; Alfred Philippson, *Das Mittelmeergebiet: Seine geographische und kulturelle Eigenart* (Hildesheim, 1974), p. 161 f.; Victor D. Hanson, "Practical Aspects of Grape-Growing and the Ideology of Greek Viticulture," in *Agriculture in Ancient Greece*, ed. Berrit Wells (Stockholm, 1992), p. 161; Goudineau and Guilane, *Lascaux* (note 32), p. 52 f., 101; Guy Fourquin, in Duby and Wallon, *France rurale* (Chap. 1, note 67), vol. I, pp. 466, 470, 473; Marie-Claire Amouretti and Georges Comet, *Le livre de l'olivier* (Aix-en-Provence, 1985), pp. 64 f., 94, 97 f., 137; Le Roy Ladurie, *Peasants* (Chap. 1, note 5), p. 272 f.; Glacken, *Traces* (Chap. 1, note 25), p. 130; Marcel Lachiver, *Vins, Vignes et Vignerons: Histoire du vignoble français* (Paris, 1988), p. 164.

65. Philippson, *Mittelmeergebiet* (note 64), pp. 160 ff.; Claude Royer, *Les Vignerons: Usages et mentalités des pays de vignobles* (Paris, 1980), 16; Braudel, *France* (note 57), pp. 325 ff.; Jacqueline Waldren, *Insiders and Outsiders: Paradise and Reality in Mallorca* (Oxford, 1996), p. 107; Jorge F. Branco, *Bauernarbeit im mediterranen Alltag: Agrikultur und Umweltgestaltung auf der Inselgruppe Madeira (1750–1900)* (Berlin, 1984), p. 4. Brazil: Carl D. Goerdeler in *Die Zeit*, January 4, 1991, p. 10 f. Using Siam as an example, Pierre Poivre showed that fruit trees could not last without individual usufruct rights: *Travels of a Philosopher or, Observations on the Manners and Arts of Various Nations in Africa and Asia* (Augusta, Maine, 1797), p. 35; Hans Lohmann, *Atene* [*sic!*] (Cologne, 1993), vol. I, p. 210: when Herodotus emphasizes that "Athens was the only place in the world where olive trees existed at the time," his words reflect pride of the cultural continuity without which olive cultures cannot flourish. Ibid., pp. 196 ff.: many details on the basis of archaeology.

66. Radkau and Schäfer, *Holz* (Chap. 1, note 50), p. 55.
67. Pott and Hüppe, *Hudelandschaften* (Chap. 1, note 51), p. 61; on the other hand, oak forests invited clearing, since oak groves are a sign of good agricultural soil: Friedrich Mager, *Der Wald in Altpreußen als Wirtschaftsraum*, II (Cologne, 1960), pp. 147 ff. Hans Hausrath, *Geschichte des deutschen Waldbaus von seinen Anfängen bis 1850* (Freiburg, 1982), p. 91. Thoreau said: "I think it is Linnaeus who says that while the swine is rooting for acorns he is planting acorns": *The Writings of H. D. Thoreau* (Boston, 1899), vol. IX, p. 248. Diamond, *Guns* (Chap. 1, note 78), p. 129.
68. Reinhardt, *Nutzpflanzen* (note 63), p. 216; James J. Parsons, "Die Eichelmast-Schweinehaltung in den Eichenwäldern Südwestspaniens (1962)," in *Beiträge zur Geographie der Wald- und Forstwirtschaft*, ed. Hans-Wilhelm Windhorst (Darmstadt, 1978), pp. 157, 164, 172. J. Russell Smith, "The Oak Tree and Man's Environment," *Geographical Review* 1 (1916): 3–19; Radkau and Schäfer, *Holz* (Chap. 1, note 50), p. 28.
69. Per Eliasson, *Skogt, makt och människor: En miljöhistoria om svensk skog 1800–1875* (Malmö, 2002), pp. 375 ff. (English summary).
70. Diego Moreno, "Châtaigneraie 'historique' et chatâgneraie 'traditionelle,'" *Médiévales* (Université Paris VIII) (1989): 153, 160. An excursion into Catalan forests with Diego Moreno in June 1991 made me aware of the historical importance of chestnut cultivation. Ariane Bruneton-Governatori, Châtaignes (Paris, 1991), p. 11; Moreno, *Le pain de bois: Ethnohistoire de la châtaigne et du châtaignier* (Toulouse, 1984), p. 450 and elsewhere; Philippe Joutard et al., *Les Cévennes: De la montagne à l'homme* (privately published, 1979), pp. 25 ff.; Le Roy Ladurie, *Peasants* (Chap. 1, note 5), pp. 66 ff; Vito Fumagalli, *Mensch und Umwelt im Mittelalter* (Berlin, 1992), p. 29. Jacques Blondel and James Aronson, *Biology and Wild Life in the Mediterranean Region* (Oxford, 1999), p. 230 f.
71. A list of the advantages and disadvantages of an agro-silvo-pastoral system of cultivation in Rainer Droste, *Möglichkeiten und Grenzen des Anbaus von Johannisbrot als Bestandteil eines traditionellen Anbausystems im Algarve* (Göttingen, 1993), p. 189.
72. As late as the 1990s, according to an Allensbach poll, the desire for "order" in the garden was far ahead of the ideal of the "natural garden" among German gardeners: Renate Köcher, *Garten & Glück* (Constance, 1999), p. 17 f.
73. A critical review of the scholarship on this question: David Harris, "Agricultural Origins, Beginnings and Transitions: The Quest Continues," *Antiquity* 68 (1994): 873–7. Harris's remark that the relevant literature makes only passing reference to animals (p. 876) is peculiar.
74. Jefferson Reid and Stephanie Whittlesey, *The Archaeology of Ancient Arizona* (Tucson, Ariz., 1997), p. 64.
75. Virgil: see note 62. Netting, *Smallholders* (note 6), pp. 13, 266, and elsewhere.
76. Markl, "Dynamik" (Chap. 1, note 18), p. 96.
77. Smith, *Emergence* (note 28), pp. 211 ff.; Karl W. Butzer, *Environment and Archaeology: An Ecological Approach to Prehistory* (London, 1971), p. 562; Diamond, *Guns* (Chap. 1, note 78), e.g., pp. 102 f., 112, 195.
78. Marija Gimbutas believes that the Indo-Europeans, too, were originally warlike steppe peoples, who – "restless and predatory" – conquered the peaceful farming cultures of Europe: "Die Indoeuropäer: Archäologische Problems (1963)," in *Die Urheimat der Indogermanen*, ed. Anton Scherer (Darmstadt, 1968), pp. 555 ff., 565.
79. Diamond, *Guns* (Chap. 1, note 78), p. 205.
80. Hansjörg Küster, "Mittelalterliche Eingriffe in Naturräume des Voralpenlandes," in *Umwelt in der Geschichte*, ed. Bernd Herrmann (Göttingen, 1989), p. 63 f.; on Tacitus's comment about the Germanic peoples, "Arva per annos mutant, et superest ager" [The tillage plots are changed from year to year, and there is land to spare], see Kerridge, *Common Fields* (note 6), p. 125 f.
81. Franz, *Quellen* (note 61), p. 9; Xavier de Planhol, *Kulturgeographische Grundlagen der islamischen Geschichte* (Zurich, 1975), p. 343.
82. Lynn White, Jr., *Medieval Technology and Social Change* (Oxford, 1962), pp. 41 ff.

83. Pliny, *Natural History*, trans. H. Rackham (Cambridge, Mass., 1950), 18.48, 17.3; *Propyläen Technikgeschichte* (Frankfurt a. M., 1991), vol. I, pp. 84 ff. (Helmuth Schneider) and 386 ff. (Dieter Hägermann); Joachim Hans Weniger, "Die Erfindung der Agrikultur," in Markl, *Natur* (Chap. 1, note 18), p. 183 f.; Gottfried Zirnstein, *Ökologie und Umwelt in der Geschichte* (Marburg, 1994), p. 221 f.

84. White, *Medieval Technology* (note 82); Bentzien, *Bauernarbeit* (note 57), p. 147.

85. Jacques Le Goff, *Das Hochmittelalter* (Frankfurt a. M., 1965), p. 277 f.; Roscher, *Ackerbau* (Chap. 1, note 29), p. 19. Stefan Ludwig Roth, *Schriften, Briefe, Zeugnisse* (Bucharest, 1971), p. 153; Braudel, *France* (Chap. 1, note 53), vol. II, p. 315. For Italy see Fumagalli, *Mensch und Umwelt* (note 70), pp. 46, 51; Roger Dion, *Essai sur la formation du paysage rural français* (Tours, 1934).

86. Jacubeit, *Schafhaltung* (Chap. 1, note 60), p. 102; Feio, *Alentejo* (note 7), p. 100, 122; Piers Blaikie and Harold Brookfield," Questions from History in the Mediterranean and Western Europe," in Blaikie and Brookfiled, *Degradation* (Chap. 1, note 80), p. 124.

87. Rudolf von Albertini, *European Colonial Rule, 1880–1940: The Impact of the West on India, South-East Asia, and Africa*, trans. John G. Williamson (Westport, Conn., 1982), pp. 354–5.

88. Walther Heissig, *Die Mongolen: Ein Volk sucht seine Geschichte* (Munich, 1978), p. 204. Ibn Khaldûn, *The Muqaddimah: An Introduction to History*, trans. Franz Rosenthal (Princeton, N.J., 1967), vol. I, pp. 177 ff., 302 f.

89. Campbell, *Human Ecology* (note 15), pp. 157–8; Planhol (note 81), pp. 8 f., 16 f.

90. Horst G. Mensching, "Die Verwüstung der Natur durch den Menschen in historischer Zeit: Das Problem der Desertifikation," in Markl, *Natur* (Chap. 1, note 18), p. 164 f.

91. Steven Runciman, *A History of the Crusades* (Cambridge, 1954), vol. III, p. 242.

92. H. F. Lamprey, "Pastoralism Yesterday and Today: The Over-Grazing Problem," in *Tropical Savannahs*, ed. François Bourlière (Amsterdam, 1983), pp. 645 ff.; Louise E. Sweet, "Camel Pastoralism in North Arabia and the Minimal Camping Unit," in Leeds and Vayda, *Man, Culture, and Animals* (note 33), pp. 129 ff.; Brent D. Shaw, *Environment and Society in Roman North Africa* (Aldershot, 1995), pp. 663 ff., 700 ff.; Marshall G. P. Hodgson, *The Venture of Islam* (Chicago, 1974), vol. II, p. 391; Planhol (note 81), pp. 50 f., 150 f., 214 ff. Nomads as the creators of the steppe: *The Secret History of the Mongols* leaves one with the impression that Mongolia was more forested back then than it is today – that the forest was not a foreign element to the Mongols; see *The Secret History of the Mongols*, trans. Igor de Rachewilt (Leiden, 2004), vol. I, pp. 2, 12, 22, 32, 58, 166, 195. According to one son, Genghis Khan and his companions had "the trees as their protective cover."

93. Neeladri Bhattacharya, "Pastoralists in a Colonial World," in Arnold and Guha, *Nature* (note 63), p. 50; Herodotus IV.46 f.

94. Criticism of ecological determinism in the interpretation of pastoralism: Hjort (Chap. 1, note 68); Karl Jettmar, "Die Bedeutung politischer Zentren für die Entstehung der Reiternomaden Zentralasiens," in *Die Nomaden in Geschichte und Gegenwart* (Berlin, 1981) (Veröffentlichungen des Museums für Völkerkunde Leipzig 33), pp. 49, 62; Melvyn Goldstein and Cynthia M. Beall, *The Nomads of Western Tibet* (London, 1991), pp. 69 ff. See also their book *The Changing World of Mongolia's Nomads* (Los Angeles, 1994), Introduction and the chapter on the *negdel*: until 1990, the "negdel" herders' collective kept the number of grazing animals fairly constant, even if it did so unintentionally by paralyzing individual initiative. The liberalization introduced since then has made the problem of overgrazing acute. E. Erdenijab: "The struggle between the limitations of pastures and the breeding of livestock is the fundamental conflict of the pastoral economy." Goldstein and Beall, "An Economic Assessment of Pasture Degradation," in *Culture and Environment in Inner Asia*, ed. Caroline Humphrey and David Sneath (Cambridge, 1996), vol. I, p. 189; *Fischer Weltgeschichte*, vol. XVI, p. 22 (Gavin Hambly). B. Tseren ("Traditional Pastoral Practice of the Oirat Mongols and Their Relationship with the Environment," in Humphrey and Sneath, vol. II, p. 153) says that the Mongols had "invisible fences" in their grazing ranges. And William of Rubruck said of the Tartars around 1250 that "every commander, according

to whether he has a greater or smaller number of men under him, is familiar with the limits of his pasturelands and where he ought to graze in summer and winter, in spring and autumn": William of Rubruck, *The Mission of Friar William of Rubruck*, trans. Peter Jackson (London, 1990), p. 72. Nevertheless, one should hardly picture these limitations as precise and stable over time, since there was no superordinate authority that could have enforced them. Ferdinand v. Richthofen, *China* (1877; reprint, Graz, 1971), vol. I, p. 45. In 1631/32, the Manchu emperor fixed the boundaries of the Mongol pasture land: Udo B. Barkmann, *Geschichte der Mongolei* (Bonn, 1999), p. 25.

95. In a conversation with the author (August, 3, 1999), Walther Heissig, a scholar of the Mongols, argued vehemently against the common notion of a mobile pastoralism without boundaries. Johannes Esser, *Lebensraum und soziale Entfremdung (am Beispiel der Oase Brezina, Algerien)* (Frankfurt a. M., 1984), pp. 97 ff.; McNeill, *Mountains* (Chap. 1, note 16), p. 279.

96. Bhattacharya, "Pastoralists" (note 93), pp. 64 ff.; Marvin Harris and Eric B. Ross, eds., *Death, Sex, and Fertility: Population Regulation in Preindustrial and Developing Societies* (New York, 1987), p. 45 f.; B. O. Gomboev, "The Structure and Process of Land-Use in Inner Asia," in Humphrey and Sneath, *Culture and Environment* (note 94), vol. I, p. 50; Rolf Herzog, "Auswirkung der letzten Dürre auf die Sahel-Nomaden," in *Nomaden in Geschichte* (note 94), p. 138; David Western and Virginia Finch, "Cattle and Pastoralism: Survival and Production in Arid Lands," *Human Ecology* 14 (1986): 89; Lamprey, "Pastoralism" (note 92), p. 658; critical response by Monique Mainguet, *Desertification* (Berlin, 1991), p. 13. According to F. Clark Howell (in *Cambridge History of Africa* [Cambridge, 1982], vol. I, p. 572) and Raymond Mauny (ibid., vol. II, pp. 272 ff.), scholarship today is dominated by the assumption that animal herds – which are documented here earlier than anywhere else in the Near East – have contributed substantially to the formation of the desert in the Sahara. Worster, in Merchant, *Major Problems* (note 56), p. 317 f. Thomas E. Lawrence, *Seven Pillars of Wisdom: The Complete 1922 Edition* (London, 2004), p. 16.

97. Grigorij F. Dachslejger, "Seßhaftwerdung von Nomaden," in *Nomaden in Geschichte* (note 94), p. 109 f. Israelites: Jacques Le Goff, "La désert-forêt dans l'occident médiéval," 19 (1980): 23: "In ancient Israel, the desert long maintained its renown vis-à-vis the city, the creation of Cain." Thomas Allsen (in *Cambridge History of China* [Cambridge, 1994], vol. VI, p. 328) goes so far as to say: "Indeed, pure nomadism is a hypothetical construct, not a social reality." The Romanian philosopher Lucian Blaga saw the Romanian essence embodied in the shepherds moving across the mountains (many Saxons of Transylvania have a similar, if less affectionate, view), while Nicolae Iorga, the most famous Romanian historian, wanted the Rumanians to be seen as a people of farmers devoted to "the heavy, sacred cultivation of the soil": Nicolae Iorga, *Schriften und Briefe* (Bucharest, 1978), pp. 47 ff. Tibet: James F. Downs and Robert B. Ekvall, "Animals and Social Types in the Exploitation of the Tibetan Plateau," in Leeds and Vayda, *Man, Culture, and Animals* (note 33), pp. 180 ff. On the farming element and the Tibetans' highly developed awareness of fertilization, see Rolf A. Stein, *Die Kultur Tibets* (Berlin, 1989), pp. 117 f., 132 ff. In the wealth of contemporary writings celebrating the spiritual harmony of Tibetan Buddhism with nature, this concrete and mundane aspect is usually not considered. Max Weber, *Ancient Judaism*, trans. Hans H. Gerth and Don Martindale (New York, 1952), pp. 154 ff., 189 f.

98. Bhattacharya, "Pastoralists" (note 93), p. 67. Since nomads were dependent on trade with agricultural regions, it makes little sense to attribute the downfall of many Central Asian irrigation cultures, whose ruins can be seen today in the desert, without closer examination to nomadic incursions, rather than the inherent ecological instability of irrigation agriculture in arid regions.

99. Josef H. Reichholf in *Süddeutsche Zeitung*, March 27/28, 1999. James Lovelock, *Das Gaia-Prinzip* (Frankfurt a. M., 1993), p. 233; see Robert Lawlor, *Voices of the First Day: Awakening in the Aboriginal Dreamtime* (Rochester, Vt., 1991), pp. 150–1, for whom this is an "appalling example" of a "one-eyed" vision of global ecological planning. Jeremy Rifkin, *Beyond Beef: The Rise and Fall of the Cattle Culture* (New York, 1992).

100. Garret Hardin, "The Tragedy of the Commons," *Science* 162 (1968): 1243–8. Discussion in John A. Baden and Douglas P. Noonan, eds., *Managing the Commons* (Bloomington, Ind., 1998 [1977]); Herman P. J. Cesar, *Control and Game Models of the Greenhouse Effect: Economic Essays on the Comedy and Tragedy of the Commons* (Berlin, 1994). The discussion is conducted largely on a theoretical level; historians are hardly involved at all.

101. Johann Nepomuk v. Schwerz, *Beschreibung der Landwirtschaft in Westfalen* (1836) (reprint, Münster-Hiltrup, no date), p. 321; similar reports from France: Josef Kulischer, *Allgemeine Wirtschaftsgeschichte des Mittelalters und der Neuzeit* (Munich, 1965), pp. 53 ff. Reiner Prass, *Reformprogramm und bäuerliche Interessen: Die Auflösung der tradititionellen Gemeindeökonomie im südlichen Niedersachsen* (Göttingen, 1997), p. 93; Rainer Beck, *Unterfinning: Ländliche Welt vor Anbruch der Moderne* (Munich, 1993), p. 85. Stefan Brakensiek, *Agrarreform und ländliche Gesellschaft: Die Privatisierung der Marken in Nordwestdeutschland 1750–1850* (Paderborn, 1991): although he states (p. 45) that "the commons were ecologically finished," he notes (p. 319) that the heath commons, when they were planted, soon yielded no less than the old agricultural fields. Johann Moritz Schwager in *Westfälischer Anzeiger* 1409 (1801), p. 105: "On heaths where the animals, driven out too often, used to fight for every sparse blade of grass, there now waved rich harvests of grain." If that was the case, the soil could not possibly have been destroyed! Reinhold Tüxen, *Die Haselünner Kuhweide: Die Pflanzengesellschaften einer mittelalterlichen Gemeinweide* (Göttingen, 1974) (*Mitteilungen der floristisch-soziologischen Arbeitsgemeinschaft in Niedersachsen*, N. F., no. 17).

102. A. T. Grove and Oliver Rackham, *The Nature of Mediterranean Europe: An Ecological History* (New Haven, Conn., 2001), p. 88; Netting, *Smallholders* (note 6), p. 173, note; K. William Kapp, *Soziale Kosten der Marktwirtschaft* (Frankfurt a. M., 1988 [orig. 1950]), p. 73; Gustav Engel, *Die Westfalen* (Bielefeld, 1987), p. 196; Jon Mathieu, *Bauern und Bären: Eine Geschichte des Unterengadins von 1650 bis 1800* (Chur, 1987), p. 39; Bätzing, *Alpen* (Chap. 1, note 54), pp. 46, 22 f. (protection against erosion); Winfried Schenk, *Waldnutzung, Waldzustand und regionale Entwicklung in vorindustrieller Zeit im mittleren Deutschland* (Stuttgart, 1996), p. 297 f.; Andreas Ineichen, *Innovative Bauern: Einhegungen, Bewässerung und Waldteilungen im Kanton Luzern im 16. u. 17. Jh.* (Lucerne, 1996), pp. 68 ff., 74.

103. Radkau and Schäfer, *Holz* (Chap. 1, note 50), p. 54 f.; Margaret A. McKean, "The Japanese Experience with Scarcity: Management of Traditional Common Lands," in *Environmental History: Critical Inssues in Comparative Perspective*, ed. Kendall E. Bailes (Lanham, 1985) pp. 358, 362 (one of the few historical studies that deal explicitly with Hardin). Martin Stuber, *'Wir halten eine fette Mahlzeit, denn mit dem Ei verzehren wir die Henne': Konzepte nachhaltiger Waldnutzung im Kanton Bern 1750–1880* (Zurich, 1997), p. 167; Jeremias Gotthelf, *Die Käserei in der Vehfreude* (Basel, 1978 [orig. 1850]), p. 133; François Walter, *Bedrohliche und bedrohte Natur: Umweltgeschichte der Schweiz seit 1800* (Zurich, 1996), p. 58 f. Johann Stehrer, "Der Wandel in der Almwirtschaft," in *Strobl am Wolfgangsee*, ed. Johann Stehrer (Strobl, 1998), p. 407. Ibid., p. 393 (Johannes Lang): The farmers in Strobl always had a prescribed number of animals for the mountain pasture, and this number hardly changed from the late Middle Ages to the nineteenth century.

104. Roscher, *Nationalökonomik* (Chap. 1, note 29), p. 351; Bhattacharya, "Pastoralists" (note 93), pp. 49 ff.; Guha, *Unquiet Woods* (Chap. 1, note 12), p. 56 f.; Bruce Rich, *Mortgaging the Earth* (Boston, 1994), p. 47 f. In China, Mark Elvin sees in the absence of any counterpart to the European "common lands" an element of instability, namely the lack of ecological reserves: "The environmental history of China: an agenda of ideas," *Asian Studies Review* 14 (1990): 48.

105. Albrecht Thaer, *Grundsätze der rationellen Landwirtschaft*, 9th ed. (Berlin, 1837), vol. I, pp. 85 ff.

106. B. H. Slicher van Bath, *The Agrarian History of Western Europe A.D. 500–1850* (London, 1963), p. 245; Julius Adolph Stöckhardt, *Chemische Feldpredigten für deutsche Landwirthe*, 2. Abt. (Leipzig, 1856), p. 185.

107. Georg Niemeier and Willi Faschenmacher, *Plaggenböden: Beiträge zu ihrer Genetik und Typologie* (Münster, 1939) (Westf. Forschungen 2 H. 1), pp. 32 ff.; Brakensiek, *Agrarreform*

(note 101), p. 43 f.; Christopher Smout, *Nature Contested: Environmental History in Scotland and Northern England since 1600* (Edinburgh, 2000), p. 70. Nineteenth-century accounts reports that in heath farms, the procurement of plaggen and litter consumed half of all manual and draught labor: Hermann Cordes et al., *Naturschutzgebiet Lüneburger Heide* (Bremen, 1997), p. 69. Amtmann Tiemann of Brackwede, who was eager to get the Alpine farmers to stop cutting plaggen sod, described this work as terrible drudgery and assured his readers that the word "plaggen" was derived from "plague": Horst Wasgindt and Hans Schumacher, *Bielefeld Senne* (Bielefeld, 1989), vol. II, p. 41; Werner Franke et al., *Wald im Emsland* (Sögel, 1981), p. 50.

108. Heinz Ellenberg, *Bauernhaus und Landschaft in ökologischer und historischer Sicht* (Stuttgart, 1990), p. 127; Karl-Ernst Behre, "Zur mittelalterlichen Plaggenwirtschaft in Nordwestdeutschland und angrenzenden Gebieten nach botanischen Untersuchungen," in *Untersuchungen zur eisenzeitlichen und frühmittelalterlichen Flur in Mitteleuropa*, ed. Heinrich Beck et al. (Göttingen, 1980), pp. 32 ff., 42. Schwerz, *Beschreibung der Landwirtschaft* (note 101), pp. 121 ff., 209 ff.; Dieter Brosius et al., *Die Lüneburger Heide* (Hannover, 1984), pp. 19, 28.

109. Liebig, *Briefe* (Chap. 1, note 26), p. 474, letter 46.

110. Walter Kremser, *Niedersächsische Forstgeschichte* (Rotenburg, 1990), pp. 769 f., 781; Pott and Hüppe, *Hudelandschaften* (Chap. 1, note 51), pp. 50, 69; Vandana Shiva, *Staying Alive: Women, Ecology, and Development* (London, 1988), p. 65 f.

111. The saying about rich fathers and poor sons was also quoted as German peasant wisdom in the United States around 1800: James T. Lemon, *The Best Poor Man's Country* (Baltimore, Md., 1972), p. 173. Thorkild Kjaergaard, *The Danish Revolution 1500–1800: An Ecohistorical Interpretation* (Cambridge, 1994), pp. 49 ff.; Schwerz, *Beschreibung* (note 101), pp. 60 f., 96; Stöckhardt, *Chemische Feldpredigten* (note 106), p. 65; Carl Sprengel, *Die Lehre vom Dünger* (Leipzig, 1845), pp. 347, 365 f. "Goldgrube": Hamm, *Landwirtschaft* (note 56), p. 170.

112. Steven Stoll, *Larding the Lean Earth: Soil and Society in 19th-Century America* (New York, 2002), pp. 150 ff.

113. Gertrud Schröder-Lembke, "Die Hausväterliteratur als agrargeschichtliche Quelle," *Zeitschrift für Agrargeschichte und Agrarsoziologie* 1 (1953): 115.

114. Niklas Luhmann, *Ecological Communication*, trans. with an introduction by John Bednarz, Jr. (Oxford, 1989), p. 32.

115. Roy A. Rappaport, *Pigs for the Ancestors: Ritual in the Ecology of a New Guinea People* (New Haven, Conn., 1968); Reinhardt, *Nutzpflanzen* (note 63), pp. 140 ff.; James G. Frazer, *The Golden Bough: A Study in Magic and Religion* (London, 1978 [1922]), p. 147; Peter E. Stüben, "Pioniermission und die Zerstörung indigener Tabus: Folgen für die Umwelt?" in *Seelenfischer: Mission, Stammesvölker und Ökologie*, ed. Peter E. Stüben (Gießen, 1994), p. 193: "At least they have lost their fear of evil spirits – but their trees are gone, as well." Tsui Yenhu, in Humphrey and Sneath, *Culture and Environment* (note 94), vol. II, p. 7.

116. Axel Michaels, "Sakralisierung als Naturschutz? Heilige Bäume und Wälder in Nepal," in *Natur-Bilder: Wahrnehmungen von Natur und Umwelt in der Geschichte*, ed. Rolf-Peter Sieferle and Helga Breuninger (Frankfurt/New York, 1999), pp. 117, 124 ff.

117. Harris, *Cannibals* (Chap. 1, note 47), p. 89.

118. Stein, *Kultur Tibets* (note 97), pp. 293–6.

119. Tacitus, *The Annals*, trans. John Jackson, in Tacitus, vol. III, *Histories IV–V, Annals I–III* (Cambridge, Mass., 1969), p. 379. Klaus Grewe, *Licht am Ende des Tunnel: Planung und Trassierung im antiken Tunnelbau* (Mainz, 1998).

120. Duerr: *Der Spiegel* 50 (1996): 223 f. Clifford Geertz, "Religion as a Cultural System," in *Anthropological Approaches to the Study of Religion*, ed. M. Banton (London, 1966), pp. 35, 36. In a conversation with the author (November 12, 1998), the ethnologist Ute Luig emphasized the "enormous pragmatism" of Africans in their handling of norms: even sacred groves can be cut down if needed once certain rituals had been performed.

121. Frazer, *Golden Bough* (note 115), pp. vii, 389 ff., 149 f., 113.

122. Ibid., pp. 148 ff.; Schubert, *Alltag im Mittelalter* (Chap. 1, note 38), p. 101; Albert Hauser, *Wald und Feld in der alten Schweiz* (Zurich, 1972), p. 79 f.; Schele and Freidel, *Maya* (Chap. 1, note 71), p. 84 f.

123. Roy Pascal, *The German Sturm und Drang* (Manchester, 1953), p. 214 (on Shaftesbury); McNeill, *Mountains* (Chap. 1, note 16), p. 272.

124. Glacken, *Traces* (Chap. 1, note 25), p. 14.

125. Oswald Spengler, *The Decline of the West*, trans. C. F. Atkinson (New York, 1928), vol. II, pp. 89–90. Herbert Kühn, Erwachen und Aufstieg der Menschheit (Frankfurt a. M., 1966), p. 257; Ferdinand Herrmann, "Die religiös-geistige Welt des Bauerntums," in *Handbuch der Urgeschichte*, ed. Karl J. Narr (Bern, 1975), vol. II, pp. 650, 662.

126. Hahn, *Haustiere* (note 49), p. 101: Walter Heissig, "Der 'Dank an die Mutter' und seine mongolischen Varianten," in *Memoriae munusculum*, ed. Klaus Röhrborn et al. (Wiesbaden, 1994), p. 65. Erich Neumann, *Die große Mutter* (Darmstadt, 1957), p. 229; Walter Heissig, ed., *Dschingis Khan: Ein Weltreich zu Pferde* (Cologne, 1981), p. 42; Bauer, *China* (Chap. 1, note 39), p. 211.

127. Sam D. Gill, *Mother Earth* (Chicago, 1987); Karl-Heinz Kohl, "Der postmoderne Wilde," *Psychologie heute* (Feb. 1998): 60 f.; Bob Blaisdell, ed., *Great Speeches by Native Americans* (Mineola, N.Y., 2000), p. 166. William Arrowsmith and Michael Korth, *Die Erde ist unsere Mutter: Die großen Reden der Indianerhäuptlinge* (Munich, 1995), p. 51, similarly pp. 30 ff.

128. Eugen Drewermann, *Der tödliche Fortschritt*, 5th ed. (Freiburg, 1991), pp. 74, 160 ff.; Blaisdell, *Great Speeches* (note 127), p. 41. According to the New Testament scholar Andreas Lindemann, the supposed Essene hymn to Mother Earth one finds repeatedly in the ecological literature (e.g. in Peter-Cornelius Mayer-Tasch, ed., *Natur denken: Eine Genealogie der ökologischen Idee*, I [Frankfurt a. M., 1991], pp. 128 ff.), is also a forgery.

129. This is also emphasized by Peter Gerlitz, *Mensch und Natur in den Weltreligionen* (Darmstadt, 1998), p. xi, even though he assembles everything that could create the impression that religion contains an ecological message.

130. Thomas, *Man and the Natural World* (note 49), p. 154; Glacken, *Traces* (Chap. 1, note 25), p. 197; Brown, *Augustine* (note 61), p. 143; Mayer-Tasch, *Natur denken* (note 127), p. 141.

131. *Die Religion in Geschichte und Gegenwart*, 2nd ed. (Tübingen, 1931), vol. V, col. 1788.

132. Manfred Höfler, *Wald- und Baumkult in Beziehung zur Volksmedicin Oberbayerns* (Munich, 1892), p. 3 f.; Thomas, *Man and the Natural World* (note 49); Glacken, *Traces* (Chap. 1, note 25), pp. 214 ff.; Werner Müller, *Geliebte Erde* (Bonn, 1982), p. 35; Helmut Feld, *Franziskus von Assisi und seine Bewegung* (Darmstadt, 1994), p. 224. Opinions diverge on how representative or unique Saint Francis was in his brotherly gesture toward nature. Henry Thode, *Franz von Assisi* (Vienna, 1934), p. 149: "The old biographers are inexhaustible in their stories of the tender love with which Francis embraced all animals as God's creatures." Such views were not foreign even to Luther, as when he takes the side of birds hounded by man in his tractate: "Klage der Vögel an D. Martinum Luthern über Wolfgang Siberger seinen Diener." However, he excludes the sparrow as a pest. Christoph Gasser, "Vogelschutz zwischen Ökonomie und Ökologie: Das Beispiel der Sperlingsverfolgungen (17.–20. Jh.)," in *Mensch und Tier* (Marburg 1991) (Hessische Blätter für Volks- und Kulturforschung N. F. 27), p. 42.

133. Glacken, *Traces* (Chap. 1, note 25), pp. 205 f., 379 ff.

134. René Grousset, *Die Reise nach Westen oder wie Hsüan Tsang den Buddhismus nach China holte* (Cologne, 1986), p. 109; Planhol, *Kulturgeographische Grundlagen* (note 81), pp. 8 f., 39 f., 51 f., 74 f., 90 f. For an opposing view Peter Christensen, *The Decline of Iranshahr* (Copenhagen, 1993), pp. 2, 10, 12, 186, 324. Clifford Geertz, *Islam Observed: Religious Developments in Morocco and Indonesia* (Chicago, 1971). The distance between humans and animals appears to be even greater in Islam than it is in Christian culture: Herbert Eisenstein, "Mensch und Tier im Islam," in Münch, *Tiere* (note 52), p. 137 and elsewhere. On laborious modern attempts to ecologize Islam see Poul Pederen in *Asian Perceptions of Nature: A Critical Approach*, ed. Ole Bruun and Arne Kalland (Richmond, Va., 1995), p. 263.

135. Gadgil and Guha, *Fissured Land* (Chap. 1, note 48), pp. 81 f., 103 f.
136. Udo B. Barkmann, *Landnutzung und historische Rahmenbedingungen in der Äußeren Mongolei/Mongolischen Volksrepublik (1691–1940)* (Osaka, 2000) (Senri Ethnological Reports 17), pp. 51 ff.
137. Redemption of humanity: Tenzin Choegyal, the brother of the Dalai Lama, made this point emphatically in a conversation with the author when asked about elements of environmental awareness in Buddhism (November 23, 1996). He added that it was a waste of time to talk about tree cults. He evidently felt that the ecological interpretation of Buddhism was a western fad. Rich, *Mortgaging the Earth* (Chap. 1, note 7), pp. 15–17; David Feeny, "Agricultural Expansion and Forest Depletion in Thailand, 1900–1975," in *World Deforestation in the 20th Century,* ed. John F. Richards and Richard P. Tucker (Durham, N.C., 1988), pp. 112 ff. Leslie E. Sponsel and Poranee Natadecha, "Buddhism, Ecology, and Forests in Thailand: Past, Present, and Future," in *Changing Tropical Forests,* ed. John Dargavel et al. (Canberra, 1988), pp. 305 ff. It would appear that Buddhism as an ecological inspiration is only a very recent phenomenon.
138. Donald Quataert in *An Economic and Social History of the Ottoman Empire,* ed. Donald Quataert and Halil Inalcik (Cambridge, 1994), p. 790; Graham E. Clarke, "Thinking through Nature in Highland Nepal," in Bruun and Kalland, *Asian Perceptions of Nature* (note 134), p. 101.
139. Kristine Kern, "Politische Kultur und Umweltpolitik. Amerikanische Erfahrungen und europäische Perspektiven," in *Europas Kulturen und ihr Umgang mit der Natur, Insel Mainau 1999* (= Mainauer Gespräche 14), p. 39. Some references in this direction can also be found in Mark Stoll, *Protestantism, Capitalism, and Nature in America* (Albuquerque, N.M., 1997).

3. WATER, FORESTS, AND POWER

1. Schubert, *Alltag im Mittelalter* (Chap. 1, note 38), p. 45.
2. Anne-Marie Cocula-Vaillières, *Un fleuve et des hommes: Les gens de la Dordogne au XVIIIe siècle* (Paris, 1981), p. 55. James C. Scott, *Seeing like a State: How Certain Schemes to Improve the Human Condition Have Failed* (New Haven, Conn., 1998).
3. Ian Burton et al., *The Environment as Hazard* (New York, 1978), p. 2.
4. Garcilaso de la Vega, *The Incas: The Royal Commentaries of the Inca,* ed. Alain Gheerbrant (New York, 1964), p. 156; we are told something similar in the other "classic" account of the Inca empire: *The Incas of Pedro de Cieza de León,* ed. Victor W. v. Hagen (Norman, Okla., 1959), p. 15.
5. Pierre-Étienne Will, "Un cycle hydraulique en Chine: La province du Hubei du XVIe au XIXe siècles," *Bulletin de l'École Française d'Extrême-Orient* 68 (1980), p. 267 f. In ancient China, water wisdom reflected back upon political and worldly wisdom. In the sixth century B.C.E., Zi Chan, the prime minister of Zhen, dismissed a suggestion to suppress criticism of the government by invoking an argument from hydraulic engineering: "It was like blocking a stream with a dam, behind which the pressure grew until it was swept away. It was better to make small breaches and to let the water trickle through": Caroline Blunden and Mark Elvin, *China: A Cultural Atlas* (Oxford, 1983), p. 64.
6. Tyrrell, *True Garden of the Gods* (Chap. 1, note 50), 152.
7. Hans W. Schumann, *Der historische Buddha* (Cologne, 1982), p. 136 f. Hardly ever wars over water: J. A. Allen, "'Virtual Water': An Essential Element in Stabilizing the Political Economies of the Middle East," in *Transformations of Middle Eastern Natural Environments: Legacies and Lessons,* ed. Jeff Albert et al. (New Haven, Conn., 1998). Even a book on "water wars" contains the observation that "history still reveals a fear of full-scale wars fought over water": Diane Raines Ward, *Water Wars: Drought, Flood, Folly, and the Politics of Thirst* (New York, 2002), p. 195; V. O. Kluchevsky, *A History of Russia,* trans. C. J. Hogarth (New York, 1960), vol. V, Appendix, p. 248.

8. He Bochuan, *China on the Edge: The Crisis of Ecology and Development* (San Francisco, 1991), p. 22; Thomas and Middleton, *Desertification* (Chap. 1, note 83), p. 18; a similar argument was already advanced by Ferdinand v. Richthofen, *China* (Chap. 2, note 94), p. 124 f. The climate hypothesis of Ellsworth Huntington, mentioned by Gavin Hambly in *Fischer Weltgeschichte*, vol. XVI, p. 15, is considered outdated. Peter Christensen, "Middle Eastern Irrigation: Legacies and Lessons," in Albert et al., *Transformations* (note 7). That irrigation systems in arid regions damage areas located downstream was, in principle, evident and well known. In 1558 Anthony Jenkins wrote about Chwaresm: "The water that serves this entire land is drawn from the Oxus river through ditches, to the great detriment of said river, for which reason it does not flow into the Caspian Sea, as it used to, and this entire land will shortly be destroyed and become a wilderness for lack of water, when the Oxus river dries up": Edgar Knobloch, *Turkestan*, 4th ed. (Munich, 1999), p. 125 f.

9. Carl Troll, "Qanat-Bewässerung in der Alten und Neuen Welt," *Mitteilungen der Österreichischen Geographischen Gesellschaft* 105 (1963): 255–72; Michael Bonine, "Qanats and Rural Societies: Sustainable Agricultur and Irrigation, Cultures in Contemporary Iran," in *Canals and Communities: Small-Scale Irrigation Systems*, ed. Jonathan B. Mabry (Tucson, Ariz., 1996), pp. 183–209 (pp. 187 ff.: decline only in the 1960s and 1970s; apparent revival under the Islamic Republic); Norman Smith, *Man and Water: A History of Hydro-Technology* (London, 1976), pp. 69 ff.; Thomas F. Glick, *Irrigation and Society in Medieval Valencia* (Cambridge, Mass., 1970), pp. 182 ff. Günther Garbrecht, *Wasser: Vorrat, Bedarf und Nutzung in Geschichte und Gegenwart* (Reinbek, 1985), pp. 45 ff. Christensen, *Decline of Iranshahr* (Chap. 2, note 134), p. 122: thanks to the Qanats, agriculture on the Iranian Plateau was far more resilient than in Mesopotamia, even though the Qanats, too, were vulnerable to disruption and promoted the spread of malaria.

10. Horst G. Mensching, *Desertifikation* (Darmstadt, 1990), pp. 46 ff.; Hansjörg Küster, "Technik und Gesellschaft in frühen Kulturen der Menschheit," in *Technik und Kultur* (Düsseldorf, 1993), vol. X, p. 49 f.

11. Mensching, *Desertifikation* (note 10), p. 84; Garbrecht, *Wasser* (note 9), p. 74; Schwerz, *Beschreibung* (Chap. 2, note 101), p. 331. I would like to thank Hans-Karl Barth (Paderborn) for important pointers on the problem of drainage.

12. Ian Stone, *Canal Irrigation in British India* (Cambridge, 1984), p. 138. Ellsworth Huntington reported that between 1884 and 1904, a Chinese governor (Amban) on three successive occasions had cities with irrigation networks constructed in the Tarim basin, which failed every time within a few short years from salinization. This is how little even a country with China's hydraulic tradition was set up to deal with the problem of salinization. Huntington himself was so fixated on his theory of climate change that even these instances never made him think that the historical desertification processes he observed in wide sections of the globe could have been, in part, anthropogenic in origin. Instead, he also enthusiastically embraces the idea of irrigating the deserts of Central Asia! Ellsworth Huntington, *Across Central Asia* (Travel account of 1905) (reprint, New Delhi, 1996), pp. 266 ff., 237 f. Zhang Li (Xi'an), who has been studying the environmental history of the region around Urumchi, confirmed to the author that the problem of salinization was traditionally neglected in China.

13. Glick, *Irrigation and Society* (note 9), p. 22 f.

14. R. W. Dennell, "Archaeology and the Study of Desertification," in Spooner and Mann, *Desertification* (Chap. 1, note 56), p. 54.

15. Karl A. Wittfogel, *Oriental Despotism* (New Haven, Conn., 1957), p. 257.

16. Gary L. Ulmen, *The Science of Society: Toward an Understanding of the Life and Work of Karl August Wittfogel* (The Hague, 1978), p. 289: On August 7, 1951, Wittfogel testified before the Internal Security Subcommittee (the so-called McCarran Committee) of the U.S. Senate that "a consistent pro-Soviet pattern had developed" in the work of the prominent American East Asian expert Owen Lattimore. In so doing he provided McCarthy ammunition for his contention that crypto-Communists in influential positions within the American

government had caused the loss of China to the Communists; see the best-seller by John T. Flynn at the time, *The Lattimore Story* (New York, 1953). Of course it was absurd to attribute Mao's victory to individual American experts. However, Udo B. Barkmann (Berlin), once a leading Mongolist in East Germany, has repeatedly assured me that Wittfogel's statement was entirely true.

17. One extreme example: in his 450-page opus on the "Asiatic mode of production," Lawrence Krader, Wittfogel's assistant from 1948–51, devotes only a single – though page-long – footnote to his former teacher, whose invisible presence pervades the entire work: *The Asiatic Mode of Production* (Assen, 1975), pp. 115 ff., note. A broad survey of the discussion around the world in Anne M. Bailey and Josep R. Llobera, eds., *The Asiatic Mode of Production* (London, 1981). "We all copied from you," Rudi Dutschke repeatedly confessed to Wittfogel when he visited him in person in 1979 (*taz*, May 30, 1988). On Wittfogel's political conversion and the reception of his theory see Joachim Radkau, "Der Emigrant als Warner und Renegat: K. A. Wittfogels Dämonisierung der 'asiatischen Produktionsweise,'" *Exilforschung: Internationales Jahrbuch*, vol. I (Munich, 1983): 73–94.

18. Peter C. Perdue, *Exhausting the Earth: State and Peasant in Hunan, 1500–1850* (Cambridge, Mass., 1987), p. 5: "Paradoxically, as Western and Japanese scholars have turned away from Oriental Despotism, Chinese scholars have turned toward it." On the influence of the later Wittfogel on the ecologization of American Anthropology, in part in a critical light, see Barry L. Isaac, "AMP (Asiatic Mode of Production), HH (Hydraulic Hypothesis) & OD (Oriental Despotism): Some Comments," *Research in Economic Anthropology*, Suppl. 7 (1993): 464 and elsewhere; Mark Elvin to the author, October 6, 1999.

19. Donatella Mazzeo and Chiara Silvi Antonini, *Angkor* (Wiesbaden, 1974), pp. 59 ff., 62 ff., 173; Jan Myrdal, *Kunst und Imperialismus am Beispiel Angkor* (Munich, 1973), p. 95; *Fischer Weltgeschichte*, vol. XVIII (Frankfurt a. M., 1965), pp. 226 ff. (John Villiers); John Audric, *Angkor and the Khmer Empire* (London, 1972): Angkor's fate as a warning against the ecological risks of large-scale irrigation in the tropics. Teotihuacán: Hanns J. Prem and Ursula Dyckerhoff, *Das alte Mexiko* (Munich, 1986), p. 149 and elsewhere; Donald W. Kurtz, "The Economics of Urbanization and State Formation at Teotihuacan," *Current Anthropology* 28 (1987): 329–53 (controversy between economists and ecologists). Susan H. Lees, "Hydraulic Development as a Process of Response," *Human Ecology* 2 (1974): 159–75 (central guidance of hydraulic engineering in the Oaxaca valley as a response to signs of ecological crisis). William Doolittle, *Canal Irrigation in Prehistoric Mexico: The Sequence of Technological Change* (Austin, Tex., 1990), p. 151. Douglass C. North, *Structure and Change in Economic History* (New York, 1981), pp. 26, 117 note, takes Wittfogel's "hydraulic society" as a paradigm for the achievements of institutions in economic history, though he posits an excessive harmony between hydraulic institutions and natural conditions.

20. Harris, *Cannibals and Kings* (Chap. 1, note 47), pp. 155 ff., 161 ff.

21. Herodotus I.193; Garbrecht, *Wasser* (note 9), p. 62; J. H. Breasted, *A History of Egypt* (London, 1950), p. 5; Julian Rzóska, *Euphrates and Tigris, Mesopotamian Ecology and Destiny* (The Hague, 1980), pp. 44, 52; Karl W. Butzer, *Early Hydraulic Civilization in Egypt: A Study in Cultural Ecology* (Chicago, 1976), p. 109 and elsewhere.

22. Butzer, *Early Hydraulic Civilization* (note 21), pp. 12 ff., 47; Herodotus II.99; Lutz Knörnschild, *Zur Geschichte der Nilwassernutzung in der ägyptischen Landwirtschaft von den Anfängen bis zur Gegenwart* (Frankfurt a. M., 1993), p. 58, note 63.

23. Herodotus II.13–14; Adrian Balbi, *Allgemeine Erdbeschreibung*, 8th ed. (Vienna, 1893), vol. I, pp. 1049 ff.

24. Knörnschild, *Nilwassernutzung* (note 22), pp. 60 ff., 64, 259; Butzer, *Early Hydraulic Civilization* (note 22), pp. 28, 33, 82; Breasted, *History of Egypt* (note 22), p. 195; Herodotus II.108; Wolfgang Schenkel, *Die Bewässerungsrevolution im alten Ägypten* (Mainz, 1978), p. 67; in the end, Schenkel questions the validity of the idea of "revolution" (p. 73 f.).

25. Herodotus II.149; Garbrecht, *Wasser* (note 9), pp. 80 ff.; *Fischer Weltgeschichte*, vol. II (Frankfurt a. M., 1965), pp. 337 ff. (Jean Vercoutter); William Tarn, *Hellenistic Civilisation* (New

York, 1961), p. 183. During the time of colonial planning of canals and dammed lakes, the experience of ancient Egypt was reinterpreted: not the Nile as such, but the "dam basins and canals" had produced Egypt's wealth! *Prometheus* 23 (1912): 406.

26. William Willcox, *Sixty Years in the East* (Edinburgh, 1935), pp. 156, 37; J. Donald Hughes, *An Environmental History of the World* (London, 2001), pp. 162 ff.

27. Clive Ponting, *A Green History of the World* (London, 1991), p. 43 f., 61, 69 ff.; Thorkild Jacobsen and Robert M. Adams, "Salt and Silt in Ancient Mesopotamian, Agriculture: Progressive Changes in Soil Salinity and Sedimentation Contributed to the Breakup of Past Civilizations," *Science* 128 (1958): 1251–58; Adnan Hardan, "Archaeological Methods for Dating of Soil Salinity in the Mesopotamian Plain," in *Paleopedology*, ed. Dan H. Yaalon (Jerusalem, 1971), p. 181 f.

28. Jacobsen and Adams, "Salt and Silt" (note 27), p. 1252; Hardan, "Archeaological Methods" (note 27), pp. 181 ff., 186; Hans Helbaek, "Ecological Effects of Irrigation in Ancient Mesopotamia," *Iraq* 22 (1960): 194 ff.; Herbert Sauren, "Topographie der Provinz Umma nach den Urkunden der Zeit der III. Dynastie von Ur, Teil I: Kanäle und Bewässerungsanlagen," dissertation, University of Heidelberg, 1966, pp. 66 ff.; Smith, *Man and Water* (note 9), p. 10.

29. Robert McC. Adams, "Historic Patterns of Mesopotamian Irrigation Agriculture," in *Irrigation's Impact on Society*, ed. Theodore E. Downing and McGuire Gibson (Tucson, Ariz., 1974), pp. 1–19, esp. p. 3 f.; by contrast, indications of irrigation systems on a larger scale in the Middle Assyrian period in Hartmut Kühne, "The Effects of Irrigation Agriculture: Bronze and Iron Age Habitation along the Khabur, Eastern Syria," in *Man's Role in the Shaping of the Eastern Mediterranean Landscape*, ed. S. Bottema et al. (Rotterdam, 1990), p. 21 and elsewhere. Garbrecht, *Wasser* (note 9), p. 72, on "giant canals" of the Chaldeans. Christensen, *Decline of Iranshahr* (Chap. 2, note 134), pp. 4, 19 f.

30. Mohammed El Faiz, *L'agronomie de la Mésopotamie antique: Analyse du "Livre de l'agriculture nabatéenne" de Qûtâmâ* (Leiden, 1995), pp. 78 ff., 97.

31. Christensen, *Decline of Iranshahr* (Chap. 2, note 134), pp. 73, 104, 252 ff.; Adams, "Salt and Silt" (note 29), pp. 7 ff.; Rzóska, *Euphrates and Tigris* (note 21), p. 59; Andrew W. Watson, *Agricultural Innovation in the Early Islamic World: The Diffusion of Crops and Farming Techniques, 700–1100* (Cambridge, 1983), p. 104, 108, 125, 140; Marshall G. S. Hodgson, *The Venture of Islam* (Chicago, 1974), vol. I, pp. 483 ff.

32. Homer, *Iliad* XXI.257 f. Virgil, *Georgics* I. V.108 f. praises the man who brings the river to the parched fields through canals. V.269 f.: "No scruples ever forbade us to guide down the rills." Michel Sivignon, *La Grèce sans monuments* (Paris, 1978), pp. 37, 110, 248; Gilbert Argoud, "Le problème de l'eau dans la Grèce antique," in *L'eau et les hommes en Méditerranée*, published by CNRS (Paris, 1987), pp. 205 ff. Oliver Rackham and Jennifer Moody, *The Making of the Cretan Landscape* (Manchester, 1996), pp. 210 ff.

33. Gudrun Vögler, *Öko-Griechen und grüne Römer?* (Düsseldorf, 1997), p. 83 f.; Werner Eck, "Organisation und Administration der Wasserversorgung Roms," in *Sextus Iulius Frontinus: Wasserversorgung im antiken Rom* (Munich, 1983), pp. 63 f., 71.

34. Before the ecological era, the Indus culture of Mohenjo-Daro and Harappa was already considered a prime example of a culture that was presumably destroyed by undermining its own ecological basis. "Mohenjo-Daro was wearing out its landscape" was a classic statement by Mortimer Wheeler, the founding father of Indus archaeology (quoted in J. V. Thirgood, *Man and the Mediterranean Forest* [London, 1981], p. 63). For James Lovelock, the Indus civilization was probably the best historical example of how a culture destroyed itself by cutting down its forests: *Gaia: The Practical Science of Planetary Medicine* (London, 1991), p. 157. However, more recent paleo-botanical studies found no significant difference in the vegetation of that region between the Harappa period and today! See Gregory L. Possehl, ed., *Harappan Civilization* (Warminster, 1982), p. 225 f.; also pp. 417 ff.: Robert H. Dyson, "Paradigm Changes in the Study of the Indus Civilization." Is this a warning that we should be cautious about theories of deforestation that are derived from preconceived models? Or

are the – necessarily limited – findings of pollen researchers misleading, especially since the Indus civilization, according to what we know today, extended over an area of a million square kilometers?

35. Régis Ambroise et al., *Paysages de terrasses* (Aix-en-Provence, 1989), p. 11; similarly J. E. Spencer and G. A. Hale, "The Origin, Nature, and Distribution of Agricultural Terracing," *Pacific Viewpoint* 2 (1961): 1 f. Tuscany: scholars today are puzzling over the motivation behind such a soil-destroying method: was it perhaps the horror of standing water, of malaria? Henri Desplanques, "I paesaggi collinari tosco-umbro-marchigiani," *I paesaggi umani* (Milan, 1977), p. 104.

36. Rackham and Moody, *Cretan Landscape* (note 32), pp. 144, 145: "Terraces are the greatest outstanding problem in Greek landscape archaeology." Similarly Rackham and Moody, "Terraces," in *Agriculture in Ancient Greece*, ed. Berrit Wells (Stockholm, 1992), pp. 123–33. Lin Foxhall, "Feeling the Earth Move: Cultivation Techniques on Steep Slopes in Classical Antiquity," in *Human Landscapes in Classical Antiquity: Environment and Culture*, ed. Graham Shipley and John Salmon (London, 1996), pp. 44 ff. Eberhard Zangger, "Neolithic to Present Soil Erosion in Greece," in *Past and Present Soil Erosion*, ed. Martin Bell and John Boardman (Oxford, 1992), pp. 144 ff., 158. Tjeerd H. van Andel and Curtis Runnels, *Beyond the Acropolis: A Rural Greek Past* (Stanford, Calif., 1987), p. 145. More recent studies have found ancient terraces for olive tree cultivation at least in Attica: Helmut Brückner, "Changes in the Mediterranean Ecosystem During Antiquity," in Bottema, *Man's Role* (note 29), p. 130 f.; Hans Lohmann, *Atene [sic!]*, Part I (Cologne, 1993), p. 194.

37. J. Despois, "La culture en terrasses dans l'Afrique du Nord," *Annales E. S. C.* (1956): 48; Le Roy Ladurie, *Paysans de Languedoc* (Chap. 1, note 5), pp. 56 ff., 309. Jorge F. Branco, *Bauernarbeit im mediterranen Alltag: Agrikultur und Umweltgestaltung auf der Inselgruppe Madeira (1750–1900)* (Berlin, 1984), pp. 9 f., 175 ff., 283; Geertz, *Agricultural Involution* (Chap. 1, note 59), p. 34.

38. Ambroise, *Paysages* (note 35), pp. 35, 18; Clifford Geertz, "The Wet and the Dry: Traditional Irrigation in Bali and Morocco," *Human Ecology* 1 (1972): 27; Geertz, "Organization of the Balinese Subak," in *Irrigation and Agricultural Development in Asia*, ed. E. Walter Coward (Ithaca, N.Y., 1980), pp. 70 ff., 78 f.; Planhol, *Kulturgeographische Grundlagen* (Chap. 2, note 81), pp. 93, 165, 246, 250; Branco, *Bauernarbeit* (note 37), p. 9.

39. Ambroise, *Paysages* (note 35), pp. 21, 71; Spencer and Hale, "Agricultural Terracing" (note 35), p. 12; Despois, "Culture en terrasses" (note 37), pp. 45, 47, 50; Geertz, "Wet and Dry" (note 38), p. 29; Philippe Blanchemanche, *Bâtisseurs de paysages: Terrassement, épierrement et petite hydraulique agricoles en Europe XVIIe–XIXe siècles* (Paris, 1990), p. 8; D. H. Grist, *Rice*, 5th ed. (London, 1975), p. 87 f.; Yi-fu Tuan, *China* (Chicago, 1969), p. 197; Judith Shapiro, *Mao's War against Nature: Politics and the Environment in Revolutionary China* (Cambridge, 2001), pp. 106 ff.

40. Clifford Geertz, "Two Types of Ecosystems," in *Environment and Cultural Behavior*, ed. Andrew S. Vayda (New York, 1969), p. 18. A less stable picture is in N. C. van Setten van der Meer, *Sawah Cultivation in Ancient Java: Aspects of Development during the Indo-Javanese Period, 5th to 15th Century* (Canberra, 1979), pp. 16 f., 20 ff.; Ambroise, *Paysages* (note 35), pp. 25, 40; Blanchemanche, *Bâtisseurs de paysages* (note 39), pp. 171, 149; Netting, *Smallholders* (Chap. 2, note 6), p. 30 f. Mallorca: Jacqueline Waldren, *Insiders and Outsiders* (Oxford, 1996), p. 223; R. A. Donkin, *Agricultural Terracing in the Aboriginal New World* (Tucson, Ariz., 1979), p. 132; Johannes Müller, *Kulturlandschaft China* (Gotha, 1997), p. 33.

41. Rackham and Moody, "Terraces" (note 36), p. 124 f.; Ambroise, *Paysages* (note 35), p. 46; Geertz, "Two Types" (note 40), pp. 18, 21; Spencer and Hale, "Agricultural Terracing" (note 35), p. 10; Jonathan A. Sandor, "Long-Term Effects of Prehistoric Agriculture on Soils: Examples from New Mexico and Peru," in *Soils in Archaelogy*, ed. Vance T. Holliday (Washington, D.C., 1992), pp. 227 f., 237, 241; Garcilaso (Anm. 3), p. 158 f.

42. Bruno Strebel, "Kakteenbauern und Ziegenhirten in der Buknaiti Are (Nordäthiopien)," dissertation, University of Zurich (1979), p. 77.

43. See Christian Küchli, *Wälder der Hoffnung* (Zurich, 1997), pp. 86 ff. on a cooperative in Kenya, "The Women's Group under the Acacia."

44. Branco, *Bauernarbeit* (note 37), pp. 177, 180; Lucien M. Hanks, *Rice and Man: Agricultural Ecology in Southeast Asia* (Honolulu, 1992 [1972]) pp. 34, 65; Robin Clarke, *Water: The International Crisis* (London, 1991), p. 151; Gregory Bateson, *Steps to an Ecology of Mind* (London, 1972), p. 174; McNeely and Sochaczewski, *Soul of the Tiger* (Chap. 1, note 7), p. 40. Attempted introduction of irrigation terraces in northern Kenya as a catastrophic failure: W. K. Lindsay, "Integrating Parks and Pastoralists," in *Conservation in Africa*, ed. David Anderson and Richard Grove (Cambridge, 1989), p. 304. Similarly Peter Ondiege, "Land Tenure and Soil Conservation," in *In Land We Trust: Environment, Private Property and Constitutional Change*, ed. Calestous Juma and J. B. Ojwang (Nairobi, 1996), p. 133 f., even though there have also been successes over the course of time, especially in Kenya (p. 138 f.). Currently, about 40 percent of the strongly degraded soil in the world is found in Africa: Friedrich Beese, "Böden und globaler Wandel," *Spektrum der Wissenschaft, Dossier* 2 (1997): 75; Christian Küchli, *Wälder der Hoffnung* (Zurich, 1997), pp. 74 ff., 81 ff. I would like to thank Andrea Queiroz de Souza for information on terracing in East Africa.

45. Geertz, "Wet and Dry" (note 38), p. 26; also Geertz, *Involution* (Chap. 1, note 59), pp. 28, 33; Adrian Vickers, *Bali: A Paradise Created* (New York, 1994), p. 203.

46. Harold Brookfield, "Landscape History: Land Degredation in the Indonesian Region," in *Paper Landscapes: Explorations in the Environmental History of Indonesia*, ed. Peter Boomgaard et al. (Leiden, 1977), p. 29; Herbert Wilhelmy, *Reisanbau und Nahrungsspielraum in Südostasien* (Kiel, 1975), pp. 10–14, 34.

47. Robert B. Marks, *Tigers, Rice, Silk and Silt: Environment and Economy in Late Imperial South China* (Cambridge, 1998), p. 341; Zhong Gongfu, "The Mulberry Dike-Fish Pond Complex: A Chinese Ecosystem of Land-Water Interaction on the Pearl River Delta," *Human Ecology* 10 (1982): 191–202.

48. Alfred Weber, *Kulturgeschichte als Kultursoziologie* (Munich, 1950), p. 72 f.; Eva Sternfeld, *Umweltpolitik und Industrialisierung in der Volksrepublik China (1949–1985)*, p. 91; Shapiro, *Mao's War against Nature* (note 39), p. 208.

49. Liebig, *Chemische Briefe* (Chap. 1, note 26), pp. 498, 500 f.; Richard A. Wines, *Fertilizer in America* (Philadelphia, 1985), pp. 25 ff.; Steven Stoll, *Larding the Lean Earth* (New York, 2002), pp. 37 ff.

50. George Varrentrapp, *Über die Entwässerung der Städte: Über Werth und Unwerth des Wasserclosetts* (Berlin, 1868), pp. 20, 22, 24 f. Werner Pieper, *Das Scheiss-Buch: Entstehung, Nutzung, Entsorgung menschlicher Fäkalien* (Löhrbach, 1987), pp. 118 ff., 140. Bernhard Glaeser, *Umweltpolitik in China* (Bochum, 1983), p. 184; Jonathan D. Spence, *The Search for Modern China* (New York, 1990), p. 563. Mark Elvin takes a less positive view of the zealous use of "night soil," arguing that it promoted the spread of incurable worm diseases: "The Environmental Legacy of Imperial China," *China Quarterly* (Dec. 1998, no. 156) (issue devoted to "China's Environment"): 734. The Malays used to say, mockingly, that the Chinese fertilized their vegetable beds with feces and in this way ate their own excrement, as it were: Oskar Weggel, *Die Asiaten* (Munich, 1994), p. 85. Decidedly in favor of the hygienic character of the way the Chinese dealt with excrement: F. H. King, *Farmers of Forty Centuries* (London, 1989 [orig. 1911]), p. 175.

51. Yi-fu Tuan, *China* (note 39), p. 142.

52. Netting, *Smallholders* (Chap. 2, note 6), p. 236 and elsewhere; Qu Geping and Li Jinchang, *Population and the Environment in China* (Boulder, Colo., 1994), p. 4; Thomas Malthus, *An Essay on the Principle of Population* [1798] (Harmondsworth, 1970), pp. 30, 88 f.; Barrington Moore, *Social Origins of Dictatorship and Democracy* (Boston, 1966), pp. 219–20. While such concerns were long denounced as reactionary Malthusianism in Mao's China, since around 1980 population pressure has been recognized as an economic-ecological problem of the highest order also within circles of the Chinese government: Spence, *Modern China* (note 51), pp. 687 ff.

53. Richthofen, *China* (Chap. 2, note 94), p. 70; Richthofen, *Tagebücher aus China* (Berlin, 1907), vol. I, pp. 151 f., 163, 167 f., 207, 254, 333 f., 561 f.; Gudula Linck, "'Die Welt ist ein heiliges Gefäß, wer sich daran zu schaffen macht, wird Niederlagen erleiden': Konfliktaustragung an der Natur während der Umbrüche in der chinesischen Geschichte," in Calließ, *Mensch und Umwelt* (Preface to German edition, note 6), p. 334. Bruno Baumann, *Gobi* (Munich, 1995), pp. 116 f., 123.

54. Herbert Franke, "Geschichte und Natur: Betrachtungen eines Asien-Historikers," in Markl, ed., *Natur und Geschichte* (Chap. 1, note 18), pp. 55, 63; similarly Ole Bruun, "Fengshui and the Chinese Perception of Nature," in *Asian Perceptions of Nature: A Critical Approach*, ed. Ole Brunn and Arne Kalland (Richmond, Va., 1995), pp. 173 ff.

55. Linck, "Heiliges Gefäß" (note 53), pp. 327, 346, and elsewhere. For a general discussion of this issue see Yi-fuTuan, "Discrepancies between Environmental Attitude and Behavior: Examples from Europe and China," *Canadian Geographer* 12, no. 3 (1986): 176–91.

56. Fundamental for the following discussion of China is Mark Elvin and Liu Ts'ui-jung, eds., *Sediments of Time: Environment and Society in Chinese History* (Cambridge, 1998). This massive (820 pages) collaborative work surpasses all other existing publications on non-Western environmental history in length, quality, and empirical grounding, thanks not least to the unmatched Chinese sources. I would like to thank Jürgen Osterhammel for helpful pointers. Elvin, "Environmental Legacy" (note 50), p. 43; also his essay "3000 Years of Unsustainable Growth: China's Environment from Archaic Times to the Present," *East Asian History* 6 (1993): 7–46; Elvin, "The Environmental History of China: An Agenda of Ideas," *Asian Studies Review* 14 (1990): 39–53. In reply to the title of Pearl S. Buck's book, *The Good Earth*, see Vaclav Smil, *The Bad Earth: Environmental Degradation in China* (New York, 1984), p. 3 f., against an exaggerated cultural approach that has glossed over the environmental degradation in that country. On this issue see J. Baird Callicott and Roger T. Ames, "Epilogue: On the Relation of Idea and Action," in *Nature in Asian Traditions of Thought*, ed. J. Baird Callicott and Roger T. Ames (Albany, 1989), pp. 279–89; Yi-Fu Tuan, "Discrepancies between Environmental Attitude and Behaviour: Examples from Europe and China," *Canadian Geographer* 12 (1968): 176–91; Yi-Fu Tuan, *China* (note 39), pp. 29 ff., 127 ff. (findings of historical geography on anthropogenic environmental changes). Joseph Needham, "Science and Society in East and West," in his *The Grand Titration* (London, 1972), pp. 190–217; Bauer, *China* (Chap. 1, note 39), p. 227.

57. Needham, *Grand Titration* (note 56), p. 181; Needham, *Science and Civilization in China*, IV, part 3 (Cambridge, 1971), p. 234 f.; R. Keith Schoppa, *Xiang Lake: Nine Centuries of Chinese Life* (New Haven, Conn., 1989), p. 121 f. On the practical significance of the Chinese philosophy of nature and geomancy see Johannes Müller, *Kulturlandschaft China* (Gotha, 1997), pp. 71 ff. On the nature and diffusion of the Chinese feeling for nature see Lin Yutang, *Mein Land und mein Volk* (Stuttgart, n.d. [ca. 1935]), pp. 56 f., 154, 314 ff. Max Weber, *Max Weber Gesamtausgabe* (MWG) I/19, pp. 406 ff., 450 ff.

58. He Bochuan, *China on the Edge* (note 8), p. 30 f.; Needham, *Science* (note 57), p. 224 f.; Tuan, *China* (note 39), p. 29 f. Kevin Sinclair, *The Yellow River = Huang He: A 5000 Year Journey through China* (McMahon's Point, N.S.W., 1987), pp. 105 ff.; Ludwig Reinhardt, *Kulturgeschichte der Nutzpflanzen* (Munich, 1911), p. 46. According to Jung Chang, *Wild Swans* (1991), p. 65, under Japanese occupation, the Chinese were forbidden in 1939 to eat rice, as a result of which they had to live chiefly on sorghum.

59. Needham, "Thoughts on the Social Relations of Science and Technology in China," and "Science and Society in East and West," in *Grand Titration* (note 56), pp. 177–89, and 190–217. In general, he speaks approvingly of Wittfogel, even though elsewhere he dismisses his "Oriental despotism" as "fundamental nonsense." See Ulmen, *Science of Society* (note 16), p. 374.

60. Isaac, "AMP" (note 18), p. 452 f.; Arthur Cotterell and Yong Yap, *The Early Civilization of China* (London, 1975); Walter Böttger, *Kultur im alten China* (Leipzig, 1977), p. 51.

61. *Records of the Historian: Chapters from the Shih chi of Ssu-ma Ch'ien*, trans. Burton Watson (New York, 1969), p. 230 f.; Richthofen, *China* (note 8) p. 285 f.

62. Shapiro, *Mao's War* (note 39), p. 59. Today, the mistakes that were made in the building of the Sanmexia dam are admitted; at the same time, however, the government insists that the problem of siltification has been solved after repeated rebuilding of the dam: Zheng Ping, *Chinas Geographie* (Beijing, 1999), p. 67.

63. *Records* (note 61), pp. 236, 231 f.; Needham, *Science* (note 57), 4/III, p. 285 f.

64. Tsui Chi, *Geschichte Chinas und seiner Kultur* (Zurich, 1946), pp. 166 ff. Needham, *Science* (note 57), 4/III, pp. 306 ff., 319; Pierre-Étienne Will, "Un cycle hydraulique en Chine: La province du Hubei du XVIᵉ au XIXᵉ siècles," *Bulletin de l'École Française d'Extrême-Orient* 68 (1980): 267 f.; Zuo Dakang and Zhang Peiyuan, "The Huang-Huai-Hai Plain," in Turner, *Earth* (Chap. 1, note 80), pp. 473 ff.; Jacques Gernet, *A History of Chinese Civilization*, trans. J. R. Foster (Cambridge, 1972), pp. 491 ff., 356 ff.; Rolf Trauzettel, "Die Yüan-Dynastie," in *Die Mongolen*, ed. Michael Weiers (Darmstadt, 1986), p. 250; Klaus Flessel, "Der Huang-ho und die historische Hydrotechnik in China," dissertation, University of Tübingen, 1974, pp. 103, 87 ff.

65. *Europa und die Kaiser von China* (Frankfurt a. M., 1985), pp. 116 ff., 129 ff., 289 f.; Gernet, *Chinese Civilization* (note 64), pp. 548 ff.; Spence, *Modern China* (note 50), pp. 185, 489; Richthofen, *China* (note 8), p. 420 f.; Will, "Cycle Hydraulic" (note 64), p. 268. As late as the 1930s, flooding and drought catastrophes, which were attributable to the failure of state supervision of hydraulic works, contributed to the downfall of the Chiang Kai-shek government: Jürgen Osterhammel, *Shanghai 30. Mai 1925: Die chinesische Revolution* (Munich, 1997), p. 182. Sinclair, *Yellow River* (note 58), pp. 172, 180.

66. Bao Maohong, "Environmental History in China," manuscript, University of Peking, History Department, 2003.

67. Jonathan B. Mabry, "The Ethnology of Local Irrigation," in Mabry, *Canals* (note 9), p. 6. It has been claimed that even under Communist rule in China, "thousands of small artificial lakes" were constructed, which were "maintained by the local populations on their own": Siegfried Pater/Einhard Schmidt-Kallert, *Zum Beispiel Staudämme* (Göttingen, 1989), p. 14; Clarke, *Water* (note 44), p. 163. Schoppa, *Xiang Lake* (note 57).

68. Herbert Franke and Rolf Trauzettel, *Das Chinesische Kaiserreich* (Frankfurt a. M., 1958) (*Fischer Weltgeschichte*, vol. 19), pp. 162 ff.

69. Pierre-Étienne Will, "State Intervention in the Administration of a Hydraulic Infrastructure: The Example of Hubei Province in Late Imperial Times," in *The Scope of State Power in China*, ed. Stuart R. Schram (London, 1985), pp. 295–347. Siltification of canals and artificial lakes as a social problem arising from the pressure of individual landhunger on the public bodies of water: Pierre-Étienne Will, "The Zheng-Bai Irrigation System," in Elvin and Liu, *Sediments of Time* (note 56), p. 325.

70. Elvin, "3000 Years" (note 56). It is clear from Elvin and Liu, *Sediments of Time* (note 56) that an ecological crisis can be broadly documented only since the eighteenth century. Ma Yinchu: Shapiro, *Mao's War against Nature* (note 39), pp. 34–48.

71. Poivre, *Travels of a Philosopher* (Chap. 2, note 65), p. 75; Tuan, *China* (note 39), p. 139 f.; Müller, *Kulturlandschaft China* (note 40), p. 124; Hans-Rainer Kämpfe, "Die Innere Mongolei von 1691 bis 1911," in Weiers, *Mongolen* (note 64), p. 431; Li Wen, "China's Environmental Conditions in 1998," *Beijing Review*, July 12, 1999, p. 17. Growing meat consumption has led to an overuse also of the last reserves of pastureland.

72. Franke: *Fischer Weltgeschichte*, vol. XIX (Frankfurt a. M., 1968), p. 212; Jean-Claude Debeir, Jean-Paul Deléage, and Daniel Hémery, *In the Servitude of Power: Energy and Civilization through the Ages*, trans. John Bartman (London, 1990), chap. 3, "The Chinese Energy Model;" Smil, *Bad Earth* (note 56), p. 9. Caroline Blunden and Mark Elvin, *Cultural Atlas of China* (New York, 1983), pp. 37 ff.

73. Liu Ts'ui-jung, "Rice Culture in South China, 1500–1900: Adjustment and Limitation in Historical Perspective," in *Economic and Demographic Developments in Rice-Producing Societies: Some Aspects of East Asian Economic History (1500–1900)*, ed. Akira Hayami and Yoshihiro Tsubouchi (Leuven, 1990), pp. 51 ff.; Shi Zhihong, "The Development and Underdevelopment of Agriculture during the Early Qing Period," ibid., pp. 69 ff. Perdue, *Exhausting the Soil*

(note 18), p. 19 f.; Will, "Cycle Hydraulic" (note 5), p. 279; Anne Osborne, "Economic and Ecological Interactions in the Lower Yangzi Region under the Qing," in Elvin and Liu, *Sediments of Time* (note 56), p. 212 (complaint in the nineteenth century that maize was ruining the mountains, as a result of which one could grow neither bamboo nor forests there); Joachim H. Schultze, "Das Wesen der Bodenerosion," in *Bodenerosion in Mitteleuropa*, ed. Gerold Richter (Darmstadt, 1976), p. 57; Georg Borgstrom, *Der hungrige Planet* (Munich, 1967), p. 74; Wen Dazhong and David Pimentel, "17th Century Organic Agriculture in China: Energy Flows through an Agroecosystem in Jiaxing Region," *Human Ecology* 14 (1986): 26 f. Mark Elvin has also emphasized deforestation in general as a key factor in China's ecological decline: "3000 Years" (note 56), pp. 29 ff. and elsewhere. Hartmut Graß, "Brisante Mischung," in Kümmerer, *Bodenlos* (Chap. 1, note 80), p. 16.

74. Needham, *Science* (note 57), pp. 241, 244.

75. Ibid., p. 245; John F. Richards, *The Unending Frontier: An Environmental History of the Early Modern World* (Berkeley, Calif., 2003), p. 131; Linda Hershkovitz, "Political Ecology and Environmental Management in the Loess Plateau, China," *Human Ecology* 21 (1993), p. 327; Linck, "Heiliges Gefäß" (note 53), pp. 343, 345; Müller, *Kulturlandschaft* (note 40), p. 186 f.; scattered indications for a forest awareness among villagers in Yunnan: Nicholas K. Menzies, "The Villagers' View of Environmental History in Yunnan Province," in Elvin and Liu, *Sediments* (note 56), p. 113.

76. David Farrelly, *The Book of Bamboo* (San Francisco, 1984), pp. 301 f., 285; Lin Yutang, *Mein Land* (note 57), pp. 59, 155; Marianne Beuchert, *Die Gärten Chinas* (Frankfurt a. M., 1998), p. 70 f.; Karl August Wittfogel, *Wirtschaft und Gesellschaft Chinas* (Leipzig, 1931), p. 490.

77. Gernet, *Chinese Civilization* (note 64), p. 391; Beuchert, *Gärten Chinas* (note 77), p. 128.

78. Several publications by Nicholas K. Menzies: "Villagers' View" (note 74); *Forest and Land Management in Imperial China* (New York, 1994), esp. pp. 95 ff., 120, 132; "300 Years of Taungya: A Sustainable System of Forestry in South China," *Human Ecology* 16 (1988): 367; "Sources of Demand and Cycles of Logging in Pre-Modern China," in *Changing Pacific Forests*, ed. John Dargavel and Richard Tucker (Durham, N.C., 1992), pp. 64 ff.

79. Tuan, *China* (note 39), p. 142.

80. Menzies, *Forest and Land Management* (Anm. 68), p. 44. The work of Elvin (note 56) also makes clear that forest protection was not a traditional function of the ruler in China. We can gather the same impression from Elvin and Liu, *Sediments* (note 56). Ibid., p. 247 (Eduard B. Vermeer, "Population and Ecology along the Frontier in Quing China"): "Traditional Chinese thought exhibited a definite bias against forests and the cultivation of trees"; also p. 279. Otto Fischer, "Der Baum in der Kultur Chinas," *Intersilva* 2 (1942): 348; Edward H. Schafer, "The Conservation of Nature under the T'ang Dynasty," *Journal of the Economic and Social History of the Orient* 5 (1962): 303 ff.; Debeir, *Servitude of Power* (note 73), pp. 99 ff.; Yoshida Tora, *Salt Production Techniques in Ancient China* (Leiden, 1993). It is a common view among the nations of China, India, and Southeast Asia that mountain forests are home to wild peoples and potential troublemakers; from this side, too, there is a negative relationship between dominion and the forest. On this see Weggel, *Asiaten* (note 50), pp. 83 ff.

81. Patrick J. Caffrey, "Toward Wise Use: The People's Republik of China and Forest Management in Northeastern China, 1949–1953," paper delivered at the ASEH Conference in Baltimore, 1997; S. D. Richardson, *Forestry in Communist China* (Baltimore, Md., 1966); Jan Myrdal, *Report from a Chinese Village*, trans. Maurice Michael (London, 1965); Li Jinchang et al., "Price and Policy: The Keys to Revamping China's Forestry Resources," in *Public Policies and the Misuse of Forest Resources*, ed. Robert Repetto and Malcolm Gillis (Cambridge, 1988), p. 212. Message of the Dalai Lama on March 10, 1999: "It is sad and regrettable that it has taken the terrible flooding of last year for the Chinese government to realize the usefulness of environmental protection." In *Tibet und Buddhismus* 13 (1999), no. 49, p. 32.

82. Smil, *Bad Earth* (note 56), pp. 49 f. National Research Council, *Grasslands and Grassland Sciences in Northern China* (Washington, D.C., 1992), p. 31. Heissig, *Mongolen* (Chap. 2, note 88), pp. 193, 208.

83. Bo Gunnarsson, *Japans ökologischer Harakiri oder Das tödliche Ende des Wachstums* (Reinbek, 1974 [1971]); Shigeto Tsuru and Helmut Weidner, *Ein Modell für uns: Die Erfolge der japanischen Umweltpolitik* (Cologne, 1985); *Der Spiegel* (Feb. 6, 1989): 139 ff. Arnold Toynbee and Daisaku Ikeda, *Choose Life: A Dialogue*, ed. Richard L. Gage (Oxford, 1989). Ikeda believes that Toynbee overstimates the ecological merits of Shintoism, though otherwise the dialogue is more like an antiphony of mutual confirmation.

84. The following discussion is based primarily on the books of Conrad Totman with their ecological interpretation of early modern Japanese history: *Early Modern Japan* (Berkeley, Calif., 1993), pp. 229 f., 268 f.; *The Green Archipelago: Forestry in Preindustrial Japan* (Berkeley, Calif., 1989), pp. 182 f., 187, and elsewhere; *The Lumber Industry in Early Modern Japan* (Honolulu, 1995), pp. 103, 110, and elsewhere. Also, Masako M. Osako, "Forest Preservation in Tokugawa Japan," in *Global Deforestation and the 19th-Century World Economy*, ed. Richard S. Tucker and J. F. Richards (Durham, N.C., 1983), pp. 129 ff., 134.

85. John B. Cornell, "Three Decades of Matsunagi: Changing Patterns of Forest Land Use in an Okayama Mountain Village," in *History of Sustained-Yield Forestry*, ed. Harold K. Steen (Portland, Ore., 1984), pp. 237, 257 ff.; Helmut Erlinghagen, *Japan* (Munich, 1976), p. 238 f. Radkau and Schäfer, *Holz* (Chap. 1, note 50), p. 260 f.; Owen Cameron, "Japan and South-East Asia's Environment," in *Environmental Change in South-East Asia*, ed. Michael J. G. Parnwell and Raymond L. Bryant (London, 1996), pp. 67 ff. In Japan, irrigation systems remained under local control more so than in many other regions of Asia; see Randolph Barker et al., *The Rice Economy of Asia* (Washington, D.C., 1985), p. 95.

86. McNeill, *Something New* (Chap. 1, note 7), pp. 92–99.

87. I am grateful to Klaus Bergdolt, Piero Bevilacqua, Rolf Petri, and Ingrid Schäfer for pointing the way on Venetian environmental history. See Piero Bevilacqua, *Venezia e le acque: Una metafora planetaria* (Rome, 1995), pp. 13, 21; Pietro Zampetti, *Il problema di Venezia* (Florence, 1976), p. 22 f.; Bernd Roeck, "Wasser, Politik und Bürokratie: Venedig in der frühen Neuzeit," *Die alte Stadt* 20 (1993): 214, 218; Elisabeth Crouzet-Pavan, *'Sopra le acque salse': Espaces, Pouvoir et société à Venise à la fin du Moyen Âge* (Rome, 1992), vol. I, p. 315; Nelli-Elena Vanzan Marchini, *Venezia de laguna a città* (Venice, 1985), p. 115 f.; Alvise Zorzi, *Venedig* (Frankfurt a. M., 1987), p. 137 f.; Rolf Petri, *Venedig* (Hamburg, 1986), p. 65.

88. Bevilacqua, *Venezia* (note 88), pp. 24, 26 f.

89. Crouzet-Pavan, *Acque Salse* (note 88), vol. I, p. 291; Frederic C. Lane, *Venice: A Maritime Republic* (Baltimore, Md., 1973), pp. 3–4, 16, 58; Zorzi, *Venedig* (note 88), p. 183; Bevilacqua, *Venezia* (note 88), pp. 47, 50.

90. Crouzet-Pavan, *Acque Salse* (note 88), vol. I, p. 317 and elsewhere; Bevilacqua, *Venezia* (note 88), pp. 95 ff., 100 ff.; Archivio di Stato di Venezia, *Ambiente e risorse nella politica veneziana* (Venice, 1989), p. 40 f.; Roeck, "Wasser" (note 88), p. 209 f.; Christian Mathieu, "'Indubitata invenzione di capo.' Zur gesellschaftlichen Konstruktion ökologischer Risiken im frühneuzeitlichen Venedig," *traverse* 3 (2003): 81; Alvise Zorzi, *Canal Grande* (Hildesheim 1993), p. 254.

91. Philippe Braunstein and Robert Delort, *Venise: porträt historique d'une cité* (Paris, 1971), pp. 16 ff.; Freddy Thiriet, *Storia della Repubblica di Venezia* (Venice, 1981 [1952]), p. 28; Mathieu, "Indubitata" (note 91), pp. 75 ff. "Destruction": Archivio di Stato di Venezia, *Laguna, lidi, fiumi: Cinque secoli di gestione delle acque* (Venice, 1983), p. 26.

92. Lane, *Venice* (note 90), pp. 35, 415 f.; *Laguna, lidi* (note 92), p. 27 f.; Zorzi, *Canal* (note 91), p. 253; Roeck, "Wasser" (note 88), p. 212 f.; Vanzan Marchini, *Venezia* (note 88), p. 33.

93. Wittfogel, *Oriental Despotism* (note 15), p. 263; Petri, *Venedig* (note 88), p. 65.

94. Michelangelo Muraro and Paolo Marton, *Villen in Venetien* (Cologne, 1996), p. 37; Zorzi, *Venedig* (note 88), p. 364.

95. Alvise Cornaro, *The Art of Living Long* (New York, 2005); Muraro and Marton, *Villen* (note 95), p. 53 f.; *Laguna, lidi* (note 92), p. 54; Lane, *Venice* (note 90), pp. 307, 452 ff.; Vanzan Marchini (Anm. 75), p. 34 f.; Emanuela Casti Moreschi, *L'analyse historique de l'utilisation des eaux dans la lagune de Venise*, in CNRS, L'eau (Anm. 28), p. 78; Mathieu, *Indubitata* (note 90), p. 80.

96. Bevilacqua, *Venezia* (note 88), p. 14 f.; Vanzan Marchini, *Venezia* (note 88), pp. 33 ff. Roeck, "Wasser" (note 88), pp. 207 ff., 218 ff., believes, however, that Sabbadino suffered an "ecological" defeat over the long term, since the problem of reconciling the intact nature of the lagoon with the economy found no lasting solution. Rolf Petri to the author, December 18, 1998: in the nineteenth century there were renewed pleas for draining the lagoon, but this was blocked by a "powerful hotel lobby." However, by promoting industrialization on the mainland, that lobby contributed indirectly to upsetting the hydrological balance of the lagoon. Venice offers a prime example of the problem of ecological value judgments.

97. Vanzan Marchini, *Venezia* (note 88), pp. 141, 38; Archivio di Stato di Venezia, *Boschi della Serenissima: Storia di un rapporto uomoambiente* (Venice, 1988), p. 24; Bruno Vecchio, *Il bosco negli scrittori italiani del settecento* (Turin, 1974), p. 30 f.

98. *Boschi* (note 98), pp. 11 f., 55 ff., 69 ff.; Archivio di Stato di Venezia, *Boschi della Serenissima: utilizzo e tutela* (Venice, 1987), p. 31 f.; *Ambiente* (note 91), p. 73 f.

99. Herbert Hesmer, *Leben und Werk von D. Brandis* (Opladen, 1975), p. 144; Harrison, *Forests* (Chap. 2, note 46), pp. xi, 92, 241, 249, 258, 265.

100. Goethe: diary entry of October 9, 1786; Lane, *Venice* (note 90), p. 453; Vanzan Marchini, *Venezia* (note 88), pp. 77, 155; Albrecht Hoffmann, "Wassernöte und technischer Wandel in der frühen Neuzeit," in *Die Wasserversorgung in der Renaissance*, ed. Frontinus-Gesellschaft (Mainz, 2000), p. 20.

101. *L'Ambiente nella storia d'Italia* (Venice, 1989), p. 29 (Gabriella Bonacchi/Margherita Pelaja); Piero Bevilacqua, "Le rivoluzioni dell'acqua," in *Storia dell'agricoltura italiana in età contemporanea*, vol. I, p. 255 f.; Friedrich Wilhelm Toussaint, *Die Bodencultur und das Wasser* (Breslau, 1872), p. 20; Charles Wilson, *The Dutch Republic and the Civilisation of the Seventeenth Century* (London, 1968), pp. 74 ff.

102. Marc Bloch considered it a key historical insight to see the silting up of the harbor of Brugges not as a natural event, but as the reflex of societal conditions: *The Historian's Craft*, trans. Peter Putnam (New York, 1953), p. 24; it is likely that he went too far in trivializing the inherent power of nature. Paul Zumthor, *Daily Life in Rembrandt's Holland*, trans. Simon Watson Taylor (Stanford, Calif., 1994), p. 312.

103. Simon Schama, *The Embarrassment of Riches: An Interpretation of Dutch Culture in the Golden Age* (Berkeley, Calif., 1988), p. 42 f.; Dietrich Ebeling, *Der Holländer-Holzhandel in den Rheinlanden* (Stuttgart, 1992), esp. pp. 60 ff., 84 ff.; Radkau and Schäfer, *Holz* (Chap. 1, note 50), p. 138 f. Johann Kramer and Hans Rohde, *Historischer Küstenschutz: Deichbau, Inselschutz and Binnenentwässerung an Nord- und Ostsee* (Stuttgart, 1994), p. 137.

104. Wittfogel, *Oriental Despotism* (note 15), p. 36; Johan Huizinga, *Dutch Civilisation in the Seventeenth Century*, trans. Arnold J. Pomerans (New York, 1968), p. 16; Jan de Vries, *The Dutch Rural Economy in the Golden Age, 1500–1700* (New Haven, Conn., 1974), p. 197; Audrey M. Lambert, *The Making of the Dutch Landscape: An Historical Geography of the Netherlands* (London, 1971), p. 113 f. (inconsistent statements about the extent to which work on the dikes strengthened self-government or higher authorities); Horst Johannes Tümmers, *Der Rhein: Ein europäischer Fluß und seine Geschichte*, 2nd ed. (Munich, 1999), pp. 368 ff.; *Die Landschaften Niedersachsens*, 3rd ed. (Hannover, 1965), no. 50.

105. Schama, *Embarrassment of Riches* (note 104), pp. 34 ff., 44, 266; Zumthor, *Daily Life* (note 103), pp. 302 ff.; van Bath, *Agrarian History* (Chap. 2, note 106), p. 213; Hans Walter Flemming, *Wüsten, Deiche und Turbinen* (Göttingen, 1957), p. 159; Sheila Jasanoff et al., *Handbook of Science and Technology Studies* (Thousand Oaks, Calif., 1995), pp. 342 ff. (Wiebe E. Bijker); *Das neue Buch der Erfindungen, Gewerbe und Industrien*, 6th ed. (Leipzig, 1872), vol. II, pp. 172 ff.

106. Hans-Jürgen Nitz, "Mittelalterliche Moorsiedlungen: Agrarische Umweltgestaltung unter schwierigen naturräumlichen Voraussetzungen," in Herrmann, *Umwelt* (Chap. 2, note 80), p. 54; Lambert, *Dutch Landscape* (note 105), pp. 210, 239; Petra van Dam to the author, June 14, 1999. I would also like to thank her for additional pointers on Dutch environmental history.

107. Nitz, "Moorsiedlungen" (note 107), pp. 56, 60; de Vries, *Rural Economy* (note 105), p. 202; van Bath, *Agrarian History* (Chap. 2, note 106), p. 162; Lambert, *Dutch Landscape* (note 105), pp. 208 ff.; J. W. de Zeeuw, *Peat and the Dutch Golden Age* (Wageningen, 1978), pp. 21 ff.

108. Heinrich Hoops, *Geschichte des Bremer Blocklandes* (Bremen, 1984 [1927]), pp. 9f., 16 f., 35 f., 45.

109. Uwe Pörksen, *Die politische Zunge* (Stuttgart, 2002), p. 84.

110. Fridrich Arends, *Abhandlungen vom Rasenbrennen und dem Moorbrennen* (Hannover, 1826), pp. 3 ff., 8 f.; a Hannoverian protest against peat-burning from 1836, which already anticipated the theme of "silent spring," in Bayerl and Troitzsch, eds., *Quellentexte* (Chap. 1, note 28), p. 258. Karlhans Göttlich, ed., *Moor- und Torfkunde* (Stuttgart, 1990), p. 394 f.; Josef Kulischer, *Allgemeine Wirtschaftsgeschichte des Mittelalters und der Neuzeit*, II (reprint, Munich, 1965), pp. 39, 44 ff.; Klaus Herrmann, *Pflügen, Säen, Ernten* (Reinbek, 1985), pp. 117 ff.

111. This was the assessment in 1988 by the Dutch National Institute for Public Health and the Environment (Rijksinstitut voer Volksgezondheit en Milieu) in a study entitled *Sorgen für morgen – Niederlande im Jahr 2000* (Helmut Hetzel in *VDI-Nachrichten* 52 [1988]: 17). However, the study presented in 1992 by the Dutch environmental group Milieudefensie, *Sustainable Netherlands*, which became the model for the Wuppertal study "Zukunftsfähiges Deutschland," warned against reducing the problem of the nonsustainability in agriculture to the excess of liquid manure, and it pointed, among other things, to the extremely high energy consumption of the greenhouses: *Sustainable Netherlands*, pp. 158, 162.

112. See L. W. Hackett, *Malaria in Europe: An Ecological Study* (London, 1937).

113. August Bebel, *Woman under Socialism*, trans. Daniel De Leon (New York, 1904), p. 288.

114. Angelo Celli, *The History of Malaria in the Roman Campagna from Ancient Times* (London, 1933), p. 10; similarly the newer malaria classic: Leonard J. Bruce-Chwatt and Julian de Zulueta, *The Rise and Fall of Malaria in Europe: A Historico-Epidemiological Study* (Oxford, 1980), pp. 17 ff., 89 ff. I would like to thank Neithard Bulst for pointing out ecological aspects of the history of endemic diseases. Nomadism: Henry Hobhouse, *Seeds of Change: Five Plants That Transformed Mankind* (New York, 1985), p. 8.

115. Cicero, *De re publica* 2.11; Celli, *Malaria* (note 115), pp. 12 f., 19 ff., 66 ff; on this see Erwin Schimitschek and Günther T. Werner, *Malaria, Fleckfieber, Pest: Auswirkungen auf Kultur und Geschichte, medizinische Fortschritte* (Stuttgart, 1985), pp. 15 ff.; Jacques Ruffié and Jean Charles Sournia, *Die Seuchen in der Geschichte der Menschheit* (Munich, 1992), pp. 152 ff.; Stefan Winkle, *Geißeln der Menschheit: Kulturgeschichte der Seuchen* (Düsseldorf, 1997), pp. 261 f., 270.

116. Braudel, *Mediterranean* (Chap. 2, note 5), p. 65; similarly Rhoads Murphey, "The Decline of North Africa since the Roman Occupation: Climatic or Human?" *Annals of the Association of American Geographers* 41 (1951): 127. Hackett, *Malaria* (note 113), p. xiv, invokes an Italian saying: "Malaria flees before the plow." However, on p. 18 he provides indications that irrigation networks make malaria worse. Similarly Winkle, *Geißeln* (note 116), pp. 709 ff., 751 f.; Mart A. Stewart, *"What Nature Suffers to Groe": Life, Labor, and Landscape on the Georgia Coast, 1680–1920* (Athens, Ga., 1996), pp. 140 f., 280; George S. Marsh, *Man and Nature* (Cambridge, Mass., 1965 [1864]), p. 323; Neithard Bulst, "Alte und neue Krankheiten: Seuchen, Mensch und Umwelt," in *Milieux naturels, espaces sociaux*, ed. Élisabeth Mornet and Franco Morenzoni (Paris, 1997), p. 755.

117. Celli, *Malaria* (note 115), p. 21; Winkle, *Geißeln* (note 116), pp. 718, 720, 728; Marks, *Tigers* (note 47), p. 334; Jonathan S. Adams and Thomas O. McShane, *The Myth of Wild Africa* (Berkeley, Calif., 1996), p. 5.

118. Piero Bevilacqua, *Tra natura e storia: Ambiente, economie, risorse in Italia* (Rome, 1996), pp. 39 ff.; Rosaria Mancino, "Una coltura dilagante. Le risaie vercellesi nel '700," in *L'Ambiente nella Storia d'Italia*, published by the Fondazione Lelio e Lisli Basso Isocco (Venice, 1989), pp. 138 ff.; *Das Buch der Erfindungen, Gewerbe und Industrien*, 8th ed. (Leipzig, 1885), vol. III, p. 275; Winkle, *Geißeln* (note 116), p. 766; Ian Stone, *Canal Irrigation in British*

India (Cambridge, 1984), pp. 144 ff. Still today, malaria does not appear in the textbooks on irrigation technology: it is not a problem for the engineers.

119. Winkle, *Geißeln* (note 116), pp. 712ff., 724; May R. Berenbaum, *Bugs in the System: Insects and Their Impact on Human Affairs* (Reading, Mass., 1995), pp. 230 ff.; Mark Elvin, *The Pattern of the Chinese Past* (Stanford, Calif., 1973), pp. 185 ff.; Paola Corti, "Le paludisme et le pouvoir pontifical: Pie VI et les marais pontins (XVIIIe siècle)," in *Maladies et société (XIIe-XVIIIe siècles)*, ed. Neithard Bulst and Robert Delort (Paris, 1989), pp. 215 ff.

120. Winkle, *Geißeln* (note 116), p. 772; Hackett, *Malaria* (note 113), p. 10; McNeill, *Something New* (Chap. 1, note 7), p. 131 f.; Ruffié and Sournia, *Seuchen* (note 116), p. 150.

121. Poivre, *Travels* (note 72); Johan Leonard Blussé van Oud-Alblas, "The Story of an Ecological Disaster: The Dutch East India Company and Batavia (1619–1799)," in his *Strange Company: Chinese Settlers, Mestizo Women and the Dutch in VOC Batavia* (Dordrecht, 1986), pp. 15–35.

122. Corti, "Le paludisme" (note 120), pp. 215 ff., 245. More recent eco-revisionists defended the passive resistance of the old established inhabitants to the *bonifica*: the fish yield of the swamps was supposedly greater than what agriculture would yield on the reclaimed land. See Antonio Cederna, *La distruzione della natura in Italia* (Turin, 1975), p. 56.

123. Olivier Balabanian and Guy Bouet, *L'eau et la maitrise de l'eau en Limousin* (Treignac, 1989), p. 207.

124. Horst G. Mensching, "Ökosystem-Zerstörung in vorindustrieller Zeit," in Lübbe and Ströker, *Ökologische Problems* (Chap. 1, note 40), p. 19 f.; Diamond, *Guns* (Chap. 1, note 78), p. 411.

125. Fraas, in Schramm, *Ökologie-Lesebuch* (Chap. 2, note 67), pp. 61, 112 f.; Fritz Andreas Zehetmair, *Carl Nikolaus Fraas* (Munich, 1995); *Buch der Erfindungen* (note 106), vol. III, p. 347; Johannes Gaitanides, *Griechenland ohne Säulen* (Frankfurt a. M., 1980 [1955]), p. 76.

126. Cederna, *Distruzione della natura* (note 123), Part II (pp. 223 ff.): "quello che fu il giardino d'Europa"; Varro, *Marcus Teretius Varro on Agriculture*, trans. William Davis Hooper (Cambridge, Mass., 1936), I.1:3–7, p. 171: "Is not Italy so covered with trees that the whole land seems to be an orchard?"; Dionysius of Halicarnassus, *Roman Antiquities*, trans. Earnest Cary (Cambridge, Mass., 1937), vol. I, I.37: "But most wonderful of all are the forests growing upon the rocky heights, in the glens, and on the uncultivated hills, from which the inhabitants are abundantly supplied with fine timber suitable for the building of ships as well as for all other purposes." Victor Hehn, *Olive, Wein und Feige* (Frankfurt a. M., 1992 [1870]), p. 14 f.

127. Plato, *Critias*, trans. A. E. Taylor, in *The Collected Dialogues of Plato*, ed. E. Hamilton and Huntington Cairns (Princeton, N.J., 1961), p. 1216; on this see Glacken, *Traces* (Chap. 1, note 25), p. 120 f.; Karl-Wilhelm Weeber, *Smog über Attika: Umweltverhalten im Altertum* (Reinbek, 1993), p. 21 f.

128. J. V. Thirgood, *Cyprus: A Chronicle of its Forests, Land and People* (Vancouver, 1987), p. 71 f.

129. Russell Meiggs, *Trees and Timber in the Ancient Mediterranean World* (Oxford, 1982), pp. 371 ff. on the question of deforestation.

130. Claudia Honegger, in *Schrift und Materie der Geschichte*, ed. Claudia Honegger (Frankfurt a. M., 1977), p. 24; Fernand Braudel et al., *Die Welt des Mittelmeeres*, (Frankfurt a. M., 1997), pp. 21 f., 31.

131. Rackham and Moody, *Cretan Landscape* (note 32), pp. 18, 21; Rackham, "Ecology and Pseudo-ecology: The Example of Ancient Greece," in *Human Landscapes in Classical Antiquity*, eds. Graham Shipley and John Salmon (London, 1996), p. 25; Rackham and Moody, "Terraces" (note 36), pp. 123, 133. For McNeill, *Mountains of the Mediterranean* (Chap. 1, note 16), Rackham's position is a "maverick opinion" (p. 311, note). Even to Jacques Blondel und James Aronson, who portray the relationship between humans and their environment in the Mediterranean as a "thousand-year love story," the process of deforestation is a fact: *Biology and Wildlife in the Mediterranean Region*, (Oxford, 1999), pp. 197, 201, 206, except that from the perspective of biodiversity, they do not necessarily regret

that process. But Andel and Runnels, *Beyond the Acropolis* (note 36) also note that Mediterranean vegetation recovers quickly after being disturbed and impeded erosion (pp. 140, 142). Meiggs, *Trees and Timber* (note 130), p. 385 f.: the Romans knew how to keep their sheep and goats under control.

132. Andel and Runnels, *Beyond the Acropolis* (note 36), pp. 113, 116 f., 120 ff., 139 f., 152; Curtis N. Runnels, "Umweltzerstörung im griechischen Altertum," in *Frühe Stadtkulturen*, ed. Wolfram Hoepfner (Heidelberg, 1997), pp. 138, 142; Tjeerd H. van Andel and Eberhard Zangger, "Landscape Stability and Destabilisation in the Prehistory of Greece," in Bottema, *Man's Role* (note 29), pp. 139, 147; Eberhard Zangger, "Neolithic to Present Soil Erosion in Greece," in *Past and Present Soil Erosion*, ed. Martin Bell and John Boardman (Oxford, 1992), pp. 133–42, 146.

133. McNeill, *Mountains* (Chap. 1, note 16); Eugen Wirth, *Syrien: Eine geographische Landeskunde* (Darmstadt, 1971), pp. 124 f., 131 f.; Thirgood, *Cyprus* (note 129), p. 74; *Ambiente Italia* (note 102), pp. 40, 42 f. (Sergio Anselmi): progressive deforestation, especially since the sixteenth century, was accelerated in the nineteenth by the cultivation of maize, since it can also be done on slopes; Bruno Donati and Alice Lang, *La Valle Maggia* (Bellinzona, 1983), pp. 9 ff.; G. H. Willcox, "A History of Deforestation as Indicated by Charcoal Analysis of 4 Sites in Eastern Anatolia," *Anatolian Studies* 24 (1974): 123; Brent D. Shaw, *Environment and Society in Roman North Africa* (Aldershot, 1995), pp. 392 ff.; Moses I. Finley et al., *A History of Sicily* (New York, 1968), vol. I, p. 157; Braudel, *Mediterranean* (Chap. 2, note 5), vol. I, pp. 602 ff.; Meiggs, *Trees and Timber* (note 130), p. 392; Kolokotronis: McNeill, *Mountains* (Chap. 1, note 6), p. 300, note; Alfred Philippson, *Das Ägäische Meer und seine Inseln* (Frankfurt a. M., 1959), p. 46.

134. Maurice Lombard, *Blütezeit des Islams* (Frankfurt a. M., 1992 [1971]), pp. 177 ff.; Lombard, "Les bois dans la Méditerranée musulmane (VII–XIᵉ siècles)," *Annales ESC* (1959): 234–54; Wilhelm Wölfel, *Wasserbau in den Alten Reichen* (Berlin, 1990), p. 19; Radkau and Schäfer, *Holz* (Chap. 1, note 50), p. 21; Johannes Koder, *Der Lebensraum der Byzantiner* (Graz, 1984), p. 53 f.; Eugen Wirth, *Syrien* (Darmstadt, 1971), p. 125.

135. Piers Blaikie and Harold Brookfield, "Questions from History in the Mediterranean and Western Europe," in Blaikie and Brookfield, *Land Degradation* (Chap. 1, note 80), p. 122 f.; Claudia Vita-Finzi stimulated the discussion with his climate change hypothesis: *The Mediterranean Valleys: Geological Changes in Historical Times* (Cambridge, 1969), p. 115 and elsewhere. Vita-Finzi notes that the Romans were interested in erosion on the mountain slopes, since the soil was easier to cultivate in the valleys, "although the Romans fully deserve to be regarded as conservation minded" (p. 117). Staking out a middle ground is Alfred Philippson, *Das Mittelmeergebiet* (Hildesheim, 1974), pp. 133 ff.; p. 141: "Thus, while the characteristic landscape picture of the Mediterranean countries is essentially the product of the climate, human culture has significantly accentuated it."

136. Neil A. Wells and Benjamin R. Andriamihaja, "Extreme Gully Erosion in Madagascar and Its Natural and Anthropogenic Causes," in *Natural Change and Human Impact in Madagascar*, ed. Steven M. Goodman and Bruce D. Patterson (Washington, D.C., 1997), p. 70.

137. Bruno Vecchio, *Il bosco negli scrittori italiani del settecento e dell'età napoleonica* (Turin, 1974), pp. 151 ff., 194 ff.

138. Aristotle, *The Politics of Aristotle*, ed. and trans. Ernest Barker (New York, 1962), Book 7, 1331 b, p. 310. Thérèse Sclafert, *Cultures en Haute-Provence; Déboisement et pâturages au Moyen Age* (Paris, 1959), pp. 170 f.

139. Piero Bevilacqua, "Acque e terre nel Regno di Napoli," *Ambiente Italia* (note 102), pp. 78 ff.

140. Hansjörg Köster, *Geschichte der Landschaft in Mitteleuropa* (Munich, 1995), pp. 219, 224; Martin Born, *Die Entwicklung der deutschen Agrarlandschaft* (Darmstadt, 1974), pp. 28, 38; Hans-Jürgen Nitz, "Regelmäßige Langstreifenfluren und fränkische Staatskolonisation," in *Historisch-genetische Siedlungsforschung*, ed. Hans-Jürgen Nitz (Darmstadt, 1974), p. 358. For France, with reference to oustanding questions, see Duby and Wallon, *France Rurale* (Chap. 1, note 67), vol. I, pp. 426 ff. (Guy Fourquin). It would appear that virtual

forest-clearing contracts between manorial lords and those willing to undertake the work are far more rare in France than in Germany.

141. Helmut Hildebrandt, "Siedlungsgenese und Siedlungsplanung in historischer Zeit," in *Historische Kolonisation und Plansiedlung in Deutschland*, ed. Hans-Jürgen Nitze (Berlin, 1994), p. 21; *Fischer Weltgeschichte*, XI (Frankfurt a. M., 1965), p. 72 (Jacques Le Goff); Heide Wunder, *Die bäuerliche Gemeinde in Deutschland* (Göttingen, 1986), p. 41.

142. Franz, *Quellen* (Chap. 2, note 61), pp. 48 f., 182 f.; Schubert, *Alltag im Mittelalter* (Chap. 1, note 38), p. 44; *Die Landschaften Niedersachsens*, 3rd ed. (Hannover, 1965), no. 94; Simone Lefèvre, "La politique forestière des monastères de l'Ile-de-France," *Actes du symposium international d'histoire forestière* (Nancy, 1979), vol. I, p. 20.

143. Louis Badré, *Histoire de la forêt française* (Paris, 1983), p. 46 f.; similar examples from the sources: Ernst Schubert, "Scheu vor der Natur – Ausbeutung der Natur: Formen und Wandlungen des Umweltbewußtseins im Mittelalter," *Von der Angst zur Ausbeutung: Umwelterfahrung zwischen Mittelalter und Neuzeit* (Frankfurt a. M., 1994), p. 22.

144. Marc Bloch, *French Rural History: An Essay on Its Basic Characteristics*, trans. Janet Sondheimer (Berkeley, Calif., 1966), p. 17; Glacken, *Traces* (Chap. 1, note 25), pp. 327 f., 332 f., 336 ff.; Radkau and Schäfer, *Holz* (Chap. 1, note 50), p. 53 f.; Karl Hasel, *Forstgeschichte* (Freiburg, 1985), p. 52; Abel, *Agricultural Fluctuations* (Chap. 1, note 30), p. 83; Helga Knoke, *Wald und Siedlung im Süntel* (Rinteln, 1968), p. 37; Alfred Bonnemann, *Der Reinhardswald* (Hann. Münden, 1984), p. 236.

145. Hans-Rudolf Bork, *Bodenerosion und Umwelt: Verlauf, Ursachen und Folgen der mittelalterlichen und neuzeitlichen Bodenerosion* (Braunschweig, 1988), pp. 34 ff., 43 f., 47 f., 198; Bork, *Landschaftsentwicklung* (Chap. 1, note 14), pp. 31 ff.

146. Radkau and Schäfer, *Holz* (Chap. 1, note 50), p. 58 f.; Hasel, *Forstgeschichte* (note 145), p. 108 f.

147. Charles R. Young, *The Royal Forests of Medieval England* (Leicester, 1979), p. 7.

148. Schubert, *Alltag im Mittelalter* (Chap. 1, note 38), pp. 48 ff.

149. Joachim Radkau, "Vom Wald zum Floß – ein technisches System? Dynamik und Schwerfälligkeit der Flößerei in der Geschichte der Forst- und Holzwirtschaft," in *Auf den Spuren der Flößer*, ed. Hans-Walter Keweloh (Stuttgart, 1988), pp. 21 ff.; Theodor Müller, *Schiffahrt und Flößerei im Flußgebiet der Oker* (Braunschweig, 1968), p. 85; Radkau and Schäfer, *Holz* (Chap. 1, note 50), pp. 99 ff.; Robert G. Albion, *Forests and Sea Power* (Cambridge, 1926), p. 183.

150. Michel Devèze, *La grande réformation des forêts sous Colbert* (Nancy, 1962); Andrée Corvol, *L'homme et l'arbre sous l'Ancien Régime* (Paris, 1984), pp. 178, 185; Corvol, *L'Homme aux Bois: Histoire des relations de l'homme et de la forêt XVIIᵉ-XXᵉ siècle* (Paris, 1987), p. 305.

151. Oliver Rackham, *Trees and Woodland in the British Lanscape* (London, 1976), p. 85; Rackham, *Ancient Woodland, Its History, Vegetation and Uses in England* (London, 1980), p. 153; on the other hand, see his *The Illustrated History of the Countryside* (London, 1994), p. 48: "In France, Germany and Switzerland, ancient woods are everyone's heritage; in Britain alone have we lost that birthright, and with it the knowledge and love of woods." He is doubtful, however, whether the cruel punishments of the Middle Ages were ever imposed: Rackham, *The Last Forest: The Story of Hatfield Forest* (London, 1989), p. 60 f. Charles R. Young, *The Royal Forests of Medieval England*, (Leicester, 1979), pp. 7, 11, 65, 147; Thomas, *Man and the Natural World* (Chap. 2, note 39), pp. 194 ff., 198 ff.

152. Radkau and Schäfer, *Holz* (Chap. 1, note 50), p. 145.

153. Dorothea Hauff, *Zur Geschichte der Forstgesetzgebung und Forstorganisation des Herzogtums Württemberg im 16. Jahrhundert* (Stuttgart, 1977), p. 31.

154. Radkau and Schäfer, *Holz* (Chap. 1, note 50), pp. 59 ff., 64 f.; Knoke, *Wald und Siedlung* (note 145), pp. 51, 63 f.

155. Radkau and Schäfer, *Holz* (Chap. 1, note 50), pp. 54 f., 170 ff.; Heinrich Oberrauch, *Tirols Wald und Waidwerk* (Innsbruck, 1952), p. 21. Rocquelet: *Histoire des forêts française: Guide de recherche* (Paris [CNRS], 1982), p. 135; Christian Fruhauf takes a different view: *Forêt et société: De la forêt paysanne à la forêt capitaliste en pays de Sault sous l'ancien régime* (Paris,

1980). A peculiar consensus on forest policy is reported from Kurtrier by Christoph Ernst, "Den Wald entwickeln: Ein Politik- und Konfliktfeld in Hunsrück und Eifel im 18. Jh.," dissertation, University of Trier, 1998, pp. 247 ff.: there the efforts of the territorial estates to "get rid of the Forestry Office," which was dominated by the hunters, were supported by the government, which abolished the Forestry Office in 1783! In all of this, the wood shortage argument is tossed back and forth.

156. Ingrid Schäfer, *"Ein Gespenst geht um": Politik mit der Holznot in Lippe, 1750–1850* (Detmold, 1992), pp. 62 ff.

157. Josef Mooser, "'Furcht bewahrt das Holz.' Holzdiebstahl und sozialer Konflikt in der ländlichen Gesellschaft 1800–1850 an westfälischen Beispielen," in *Räuber, Volk und Obrigkeit*, ed. Heinz Reif (Frankfurt a. M., 1984), p. 77 f.

158. Max Weber, *Wirtschaftsgeschichte*, ed. S. Hellmann and M. Palyi, 5th ed. (Berlin, 1991), p. 271 f.

159. Richard M. Allesch, *Arsenik: Seine Geschichte in Österreich* (Klagenfurt, 1959); Helfried Valentinitsch, *Das landesfürstliche Quecksilberbergwerk Idria 1575–1659* (Graz, 1981), p. 202; Maria Barbara Rößner, "Gesundheitsgefährdung durch Umweltverschmutzung: Vorindustrielles Umweltbewußtsein in Köln," *Jahrbuch des kölnischen Geschichtsvereins* 66 (1999): 69 ff.

160. Peter Brimblecombe, *The Big Smoke: A History of Air Pollution in London since Medieval Times* (London, 1987).

161. John Evelyn, "Fumifugium: or the Inconvenience of the Aer and Smoake of London," in *The Smoke of London: Two Prophecies*, ed. Robert Barr (Elmsford, n.d.), pp. 20 f., 24; Evelyn, *Sylva or a Discourse on Forest Trees* (London, 1664).

162. André Guillerme, *Les temps de l'eau: La cité, l'eau et les techniques* (Seyssel, 1983), pp. 63 ff., 74, 101 f.

163. Elisabeth Suter, *Wasser und Brunnen im alten Zürich* (Zurich, 1981), p. 113 f.; *Die Wasserversorgung im Mittelalter* (Mainz, 1991), pp. 53, 55 f. (Klaus Grewe); Ulf Dirlmeier, "Zu den Lebensbedingungen in der mittelalterlichen Stadt: Trinkwasserversorgung und Abfallbeseitigung," in *Mensch und Umwelt im Mittelalter*, ed. Bernd Herrmann (Stuttgart, 1986), p. 152 f.; *Von der Schîssgruob zur modernen Stadtsanierung* (Zurich, 1987), pp. 41 f., 57 f.

164. *Wasserversorgung im Mittelalter* (note 163), p. 96 f. (Clemens Kosch). Martin Illi, "Wasserentsorgung in mittelalterlichen Städten," *Die alte Stadt* 20 (1993): 223 (here once again using Zurich as an example): as a rule the authorities made sure that only "pure" dishwater, or at most urine, could be emptied into the gutter.

165. Horst Dreitzel, "Johann Peter Süßmilchs Beitrag zur politischen Diskussion der deutschen Aufklärung," in *Ursprünge der Demographie in Deutschland*, ed. Herwig Birg (Frankfurt a. M., 1986), p. 91; Hufeland, *Makrobiotik* (Frankfurt a. M., 1984 [1796]), p. 131.

166. J. H. Vogel, *Die Verwertung der städtischen Abfallstoffe* (Berlin, 1896).

167. Sabine Barles, "L'invention des eaux usées: l'assainissement de Paris, de la fin de l'Ancien Régime à la seconde guerre mondiale," in *Le Démon moderne: La pollution dans les sociétés urbaines et industrielles d'europe*, ed. Christoph Bernhardt and Geneviève Massard-Guilbaud (Paris, 2002), pp. 129–56.

168. Wines, *Fertilizer in America* (note 49), pp. 3, 11 f.; Maria Curter, *Berliner Gold: Geschichte der Müllbeseitigung in Berlin* (Berlin, 1996), pp. 32 ff.

169. *Schîssgruob* (note 163), p. 44; Peter Reinhart Gleichmann, "Die Verhäuslichung körperlicher Verrichtungen," in *Materialien zu N. Elias' Zivilisationstheorie*, ed. Peter Reinhart Gleichmann et al. (Frankfurt a. M., 1977), pp. 261 ff. Berlin passed an ordinance in 1671 that "every peasant who comes to market shall take one load of excrement out of the city" (Marie-Elisabeth Hilger, "Umweltprobleme als Alltagserfahrung in der frühneuzeitlichen Stadt?" *Die alte Stadt* 11 [1984]: 132), a sign that even back then, the problem of the disposal of excreta that the cities faced did not resolve itself through the peasants' hunger for fertilizer. Dirlmeier, "Lebensbedingungen" (note 64), p. 158; Jürgen Hagel, "Mensch und Wasser in der alten Stadt: Stuttgart als Modell," *Die alte Stadt* 14 (1987): 135 f. In a city like

Freiburg, which had numerous streams with a strong gradient, the "water closet" – the latrine over a brook or ditch – was already widespread in the late Middle Ages: Werner Konold and Katrin Schwinekörper, "Wasser und Abwasser in der Stadtwirtschaft," *Der Bürger im Staat* 46, no. 1 (1996): 15. It would appear that the earliest place where latrines located above a flowing body of water were the usual standard was in remote Cistercian monasteries that had plenty of water and few neighbors.

170. *Minden – 1200 Jahre Stadtgeschichte* (Minden, 1998), p. 34.

171. On this and the following discussion: Joachim Radkau, "Das Rätsel der städtischen Brennholzversorgung im 'hölzernen Zeitalter,'" in *Energie und Stadt in Europa: Von der vorindustriellen 'Holznot' bis zur Ölkrise der 1970er Jahre,* ed. Dieter Schott (Stuttgart, 1997), pp. 43–75.

172. Heinz-Dieter Heimann, "Der Wald in der städtischen Kulturentfaltung und Land-schaftswahrnehmung," in *Mensch und Natur im Mittelalter,* ed. Albert Zimmermann and Andreas Speer (Berlin, 1991), vol. I, p. 871; *Histoire des forêts* (note 156), p. 76; as late as 1830, the forest villages of Ariège were engaged in a virtual war against the iron works and charcoal-makers in an effort to preserve their forest rights: *Peter Sahlins, Forest Rites: The War of the Demoiselles in 19th Century France* (Cambridge, Mass., 1994). Antje Sander-Berke, "Spätmittelalterliche Holznutzung für den Baustoffbedarf, dargest. am Beispiel norddeutscher Städte," in *Bergbau, Verhüttung und Waldnutzung im Mittelalter: Auswirkungen auf Mensch und Umwelt,* ed. Albrecht Jockenhövel (Stuttgart, 1996), p. 197. Another impor-tant topic that is not dealt with here is the effect of cities on the surrounding agriculture; on this see Franz Irsigler, "Die Gestaltung der Kulturlandschaft am Niederrhein unter dem Einfluß städtischer Wirtschaft," in *Wirtschaftsentwicklung und Umweltbeeinflussung,* ed. Hermann Kellenbenz (Wiesbaden, 1982), pp. 173–95. The urban market often led to an intensification of nearby agriculture, as in the form of garden cultivation, but also to the one-sided cultivation of industrial plants, in which case, especially, there was a danger of exhausting the soil.

173. Erich Egg et al., *Stadtbuch Schwaz* (Schwaz, 1986), pp. 97, 101.

174. Radkau, "Rätsel" (note 172), p. 56 f.

175. Eugen Wagner, *Die Holzversorgung der Lüneburger Saline in ihrer wirtschaftsgeschichtlichen und kulturgeographischen Bedeutung* (Düsseldorf, 1930); Christian Lamschus, "Die Holzvers-orgung der Lüneburger Saline in Mittelalter und Früher Neuzeit," in *Recht und Alltag im Hanseraum,* ed. Silke Urbanski et al. (Lüneburg, 1993), pp. 321–32; Radkau and Schäfer, *Holz* (Chap. 1, note 50), pp. 91–5, 131 ff., 196 f.; Götz v. Bülow, *Die Sudwälder von Reichen-hall* (Munich, 1962), p. 159 f.; on this see J. Radkau in *Geschichte in Wissenschaft und Unterricht* 50 (1999): 256.

176. Joachim Radkau, "Holzverknappung und Krisenbewußtsein im 18. Jh.," *Geschichte und Gesellschaft* 9 (1983): 515 and elsewhere; Denis Woronoff, *L'industrie sidérurgique en France pendant la révolution et l'Empire* (Paris, 1984); Arlette Brosselin et al., "Les doléances contre l'industrie," in *Forges et forêts,* ed. Denis Woronoff (Paris, 1990), p. 13.

177. Rackham (note 152, first two references); also, Radkau, "Holzverknappung" (note 177), p. 526, note 54. Radkau and Schäfer, *Holz* (Chap. 1, note 50), pp. 107 ff.

178. Oberrauch, *Tirols Wald* (note 156), p. 49 f.

179. Mircea Eliade, *The Forge and the Crucible,* trans. Stephen Corrin (Chicago, 1962), p. 43 f.; Georg Agricola, *Vom Berg- und Hüttenwesen* (Munich, 1977 [1556]), p. 3; Bünting: Günter Bayerl and Ulrich Troitzsch, eds., *Quellentexte zur Geschichte der Umwelt von der Antike bis heute* (Göttingen, 1998), pp. 187 ff.

180. Vögler, *Öko-Griechen* (note 33), p. 79; Pliny (Chap. 2, note 83), 33.21.

181. Paulus Niavis, *Judicium Jovis oder Das Gericht der Götter über den Bergbau* (Berlin, 1953) (Freiberger Forschungshefte D 3).

182. Joachim Radkau, *Technik in Deutschland: Vom 18. Jahrhundert bis zur Gegenwart* (Frankfurt a. M., 1989), p. 112.

183. Eliade, *Forge and Crucible* (note 179), p. 67; Pliny (Chap. 2, note 83), 33, 21.

4. COLONIALISM AS A WATERSHED IN ENVIRONMENTAL HISTORY

1. Elizabeth Dore, "How Sustainable Were Pre-Columbian Civilizations?" in *Green Guerillas: Environmental Conflicts and Initiatives in Latin America and the Caribbean*, ed. Helen Collinson (London, 1996), p. 49; David Watts, *The West Indies: Patterns of Development, Culture and Environmental Change since 1492* (Cambridge, 1987); *HB Bildatlas Dominikanische Republik – Haiti* (Hamburg, 1999), p. 87; Rudolf Borchardt, ed., *Der Deutsche in der Landschaft* [1925] (Frankfurt a. M., 1989), pp. 215 ff.; Marc Aurele Holly, *Agriculture in Haiti* (New York, 1955), p. 217; India: personal communication from Michael Mann.

2. George P. Marsh, *Man and Nature: Or, Physical Geography as Modified by Human Action* [1864] (Cambridge, Mass., 1965), p. 11; Horst G. Mensching, "Ökoystem-Zerstörung in vorindustrieller Zeit," in Lübbe and Ströker, *Ökologische Probleme* (Chap. 1, note 30), p. 20 f.

3. On the statement "latifundia perdidere" see René Martin, "Plinius d.J. und die wirtschaftlichen Probleme seiner Zeit," in *Sozial- und Wirtschaftsgeschichte der römischen Kaiserzeit*, ed. Helmuth Schneider (Darmstadt, 1981), pp. 199 ff.; Moses I. Finley dismisses Pliny's words as a moralizing generalization: *Ancient Slavery and Modern Ideology* (New York, 1980), p. 92. All these discussions, however, are characterized by an absence of any ecological examination of agriculture. By contrast, see Cedric Yeo, "The Overgrazing of Ranch-Lands in Ancient Italy," *Transactions of the American Philological Association* 79 (1948): 292 ff.; *Propyläen-Technikgeschichte*, I (Frankfurt a. M., 1991), pp. 214 ff. (Helmuth Schneider). C. R. Whittaker, "Agri deserti," in *Studies in Roman Property*, ed. M. I. Finley (Cambridge, 1976), pp. 137–65. Ellsworth Huntington," Climate Change and Agricultural Exhaustion as Elements in the Fall of Rome," *Quarterly Journal of Economics* 31 (1917): 173–208; on this see Rhoads Murphy, "The Decline of North Africa since the Roman Occupation: Climatic or Human?" *Annals of the Association of American Geographers* 41 (1951): 116–32. Max Weber, *Die römische Agrargeschichte in ihrer Bedeutung für das Staats- und Privatrecht* [1891] (Tübingen, 1988), p. 131; Weber, *Gesammelte Aufsätze zur Sozial- und Wirtschaftsgeschichte* (Tübingen, 1988), p. 310. Unlike other scholars, Lynn White, Jr. (*Medieval Technology and Social Change*, [Oxford, 1962], pp. 70, 75), believes that there was no regular field and crop rotation in Roman agriculture, in spite of relevant ideas in the agrarian writings. If he is correct, it would mean that an essential element of stability was missing.

4. Hodgson, *Venture of Islam* (Chap. 2, note 92), vol. II, pp. 396, 402 f.; Cotterell and Yap, *Early Civilization of China* (Chap. 3, note 60), p. 221. When Mongol rule was overthrown in China in 1368, and the Mongols flooded back to their ancestral lands, the conflict over pastureland grew more intense, and there were growing signs of overuse: Udo B. Barkmann, *Geschichte der Mongolei* (Bonn, 1999), pp. 21, 25 f. (immoral killing of refugees of one's own people as an "emergency brake for population policy").

5. McNeill, *Plagues* (Chap. 3, note 117), p. 147; Klaus Bergdolt, *Der Schwarze Tod in Europa: Die Große Pest und das Ende des Mittelalters* (Munich, 1994), pp. 34 ff.

6. Ulrich Raulff, "Die Schule der Ratten gegen die Schule der Flöhe: Über Menschen- und Naturgeschichten," in *Vom Umschreiben der Geschichte*, ed. Ulrich Raulff (Berlin, 1986), p. 18.

7. Bergdolt, *Schwarze Tod* (note 5), pp. 14 ff.; McNeill, *Plagues* (Chap. 3, note 117) pp. 103 f., 106; Ruffié and Sournia, *Seuchen* (Chap. 3, note 116), pp. 25 ff.; Winkle, *Geißeln* (Chap. 3, note 116), pp. 436 ff.

8. Bergdolt, *Schwarze Tod* (note 5), pp. 17, 34; McNeill, *Plagues* (Chap. 3, note 116), chap. III.

9. Michael M. Postan, *The Medieval Economy and Society* (London, 1972), pp. 26 f., 63 ff.; William Chester Jordan, *The Great Famine: Northern Europe in the Early 14th Century* (Princeton, N.J., 1996), pp. 26 f., 200 f.; Joan Thirsk, *Alternative Agriculture: A History from the Black Death to the Present Day* (Oxford, 1997), p. 254 f., emphasizes, against the "Postan orthodoxy," more strongly the flexibility of peasants and their capacity for innovation in times of crisis; J. D. Chambers and G. E. Mingay, *The Agricultural Revolution 1750–1880* (London,

1966), p. 6. The great French medievalist Jacques Le Goff believed – even before the ecological era – that he could detect an ecologial crisis in Europe around 1300: a vicious
cycle of overpopulation, deforestation, overuse of the soil, and soil erosion: *Das Hochmittelalter* (Frankfurt a. M., 1965) (= *Fischer Weltgeschichte*, vol. XI), p. 277 f.

10. Daniel Defoe, *A Journal of the Plague Year* [1723] (New York, 1960), p. 101. The "Black
Death" as the savior from a vicious ecological cycle: Charles R. Bowlus, "Die Umweltkrise
im Europa des 14. Jahrhunderts," in *Fortschritte der Naturzerstörung*, ed. Rolf Peter Sieferle
(Frankfurt a. M., 1988), pp. 13 ff. Neithard Bulst, "Krankheit und Gesellschaft in der
Vormoderne: Das Beispiel der Pest," in Bulst and Delort, *Maladies* (Chap. 3, note 120), p. 29.
Even Marsilius von Padua, though an advocate of peace at heart, mentions in his *Defensor Pacis*
(1324) wars and epidemics as the steps that Heaven and nature took against overpopulation
(ne hominum superflua propagatio fiat): Dictio I, cap. 17, no. 10. Overpopulation was thus
already perceived to be a danger before the first great plague epidemic. I would like to thank
Horst Dreitzel for calling my attention to this passage in Marsilius.

11. Johan Goudsblom, "Zivilisation, Ansteckungsangst und Hygiene: Betrachtungen über
einen Aspekt des europäischen Zivilisationsprozesses," in Gleichmann, *Materialien* (Chap. 3,
note 170), pp. 215 ff. See ibid., p. 222: Elias himself would not accept such a trivial, rational
explanation, which would have made sociological-anthropological explanations unnecessary.

12. Bulst, "Krankheit und Gesellschaft" (note 10), pp. 28, 32, 13; Paul Slack, "The Disappearance
of Plague: An Alternative View," *Economic History Review*, 2nd Ser. 34 (1981): 475: "It *was*
human action which freed Western Europe from plague in the later 17th century and
early 18th century." Erna Lesky, "Die österreichische Pestfront an der k.k. Militärgrenze,"
Saeculum 8 (1957): 104 f. (arguments for its effectiveness). Peter Frey in *Die Rückkehr der
Seuchen*, ed. Hans Schadewaldt (Cologne, 1994), p. 41: "There is a good deal of evidence
that the plague pathogen itself underwent a mutation that made it less aggressive."

13. Alfred W. Crosby, *Ecological Imperialism: The Biological Expansion of Europe, 900–1900* (Cambridge, 1986). Methodological critique of Crosby: William Cronon, *Changes in the Land:
Indians, Colonists, and the Ecology of New England* (New York, 1983), p. 14. More fundamental still: David Arnold, *The Problem of Nature: Environment, Culture and European Expansion*
(Oxford, 1996), pp. 80 ff., 87 ff. (on biological determinism and Social Darwinism in
Crosby), p. 91: "Crosby marches with the armies of conquest; he does not tarry with
nature's losers."

14. In an earlier book, Crosby himself pointed to such reciprocal effects of colonialism: *The
Columbian Exchange: Biological and Cultural Consequences of 1492* (Westport, Conn., 1972),
p. 176 f. and elsewhere. But this book, which still presented the ecological story without the
word "imperialism" and on the model of "reciprocal effects" did not have nearly the impact
of his *Ecological Imperialism!* Indios and sheep: Daniel W. Gade, "Landscape, System, and
Identity in the Post-Conquest Andes," in *Agriculture, Resource Exploitation, and Environmental
Change*, ed. Helen Wheatley (Aldershot, 1997), p. 36. The beginnings of wheat cultivation
in the states of New England were difficult and involved severe setbacks (Cronon, *Changes*
[note 13], pp. 153 ff.), whereas maize spread much more rapidly in the Mediterranean regions:
Johannes Zscheischler et al., *Handbuch Mais*, 4th ed. (Frankfurt a. M., 1990), pp. 15 ff. In
Germany, the era of maize cultivation, in spite of numerous older efforts, did not begin
until the 1970s, on the basis of new hybrids.

15. William N. Denevan, "Estimating the Unknown," in *The Native Population of the Americas in 1492*, ed. William N. Denevan (Madison, Wisc., 1976), pp. 3 ff.; Denevan, "The
Pristine Myth: The Landscape of the Americas in 1492," *Annals of the Association of American Geographers* 82 (1992): 379; Gordon M. Day, "The Indian as an Ecological Factor in
the Northeastern Forest," *Ecology* 34 (1953): 330. Outside of the well-known high civilization of ancient America, the Hohokam of the Sonoran Desert (Arizona) and the mysterious collapse of their irrigation culture have long been an especially interesting and
debated case. There is some indication that salinization was a decisive factor. On this see

Shepard Krech III, *The Ecological Indian: Myth and History* (New York, 1999), pp. 47–61. This too, is evidence of a high population density in some regions outside of the high civilizations.

16. Crosby, *Ecological Imperialism* (note 13), chap. 8; Marvin Harris, "Why the First Earth Conquered the Second," in his *Our Kind: Who We Are, Where We Came From, Where We Are Going* (New York, 1989), pp. 488–91; hoe: Albert Wirz, *Sklaverei und kapitalistisches Weltsystem* (Frankfurt a. M., 1984), p. 111; David Watts, *The West Indies* (Cambridge, 1987), p. 429.

17. Elinor G. K. Melville, *A Plague of Sheep: Environmental Consequences of the Conquest of Mexico* (Cambridge, Mass., 1994), pp. 56 ff., 164; Melville, "The Long-Term Effects of the Introduction of Sheep into Semi-Arid Sub-Tropical Regions," in *Changing Tropical Forests: Historical Perspectives on Today's Challenges in Central & South America*, ed. Harald K. Steen and Richard S. Tucker (Durham, N.C., 1992), pp. 147 and elsewhere. At the ASEH Conference in Tucson (1999), however, Elinor Melville remarked that at the time she was too fixated on the concept of "colonialism" and had therefore not been receptive enough to Indian continuities. See Gade, "Landscape" (note 14), p. 36. Karl W. Butzer, "The Americas before and after 1492," *Annals of the Association of American Geographers* 82 (1992): 354: "In sum, there was a considerable degree of continuity in terms of Indian ownership." Eric R. Wolf, "Aspects of Group Relations in a Complex Society: Mexico," in *Peasants and Peasant Societies*, ed. Theodor Shanin (New York, 1971), pp. 57 ff.: "hostile symbiosis" of the Indian villages with the haciendas. Green Revolution: Veronika Bennholdt-Thomsen, *Subsistenzkultur und bäuerliche Ökonomie* (Bielefeld, 1999) (*Diskussionsbeiträge zur Subsistenz* 7), p. 2.

18. Juan Carlos Garavaglia, "Atlixco: L'eau, les hommes et la terre dans une vallée mexicaine (15e–17e siècles)," *Annales HSS* (Nov./Dec. 1995): 1345; Herman W. Konrad, "Tropical Forest Policy and Practice during the Mexican Porfiriato, 1876–1910," Steen and Tucker, *Tropical Forests* (note 17), p. 131; Joel Simon, *Endangered Mexico: An Environment on the Edge* (San Francisco, 1997), pp. 93 f., 140, 238; Lane Simonian, *Defending the Land of the Jaguar: A History of Conservation in Mexico* (Austin, Tex., 1995), pp. 3, 62, 90 ff., 173; Paul F. Starrs, "California's Grazed Ecosystems," in *Green versus Gold: Sources in California's Environmental History*, ed. Carolyn Merchant (Washington, D.C., 1998), p. 200. In Central America, too, the great waves of deforestation evidently occurred only after independence, if not until after 1945: Stanley Heckadon-Moreno, "Spanish Rule, Independence, and the Modern Colonization Frontiers," in *Central America: A Natural and Cultural History*, ed. Anthony G. Coates (New Haven, Conn., 1997), pp. 185 ff. In 1938, at the time of the Dust Bowl, Carl Sauer, one of the founding fathers of cultural geography in America, wrote: "The United States heads the list of exploited and dissipated land wealth. Physically, Latin America is in much better shape than our own Country." Quoted in Donald Worster, *Dust Bowl* (Oxford, 1979), p. 206 f.

19. Hobhouse, *Seeds of Change* (Chap. 3, note 115), p. 52.

20. Wirz, *Sklaverei* (note 16), pp. 93, 193, 218; Anthony Luttrell, "The sugar industry and its importance for the economy of Cyprus during the Frankish period," in *The Development of the Cypriot Economy*, ed. V. Karageorghis (Nicosia, 1996), p. 165; Watts, *West Indies* (note 1), pp. 393–400; Hobhouse, *Seeds of Change* (Chap. 3, note 115), p. 52; Heinrich Handelmann, *Geschichte von Brasilien* (Zurich, 1987 [1860]), p. 414; Gilberto Freyre, *The Mansions and the Shanties (Sobrados e mucambos): The Making of Modern Brazil*, trans. and ed. Harriet de Onís, with an introduction by Frank Tannenbaum (New York, 1963), chap. 10; Al Imfeld, *Zucker* (Zurich, 1983); Sidney W. Mintz, *Sweetness and Power: The Place of Sugar in Modern History* (New York, 1985).

21. Handelmann, *Brasilien* (note 19), p. 410; see also Fernando Ortiz, *Tabak und Zucker: Ein kubanischer Disput* (Frankfurt a. M., 1987). Freyre, *Mansions and Shanties* (note 19), p. 433 f. Poivre, *Travels* (Chap. 2, note 62), p. 18 ff.; Ghana: information kindly provided by Christfried Döring.

22. *Fischer Weltgeschichte,* XXII (Frankfurt a. M., 1965), p. 307 (Richard Konetzke); Horst G. Mensching, "Natur als Ressource = Naturzerstörung?" in *Zum Naturbegriff der Gegenwart* (Stuttgart, 1994), vol. I, p. 178; Franz Thorbecke, "Waldnutzung und Waldschutz im tropischen Westafrika," in *Beiträge zur Geographie der Wald- und Forstwirtschaft,* ed. Hans-Wilhelm Windhorst (Darmstadt, 1978), pp. 39 ff.

23. For information on Haiti I am grateful to Heike Bienefeld. Wolf Donner, *Haiti: Naturraumpotential und Entwicklung* (Tübingen, 1980), pp. 153, 190 ff., 206 ff. Erosion also as a social problem: "As a rule, the person who causes erosion does not suffer from its effects," and nothing was more "alien" to the Haitian peasant "than the spirit of solidarity" (p. 208). Anthony V. Catanese, *Rural Poverty and Environmental Degradation in Haiti* (Bloomington, Ind., 1991), p. 36: "pervasive rural individualism" as a cause of erosion, no thought given to terracing. Walther L. Bernecker, *Kleine Geschichte Haitis* (Frankfurt a. M., 1996), pp. 7, 133, 193 f.

24. James C. McCann, *People of the Plow: An Agricultural History of Ethiopia, 1800–1990* (Madison, Wisc., 1995), pp. 33 note ("drought follows the plow"), 93, 133, 145, 263. The findings are not entirely clear, however.

25. Leroy Vail, "Ecology and History: The Example of Eastern Zambia," *Journal of Southern Africa Studies* 3 (1977): 138 ff.; Helge Kjekshus, *Ecology Control and Economic Development in East African History: The Case of Tanganyika 1850–1950* (London, 1977), pp. 126, 181, and elsewhere. With a somewhat qualifying perspective: John McCracken, "Colonialism, capitalism and the ecological crisis in Malawi: A Reassessment," in *Conservation in Africa,* ed. David Anderson and Richard Grove (Cambridge, 1989), pp. 63, 68, 71 ff.; John Ford, *The Role of the Trypanosomiases in African Ecology: A Study of the Tsetse Fly Problem* (Oxford, 1971), esp. pp. 488–93; John M. MacKenzie, *The Empire of Nature: Hunting, Conservation and British Imperialism* (Manchester, 1988), pp. 225 ff.: Reserves and the tsetse controversy. It is peculiar how little attention this highly explosive controversy has received in the discussion of the Crosby thesis. On the deeply emotional connection between imperialism and big-game hunting see also William Beinart, "Empire, Hunting and Ecological Change in Southern and Central Africa," *Past & Present* 128 (1990): 162–86. Imperialists and hunters were already subjected to criticism from contemporaries: the wildlife reserves were a means of disarming critics. Sympathies for the tsetse fly: Jonathan S. Adams and Thomas O. McShane, *The Myth of Wild Africa: Conservation without Illusion* (Berkeley, Calif., 1992), pp. 49, 59 ff.; Bernhard Grzimek, *Kein Platz für wilde Tiere* (Munich, 1973), p. 16; Grzimek, *Serengeti darf nicht sterben* (Berlin, 1964), p. 242; Anton Metternich, *Die Wüste droht* (Oldenburg, 1949), p. 176. By contrast, Paul Rohrbach, an early thinker of Wilhelmenian "world politics," prophesied that if German science were able to conquer the "tsetse evil," the "curse of the black continent," all of Africa would willingly submit to the Germans: *Weltpolitisches Wanderbuch* (Leipzig, 1916), p. 216 f. The emergence of a "siege mentality" among the early proponents of African national parks: Robert W. Sussmann et al., "Satellite Imagery, Human Ecology, Anthropology, and Deforestation in Madagascar," *Human Ecology* 22 (1994): 340. Nancy Langston in personal communication with the author (April 15, 1999), based on personal research in Zimbabwe: as long as the Africans were in a sense part of the animal world, they were allowed to remain within the animal reservations. But when they became fully human, their presence was considered unnatural!

26. John M. MacKenzie, *Empires of Nature and the Natures of Empires: Imperialism, Scotland and the Environment* (East Linton, 1997), p. 18. MacKenzie also offers an especially competent discussion of Grove's theses (pp. 18 f. and 70 f.), for if there is anyone whose scholarly travels match those of Grove, it is MacKenzie.

27. Richard H. Grove, *Green Imperialism: Colonial Expansion, Tropical Island Edens, and the Origins of Environmentalism, 1600–1860* (Cambridge, 1995); on the controversial question of the practical influence of this "environmentalism" see ibid., pp. 427, 484. A brief summary of his argument in "Origins of Western Environmentalism," *Scientific American* 267, no. 1 (1992): 42–7. There the quest is for the Arcadian utopia at the beginning, though in the end economic interests are decisive.

28. Wilhelm Windelband, *Lehrbuch der Geschichte der Philosophie*, 14th ed. (Tübingen, 1950), p. 331 f.; Duhamel: Walter Kremser, *Niedersächische Forstgeschichte* (Rotenburg, 1990), p. 749; Gerold Richter in *Bodenerosion in Mitteleuropa*, ed. Gerold Richter (Darmstadt, 1976), pp. 1 and 23 ff.: Paul Ehrenberg, the first detailed German indications about soil loss (erosion); an *Ökonomierat* by name of Löll wrote in 1848 about the German peasants "that the mud of the brooks and rivers is nothing other than their topsoil washed away by rainwater, it doesn't occur to these good people." It was only wind erosion that drew a reaction in northern Germany and Jütland as early as the seventeenth century: Hans Hausrath, *Geschichte des deutschen Waldbaus* (Freiburg, 1982), pp. 179 ff.

29. Glacken, *Traces* (Chap. 1, note 25), pp. 429 ff.; bumblebees: *Urania Tierreich, Insekten* (Leipzig, 1994), p. 465 f. Especially New Zealand, whose native flora and fauna was not very resistant to neophytes, became the ideal field of experimentation for the "acclimatization" of European species. For a wealth of documentation see Bernhard Kegel, *Die Ameise als Tramp: Von biologischen Invasionen* (Zurich, 1999). That is why New Zealand is the ideal type for the Crosby thesis.

30. Grove, *Green Imperialism* (note 26), p. 174; Poivre, *Travels* (Chap. 2, note 62), pp. 20 ff.

31. Charles R. Redman, *Human Impact on Ancient Environments* (Tucson, Ariz., 1999), p. 193; Roscher, *Ackerbau* (Chap. 1, note 29), p. 838 f.; Pfister, "Patterns" (Chap. 1, note 86), pp. 303, 308. Iceland as a "laboratory" for the influence of environmental change on population development: Arthur E. Imhof, "Mensch und Natur: Züge aus der Bevölkerungsgeschichte der Neuzeit," in Markl, *Natur und Geschichte* (Chap. 1, note 17), pp. 212 ff.; Hans Kuhn, *Das alte Island* (Düsseldorf, 1971), pp. 15 ff., 66, 268; Jesse L. Byock, *Medieval Iceland* (Berkeley, Calif., 1988), p. 95 f. (export and not subsistence-oriented sheep rearing). Thomas H. McGovern et al., "Northern Islands, Human Error, and Environmental Degradation: A View of Social and Ecological Change in the Medieval North Atlantic," *Human Ecology* 16 (1988): 231 f., 245, 248, 261, 264; Daniel E. Vasey, "Population, Agriculture, and Famine: Iceland, 1784–85," *Human Ecology* 19 (1991): 323–50, however, emphasizes the disastrous effect of the volcanic eruption of 1783. Sturla Fridriksson, "Grass and Grass Utilization in Iceland," *Ecology* 53 (1972): 784–96, esp. p. 791.

32. Easter Island as a prime example time and again: Paul R. Ehrlich (author of *Population Bomb*) and Anne H. Ehrlich, *Betrayal of Science and Reason: How Anti-Environmental Rhetoric Threatens Our Future* (Washington, D.C., 1996), pp. 84 ff.; Jared Diamond, "Easter's End," *Discover* 16 (1995), no. 8, pp. 63–9; Ponting, *Green History* (Chap. 3, note 27), pp. 1 ff. (The Lessons of Easter Island); Timothy F. Flannery, *The Future Eaters: An Ecological History of the Australasian Lands and People* (Chatswood, 1994), pp. 254–8. This view is based above all on Paul Bahn and John Flenley, *Easter Island, Earth Island* (London, 1992), pp. 164–218, and was popularized by Kevin Costner's "eco-movie" *Rapa Nui*. For a critical perspective see Jo Anne Van Tilburg, *Easter Island: Archaeology, Ecology and Culture* (London, 1994), esp. p. 164. Roggeveen: Carl Friedrich Behrens, *Der wohlversuchte Südländer: Reise um die Welt 1721/22* (reprint Leipzig, 1925), p. 67. In actuality, Easter Island seems to be a paradigm for the necessity of a critical stance toward deforestation-catastrophe scenarios. The island-ecological collapse paradigm has a theoretical background: namely in the theory – vigorously discussed in the 1970s and 1980s – that ecosystems become stable only once they reach a certain size. This thesis grew out of the growth ambitions of many national parks. On this see David Quammen, *The Song of the Dodo: Island Biogeography in an Age of Extinctions* (London, 1996), pp. 444 ff.

33. Wildlife preserves: MacKenzie, *Empires of Nature* (note 26). Rathenau: "Deutsche Gefahren und neue Ziele," *Neue Freie Presse* (Vienna), December 25, 1913 (*Gesammelte Schriften*, vol. I, pp. 276 ff.); Michael Mann, *Flottenbau und Forstbetrieb in Indien, 1794–1823* (Stuttgart, 1996), pp. 18 ff.; Franz Heske, *Im heiligen Lande der Gangesquellen* (Neudamm, 1937), p. 123; William Beinart and Peter Coates, *Environment and History: The Taming of Nature in the USA and South Africa* (London, 1995), p. 39.

34. Isabelle Knap, "Die Entstehung von Umweltbewußtsein in Kolonialgebieten? Eine Untersuchung des Umgangs der europäischen Kolonialmächte mit Natur und Umwelt in der

frühen Neuzeit am Beispiel von Mauritius, Java, Ambon und Südafrika," Master's Thesis, University of Bielefeld, 2003.

35. In the case of Cleghorn, a pioneer of forest awareness in British India who was harshly critical of the British negligence in matters of forestry, Grove emphasizes his Scottish background: he came from a country that was once treated by England as a quasi colony and ruthlessly deforested. In fact, Grove believes he can detect a specific Scottish environmental consciousness: Richard Grove, "Scotland in South Africa: John Crumbie Brown and the Roots of Settler Environmentalism," in *Ecology and Empire: Environmental History of Settler Societies*, ed. Tom Griffiths and Libby Robin (Seattle, Wash., 1997), pp. 139 ff. Acclimatization: Michael A. Osborne, *Nature, the Exotic, and the Science of French Colonialism* (Bloomington, Ind., 1994), pp. 159 ff.

36. Herbert Scurla, *Alexander v. Humboldt* (Frankfurt a. M., 1984 [1955]), p. 53 f.; Adrian Desmond and James Moore, *Darwin* (New York, 1991), p. 91: "He tore through Humboldt... and everything fell into place." Grove, *Green Imperialism* (note 27), pp. 364 ff., 382; A. v. Humboldt, *Die Reise nach Südamerika* (Göttingen, 1990), p. 286 f.

37. Georg Forster, *A Voyage Round the World*, ed. Nicholas Thomas and Oliver Berghof (Honolulu, 2000), vol. I, pp. 105, 134; Forster, *Ansichten vom Niederrhein* (Stuttgart, 1965 [1791]), pp. 56 ff.; Scurla, *Humboldt* (note 35), p. 39; Beinart and Coates, *Environment and History*, p. 38.

38. Charles Darwin, *The Voyage of the Beagle* (New York, 1909), p. 459; Desmond and Moore, *Darwin* (note 36), p. 266 f.; Grove, *Green Imperialism* (note 27), p. 484, note.

39. Berenbaum, *Bugs in the System* (Chap. 3, note 120), p. 184.

40. Hansjürg Steinlin, "Globale und volkswirtschaftliche Aspekte der Forstwirtschaft," in *Mainauer Gespräche*, vol. X (*Wozu braucht der Mensch den Wald?*) (Mainau, 1994), p. 18 f. France established its first national parks in the African colonies: Emile Leynaud, *L'Etat et la nature: L'exemple des parcs nationaux français* (Florac, 1985), p. 21 f.

41. Jawaharlal Nehru, *Gimpses of World History: Being Further Letters to His Daugher, Written in Prison, and Containing a Rambling Account of History for Young People* (Delhi, 1989), p. 58. In the same year (1989) in which the magnum opus of China's environmental history appeared (Evlin and Liu, *Sediments of Time* [Chap. 3, note 56]), a similarly extensive anthology on the environmental history of Indo-Asia was published: Richard H. Grove, Vinita Damodaran, and Satpal Sangwan, eds., *Nature and the Orient: The Environmental History of South and Southeast Asia* (Delhi, 1998). Its sources, however, reach back only sporadically before the colonial period. One handicap seems to be the fact that most Indian historians are not able to read the Persian sources of the Mughal period. I am grateful to Ravi Rajan for information about the current state of scholarship. Gadgil and Guha, *This Fissured Land* (Chap. 1, note 48), p. 107 f.; elsewhere, however, Guha, too, emphasizes the western origins of India's modern environmental consciousness; see Grove et al. (above), p. 23, note 54. Irfan Habib, *The Agrarian System of Mughal India (1556–1707)* (London, 1963), p. 1. This book, written by a lecturer at the Aligarh Muslim University, seems to be the only larger work based on Mughal archival sources.

42. According to Hegel, the "quest for India is a moving force of our whole history. Since ancient times all nations have directed their wishes and desires to that miraculous country whose treasures they coveted": Hermann Kulke and Dietmar Rothermund, *A History of India*, 4th ed. (New York, 2004), p. 105; François Bernier, *Travels in the Mogul Empire 1656–1668*, ed. Archibald Constable (New Delhi, 1972), pp. 230, 437; Pierre Poivre, *Reisen eines Philosophen 1768*, ed. Jürgen Osterhammel (Sigmaringen, 1997), p. 221 (J. Osterhammel). Christopher A. Bayly, *Rulers, Townsmen and Bazaars: North Indian Society in the Age of the British Expansion, 1770–1870* (Cambridge, 1983), p. 79: Blayly argues that the nineteenth century saw the creation of a "black legend" about the eighteenth century, with observers seeing human-caused destruction even in areas that were barren by nature. India underpopulated: Landes, *Wealth and Poverty* (Chap. 1, note 84), p. 156; a different view in Harris, *Cannibals and Kings* (Chap. 1, note 47), pp. 146–7.

43. Ludwig Reiners, *Roman der Staatskunst* (Munich, 1951), p. 41; Kulke and Rothermund, *History of India* (note 41), p. 7. Grove, *Nature* (note 40), p. 13: "new environmental history" contributes to relativizing British colonialism as a turning point, in contrast to the "old" environmental history à la Gadgil and Guha, *Fissured Land* (note 40). Tea: Reinhardt, *Nutzpflanzen* (Chap. 2, note 63), pp. 475 ff.

44. Stone, *Canal Irrigation* (Chap. 3, note 119), pp. 32 ff.; Edward J. Vander Velde, "Local Consequences of a Large-Scale Irrigation System in India," in *Irrigation and Agricultural Development in Asia*, ed. E. Walter Coward (Ithaca, N.Y., 1980), p. 311; Dietmar Rothermund, ed., *Indien: Ein Handbuch* (Munich, 1995), pp. 29, 33, 35 (Hans-Georg Bohle).

45. Hans Walter Flemmig, *Wüsten, Deiche und Turbinen* (Göttingen, 1957), p. 46 f.; Kulke and Rothermund, *History of India* (note 41), p. 100; Ranabir Chakravarti, "The Creation and Expansion of Settlements and Management of Hydraulic Resources in Ancient India," in Grove, *Nature* (note 40), p. 100. However, archeological excavations near Allahabad have "yielded remains of large hydraulic projects assigned to the period circa 200 BC to AD 200" (p. 98). The Indian Mughal emperor Babar, for whom, given his background, Samarkand was the ideal city, thought it noteworthy that if the inhabitants of Hindustan wanted to establish a settlement, "[e]ven where, as for some towns, it is practicable to convey water by digging channels, this is not done. For not doing it there may be several reasons, one being that water is not at all a necessity in cultivating crops and orchards": *Babur-Nama (Memoirs of Babur)*, trans. Annette Susannah Beveridge (reprint, New Delhi, 1979 [orig. 1922]), vol. I, p. 486. Furthermore: "It always appears to me that one of the chief defects of Hindustan is the want of artificial water courses": ibid., vol. II, p. 194.

46. Friedrich Engels, *Herr Eugen Dühring's Revolution in Science (Anti-Dühring)*, trans. Emile Burns and C. P. Dutt (New York, 1939), p. 139.

47. Damodar D. Kosambi, *An Introduction to the Study of Indian History* (Bombay, 1975 [1956]), p. 74 f.; Wittfogel, *Oriental Despotism* (Chap. 3, note 15), p. 107; Romila Thapar and Percival Spear, *A History of India* (Harmondsworth, 1966), p. 77; Habib, *Agrarian System* (note 40), p. 35 f.; Bayly, *Townsmen and Bazaars* (note 41) pp. 84 ff. on the instability and decline of the hydraulic works of the Mogul Empire. Stone, *Canal Irrigation* (Chap. 3, note 119), p. 13 f.; Bernier, *Travels* (note 41), p. 226 f.; Vandana Shiva, *Staying Alive: Women, Ecology and Development* (New Delhi, 1988), p. 179 f.

48. Toynbee, *Study of History* (Chap. 1, note 4), vol. I, p. 257; Elizabeth Whitcombe, *Agrarian Conditions in Northern India*, I (Berkeley, Calif., 1972), pp. 70, 285 ff.; Bayly, *Townsmen and Bazaars* (note 41), p. 79 and elsewhere; Stone, *Canal Irrigation* (Chap. 3, note 119), pp. 9, 68 ff., 141 ff.; David Gilmartin, "Models of the Hydraulic Environment: Colonial Irrigation, State Power and Community in the Indus Basin," in Arnold and Guha, *Nature, Culture, Imperialism* (Chap. 2, note 63), p. 229; "David Hardiman, Small-Dam Systems of the Sahyadris," in ibid., p. 204 f.; A. Dieck, *Die naturwidrige Wasserwirthschaft der Neuzeit* (Wiesbaden, 1879), p. 47 f.; Eric Stokes, *The Peasant and the Raj* (Cambridge, 1978), p. 233.

49. Needham, *Science* (Chap. 3, note 57), 4/III, pp. 368 ff.; R. A. L. H. Gunawardana, "Irrigation and Hydraulic Society in Medieval Ceylon," *Past & Present* 53 (1971): 3–27; Edmund R. Leach, "Village Irrigation in the Dry Zone of Sri Lanka," in Coward, *Irrigation* (note 43), pp. 91 ff.; Leach, "Hydraulic Society in Ceylon," in Bailey and Llobera, *Asiatic Mode of Production* (Chap. 3, note 17), pp. 207 ff.; Pamela C. Stanbury, "The Utility of Tradition in Sri Lankan Bureaucratic Irrigation," in Mabry, *Canals* (Chap. 3, note 9), pp. 210 ff.

50. Gadgil and Guha, *Fissured Land* (Chap. 1, note 48), p. 78 f.; Kosambi, *Indian History* (note 46), p. 123; Shiva, *Staying Alive* (note 46), p. 195; Thapar and Spear, *History of India* (note 46), pp. 33, 35; Schumann, *Buddha* (Chap. 3, note 7), pp. 285 ff.; George Erdosy, "Deforestation in Pre- and Protohistoric South Asia," in Grove, *Nature* (note 40), pp. 62–65: pollen analysis indicates deforestation in the Ganges plain for millennia, although "significant stretches of forest" still remained in the nineteenth century. N. J. Allen, "Hinduization: The Experience of the Thulung Rai," in *Nationalism and Ethnicity in a Hindu Kingdom (Nepal)*, ed. David

N. Gellner et al. (Amsterdam, 1997), p. 306: "The definite destruction of the jungle seems to me central to the experience of becoming a Hindu."

51. Gadgil and Guha, *Fissured Land* (Chap. 1, note 48), p. 81 f.; Mahesh Rangarajan, "Environmental Histories of South Asia: A Review Essay, *Environment and History* 2 (1996) (no. 2, special issue: South Asia); Madhav Gadgil, "Deforestation: Problems and Prospects," in *History of Forestry in India*, ed. Ajay S. Rawat (New Delhi, 1991), pp. 13–15; Dharmashastra: Mazzeo and Antonini, *Angkor* (Chap. 3, note 19), p. 63; Chetan Singh, "Forests, Pastoralists and Agrarian Society in Mughal India," in Arnold and Guha, *Nature, Culture, Imperialism* (Chap. 2, note 63), pp. 27, 38; Christian Sigrist et al., *Indien: Bauernkämpfe* (Berlin, 1976), pp. 77 ff. It would appear that a tradition of forest protection that grew out of hunting privileges for the rulers existed only sporadically in India: according to Hindu rules, hunting was a matter for pariahs. Thapar and Spear, *History of India* (note 46), p. 56. The Brahmins disapproved of hunting; an ancient Indian praise of royal hunting was intended to bring ruin upon the king: Robert Krottenthaler, *Die Jagd im alten Indien* (Frankfurt a. M., 1996), p. 18 f. Grove, *Imperialism* (note 26) mentions some scattered Indian origins of forest protection (pp. 84 ff., 418 f.). Dietrich Brandis, *Indian Forestry* (Woking, 1897), pp. 12 ff. Although the Mughal emperors had their hunting preserves, this does not appear to have given rise to a forest protection policy: on the contrary, the Mughal army was accompanied by woodcutters. Mahesh Rangarajan, *Fencing the Forest: Conservation and Ecological Change in India's Central Provinces 1860–1914* (New Delhi, 1996), p. 12. Shivaji, on the other hand, was at times allied with forest peoples: Ajay Skaria, *Hybrid Histories: Forest, Frontiers and Wildness in Western India* (New Delhi, 1999), p. 128. Many forest peoples and forests were able to survive longer in India than in China.

52. Mann, *Flottenbau* (note 32); Richard Haeuber, "Indian Forestry Policy in Two Eras: Continuity or Change?" *Environmental History Review* 17 (1993): 52; Gadgil, "Deforestation" (note 50), pp. 25, 33; M. D. Upadhyaya, "Historical Background of Forest Management and Environmental Degradation in India," in ibid., p. 117 f.; Guha, *Unquiet Woods* (Chap. 1, note 112), pp. 37, 39 f.; Grove, *Imperialism* (note 27), pp. 451 ff.; Hugh Cleghorn, *The Forests and Gardens of South India* (London, 1861), pp. ix, 118; Richard S. Tucker, "The British Colonial System and the Forests of the Western Himalayas, 1815–1914," in *Global Deforestation and the 19th-Century World Economy*, ed. Richard S. Tucker and J. F. Richards (Durham, N.C., 1983), pp. 158 ff.

53. Mann, *Flottenbau* (note 26), pp. 46 f., 109, 132 ff.; Grove, *Green Imperialism* (note 27), pp. 380 ff., 395 f.; Adam Smith, *An Inquiry into the Nature and Causes of the Wealth of Nations*, 2 vols. in 1 (Chicago, 1976), vol. 2, p. 154. Similarly Brandis, *Indian Forestry* (note 50), p. 36. Richard S. Tucker, "The Historical Context of Social Forestry in the Kumaon Himalayas," *Journal of Developing Areas* 18 (1984): 343. Herbert Hesmer, *Leben und Werk von Dietrich Brandis, 1824–1907* (Opladen, 1975), pp. 40, 109 f., 165, 205, 278 f., 287; Brandis, *Indian Forestry* (note 50), pp. 53, 84, 90. Raymond L. Bryant, "Shifting the Cultivator: The Politics of Teak Regeneration on Colonial Burma," *Modern Asian Studies* 28 (1994): 244 ff.; Bryant, "Rationalizing Forest Use in British Burma 1856–1942," in Grove et al., *Nature* (note 40), pp. 842, 845; Gadgil, "Deforestation" (note 50), pp. 22 f., 40 ("battle against bamboos" by the Forst Department of the late colonial period into the 1950s). Küchli, *Wälder der Hoffnung* (Chap. 3, note 43), p. 159 f.; MacKenzie, *Empires of Nature* (note 26), p. 71. Rangarajan, *Fencing the Forest* (note 50), pp. 86 ff., points out that the nature of many Indian forests is inherently not unfavorable for a consensus between local peoples and British rule, for the "cash trees" and the "people's trees" were often times identical, especially in the case of the teak tree. The situation was different in the higher elevations, which favored coniferous woods, and in the moist plains, which favored eucalyptus plantations.

54. Tucker, "Historical Context" (note 52), p. 346 f.; Guha, *Unquiet Woods* (note 51), p. 116. Skaria (*Hybrid Histories* [note 50], p. 275, note), doubts Guha's thesis of the ecological rationality of these cases of arson and believes they also destroyed forests that were useful to the local population.

55. B. B. Vohra, "The Greening of India," in *India's Environment: Crises and Responses*, ed. J. Bandyopadhyay (Dehra Dun, 1985), p. 29; Gadgil, "Deforestation" (note 50), p. 15 f.; Clearcutting: communication by Vandana Shiva to the author, June 26, 1993; Mark Poffenberger, "The Resurgence of Community Forest Management in the Jungle Mahals of West Bengal," in Arnold and Guha, *Nature* (note 63), pp. 356 ff.; Guha, *Unquiet Woods* (note 51), pp. 155 ff., 168. The slogan of the Chipko movement is: "What are the blessings of forests? Soil, water and air, Soil, water and air are the essentials of human life." M. S. S. Rawat, "Social und Cultural Functions of Trees and Forests in the Garhwal Himalaya," in *Himalaya: A Regional Perspective*, ed. M. S. S. Rawat (Delhi, 1993), p. 43. Bertrand Schneider, *The Barefoot Revolution* (London, 1988), pp. 6–7; Tirunellai N. Seshan and Sanjoy Hazarika, *The Degeneration of India* (New Delhi, 1995), p. 128; John McNeill, *Something New under the Sun* (Chap. 1, note 7), p. 161.

56. Neil Charlesworth, *British Rule and the Indian Economy 1800–1914* (London, 1982), pp. 32 ff.; Stokes, *Peasant* (note 47), p. 267 f.; M. K. Gandhi, *Non-Violence, Weapon of the Brave* (Ahmedabad, n.d.), p. 8; a contrarian view by Kosambi, *Indian History* (note 46), p. 258; Singh, "Forests" (note 50), pp. 44, 47; Jawaharlal Nehru, the first prime minister of independent India, claimed that British colonial policy was leading to an increasing "ruralization" of India, as "people were leaving the towns and going to the village and the land." Although he venerated Gandhi, he regarded the glorification of the Indian village as British romanticism: *Glimpses of World History* (note 41), pp. 422, 621. Eric L. Jones, *The European Miracle: Environments, Economies, and Geopolitics in the History of Europe and Asia* (Cambridge, 1981), chap. 10; Richard B. Reidinger, "Water Management by Administrative Procedures in an Indian Irrigation System," in Coward, *Irrigation* (note 43), pp. 263, 267, 283, 285; R. S. Dhir, "The Human Factor in Ecological History," in Spooner and Mann, *Desertification* (Chap. 1, note 56), p. 331; Kulke and Rothermund, *History of India* (note 41), p. 404; Rothermund, *Indien* (note 43), pp. 37, 492. A. M. Michael, *Irrigation* (New Delhi, 1978), p. 52, on the systemic leap from previous "protective irrigation" (water reserves for periods of drought) to constant irrigation in the wake of the intensification of agriculture. Howard: Shiva, *Staying Alive* (note 46), pp. 118 ff.; Joan Thirsk, *Alternative Agriculture: A History from the Black Death to the Present Day* (Oxford, 1997), p. 224. Michael Mann, *British Rule on Indian Soil: North India in the First Half of the 19th Century* (New Delhi, 1999), pp. 153 ff.; Heske, *Gangesquellen* (note 32), p. 164 f.

57. Kailash Sankala, *Der indische Tiger und sein Reich* (Augsburg, 1997), pp. 7, 86; Richard H. Grove, "Colonial Conservation, Ecological Hegemony and Popular Resistance: Towards a Global Synthesis," in *Imperialism and the Natural World*, ed. John M. MacKenzie (Manchester, 1990), p. 35.

58. At the beginning of the criticism stand the travel reports of the Swedish naturalist Peter Kalm (around 1750): see Cronon, *Changes in the Land* (note 13), pp. 120, 122, 168 f. Harry J. Carman, ed., *American Husbandry* (Port Washington, N.Y., 1939), pp. 57, 61, 93, 106; Hobhouse, *Seeds of Change* (Chap. 3, note 115), p. 157; Carolyn Merchant, ed., *Major Problems in American Environmental History* (Lexington, Ky., 1993), p. 112 (Thomas Jefferson on soil exhaustion from tobacco cultivation), pp. 94 ff.; Seymour and Girardet, *Far from Paradise* (Chap. 2, note 28), p. 133; Gordon G. Whitney, *From Coastal Wilderness to Fruited Plain: A History of Environmental Change in Temperate North America 1500 to the Present* (Cambridge, Mass., 1994), pp. 227 ff. John Opie, *Nature's Nation: An Environmental History of the United States* (Fort Worth, Tex., 1998), pp. 68 f., 348; John Steinbeck, *The Grapes of Wrath* (New York, 1976), p. 41. A first critical review of the soil exhaustion theses, though without denying them entirely: Abbot S. Usher, "Soil Fertility, Soil Exhaustion, and Their Historical Significance," *Quarterly Journal of Economics* 37 (1923): 385–411. Walter Edgar, *South Carolina: A History* (Columbia, S.C., 1998), pp. 275 ff.; Lacy K. Ford, Jr., "Self-sufficiency, Cotton and Economic Development," *Journal of Economic History* 45 (1985): 261–7; Carolyn Merchant, *The Columbia Guide to American Environmental History* (New York, 2002), p. 48.

59. Avery O. Craven, *Soil Exhaustion as a Factor in the Agricultural History of Virginia and Maryland, 1606–1860* (Urbana, Ill., 1926), pp. 9 ff., 19. Warren S. Scoville, "Did Colonial Farmers

'Waste' Our Land?" *Southern Economic Journal* 20 (1953): 178 ff. mentions Craven's idea critically as the prevailing opinion, though he counters it merely with the economic rationale of the wasteful use of land. More recent criticism of Craven: Merchant, *Guide* (note 54), p. 48, but see also p. 53; Carville Earle, "The Myth of the Southern Soil Miner: Macrohistory, Agricultural Innovation and Environmental Change," in *The Ends of the Earth*, ed. Donald Worster (Cambridge, 1988), pp. 175–210. In my view, Earle falsely turns the thesis that Craven presented in a rather objective and dry manner into a myth, and he also imparts to this thesis an ideological slant directed against the South, which I do not detect in Craven. He counters Craven with scattered findings and on the whole more with general observations. Many recent findings are in line with Craven's thesis: Jack T. Kirby, *Poquosin: A Study of Rural Landscape and Society* (Chapel Hill, N.C., 1995), pp. 116 ff.; Willard W. Cochrane, *The Development of American Agriculture: A Historical Analysis* (Minneapolis, Minn., 1979), pp. 74 ff.; Timothy Silver, *A New Face on the Countryside: Indians, Colonists, and Slaves in South Atlantic Forests, 1500–1800* (Cambridge, Mass., 1990), pp. 163–70; R. Douglas Hurt, *American Agriculture: A Brief History* (Ames, Iowa, 1994), pp. 23, 91, 120; Michael S. Conzen, ed., *The Making of the American Landscape* (New York, 1990), pp. 108 f., 118 ff., 121 (Sam B. Hillard on plantations in the South); Stoll, *Lean Earth* (Chap. 2, note 112), p. 45 f.

60. Silver, *A New Face* (note 58), pp. 139 ff.; Cronon, *Changes* (note 57), p. 127; Lorena S. Walsh, "Land Use, Settlement Patterns, and the Impact of European Agriculture, 1620–1820," in *Discovering the Chesapeake*, ed. Philip D. Curtin et al. (Baltimore, Md., 2001), p. 235.

61. Johannes Gillhoff, *Letters of a German American Farmer: Jürnjakob Swehn travels to America*, trans. Richard Lorenz August Trost (Iowa City, Iowa, 2000), p. 29.

62. On the controversies between "improvers" und "emigrants" see Stoll, *Lean Earth* (Chap. 2, note 112), pp. 25 ff., 84 ff. In his critique of the Craven thesis, the geographer Carville Earle has emphasized: "Neither history nor environmental history is linear." Earle, "The Myth of the Southern Soil Miner: Macrohistory, Agricultural Innovation, and Environmental Change," in Worster, *Ends of the Earth* (note 58), p. 208.

63. This is the main thesis of Richard A. Wines, *Fertilizer in America: From Waste Recycling to Resource Exploitation* (Philadelphia, 1985). On nineteenth-century "dunghill doctrines" see Stoll, *Lean Earth* (Chap. 2, note 112), pp. 49 ff.

64. Martin V. Melosi, *The Sanitary City* (Baltimore, Md., 2000), p. 167.

65. Donald Worster, "Dust Bowl," in Sieferle, *Naturzerstörung* (note 10), p. 135; Worster, "Cowboy Ecology," Merchant, in *Major Problems* (note 58), pp. 319 ff.; Richard White, *"It's Your Misfortune and None of My Own": A New History of the American West* (Norman, Okla., 1991), pp. 135, 152, 226, 353.

66. Thomas and Middleton, *Desertification* (Chap. 1, note 83), pp. 21 ff. Already immediately following the Dust Bowl, Hugh H. Bennett, *Soil Conservation* (New York, 1939), with a global perspective reaching far back in history, p. 54: "The current erosion crisis in North America can be definitely attributed to the exploitation of the land that followed European settlement.... The causes ... lie in the distant past and in those countries in which our crops and farm practices originated" (which deflects responsibility from specifically American negligence!). Donald Worster, *Dust Bowl* (Oxford, 1979), p. 56. William Lockeretz, "The Lessons of the Dust Bowl," *American Scientist* 66 (1978): 560 ff. David E. Lilienthal, *TVA – Democracy on the March* (New York, 1944), p. 26. The Dust Bowl gave rise worldwide to a type of environmental awareness that was influential for decades, especially in a desert country like Australia, which in the aftermath experienced a wave of soil conservation enthusiasm. On this see Roland Breckwoldt, *The Dirt Doctors: A Jubilee History of the Soil Conservation Service of New South Wales* (Candelo, N.S.W., 1988), pp. 132 ff. By contrast, the book by the botanist Paul Sears, *Deserts on the March*, published at the height of the Dust Bowl, was already pervaded by a universal ecological pessimism. However, that pessimism had no effect in the atmosphere of the New Deal era.

67. Seymour and Girardet, *Far from Paradise* (Chap. 2, note 28), p. 134; Worster, *Dust Bowl* (note 65), p. 53; Henry L. Mencken, "The Dole for Bogus Farmers," *American Mercury* 39 (1936): 400 ff.

68. William Cronon, "Telling Stories about Ecology," in Merchant, *Major Problems* (note 58), pp. 323 ff.; Peter J. Bowler, *The Environmental Sciences* (London, 1992), pp. 523 ff.; James C. Malin, *The Grassland of North America: Prolegomena to Its History* (Gloucester, Mass., 1967), pp. 413, 423, 426 f.; on this see Donald Worster, *Under Western Skies: Nature and History in the American West* (New York, 1992), pp. 95 ff. Conzen, *Landscape* (note 58), pp. 20 f., 172, 176. Native American fire-clearance cultivation: Omer C. Stewart, "Why the Great Plains Are Treeless," *Colorado Quarterly* 2 (1953): 40–50.

69. Reisner, *Cadillac Desert* (Chap. 1, note 69), p. 141: "Worst perversion of New Deal ideas"; pp. 39 ff. The tradition, however, is much older than the New Deal: already around 1790, an English observer noted that "the Americans seem more alive to the benefit of irrigation than any other kind of agricultural improvement": Lemon, *Poor Man's Country* (Chap. 2, note 111), p. 175. Georg Borgstrom, *Too Many* (London, 1969), quoted in Smith, *Man and Water* (Chap. 3, note 9), p. 208: "Evaporation losses...mean that desert irrigation can require anything between ten and fifty thousand times the water needed in those humid regions where irrigation is at its most efficient." Another example, then, of a disastrous technology transfer from humid to dry regions.

70. Hurt, *American Agriculture* (note 58), pp. 36, 54; Conzen, *Landscape* (note 58), pp. 88 ff. (Peirce F. Lewis); Merchant, *Major Problems* (note 58), p. 143 f. (Benjamin Rush, 1789); John R. Stilgoe, *Common Landscape of America, 1580 to 1845* (New Haven, Conn., 1982), pp. 191, 282 ff.; Beinart and Coates, *Environment and History* (note 32), p. 38; Stoll, *Lean Earth* (Chap. 2, note 112), pp. 73–91.

71. Barbara Novak, *Nature and Culture: American Landscape and Painting 1825–1875* (London, 1980), p. 147; ibid., p. 157: this was demonstratively true for the Romantic landscape painter Thomas Cole.

72. Gerold Tanquary Robinson, *Rural Russia under the Old Regime* (Berkeley, Calif., 1969), p. 97 f.; Jerome Blum, *Lord and Peasant in Russia: From the 9th to the 19th Century* (Princeton, N.J., 1961), pp. 336 ff.; Kluchevsky: Richard Pipes, *Russia under the Old Regime* (New York, 1974), p. 12. The lack of a relationship to the soil on the part of the serfs: Kluchevsky, *History of Russia* (Chap. 3, note 7), vol. III, chap. 10. Damage in southern Russia: Heiko Haumann, *Geschichte Rußlands* (Munich, 1996), p. 22; Roscher, *Nationalökonomik* (Chap. 1, note 29), pp. 107, 109. Slash-and-burn cultivation: Pyne, *Vestal Fire* (Chap. 2, note 12), pp. 274 ff., 310 f. Maxim Gorki wrote in 1922 about the Russian peasant that in him "the instinct of the nomad had not died off: he sees in the work of the farmer almost a curse of God, he suffers from the 'urge to change location.'" In Krisztina Mänicke-Gyöngyösi, ed., *A. W. Tschajanow, Reise ins Land der bäuerlichen Utopie* (Frankfurt a. M., 1981), p. 90 f. According to other reports, however, the three-field system was already widespread in the nineteenth century, and even more so after the peasant liberation of 1861: Mary Matossian, "The Peasant Way of Life," in *The Peasant in 19th-Century Russia*, ed. Wayne S. Vucinich (Stanford, Calif., 1968), p. 9. On the Soviet side the strength of this tradition was overemphasized; see E. B. Alayev et al., "The Russian Plain," in Turner, *Earth* (Chap. 1, note 80), p. 558. Max Weber, "Zur Russischen Revolution von 1905," *MWG* I/10, p. 506 f.; Harry T. Willets, "Die russische Agrarfrage nach der Bauernreform," in *Wirtschaft und Gesellschaft im vorrevolutionären Rußland*, ed. Dietrich Geyer (Cologne, 1975), p. 174; Anton Metternich, *Die Wüste droht* (Bremen, 1947), pp. 184 ff. (soil research). The most recent and most thorough regional study is David Kerans, *Mind and Labor on the Farm in Black-Earth Russia, 1861–1914* (New York, 2001), esp. pp. 37–41. For Kerans, as well, there is no doubt that the degradation of the soil was real. He sees the cause in rural overpopulation, combined with the transmission of agricultural practices (pasturing of the fallow) that were adapted to the heavy forest soils of the north, but not to the soil of the steppe.

73. Anton Metternich, *Die Wüste droht: Die gefährdete Nahrungsgrundlage der menschlichen Gesellschaft* (Bremen, 1949), p. 184 f.; Philipp R. Pryde, *Environmental Management in the Soviet Union* (Cambridge, 1991), p. 198 f.; David Moon, "Were the Steppes Ever Forested? Science, Economic Development, and Identity in the Russian Empire in the 19th Century," in *Dealing with Diversity: 2nd International Conference of the European Society for Environmental*

History, Prague 2003, Proceedings, pp. 206 ff.; D. G. Wilenski, *Bodenkunde* (Berlin, 1957 [orig. Russian 1954]), pp. 30 ff., 344 ff.; Douglas R. Weiner, *A Little Corner of Freedom: Russian Nature Protection from Stalin to Gorbachev* (Berkeley, Calif., 1999), pp. 222, 241; Stefan Merl, "Entstalinisierung, Reformen und Wettlauf der Systeme," in *Handbuch der Geschichte Rußlands*, ed. Stefan Plaggenborg (Stuttgart, 2002), vol. V, pp. 215 ff. *After Chernobyl: Offene Worte: Gorbatschow, Ligatschow, Jelzin und 4991 Deligierte diskutieren über den richtigen Weg* (= *Protokoll der 19. Gesamsowjetischen Konferenz der KpdSU im Sommer 1988*), p. 390 f.

74. Harris, *Our Kind* (note 16), pp. 115 ff., 487 ff.; Diamond, *Guns* (Chap. 1, note 78), pp. 157 ff. and elsewhere.

75. Max Weber, *General Economic History*, trans. Frank H. Knight (New Brunswick, N.J., 1981), p. 312; J. B. Ojwang and Calestous Juma, "Towards Ecological Jurisprudence," in Ojwang and Juma, *In Land We Trust* (Chap. 3, note 44), p. 321.

76. Wolfgang Reinhard, *Geschichte der Staatsgewalt: Eine vergleichende Verfassungsgeschichte Europas von den Anfängen bis zur Gegenwart* (Munich, 1999), p. 15.

77. Peter Häberle, *Europäische Rechtskultur* (Frankfurt a. M., 1994), pp. 323, 336. Eugen Wirth, *Syrien* (Darmstadt, 1971), p. 143; Lin Yutang, *Mein Land* (Chap. 3, note 77), pp. 217 ff., 231.

78. Winfried Schenk, *Waldnutzung, Waldzustand und regionale Entwicklung in vorindustrieller Zeit im mittleren Deutschland* (Stuttgart, 1996), p. 297 f. Compare, by contrast, Dietmar Rothermund's explanation why in Indian villages agrarian credit associations on Raiffeisen's model were never able to play the role intended for them: "What was missing was the incorruptible village teacher, without whom the Raiffeisen system would not have worked in Germany, either." In *Markt und Macht in der Geschichte*, ed. Helga Breuninger and Rolf Peter Sieferle (Stuttgart, 1995), p. 188. Oskar Weggel's explanation for the failure of the Raiffeisen cooperatives in the Indian villages (*Die Asiaten* [Munich, 1994], p. 176) is that "the peasants used to a subsistence economy were unable to grasp the meaning of a community of solidarity." Ibid., p. 295: a "struggle over law" runs counter to most Asian cultures.

79. Jones, *European Miracle* (note 56), p. 227; Angus MacLaren, *A History of Contraception from Antiquity to the Present Day* (Oxford, 1990), pp. 141 ff.; David Grigg, *Population Growth and Agrarian Change: A Historical Perspective* (Cambridge, 1930), p. 289; Braudel, *France* (Chap. 1, note 53), pp. 188 ff. A key problem, and at the same time one of the great mysteries of history, is the question of what kind of mental manifestations accompanied this limitation on the number of children, and to what extent this takes us into a dark world of repression and hidden infanticide, or into a pleasurable world of the art of love without conceiving. Justus Möser, *Patriotische Phantasien*, vol. IV, 15, "Thus one should entirely prohibit inoculation with smallpox": "A good mother used to thank God if he shared fairly with her and also took one sheep more." But people no doubt relied not only on smallpox to limit the number of children. Around 1900, many physicians warned that "marital Malthusianism" – contraceptive sexual practices – caused "nervousness"; but it would seem that common people, especially, did not believe this: Joachim Radkau, *Das Zeitalter der Nervosität* (Munich, 1998), pp. 160 ff.

80. Julius Klein, *The Mesta: A Study in Spanish Economic History 1273–1836* (Port Washington, N.Y., 1964 [1920]), pp. 312 ff., 351–5; Hans Hausherr, *Wirtschaftsgeschichte der Neuzeit*, 2nd ed. (Weimar, 1955), p. 115.

81. Wolfgang Jacobeit, *Schafhaltung und Schäfer in Zentraleuropa bis zum Beginn des 20. Jahrhunderts* (Berlin, 1987), p. 56; Yeo, "Overgrazing" (note 3), p. 289 f. Reports from the eighteenth century state that across wide stretches of Spain, every year half the cultivated land lay fallow, and in some villages two-thirds: L. M. Bilbao and E. Fernández de Pinedo, "Wool Exports, Transhumance and Land Use in Castile in the 16th, 17th and 18th Centuries," in *The Castilian Crisis of the 17th Century*, ed. I. A. A. Thompson and Bartolomé yun Casalilla (Cambridge, 1994), p. 111.

82. Douglass C. North and Robert S. Thomas, *The Rise of the Western World: A New Economic History* (Cambridge, 1973), pp. 4, 130 f.; van Bath, *Agrarian History* (Chap. 2, note 106),

p. 168; Hausherr (Anm. 67), p. 116; Marion Hammerl and Thomas Griesinger, "Transhumanz – der große Treck für die Natur," *Globus* (May 1998): 23 ff.

83. Klein, *Mesta* (note 79), p. 320 f.; C. H. E. Frhr. v. Berg, "Die Wälder in Spanien und Portugal," in *Kritische Blätter für Forst- und Jagdwissenschaft* 46/I (1863): 233; Marsh, *Man and Nature* (note 2), p. 240.

84. J. V. Thirgood, *Man and the Mediterranean Forest: A History of Resource Depletion* (London, 1981), p. 50; Heinrich Rubner, *Forstgeschichte im Zeitalter der industrellen Revolution* (Berlin, 1967), p. 55; Erich Bauer, "Der spanische Wald in der Geschichte," in *Actes du symposium international d'histoire forestière* (Nancy, 1979), vol. I, p. 172; Henry Kamen, *Philip of Spain* (New Haven, Conn., 1997), p. 182.

85. Helen Groome, "The Evolution of Forest Policy in Spain during the 19th and 20th Centuries," *News of Forest History* 9/10 (1989): 1; Rubner, *Forstgeschichte* (note 83), pp. 55 ff.; Bauer, "Spanische Wald" (note 84), pp. 172 ff.

86. James J. Parsons, "Die Eichelmast-Schweinehaltung in den Eichenwäldern Südwestspaniens," in *Beiträge zur Geographie der Wald- und Forstwirtschaft*, ed. Hans-Wilhelm Windhorst (Darmstadt, 1978), pp. 147 ff.; Radkau and Schäfer, *Holz* (Chap. 1, note 50), p. 256.

87. Radkau and Schäfer, *Holz* (Chap. 1, note 50), p. 137; Ian Layton, "The Timber and Naval Stores Supply Regions of Northern Europe during the Early Modern World-System," in *The Early-Modern-World-System in Geographical Perspective*, ed. Hans-Jürgen Nitz (Stuttgart 1993), pp. 265–95; Thorkild Kjaergaard, *The Danish Revolution 1500–1800: An Ecohistorical Interpretation* (Cambridge, 1994), p. 90 f.

88. Rackham, *Trees and Woodland* (Chap. 3, note 152), p. 97; see also the rest of note 152.

89. Liebig, *Chemie* (Chap. 1, note 26), II, pp. 71 ff.; Scheffel: Joachim Radkau, *Mensch und Natur in der Geschichte* (Leipzig, 2002), p. 21; Wines, *Fertilizer in America* (note 62), pp. 33 ff., 54 ff.; Hinrich Hansen, "Guano ist alle! Dünger und Kunstdünger in Schleswig-Holstein im 19. Jahrhundert und einige ökologische Fragen," in *Dünger und Dynamit*, ed. Manfred Jakubowski-Tiessen and Klaus-J. Lorenzen Schmidt (Neumünster, 1999), pp. 155 ff.; Luis Martin, *The Kingdom of the Sun: A Short History of Peru* (New York, 1974), pp. 220 ff.; Smout, *Nature Contested* (Chap. 2, note 106), pp. 76 ff.

90. W. G. Hoskins, *The Making of the English Landscape* (Harmondsworth, 1970 [orig. 1955]), p. 178; J. A. Yelling, *Common Fields and Enclosure in England 1450–1850* (London, 1977), p. 214; Ernst Klein, *Die englischen Wirtschaftstheoretiker des 17. Jahrhunderts* (Darmstadt, 1973), pp. 10 ff.; Hausherr, *Wirtschaftsgeschichte* (note 79), p. 121; Josef Kulischer, *Allgemeine Wirtschaftsgeschichte des Mittelalters und der Neuzeit*, II (Munich, 1965), p. 67: the charges leveled at the enclosures at the time resembled those brought against the Spanish Mesta. For example, we are told that the "terrible enclosers" were transforming "delightful fields" into desolate wasteland. Polanyi, *Great Transformation* (Chap. 2, note 5), p. 34, ascribes to the enclosures a destructive effect on the soil resembling that of the Mesta.

91. Smout, *Nature Contested* (Chap. 2, note 106), pp. 125 f., 128 f.; C. R. Wickham-Jones, *The Landscape of Scotland: A Hidden History* (Charleston, S.C., 2001), p. 40 f.; Ian G. Simmons, *An Environmental History of Great Britain from 10,000 Years Ago to the Present* (Edinburgh, 2001), p. 159; MacKenzie, *Empires of Nature* (note 26), pp. 65 ff.

92. Texts on the history of the controversy over hedges in Radkau, *Mensch und Natur* (note 88), p. 16 f.

93. J. D. Chambers and G. E. Mingay, *The Agricultural Revolution 1750–1880* (London, 1966), pp. 48 ff., 81, 87: in the eighteenth century there were many local variations on the enclosures, as well as learning processes. Much the same was also true of the preceding common fields, however: Alan R. H. Baker and R. A. Butlin in *Studies of Field Systems in British Isles*, ed. Alan R. H. Baker and R. A. Butlin (Cambridge, 1973), pp. 619 ff.; Johann Georg Krünitz, *Oeconomische Encyclopädie* (Brünn, 1789), vol. XXIV, p. 541; J. A. Yelling, *Common Field and Enclosure in England 1450–1850* (London, 1977), pp. 187, 200. Oliver Rackham (The "Countryside: History and Pseudo-History," *The Historian* 14 [1987]: 13 f.) polemicizes

against the "Enclosure-Act Myth," as though English hedges were only invented at that time: in fact, many of them were much older. Reformers were divided in their opinions about hedges. Mayer, the "gypsum apostle" of Hohenlauhe, believed that they were "very harmful" to agriculture: "Under them gather all harmful insects: caterpillars, snails, mice, moles, rabbits, and the like." Johann Friedrich Mayer, *Lehrbuch für Land- und Haußwirthe* (reprint, Schwäbisch Hall, 1980 [orig. 1773]), p. 91. Albrecht Thaer, *Einleitung zur Kenntniß der englischen Landwirtschaft* (Hannover, 1804), vol. III, pp. 40 ff., 44, thought it was "really quite inconceivable" how far the English, though exemplary in many respects, were behind in the use of fertilizer: "Given the astonishing number of livestock that is kept in England and the rich fodder, if the dung were properly used, all of England would have to be a manure hotbed. Alas, most of it is lost in the animal and pasturing husbandry." Here the ecological drawbacks of industrialized agriculture were already beginning to become evident in England, the motherland of industrialization.

5. AT THE LIMITS OF NATURE

1. Periodization on the basis of energy: Rolf Peter Sieferle, *Der unterirdische Wald: Energiekrise und Industrielle Revolution* (Munich, 1982), esp. pp. 17–64; Debeir, *Servitude of Power* (Chap. 3, note 73); steam engine: Joachim Radkau, *Technik in Deutschland: Vom 18. Jahrhundert bis zur Gegenwart* (Frankfurt a. M., 1989), pp. 11 ff.; Radkau, "Vom Holzmangel zum Energieproblem: Abstraktionsschübe und Metaphysik in der deutschen Technikgeschichte," *Sozialwissenschaftliche Informationen* 18 (1989): 81–7; E. A. Wrighley, *Continuity and Change: The Character of the Industrial Revolution in England* (Cambridge, 1988), p. 40.
2. Carville Earle and Ronald Hoffman, "Genteel Erosion. The Ecological Consequences of Agrarian Reform in the Chesapeake, 1730–1840," in *Discovering the Chesapeake: The History of an Ecosystem*, ed. Philip D. Curtin et al. (Baltimore, Md., 2001), p. 283.
3. Young: Keith Thomas, *Man and the Natural World: Changing Attitudes in England 1500–1800* (London, 1983), p. 255. Adam Schwappach, *Handbuch der Forst- und Jagdgeschichte* (Berlin, 1886), vol. I, p. 287.
4. J. F. Richard, "World Environmental History and Economic Development," in *Sustainable Development of the Biosphere*, ed. William C. Clark and R. E. Munn (Cambridge, 1986), pp. 53 ff.; Boris Rozanov et al., "Soils," in Turner, *Earth* (Chap. 1, note 80), p. 210; Friedrich Wilhelm Toussaint, *Die Bodencultur und das Wasser* (Breslau, 1872), p. 269.
5. Rita Gudermann, *Morastwelt und Paradies: Ökonomie und Ökologie in der Landwirtschaft am Beispiel der Meliorationen in Westfalen und Brandenburg (1830–1880)* (Paderborn, 2000), pp. 432, 459. Richards, *Unending Frontier*, p. 215, noted for England as early as the seventeenth century: "Every drainage proposal met defiant criticism from opposed fen-dwellers, who feared, rightly, the irretrievable loss of their way of life."
6. Annie Antoine et al., *L'agriculture en Europe occidentale à l'époque moderne* (Paris, 2000), p. 182 f.; Nicola Iorga, *Geschichte des rumänischen Volkes* (Gotha, 1905), pp. 403 ff.; Redcliffe Salaman, *The History and Social Influence of the Potato* (Cambridge, 1985 [orig. 1949]), p. 515; Stephan Ludwig Roth, *Schriften, Briefe, Zeugnisse* (Bucharest, 1971), p. 151 (note: the Transylvanian national heroes speak of "gypsy nature" as something praiseworthy!); McNeill, *Mountains* (Chap. 1, note 16), p. 355. In Robert McC. Netting's now classic study of the community of Törbel in the Valais (*Balancing on an Alp: Ecological Change and Continuity in a Swiss Mountain Community* [Cambridge, 1981]), it is above all the potato that stimulates population growth and thereby shatters the ecological balance.
7. Paul Leser, *Entstehung und Verbreitung des Pfluges* (Münster, 1931), p. 564 f.; Gerhard Hard, "Exzessive Bodenerosion um und nach 1800," in *Bodenerosion in Mitteleuropa*, ed. Gerold Richter (Darmstadt, 1976), pp. 197 ff. Hans-Rudolf Bork, *Bodenerosion und Umwelt* (Braunschweig, 1988), p. 79, refers to the thesis – already advocated by Jean Vogt in 1953 – that this wave of erosion can be attributed to the structural change within agriculture at that time as "refuted," and demonstrates that "extremely heavy rains" were the "immediate cause."

However, these kinds of rainy phases are not all that rare in Central and Western Europe: must we not look for the *deeper* cause in the longer exposure of the soil, after all? On this see more recently Bork at al., *Landschaftsentwicklung in Mitteleuropa* (Gotha, 1998), p. 255 f. Weeds: Richard Pott, *Die Pflanzengesellschaften Deutschlands*, 2nd ed. (Stuttgart, 1995), p. 165.

8. Andreas Ineichen, *Innovative Bauern: Einhegungen, Bewässerung und Waldteilungen im Kanton Luzern im 16. und 17. Jahrhundert* (Lucerne, 1996), pp. 26, 29, 95 f.; Mayer, *Lehrbuch* (Chap. 4, note 92), p. 56: "How these (the ditches) must be laid out and managed, I do not wish to say: . . . common sense teaches all peasants one thing." Vicious circle: Dieter Hassler et al., *Wässerwiesen: Geschichte, Technik und Ökologie der bewässerten Wiesen, Bäche und Gräben im Kraichgau* (Ubstadt-Weiher, 1995), p. 42. Canals: Joachim Radkau, "Zum ewigen Wachstum verdammt? Jugend und Alter großer technischer Systeme," in *Technik ohne Grenzen*, ed. Into Braun and Berward Joerges (Frankfurt a. M., 1994), pp. 58 ff. "Canal Mania": Charles Hatfield, *British Canals* (Newton Abbot, 1979 [orig. 1950]), pp. 107 ff.; Smith, *Wealth of Nations* (Chap. 4, note 52), vol. II, 280.

9. Christoph Bernhardt, "Zeitgenössische Kontroversen über die Umweltfolgen der Ober-rheinkorrektion im 19. Jh.," *Zeitschrift für die Geschichte des Oberrheins* 146 (1998): esp. 301 ff. I am grateful to Christoph Bernhardt for many pointers on this topic in personal con-versations. Traude Löbert, *Die Oberrheinkorrektion in Baden: Zur Umweltgeschichte des 19. Jahrhunderts* (Karlsruhe, 1997), pp. 23, 40 ff., 45 f., 58; Horst-Johs Tümmers, *Der Rhein: Ein europäischer Fluß und seine Geschichte* (Munich, 1994), pp. 144 ff.; Franz Schnabel, *Deutsche Geschichte im 19. Jahrhundert* (Freiburg, 1965), vol. VI, pp. 42 ff., 91f. Oderbruch: Martina Kaup, "Die Kultivierung des Oderbruchs: Nutzungswandel eines Lebensraumes," Master's Thesis, University of Göttingen, 1992, esp. pp. 62 ff., 67 ff.; Erwin Nippert, *Das Oderbruch: Zur Geschichte einer deutschen Landschaft* (Berlin, 1995), p. 192 f. The "pike catchers" did not prevail. Still, one can see the difference between the river regulations of the eighteenth and nineteenth centuries and those of most recent times, if one compares the state of the Oder and the Elbe with that of the Rhine and the Danube.

10. Karsten Althöfer-Westenhoff and Bernd Josef Wagner, *Geschichte im Fluß: Zur Umwelt-geschichte von Werre und Else im östlichen Westfalen* (Bielefeld, 1997), pp. 28 f., 40 ff. I would like to thank Bernd J. Wagner for his stimulating ideas about environmental history.

11. Ibid., p. 42. Alwin Seifert, "Naturferner und naturnaher Wasserbau," in *Wasser – bedrohtes Lebenselement*, ed. Karl August Walther (Zurich, 1964), pp. 85–8; Seifert, however, believes that the beginnings of the progressive lowering of groundwater were already present in Tulla; the topic was later tabooed (p. 86). Jürgen Schwoerbel, "Technik und Wasser," in *Technik und Kultur* (Düsseldorf, 1994), vol. VI, p. 384 f.; *Die Donau* (exhibition catalog) (Linz, 1994), p. 221 (Werner J. Promintzer, "Donauregulierung und Hochwasserschutz"); A. Dieck, *Die naturwidrige Wasserwirtschaft der Neuzeit: Ihre Gefahren und Nachteile* (Wiesbaden, 1879), foreword and elsewhere.

12. Alois Brandstetter, *Die Mühle* (Munich, 1984) (tales of an old water miller), p. 20: "He said . . . that observation of the water had profound meaning and led to the creation of a natural understanding of water." "Unfortunately the observation of water today shows more and more signs of a lack of human understanding, indeed, of criminal negligence" (p. 37). Günter Bayerl and Karl Pichol, *Papier* (Reinbek, 1986), p. 195; Rita Gudermann, *Morastwelt und Paradies*, (Paderborn, 2000), p. 218 f.

13. Radkau and Schäfer, *Holz* (Chap. 1, note 50), pp. 129 ff., 186 ff.; attempt by the territorial authorities to set priorities in supplying wood to the trades: Ingrid Schäfer, *'Ein Gespenst geht um': Politik mit der Holznot in Lippe 1750–1850* (Detmold, 1992), pp. 74–177; Radkau, "Wachstum" (note 8), p. 68.

14. Barrington Moore, *Social Origins of Dictatorship and Democracy* (Boston, 1966), p. 506; Karl Polanyi, *The Great Transformation* (Boston, 1957 [orig. 1944]), p. 77; similarly Schnabel, *Deutsche Geschichte* (note 9), VI, p. 243: "Had democracy already existed at the beginning of the nineteenth century, it would have made modern technology impossible. Artisans,

workers, and farmers in parliament together would have voted against the machine." Ulrike Gilhaus, *'Schmerzenskinder der Industrie': Umweltverschmutzung, umweltpolitischer und sozialer Protest im Industriezeitalter in Westfalen 1845–1914* (Paderborn, 1995), pp. 36 ff., 46 ff. on convergences between premodern economic structures and a careful treatment of the environment (exaggerating somewhat). Radkau, "Gefährdung" (Chap. 1, note 41), p. 77

15. Erich Jantsch, *Die Selbstorganisation des Universums*, 4th ed. (Munich, 1988), pp. 107 ff.

16. France: Arlette Brosselin, Andrée Corvol, and Francois Vion-Delphin, "Les doléances contre l'industrie," in *Forges et forêt*, ed. Denis Woronoff (Paris, 1990), pp. 13 ff.; Radkau, "Holzverknappung" (Chap. 3, note 177), p. 529.

17. Kjaergaard, *Danish Revolution* (Chap. 2, note 111), pp. 18 ff. Stimulating reflections on an "institutional" interpretation of the wood alarm, in part as a critique of my earlier ideas," are offered by Margrit Grabas, "Krisenbewältigung oder Modernisierungsblockade? Die Rolle des Staates bei der Überwindung des 'Holzenergiemangels' zu Beginn der Industriellen Revolution in Deutschland,"*Jahrbuch für europäische Verwaltungsgeschichte* 7 (1995): 48 and elsewhere.

18. Forster, *Niederrhein* (Chap. 4, note 36), p. 48; many similar testimonials in Gerhard Huck and Jürgen Reulecke, ed., *"und reges Leben ist überall sichtbar!" Reisen im Bergischen Land um 1800* (Neustadt, 1978). Similarly in England: Hoskins, *English Landscape* (Chap. 4, note 89), pp. 214, 230.

19. Claus-Peter Hutter, ed., *Ackerland und Siedlungen: Biotope erkennen, bestimmen, schützen* (Stuttgart, 1999), p. 61.

20. "Interconnected system": very vividly described by Jeremias Gotthelf for the Swiss dairy business, *Die Käserei in der Vehfreude* (Basel, 1978 [orig. 1850]), p. 22: "for everything is interconnected and one thing arises from the next in a very strange way and often so subtly that the human eye does not even see the threads." However, the collapse of the cheese boom destroyed the socioecological harmony. Radkau and Schäfer, *Holz* (Chap. 1, note 50), p. 147; Schwerz, *Landwirtschaft* (Chap. 2, note 101), p. 319 f. A tract by the agrarian reformer Johann Christoph Schubart v. Kleefeld (1783) is entitled *Hutung, Trift und Brache, die größten Gebrechen und die Pest der Landwirtschaft* (Pasture, drifting, and fallow, the greatest ills and the plague of agriculture).

21. *Das Buch der Erfindungen*, III, 8th ed. (Leipzig, 1885), p. 307; Schwerz, *Landwirtschaft* (Chap. 2, note 101), p. 206; Toussaint, *Bodencultur* (note 4), p. 143.

22. Mayer, *Lehrbuch* (Chap. 4, note 92), p. 77 f.; Rudolf Zacharias Becker, *Noth- und Hülfsbüchlein für Bauersleute* [1788] (reprint, Dortmund, 1980), p. 274 f.; Albert Hauser, *Wald und Feld in der alten Schweiz* (Zurich, 1972), p. 263 f.; Smout, *Nature Contested* (Chap. 2, note 197), p. 65; Wines, *Fertilizer in America* (Chap. 3, note 49), p. 7; Gottfried Hösel, *Unser Abfall aller Zeiten* (Munich, 1987), p. 205 (Pettenkofer).

23. Liebig, *Chemie* (Chap. 1, note 26), p. 170; H. Großmann and W. v. Flügge, *Düngemittel im Kriege* (Berlin, 1917), p. 31, still reported that the farmer had called farmyard manure "the holy Christ or soul of agriculture." 1848: Josef Mooser, *Ländliche Klassengesellschaft 1770–1848* (Göttingen, 1984), p. 137. Young, *Voyages en France* (Chap. 2, note 12), vol. III, p. 1238; Roscher, *Nationalökonomie* (Chap. 1, note 29), pp. 128 ff.; Kulischer, *Allgemeine Wirtschaftsgeschichte* (Chap. 4, note 89), vol. II, p. 46 f.

24. Seneca, *Letters* (Chap. 1, note 25), p. 88; Liebig, *Chemische Briefe* (Chap. 1, note 26), p. 474; Johann Ernst Tiemann, "Versuch, den Eingesessenen des Kgl. Preuß. Amts Brackwede ... eine einträglichere Landeskultur beliebt zu machen," *74. Jahresbericht des Historischen Vereins der Grafschaft Ravensberg* (Bielefeld, 1982/83); Woodward, "Manuring Practices" (Chap. 1, note 28); Mingay, *Agricultural Revolution* (Chap. 4, note 9), p. 33.

25. Liebig, *Chemie* (Chap. 1, note 26), II, p. 368 f.; Julius A. Stöckhardt, *Chemische Feldpredigten für deutsche Landwirthe*, 3rd ed. (Leipzig, 1856), p. 97 f.; Woodward, "Manuring Practices" (Chap. 1, note 28), p. 103; Krünitz: Radkau, *Mensch und Natur* (Chap. 4, note 88), p. 97; Wines, *Fertilizer in America* (Chap. 3, note 49), pp. 25 ff.; Braudel, *France* (Chap. 1, note 53), vol. II, 249; Manuel Frey, *Der reinliche Bürger: Entstehung und Verbreitung bürgerlichen*

Tugenden in Deutschland, 1760–1860 (Göttingen, 1997), p. 320 f.; Thaer, *Englische Landwirtschaft* (Chap. 4, note 92), vol. III, p. 59 f.: "Remarkable and almost inexplicable" was the "amount of desolate land" in the environs of London, where excremental fertilizer existed in abundance. *Wörterbuch der deutschen Volkskunde* (Stuttgart, 1955), pp. 142 f., 436 f.; Alain Corbin, *The Foul and the Fragrant: Odor and the French Social Imagination* (Cambridge, Mass., 1986).

26. Hermann Priebe, *Die subventionierte Naturzerstörung: Plädoyer für eine neue Agrarkultur* (Munich, 1990), pp. 13 ff.

27. Antoine, *L'Agriculture en Europe* (note 6), p. 164; Mayer, *Lehrbuch* (Chap. 4, note 92), pp. 78, 81; Kulischer, *Allgemeine Wirtschaftsgeschichte* (Chap. 4, note 89), vol. II, pp. 46, 59; Schwerz, *Beschreibung* (Chap. 2, note 101), p. 86; Roscher, *Nationalökonomie* (Chap. 1, note 29), p. 128; Thaer: Hans Schlange-Schöningen, *Lebendige Landwirtschaft* (Hannover, 1947), p. 67; Kerstin Rottmann, "Der Mythos um Königin Louise," Master's Thesis, University of Bielefeld (1997); Ulrich Willerding, *Zur Geschichte der Unkräuter Mitteleuropas* (Neumünster, 1986), p. 89.

28. Rolf Peter Sieferle, *Rückblick auf die Natur* (Munich, 1997), p. 65; Schubert, *Alltag im Mittelalter* (Chap. 1, note 38), p. 143 f.; Radkau, *Mensch und Natur* (Chap. 4, note 88), p. 166 f.

29. *Buch der Erfindungen*, 8th ed. (Leipzig, 1885), vol. III, p. 261; Liebig, *Chemie* (Chap. 1, note 26), vol. I, p. 39; Kjaergaard, *Danish Revolution* (Chap. 2, note 111), pp. 56, 86.

30. Mayer, *Lehrbuch* (Chap. 4, note 92), p. 78.

31. *Der Flachsbau* (Berlin, 1935), pp. 40 ff.; ibid., p. 39: flax as the optimal crop after potatoes. Stefan Brakensiek, *Agrarreform und ländliche Gesellschaft: Die Privatisierung der Marken in Nordwestdeutschland 1750–1850* (Paderborn, 1991), pp. 103 ff. I would like to thank Stefan Brakensiek for pointing out many environmentally relevant aspects of agrarian reform. Liebig, *Chemie* (Chap. 1, note 26), vol. I, p. 39. *Produktivkräfte in Deutschland 1800 bis 1870* (Berlin, 1990), p. 283 f.

32. *Universität Hohenheim 1818–1968* (Stuttgart, 1968), p. 21 (Günther Franz); Hamm, *Landwirtschaft* (Chap. 2, note 56), p. 114. Schwerz, *Landwirtschaft* (Chap. 2, note 101), p. 53.

33. Hauser, *Wald und Feld* (note 22), p. 266 f.

34. Heinz Hamann in *Arbeitsgemeinschaft für Forschung des Landes NRW*, Heft 60 (Papers and discussions on the importance of humus to soil fertility) (Cologne, 1956), p. 31.

35. Ibid., p. 93 (Carl H. Dencker); Max Eyth, "Das verhängnisvolle Billardbein" (1863), in his *Hinter Pflug und Schraubstock* (1899, many editions).

36. Thus already Ernst Rudorff in his pioneering essay "Über das Verhältnis des modernen Lebens zur Natur," *Preußische Jahrbücher* 45 (1880): 262, 271.

37. Mario Sulli et al., "Forestry Legislation and Management in Italy, 1861–1923: Environmental Needs and Social Dynamics," in *Naturnutzung und Naturschutz in der europäischen Rechts- und Verwaltungsgeschichte*, ed. Erk Volkmar Heyen (Baden-Baden, 1999), p. 116 f.

38. Radkau and Schäfer, *Holz* (Chap. 1, note 50), pp. 149 ff., 155 ff.; Karl Hasel, *Studien über Wilhelm Pfeil* (Hannover, 1982), p. 182 f.

39. August Bernhardt, *Geschichte des Waldeigentums* (Aalen, 1966 [orig. 1874]), vol. II, p. 327.

40. Krünitz, *Oeconomische Encyclopädie* (Chap. 4, note 92), p. 532 f.; Joachim Radkau, "Ein Abgrund von 'Holzhurerei'? Der alltägliche Holzdiebstahl im alten Bielefeld," *Ravensberger Blätter* (April 1989): 12 f.

41. Schwerz, *Landwirtschaft* (Chap. 2, note 101), p. 330; Josef Mooser, "Furcht bewahrt das Holz," in *Räuber, Volk und Obrigkeit*, ed. Heinz Reif (Frankfurt a. M., 1984), p. 77; Johann Jakob Trunk, *Neuer Plan der allgemeinen Revolution in der bisherigen Forstökonomie-Verwaltung* (Frankfurt a. M., 1802), p. 29; Klaus Müller-Hohenstein, "Die anthropogene Beeinflussung der Wälder im westlichen Mittelmeerraum," in *Beiträge zur Geographie der Wald- und Forstwirtschaft*, ed. Hans-Wilhelm Windhorst (Darmstadt, 1978), p. 372.

42. Nancy Langston is critical, with some justification, of attributing erroneous developments in forestry to a fundamental ignorance in the past: *Forest Dreams, Forest Nightmares: The Paradox of Old Growth in the Inland West* (Seattle, Wash., 1995), pp. 8 ff., 296 ff.

43. Walter Kremser, *Niedersächsische Forstgeschichte* (Rotenburg, 1990), p. 481; Radkau and Schäfer, *Holz* (Chap. 1, note 50), p. 159; Schwappach, *Handbuch* (note 3), I, p. 300; Schäfer, *Holznot* (note 13), p. 225.

44. Geitel, "Das Nachhaltigkeitsprinzip," *Kritische Blätter für Forst- und Jagdwissenschaft* 46 (1863), vol. II, 187 ff.

45. Radkau and Schäfer, *Holz* (Chap. 1, note 50), p. 144 ff.; Riehl: ibid., p. 142 f.; on the many meanings of the term *sustainability* in forest science see Wiebke Peters, "Die Nachhaltigkeit als Grundsatz der Forstwirtschaft, ihre Verankerung in der Gesetzgebung und ihre Bedeutung in der Praxis," dissertation, University of Hamburg (1984).

46. Hans-Martin Blitz, "'Gieb, Vater, mir ein Schwert!' Identitätskonzepte und Feindbilder in der 'patriotischen' Lyrik Klopstocks und des Göttinger 'Hain,'" in *Machtphantasie Deutschland*, ed. Hans Peter Hermann et al. (Frankfurt a. M., 1996), pp. 97 ff. Ernst Moritz Arndt, *Ein Wort über die Pflegung und Erhaltung der Forsten und der Bauern im Sinne einer höheren, d.h. menschlichen Gesetzgebung* (Schleswig, 1820), p. 49. In this work, Arndt mentions, as though it were a well-known fact, that where "man becomes bad and miserable," "nature, too, becomes bad and miserable." Riehl, *Naturgeschichte* (Chap. 1, note 10), pp. 80, 83, 87.

47. Radkau and Schäfer, *Holz* (Chap. 1, note 50), pp. 178 ff.; Kremser, *Forstgeschichte* (note 59), p. 403.

48. Radkau and Schäfer, *Holz* (Chap. 1, note 50), p. 173; *Buch der Erfindungen* (note 21), vol. III, p. 352.

49. Corvol: *L'homme et l'arbre* (Chap. 3, note 151), p. 178. Louis Badré, *Histoire de la forêt française* (Paris, 1983), pp. 164, 197, 213 f. Marsh, *Man and Nature* (Chap. 4, note 2), p. 240. Rondeau: Philippe Jéhin, *Les hommes contre la forêt: L'exploitation des forêts dans le Val d'Orbey au XVIIIᵉ siècle* (Strasbourg, 1993), p. 126.

50. Radkau and Schäfer, *Holz* (Chap. 1, note 50), p. 172 f.; Jean Rousseau and Michel Bouvier, *La grande forêt de Chaux* (Dole, 1980), p. 40; Peter Sahlins, *Forest Rites: The War of the Demoiselles in 19th-Century France* (Cambridge, Mass., 1994).

51. Badré, *Forêt française* (note), p. 53; Corvol, *L'Homme aux Bois* (Chap. 3, note 151), p. 314; Marsh, *Man and Nature* (Chap. 4, note 2), p. 189; Radkau, "Gefährdung" (Chap. 1, note 41), pp. 66 ff.

52. I am indebted to Christian Pfister for important pointers on the importance of the forest to the hydrological cycle and on the politicization of assertions about this fact. – *Kritische Blätter für Forst- und Jagdwissenschaft* 46 (1863), vol. I, 24 ff.; Kremser, *Niedersächsische Forstgeschichte* (note 43), p. 491 f.; *Buch der Erfindungen* (note 21), vol. VII, p. 101; Roscher, *Nationalökonomie* (Chap. 1, note 29), pp. 835 ff.; Marsh, *Man and Nature* (Chap. 4, note 2), p. 335; Langston, *Forest Dreams* (note 42), pp. 142 ff.; Donald J. Pisani, "Forests and Conservation," *Journal of American History* 72 (1985): 345, 347 ff.; Pisani, *To Reclaim a Divided West: Water, Law, and Public Policy, 1848–1902* (Albuquerque, N.M., 1992), pp. 161 ff.; J. M. Powell, *Environmental Management in Australia, 1788–1914* (Melbourne, 1976), pp. 60 ff. (An Australian Awakening); Guha, *Unquiet Woods* (Chap. 1, note 112), pp. 155 ff.

53. Radkau and Schäfer, *Holz* (Chap. 1, note 50), pp. 166 ff.

54. *Kritische Blätter* (note 52), pp. 77–80; current state of knowledge: Gerhard Mitscherlich, *Wald, Wachstum und Umwelt*, vol. II: *Waldklima und Wasserhaushalt*, 2nd ed. (Frankfurt a. M., 1981), esp. pp. 180 ff., 191 ff., 242 ff., 339 f., 345 f., 350 ff. Vasant K. Saberwal, who has critically deconstructed the "desiccationist discourse" and the thesis of the forest as "sponge," has rightly pointed out (*Pastoral Politics* [Delhi, 1999], p. 123) that it is not the cutting as such but the subsequent use of the land that creates the threat of erosion and desertification. However, in more recent times, people generally do not clear the forest to let shrubs grow afterward.

55. François Walter, *Bedrohliche und bedrohte Natur: Umweltgeschichte der Schweiz seit 1800* (Zurich, 1996), pp. 55 ff.; Christian Pfister, "Häufig, selten oder nie: Zur Wiederkehrperiode der großräumigen Überschwemmungen im Schweizer Alpenraum seit 1500," *Jahrbuch*

der Geographischen Gesellschaft Bern 59 (1994–6): 139–48; Stuber, *Waldnutzung* (Chap. 2, note 103), pp. 199, 208.

56. James Fairhead and Melissa Leach, *Misreading the African Landscape: Society and Ecology in a Forest-Savanna Mosaic* (Cambridge, 1996).

57. Thomas, *Man and the Natural World* (Chap. 2, note 49); Simon Schama, *Landscape and Memory* (New York, 1995).

58. Carolyn Merchant, *The Death of Nature: Women, Ecology, and the Scientific Revolution* (San Francisco, 1990); Schama, *Landscape and Memory* (note 57); Thomas, *Man and the Natural World* (Chap. 2, note 49), pp. 109 f., 122; sharp criticism of Descartes: Paul Münch, "Die Differenz zwischen Mensch und Tier," in *Tiere und Menschen*, ed. Paul Münch (Paderborn, 1998), pp. 333 ff.: "It was pointed out early that the doctrine of animal automata mocked all everyday experience." *The Complete Essays of Montaigne*, trans. Donald M. Frame (Stanford, Calif., 1957), p. 331 (Apology for Raymond Sebond); Ruth-E. Mohrmann, "'Blutig wol ist Dein Amt, o Schlachter...' Zur Errichtung öffentlicher Schlachthäuser im 19. Jahrhundert," *Hessische Blätter* N. F. 27 (1991): 101 ff.

59. Thomas, *Man and the Natural World* (Chap. 2, note 49), p. 160; Wolfgang Krohn, *Francis Bacon* (Munich, 1987), p. 49; Johann Georg Krünitz, *Oeconomische Encyclopädie*, 14. Teil (Brünn, 1788), p. 416 f.; Emilie Fallenstein, *Erinnerungsblätter an meine Kindheit und Jugend* (Stuttgart, 1882), p. 20; Joachim Radkau, *Max Weber: Die Leidenschaft des Denkens* (Munich, 2005), p. 800.

60. Michael Niedermeier, *Erotik in der Gartenkunst: Eine Kulturgeschichte der Liebesgärten* (Leipzig, 1995), p. 162 and elsewhere; Ralph Waldo Emerson, *The Collected Works of Ralph Waldo Emerson*, vol. I: *Nature, Addresses, and Lectures* (Cambridge, Mass., 1971), p. 13; Alfred Runte, *National Parks: The American Experience* (Lincoln, Neb., 1979), p. 82. Cemeteries, too, are a characteristic component of the new nature religion: designed as lavish parks, they proclaim – contrary to Christian doctrine – the tacit message that death means rest in green nature!

61. Smith, *Wealth of Nations* (Chap. 4, note 52), p. 100; Thomas, *Man and Natural World* (Chap. 2, note 49), p. 209; Hermann Graf von Arnim and Willi A. Boelck, *Muskau: Standesherrschaft zwischen Spree und Neiße* (Frankfurt a. M., 1992), pp. 169 f., 188, 217, 320.

62. Franz Wieacker, *Privatrechtsgeschichte der Neuzeit* (Göttingen, 1952), p. 152; Hans Welzel, *Naturrecht und materiale Gerechtigkeit*, 4th ed. (Göttingen, 1962), p. 162 f.; Las Casas: Helen M. Bailey and Abraham S. Nasatir, *Latin America: The Development of Its Civilization* (Englewood Cliffs, N.J., 1960), p. 100; Hans Christian and Elke Harten, *Die Versöhnung mit der Natur: Gärten, Freiheitsbäume, republikanische Wälder, heilige Berge und Tugendparks in der Französischen Revolution* (Reinbek, 1989), pp. 110 f., 127 f.

63. Gudrun M. König, *Eine Kulturgeschichte des Spaziergangs* (Vienna, 1996), p. 11; Christa Habrich in *Deutsches Medizinhistorisches Museum Ingolstadt* (Ingolstadt, 1986), p. 36, on the "'stomach worries' that emerged in all civilized countries of Europe beginning in the seventeenth century," and that made the enema syringe "virtually the symbol of an entire social class in the eighteenth century." Niedermeier, *Erotik in der Gartenkunst* (note 60), pp. 196 ff., 201.

64. Radkau, *Technik* (note 1), p. 91; Werner Leibbrand, *Romantische Medizin* (Hamburg, 1937), p. 106; Erna Lesky, *Meilensteine der Wiener Medizin* (Vienna, 1981), p. 34 f.; Max Neuburger, *Die Wiener Medizinische Schule im Vormärz* (Vienna, 1921), pp. 24 ff.

65. Donald Worster, *Nature's Economy: A History of Ecological Ideas* (Cambridge, Mass., 1985), pp. 126 ff.; Darwin, *Voyage of the Beagle* (Chap. 4, note 37), p. 530; Wilhelm Bölsche, *Das Liebesleben in der Natur*, 3 vols. (Jena, 1898–1902); Walther Schoenichen, *Der Scheintod als Schutzmittel des Lebens* (Odenkirchen, 1903), p. 105; Ludwig Klages, *Mensch und Erde*, 4th ed. (Jena, 1933), pp. 13, 39 f.

66. Radkau, "Gefährdung" (Chap. 1, note 41), pp. 73 ff.; Hans-Liudger Dienel, *Herrschaft über die Natur? Naturvorstellungen deutscher Ingenieure 1871–1914* (Stuttgart, 1992), esp. p. 117.

67. Friedrich Meinecke, *Historism: The Rise of a New Historical Outlook*, trans. J. E. Anderson (London, 1972), p. 305.

68. Glacken, *Traces* (Chap. 1, note 25), pp. 451 ff., 621 f., 709; J. R. Hale, *The Civilization of Europe in the Renaissance* (London, 1993), p. 616.

69. Olav Wernekenschnieder, "Die Verbindung zwischen Naturschutz und nationaler Identität in der Ausbildung der Nationalkultur Norwegens," manuscript (Bielefeld, 1996); Katharine Baetjer, *Glorious Nature: British Landscape Painting 1750–1850* (Denver, Colo., 1993), pp. 47, 51; Reto Cattelan, "Wirtschaftliche und politische Prämissen des Landschaftsgartens in England und in Deutschland," dissertation, University of Zurich, 1980, pp. 12 ff.; Adrian von Buttlar, "Das 'Nationale' als Thema der Gartenkunst des 18. und frühen 19. Jahrhunderts," in *Zum Naturbegriff der Gegenwart* (Stuttgart, 1994), vol. I, pp. 327–50, describes the search for the "German" garden as the story of a failure.

70. Andreas Knaut, *Zurück zur Natur! Die Wurzeln der Ökologiebewegung* (Greven, 1993), p. 396; Konrad Buchwald, "Geschichtliche Entwicklung von Landschaftspflege und Naturschutz in Deutschland," in *Handbuch für Landschaftspflege und Naturschutz*, ed. Konrad Buchwald and Wolfgang Engelhardt (Munich, 1968), p. 99; Derek Clifford, *Gartenkunst* (Munich, 1966), p. 407; Marielouise Gothein, *Geschichte der Gartenkunst* [1926] (reprint, Munich, 1988), vol. II, p. 399; Riehl, *Naturgeschichte* (Chap. 1, note 10), pp. 75, 80; Alexandra Mittmann, "'Gott schuf die Welt, und der Mensch verschönert sie' – Naturauffassung, Gartenideal und Menschenbild in Christian Cay Lorenz Hirschfelds *Theorie der Gartenkunst*," Master's Thesis, University of Bielefeld, 2001; Rita Gudermann, *Morastwelt und Paradies* (Chap. 1, note 17), pp. 163 ff.; Tyrrell, *True Gardens* (Chap. 2, note 54).

71. Riehl, *Naturgeschichte* (Chap. 1, note 10), pp. 148 ff. Examples of how the search for a national garden style could lead to many discoveries about the habitat conditions for plants can be found in the best-sellers by William Robinson: *The Wild Garden* (1870) and *The English Flower Garden* (1883). I would like to thank Anke Kuhbier for the reference.

72. Paolo Pino wrote in his *Dialogo di Pittura* in 1548: "The Northern peoples live in wild nature. That is why their landscape pictures are interesting. We Italians live in the garden of the world, which is delightful, but not suitable for artistic representation." Quoted in Anke Repp-Eckert, *Niederländische Landschaftsmalerei* (Cologne, Wallraf-Richartz-Museum, 1989), p. 5. So old are the aesthetic ideals of wild nature – and the self-delusions about wilderness!

73. Badré, *Forêt française* (note 49), p. 168 f.; Danny Trom, "Natur und nationale Identität: Der Streit um den Schutz der 'Natur' um die Jahrhundertwende in Deutschland und Frankreich," in *Nation und Emotion*, ed. Etienne Françoise et al. (Göttingen, 1995), p. 158; Karl Hasel, *Studien über Wilhelm Pfeil* (Hannover, 1982) [*Aus dem Walde* 36], p. 137.

74. Hans Jörg Oeschger, *Douglasienanbau in Baden-Württemberg* (Stuttgart, 1975), pp. 130 ff.; Hansjörg Küster, *Geschichte des Waldes* (Munich, 1998), p. 175. Friedrich Schwabe, *Wo Vogelsang, da Erntesegen! Ein Weckruf und Hinweis auf die Notwendigkeit und den Nutzen des Vogelschutzes im Land- und Gartenbau*, 5th ed. (Mühlhausen, 1925), p. 5. "Ausschuß zur Rettung des Laubwaldes, Stimmen und ergänzende Bemerkungen zur Eingabe an das Reichsforstamt vom 16.1.1941," in the Staatsarchiv Detmold. Still today, Wolfgang Scherzinger complains (*Naturschutz im Wald: Qualitätsziele einer dynamischen Waldentwicklung* [Stuttgart, 1996], p. 335) about the "complete lack of conceptual thinking" in the choice of forest regions for German national parks; he notes with astonishment that of all the different woodlands, the mixed oak and birch forest has so far not been included in a large protected area.

75. Ludwig Klages, "Mensch und Erde," in *Hoher Meißner*, ed. Winfried Mogge and Jürgen Reulecke (1913), p. 173; crested lark: Peter Finke, ed., *Natur verstehen – Natur erhalten* (Bielefeld, 1991), p. 36 f.

76. Walther Schoenichen, *Naturschutz, Heimatschutz: Ihre Begründung durch Ernst Rudorff, Hugo Conwentz und ihre Vorläufer* (Stuttgart, 1954), pp. 231 ff., 247 ff., 275; Knaut, *Zurück zur Natur* (note 70), pp. 244, 251.

77. Raymond H. Dominick, *The Environmental Movement in Germany* (Bloomington, Ind., 1992), p. 75; Wolfgang Wippermann and Detlef Berentzen, *Die Deutschen und ihre Hunde*

(Munich, 1998), pp. 60 ff.; Roland Buchwald, *Fischland, Darß und Zingst* (Ilmenau, 1998), p. 39; Reinhard Johler, "Vogelmord und Vogelliebe: Zur Ethnographie konträrer Leidenschaften," *Historische Anthropologie* 5 (1997): 20, 23, 27; Schwabe, *Vogelsang* (note 68); Alfred Barthelmeß, *Vögel – Lebendige Umwelt: Probleme von Vogelschutz und Humanökologie geschichtlich dargestellt und dokumentiert* (Freiburg, 1981), pp. 146 ff.; Walther Schoenichen, *Naturschutz im Dritten Reich* (Berlin, 1934), p. 18: "More and more, Germany is becoming (in the nineteenth century) the motherland of bird protection." Hans Klose, *50 Jahre Staatlicher Naturschutz: Ein Rückblick auf den Weg der deutschen Naturschutzbewegung* (Gießen, 1957), p. 10. England: Christoph Spehr, *Die Jagd nach Natur* (Frankfurt a. M., 1994), pp. 139 ff.

78. Georg Bonne, *Deutsche Flüsse oder deutsche Kloaken? Eine ernste Mahnung in letzter Stunde an unsere Regierungen und unser Volk* (Hamburg, 1907), p. 3.

79. Runte, *National Parks* (note 60), pp. 11 ff., 18; Thomas Jefferson, "Notes on the State of Virginia," in *Thomas Jefferson: Writings* (New York, 1984); Robert McHenry, ed., *A Documentary History of Conservation in America* (New York, 1972), pp. 174 ff.

80. Runte, *National Parks* (note 60), pp. 48, 128–37 (Everglades); Roderick Nash, "The American Invention of National Parks," *American Quarterly* 22 (1970): 227; Karl Ditt, "Naturschutz zwischen Zivilisationskritik, Tourismusförderung und Umweltschutz: USA, England und Deutschland 1860–1970," in *Politische Zäsuren und gesellschaftlicher Wandel im 20. Jahrhundert*, ed. Matthias Frese and Michael Prinz (Paderborn, 1996), p. 505; Linda Lear, *Rachel Carson, Witness for Nature* (London, 1997), p. 137 f. In Canada, both Anglo- and Franco-Canadians identified with the national parks: the nature parks as a national unifier!

81. Stephen Fox, *John Muir and His Legacy: The American Conservation Movement* (Boston, 1981), p. 107.

82. Donald J. Pisani, "Forests and Conservation, 1865–1890," *Journal of American History* 72 (1985): 351; William Cronon, *Nature's Metropolis: Chicago and the Great West* (New York, 1991), pp. 200 ff.; Shary H. Olson, *The Depletion Myth: A History of the Railroad Use of Timber* (Cambridge, Mass., 1971).

83. Samuel P. Hays, *Conservation and The Gospel of Efficiency: The Progressive Conservation Movement 1890–1920* (New York, 1975), pp. 5 ff., 22 ff., 29; Fox, *John Muir* (note 81), pp. 126 f., 141 f.; Elmo R. Richardson, *The Politics of Conservation: Crusades and Controversies 1897–1913* (Berkeley, Calif., 1962), pp. 17, 25, 44; Gifford Pinchot, *Breaking New Ground* [1947] (Washington, D.C., 1998), pp. 79 ff. ("Public Awakening"), 147 ff. and elsewhere (the forests as the embodiment of the "public good" that had to be defended against private self-interest); Edmund Morris, *Theodore Rex* (New York, 2001), p. 486; Langston, *Forest Dreams* (note 42), p. 109 f.; Reisner, *Cadillac Desert* (Chap. 1, note 69), p. 81 and elsewhere; Donald J. Pisani, *To Reclaim a Divided West: Water, Law, and Public Policy, 1848–1902* (Albuquerque, N.M., 1992), pp. 328, 335. Coordination problems: Franklin D. Roosevelt's National Resources Planning Board, which ran into opposition from existing departments, did "most of its work in secret": *The Global 2000 Report to the President* (U.S. Department of State, 2000), Appendix A: Lessons from the Past; Michael P. Cohen, *The History of the Sierra Club 1892–1970* (San Francisco, 1988), p. 29 f.

84. Roosevelt, *Autobiography* (Chap. 2, note 46), p. 348; Worster, *Nature's Economy* (note 65), pp. 270 ff.

85. Robert G. Lee, "Sustained-Yield and Social Order," in *History of Sustained-Yield Forestry*, ed. Harold K. Steen (Portland, Ore., 1984), p. 97.

86. Schoenichen, *Scheintod* (note 65), p. 279; Knaut, *Zurück zur Natur* (note 70), p. 103.

87. Knaut, *Zurück zur Natur* (note 70), pp. 43, 106, 144 f.; Buchwald, "Landschaftspflege" (note 70), p. 103; Hermann Cordes et al., *Naturschutzgebiet Lüneburger Heide* (Bremen, 1997), p. 309 f.; Reinhard Falter, "'80 Jahre 'Wasserkrieg': Das Walchensee-Kraftwerk," in *Von der Bittschrift zur Platzbesetzung: Konflikte um technische Großprojekte*, ed. Ulrich Linse et al. (Berlin, 1988), pp. 73, 124, 126. Friedemann Schmoll, *Erinnerung an die Natur: Die Geschichte des Naturschutzes im deutschen Kaiserreich* (Frankfurt a. M., 2004), p. 13.

88. Ernst Rudorff, "Über das Verhältnis des modernen Lebens zur Natur," *Preußische Jahrbücher* 45 (1880): 270; Joachim Radkau, "Naturschutz und Nationalsozialismus – wo ist das Problem?" in *Naturschutz und Nationalsozialismus*, ed. Joachim Radkau and Frank Uekötter (Frankfurt a. M., 2003), p. 50; Walther Schoenichen, *Zauber der Wildnis in deutscher Heimat* (Neudamm, 1935), p. 53.

89. Ulrich Beck, *Risikogesellschaft* (Frankfurt a. M., 1986), p. 264; a contrary view: Anna Bramwell, *Ecology in the 20th Century* (New Haven, Conn., 1989), p. 185; Franz-Josef Brüggemeier, *Tschernobyl 26. April 1986: Die ökologischen Herausforderung* (Munich, 1998), p. 111; numerous indications of cross-links between nature protection and reform movements in Diethart Kerbs and Jürgen Reulecke, eds., *Handbuch der deutschen Reformbewegungen* (Wuppertal, 1998). Eden: Ulrich Linse, *Zurück o Mensch zur Mutter Erde: Landkommunen in Deutschland 1890–1933* (Munich, 1983), pp. 40 ff. Emissions: Jürgen Büschenfeld, *Flüsse und Kloaken: Umweltfragen im Zeitalter der Industrialisierung (1870–1918)* (Stuttgart, 1997), p. 85 f.

90. Klose, *Staatlicher Naturschutz* (note 77), p. 31 (nature protection pamphlet in 1931 was "nothing but a call for Reich law"); Chadwick: Anthony S. Wohl, *Endangered Lives: Public Health in Victorian Britain* (London, 1983), pp. 111, 142 ff.; Marjatta Hietala, *Services and Urbanization at the Turn of the Century: The Diffusion of Innovations* (Helsinki, 1987), pp. 259–305, 406; Hans-Ulrich Wehler, *Deutsche Gesellschaftsgeschichte 1849–1914* (Munich, 1995), pp. 533, 542; Raymond Tucker: Joel A. Tarr and Carl Zimring, "The Struggle for Smoke Control in St. Louis," in *Common Fields: An Environmental History of St. Louis*, ed. Andrew Hurley (St. Louis, Mo., 1997), pp. 209 ff.; Frank Uekötter, *Von der Rauchplage zur ökologischen Revolution* (Essen, 2003), pp. 187–94.

91. John v. Simson, *Kanalisation und Städtehygiene im 19. Jahrhundert* (Düsseldorf, 1983), pp. 141 ff.; Richard Evans, *Death in Hamburg* (London, 1987); later Hamburg representation volume: *Hygiene und soziale Hygiene in Hamburg* (Hamburg, 1928 [a similar, less elaborate volume had been published in 1901]). For Munich: Peter Münch, *Stadthygiene im 19. und 20. Jahrhundert* (Göttingen, 1993).

92. Martin V. Melosi, *The Sanitary City: Urban Infrastructure in America from Colonial Times to the Present* (Baltimore, Md., 2000), pp. 167, 260.

93. Klaus-Georg Wey, *Umweltpolitik in Deutschland: Kurze Geschichte des Umweltschutzes in Deutschland seit 1900* (Opladen, 1982), p. 39; Ralf Henneking, *Chemische Industrie und Umwelt* (Stuttgart, 1994), p. 421.

94. Valentin Thurn and Bernhard Clasen, eds., *Klassenfeind Natur: Die Umweltkatastrophe in Osteuropa* (Gießen, 1992), esp. pp. 27 ff.: Gianguido Piani, "Grüne Nationalisten. Aufstieg und Fall der litauischen Umweltbewegung." Alon Tal, *Pollution in a Promised Land: An Environmental History of Israel* (Berkeley, Calif., 2002), p. 409.

95. Michael Stolberg, *Ein Recht auf saubere Luft? Umweltkonflikte am Beginn des Industriezeitalters* (Erlangen, 1994), p. 310; Franz-Josef Brüggemeier and Michael Toyka-Seid, eds., *Industrie-Natur: Lesebuch zur Geschichte der Umwelt im 19. Jahrhundert* (Frankfurt a. M., 1995), pp. 153 ff.

96. Hans Wislicenus, "Zur Beurtheilung und Abwehr von Rauchschäden," *Zeitschrift für angewandte Chemie* (1901): 689.

97. Alain Corbin, *The Foul and the Fragrant* (Cambridge, Mass., 1986), p. 22 f.; Joachim Radkau, *Das Zeitalter der Nervosität* (Munich, 1998), pp. 87 ff.; Melosi, *Sanitary City* (note 92), p. 111; Marianne Rodenstein, *"Mehr Licht, mehr Luft": Gesundheitskonzepte im Städtebau seit 1750* (Frankfurt a. M., 1988).

98. Asa Briggs, "Public Health: The 'Sanitary Idea,'" *New Society* (Feb. 15, 1968): 229 ff.; on Chadwick see also Wohl, *Endangered Lives* (note 90); Scheidemann: Engelbert Schramm, *Arbeiterbewegung und industrielle Umweltprobleme* (Frankfurt a. M., 1988) (Forschungsgruppe Soziale Ökologie AP 18), p. 20.

99. J. H. Vogel, *Die Verwertung der städtischen Abfallstoffe* (Berlin, 1896), pp. 279–98; Daniel Roche, "Le temps de l'eau rare du moyen âge à l'époque moderne," *Annales ESC* 39

(1984): 386; Ignaz Zadek, *Hygiene der Städte I: Die Trinkwasser-Versorgung* (Berlin, 1909), p. 8 f.; Cairo: Uwe Tröger, "Rieselfelder – Schaden oder Nutzen?" in *Blickwechsel: Beiträge zur Geschichte der Wasserversorgung und Abwasserentsorgung in Berlin und Istanbul*, ed. Noyan Dinçkal and Shahrooz Mohajeri (Berlin, 2001), p. 179 f. Industrial waste: optimists about technology believed in the late nineteenth century that chemistry would sooner or later reuse all waste productively; Radkau, *Technik* (note 1), p. 208 f. Berlin: Susanne Hauser, "'Reinlichkeit, Ordnung und Schönheit': Zur Diskussion über Kanalisation im 19. Jahrhundert," *Die alte Stadt* 19 (1992): 311; U.S.A.: Joel A. Tarr, *The Search for the Ultimate Sink: Urban Pollution in Historical Perspective* (Akron, Ohio, 1996), pp. 323 ff.

100. Büschenfeld, *Flüsse und Kloaken* (note 89), pp. 319 f., 400, 417; Julius v. Schroeder and Carl Reuss, eds., *Die Beschädigung der Vegetation durch Rauch und die Oberharzer Hüttenrauchschäden* (Berlin, 1883; reprint Leipzig, 1986), pp. 9, 244, 276.

101. Jean-Pierre Goubert, *The Conquest of Water: The Advent of Health in the Industrial Age*, trans. Andrew Wilson (Cambridge, 1989); Heinrich Zellner, *Die Verunreinigung der deutschen Flüsse durch Abwässer der Städte und Industrien* (Berlin, 1914), pp. 16, 19. There is no permanent solution when it comes to water purification plants: the problem of the decay of treatment plants exists to this day. Reinhold Weimann, *Verschmutzte Wasserläufe* (Stuttgart, 1958), p. 9.

102. Zadek, *Hygiene* (note 99), p. 29; W. Deecke, "Zur Grundwasserfrage: Eine Warnung," *Preußische Jahrbücher* 137 (1909): 217.

103. Bonne, *Deutsche Flüsse* (note 78), p. 6.

104. Büschenfeld, *Flüsse und Kloaken* (note 89), pp. 298 ff., 308 ff.; Ulrich Eisenbach, "Kaliindustrie und Umwelt," in *Die Kaliindustrie an Werra und Fulda: Geschichte eines landschaftsprägenden Industriezweigs*, ed. Ulrich Eisenbach and Akos Paulinyi (Darmstadt, 1998), pp. 200 ff.

105. Louis C. McCabe, ed., *Air Pollution*, Proceedings of the U.S. Technical Conference on Air Pollution (New York, 1952), pp. 453, 482.

106. W. C. Hueper, "Environmental Cancer Hazards Caused by Industrial Air Pollution," in McCabe, *Air Pollution* (note 105), p. 482, and the subsequent discussion; Hahnemann: Radkau, *Mensch und Natur* (Chap. 4, note 88), p. 99; "smoke farmers": personal communication from Frank Uekötter; Heinrich Rubner, *Deutsche Forstgeschichte 1933–1945* (St. Katharinen, 1985), p. 33 f.

107. Arne Andersen and Franz-Josef Brüggemeier, "Gase, Rauch und Saurer Regen," in *Besiegte Natur*, ed. Franz-Josef Brüggemeier and Thomas Rommelspacher (Munich, 1987), p. 66; Gerd Spelsberg, *Rauchplage: 100 Jahre Saurer Regen* (Aachen, 1984), p. 172.

108. William Morris, "The Beauty of Life," in *The Collected Works of William Morris*, vol. XXII (New York, 1966), p. 71; Frank Uekötter, "Eine lange Tradition des Nicht-Handelns: Der Bremer Umgang mit der Luftverschmutzung 1880–1956," *Bremisches Jahrbuch* 77 (1998): 224–46; Uekötter, "Confronting" (Preface to the German edition, note 5). I am grateful to Frank Uekötter for a good deal of information on the history of how humans have dealt with the problem of smoke.

109. Arne Andersen, *Historische Technikfolgenabschätzung am Beispiel des Metallhüttenwesens und der Chemieindustrie 1850–1933* (Stuttgart, 1996), pp. 45–225.

110. Arthur Shadwell, *Industrial Efficiency: A Comparative Study of Industrial Life in England, Germany and America* (London, 1913), p. 145.

111. Frank Uekötter, *Von der Rauchplage zur ökologischen Revolution: Eine Geschichte der Luftverschmutzung in Deutschland und den USA 1880–1970* (Essen, 2003).

112. Heide Berndt, "Hygienebewegung des 19. Jahrhunderts als vergessenes Thema von Stadt- und Architektursoziologie," *Die alte Stadt* 14 (1987): 140–63; John v. Simson, *Kanalisation und Städtehygiene im 19. Jahrhundert* (Düsseldorf, 1983), p. 5; Rodenstein, *Mehr Licht* (note 97); Jürgen Reulecke and Adelheid Gräfin zu Castell Rüdenhausen, eds., *Stadt und Gesundheit* (Stuttgart, 1991); Dittmar Machule et al., eds., *Macht Stadt krank?* (Hamburg, 1996). As one can see, the sanitation movement can be discerned especially within the

context of the history of urbanization. Radkau, *Nervosität* (note 97), pp. 321 ff. In France, the sanitation movement has had a longer presence, since it had a great man and dominant actor in Louis Pasteur; see Bruno Latour, *The Pasteurization of France* (Cambridge, Mass., 1988). However, it seems to have been fixated more one-sidedly on the fight against microbes than was the case in Germany.

113. Peter Krautwig, "50 Jahre hygienische Entwicklung, mit besonderer Berücksichtigung der Cölner Verhältnisse," *Centralblatt für allgemeine Gesundheitspflege* 30 (1911): 32 f.; Johanna Bleker, "Die Stadt als Krankheitsfaktor: Eine Analyse ärztlicher Auffassungen im 19. Jahrhundert," *Medizinhistorisches Journal* 18 (1983): 130 f.; Bonne, *Deutsche Flüsse* (note 78), p. 13 f.

114. James Hobrecht, *Die Kanalisation von Berlin* (Berlin, 1884), p. 302; John v. Simson, *Kanalisation und Städtehygiene im 19. Jahrhundert* (Düsseldorf, 1983), p. 24.

115. Ibid., p. 7 f.; on the controversy over combined sewerage see Simson, *Kanalisation* (note 91); Alfred Grotjahn, *Die hygienische Kultur im 19. Jahrhundert* (Berlin, 1902), pp. 11 ff.; Alwin Seifert, *Ein Leben für die Landschaft* (Düsseldorf, 1962), p. 128 f.; see also note 93. The fact that nature protectors today fight to preserve sewage fields that are no longer in active use reveals how ecological judgments are tied to their times. On this see Jan Dörner and Malte Redlich, *Die Rieselfelder: Ein schützenswertes Vogelreservat oder volkswirtschaftlicher Unsinn?* (Münster, 1999), prize-winning entry for the student competition in History.

116. Uekötter, *Rauchplage* (note 90), p. 508; Jürgen Büschenfeld, "Visionen des Fortschritts: Grenzwerte in der Gewässerschutzdebatte um 1900," in *Der Optimismus der Ingenieure*, ed. Hans-Liudger Dienel (Stuttgart, 1998), p. 83 f. Lovelock, *Gaia: The Practical Science of Planetary Medicine* (London, 1991), p. 174.

117. Melosi, *Sanitary City* (note 92), p. 426.

118. Gilhaus, *Umweltverschmutzung* (note 14), p. 351.

6. IN THE LABYRINTH OF GLOBALIZATION

1. Guillaume Vera-Navas, "The First Report to the Club of Rome: How It Came About and Its International Repercussions," in *Dealing with Diversity, Proceedings of the 2nd International Conference of the ESEH* (Prague, 2003), pp. 308 ff. The *Limits to Growth* impressed readers at the time especially with its large computer calculations, even though they merely confirmed the assumptions that formed the basis of the study. The success of 1972 was tied to the situation at the time, and it was not repeated with subsequent publications by the Club of Rome.

2. See Chap. 4, note 21; Albert Schweitzer, *Out of My Life and Thought*, trans. Ante Bultmann Lemke (Baltimore, Md., 1990), p. 211.

3. Frank Uekötter, "Stark im Ton, schwach in der Organisation. Der Protest gegen den frühen Automobilismus," *Geschichte in Wissenschaft und Unterricht* 54 (2003): 658–70.

4. Christian Pfister, ed., *Das 1950er Syndrom: Der Weg in die Konsumgesellschaft* (Bern, 1995); on this see Jörn Sieglerschmidt, ed., *Der Aufbruch ins Schlaraffenland: Stellen die 50er Jahre eine Epochenschwelle im Mensch-Umwelt-Verhältnis dar?* (Mannheim, 1995) (Environmental History Newsletter Special issue no. 2). Pfister derives his data on the historical development of greenhouse gas emissions from the follow-up report to *Limits to Growth*: Donella H. and Dennis L. Meadows and Jørge Randers, *Beyond the Limits: Confronting Global Collapse, Envisioning a Sustainable Future* (Post Mills, Vt., 1992), p. 94, which indicates as its source the World Meteorological Organization. However, measurements of the CO_2 concentration in the atmosphere exist only after 1958 in Hawaii and Antarctica. Still, analysis of ice core samples have shown that the concentration of greenhouse gases in the atmosphere in most recent times (even if the precise time cannot be determined) has reached "much higher values than ever before since the appearance of human beings on the earth" (ibid., p. 128). Although Pfister sees the United States as the main force behind the "50s syndrome," he sees the trigger of the collapse of oil prices in the late 1950s in the Soviet Union,

which broke the cartel of the oil magnates with its aggressive sales strategy. See Daniel Yergin, *The Prize: The Epic Quest for Oil, Money, and Power* (New York, 1991), pp. 519, 773 f. With Pfister, too, the old mentality of economizing and not throwing away anything had its unpleasant sides; for example, he quotes from a German student essay from 1948: "My best day was when my brother Friedrich died. Since then I have a coat and shoes and socks and a knit vest" (*1950er Syndrom*, p. 72). For all the environmental consciousness, one must not underestimate the liberating aspect of the ability to throw things away! I already suggested the 1950s/60s as an epochal watershed in environmental history at the conference "Mensch und Umwelt in der Geschichte" in June 1985 at the Evangelische Akademie Loccum: "Wald- und Wasserzeiten, oder: Der Mensch als Makroparasit? Epochen und Handlungsimpulse einer menschenfreundlichen Umweltgeschichte," in *Mensch und Umwelt in der Geschichte*, ed. Jörn Calließ et al. (Pfaffenweiler, 1989), pp. 161 ff.

5. William Rathje and Gullen Murphy, *Rubbish!* (New York, 1992); Norman Fuchsloch, "Recycling, Upcycling, Downcycling. Eine umwelthistorische Ist-Soll-Analyse," in *Recycling in Geschichte und Gegenwart*, ed. Roland Ladwig (Freiberg, 2003), p. 16.

6. Ulrich Petschow, "The Roaring Fifties – das Abheben der Stoffströme: Anmerkungen zur Debatte um das 1950er Syndrom," *IÖW/VÖW-Informationsdienst* 9, nos. 3–4 (1994): 20 f. Dietmar Klenke, *"Freier Stau für freie Bürger": Die Geschichte der bundesdeutschen Verkehrspolitik* (Darmstadt, 1995), pp. 63 ff. Detlef Stender, "Das bittere Ende: Ökologische Aspekte des Kühlschranks," in *"Das Paradies kommt wieder": Zur Kulturgeschichte und Ökologie von Herd, Kühlschrank und Waschmaschine* (Hamburg, 1993), p. 103.

7. Helmut Jäger, *Einführung in die Umweltgeschichte* (Darmstadt, 1994), pp. 52 ff., 66 ff. Bork, *Landschaftsentwicklung* (Chap. 1, note 22), p. 109: in the twentieth century, soil erosion in Central Europe "has increased by more than four-fold compared to previous centuries."

8. Joachim Radkau, *Aufstieg und Krise der deutschen Atomwirtschaft 1945–1975* (Reinbek, 1983), pp. 64 ff.

9. Fumagalli, *Mensch und Umwelt* (Chap. 2, note 70), p. 58. On the desolation of the landscape in central Italy from the decline of traditional polyculture see Sergio Anselmi in *Ambiente Italiana* (Chap. 3, note 102), p. 55. France: *Der Spiegel*, August 27, 1990. England: James Lovelock, *The Ages of Gaia* (New York, 1988), p. 228: "The recent act of destruction of the English countryside is a vandalism almost without parallel in modern history."

10. Conservationists: Douglas R. Weiner, *Models of Nature: Ecology, Conservation, and Cultural Revolution in Soviet Russia* (Bloomington, Ind., 1988), pp. 229 ff.; Weiner, "The Historical Origins of Soviet Environmentalism," in *Environmental History*, ed. Kendall E. Bailes (Lanham, 1985), pp. 379 ff. Erosion research: Anton Metternich, *Die Wüste droht* (Bremen, 1947), p. 184 f.; however, D. R. Weiner, when asked by the author, knew nothing about this. Aral Sea: Horst G. Mensching, *Desertifikation* (Darmstadt, 1990), pp. 110–15; Stefan Klötzli, "Wasserprobleme und Konflikte in Zentralasien," *Wechselwirkung* 67 (June 1994): 17 ff. E. B. Alayev et al., "The Russian Plain," in Turner, *Earth* (Chap. 1, note 80), pp. 553 ff. Boris Komarov (pseudonym of Zeev Wolfson), *The Destruction of Nature in the Soviet Union* (New York, 1980), pp. 3 ff., 16 (Lake Baikal as the trigger of public attention). Philip R. Pryde, *Environmental Management in the Soviet Union* (Cambridge, 1991), pp. 221 ff. Rasputin: *Der Spiegel*, April 8, 1985, pp. 126 ff.

11. Wolfgang Weischet, *Die Grüne Revolution: Erfolg, Möglichkeiten und Grenzen in ökologischer Sicht* (Paderborn, 1978), pp. 29 ff. and elsewhere; Klaus M. Leisinger, "Die 'Grüne Revolution' im Wandel der Zeit: Technologische Variablen und soziale Konstanten," *Social Strategies* 2, no. 2 (1987): 27 ff., 31; David A. Sonnenfeld, "Mexico's 'Green Revolution,' 1940–1980: Towards an Environmental History," *Environmental History Review* 16 (1992): 38 ff. "Less interesting to modern ecology": Tirunellai N. Seshan, as the Indian Environmental Secretary, saw his primary task in liberating environmental policy from the dominance of scientific experts. Brazil: José Lutzenberger from personal experience, in José Lutzenberger and Michael Schwartzkopff, *Giftige Ernte* (Greven, 1988), pp. 24 ff., 34: "When I left Brazil in 1957, the poison madness in agriculture had only just begun. But I could never

have imagined the extent to which it would run out of control." Rice: Francesca Bray in *Spektrum der Wissenschaft, Dossier* 2/97 (Welternährung): 50–3.

12. Roland Motz and Gaby Otto, *Mexiko* (Reinbek, 1986), p. 172; Shridath Ramphal, *Das Umweltprotokoll* (Frankfurt a. M., 1992), p. 63; Keith Pezzoli, "Environmental Conflicts in the Urban Milieu: The Case of Mexico City," in *Environment and Development in Latin America*, ed. David Goodman and Michael Redclift (Manchester, 1991), pp. 205 ff.

13. Radkau, *Atomwirtschaft* (note 8), pp. 67 ff., 88 f. Gerhard Merkl et al., *Historische Wassertürme* (Munich, 1985), p. 167; Th. Rehbock, *Die Talsperren* (Leipzig, 1913 [= *Der Wasserbau* II/2]), p. 80; Lewis Mumford, *Technics and Civilization* (New York, 1963 [1934]), pp. 221 ff.

14. Knaut, *Zurück zur Natur* (Chap. 5, note 69), pp. 413 ff.; Walter, *Bedrohte Natur* (Chap. 2, note 103), pp. 180 ff.; Hanspeter Kriesi, *AKW-Gegner in der Schweiz* (Diessenhofen, 1982), p. 4; Joachim Radkau in *RWE: "Ein Konzern wird transparent,"* ed. Dieter Schweer and Wolf Thieme (Wiesbaden, 1998), p. 182.

15. TVA: Rich, *Mortgaging the Earth* (Chap. 2, note 104), pp. 231–4. For a general discussion: Siegfried Pater and Einhard Schmidt-Kallert, *Zum Beispiel Staudämme* (Göttingen, 1989), pp. 42 ff.: Aswan. Schneider, *Barefoot Revolution* (Chap. 4, note 54), pp. 4 ff.: "The Big Dams – An Environmental and Human Tragedy." Groundwater: Clarke, *Water* (Chap. 3, note 44), p. 58; Russell A. Mittermeier, *Wilderness: Earth's Last Wild Places* (Chicago, 2003).

16. Siberia: Hans Walter Flemming, *Wüsten, Deiche und Turbinen* (Göttingen, 1957), pp. 119 ff.; Flemming, chief of the *Reichsverband der Deutschen Wasserwirtschaft* from 1940 to 1945, believed at the time that the Soviet Union would acquire "unimaginable wealth" after completion of this project. Alexander Gall, *Das Atlantropa-Projekt* (Frankfurt a. M., 1998). Panatomic: Arthur R. Tamplin and John W. Gofman, *Kernspaltung: Ende der Zukunft?* (Hameln, 1974), pp. 95 ff. In general: Dirk van Laak, *Weiße Elefanten: Anspruch und Scheitern technischer Großprojekte im 20. Jahrhundert* (Stuttgart, 1999).

17. On the decline in the rate of population growth see the authors of *The Population Bomb*, Paul R. and Anne H. Ehrlich, *Betrayal of Science and Reason* (Washington, D.C., 1996), p. 62 f. However, he makes this too much into a question of relevant U.S. "leadership."

18. Joachim Radkau, "Die Kernkraftkontroverse im Spiegel der Literatur. Phasen und Dimensionen einer neuen Aufklärung," in *Das Ende des Atomzeitalters? Eine sachlich-kritische Dokumentation*, ed. Armin Hermann and Rolf Schumacher (Munich, 1987), pp. 307–34.

19. Pathbreaking for the international discussion was Charles Perrow, *Normal Accidents: Living with High-Risk Technologies* (New York, 1984).

20. Juan Martinez-Alier, *Ecological Economics* (Oxford, 1987), p. 119. Even David Landes, who on the whole tends to embrace the optimistic notion that all countries of the world, given an American work ethic, can attain American levels of prosperity, notes: "The difference in income per head between the richest industrial nation, say Switzerland, and the poorest non-industrial nation, Mozambique, is about 400 to 1. Two hundred and fifty years ago, this gap between richest and poorest was perhaps 5 to 1, and the difference between Europe and, say, East or south Asia (China or India) was around 1.5 or 2 to 1." Landes, *Wealth and Poverty* (Chap. 1, note 84). Of course, with data of this kind, even an approximate statistical exactitude is impossible.

21. To what extent this statement is true of Fascism in general requires further study. So far, it would appear that German National Socialism is rather a special case. True, Mussolini and Franco undertook reforestation projects, but so did Stalin and Mao: in many countries of the world, the forest is a symbol of power. Ideologically there is a special kinship between German National Socialism and Romanian fascism of the "Legion of the Archangel Michael": not only in its intense anti-Semitism, but also in its nature romanticism. Corneliu Zelea, the founder and leader of the Legion, took the name "Codreanu," "forester," and polemicized against Jewish wood traders who were destroying the Romanian forests. A similar polemic, however, is also found in the Romanian historian Nikola Iorga, whom the fascists murdered.

22. David Schoenbaum, *Hitler's Social Revolution: Class and Status in Nazi Germany 1933–1939* (New York, 1966), p. 155. Even Simon Schama, beyond any hint of suspicion that he harbors secret sympathy for Nazism, has remarked that "it is . . . painful to acknowledge how ecologically conscientious the most barbaric regime in modern history actually was" (Schama, *Landscape and Memory* [Chap. 5, note 57], p. 119). Rolf Wiggershaus, *Die Frankfurter Schule* (Munich, 1986), p. 389.

23. Heinz Wilhelm Hoffacker, *Entstehung der Raumplanung, konservative Gesellschaftsreform und das Ruhrgebiet 1918–1933* (Essen, 1989), p. 51 f.

24. Edeltraut Klüting, "Die gesetzlichen Regelungen der nationalsozialistischen Reichs-regierung für den Tierschutz, den Naturschutz und den Umweltschutz," in *Naturschutz und Nationalsozialismus,* ed. Joachim Radkau and Frank Uekötter (Frankfurt a. M., 2003), pp. 84, 103; Wey (Chap. 5, note 86), pp. 149 ff.; Raymond H. Dominick, *The Envi-ronmental Movement in Germany* (Bloomington, Ind., 1992), pp. 106 ff.; Rainer Schröder, "Umweltschutzrecht in der Weimarer Republik und im Dritten Reich," in *Schübe des Umweltbewußtseins und der Umweltrechtsentwicklung,* ed. Michael Kloepfer (Bonn, 1995), p. 82 f.; landscape conservationists: Arne Andersen, "Naturschutz in Deutschland bis 1945," in *Der Neubeginn im Naturschutz nach 1945,* published by the Stiftung Naturschutzgesellschaft (Landau, 1998), p. 19. Michael Wettengel, "Staat und Naturschutz 1906–1945," in *His-torische Zeitschrift* 257 (1993): 389 f. concludes: "Typical for nature protection in the Nazi state were spectacular single actions that were effective as publicity, as for example in the case of the 'Hohenstoffel' in the Hegau, which had always been an ideal landscape for the youth movement." That would be in line with the style of National Socialism, but there is still a lot that needs to be examined on a regional level. Werner Ebert et al., *Natur und Geschichte der Schorfheide* (Eberswalde, 2001), p. 17.

25. Gesine Gerhard, "Richard Walther Darré – Naturschützer oder 'Rassenzüchter'?" in Radkau and Uekötter, *Naturschutz und Nationalsozialismus* (note 24), pp. 257–71; Anna Bramwell, *Blood and Soil: Richard Walther Darré and Hitler's 'Green Party'* (Abbotsbrook, 1985), begins her book with the provocative assertion that political correctness was pre-venting people from recognizing that the Nazi regime was the most successful pioneer of ecological agriculture. See also ibid., pp. 10, 21, 172, 176 ff. On the other hand, the Nazi era saw the beginning of an accelerated cultivation of maize, which German farmers had resisted for centuries: Johannes Zscheischler et al., *Handbuch Mais,* 4th ed. (Frankfurt a. M., 1990), p. 20. Karl Eckart, *Agrargeographie Deutschlands* (Gotha, 1998), pp. 130, 135.

26. Heinrich Rubner, *Deutsche Forstgeschichte 1933–1945: Forstwirtschaft, Jagd und Umwelt im NS-Staat* (St. Katharinen, 1985), pp. 54, 72 ff., 85 f., 101, 104 ff., 203; Kremser, *Niedersächsische Forstgeschichte* (Chap. 2, note 110), pp. 797 ff.; Karl Hasel, Forstgeschichte (Hamburg, 1985), p. 150 f.; Alfred Dengler, *Waldbau auf ökologischer Grundlage,* 2nd ed. (Berlin, 1935 [1929]).

27. Thomas Zeller, "'Ganz Deutschland sein Garten': Alwin Seifert und die Landschaft des Nationalsozialismus," in Radkau and Uekötter, *Naturschutz und Nationalsozialismus* (note 24), pp. 273–307; Alwin Seifert, *Ein Leben für die Landschaft* (Düsseldorf, 1962), pp. 35, 37 ff., 100 ff. (The Great Water War), 105 (opposed by Darré); Franz W. Seidler, *Fritz Todt* (Frankfurt a. M., 1988), pp. 116 ff., 279 ff.; Dietmar Klenke, "Autobahnbau und Naturschutz in Deutschland," in *Politische Zäsuren und gesellschaftliche Modernisierung im 20. Jahrhundert,* published by the Westfälisches Institut für Regionalgeschichte (Paderborn, 1995); on the desertification of Germany: *Kulturwasserbau und Heimatschutz,* special reprint from the journal *Deutsche Technik 1936–38* (Berlin, 1939), pp. 2 f., 5; Alwin Seifert, *Im Zeital-ter des Lebendigen: Natur, Heimat, Technik* (Dresden, 1941), p. 11: "All technology is a child of the fire; technology is not conceivable without fire. The bringer of fire is Prometheus, Lucifer." Alwin Seifert, *Gärtnern, Ackern – ohne Gift* (Munich, 1991 [1971]), with an insight-ful afterword by Jürgen Dahl. Bramwell, *Blood and Soil* (note 18), p. 173 f. On the room for discussion about the compatability of technology with nature see also the controversy about Werner Sombart, *Die Zähmung der Technik* (Berlin, 1935), pp. 30 ff. Johann Paul,

"Autoverkehr und Straßenprojekte im Naturschutzgebiet Siebengebirge 1918 bis 1945," *Rheinische Heimatspflege* 42, no. 3 (2005): 203.

28. Anton Lübke, *Das deutsche Rohstoffwunder*, 8th ed. (Stuttgart, 1942), pp. 502 ff., 520 ff., and elsewhere; Peter Münch, *Stadthygiene im 19. und 20. Jahrhundert* (Göttingen, 1993), pp. 105 f., 266 f., 280 f.; Seifert, *Leben* (note 27), p. 128 f.

29. Brüggemeier, *Tschernobyl* (Chap. 5, note 89), p. 163; George W. F. Hallgarten and Joachim Radkau, *Deutsche Industrie und Politik von Bismarck bis heute* (Frankfurt a. M., 1974), pp. 306 ff., 310; Hans Klose, *50 Jahre staatlicher Naturschutz* (Gießen, 1957), pp. 32, 35.

30. Joachim Radkau, "Nationalsozialismus und Modernisierung," in *Scheidewege der deutschen Geschichte*, ed. Hans-Ulrich Wehler (Munich, 1995), p. 185 f.; Werner Jochmann, ed., *A. Hitler – Monologe im Führer-Hauptquartier 1941–1944* (Munich, 1982), pp. 39, 53. "Nature" does not appear in the index to *Mein Kampf*. Hitler occasionally invoked nature in the Darwinian sense to justify the necessity of eternal struggle. In nature protection, however, nature as such remained something that was in need of protection.

31. Gert Gröning and Joachim Wolschke-Bulmahn, *Die Liebe zur Landschaft, Teil III: Der Drang nach Osten* (Munich, 1987); Klaus Fehn, "'Lebensgemeinschaft von Volk und Raum': Zur nationalsozialistischen Raum- und Landschaftsplanung in den eroberten Ostgebieten," in Radkau and Uekötter, *Naturschutz und Nationalsozialismus* (note 24), pp. 207–24.

32. Konrad Lorenz as one of the first authority figures in the Austrian environmental and anti-nuclear power movement: Otto Koenig, *Naturschutz an der Wende* (Vienna, 1990), pp. 10 f., 29, 108, 133. In 1965 Ernst Jünger professed himself an admirer of Rachel Carson, for example, in his essay "Forscher und Liebhaber," in *Sämtliche Werke*, part 2, X (Stuttgart, 1980), p. 331. Given his background in entymology, he had particular reason to reject DDT. Heidegger's critique of technology, which grew out of his fundamental distance to the technical interpretation of thinking, found broad resonance in the 1950s: Rüdiger Safranski, *Martin Heidegger: Between Good and Evil*, trans. Ewald Osers (Cambridge, Mass., 1998), pp. 382 ff. Ernst Hoplitschek even believes ("Der Bund Naturschutz in Bayern: Traditioneller Naturschutzverband oder Teil der Neuen Sozialen Bewegungen?" dissertation, Free University of Berlin, 1984, p. 55) that the "nature protection movement was never really able to recover" from being compromised by its alliance with the Nazi regime. Anna Bramwell has put forth the thesis that the stock of ideas in the contemporary environmental movement is largely derived from the German cultural sphere – from typically German holistic thinking about nature: *Ecology in the 20th Century* (New Haven, Conn., 1989), pp. 175 ff. (Ecology: A German Disease?). Donald Worster, on the other hand, who, unlike Bramwell, identifies with the environmental movement, sees almost exclusively Anglo-American origins: *Nature's Economy: A History of Ecological Ideas* (Cambridge, Mass., 1977).

33. Worster, *Nature's Economy* (note), p. 339. Metternich, *Wüste* (note 10), p. 164. At that time, Schleswig-Holstein experienced enormous dust storms when the lack of firewood led to the clear-cutting of hedges: Seifert, *Leben* (note 27), p. 124. How present apocalyptic anxieties were in postwar Germany is also reflected in the new concluding chapter that Alfred Weber added to his book *Kulturgeschichte und Kultursoziologie* in 1951: titled "Prospects," it prophesied "catastrophes" from the continued population growth and the "plundering of nature." Such warnings were not unique at the time: see J. H. J. van der Pot, *Die Bewertung des technischen Fortschritts* (Assen, 1985), vol. II, pp. 870 f., 1189.

34. Radkau, *Atomwirtschaft* (note 8), pp. 92 ff.; Robert J. Lifton, *Death in Life: The Survivors of Hiroshima* (Harmondsworth, 1967), pp. 112, 143; p. 103 f.: some Japanese even drew the experience of the industrability of nature from Hiroshima, where the vegetation reappeared. Ilona Stölken-Fitschen, *Atombombe und Geistesgeschichte* (Baden-Baden, 1995), pp. 92 ff. on the case of the "Happy Dragon." On the history of the perception of the risk of radioactivity see Catherine Caufield, *Multiple Exposures: Chronicles of the Radiation Age* (New York, 1989).

35. Claudine Herzlich and Janine Pierret, *Kranke gestern – Kranke heute: Die Gesellschaft und das Leiden* (Munich, 1991), pp. 64 ff., 74 ff., 137 f.; David L. Sills, "The Environmental

Movement and Its Critics," *Human Ecology* 3 (1975): 24; Richard E. Benedick, *Ozone Diplomacy* (Cambridge, Mass., 1991), p. 67; McCabe, *Air Pollution* (Chap. 5, note 105), pp. 453, 482; Lovelock, *Ages of Gaia* (note 9), p. 177; Daniel J. Fiorino, *Making Environmental Policy* (Berkeley, Calif., 1995), p. 128.

36. Thomas Gorsboth and Bernd Wagner, "Die Unmöglichkeit der Therapie: Am Beispiel der Tuberkulose," *Kursbuch 94* (Nov. 1988): 123–46; Radkau, *Nervosität* (Chap. 5, note 97). Beginning in the 1920s, cancer replaced tuberculosis as the most common cause of death in the industrialized states. In the 1930s Nazi Germany, where the connection between smoking and lung cancer was already drawing attention, became the world leader in cancer research: Robert N. Proctor, *The Nazi War on Cancer* (Princeton, N.J., 1999).

37. David Rosner and Gerald Markowitz, *Deadly Dust: Silicosis and the Politics of Occupational Disease in 20th-Century America* (Princeton, N.J., 1994), pp. 169, 181; Christopher C. Sellers, *Hazards of the Job: From Industrial Disease to Environmental Health Science* (Chapel Hill, N.C., 1997), pp. 1 f., 235 f.; Caufield, *Multiple Exposures* (note 34). I would like to thank Andrea Westermann (ETH Zurich) for important suggestions regarding this topic.

38. René and Jean Dubos, *The White Plague: Tuberculosis, Man, and Society* (New Brunswick, N.J., 1992 [1952]); Ramphal, *Umweltprotokoll* (note 12), pp. 43, 285; Pot, *Bewertung* (note 33), I, p. 411; II, p. 861; Donald Fleming, "Wurzeln der New-Conservation-Bewegung," in Sieferle, *Fortschritte* (Chap. 4, note 10), pp. 242 ff.

39. Lear, *Rachel Carson* (Chap. 5, note 80), p. 184 f.; Fleming, "Wurzeln" (note 38), pp. 220 f., 238 ff.

40. Constanze Eisenbart and Dieter von Ehrenstein, *Nichtverbreitung von Nuklearwaffen – Krise eines Konzepts* (Heidelberg [Forschungsstätte der evangelischen Studiengemeinschaft], 1990); ibid., pp. 63–89: Joachim Radkau, "Die Kontroverse um den Atomsperrvertrag aus der Rückschau." Contrary to what many German opponents of nuclear energy believe, the conflict of the atom was the catalyst of the environmental movement not only in Germany, but also in France (though not in England): see Brendan Prendiville, "Environmentalism in France & Britain during the 1970s," in *Dealing with Diversity, Proceedings of the 2nd International Conference of the ESEH* (Prague, 2003), pp. 136 ff.

41. Radkau, *Atomwirtschaft* (note 8), p. 436 f.; Aaron Wildavsky, *But Is It True? A Citizen's Guide to Environmental Health and Safety Issues* (Cambridge, 1995), pp. 58 ff.; Sills, "Environmental Movement" (note 35), p. 4 f.; Sheldon Novick, *Katastrophe auf Raten: Wie sicher sind Atomkraftwerke?* (Munich, 1971), pp. 42 ff.; Thomas Wellock, "The Battle for Bodegy Bay," in *Green versus Gold*, ed. Carolyn Merchant (Washington, D.C., 1998), p. 348; Anna Bramwell, *The Fading of the Greens* (New Haven, Conn., 1994), pp. 93, 203.

42. Joachim Radkau, "Hiroshima und Asilomar: Die Inszenierung des Diskurses über die Gentechnik vor dem Hintergrund der Kernenergie-Kontroverse," *Geschichte und Gesellschaft* 14 (1988): 329–63.

43. On the history of this motif see Pot, *Bewertung* (note 33), vol. II, pp. 810 ff.

44. Dominick, *Environmental Movement* (note 24), pp. 148 ff.

45. Ibid., pp. 152 ff.; Radkau, *Atomwirtschaft* (note 8), p. 445; Brüggemeier, *Tschernobyl* (Chap. 5, note 88), p. 203 f.; Günther Schwab, *Der Tanz mit dem Teufel*, 15th ed. (Hameln, 1991), pp. 281 ff.: here the chief Devil explains: "My favorite little poison, however, will always be the marvelous, splendid, and indestructible DDT."

46. David M. Raup, *The Nemesis Affair: A Story of the Death of Dinosaurs and the Ways of Science* (New York, 1986), p. 29; Peter J. Bowler, *The Environmental Sciences* (London, 1992), pp. 195, 211 f.

47. At a conference about the interaction between climate research and the media at the Bielefeld Zentrum für interdisziplinäre Forschung on November 29, 1999, Flöhl, the science editor for the *Frankfurter Allgemeine Zeitung*, polemicized: "The media are trained dogs who eat from the hands of the apocalypticists!" By now, however, the media, too, has learned. For a general discussion see most recently Frank Uekötter and Jens Hohensee, eds., *Wird Kassandra heiser? Die Geschichte falscher Ökoalarme* (Wiesbaden, 2004).

48. Walter Laqueur, *The Fate of the Revolution: Interpretations of Soviet History* (New York, 1967), p. 160.

49. Radkau, *Atomwirtschaft* (note 8), p. 453 f.

50. John M. MacKenzie, "Empire and the Ecological Apocalypse: The Historiography of the Imperial Environment," in Griffiths and Robin, *Ecology and Empire* (Chap. 4, note 34), p. 225 (Australia): "European hunters produced an apocalyptic vision which often produced equally apocalyptic solutions," namely, hunting bans and resettlement of people, which destroyed the culture of the aborigines. Pfister, "Überschwemmungen" (Chap. 5, note 55), p. 146.

51. U.S.A.: McCabe, *Air Pollution* (Chap. 5, note 105). In retrospect, many environmentalists saw the decision by the Congress in 1956 not to build Echo Dam as a milestone in the political change: Mark W. T. Harvey, "Battle for Wilderness: Echo Park Dam and the Birth of the Modern Wilderness Movement," in *A Sense of the American West*, ed. James E. Sherow (Albuquerque, N.M., 1998), pp. 181 ff. Federal Republic: Franz-Josef Brüggemeier and Thomas Rommelspacher, *Blauer Himmel über der Ruhr: Geschichte der Umwelt im Ruhrgebiet 1840–1990* (Essen, 1992), pp. 65 ff.; Wey, *Umweltpolitik* (Chap. 5, note 92), p. 177; Passage of the Water Law of 1957: Rainer Wolf, *Der Stand der Technik* (Opladen, 1986), pp. 138 ff.: 1955 establishment of the VDI-Commission "Reinhaltung der Luft" (Keeping the Air Clean), 1964 TA Luft.

52. Radkau, *Technik* (Chap. 5, note 1), p. 213; Kaibab: Flader, *Thinking like a Mountain* (Chap. 2, note 46), pp. 175 ff. Joel A. Tarr, *The Search for the Ultimate Sink: Urban Pollution in Historical Perspective* (Akron, Ohio, 1996), pp. 11 ff. (Sanitary Movement); Pittsburgh: John Opie, *Nature's Nation: An Environmental History of the U.S.* (Fort Worth, Tex., 1998), pp. 276–84; California: Merchant, *Green vs. Gold* (Chap. 4, note 18), esp. pp. 372 ff. (Barry Commoner), 399 ff.; Uekötter, *Rauchplage* (Chap. 5, note 90), p. 519 f.; Mike Davis, *Ecology of Fear: Los Angeles and the Imagination of Disaster* (New York, 1998); Charles E. Little, *Green Fields Forever: The Conservation Tillage Revolution in America* (Washington, D.C., 1987); Edward H. Faulkner, *Plowman's Folly* (1943).

53. Uekötter, *Rauchplage* (Chap. 5, note 90), p. 226 f.; Reinhold Weimann, *Verschmutzte Wasserläufe*, published by the Vereinigung Deutscher Gewässerschut (Stuttgart, 1958), p. 7 f. The representative collective work *Wasser – bedrohtes Lebenselement*, ed. Karl August Walther (Zurich, 1964) reveals the degree to which the environmental consciousness of the 1970s and 1980s already existed among those concerned about protecting the water.

54. Fiorino, *Environmental Policy* (note 35), p. 155 f.

55. Bowler, *Environmental Sciences* (note 46), pp. 507 ff., 546 ff.; Ludwig Trepl, *Geschichte der Ökologie* (Frankfurt a. M., 1987), pp. 177 ff., 183 ff.; Weinzierl: Ernst Hoplitschek, "Der Bund Naturschutz in Bayern: Traditioneller Naturschutzverband oder Teil der Neuen Sozialen Bewegungen?" dissertation, University of Berlin (1984), p. 116; Radkau, *Mensch und Natur* (Chap. 4, note 88), p. 16; Muir: Peter Davis, *Museums and the Natural Environment* (London, 1996), p. 10.

56. Douglas R. Weiner, *A Little Corner of Freedom: Russian Nature Protection from Stalin to Gorbachev* (Berkeley, Calif., 1999), pp. 83 ff., 104, 198, 225.

57. Engelbert Schramm, "Die Verwissenschaftlichung der Oppositionsbewegungen," *Prokla* 79 (June 1990): 26 f.; "know-nothingism" as a justification for inaction: Adam M. Finkel and Dominic Golding in *Worst Things First? The Debate over Risk-Based National Environmental Priorities*, ed. Adam M. Finkel and Dominic Golding (Washington, D.C., 1994), p. 326.

58. Noise: once a priority: Radkau, *Nervosität* (Chap. 5, note 97), p. 208 ff. Hermann Hasse, *Die internationale Lärmschutzbewegung* (Gautzsch, 1914); Dominick (note 17), p. 143 f.; Walter, *Bedrohte Natur* (Chap. 2, note 103), p. 174. Hermann Scheer, *Solare Weltwirtschaft: Strategie für die ökologische Moderne* (Munich, 1999), p. 301 f. Trucks: Dietmar Klenke, *Bundesdeutsche Verkehrspolitik und Motorisierung* (Stuttgart, 1993), pp. 252 ff. Ibid., p. 121: Seebohm calls commercial trucking a "wrong track of motorization." On the problem today see *Der Spiegel* 34 (1999): 62 ff.

59. Fleming, "Wurzeln" (note 38), p. 221 f.; Lear, *Rachel Carson* (Chap. 5, note 80), p. 144 f. White, "Ecological Roots" (Chapter 1 note 33). Joe D. Brown, *The Hippies* (New York, 1967), p. 7 f.; the Hippies, too, seem to be among the forgotten pasts of an environmental movement that has become mainstream. Earth Day: Samuel S. Hays, *Beauty, Health, and Permanence: Environmental Politics in the U.S., 1955–1985* (Cambridge, Mass., 1987), p. 52.

60. Merchant, *Major Problems* (Chap. 4, note 57), p. 564; Charlene Spretnak, *Green Politics* (New York, 1984), pp. 9 ff.; Petra J. Kelly, "Religiöse Erfahrung und politisches Engagement," in *Die Grünen und die Religion*, ed. Gunter Hesse and Hans-Hermann Wiebe (Frankfurt a. M., 1988), pp. 28 ff. "Fascism": Jutta Ditfurth, *Entspannt in die Barbarei: Esoterik, (Öko-)Faschismus und Biozentrismus* (Hamburg, 1996).

61. Ernst Haeckel, *The Riddle of the Universe*, trans. Joseph McCabe (New York, 1900), p. 337; Jacob von Uexküll, *Niegeschaute Welten: Die Umwelten meiner Freunde* (Berlin, 1936), p. 174; in *Wasser – bedrohtes Lebenselement* (note 53) spiritual notions of water are repeatedly invoked, e.g. pp. 91 ff. by Reinhold Weimann. See also Reinhold Weimann, *Verschmutzte Wasserläufe* (note 53), pp. 7, 111. Gründler: Joachim Radkau, "Learning from Chernobyl for the Fight Against Genetics? Stages and Stimuli of German Protest Movements – A Comparative Synopsis," in *Resistance to New Technology*, ed. Martin Bauer (Cambridge, 1995), p. 241 f. Switzerland: personal communication from Ueli Häfeli. Hermann Graf Hatzfeld in *Ökologische Waldwirtschaft*, ed. Hermann Graf Hatzfeld (Heidelberg, 1996), p. 11; Wilhelm Bode and Martin v. Hohnhorst, *Waldwende* (Munich, 1994), p. 100. Since then, the "clever laziness" that the Swiss forester Hans Leibundgut has recommended to foresters – referring to a basic attitude of intelligent laissez-faire toward the forest – has become a standard slogan within forestry circles.

62. Hays, *Beauty* (note 59), p. 53; Günter Küppers, Peter Lundgreen, and Peter Weingart, *Umweltforschung – die gesteuerte Wissenschaft?* (Frankfurt a. M., 1978), pp. 108, 114, 127 ff. Hubert Weinzierl, ed., *Natur in Not: Naturschutz – eine Existenzfrage* (Munich, 1966). Michael Kloepfer, "Umweltrechtsentwicklungen in Deutschland nach 1945," in Kloepfer, *Umweltbewußtsein* (note 24), pp. 100–9; Dietmar Klenke, "Bundesdeutsche Verkehrspolitik und Umwelt: Von der Motorisierungseuphorie zur ökologischen Katerstimmung," in Abelshauser, *Umweltgeschichte* (Preface to the German edition, note 6), pp. 184 ff.

63. Brown, *Hippies* (note 59), p. 165; Erik S. Eckholm, "The Deterioration of Mountain Environments," *Science* 189 (1975): 764; *Erhaltung und nachhaltige Nutzung tropischer Regenwälder* (Cologne, 1986), p. 59 f. Stanley F. Stevens, *Claiming the High Ground: Sherpas, Subsistence and Environmental Change in the Highest Himalaya* (Delhi, 1996), pp. 360 ff. Toni Hagen in *Mensch und Umwelt in Nepal*, ed. Susanne v. d. Heide (St. Augustin, 1992), p. 10. Prayag Raj Sharma, "Nation-Building, Multi-Ethnicity, and the Hindu State," in *Nationalism and Ethnicity in a Hindu Kingdom (Nepal)*, ed. David N. Gellner et al. (Amsterdam, 1990), p. 473. Perception of catstrophe especially from the outside: K. Panday, "Future of Nepalese Forests and Forests for Future," in v. d. Heide, *Mensch und Umwelt* (note 63), p. 59. The discussion is based in part on the author's own travels to Nepal in 1977/78 and 1999; valuable information has come from Gert and Herta Wegner, Niels Gutschow, and Peter Ottinger.

64. Egbert Pelinck (Director General of ICIMOD) in *Akzente*, published by GTZ, Nepal-Sonderheft, September 1996 (Eschborn), p. 33; Birendra Bir Basnyat, "Nepal's Agriculture: Sustainability and Intervention," dissertation, Wageningen, 1995, p. 174. S. K. Chadha, ed., *Environmental Holocaust in Himalaya* (New Delhi, 1989); the editor was influenced by Indian concerns (p. 2): "In the absence of the Himalaya, India would have been a bleak desert land, with imbalanced ecology and environment." Thomas Fricke believes that more recent ecological studies of the Himalaya region were fixated too one-sidedly on "environmental degradation," thereby neglecting human *accommodation* to the environment: "Human Ecology in the Himalaya," *Human Ecology* 17, no. 2 (1989): 133; T. B. S. Mahat et al., "An Historical Perspective of the Forests of Sindhu Palchok and Kabhre Districts of Nepal," in *Geschichte der Waldnutzung und der Forstwirtschaft in gebirgigen Regionen* (Zurich, 1985) (Beiheft zur Schweizerischen Zeitschrift für Forstwesen 74), pp. 235 ff., 242 f.; Steven

Folmar, "Variation and Change in Fertility in West Central Nepal," *Human Ecology* 20 (1992): 243 f.; David N. Zurick, "Historical Links between Settlement, Ecology, and Politics in the Mountains of West Nepal," *Human Ecology* 17 (1989): 237; Sanat K. Dhungel and Bart W. O'Gara, "Ecology of the Hog Deer in Royal Chitwan National Park, Nepal," *Wildlife Monographs* no. 119 (Oct. 1991): 36 f.

65. Keshar Man Bajracharya, "Economic and Environmental Management of Forests in Nepal: Issues and Problems," in *Environment and Sustainable Development: Issues in Nepalese Perspective*, ed. Madan K. Dahal and Dev Raj Dahal (Kathmandu, 1993), p. 48; Basnyat (note 52), p. 61 (silviculture to produce leaf fodder); Wolf Donner, "Probleme der nepalischen Bewässerungswirtschaft," in v. d. Heide, *Mensch und Umwelt* (note 63), p. 17 (argues against blaming the mountain farmers); Panday, p. 66: "deforestation" as a matter of definition; Hermann Warth, *Wer hat dich, du armer Wald . . . Die Krise in Nepal* (Bad Honnef, 1987), p. 43. J. L. Ross, "Culture and Fertility in the Nepal Himalayas: A Test of a Hypothesis," *Human Ecology* 12 (1984): 163 ff.; John J. Metz, "A Framework for Classifying Subsistence Production Types of Nepal," *Human Ecology* 17 (1989): 147 ff.; Jack D. Ives, "The Theory of Himalayan Environmental Degradation: Its Validity and Application Challenged by Recent Research," *Mountain Research and Development* 7 (1987): 189 ff., 193; Jack D. Ives and Bruno Messerli, *The Himalayan Dilemma: Reconciling Development and Conservation* (London, 1989), pp. 48, 65, 86 f. (catastrophic flooding in Bengal), 88 ff. (terraces), 92 (tourist perception), 123, 208, 217 (blaming of mountain dwellers), 205 (still, good reason to assume "that Nepal, and the entire region, *is* moving into a situation of supercrisis"). The book is dedicated to the "subsistence farmers of the mountains" as the "best hope for solving the dilemma." As Swiss, the authors are suspicious of scenarios that blame mountain farmers for flooding in the lowlands. Nigel J. R. Allan, "Human Aspects of Mountain Environmental Change, 1889–1992," in his *Mountains at Risk* (New Delhi, 1995), p. 13 f., describes how the Indians, too, are adopting the perception by European tourists of the Himalayas as a "threatened paradise." Robert Hoffpauir, "Subsistence Strategy and Its Ecological Consequences in the Nepal Himalya," *Anthropos* 73 (1978): 239 f. (awareness of fertilizer), 244 ff. (villagers aware of the ecological risks). Klaus Seeland, *Ein nicht zu entwickelndes Tal: Traditionelle Bambustechnologie und Subsistenzwirtschaft in Ost-Nepal* (Diessenhofen, 1980), p. 89. Kanat M. Dixit (Nepalese journalist), "Welchen Himalaya hätten Sie gern? Sehnsucht verklärt – oder: Über die Schwierigkeit, sich vom Himalaya das richtige Bild zu machen," in *GEO Special Himalaya* (June 1976): 24 ff. Blaikie and Brookfield, *Land Degradation* (Chap. 1, note 80), pp. 37–48. Ramphal, *Umweltprotokoll* (note 12), p. 49; Michael Thompson, "Policy-Making in the Face of Uncertainty: The Himalayas as Unknowns," in *Water and the Quest for Sustainable Development in the Ganges Valley*, ed. Michael Thompson and G. S. Chapman (London, 1995), p. 28 f. In retrospect, the activities of the World Bank in Nepal seem like a didactic play about the dilemma of a development and environmental policy from the very top down, even if the intentions are good and based on correct insights: see Rich, *Mortgaging the Earth* (Chap. 2, note 104), pp. 105, 336–43.

66. Panday in v. d. Heide, *Mensch und Umwelt* (note 63), p. 80; sherpas: Stevens, *High Ground* (note 63), pp. 10, 128 ff., 223, 413 f. Wolf Donner, *Nepal* (Munich, 1990), pp. 23 f., 106, 110.

67. No tradition of cooperation on irrigation: Donner (note 53), p. 31. Striking evidence for the lack of faith in the future of one's own land across much of the Third World is offered by Peter Grubbe, *Der Untergang der Dritten Welt* (Hamburg, 1991). Mahesh Banskota in *ICIMOD Newsletter* no. 34 (1999), p. 14. Exodus mentality: Savitri G. Burman, *The Kali Watershed: Resource Use and Environmental Degradation in the Himalayas* (New Delhi, 1999), pp. 195 ff.

68. *Biodiversität und Tourismus*, published by the Bundesamt für Naturschutz (Berlin, 1997), p. 68; Pradyumna S. Karan, *Bhutan: Environment, Culture and Development Strategy* (New Delhi, 1990), p. 79. Karan is among the very small group of scientists who have been able to do field research in Bhutan (Fricke, "Human Ecology" [note 53], p. 140 f.). A. C. Sinha, "Colonial Context and National Strategy of Forest Management in Bhutan,"

in Rawat (Preface to the German edition, note 1), p. 269 f.; Dasho C. Dorji (chief forest expert and Development Minister of Bhutan), "Bhutan Looks Ahead," in *Bhutan and Its Natural Resources* (New Delhi, 1991), pp. 41 ff., also p. 57 (Mingma Norbu Sherpa). Geoffrey Lean, "Bhutans radikale Umweltpolitik," in *Bäume – Menschen – Erosionen,* ed. Ludmilla Tüting (Löhnbach, 1987), pp. 52 ff.; Martin Brauen, *Irgendwo in Bhutan: Wo die Frauen (fast immer) das Sagen haben* (Frauenfeld, 1994).

69. D. N. S. Dhakal and Christopher Strawn, *Bhutan: A Movement in Exile* (New Delhi, 1994); E. C. Wolf, "Shangrila ohne Menschenrechte," *Südasien* 3 (1997): 57 ff.; Michael Hutt has sought to mediate between the clashing viewpoints: Michael Hutt, ed., *Bhutan: Perspectives on Conflict and Dissent* (Gartmore, 1994); see pp. 48 and 51 (Jigmi Y. Thinley, interior minister of Bhutan), pp. 106 f. and 120 (Chr. Strawn), p. 191 f. (Leo E. Rose).

70. So the argument by Michael Hutt in the introduction to *Bhutan* (note 69), p. 12, as well as Herbert Wilhelmy, *Bhutan* (Munich, 1990), p. 38. Ecological charges against immigrants can today be heard also in Western Mongolia: "The Kasaks simply came into the country uninvited, exploited nature by hunting, felling, and picking to their heart's content": Viktoria Raith and Cathleen Naundorf, *Steppen, Tempel und Nomaden: Zwei Frauen entdecken die Mongolei* (Munich, 1994), p. 229.

71. *Der Spiegel* 45 (1996): 167 f.

72. Uekötter, *Rauchplage* (Chap. 5, note 90), p. 514.

73. Erich Jantsch, *Die Selbstorganisation des Universums* (Munich, 1982), p. 116. Even the creator of the Gaia hypothesis believes that Gaia, the quasi-organism of the earth, "emphasizes most the significance of the individual organism. It is always from the action of individuals that powerful local, regional, and global systems evolve": Lovelock, *Ages of Gaia* (note 9), p. 236. Even the report *Global 2000 Report* (Chap. 5, note 83) concludes: "There is no global water economy."

74. UNEP, *Global Environment Outlook 2000* (London, 1999), p. 240.

75. Blaikie and Brookfield, *Land Degradation* (Chap. 1, note 80), p. 245: "Yet local knowledge is clearly not enough, otherwise there would be no problems."

76. Dieter Oberndörfer, *Schutz der tropischen Regenwälder durch Entschuldung* (Munich, 1989), p. 10; Marvin S. Soroos, "Trends in the Perception of Ecological Problems in the U.N. General Debates," *Human Ecology* 9 (1981): 34. For the Third World, the attraction of this role playing also lies in the fact that it can play its "biodiversity," which exists without any environmental policy, as a trump card. On this see Jessica Suplie, *"Streit auf Noahs Arche": Zur Genese der Biodiversitäts-Konvention* (Berlin, 1995), p. 54 and elsewhere. Even a state like Albania comes off well within Europe from the perspective of biodiversity.

77. Benedick, *Ozone Diplomacy* (note 35), p. 205 f. and elsewhere. However, one should bear in mind the author's own interests: he was the lead negotiator for the U.S. By contrast, Meadows and Randers, *Grenzen des Wachstums* (note 4) emphasize the accomplishment of the UN Environmental Program (UNEP), ibid., p. 191. As the "moral of the story," they conclude: "One does not need a world government to solve global problems – though one does need global scientific cooperation, a worldwide information system, and a recognized international forum with the competency to develop agreements." Scheer, *Solare Weltwirtschaft* (note 58), p. 315.

78. Ernst Ulrich v. Weizsäcker and Helmut Schreiber, "Luftreinhaltung: Der schwierige Konsens," in *Dicke Luft in Europa: Aufgaben und Probleme der europäischen Umweltpolitik,* ed. Lothar Gündling and Beate Weber (Heidelberg, 1988), pp. 163 ff. In the political controversy over acid rain, even Lovelock did not argue from the Gaia perspective, but as an outraged Britishman: *Gaia: The Practical Science of Planetary Medicine* (London, 1991), pp. 159–62. Gerald Hau and Claus-Peter Hutter, *Nördliche Sporaden* (Überlingen, 1997), p. 14. The Environmental Impact Assessment (Umweltverträglichkeitsprüfung [UVP]) is often seen as an accomplishment of the EU in environmental policy. Gertrude Lübbe-Wolff has argued, however, that the UVP is always too late where the EU has created economic background conditions with effects that are harmful to the environment (in *Mainauer Gespräche* XIV [Mainau, 1999], p. 153). Alexander Schink, "Die Umweltverträglichkeitsprüfung in einer

Bilanz," *Natur und Recht* 20 (1998): 174: "UVP has been robbed of its bite both in terms of environmental policy and in terms of environmental law."

79. *Sustainable Netherlands* (Chap. 3, note 112); Holger Krawinkel, *Für eine neue Energiepolitik: Was die B.R.D. von Dänemark lernen kann* (Frankfurt a. M., 1991); Switzerland: Hans R. Nebiker, "Umweltpolitik in einem souveränen Kleinstaat – Möglichkeiten und Grenzen," *Mainauer Gespräche* 8 (1991) ("Wenn's dem Nachbarn nicht gefällt: Umweltpolitik als europäische Aufgabe"): 43–54. Timothy F. Flannery, "The Fate of Empire in Low- and High-Energy Ecosystems," in Griffiths and Robin, *Ecology and Empire* (Chap. 4, note 34), p. 58.

80. Wolfgang Sachs, "Der blaue Planet: Zur Zweideutigkeit einer modernen Ikone," in *Natur im Kopf* (Preface to the German edition, note 6), vol. I, pp. 76 ff.; Pot, *Bewertung* (note 33), vol. II, pp. 872 f., 1189.

81. Lovelock, *Gaia* (note 5), p. 28; Claude Martin in *Kahlschlag im Paradies*, ed. Peter E. Stüben (Gießen, 1985), p. 105; Mainguet, *Desertification* (Chap. 1, note 32), p. 8.

82. Clarke, *Water* (Chap. 3, note 44), p. 155.

83. Hans-Werner Prahl and Albrecht Steinecke, *Der Millionen-Urlaub* (Bielefeld, 1989), p. 73 and elsewhere; Ralf Unkart, "Das Tourismuskonzept der Alpenkonvention 1992," *Mainauer Gespräche* 9 (1992): 16 f. (mass tourism as a plague); Janet Cochrane, "The Sustainability of Ecotourism in Indonesia: Fact and Fiction," in *Environmetal Change in South-East Asia*, ed. Michael J. G. Parnwell and Raymond L. Bryant (London, 1996), p. 240 f.; Joachim Radkau, "Aloha – Vom Abheben deutscher Eliten: Die verborgenen Inseln der Insider und die Demokratisierung der Nervosität," in *Kursbuch 139: Die neuen Eliten* (Berlin, 2000), pp. 45–58. Global overview: Ludwig Ellenberg et al., eds., *Ökotourismus* (Heidelberg, 1997).

84. Christoph Hennig, *Reiselust: Touristen, Tourismus und Urlaubskultur* (Frankfurt a. M., 1999), p. 116 and elsewhere; as early as the eighteenth/nineteenth centuries: Thomas, *Natural World* (Chap. 2, note 49), p. 261: "It has even been suggested that the appreciation of sublime scenery increased in direct ratio to the number of turnpike acts."

85. Ernst Rudorff, "Über das Verhältniß des modernen Lebens zur Natur," *Preußisches Jahrbuch* 45 (1880): 261 ff.: "People celebrate nature, but they do so by prostituting it." Walter, *Bedrohte Natur* (Chap. 2, note 103), p. 85; Knaut, *Zurück zur Natur* (Chap. 5, note 70), p. 407.

86. Jost Krippendorf, *Alpsegen, Alptraum: Für eine Tourismus-Entwicklung im Einklang mit Mensch und Natur* (Bern, 1986), p. 23 f.

87. A detailed and sympathetic account in Sterling Evans, *The Green Republic: A Conservation History of Costa Rica* (Austin, Tex., 1999); Michael Dutschke, *Financing Sustainable Development: The Case of Costa Rica* (Hamburg, 1998). Meadows and Randers (note 2), p. 84 f. still pointed to Costa Rica as a deterrent example of the "worst forestry sins"; similarly Jean Carriere, "The Crisis in Costa Rica: An Ecological Perspective," in Goodman and Redclift, *Latin America* (note 12), pp. 184 ff. For John Vandermeer and Ivette Perfecto, *Breakfast of Biodiversity: The Truth about Rain Forest Destruction* (Oakland, Calif., 1995), pp. 105 ff., the "Greening of Costa Rica" is not a victory for ecology, but for the tourism interests, at times over the vital needs of the locals, who need better banana plantations instead of nature parks. On the conflicts over the national parks in Costa Rica see also Peter Utting, *Trees, People and Power: Social Dimensions of Deforestation and Forest Protection in Central America* (London, 1993), pp. 105 ff. Ellenberg, *Ökotourismus* (note 83), p. 273: "Costa Rica is considered a pioneer in eco-tourism and is in many respects merely a successful environmental hypocrite."

88. Haiti: Chap. 4, note 22. Norman Myers (editor of *Gaia Atlas of Planet Management*, 1985), "The Environmental Dimension to Security Issues," *Environmentalist* 6, no. 4 (1996): 253 f. In his view, the nearly one million "boat people" that left Haiti are primarily "environmental refugees."

89. *Der Spiegel* 32 (1997): 82 f. (Michael Miersch); Jonathan S. Adams and Thomas O. McShane, *The Myth of Wild Africa* (Berkeley, Calif., 1996), pp. 194 f., 202: tourism saved the mountain gorillas, while the legendary Dian Fossey, whose murder brought her worldwide fame, made the protection of the gorillas hated by the locals.

90. *Der Spiegel* 6 (1997): 162 f. Herbert Hesmer, *Der kombinierte land- und forstwirtschaftliche Anbau*, 2 vols. (Stuttgart, 1966). Vandana Shiva, "Einige sind immer globaler als andere," in *Der Planet als Patient: Über die Widersprüche globaler Umweltpolitik*, ed. Wolfgang Sachs (Berlin, 1994), p. 176.

91. Russia: personal communication from Marina Kuzmenok (Pensa); Tuva: Caroline Humphrea and David Sneath, in *Culture and Environment in Inner Asia*, vol. I, ed. Caroline Humphries and David Sneath (Cambridge, 1996), p. 8.

92. Ellis, *Men and Whales* (Chap. 2, note 38), pp. 434, 445; Mountain gorillas: note 89; Robben: Henry Makowski, *Nationalparke in Deutschland: Schatzkammern der Natur – Kampfplätze des Naturschutzes* (Neumünster, 1997), p. 36 f. Panda: Ludmilla Tüting in *Tibet – Ein vergewaltigtes Land*, ed. Petra K. Kelly and Bert Bastian (Reinbek, 1988), p. 153.

93. Joachim Scharioth (Battelle Institut Frankfurt), while discerning learning processes in the wake of the controversy over nuclear energy, believes nevertheless that the discussion of risk has the "function of a ritual": "it serves the ritualized management of potential dangers that cannot be eliminated in real life." Gesellschaft für Sicherheitswisschenscahft, ed., *Probabilistische Risikoanalyse* (Wuppertal, 1984), p. 314 f. However, one should not rule out the possibility that in certain situations, rituals promote a real and effective engagement with the problems. Skepticism predominates in Bernd Hansjürgens and Gertrude Lübbe-Wolff, eds., *Symbolische Umweltpolitik* (Frankfurt a. M., 2000).

94. For some time now, there has been a counterattack by eco-optimists or eco-revisionists against what they like to call ecological "apocalypticists." In Germany: Dirk Maxeiner and Michael Miersch, *Öko-Optimismus* (Munich, 1996); in the United States earlier, Aaron Wildavsky, *But Is It True?* (Cambridge, Mass., 1995); Gregg Easterbrook, *A Moment on the Earth: The Coming Age of Environmental Optimism* (New York, 1995). To some extent the two camps stake out their positions more for show than substance, since the optimists often argue on the basis of the successes achieved by the concerned environmental movement, while some of the prophecies of doom reflect a calculated pessimism intended to galvanize the public. In the final analysis, however, another background to this controversy is the philosophical problem of what kind of practical conclusions we should draw from the infinite complexity of nature and the inadequacy of our knowledge about many interrelationships.

95. Al Gore, *Earth in the Balance: Ecology and the Human Spirit* (New York, 1992), p. 141; Radkau, *Technik* (Chap. 5, note 1), p. 368.

96. UNEP, *GEO 2000*, pp. 56, 67.

97. Fritz Vorholz in *Die Zeit*, October 11, 1996, p. 24.

98. Michael Dutschke and Axel Michaelowa, *Der Handel mit Emissionsrechten für Treibhausgase* (Hamburg, 1998 [HWWA-Report 187]), p. 29 f.

99. Niklas Luhmann, *Ecological Communication*, trans. John Bednarz, Jr. (Cambridge, 1986). On this see Joachim Radkau, "Aussichtslosigkeit von Umweltpolitik" (Preface to the German edition, note 6), pp. 25 ff.

100. Myers, "Security Issues" (note 88); *Wechselwirkung* 67 (June 1994), special issue on ecological conflicts (especially over water resources), p. 22 f.: Volker Böge, "Die Militarisierung der Umweltpolitik. Ulli Kulke, Krieg ums Wasser: Die Gefährdung der globalen Lebensgrundlagen – Ursache für die Waffengänge der Zukunft," *Natur* 2 (1991): 21 ff. Joachim Hoelzgen on "Anatolia's dams and water as a weapon": *Der Spiegel* 3 (1991): 142 ff. So far, however, war has never been the ultima ratio of environmental policy. Does the ecological discourse as such promote peaceful reason, even if it stirs up fear?

101. Joachim Raschke, *Die Grünen: Wie sie wurden, was sie sind* (Cologne, 1993). Only twelve pages in this large tome of 960 pages deal with "ecology."

102. See note 95.

103. Günther Rüther and the Konrad-Adenauer-Stiftung, *Rettungsaktion Planet Erde* (Wesseling, 1995), p. 2.

104. *Sonnenenergie – Schlüssel zur Zukunft?* published by the Evangelische Akademie Mülheim (1995), p. 37 f.

105. *Der Spiegel* 10 (1999): 174 (Jochen Bölsche). Frank Hoffmann and Theo Romland, *Die Recycling-Lüge* (Stuttgart, 1993).

106. Peter Knoepfel and Helmut Weidner, *Luftreinhaltungspolitik im internationalen Vergleich* (Berlin, 1985), vol. I, p. 215 f.: "In terms of the mountain of existing law" on keeping the air clean, the Federal Republic "clearly holds a leading position." But quantity does not equal quality; instead, there is a tendency to "move into secondary areas that increase the administrative expense and effort." R. Steinberg and D. Schütze, "Umweltverträgliche Technikgestaltung durch Recht," *Kritische Vierteljahresschrift für Gesetzgebung und Rechtstheorie* (1998): 255 f. I would like to thank Gertrude Lübbe-Wolff and Martin Stock for references to environmental law.

107. Radkau, *Atomwirtschaft* (note 8), pp. 366 ff., 388 ff. Labisch: in *Maladies et société*, ed. Neithard Bulst and Robert Delort (Paris 1989), p. 410. Fiorino, *Environmental Policy* (note 35), p. 223.

108. Through conversations with the environmental lawyer Gertrude Lübbe-Wolff and her father, the philosopher Hermann Lübbe, I have come to realize that pioneering thinkers of the environmental movement are usually too Kantian in their argumentation – arguing from an Ought, from an ecological imperative – and not Hegelian enough, which would mean basing the argument on the potential for reason inherent in real developments. Here, precisely, seems to lie one task of environmental history.

109. For that reason it seems to me ill-considered when social scientists dismiss the notion of "overpopulation" as "biologism" or worse, and calculate that the earth could support several times the current population if people gave up cars and meat and moved into energy-saving homes. Guaranteeing a sustainable ecological balance under such conditions presupposes an effective global eco-dictatorship that is neither desirable nor to be expected in the future. Still, German Greens have traditionally rejected any kind of birth control in the Third World, since – according to a campaign platform of the Greens from 1989 – birth control follows the "erroneous doctrine of a causal link between population growth, ecological destruction, and social misery (Raschke, *Die Grünen* [note 101], p. 126, note). By now, however, it would appear that some perceive a feminist dimension in the population problem, for it would seem that an improvement in the social status and education of women usually leads to a drop in the birth rate.

110. Bruce Rich, *Die Verpfändung der Erde* (Stuttgart, 1998), 386.

111. Maurice Agulhon, *Der vagabundierende Blick* (Frankfurt a. M., 1995); revealing examples of "ecological surprises" in Josef H. Reichholf, *Comeback der Biber* (Munich, 1993), and Reichholf, *Der blaue Planet* (Munich, 1998). Time and again, the point is that even so-called environmental pollution benefits some species. But what are we to conclude from that? Reichholf himself does not wish to give emissions the green light.

112. The Indian environmental historian Vasant K. Saberwal has aptly described the basic problem in the context of his criticism of the hostile way in which the (British) Indian forestry administration dealt with shepherds: "Within certain political contexts, foresters and conservationists in general have lacked the institutional space within which to acknowledge the uncertainty inherent to our understanding of ecological phenomenon." See his *Pastoral Politics: Shepherds, Bureaucrats and Conservation in the Western Himalaya* (Oxford, 1999), p. 207.

EPILOGUE: HOW TO ARGUE WITH ENVIRONMENTAL HISTORY IN POLITICS

1. Sam Whimster, ed., *Max Weber and the Culture of Anarchy* (New York, 1998). On the meeting itself: PSE (Paul Scherrer Institut), ed., *Proceedings of the Workshop on Risk Perception as Initiator and Steering Instrument of Innovative R&D, Ascona, April 1–3 1998*, PSI Proceedings 99-02.

2. The authors of two pioneering German studies on energy conservation and on solar energy were at the time of writing top managers at RWE, Germany's largest producer of electricity:

Bernd Stoy, *Wunschenergie Sonne*, 3rd ed. (Heidelberg, 1980), and Bernd Soy and Werner Müller, *Entkopplung: Wirtschaftswachstum ohne mehr Energie?* (Stuttgart, 1978). Both books are excellent and their authors were without doubt serious about what they wrote. However, no significant influence by these ideas on the strategy of RWE has been discernible so far.

3. That is one of the main theses of Uekötter, *Rauchplage* (Chap. 5, note 90).

4. Elisabeth Dore, "Capitalism and Ecological Crisis: Legacy of the 1980s," in *Green Guerillas: Environmental Conflicts and Initiatives in Latin America and the Caribbean*, ed. Helen Collinson (London, 1996), p. 16 f.

5. James Fairhead and Melissa Leach, *Misreading the African Landscape: Society and Ecology In a Forest-Savanna Mosaic* (Cambridge, 1996), p. 253.

6. One environmentalist in Thuringia confessed to me that in trying to explain the FFH guidelines of the EU to his farmers, he told them, counting on their faulty orthography, that FFH stood for "Pflanzen, Viecher, Heimat" (plants, animals, homeland). If he started talking to them about "Fauna, Flora, Habitat," they didn't want to hear any more!

7. Radkau and Uekötter, *Naturschutz und Nationalsozialismus* (Chap. 6, note 24).

8. Radkau and Schäfer, *Holz* (Chap. 1, note 50), pp. 271 ff.

9. Uekötter, *Rauchplage* (Chap. 5, note 90), p. 513 f.

10. Milton Osborne, *The Mekong: Turbulent Past, Uncertain Future* (New York, 2000).

11. Radkau, *Atomwirtschaft* (Chap. 6, note 8), pp. 360 ff.; Radkau, "Sicherheitsphilosophien in der Geschichte der bundesdeutschen Atomwirtschaft," in *Atomwirtschaft und innere Sicherheit*, ed. Wolfgang Gessenharter and Helmut Fröchling (Baden-Baden, 1989), pp. 101 ff.

12. At the conclusion of a lecture series at the University of Basel on environmental history, two students put this provocative question to the participants (of which I was one): "Why is environmental history boring?" (Monica Kalt and Jan Hodel in *Environmental History Newsletter Special Issue* no. 1 [1993]: 108–25). They were complaining that the existing literature on environmental history was for the most part a mere appendix to the environmental movement, which is why one always knew at the outset what the result of the historical studies would be. I have taken this criticism to heart! Specifically as a response to this challenge, I wrote the article "Unbekannte Umwelt. Von der altklugen zur neugierigen Umweltgeschichte," *Praxis Geschichte* 11, no. 4 (1997): 4–10, which was at the same time the program for the German edition of this book.

13. Ian Tyrrell (Sydney), in response to my question why the topic of "salinization" hardly appeared in his book *True Gardens of the Gods*, even though it dealt extensively with irrigation and salinization was one consequence in Australia and Calfornia, wrote on December 12, 2003: "They did mainly neglect the problem of salinization, and where it was mentioned it was in the context of saying that such things happened under different soil conditions: namely that the soils were superior to those of California or India. California's irrigating areas were often said to be desert whereas the Australian (deserts) were not in the areas where irrigation was promoted. Of course these ideas were ill-informed and also self-serving, but the problem of salinization did not emerge as a major one at that time up to the 1920s in Australia. A good deal though not all of the current problem is, furthermore, dry-land salinity due to the removal of forest cover . . . , a situation that irrigators claimed to deal with through reforestation and afforestation."

14. Friedrich Münzinger, *Atomkraft*, 3rd ed. (Berlin, 1960).

15. Joachim Radkau, "Sicherheitsphilosophien" (note 11), pp. 98 ff.

16. Wolf Häfele, *Hypotheticality and the New Challenges: The Pathfinder Role of Nuclear Energy* (IIASA Research Report 73–14) (Laxenburg, 1973).

17. Tom R. Burns and Reinhard Ueberhorst, *Creative Democracy: Systematic Conflict Resolution and Policymaking in a World of High Science and Technology*, with a Foreword by Willy Brandt (New York, 1988).

18. Joachim Radkau, "Schlußkommentar," in *Perspektiven einer zivilen Nutzung der Kernenergie: Energiepolitisches Kolloquium der Evangelischen Akademie Loccum vom 24–26. 6. 1994*, ed. Andreas Dally (Loccum, 1994), p. 644.

19. One of these global strategists assured me that the solution to global environmental problems was not difficult. Population growth would come to an end on its own within two or three generations; such forecasts could be made with certainty. The world had plenty of fresh water, one simply had to use pipelines to bring it from water-rich regions into thirsty regions. And the political problems that such a gigantic project would pose? Well, that was all very easy, really: the United States has the power, it simply has to make the unreasonable states see the light, just as they did with Iraq. This man's background was in the sciences. As a historian, I do not find this path easy at all.

20. Hans-Ulrich Wehler, "Moderne Politikgeschichte exemplarisch: Aufstieg und Krise der westdeutschen Atomwirtschaft 1945–1975," in his *Aus der Geschichte lernen?* (Munich, 1988), pp. 91–7.

21. Dietmar Klenke, *"Freier Stau für freie Bürger": Die Geschichte der bundesdeutschen Verkehrspolitik* (Darmstadt, 1995), p. 63.

22. Joachim Radkau, "Hiroshima und Asilomar. Die Inszenierung des Diskurses über die Gentechnik vor dem Hintergrund der Kernenergie-Kontroverse," *Geschichte und Gesellschaft* 14 (1988): 329–63.

23. Radkau, *Technik* (Chap. 5, note 1), p. 345.

24. For example, Rolf Peter Sieferle, *Der unterirdische Wald: Energiekrise und Industrielle Revolution* (Munich, 1982); Debeir, Deléage, and Hémery, *Power* (Chap. 3, note 73). When I asked Deléage about French environmental history back then, he responded that in France the historical study of the environment consisted almost entirely of himself: at the beginning, then, there was the energetic picture of history. Since then, that has changed dramatically.

25. Joachim Radkau, "Vom Holzmangel zum Energieproblem: Abstraktionsschübe und Metaphysik in der deutschen Technikgeschichte," *Sowi/Sozialwissenschaftliche Informationen* 2 (1989): 81–7.

26. Reimar Gilsenbach, *Die Erde dürstet: 6000 Jahre Kampf ums Wasser* (Leipzig, 1961), pp. 33 ff.

27. René Létolle and Monique Mainguet, *Der Aralsee: Eine ökologische Katastrophe*, (Heidelberg, 1996), pp. 387 ff.; Nikita F. Glazovsky, "The Aral Sea Basin," in *Regions at Risk: Comparisons of Threatened Environments*, ed. Jeanne X. Kapserson et al. (Tokyo [UNO], 1995), pp. 92–139.

28. UNEP, ed., *Global Environment Outlook* (London, 1999), p. 337 f.

29. Gary Paul Nabhan, "Cultural Parallax in Viewing North American Habitats," in *Reinventing Nature? Responses to Postmodern Deconstruction*, ed. Michael Soulé and Gary Lease (Washington, D.C., 1995), pp. 87–101.

30. As was asserted, for example, at a conference titled "Fit for Sustainability?" organized by the Deutsche Gesellschaft für Umwelterziehung (DGU, German Society for Environmental Eucation) at the Berlin Federal Office for the Environment in February 2001. The major thrust of the discussion was that humanity, as a result of its evolution and the process of natural selection, in keeping with the law of the survival of the fittest, is "unfit" for sustainability: Axel Beyer, ed., *Fit für Nachhaltigkeit? Biologisch-anthropologische Grundlagen einer Bildung für nachhaltige Entwicklung* (Opladen, 2002).

31. Joachim Radkau, "Exceptionalism in European Environmental History," *Bulletin of the German Historical Institute* (Washington, D.C.) 33 (2003): 23–44, with commentary by John R. McNeill, pp. 45–52.

32. McNeill, *Something New* (Chap. 1, note 7), p. 358.

33. Even the first German introduction to environmental history, written by a geographer, considered *Nachhaltigkeit* a German translation of "sustainability" and knew nothing about the German history of the concept. This is one indication of just how much *Nachhaltigkeit* remained an insider-term within forestry: Helmut Jäger, *Einführung in die Umweltgeschichte* (Darmstadt, 1994), p. 231.

34. Wiebke Peters, "Die Nachhaltigkeit als Grundsatz der Forstwirtschaft. Ihre Verankerung in der Gesetzgebung und ihre Bedeutung für die Praxis. Die Verhältnisse in der Bundesrepublik

Deutschland im Vergleich mit einigen Industrie- und Entwicklungsländern," dissertation, University of Hamburg (1984).

35. On Emerson see Carolyn Merchant, *The Columbia Guide to American Environmental History* (New York, 2002), p. 71 f.

36. This is the finding of a study commissioned by the German Bundesamt für Naturschutz: Uwe Brendle, *Musterlösungen im Naturschutz – Politische Bausteine für erfolgreiches Handeln* (Bonn, 1999), p. 25.

37. Ortwin Renn et al., "Wege in eine nachhaltige Zukunft," in *Agenda 21, Vision: Nachhaltige Entwicklung*, ed. Birgit Breuel (Frankfurt a. M., 1999), 33; Jürgen Gaulke, *John Stuart Mill* (Reinbek, 1996), 80 f.

38. Vilém Flusser, "Alte und neue Codes: Sao Paulo," in *Städtische Intellektuelle: Urbane Milieus im 20. Jahrhundert*, ed. Walter Prigge (Frankfurt a. M., 1992), 199, 197.

39. Uekötter, *Rauchplage* (Chap. 5, note 90), p. 507 f.

40. Antoinette M. Mannion, *Global Environmental Change: A Natural and Cultural Environmental History*, 2nd ed. (Harlow, 1997), Preface.

41. "Doing Environmental History," in Worster, *Ends of the Earth* (Chap. 4, note 58), p. 289.

42. Documentation: Kulturamt Stuttgart, ed., *Zum Naturbegriff der Gegenwart*, 2 vols. (Stuttgart, 1994).

43. It is also not that rare in papers on nature that various nature concepts get jumbled together: nature as goddess, nature as construct. At an international conference on environmental history in Lammi (Finland) in September 1992, several speakers talked about "conceptual pollution" (by analogy to "environmental pollution") in scholarship on environmental history. There is no doubt that this is indeed a problem! On this see Joachim Radkau, "Wood and Forestry in German History: In Quest of an Environmental Approach," *Environment and History* 2, no. 1 (1996): 63 ff.

44. On this controversy see my web site: www.joachim/radkau.de. The sharpest attack came from Wolfgang v. Stromer, who denounced my research project on the history of wood scarcity as a prime example of the waste of research funding: see his "Gewerbereviere in Spätmittelalter und Frühneuzeit," in *Gewerbe- und Industrielandschaften vom Spätmittelalter bis ins 20. Jahrhundert* (Vierteljahrschrift für Sozial- und Wirtschaftsgeschichte, Supplement 78) (Stuttgart, 1986). Stromer is a descendant of the *Waldstromer* who, beginning in 1368 in the imperial forest of Nuremberg, undertook the first coniferous afforestation in world history that is documented in the sources. With the traditional picture of forest history, Stromer is defending the reputation of his ancestors as (alleged) saviors of humankind.

45. Runte, *National Parks* (Chap. 5, note 60), p. 82.

46. Adolf Hitler, *Mein Kampf* (Munich, 1937), p. 144.

47. Paul Shepard, "Virtually Hunting Reality in the Forests of Simulacra," in *Reinventing Nature? Responses to Postmodern Deconstruction*, ed. Michael E. Soelé and Gary Lease (Washington, D.C., 1995), p. 20.

48. Didier Eribon, *Michel Foucault – Eine Biographie* (Frankfurt a. M., 1991), p. 472.

49. Jacob von Uexküll, *Niegeschaute Welten* (Chap. 1, note 65).

50. *Max Weber Gesamtausgabe* I/20, p. 96.

Index